India[n]
Literary
Criticism

Theory and Interpretation

Also by G.N. Devy

G.N. DEVY Reader

A NOMAD CALLED THIEF
Reflections on Adivasi Voice and Silence

Indian Literary Criticism

Theory and Interpretation

Edited by

G.N. Devy

Orient BlackSwan

ORIENT BLACKSWAN PRIVATE LIMITED

Registered Office
3-6-752 Himayatnagar, Hyderabad 500 029 (A.P.), INDIA
e-mail: centraloffice@orientblackswan.com

Other Offices
Bangalore, Bhopal, Bhubaneshwar, Chandigarh, Chennai, Ernakulam, Guwahati,Hyderabad, Jaipur, Kolkata, Lucknow, Mumbai, New Delhi, Noida, Patna

First published by Orient Longman Private Limited 2002
Reprinted 2004
Second Edition Published by Orient Blackswan Private Limited 2010
Reprinted 2011

ISBN: 978 81 250 3952 5

Typeset by
Le Studio Graphique, Gurgaon 122 001

Printed in India at
B.B. Press, Noida

Published by
Orient Blackswan Private Limited
1/24 Asaf Ali Road, New Delhi 110 002
e-mail: delhi@orientblackswan.com

For

Prakash and Anagha

CONTENTS

Part II: Interpretation

ACKNOWLEDGEMENTS

For copyright material included in this book, the editor and publishers are grateful to the following:

Bhandarkar Oriental Research Institute, Pune, for the passages from *Bharata Nāṭya Manjiri* by G.K. Bhatt, and from *Śantarasa and Abhinava's Philosophy* by J.L. Masson and M.V. Patwardhan; Kural Neri Publishing House, Madurai, for the passage from *Tholkāppiyam in English with Critical Studies* by S. Ilakkuvanar; Motilal Banarsidass Publishers for the excerpts from *Vākyapadiya* translated by K. Raghavan Pillai, from *The Daśarupa: A Treatise on Hindu Dramaturgy*, translated by George Hass, and from *The Rasikapriyā of Keshavadasa*, translated by K.P. Bahadur; Ramaswamy Sastrulu & Sons for the passage from Dandin's *Kāvyādarśa*, translated by Vavilla Venkateswara Sastrulu; Professor K. Krishnamoorthy for the passages from his books *Dhavanyāloka of Anandavardhana* and *Valkroktijivita of Kuntaka*, and from his chapter 'Introduction to Sanskrit Criticism' in *Comparative Indian Literature—II*, edited by K.M. George; Samata Books, Chennai, for the passage from *Bhāvārthadīpikā* translated by R.K. Bhagwat; the Historical Research and Documentation Programme, Jaipur, for the excerpts from *India as seen by Amir Khusrau in 1318 A.D.*; the Institute of Oriental Philosophy, Brindavan, for the passage from *Sri Rupa Goswami's Bhaktirasamṛtasindhuh*, translated by Tridandi Swami Hṛdaya Bon Maharaja; the Asiatic Society of Bengal for the passage from the *Muntakhabu-t-Tawārīkh*, translated by Sir Wolseley Haig; Sardar Jafri and Qurratulain Hyder for the excerpt from *Ghalib and His Poetry*; Vishwabharati for the excerpt from *Personality: Lectures Delivered in America* by Rabindranath Tagore; the Sri Aurobindo Ashram Trust, for the passages from *The Harmony of Virtue and Future Poetry* by Sri Aurobindo; Popular Prakashan, Mumbai for the excerpt from *Arts and Man* by B.S. Mardhekar; the author, for the excerpt from *Sahitya: a Theory* by Krishna Rayan; Smt Ushaben Joshi and Shri Upendra Nanavaty for the excerpt from *Chintayami Manasa* by Suresh Joshi (translated by Upendra Nanavaty); the author for the essay 'The Marathi Novel 1950–1975' by Bhalchandra Nemade, translated by G.N. Devy;

Oxford University Press, New Delhi for the article by Gayatri Chakravorty Spivak from *Subaltern Studies Vol. V*, edited by Ranajit Guha, for the excerpts from *Poems of Love and War* by A.K. Ramanujan, from *The World and the World* by B.K. Matilal, and from *The Inner World* by Sudhir Karkar; the author and the *Economic and Political Weekly* for the article 'Orientalism and After' by Aijaz Ahmad; Kavyalaya Publishers, Mysore for the excerpt from *Art Experience* by M.K. Hiriyanna; the *Journal of Art and Ideas* and the author for the article 'Aesthetics: Some Important Problems' by R.B. Patankar.

All efforts have been made to contact the correct copyright holders of the passages, and the publishers would be happy to hear from one or two who have not responded, so that suitable arrangements can be made.

INTRODUCTION TO SECOND EDITION

Language is, perhaps, the most distinguishing feature of the human species, the most marked difference between other forms of life and the human consciousness. Language itself is made of such ephemeral material such as the verbal modulations and entirely arbitrarily generated signs that, by its very nature, it is not capable of functioning within a framework of fixed correspondence between forms and significance. The perpetually shifting relationship between the verbal container and the content it is supposed to hold, as well as the semblance of a predictable relationship between them, provide human language their innate ability to be a versatile medium of creative expression. Thus, practically every linguistic utterance is 'creative' in essence. The marvel that is human speech largely vanishes into thin air, while some of it manages to remain embedded in the collective reception by a given speech community. A small part of this acquires staying power not only in its own time and context but beyond. Expression which is capable of transcending culture and time comes to be recognised as 'literature'. The notion of what constitutes literature keeps changing from one era to another, from one culture to another. 'The notion of what constitutes literature' should probably be the most rudimentary definition of 'Literary Criticism'. But since the perception of what makes literature keeps changing, the norms and the idiom of literary criticism also continue to change from period to period; and there can be very distinct differences between the idea of literary criticism prevailing in one culture and that prevailing in another culture within the same historical period. This is not to say that there are no points of convergence and accidental or justified similarities between a given set of period-styles or cultural-styles of critical idioms. Such convergences or similarities are natural since the interdependence between the human consciousness and the external world, which language attempts to describe, is the very essence of human existence. Hence, while approaching any specific tradition of literary criticism it is desirable to keep in view the large backdrop of the relation between reality, language, literature and criticism.

Indian students of literature, particularly those who are exposed to western traditions of literary criticism, generally tend to think that there are, or should be, points of convergence between one or many of the western traditions of literary criticism and the one or many Indian traditions. Since higher education in India as it exists at present was shaped within the crucible of the colonial transactions of knowledge, Indian students of literature in English, as well as students of Bhasha literature to an extent, come to expect that the transition of the idiom of criticism from ancient times to our time in India has been akin to the transition in western tradition(s). If dissimilarities are noticed, they are read more as indicative of philosophical flaws or cultural inadequacies within the Indian tradition(s). Historians of ideas have pointed out that within the tradition conceived by ancient Greek philosophers like Plato, and Aristotle and partially revived and modified by British thinkers like Dryden, Coleridge, Arnold, Eliot, etc., literary criticism has run through four major phases: the mimetic phase, the didactic phase, the expressive phase, and the autonomous phase (M.H. Abrams, *The Mirror and the Lamp*, 1953). It would be a frustrating task to figure out if literary criticism in Arabic, Chinese, Tamil or Hebrew has precisely the same progression. Clearly, it will be inappropriate to read a given tradition of literary criticism in terms of the progression of another tradition, however rich in thought or dominant in terms of its influence the one or the other may have been.

I was required to reflect on these issues as someone engaged professionally with the field of literature teaching and research. As a young scholar of literature, I started thinking some there decades ago about the nature of literary criticism appropriate for Bhasha literature. At that time, I was not quite aware of how numerous the literary traditions and the speech communities have been in the Indian sub-continent. Though I had gone through the Census statistics on mother tongues (1652 as in the 1961 Census data), I had not quite imagined that many among those would really be surviving in our time as literary languages. Hence, I had no hesitation in arguing that an Indian student can propose for herself or himself an Indian intellectual tradition that would provide her or him a cultural space to engage in creative expression. In order to assess the viability of the enterprise, I undertook a scrutiny of the resources available in the library collection at the Baroda University. Fortunately, as I thought at that stage in my life, the Baroda University library had a rich enough stock of works in the field to keep me thrilled over several years.

During those years, I undertook to gather similar materials from other libraries in India, particularly those specialising in Oriental Studies, and in Britain and the United States whenever I visited those countries. As the material started piling up on my desk, I began to realise that the field had far too many challenges, and that it would be unwise to postulate any single tradition of literary criticism for the entire gamut of Bhasha literature. The realisation prompted me to write a long essay discussing the complexities involved in the enterprise, which appeared in the form of a book under the title *After Amnesia* (Orient Longman, 1992). However, I felt that it would not be inappropriate to select some of the texts out of the materials I had gathered and share them with other Indian teachers of literature who may have gone through a similar process of reflection and doubt. Therefore, I spent two long summers in preparing a typescript. When I typed the manuscript of this anthology, I had no idea as to its fate. For various reasons the actual publication got delayed. Therefore, though this anthology was first published at the beginning of the twenty-first century, I appeal to the reader not to overlook the fact that it is a twentieth century work by a young teacher of literature trying to define his own tradition of literary thought for himself. If I had compiled the volume when it was published, it would have been somewhat different in its orientation. In my 'Preface', to the first edition of the anthology, written in 1993, I had stated:

> It is hoped that the reader will find this volume useful, if not completely satisfactory, and that some other critic-editor will bring out an improved and more inclusive version as a sequel to it. It is also hoped that this volume contributes, in however modest a measure, to curing our collective cultural amnesia.

Since the publication of the anthology, it has been reprinted twice, and is now being issued once more in a slightly modified format. One may be permitted to see this as an indication that there still is a need for a volume of this kind, at least for post-graduate students and college teachers of literary criticism.

As the editor of the anthology I feel pleased that it is being used today, but I would like to state that I am acutely aware of the major literary and contextual changes that have occurred during the two decades since I prepared the volume. Of these, one is a literary change, the second pertains to the structure of higher education, and the third is related to the political context. During the 1980s, Indian departments of literature had not as yet been fully exposed to post-structural and post-modern theory. The English translations of Jaques Derrida, Michael Foucault, Jaques Lacan, Roland Barthes, Louis Althusser, Jean Baudrillard, Gilles Deleuze and Jean-Francois Lyotard had just started appearing; and Indian departments of literature had not as yet introduced their ideas in the curriculum. Those were the years when English Studies, in India as well as in other post-colonial countries, had started making initial moves towards decolonising literary studies. Obviously, the focus in criticism courses had not yet started moving from England and the United States to France, Germany and Italy. That change, and a truly substantial change, occurred in India mainly during the last decade of the twentieth century. As it happens, whenever a new philosophical or literary trend emerges with originality and force, several path-breaking studies written by Indian scholars start appearing during that decade. Moreover, as the disciplinary boundaries blurred, the critical idiom started receiving fresh concepts and insights from the fields of cinema and media studies, painting and sculpture, psychology and political thought. A future edition of the anthology stands to gain immensely by the inclusion of a whole section drawn from the rich wealth of criticism produced in India since the 'nineties.

Another contextual change that has occurred since I first made this compilation is related to the near disappearance of scholarship in the classical Indian languages. During my student days, at least some of my teachers had an acquaintance with Sanskrit and a few had learnt Pali. Besides, a majority of literature teachers in English departments had an intimate involvement with the literature in their own languages. As a result, it was not uncommon among academics to allude to the *rasa* or *dhvani* theory without any sense of unease. Though it is possible to raise serious questions about the propriety of speaking of Bharat Muni and Aristotle in a single breath — and I have myself questioned this practice — the teachers of literature during the first two or three decades after independence were able to pass on to their students at least some awareness about the ancient and medieval Indian texts in literary theory. That situation has changed substantially. It is rare to find a literature teacher in India now who can offer students any sustained discourse or analysis of the texts in Sanskrit or Pali. One notices that the tremendous gain in the form of exposure to the post-modern post-structural theory is sadly offset by an equal loss of access to parts of the Indian intellectual tradition(s). In this changed context, I tend to think that there is an enhanced justification for an anthology such as the present one.

The most notable change, however, is neither pertaining to theory nor to the system of higher education. It comes from the political ethos. When I was struggling to gather texts from various ancient, medieval and modern sources and put them together in a single volume, I did not have to think it a given thinker would be labelled as a Hindu thinker (or otherwise). I am not able to say with any certainty if I was politically naïve or if the cultural atmosphere in India a quarter century ago was more liberal. My aim in presenting a volume of Indian thinkers on literature was primarily aimed at rescuing the field of literary studies from the undue dominance of irrelevant colonial baggage. But, now I fear that my idea of tracing the literary thought back to ancient times may stand the risk of being seen in part as politically retrogressive. Therefore, I would like the user of this volume to bear in mind that I have neither included in this volume nor excluded from it any thinker for reasons of his/her religious affiliation. I do not think of religion as a matter of 'affiliation' but as a matter of purely personal pursuit. Besides, the rich tapestry of Indian literary traditions over the last three thousand years stands out for its profound spirit of tolerance and its immense ability to accept and nurture diversity.

It is important for Indian students of literature to know that most of the seminal theoretical positions proposed by thinkers in the Indian past had drawn upon a variety of linguistic, cultural and spiritual traditions. Beginning with Bharat Muni's description of *natya*, Dandin's theory of *riti* and Abhinava's concept of *rasa-dhvani* to Aurobindo's understanding of 'aesthesis' and Bhalchandra Nemade's definition of the novel, the theorists have invariably invoked the plurality of voices, tones, world-views, languages and styles as a value in creative expression. In preparing an anthology of an extremely complex and varied intellectual spectrum it is almost impossible to follow rigid guidelines. I was aware of the difficulties when I set out to make my choices. I had stated the difficulties in making the choices I made in the Preface to the first edition:

In our own times, quite often the contemporary critical texts of significance tend to remain hidden in the pages of obscure periodicals, or are blocked by obscure publishers. Added to this is the problem of availability of good translations of critical materials. In a country where even literary works do not get translated in good time into all Indian languages, it is too much to expect to find translators committed to such a specialised activity as literary criticism. The combined result of this situation is that an Indian student of literature does not have easy access to India's critical tradition. She may show an emotional solidarity with the cause of Indian criticism, but may not be able to mention even one Indian text of literary criticism with any degree of familiarity, excepting those texts which are the most contemporary. Therefore, many of us have wished that there was a series of volumes giving Indian students modern renderings, of important Indian critical texts from the past, to be put to use in the present. To prepare such a series of scholarly volumes would be a project worthy of being taken up by a committee of scholars or a literary academy. The volume being offered here is a small substitute aimed at fulfilling that long-felt need. This volume tires to bring under one cover some of the most significant literary thinkers in the Indian tradition of the last two millennia. It is being offered in the hope that it will provide teachers, students and scholars-in-the-making easy access to some of the key concepts, terms and ideas from various Indian traditions of literary theorising. Besides, it will give students a convenient text in which they can find first-hand some of the most significant literary thinkers. It is with these modest aims that the present volume is put together though I am fully aware of its deficiencies.

Having said that, I will at once point out the deficiencies in this volume. The most striking one is that the excerpts selected from the Tamil classic *Tolkappiyam* are all too brief. Unfortunately, the translation of order relevant sections available to us is so poor in quality that however sympathetically I looked at it, it was impossible to decide in favour of its inclusion. The parts translated by Prof. Zvelebil of Holland, though the translation is very lucid, would not have fitted into the present scheme of the volume. Next, no text from Pali or Prakrit has been included. Two very able candidates that merited consideration were Ananda Coomaraswamy's translation of Milinda, and Nagnajita's treatise on structural aesthetics. Coomaraswamy's rendering of the concept of samvega is erudite; but the original is difficult to extricate from the translator's comments. On the other hand, Nagnajita's treatise on painting, which has so miraculously survived translation from Pali to Chinese to German to English would have been quite a valuable addition to this volume. However, the difficulty comes from the fact that not even one historian of ancient Indian poetics/aesthetics takes it into cognisance. In our collective amnesia it still exists at the level of fantasy! I decided to go by consensus. Except for Rupa Goswami, no other Sanskrit critic of the post-Abhināva period is included here. Though Abhinavagupta completed his life-mission by the first quarter of the eleventh century, the tradition of Sanskrit poetics continued till the middle of the seventeenth century. Jagannatha was, probably, the last important theorist in that tradition. However, the post-Abhinava theory was an abstract exercise with little reference to any contemporary living literature in modern Indian languages and not in Sanskrit. Rupa Goswami deserved inclusion in this volume, because he alone among the post-Abhinava critics tried to 'modernise' Sanskrit poetics by conceptualising Bhakti as a rasa. Perhaps, Madhusudan Saraswati is as important; however, having included Rupa Goswami, it was felt that the inclusion of Madhusudan Saraswati would have been superfluous here.

When one thinks of literary criticism in medieval India, one experiences the difficulty caused by a relative absence of theoretical documents. What the medieval poets created was a fresh and powerful set of conventions, styles and metres; but they do not indicate that they felt the need to articulate the literary and theoretical premises guiding these styles, metres and conventions. Several passages from Jnanadeva's Bhavarthadipika are included to exemplify the manner in which the orientation of creative literature was shifting during the medieval centuries. I am happy that an excerpt from Amir Khusrau and three passages from Badaoni's literary history could be included here. However, it was not possible to include examples of the work of Hemachandra, the thirteenth century lexicographer and bilingual critic, for want of a suitable English translation. The availability of translations has in fact been one of the major limiting factors of this anthology.

Many texts included are translations from Sanskrit, Persian, Hindi, Marathi and Gujarati. Translations always have a way of misbehaving. They may say more than the original, or even less than the original; but they rarely say exactly what the original says. The difficulty is greater with English translations of ancient and medieval Indian texts, for they have a long and entrenched habit of being obscure and unreadable. I have retained most of the translations used here in their exact form, since they are done by eminent scholars. And, in a form of literature where ideas are more important than the way in which they are presented, it is preferable to have 'faithful' translations even if they are not charming. Yet, occasionally, I have touched up the translated versions so that they do not become entirely unintelligible.

In our times, Indian literary criticism seems to have been facing a profound crisis of identity. Philosophically speaking, this crisis originates in the uncertainty of perspective about basic aesthetic premises: should they be 'logical' and 'universal', or should they be 'native' and 'relevant'? These questions cannot be answered with any degree of certitude in the context of a multi-ethnic, post-colonial culture. Historically speaking, the crisis in criticism can be traced back to the beginning of the last millennium, to those pre-colonial centuries when Bhashas were emerging as languages of literary expression. In those new languages, and in literature written in them, there was a richness of creative expression but practically no critical writing and articulation. The split was perhaps a matter of a conscious cultural decision by the heterogeneous community of writers. There is no evidence that the decline of literary criticism was ever perceived as a crisis in any of the Bhashas during the pre-colonial centuries. The awareness of an imaginary or a real crisis in criticism in perhaps a gift of the colonial experience. During the last hundred and fifty years there has been an unprecedented rise in the status of criticism as an essential aspect of literary culture.

The importance of literary criticism increases when literary education becomes institutionalised and literature becomes a 'subject' in schools and universities. A natural consequence of this shift is the increase in importation of critical concepts, tools and perspectives. Another consequence is the spread of revivalist tendencies. At the time of inception of colonial education in India during the early nineteenth century, the debate between the Orientalists and the Anglicists occupied the centre-stage of the elite culture in India. The same debate, in infinite new varieties, continued to control and guide critical and meta-critical thought in India throughout the twentieth century. Quite often the fact is completely overlooked that the two positions are non-starters in the context of modern Indian literature. The result is that we have critics who wish to modernise and westernise criticism, as well as critics who wish to purify and revive the mainstream native tradition of criticism. Considering that criticism, at its best, is produced for and by specific periods and styles in a literary tradition, this turning away, or turning back has not resulted in any significant contribution to the upkeep of contemporary creative literature in Indian languages. As such, literary history, practical criticism, theoretical formulation and the related philosophical speculation have remained inadequately developed in modern India. In any case, the development in these areas has not equaled, during any decade of the twentieth century, that in the field of creative writing.

Whether as a cause or a consequence of the above, contemporary Indians seem to be afflicted by a sense of amnesia in relation to literary history. Within the sphere of literary criticism, the affliction becomes more severe owing to the general unavailability of the older critical texts, and, in part, due to the alienation from the intellectual ethos within which these texts were generated. To a large extent, modern India has lost touch with the Sanskrit language. Similarly, there is not much awareness, outside the small circle of specialists, of the literary and critical texts produced in medieval India. And, though many of the texts continue to survive through oral transmission in the cultural transactions of sects founded upon those texts, there is little rapport between the classes involved in the sects and the class of intellectuals that has monopolised the contemporary literary culture.

The more debatable sections of this anthology are those in which the reader finds materials from the twentieth century. As we move closer to our own times, the difficulties in making the best choice increase. Should one include literary credos by creative writers? Should the views on art and literature of a philosopher like J. Krishnamurti be included? Which of the twenty or so languages used for creative expression should be given representation? Should one represent literary movements such as the Progressive Movement, Dalit literature, Nava-Kavya, Magical Realism, etc.? And finally, the most tricky of all questions, how much and whether any space should be given to modern Indian thinkers like Ashis Nandy, M.N. Srinivas, Sudhir Kakar and so on? In the face of all these questions, I have used my own judgement, inevitably with its subjective preferences, in selecting the more significant critics of this century: Sri Aurobindo, Tagore, B.S. Mardhekar, Krishna Rayan, Suresh Joshi, Bhalchandra Nemade, Gayatri Spivak and Aijaz Ahmad. There can be little doubt that each one of them has made a significant contribution to the modern critical discourse in India. Some more thinkers could have been included. In particular, I was keen on including a translation of Ram Vilas Sharma's writing on literary history. However, for entirely non-academic reasons this did not become possible. Similarly, I should have liked to reproduce one of Homi Bhabha's essays here. I tend to think that he has been among the post-independence Indian literary critics one highly original in his arguments. A translation of his work in a few major Indian languages may cause a deep impact on critical writings in those languages. Yet, Bhabha's intellectual engagement has been primarily with post-structural theory in the context of post-modernism rather than with Bhasha literature. However, at a future date, when diaspora literature has received a greater acceptance within Bhasha literature, an extended version of this anthology, or another anthology such as this one, needs to include Homi Bhabha's work as an important contribution to 'Indian' literary criticism. I also have a feeling that a quarter century from now if a similar anthology of criticism is to be compiled, it will be necessary to include in it the activist writings of Mahasweta Devi, Arundhati Roy and cultural essays by Sivram Karanth and Dilip Chitre. The overlap between literature and history is overwhelmingly transforming our perception of creativity.

It has been the attempt here to represent the work of every Indian critic who can be claimed to have founded a school of thought or a literary trend: Rasa (Bharatamuni), riti (Dandin), dhvani (Anandavardhana), vakrokti (Kuntaka). Abhinavagupta is included as a great philosopher with an original interpretation of the rasa theory. Jnanesvara was the founder of the Marathi tradition of poetry, and an able spokesman for bhakti poetics. Rupa Goswami in Sanskrit and Keshavadasa in Hindi continue his work, but with significantly differing emphasis. Al Badaoni represents the movement towards literary historiography in Persian. Besides, his text should show the reader that, contrary to the generally held assumption, literary history is not entirely of Western origin. Sri Aurobindo represents the most idealistic in Indian Romanticism. Tagore stands as a colossus among modern Indian writers. Mardhekar is, probably, the first Indian critic to turn to the area of pure aesthetics. Aijaz Ahmad indicates the directions in which Marxism was and is put to use in Indian literary history and criticism. Nemade is the founder of the Nativism movement, and Suresh Joshi is perhaps the most remarkable among Indian Formalists. Gayatri Spivak is the chief exponent of subaltern gender-justice. All of them, together, should provide very exciting reading to Indian students of literary criticism.

The second part of this volume, entitled 'Interpretation', consists of celebrated comments on Indian criticism. Not all of them were written as essays in literary criticism. Sudhir Kakar's analysis of the psychology of bhakti, and B.K. Matilal's commentary on Bhartrhari belong to other discourses; but they are included in this volume as they illuminate some of the texts included in the first part of the volume. K. Krishnamoorthy, Ananda Coomaraswamy and

M. Hiriyanna have been the most significant interpreters of Sanskrit poetics during the twentieth century. Their commentaries should make a student's passage to Sanskrit poetics much less difficult. R.B. Patankars' provocative essay on modern Marathi aesthetics is included for two reasons. One, his contribution to the field of aesthetics in India is so significant that no anthology of this nature can overlook it; and two, his analysis of the situation in Marathi should be applicable with varying degrees to criticism in other Indian languages. However, the section on interpretation has been kept somewhat exclusive by bringing in it only the most essential and the most celebrated of commentaries. This is, of course, not to deny that a great wealth of comments on ancient and modern Indian criticism exists today, though it is not properly classified in anthologies and bibliographies so far.

October 2009 G.N. Devy

Part I

Theory

BHARATAMUNI

Tradition considers the *Nāṭyaśāstra* as an additional Veda, so important has it been in the history of Indian literary thought. A version of the *Nāṭyaśāstra* had been in existence before the third century; but by the third century, it had taken a definitive shape, as the references of later critics indicate. The authorship of *Nāṭyaśāstra* is ascribed to Bharatamuni. Our knowledge of him is so little that it is impossible to think of his literary philosophy in the context of his other probable works. It is not even certain whether or not he, the author of this great work, ever existed.

The *Nāṭyaśāstra* is a compendium of performed arts: drama, music, dance. It presents in a great wealth of detail descriptions of the prevalent modes of these art performances; and the extraordinary precision with which the multiple facets of these arts have been defined and analysed is indicative of the sophistication of the art practices as well as art-criticism of Bharata's age. The *Nāṭyaśāstra* was used through the fifteen hundred years of Sanskrit literary thought as the bedrock of literary theory. Whether it was Abhinavagupta, Mammata, or Viśwanath, discussing poetry and literature during the subsequent centuries, they inevitably turned to Bharata's formulations as the polar star of Indian aesthetics.

To many revivalistic Indian critics during the last two hundred years, Bharata has been the maker of the *rasa* theory. While there is no denying that his fascinating insight in the psychology of aesthetic reception was a phenomenal triumph of intellect, it is necessary to remind ourselves that the *Nāṭyaśāstra* is not devoted solely to the exposition of *rasa* theory. That is but a fragment of the entire compendium. It is also necessary to remember that the intervening centuries have altered both the concept of *rasa* (as in *bhaktirasa* during the middle ages) as well as the philosophic context within which it was originally couched. Hence, any easy revival may be impracticable.

There are many renderings of the *Nāṭyaśāstra* or parts of it in modern Indian languages, translation of concepts and terminology being easier in these languages. However, there is no satisfactory rendering of it in English. It must be added, immediately, that Monomohan Ghosh's rendering, which is its only available translation in English, has generally been praised by modern Sanskrit scholars. But it does not make easy reading for the non-Sanskritists. A quarter-century ago, G.K. Bhatt produced a *Bharata-Natya-Manjiri* (1975). It is a digest of the great work, and is aimed at the beginner, probably the undergraduate students of Sanskrit poetics. However, it is built upon Monomohan Ghosh's translation, and is slightly less archaic. Excerpts from it are used here, with occasional syntactic modifications. The materials used are the English sections from pages 11–16, 75–107, 153–154 & 265–268 of the *Bharata Natya Manjiri* (1975, Bhandarkar Institute, Pune.)

On *Nāṭya* and *Rasa*: Aesthetics of Dramatic Experience

.... The *nāṭya* (in fact) is depiction and communication pertaining to the emotions of the entire triple world:

Occasionally piety, occasionally sport, occasionally wealth, occasionally peace of mind, occasionally laughter, occasionally fighting, occasionally sexual passion, occasionally slaughter;

the pious behaviour of those who practise religion, the passion of those who indulge in sexual pleasure, the repression of those who go by a wicked path, the act of self-restraint of those who are disciplined;

creating boldness among those who are impotent, enthusiasm among those who consider themselves brave, comprehension among those who lack understanding, as also wisdom among the learned;

graceful pleasures for those who wield power, steadiness and comfort for such as are afflicted with pain and misery, the ways of earning wealth for those who live by money, courage for those whose mind is despondent;

rich with different kinds of emotions, built on the stuff of many stages and situations (*avasthā*) and imitating the conduct of the world: that is what this *nāṭya* is, which I have produced.

Based on the actions of men, high, middling and low, this *nāṭya* will produce wholesome instruction, create courage, pastime, entertainment and pleasure.

This *nāṭya* will be instrumental in producing restfulness, at the proper time, for such as are afflicted with misery, fatigue and sorrow and for poor wretches (*tapasvin*).

It will conduce to piety, glory, healthy life; it will be beneficial, promote intellectual growth. The *nāṭya*, in brief, will be the instrument of instruction for the world.

There is hardly any knowledge, any artist's craft, any lore, any fine art, any design, in which art, lore and emotions are interconnected, any activity, that will not be seen in this *nāṭya*.

So, you should not entertain any sense of resentment towards the gods. The *nāṭya*, I assure you, will be an imitative presentation of all the Seven Islands.

The *nāṭya* should be understood to be an indicator of happenings in the life of gods, demons, kings, family men and sages who have spiritual knowledge.

In fact the nature and behaviour (*svabhāva*) of the world, intimately connected with happiness and misery, as rendered by physical and other forms of acting, is to be called *nāṭya*.

The eight rhetorical Sentiments (*Rasas*) recognised in drama and dramatic representation are named as follows: the Erotic, Comic, Pathetic, Furious, Heroic, Terrible, Odious, Marvellous.

The high-souled Druhina (*Brahmā*) proclaimed these eight rhetorical sentiments.

I shall now mention the emotional states (*Bhāva*) as arising from the abiding (*Sthāyin*), the transient (*Sancāri or Vyabhicāri*) and the psycho-physical conditions (*Sāttvīka*) of the mind.

The abiding mental conditions (*Sthāyibhāva*) are mentioned as follows: love, laughter, sorrow, anger, energy, fear, disgust and astonishment.

Despondency, sinking or weakness (*glāni*), apprehension, jealousy or envy (*asūyā*), intoxication or pride (*mada*), fatigue, indolence, depression (*dainya*), anxiety, infatuation or distraction (*moha*), recollection, steadiness or courage (*dhṛti*), shame, impulsiveness or inconstancy (*capalatā*), exhilaration or joy (*harṣa*), agitation or impetuousness (*āvega*), stupor or inactivity (*jaḍatā*), conceit, despair (*viṣāda*), eagerness or impatience (*autsukya*), sleep, epilepsy (*apasmāra*), dreaming (*suptam*), awakening inner emotion or dissimulation (*avahittha*), menace, ferocity or cruelty (*ugratā*), thoughtfulness (*mati*), disease or sickness, madness or insanity (*unmāda*), death, fright (*trāsa*), wavering or hesitation (*vitarka*): these thirtythree emotional states are enumerated by their names (as transient mental states).

Paralysis (*stambha*), perspiration, horripilation, voice-breaking, tremor, change of colour (*vaivarṇya*), tears, complete loss of consciousness or fainting (*pralaya*): these eight are spoken as *sāttvika* or psycho-physical conditions.

Four kinds of *Abhinaya* or histrionic representations are recognised in *nāṭya*: they are: physical gestures, expressions and movements (*āṅgika*); voice-modulation in delivery of dramatic speeches (*vācika*); costume and make-up (*āhārya*) as also props and drapery; and *sāttvika* conveyed by physical reactions of inner emotional states.

The *Dharmi*, or the mode of dramatic representation, is recognised as twofold: *Lok-dharmi*, following the practice of peoples, or realistic, and *Nāṭya-dharmi*, following theatrical modes, or conventional, symbolic.

The four styles in which dramatic representation is established are: *Bhārati* or Verbal; *Sāttvatī* or Grand; *Kaiśikī* or Graceful; and *Ārabhatī* or Energetic.

The success of dramatic representation is twofold: heavenly and human.

The musical notes like *ṣaḍja* etc., are seven and belong to two groups: produced from the human voice (*śārīra*, literally, from the body) and from musical instruments like *vīṇā* (*vaiṇa*).

The musical instruments (*ātodya*) are of four kinds. Their characters are: stringed (*tata*), covered (*avanaddha*), solid (*ghana*) and with holes (*suṣira*). *Tata* is known to be connected with the stringed lyre; *Avanaddha* is connected with drum; *Ghana* is cymbal or gong; and *Suṣira* is flute.

The songs pertaining to the Dhruvās sung in the course of dramatic representation are of five kinds: songs to indicate entering (*praveśa*), unexpected or interposed happening (*ākṣepa*), leaving (*niṣkrāma*), propitiating or pleasing (*prāsādika*), filling the gap (*āntara*).

The theatre is defined as square-shaped, oblong and triangular.

* * *

[Tr.n.: The term *rasa* has a twofold significance: It means the 'aesthetic content' of literary art and also 'aesthetic relish' which the reader-spectator enjoys.]

... we shall first of all explain the rhetorical sentiments (*Rasas*). No literary import can ever proceed without rhetorical sentiment and aesthetic relish. Now, *Rasas* arise from a proper combination of the stimulants (*vibhāva*), the physical consequents (*anubhāva*), and the transient emotional states (*vyabhicāri bhāva*).

What is the illustrative case? There we say: Just as by a proper combination of different spicy foodstuffs (*vyānjana*), leafy vegetables (*ausadhi*) and other articles of food (*dravya*), there is a flavour and taste (*rasa*) produced, in the same way when different emotional states come together, aesthetic flavour and relish are produced. Just as again, on account of such articles of food as molasses, and spicy and vegetable-stuff, the six (food) flavours and tastes are produced, in the same way when various emotional states reach the abiding mental conditions, the latter attain the quality of rhetorical sentiment, or become aesthetically relishable.

Now, one may ask: what is this thing that you call 'rasa'? We say: it is so called because it is capable of being tasted or relished. How is *rasa* tasted? Just as people in a contented state of mind (*sumanasah*), eating the food prepared well (*samskṛta*) with various spicy things taste the (*various*) flavours (enjoy the various tastes) and obtain delight and satisfaction (*harṣādin*), in the same manner spectators, in the right (receptive) frame of mind (*sumanasah*), taste the permanent mental conditions, suggested (*vyānjita*) by the representation (*abhinaya*) of various emotional states, the *abhinaya* carried out by speech-delivery (*vāc*), physical gestures and movements (*anga*), and by the physical acting of physical impacts (*sattva*), and obtain pleasure and satisfaction. It is for this reason that they have been explained as *nāṭya-rasa*: aesthetic contents and their relish arising from dramatic representation.

In this context there are two traditional couplets:

> Just as connoisseurs of cooked rice or food (*bhakta*), when they eat it as prepared with many articles of food and with many different spicy things enjoy the flavour and taste,
>
> in like manner, the wise (spectators) taste and enjoy in their mind the permanent mental conditions rendered through [lit. well-connected with] the acting of emotional states (*bhāvābhinaya*).

Inter-relation of Bhāva and Rasa

One may ask: Are the emotional states turned out from the rhetorical sentiments, or is it that the sentiments are turned out of the emotional states? Some opine that they arise from mutual contact. But this is not so. Why? Because, it is a matter of actual perception that the rhetorical sentiments are turned out of the emotional states, and not that emotional states are turned out of the sentiments.

There are traditional couplets about this:

> The emotional states are so known by the designers of dramatic art because they (the *bhāvas*) bring to the spectators (*imān*) an emotional awareness (*bhāvayanti*) of the sentiments as connected with various modes of acting or dramatic representation.
>
> Just as, by many articles of food (*dravya*) of various kinds, the spicy foodstuff (*vyañjana*) like vegetables, meat, fish is brought to a distinct flavour (*bhāvayate*), in the same way, the emotional states bring the sentiments to the level of actual experience (*bhāvayanti*) when helped by different kinds of acting or histrionic representation (*abhinaya*).

There can hardly be the experience of sentiment without the previous presentation of an emotional state; nor can there be an emotional state which does not lead to the experience of a sentiment. During the process of histrionic representation the two (*bhāva* and *rasa*) accomplish their status and function by dual interaction.

As the combination of spicy foodstuffs and vegetables lends the cooked food a distinct relishable taste (*svāduta*), in the same way the emotional states and sentiments lead each to the distinct level of an experience.

As from a seed a tree grows, and from the tree flower and fruit, so all the sentiments stand as the root; the emotional states have their settled position for the sake of (*tebhyāh*: i.e. for the purpose of manifesting) the sentiments.

Now we will expound the origin, colours, (presiding deities) and illustrations of these Rhetorical Sentiments. The sources of origin of these (Sentiments) are the four basic sentiments: these are as follows: the Erotic, the Furious, the Heroic and the Odious.

The Comic Sentiment becomes possible from the Erotic, and the Pathetic from the Furious; the origin of the Marvellous is from the Heroic, and of the Terrible from the Odious.

A mimicry or imitation of the Erotic is fittingly (*tu*) described as the Sentiment of Laughter. And the consequence of the Furious is to be known as the Pathetic Sentiment.

In the same way the consequence of the Heroic is properly described as the Marvellous. And the presentation of the Odious is to be known likewise as the Terrible.

Now the colours:

The Erotic Sentiment is light-green (*śyāma*); the Comic is described as white (*sita*); Pathetic is grey (*kapota*) and the Fearful is described as red (*rakta*). The Heroic is to be known as yellow-red (*gaura*); the Terrible as black; the Odious on the contrary is blue (*rāla*) and the Marvellous is yellow.

Now the Deities:

The Erotic (Sentiment) has Viṣṇu as its presiding deity; the deity of the Comic is Pramatha; the deity of the Furious is Rudra; the Pathetic has Yama as its deity. The deity of the Odious is Mahakāla; the Terrible has Kāla as the god; the Heroic, the god Mahendra; the Marvellous has Brahma as its deity.

* * *

Bhāva

We shall now explain the emotional states (*Bhāvas*):

One may ask here: why are the *bhāvas* so called? Are they so called because they exist, denote existence of things (*bhavanti*), or because they bring about the existence of something (*bhavayanti*)? We reply: The *bhāvas* bring about poetic contents (*kāvyārtha*) through words, physical gestures and movements and psycho-physical representations; hence, the name *bhāvas*.

'*Bhu*' is a root denoting instrumentation or causation (*kāraṇa*); it follows that *bhāvita*, caused to be made, brought about, *vasita*, made to live, *kṛta*, caused to be made or produced, are synonyms. Such expression as the following is quite well-known even among common folk: 'Oh, all this is *bhāvita* (made to possess, infused or pervaded) by this fragrance or juicy taste!' The meaning in such expressions is that of 'pervading'.

About this there are some traditional verses:

(1) The content which is brought forth by the stimulants (*vibhāva*) becomes a matter of awareness (*gamyate*) to the spectators by the manifestation of the consequents (physical impacts produced, *anubhāva*) and by the concentrated acting modes (*sattva-abhinava*) of words and physical gestures: such content is given the name *bhāva* or emotional state.

(2) The *bhāva* is so called as it brings about (reveals, *bhāvayan*) the inner idea of the poet and makes it pervade (*bhāvayan*) the mind of the spectator through the representation of words, physical gestures, colour or emotional expression of the face, and through the acting (*abhinaya*) which is the result of complete concentration and absorption (*sattva*).

* * *

Vibhāva

Now, why the term *Vibhāva*? This is answered (as follows): *Vibhāva* has the meaning of distinct, specific knowledge. *Vibhāva, kāraṇa* (cause), *nimitta* (instrument), *hetū* (reason) are synonyms. As words, physical gestures and the psycho-physical acting connected with the representation of stable and transitory mental states are specifically determined by this (*vibhāvyante*), it is therefore called *Vibhāva*: Determinant or Stimulant. So that, *vibhāvita* has the same meaning as *vijnāta* (clearly known, determined).

Here, there is a verse:

As many matters based on verbal and physical acting are determined by this for the actor, and as many matters arising through the verbal and physical acting are distinctly comprehended by the spectator, this causative, stimulating or determining factor is given the name *Vibhāva*.

* * *

Anubhāva

Now, wherefore the name *Anubhāva*? The reply is: by it the particular acting rendered through words, physical gestures and *sattva* is made to be felt (*anu-bhāvyate*) as an after-effect (*anu*) of the impact of the emotional stimulant.

There is a verse about this:

> Since the emotional content of art (*artha*) is made to be felt by the particular acting through words and physical gestures, the term *anubhāva* (consequents or physical reactions) is therefore used; it is connected with the flourish of hand-gestures (*sakha*) as well as the gestures of the major and minor limbs of the body.

[Tr. note: *sakha* is a technical term of *āṇgika abhinaya*: it denotes the flourish of hand-gestures ... which an actor makes before reciting a particular dramatic speech.]

* * *

Emotional States and *Rasa*:

The emotional States (*bhāvas*) are explained in this manner as connected with Determinants or Stimulants (*vibhāva*) and Consequents (*anubhāva*). These emotional states achieve their existence only thus. Therefore we shall explain the characteristics and examples of these emotional states connected with Determinants and Consequents.

In this connection the *Vibhāva* and the *Anubhāva* are quite familiar among the common people. Besides, as they closely follow human nature their characteristics are not defined; and this is for avoiding verbal prolixity.

There is however a verse in this connection:

> The wise should know that the *Vibhāva* and the *Anubhāva* are such matters in the art of acting as are actually created (*sam-siddha*) by human nature and as closely follow the ways of human nature and worldly conduct (*lokatraya*).

Now in the matter of emotional states, the Stable or Permanent mental states (*sthāyinah*) are eight and the Transitory states (*vyabhicārinah*) are thirtytwo. There is a further separate group of eight psycho-physical states (*sāttvikah*). These fortynine emotional states should thus be recognised as the casual factors for the artistic revelation (*abhivyakti*) of the poetic content (*kriya-rasa*: its charm and relish). From these arise the *rasas* by (i.e. when the presentation acquires) the quality of universality.

The verse in this connection is:

> The emotional state pertaining to the art-content (*artha*) which evokes a hearty communion is the source of *rasa*; by it the body is pervaded as dry wood is enveloped by fire.

A question is asked in this connection: If the *rasas* are turned out by the fortynine emotional states which are connected with the content of poetic compositions and which are manifested or suggestively conveyed (*vyānjita*) through the Stimulants and Consequents, and by the fact of the presentation acquiring the quality of universality, how is it that the Permanent mental states (*sthāyinah bhāvah*) alone are said to obtain the status of *Rasa* (aesthetic charm and relish)? This is to be said in reply: Just as some particular human beings, though they have common characteristics, similar hands, feet, bellies and bodies, and major and minor limbs common with everyone else, acquire the status of king on account of their excellence (*vilakṣaṇatva*) of birth or family, moral character, learning and skill in arts (*karma*) and crafts (*śilpa*), while there, among the human beings, others possessed of limited intellect become attendants of those very beings who attain kingship: in a similar manner the Determinants, Consequents and the Transitory states remain under the wing of the Permanent mental states. Being the shelter of many mental states, the Permanent mental states appear as masters. Like the men who become subordinate (*guṇabhuta*) to the human being who occupies the position of a master commanding them (*tadvatsthāniya-puruṣa*) the other emotional states take the shelter of the Permanent states by being subordinate to them (*guṇataya*) and on account of their (i.e., of the *Sthāyibhāvas*) excellence (*guṇataya*). The Permanent states attain the status of *Rasa*. The Transitory emotional states become their retinue.

One may ask: Is there any illustrative example? Yes. Just as the Lord of men, although surrounded by a retinue of many men, alone gets the name (king), and no one else however great he may be, in a similar manner the Permanent mental state surrounded by Stimulants, Consequents and Transitory states gets the name of *Rasa*.

There is a verse in this connection:

> Just as the king is great among men and the preceptor among the pupils, likewise among all emotional states, in the context of art (*iha*), the Permanent mental state is decidedly (*hi*) great.

Vyabhicārī-bhāvas

We will now explain the transient emotional states. One may ask here: wherefore are they called *vyabhicārīns*? It may be replied: *vi* and *abha* are two prepositions;

car is a root employed in the sense of movement or motion. The *vyabhicārīns* are so called because they (the transient emotional states) move (*caranti*) prominently towards (*abhi*: *abhimukhyena*) creating the poetic sentiments in a variety of ways (*vi*: *vividham*). Equipped with the acting based on speech, body and concentrated mind, these lead or carry the spectator, in actual dramatic performance, to the poetic sentiments; hence they are called *vyabhicārīns*.

Here one may ask: how do they carry him? The reply is: this is a proven matter in the world. Just as when people say: 'The Sun carries this day or the constellation of stars', it is not meant by that statement that these are carried on arms or shoulders. However, this is a well-known saying among the people of the world. Just as the Sun is supposed to carry the constellation of stars or the day, in the same way these *Vyabhicārīns* should be understood to carry the sentiments and lead the spectators to them.

Sāttvika bhāvas

Here one may ask: are these states called *Sāttvika*, because others (like *Vibhāva, Anubhāva, Vyabhīcārī*) are represented on the stage without *sattva*? The reply is as follows:

In the context of our discussion *sattva* is something that originates in the mind. It is so called on account of the equipoised state of mind. When the mind attains perfect concentration *sattva* is produced. Now, whatever its nature, manifesting itself as horripilation, tears, loss of colour and the like, according to the association with a particular emotional state, that cannot be represented by one whose mind is distracted. And *sattva* is desired for *nāṭya* as the latter imitates human nature.

Any example to illustrate this? Here the emotional states produced by the experience of happiness and misery are set in accordance with the theatrical conventions; they should be so rendered with pure *sattva* as to be identical with emotional states in real-life experience. Now sorrow or misery is in the main weeping; how could it be acted on the stage by one who is not sorrowful, and happiness which is mainly joy be acted by one who is not happy? This, in fact, is the actor's (*tasya*) *sattva*, engrossment or concentration of mind, that, whether he be really sorrowful or happy, he should be in a position to show tears and horripilation. Having regard to this aspect of stage presentation the emotional states are expounded as *sāttvika bhāvas*.

These *sāttvika bhāvas*, which are substantially connected with different kinds of histrionic representation, are all to be included (lit., understood) in these poetic sentiments by the producers of plays. A poetic composition cannot ever be supposed to arise out of one sentiment only. Whether it is an Emotional State, a Sentiment, Dramatic Style or Local Usage (*pravṛtti*): when many of these are assembled together, the one which is represented in many ways should be considered as the dominating sentiment, the rest as transitory states.

... Those emotional states should be regarded as Transitory (*sancārībhāvah*) which move pointedly illuminating the dominating sentiment; they have reached stability (in the sentiment).

The *Bhāva* is to be presented through the single character of *Dhurta* or *Vita* and is to comprise his various conditions. The wise should always construct the *Bhana* as depicting varied activities but having only one act.

The entire character of *Bhana* has been explained by me as it has come down by tradition (*agama*).

Now, O Brahmins, I will state in due order the whole character of *Vithi.*

Vithi:

The *Vithi* should have one act; it has the character of all the sentiments and it comprises thirteen aspects (lit., limbs); it is to be acted by one or two characters; it may include three kinds of dramatic *prakṛti*, high, middling and low.

The thirteen limbs of the *Vithi* are stated as follows: *uddhatyaka, avalagita, avaspandita, nali, asat-pralāpa, vāk-keli, prapanca, mṛdava, adhibala, chala, trigata, vyahara, ganḍa.*

I have spoken about the *Vithi.* I will now explain the characteristics of these thirteen aspects.

When dramatic characters (lit., men) connect words, uttered out of due respect but not understood in their correct meaning, with other words not intended by the original speaker that is called *Uddhatyaka*: Thrust interpretation.

Something connected with another context serves to accomplish some other result, that is to be known as *Avalagita*: Transferred connection by the designers of drama.

When a certain matter (*artha*) which has been stated (*ākṣipta*) from which good or evil may arise unintentionally, is skilfully interpreted to give another meaning, that will be *Avaspandita:* Ominous suggestion.

When a riddle-like, enigmatic reply is followed by laughter, that is to be known as *Nalika* (or *Nali*: Riddle and laughter).

That is *Asat-pralāpa* (incoherent chatter) where the statement or question and the reply are both inconsistent, where the statement made by a learned man in the presence of fools, although beneficial, is not accepted.

In this representation (of *Vithi*), the *Vikheli* (Sportive speech, Repartee) is a single or twofold reply.

A statement which is untrue but which looks like mutual praise of two, which is intended in the interest of one of the two and which evokes laughter, will be *Prapanca:* Comic exposure.

* * *

Model Spectator

A person who can watch the dramatic performance with all his senses undistracted, is pure and honest, is expert in judging the pros and cons, who can ignore a fault, and lovingly appreciate merit is to be regarded as a spectator in a dramatic performance.

All those qualities can never be properly expected in every single spectator.

Since the topics of knowledge are unlimited, from among the mixed crowd in the assembly of spectators, whatever particular craft, costume, deed or action a person is familiar with, that, with reference to his own activity, he should try to witness and judge.

Men have different characters and natures. The drama is created in (i.e., on the basis of) human character as belonging to old and child-like men and women, and of high, low and middling status.

Young men derive satisfaction in the representation of love, the learned in things based on some religious or philosophical principle, those intent on money, in wealth, and the passionless, in topics concerning spiritual salvation.

Brave men delight always in personal combat and armed fight (*ahava*) and thus in the representation of Heroic and Terrible sentiments; and the aged people in religious stories and *purāṇas.*

It is not possible for the low people to understand the actions and behaviour of exalted persons. The wise are always pleased with (the representation of) all matters of principle. Children, untutored men (*murkha*) and women are always pleased with things evoking laughter and with costumes, make-up and scenery (*nepathya*).

One who experiences delight (lit., satisfaction; *tuṣṭi*) when he sees the delightful, experiences sorrow when pathetic things are presented (śoke), anger in the presentation of anger, fear in fear, such a person is to be known as the ideal (lit., most superior) spectator. Thus, a person who is able to enter in the particular imitation (*anukaraṇa*, i.e., dramatic representation) of an emotional state, and is endowed with these qualities, is to be known as a 'spectator' of that particular presentation.

In the stage performance of the ten types of drama, the spectators are to be recognised in this manner.

Bharatamuni, from the Nāṭyaśāstra

translated by G.K. Bhatt

THOLKĀPPIYAR

Tholkāppiyar, conventionally considered the author of the first Tamil grammar, is more a name used for historiographical convenience rather than the name of a person. The historical truth as well as the cultural importance of this personage are comparable to that of Vyasa in the tradition of Sanskrit literature. It is the work, *Tholkāppiyam*, which has given its supposed author his name, Tholkāppiyar. One modern commentator, S. Ilakkuvanār, likes to fix the date of its composition as being somewhere between the sixth century B.C. to the tenth century B.C. On the other hand, Kamil Zvelebil, another sympathetic commentator, likes to think of the text of the *Tholkāppiyam* in terms of a gradually growing body, which took, after the initial nucleus was formed, about eight centuries to acquire the final shape. In Zvelebil's account, the sections dealing with prosody and diction belong to the fourth to the fifth century A.D. Probably, the latter account seems closer to the truth of the matter, for there are distinct echoes of the *rasa* theory of Bharata, together with the description of a *sahṛdaya rasika*, in the *Tholkāppiyam*. What is important, of course, is not the comparative historical placement of it, but its place in the tradition of Tamil poetic literature and the Dravidian poetic sensibility. Unfortunately, it has not been available to students of literature outside Tāmilnādu: the translations that have been attempted so far are either incomplete or inadequate. In this respect too, *Tholkāppiyam* vies with the *Nāṭyaśāstra*.

The main bulk of the *Tholkāppiyam* is concerning the descriptive linguistics of Tamil. The descriptive apparatus appears to be far too sophisticated to be neglected by any modern linguist. A small, but by no means insignificant, part of it is devoted to the discussion of styles, metres, diction, and poetic sentiments. Much of these chapters involve meticulous cataloguing of themes, locales, conventions and symbols. Leaving these aside, the most original contribution to the field of literary theory that the *Tholkāppiyam* makes is in developing the antithesis between the poetry dealing with the themes of the 'interior' and the poetry dealing with the themes of the external world. The corresponding terms used in the original are *Aham* and *Puṛam*. It is impossible to bring out the fascinating psychological insight and the intellectual sophistication displayed by the author of this theory, for want of a lucid English translation. However, the essay by A.K. Ramanujan included in the present volume, together with Kamil Zvelebil's *The Smile of Murugan: On Tamil Literature of South India,* (E.J. Brill, Leiden, 1973, pp. 131–154), will be found useful in understanding the intricacies of the founding text in Tamil poetics. It must be added immediately, however, that it is somewhat surprising that the *Tholkāppiyam* did not exert much influence on the prosody and diction of the three major languages that branched off from Tamil, namely, Kannada, Malayalam and Telugu. Yet, it is certain that it has a vital link with the *Nātyaśāstra;* perhaps, the two share a now missing common ancestor? At the present stage of our knowledge about India's literary past, one must inevitably stop at that question.

The translation used here is by S. Ilakkuvanār, from his *Tholkāppiyam in English with Critical Studies*, Kuṛaḷ Ṉeṛi Publishing House, Madurai, 1963.

Excerpts used are: *Ecca Iyal*, 397–409; *Ahaththiṇai Iyal*, 3–13 & 53–55; selections from *Puraththiṇai Iyal*; *Meyppāttu Iyal*, 249–259 & 275.

On Diction and Syntax

Words used in poetry are *Iyaṛcol, Thirisol, Thisaiccol* and *Vadasol.* Of them, the *Iyaṛcol* words are those which are used in conformity with the usage of Tamil and without change in their meanings. The *Thirisol* words are of two kinds which are synonyms and homonyms. *Thisaiccol* or the dialectal words are those which are spoken with their meanings unchanged in the twelve divisions of Tamil land where correct Tamil is in use. The words of Northern language, *Vadasol,* become fit to be used in Tamil when they adopt the Tamil phonetics discarding their northern ones. Even if they become deformed in usage to suit the Tamil phonetics, they are not excluded. The poets say that when those four kinds of words are used in construction of poetry, sonant may change into surd and vice versa, phoneme may be added or elided, and phoneme may be lengthened or shortened; these changes are inevitable. The scholars say that the syntax in poetry is of four kinds which are *Niral Niṛai, Suṇṇam, Adimaṛi* and *Moḻimaṟṟu.* Of them, *Niral Niṛai* is the mode in which the words stand in a group of verbs and nouns separately in such a way as to join the predicates or governing words to the subjects or the words governed in respective order. *Suṇṇam* is the mode in which two lines of eight *sir* (measured word) grammatically formed may split up and join in such a way as to express the proper meaning of poetry. *Adimari* is the mode in which the position of the lines may be altered without changing the place of the *sirs* (measured words) and the lines may exchange places. When knowing the meaning of the stanza it is not forbidden that the final *sir* of the last line of the stanza may be connected with the penultimate line of the stanza. The mode of *moḻimaṟṟu* is changing the position of words to bring out the correct meaning of the stanza and placing them before and after as need be.

... On examining the content of poetry, it is found, *Muthal, Karu* and *Uri* are the three which excel in order in the act of composing. Space and Time are said to be *Muthal* by scholars who know their nature. Forest World occupied by *Māyōn*, mountainous world occupied by *Seyon*, water-logged world occupied by *Veṇdhan*, sea-shore world occupied by *Varunan*, these are said to be *Mullai, Kuṛinji, Murutham* and *Neythal*, respectively. The rainy season and evening belong to *Mullai* and the cold season and midnight to *Kuṛinji*. The dewy season also belongs to *Kuṛinji*, say the scholars. The last hours of the night and the dawn belong to *Murutham* and the sunset to *Neythal*. The middle placed *thinai* is being thought of when the midday and summer occur jointly. The scholars say that the later part of snow-season also belongs to it. The scholars say that when two kinds of separation take place permanently it is suitable. The intermingling of *thinai* is not prevented. The intermingling of regions is not allowed — poets well versed in literature say so. Those other than *Uripporuḷ* may overlap.

... The poets say that the usage of poets which consists of imaginary usage and factual usage as found in day-to-day life will have *kali* and *paripādal* as the metre-forms (which are specially suitable for describing the love aspects). In the literature of five love-aspects belonging to *Aham* having people as objects, the name of any particular person finds no place. The mentioning of any particular person by name may take place in *Puṛam* only ....

... *Vetci* is the *Puṛam* of *Kuṛinji;* it has fourteen divisions of dreadful nature ... *Vañji* is the *Puṛam* of *Mullai*. It is aimed at marching in advance to frighten and conquer the king who is greedy to have lands of others ... *Ulināi* is the *Puṛam* of *Murutham*. They say that to besiege a well-guarded fort and to have it conquered, is the feature of the theme of *Ulināi* ... *Thumbai* is the *Puṛam* of *Neythal*. It is the greatness of a king who comes to fight having the object of exhibiting his might ... *Vāhai* is the *Puṛam* of *Pālai*. It is said to be one which is to improve one's own avocation, with great distinction without being a hindrance to others ... *Kānji* is the *Puṛam* of *Peruñthinai*. It is the ephemeral nature of the world in all phases of life... *Pādañ* is the *Puṛam* of *Kaikkiḷai*... .

They say that thirty-two concepts, evolved out of plays, may be calculated into sixteen. They may be calculated into eight also. They say laughter, weeping, despisedness, wonder, fear, fortitude, anger and delight are the eight *meyppādus*. They say that laughter has reproach, youth, foolishness and feigned ignorance — these four, as its source.

Weeping has inferiority, loss, suffering and poverty — these four, as its source. Despisedness has agedness, illness, pain and weakness — these four, as its source. Fear has the objects of fear, beasts, thieves and the king — these four, as its source. The much praised fortitude has education, fearlessness, fame and sacrifice — these four, as its source. Anger, born of hatred, has cutting the limbs, conspiracy, inflicting injury and speaking ill — these four, as its source. The delight freed from trouble, has enjoyment of wealth, knowledge, intercourse, and plays and games — these four, as its source.

It is difficult to understand the significance of *meyppādu* for the people other than those who have the capacity of understanding well by means of eyes and ears.

Tholkāppiyar, from the Tholkāppiyam
translated by S. Ilakkuvanār

BHARTṚHARI

The most impressive achievement of ancient Indian thinkers, perhaps, was in the field of linguistics. Pāṇini has already been universally recognised as a phenomenon in the history and development of linguistics. Following Pāṇini, there was a long and rich tradition of linguistics till the period of emergence of the modern Indian languages. In this post-Pāṇini tradition, probably the most memorable contribution was by Bhartṛhari. His opus, the *Vākyapadiya* is the earliest scientific work on syntax. Scientific rigour and precision are evident in his presentation of the concepts of *sphoṭa* and *dhvani* included here. The concept of *sphoṭa,* which forms the basis of Indian Semantics, was also to become the cornerstone of Śaṅkara's Vedantic philosophy, for he perceived the relationship between the visible and the invisible universe in terms of *sphoṭa.* On a comparable scale, the concept of *dhvani* was used by literary critics and poets. Anandavardhana's entire theory of poetry was based on Bhartṛhari's interpretation of the concept of meaning. Thus, Bhartṛhari's contribution to literary criticism, and to metaphysics which formed the context of the post-classical aesthetics, can hardly be overstated.

His work has attracted so much scholarly attention that the *Vākyapadiya* is high among the much translated Sanskrit works. In recent years, Western philosophy too has started taking interest in Bhartṛhari's linguistics as may be evidenced from B.K. Matilal's publication, *The Word & The World* (OUP, 1991). The selection presented here is from the translation of *Vākyapadiya* by K. Raghavan Pillai (Motilal Banarsidass, 1971). It may be necessary to note for those readers who may not be familiar with the ancient Indian style of discursive writing that all philosophical texts had a two-tier system of presentation. The main formulas were called *kārikās* or *sutras* and the elaboration on them or a subsequent commentary was called *vritti.* Included here are only the *kārikās* (44–132 from Canto I & II) without their *vrittis.*

On Syntax and Meaning

Grammarians consider that there are two 'word-entities' in functional words; one, i.e., the *sphoṭa,* is the cause of the production of words and the other, the speech-sound, is used in connection with meanings. Some, among the teachers of old, considered that there was a difference in essence between these two. Others on the other hand speak of the same undivided entity being thought various, through a difference in conceiving it. Just as the light which is in the fire-stick acts as the cause for further lights, similarly the Word (*Om*) which is in the mind is the cause of speech-sounds. The Word is examined in the mind, is then fixed to a specific meaning and then through the instrumentality of the speech-sounds produced through their causes. The Word is neither a 'previous' nor 'a subsequent', because it is the speech-sounds which are produced in sequence.

But the non-sequential is revealed as sequential as if it were divided. Just as a reflection formed elsewhere appears, due to the activities of the water, to partake of the movements of the water, similar is the relationship between the Word and the speech-sound. Just as in perceptual knowledge, there can be seen both itself, i.e., the act of perceiving, and the object of knowledge, the thing perceived, so in the Word there appears the meaning-element and the formal element.

The inner principle called 'speech' which exists egg-like, evolving into speech-activity, assumes sequence through its parts. Just as a shape which is a copy of another shape, after it has become the object of a unified perception having been first received by the senses as a complex-pattern of parts, is then painted in stages on the canvas, so likewise there are seen in the comprehension of speech. Just as the mind of the speaker first dwells on the words, and not on their parts when he wants to convey their meaning, similarly, the activity of the hearer first arises out of the words and not their parts in his attempt to understand their sense. When certain meanings are conveyed the forms which convey them, having thus become accessories to such meanings, and having their purpose thus fulfilled, they are not perceived as accessories to action, because they are uttered for the sake of another meaning. Just as light has two powers, namely, the power of being perceived and the power of causing perception of objects, similarly all words have these two distinct powers. Meaning is not understood from words which themselves have not become objects of the sense of hearing. Without being thus received, they do not express meaning by their mere existence. Therefore when the form of the uttered word is not clear, the question 'what did you say' is asked of the speaker. But the nature of the sense-faculties is not similarly grasped when an object has to be revealed by them. These two aspects of the word, analysed and comprehended separately, act without mutual opposition as causes of different effects. Just as the words *'vṛddhi'* and the like besides expressing their own form are also related to the sounds named by them ... so the word 'agni', besides being related to the word *'agni'* (meaning fire) is also related to that referred to by the word *'agni'*, namely the form *agni*. A word which is uttered in everyday use is never linked with grammatical operations. But its capacity to convey that other form, that is, its own form as the meaning, is not obstructed. The word which is pronounced in ordinary speech being secondary, since it is for the sake of the other, namely, the thing-meant, is not linked with grammatical operations; and hence we adopt the convention that the grammatical operations are attached to words which symbolise themselves. Whatever common attributes there exist in the object with which anything is compared and the thing which is compared to it, some attributes other than them also exist in the object to which the comparison is made. Whatever quality which is the cause of the excellence of an object is itself mentioned in the form of an object, its own excellence is caused by the qualities residing in it. When a word (like *'agni'* in the Sutra *agnerḍhak*) which has its own form as its meaning is pronounced for conveying its form, then from that word is discriminated another word (namely, the word *'agni'* which has 'fire' as its meaning). Before being connected to the thing it means, a name is capable of genitive and nominative constructions, because it has its own form as its meaning. The nominative is prescribed to a name because it is meaningful with its form as its meaning, and it is from the same meaning that the genitive construction in the form 'of it' arises. Some consider that in the Sutra '*svam rupam*' a name as a particular is meant; the universal attached to the particular undergoes grammatical operation. Others think that what is meant by the Sutra is a particular instance of the named, and that it is the class which is the name, and that in any given instance one finds only a particular, the understanding of which is brought about by the universal. Both among those who uphold the eternity theory of words, and those who hold that words are created, there are some who uphold its sameness in all instances of its occurrence. Again among the upholders of the doctrine of eternity and of the doctrine that words are created there are those who uphold the plurality of words, i.e., that every occurrence of apparently the same word is really the occurrence of a different word.

(The doctrine of an opponent school is stated regarding the comparative reality of letters, words and sentences): Even when the word is a different word, the identity of the letters is not impaired; and in the same way in different sentences the same word is observed. Therefore the word does not exist as more than its letters; nor is there a sentence existing as more than letters and the words. (The grammarian's doctrine is given): Just as there are no parts in letters, there are no letters in the word. Nor is there any reality in abstracting the word from the sentence. People follow customary usage and talk of 'words' and 'letters' though basing their theories on different views and on this question what is considered as primary by one school is taken as an opposite way by others. People talk of difference of diction as belonging to the utterance of the Word, which itself is of undivided time, but appears to follow the time-pattern of the speech-sounds, in accordance with the differences in the causes of its being perceived. With regard to the short, long and prolated vowels, since a speech-unit is essentially timeless, and therefore fundamentally different from the speech-sound which reveals it, it is the time of the primary sound which is metaphorically considered as belonging to the speech-unit. It is however after the word has been revealed by the primary sound that the modified sounds are presented to the mind as distinctions of diction, and hence *a fortiori* the self of the Word is not divided into parts by them.

There are three views among those who hold the theory that words are manifested: (1) the sounds act upon the sense-faculty; or (2) they act upon the word or, (3) they act upon both. The first theory would be analogous to the theory of sight-perception which held that only the sense faculty of sight is acted upon, namely, by attention and application of ointment. The second theory would be analogous to a theory of smell-perception which held that only the thing (for instance, the earth) is acted upon in order that its smell might be received. According to the third theory, where however, the eye effects the reception of a cognition, it is clear that both the object and the sense-faculty are acted upon by the light; and speech-sounds operate in the same form. Certain theorists maintain that reception of the sound takes place without any separation of it from the form of the Word (*sphoṭa*); others hold that the sound is not perceptible. According to yet others it is an independent manifesting agent. Just as a chapter or a single verse is apprehended as a unit by means of saying over its component parts in order, but of course the book is not defined at each component part, so likewise the form of a word is apprehended as a unity when the word is revealed by the sound through the agency of causal factors which are appropriate to the cognition of the word, but which are not themselves as such apprehended. Simultaneously with the last sound, the word is apprehended by the mind in which the seed has been sown by the physical sounds, and in which ripening of the speech has been brought about by the telling over of the sounds. As far as the non-existent forms, which a hearer considers as existing in the interval before the complete word has been pronounced, are concerned, this is merely incapacity on the part of the hearer; they are in fact only means to the apprehension of the complete word. There is the semblance of distinction in cognition; similarly the attributing of distinctions on words is always seen. The word appears to be produced in stages and cognition seems to be dependent on the cognised. Just as earlier numbers in a series should be apprehended for the apprehension of subsequent ones, although the latter are different from the former, so is the apprehension of parts in a unit of speech an aid to the apprehension of the whole.

When in reality revealing units in the syllable, word and sentence function independently of each other, they appear to function in combination, although they are entirely different. Just as looking from a distance or in the dark, one at first misunderstands an object, and later on understands it otherwise in its true nature, similarly during the manifestation of the sentence by its causes, namely, the smaller units like letters and words, the mind first functions as comprehending the component units as real units. Just as there is a fixed sequence in the stages of the transformation of milk into curds and the seed into the tree, similarly there is a fixed sequence in the series of the hearer's perception of the intervening words, phrases, etc. And when they are made up of real parts, the difference in form is really due to the sequence of their sounds. And where words, etc., are considered as not made up of real parts the fancying of parts is a means to the realisation of the total unit.

It is considered by some that the Word is a universal suggested by a number of individuals and these individual speech-sounds, according to them, constitute the sound-pattern of the Word. Just as light reveals objects, the speech-sounds produced by their causes become the cause of the immutable Word. If the Word is revealed like this, does it not mean that it is not eternal? The answer is in the negative: Being revealed is not established as invariably pertaining to non-eternal things. Universals which are eternal are also considered to be revealed by those in which they inhere. In life only concrete objects are found to have relation to place and the like (for instance, time). And even accepting the alternative — that difference in place, etc., applies also to those that are not concrete objects — there is no such difference between the speech-sound and the word it reveals.

Just as there exists an inevitable competence of the revealed and the revealer between a perceiving sense-organ and the things it perceives, so does it exist between the word and the speech-sounds. And it is seen that in the case of various smells and the like which are perceived by the same sense-organ, there is a separate causal factor for each substance. ... The object revealed partakes of the attributes of the reflecting medium. This is obvious in oil, water and the like. And surely, concrete objects of the type of mountains cannot have existence except as their reflections in stones, a mirror-surface and the like of incompatible size. Therefore the period of the speech-sounds and of their secondary variations in the form of diction is assigned to the syllable, word and sentence which are themselves without time-distinctions.

The definitions of *sphoṭa* and *dhvani* by another school are given:

The *sphoṭa* is that which is produced by the union and disunion of the speech-organs like the vocal cords. And *dhvanis* are sounds born of this *sphoṭa*. Whether the speech-sound is short or long, the measure of the word does not change. The subsequent sound, i.e., the modified speech-sound, which arises out of the primary speech-sounds is expanded or contracted in its form. Like light from a lamp, merely the speech sound undifferentiated as primary and modified is heard from a distance. But in the sound of a bell and the like the distinction is clearly noticed. The long and prolated sounds which are different from the short sounds are produced by the striking of the organs of speech. And the sounds which modify diction arise after the cessation of the movements of the organs. Another school holds that even before the vibrations of the speech-organs have subsided, other sounds are formed from the word as *sphoṭa* itself, as one flame from another.

Now regarding what constitutes the substance of speech: It is held by some that air, the atoms or consciousness become speech. There is an endless number of variant views in this matter. The air which is stirred by the speaker's effort following his desire to speak strikes the speech centres and produces speech. Even powerful objects are broken by air which possesses the attributes of speed and accumulation, blowing with the capacity to cause such breaking. The atoms, which unite and separate, transform themselves into shadows, light, and darkness and also into speech on account of their possessing all possible capacities, i.e., capacities to be transformed into all things. When their capacity is being revealed these atoms which are called speech, prompted by the effort of the speaker, collect together like clouds in the sky. Finally, regarding the consciousness theory: Again, the inner knower who exists in the subtle quintessential speech transforms himself into audible speech for the purpose of revealing his nature. It, taking the form of the mind and ripening in the fire of the stomach enters the life-breath, and it is then uttered. The breath which has become the substratum of the mental principle is suffused with the mind's attributes and manifested after it passes through the fire of the stomach. Breaking up its inherent knots, i.e., its continuous currents, the breath reveals the syllables through different and distinct speech-sounds and merges into those syllables themselves. Yet another view about sound ... Sound, though it is ever existing, is not experienced because it is too subtle. It is realised through the appropriate causal factors just as air is through fanning.

The view of yet another school is that the powers of speech resident in the breath and in the mind undergo transformation into speech at the centres of speech-production and assume the distinctions of revealed speech. The power which is based on words controls this universe. This universe which has a single Intelligence as its soul is perceived as manifold through the word as the eye. Since it is seen that distinctions between two things, for instance between a *ṣaḍja* and another musical note become clear when explained in words, therefore all manner of things are determined as being only understood through words. Those who are versed in the *Vedas* know that this Universe is the transformation of speech. It was out of the *Vedas* that this universe was first evolved. In this world the knowledge of the proper action entirely depends on speech. Even a boy has this knowledge of the proper action, having in him the accumulated experience of the past. That first movement of the organs of speech, the upward sending of the breath and its contact with the centres — these would not be possible but for verbal imagination in the child. In this world no comprehension is possible except as accompanied by speech. All knowledge shines as permeated by speech. If it is denied that the permanent stuff of knowledge is speech, then that light, namely knowledge, will not shine in the form of recollection. It is speech which makes recollection possible. It is speech which binds all branches of knowledge of arts and crafts. Everything, when it is produced, is classified through it. This speech exists within and outside all living beings. Consciousness can exist in all creatures only after it is preceded by speech. It is speech which prompts all mankind to activity. When it is gone, man, dumb, looks like a log of wood or a slab of stone. It is when the distinctions such as subject versus object obtain in the state of wakefulness that the agent functions in connection with an object. But when such distinctions do not obtain, in the state of sleep, speech itself remains in the form of an object.

Whether things are identified with the self, or with the Supreme, they become established in the form in which they are introduced by words. It is words which establish things. Even when the cause for verbal expression, i.e., an object, is entirely non-existent, descriptions of the forms of such a thing through words is found, as in the case of a circle made by a fire-brand. Further, speech which exists within the speaker as his self is said to be the great Bull, identity with which is desired. Therefore, attainment of faultless speech is the attainment of Brahman. He who knows the secret of its functioning enjoys the immortal Brahman.

Bhartṛhari, from the Vākyapadiya
translated by K. Raghavan Pillai

DAṆḌIN

Daṇḍin's *Kāvyādarśa* is considered to be one of the very earliest texts in literary theory. Edwin Gerow argues in his critique of Sanskrit poetics that Daṇḍin is the pioneer of Sanskrit literary theory. The claim is difficult to establish, but cannot be brushed aside lightly. Whatever the chronological eminence, *Kāvyādarśa* is certainly an illuminating text, mainly on account of its clarity of exposition of the idea of *Alaṅkāra.* Daṇḍin's text offers a minutely detailed catalogue of the linguistic virtues of poetry, giving closely discussed illustrations for each type and sub-type of *Alaṅkāra.* It is impossible in the space available here to indicate how exhaustive his treatment of the subject is. The main contribution of Daṇḍin is the concept of *mārga-rīti*, regional variations of poetic language, and the description of the *Gauḍa* and *Vaidarbha* varieties of literary diction. Another major contribution of his, which was later elaborated upon by Bhoja in the eleventh century, is the definition of epic poetry that Daṇḍin proposes. Sanskrit literature abounds in examples of epic and episodic poetry. Daṇḍin, therefore, did not have a single prescriptive idea of epic. Apart from his comments on the subject matter and the hero of epic, he also comments on the structural principles of the genre, a unique achievement for him. In the selections presented here, I have used the translation of *Kāvyādarśa* by Vavilla Venkateswara Sastrulu (Madras, 1952). While the first two passages have been retained in their original form, the third passage is a closely edited version of the original translation.

Sarga-bandha: Epic Poetry

A *Sarga-bandha* is a *Mahā-kāvya.* Its characteristics are told here. Its beginning (mouth) or preface is either a blessing or a dedication or an indication of the contents.

It has its source either in a story told in the *Itihāsas* or other good (true) material. It deals with the fruit (or goal) of the four kinds (*Dharma, Artha, Kāma* and

Moksha). It has a great and generous person as the hero. It is embellished with descriptions of cities, oceans, hills, the seasons, the moonrise, the sunrise, of sports in the garden and of sports in the waters, of drinking scenes, of festivals, of enjoyment (love), of separation (of lovers), of (their) marriage and their nuptials and birth of princes, likewise of consultation with the ministers, of sending messengers or ambassadors, of journeys (royal progress), of war and the Hero's victories; dealing with these at length and being full of *Rasa* and *Bhāva* (flavour and suggestion): with *sargas* (chapters) which are not very lengthy and which are well formed with verse measures pleasing to the ear; everywhere dealing with a variety of topics (in each case ending each chapter in a different metre). Such a poem being well-embellished will be pleasing to the world at large and will survive several epochs (*kalpas*).

A poem does not become unacceptable even when some of these parts are wanting, if the structure of the parts incorporated in the poem is pleasing to those who know how to judge.

At first describing the hero by his good qualities and by that very description despising his enemies; this method is naturally beautiful.

After describing the lineage, prowess and scholarship etc., of even the enemy, depiction of the excellences of the hero by his victory over such an enemy is in our opinion also pleasing.

* * *

(On Regional Styles in Poetry)

... literature, the great men say, is divisible into four classes — *Samskritam, Prākritam, Apabhramśa*, and *Miśra*. Samskritam is the name of the celestial language which has been used by the great sages; Prākritam is divided into many ways as *Tadbhava, Tatsama* and *Deśi*. They consider the language pertaining to the *Mahārāshtra* as the best *Prākritam*. In such language is the ocean of gem-like sayings, *Setubandha* and other works. Similar languages are Souraseni, Goudi, Lati and the rest. In discussions, these are treated as *Prākritam* itself. In poems, languages like the *Abhira* and the like are considered as *Apabhramśa*; but in the *Śāstras* (grammars) any language other than Samskritam is considered as Apabhramsical. *Sarga-bandha* and other such are *Samskritam*; *Skandha* and other such are *Prākritam*; *Asara* and other such are *Apabhramśa*; *Nāṭaka* and other such are *Miśrakam*. *Kathā* may be composed in all languages as well as in Samskrit; they say that the *Bṛhatkathā* which is in the *Bhuta* language is of wonderful merit. The twofold classification that *Prekṣārtham* and *Śrāvyam* is illustrated by *Lasya, Chalika* and *Śalya* and such like on the one hand and on the other hand by the rest. Manifold is the path of words. And their mutual distinctions are very fine; therefore these two alone, — the path of *Vidarbha* and the path of *Gouḍa* are here described, as they have radical differences. *Śleṣa* (compact), *pasada* (clarity), *samatā* (evenness), *mādhuryam* (sweetness), *sukumārata* (elegance), *artha-vyakti* (expressiveness), *udāratvam* (excellence), *Ojas* (vigour), *kānti* and *samādhi* (structure) — these ten characteristics are considered to belong to the *vidarbha* path. In the *Gouḍa* path, the opposite of these characteristics is often found.

* * *

(On *Alaṇkāra*)

They give the names of *alaṇkāras* to the characteristics which render *kāvyas* attractive. These characteristics are even today diversified anew; who then can treat of them exhaustively?

But the rudiments of these divergent characteristics have been indicated by the old masters. This our effort is merely to formulate those rudiments again.

Some *alaṇkāras* have already been mentioned by us for the purpose of distinguishing between the *mārgas* (schools). The entirety of the remaining *alaṇkāras* which are common to all the schools is now expounded.

The old masters have shown the following *alaṇkāras* (figures of speech): Realistic expression, simile, metaphor, light, repetition, objection, illustrative citation, differentiation, cause, terseness, hyperbole, conceit, reason, subtlety, minuteness, sequence, felicity, provoking sentiment, vigour, paraphrase, unison, sublimity, denial, paronomasia, speciality, equation, direct praise, concealed praise, conjunctive expression, exchanges, benediction, confusion and expressiveness.

Realistic expression, also called *jāti* or group description, is the first *alaṇkāra* and describes the actual forms of different conditions of objects ... it alone is supreme in the fields of sciences (*śāstras*), and it is desired even in literature (*kāvyas*).

Where any kind of similarity is felt in anything that *alaṇkāra* is called simile ... simile itself, where the difference is implicit, is called metaphor ... There are two classes of metaphors desired (by poets) which are known as metaphor stating similarity and metaphor stating contrast, because they indicate respectively the similarity and the contrast between the principal and the secondary objects ... If by remaining in one place, a word, indicating *jāti* (the genus), *kriyā* (action), *guṇa* (quality) or *dravya* (the subject matter), can help the entire sentence, then it is called *dīpakam* (light).

... The repetition in meaning, the repetition in word, the repetition in both, — these three *alaṇkāras* are desired in the place of *dīpakam*. *Ākṣepa* (or objection) is a statement of denial and according to the three divisions of time (past, present and future) it is divided three-fold; and again its variety is endless, if the difference in the objection is considered .... In desiring a certain object, the citation of another object which is capable of conveying the same meaning as the original object must be considered *arthāntara-nyāsa* or illustrative citation .... When the similarity between two objects has been suggested or expressed in words, a statement of the difference between them is called *vyatireka* or differentiation .... Where, after denying the generally accepted causes, another cause is stated, whether that cause is stated as natural or whether it is attributed, then that *alaṇkāra* is called *vibhāvana* or attributed cause. Having in mind a certain object, the statement about another object which is similar to it is because of its making for terse expression called 'terseness in expression' or *samāsokti* .... Expression transgressing the limits of usage about a particular thing is *atiśayokti* or hyperbole .... When the condition or action of an animate or inanimate object is in a particular manner and it is fancied by the poet in a different manner they call that figure of speech *Utprekṣā* or conceit. Reason (*hetū*) and subtlety and minuteness (*sukṣma* and *lesa*) constitute the best *alaṇkāras* of words; the *hetū* is twofold, *kāraka* and *jñāpaka* or causal reason and reason which helps to know .... Where the meaning is indicated by *ingita* or facial gesture and *ākāra* or the condition of the body then it is considered to be *sukṣma* or subtlety .... *Samkhyanam* or *Krama* or sequence is where the intended words follow in their proper order. It is also called *Yathāsamkhyām* .... *Preya* or felicity is felicitous expression and *Rasavant* (or provoking sentiment) where *Rasa* (sentiment) abounds; *Urjasvi* is where pride dominates or where vigour or excellence is appropriate. Without stating directly a particular meaning, for the accomplishment of that very meaning what is told in another manner is considered to be *Paryāyoktam* or paraphrase. When a person is about to commence a piece of work, he gets an additional ally for the accomplishment of that object by good fortune; that they say is *samahitam* or union. Wise men call that alaṇkāra *Udattam* or sublimity which expresses the pre-eminent greatness of a person either in the qualities of his heart or in his riches .... Where something is denied and another meaning is made clear, then it is *Apahnuti* or denial. *Sliṣtam* or paronomasia is defined as a group of words which have one form but many meanings .... When in the quality, genus, predicate etc., an alteration or variation is shown, that makes for the pointing out of its speciality and is known as *Viśeṣokti* or speciality .... That is considered *Tulyayogita* or equation where, for the sake of praising or blaming a thing, a statement is made making it equal with things possessing the particular quality pre-eminently .... Where opposed objects are mentioned together with a view to emphasise their specialities, then it is considered *Savirodha* or opposition. Where the praise of an object with which one is not concerned is made then it is *Aprastuta-Praśamsā* or indirect praise .... If there be praise in the form of despair, it is considered to be *Vyājastuti* or concealed praise; here virtues appear in the form of vices. Where a similar good or bad consequence is exhibited by connecting a thing with another object, then it is *Nidarśanam* or illustrative example. *Sahokti* is the statement conjunctively of the qualities and actions of things; where there is an exchange of things, that (figure of speech) is *Parivṛtti* or exchange. *Asih* or benediction is where the desired object is extolled .... Of the *alaṇkārasamsṛṣṭi* or confusion of *alaṇkāras* there are two modes to be seen: (1) where there is a relationship of part (*anga*) and whole (*angi*) between the *alaṇkāras* and (2) where there is no interdependence among the *alaṇkāras*.

Daṇḍin, from the Kāvyādarśa
translated by Vavilla Venkateswara Sastrulu

ANANDAVARDHANA

The *Dhvanyāloka* of Anandavardhana (8th Century A.D.) is, with Bharata's *Nāṭyaśāstra*, the most central theory of literature in Indian tradition. *Dhvanyāloka* itself is a huge compendium of poetry and poetic styles, which refers to numerous views, scholars and poetic texts, mostly by way of illustration. The theory proposed by Anandavardhana is known by the name *Dhvani*, which means the suggestive quality of poetic language. He has the distinction of introducing in Sanskrit poetics the semantics of poetic language; but more important is the contribution in terms of turning the focus of critical discussion from the outward linguistic style and poetic embellishment to the more complex issue of linguistic structure in poetry. In Anandavardhana's view it is this structure, which is the total effect of the suggestive quality of language, that distinguishes poetry from the ordinary usage of language. His theory, appropriately, exerted an abiding influence on the succeeding generations of theoreticians in India. Among those who attempted re-statement of Anandavardhana's views in one form or the other were Bhattanayaka, Kuntaka, Mahimbhatta, Dhananjaya, Bhoja, Pratiharenduraja, Rajasekhara, Viśwanatha. In the twentieth century, Anandavardhana's theory has found a new lease of life, mainly under the impact of Western stylistics and Structuralism. Critics like Krishna Rayan and C.D. Narasimhaiah have been very enthusiastic about the practical utility of the *Dhvani* theory in the context of modern Indian literature. Though Anandavardhana has been a theoretician of such a crucial importance, a good translation of his work was not easily available until Prof. K. Krishnamoorthy published his critical edition with translation of *Dhvanyāloka* (Karnataka University, Dharwar, 1974). The text included here is selected from this translation by bringing together in their proper sequential order the main principles (i.e. the *Karikas*) propounded by Anandavardhana.

Dhvani: Structure of Poetic Meaning

Though the learned men of yore have declared time and again that the soul of poetry is suggestion, some would aver its non-existence, some would regard it as something (logically) implied and some others would speak of its essence as lying beyond the scope of words. We propose, therefore, to explain its nature and bring delight to the hearts of perceptive critics.

That meaning which wins the admiration of refined critics is decided to be the soul of poetry. The 'explicit' and the 'implicit' are regarded as its two aspects.

Of these, the explicit is commonly known and it has been already set forth in many ways through figures of speech such as the simile by other writers; hence it need not be discussed here at length.

But the implicit aspect is quite different from this. In the words of first-rate poets it shines supreme and towers above the beauty of the striking external constituents even as charm in ladies.

That meaning alone is the soul of poetry; and so it was that, of yore, the sorrow of the First Poet (i.e. Valmiki) at the separation of the curlew couple took the form of a distich.

The speech of first-rate poets streaming forth that sweet content reveals clearly their extraordinary genius which is as unearthly as it is ever bright.

It is not understood by a mere learning in grammar and in dictionary. It is understood only by those who have an insight into the true significance of poetry.

That meaning, and that rare word which possesses the power of conveying it, only these two deserve the careful scrutiny of a first-rate poet.

Just as a man interested in perceiving objects (in the dark) directs his efforts towards securing a lamp since it is a means to realise his end, so also does one who is ultimately interested in the suggested meaning proceed by first evincing interest in the conventional meaning.

Just as the purport of a sentence is grasped through the meaning of individual words, the knowledge of that sense is got at only through the medium of the explicit sense.

Though by its own power the word-import is responsible for conveying the sentence-import, just as it escapes notice once its purpose is served — So also that suggested meaning flashes suddenly across the truth-perceiving minds of perceptive critics when they turn away from the literal meaning.

That kind of poetry, wherein the (conventional) meaning renders itself secondary or the (conventional) word renders its meaning secondary and suggests the (intended or) implied meaning, is designated by the learned as *dhvani* or 'Suggestive Poetry'.

Suggestion does not bear identity with indication because there is a difference between the two.

Nor is this a differentia of that as both the fallacies of Too Wide and Too Narrow would result (if one were to hold such a view).

Only that word, which conveys a charm incapable of communication by any other expression and which is pregnant with suggestive force, becomes a fit instance for the title 'Suggestive'.

Words which signify by common usage meaning other than what they primarily denote, as for instance the word *lāvanya*, do not become instances of Suggestion.

If one gives up the primary denotative power of a word and understands a sense (secondarily conveyed by it) through its indicative power, it is because of a purpose. In conveying this purpose, the word does not move falteringly at all (as it moves falteringly when indicating a meaning secondarily).

The fact is that indication is grounded on the primary denotative force of words. How can it ever be a definition of suggestion whose sole support is suggestivity?

At the most, it might serve as pointer to one of the aspects of suggestion.

If one were to say that the definition of suggestion has already been propounded by others, it would only substantiate our own position.

II

'Merged in the other meaning' and 'Completely lost' — these are the two kinds of the expressed in 'Suggestion with intended literal import'.

The nature of suggestion 'with intended literal import' is also two-fold: (i) 'of discernible sequentiality' and (ii) 'of undiscernible sequentiality'.

Sentiment, emotion, the semblance of sentiment or mood and their (rise and) cessation etc., are all of 'undiscerned sequentiality'. It is decided that when we have the prominent presence of this variety, we are having the very soul of suggestion.

Only that, wherein all the several beautifiers of the expressed sense and the expression exist with the single purpose of conveying sentiment and so on, is to be regarded as coming under the scope of suggestion.

But if in a poem the chief purport of the sentence should relate to something else, and if sentiment and so on should come in only as auxiliaries to it, it is my opinion that sentiment and so on are figures of speech in such a poem.

Those which inhere in this principal element are regarded as qualities. And figures are to be known as those that are associated with its parts even like ornaments such as the bracelet.

The Erotic indeed, is the sweetest and the most delectable of all sentiments. The quality of sweetness is grounded securely on poetry which is full of this sentiment.

In sentiments viz., Love-in-separation and the Pathetic, sweetness will be uppermost. It is so because the mind is moved very much in such instances.

Sentiments like the Furious are characterised by great exciting power in poetry. The quality of forcefulness is that which inheres in sound and sense which produce this effect.

That quality in poetry by which poetry throws itself open to the entry of all sentiments may be taken as perspicuity. Its applicability is universal.

Defects like 'indelicacy' which have been shown to be impermanent (by the ancient writers) have been in fact illustrated as blemishes only with reference to the erotic sentiment when its nature is suggestion.

The sub-division of its parts and its own sub-divisions become endless indeed if one were to take into account their mutual permutations also.

Hence their broad indications only will be given here. But it should be enough to educate refined critics. Their minds will have received the light which would enable them to guess aright everywhere.

In none of the varieties of the principal erotic sentiment does alliteration become a source of suggestion since it involves great effort at achieving similarity.

Even if the poet should be an expert in the use of figures like assonance, his employment of them in the erotic sentiment which is of the nature of suggestion, and particularly in that love-in-separation, would amount only to a lapse on his part.

Only that is admitted as a figure of suggestive poetry whose employment is rendered possible just by the emotional suffusion of the poet and which does not require any other extra effort on his part.

The galaxy of figures like metaphor becomes truly significant (i.e. will be real ornaments) when they are employed with great discrimination in instances of the Erotic Sentiment which is intrinsic to *dhvani*.

The sole consideration that it is only a means to the delineation of sentiment and never an end in itself, the necessity of employing it at the right time and of abandoning it at the right time; the absence of over-enthusiasm on the poet's part in pressing it too far, and finally, his keen watchfulness in making sure that it remains a secondary element only — these are the various means by which figures like metaphor become accessories (of the suggested sentiment).

The other element of this suggestion manifests itself in the same way as resonance and the temporal sequentiality of the two meanings will be discernible.

It is also two-fold: — 'that which is based on the power of the word' and 'that which is based on the power of sense'.

Only that instance wherein is present a figure that is not expressed directly by any word but conveyed solely by the suggestive power of the word itself, should be regarded as suggestion based on the power of the word.

The other variety of suggestion is based upon the power of sense and it is instanced in places where the second meaning is conveyed only by way of implication by the first meaning and not by the expressed words at all.

A context wherein even an idea suggested by the power of the word and sense is again expressed directly in so many words by the poet, will instance only a figure far removed from suggestion. The sense which suggests another sense is also two-fold: 1. Existing only in ornate expression and 2. Naturally existing.

Contexts where a new figure of speech is seen to result from the mere power of sense and is suggested in the form of resonance should be deemed as instances of another variety of suggestion.

It has been shown effectively (even by the ancient writers) that the assemblage of figures like metaphor though generally found to be expressed only, also become suggested quite often.

Even if there should be found a suggested figure, unless there is also a singleness of aim towards it on the part of the expressed, it cannot be considered as a mode of suggestion.

Those very figures which do not possess invariably even the capacity of forming the body of poetry when they appear in their expressed state, will be found to assume extraordinary beauty when they become participants of suggestion.

When figures are suggested only by the idea itself, they are invariably participants of suggestion; for the very procedure of poetry is dependent upon it.

If other figures are suggested they will become participants of suggestion in case the principal importance of the suggested is discernible in respect of extraordinary charm.

If an instance of the implied sense is such that it can be caught only with great difficulty or if it is only subordinate to the expressed sense, in either case, it will not be an instance of suggestion.

The usage of a word with faltering denotation either because of the poet's want of education or because of his lack of genius, should not be regarded by the learned as a way of suggestion.

The full definition of suggestion in all its varieties includes clarity of manifestation and principal importance of the suggested element.

III

Both the varieties of suggestion with unintended literal import and resonance-like suggestion are suggested by individual words and by whole sentences.

Suggestion with undiscerned sequentiality will flash forth in letter, word etc., sentence, composition, and finally the work as a whole.

The (Sanskrit) letters 'ś', and 'ṣ' letters conjunct with 'r' and 'ḍh' — all these become deterrents of the erotic sentiment. Hence those letters are not conducive to a particular sentiment.

When these very letters are employed in relation to the sentiment of disgust and so forth, they will only intensify them. Hence also letters suggest sentiments.

'Texture' is said to be of three kinds: (1) without compounds (2) with medium-sized compounds, and (3) with long compounds.

The propriety or decorum of the speaker and the spoken is the consideration which governs it.

Another consideration which governs the usage of a texture is its decorum with regard to the literary medium adopted. Texture thus becomes different in different forms of literature.

The consideration of decorum detailed above will also govern all prose works which are not governed by the rules of metre.

Texture with decorum in the delineation of sentiments will shine out wherever it might be found. It will, however, assume a shade of variation coupled with the decorum of literary medium.

Construction of only such a plot, either traditional or invented, as is charming with its decorum of (the accessories of sentiment, viz.,) stimuli of setting, abiding emotions, emotional response, and passing moods:

If, in a theme, adapted from a traditional source, the poet is faced with situations conflicting with the intended sentiment, his readiness to leave out such incidents and inventing in their place even imaginary incidents with a view to delineating the intended sentiment:

The construction of divisions and sub-divisions of the plot only with a view to delineating sentiments and not at all with a desire for mere conformity to rules of poetics:

Bringing about both the high tide of sentiment and its low ebb appropriately in the work; preserving the unity of the principal sentiment from beginning to end:

A discreet use of figures of speech even when the poet is capable of using them in any number;

Such are the conditions which underlie the suggestiveness of a whole work of literature in regard to sentiments, etc.

Of this suggestion, the variety which is of the form of resonance and which has been already illustrated is found often in entire works of literature also.

Case-terminations, conjugational terminations, number, relation, accidence, primary affixes, secondary affixes, and also compounds — all these become conveyers of suggestion with undiscerned sequentiality.

Whether it is the whole work or a single stanza, a good poet who is desirous of incorporating sentiments etc., in what he writes should take pains to avoid hindrances to them.

Sketching the setting etc., of an opposite sentiment, describing something whose connection with the subject on hand is only very remote.

Stopping the delineation of sentiment abruptly as also elaborating it when not required; over-elaborating it again and again though it has already received sufficient elaboration, and indecorum in respect of behaviour — all these hinder the course of sentiment.

After the intended leading sentiment has been established on a secure footing, there will be no defect in including even hindrances provided that these come either as foils or as ancillaries.

Though there is a convention that more than one sentiment should find a place in entire works of literature, one of them alone should be made principal by the poet who aims at greatness in his works.

The importance of an intended sentiment which is shining throughout the work abidingly cannot be marred by the inclusion of other sentiments.

Just as one plot is made to remain major in a work as a whole, so also one sentiment can be made to remain major and it will not at all lead to a discrepancy.

When a sentiment is delineated in a work as the principal one, no other sentiment, whether unopposed or opposed to it, should be treated elaborately. This will ensure one that no opposition between them will remain any more.

If a sentiment opposed to the principal one happens to occur in the same substratum as that of the latter itself, the opposed sentiment should be given a different substratum; (once this is done) there will be no defect even if it should be treated in full.

A sentiment which has no opposition due to the sameness of substratum but which becomes an opposite of another (i.e. principal) sentiment coming closely beside it should be so conveyed by the intelligent poet that a third sentiment will intervene between the conflicting ones.

By the intervention of another sentiment, even the opposition of two sentiments in the same sentence will disappear.

The opposition and non-opposition of sentiments should be clearly noticed in the above manner, particularly so in the Erotic sentiment, for it happens to be the most delicate of all (sentiments).

A good poet should be extremely careful so far as that sentiment is concerned. Otherwise, the slightest inattention (or lapse) on his part will appear glaring at once.

Either for the sake of winning the attention of people who deserve to be instructed or for the sake of endowing the work with unique charm, a touch of the opposite sentiments may be brought into the accessories of the Erotic sentiment. It will not then be a fault.

When a good poet composes his poem bearing in mind these concepts of non-opposition and opposition of sentiments etc., he shall never blunder.

The main task of a first-rate poet lies in a proper marshalling of all the contents and the expressions in the direction of sentiments etc.

Vṛttis (literally, Modes) are said to be of two kinds only because they relate to appropriate employment of senses and sound in keeping with sentiments, etc.

We can see another variety of poetry viz. poetry of subordinated suggestion, wherein the artistic excellence of the expressed is greater than that of the suggested, though the latter also happens to be present alongside of the former.

In all poetic compositions that look delightful by reason of their lucid and elegant words, only this variety of poetry should be recognised by the intelligent critic.

The whole host of figures is seen in many an instance to put on a new charm when it is brought into touch with the suggested element.

Even for such expressions of poets as are already adorned by figures, this shade of suggestion will be a most important ornament even as bashfulness will be for women.

Of course we see the communication of a new meaning by the agency of Ironic Tone. Even this will come within this variety of poetry so long as the suggested element happens to remain secondary.

Instances which can reasonably be brought under this class of poetry should not be classed under *dhvani* by refined critics.

This class of poetry viz., that with subordinated suggestion will also assume the form of *dhvani* or that with principal suggestion if one views it from the standpoint of exclusive purport of sentiments etc.

These two classes of poetry are decided thus on the principle of importance or unimportance of the suggested content. That which is other than both is given the name of Portrait (*Citra*).

Portrait-like poetry is also seen to be two-fold inasmuch as it is based either on word or on meaning. The first variety is word-portrait and the second, meaning-portrait.

It shines in diverse ways with its several varieties of subordinated suggestion, figures, its own sub-varieties, their inter-mingling and collocation.

Such are some of the different ways of principal suggestion and some of the minor classes of the major ways. Who can ever count them exhaustively? We have just indicated therefore, their direction only.

Principal suggestion which we have defined hitherto should be attentively studied not only by all the poets who aspire after writing good poetry but also by all the critics who aspire after understanding it well.

Those who were unable to explain properly this essential principle of poetry as they had only a glimmer of it (and nothing more), have brought into vogue the theory of styles.

Once this theory of poetry is fully understood, even the so called 'Modes' relating to the nature of sounds as well as to the nature of meanings will become intelligible.

IV

By the ways of principal suggestion as also subordinated suggestion shown thus far, the quality of creative imagination in poets will assume endlessness.

By a mere touch of even a single variety of suggestion (among the many that have been enumerated), the poet's expression will acquire novelty though it might perhaps embody only a trite idea.

The sentiments, etc. whose scope is very wide should be followed along the said course. The otherwise limited range of poetry has become so unlimited only because of their influence.

Even trite subjects in poetry will put on a new freshness if they get into touch with sentiment just as the same trees appear quite new with the advent of spring.

Though several varieties of the suggested-suggester relationship are possible, the poet should be most intent upon one of them in particular, viz., that relating to the delineation of sentiments etc.

So long as these varieties of principal and subordinate suggestion are utilised in a work and so long as the poet has the gift of creative imagination (in so utilising them), there can be no dearth of poetic themes.

Infinitude is achieved by the expressed content also even when it remains in its pure and natural state by reason of the considerations of circumstances, place, time, etc.

We find in plenty examples of utilising the expressed content with variations of circumstances etc. But it will shine out only in the association of sentiment if only the real nature of objects in the world, differing as it does according to place, time, and so on, is utilised in such a way that it is imbued with sentiment, emotion etc., and that it is in keeping with the demands of decorum.

Like the resources of primordial Nature herself, the infinite possibilities of poetic themes can never be drained off even by a million Bṛhaspatis composing with all their might simultaneously.

There are bound to be plenty of coincidences amongst great minds.

But all of them should not be regarded by the wise as being identical (in respect of plagiarism).

Coincidence means correspondence with another. It may be like that of a reflected image or like that of a painted picture or like that of two living persons resembling each other.

Of these, the first has no separate existence at all of its own; the existence of the second is no more than a non-entity; while the third has a definite existence of its own. A poet need not reject such similarity in themes.

So long as there is a separate life of its own, even a poetic theme bearing a close correspondence to an earlier one will acquire exceeding beauty; just as the delightful face of a woman will appear exceedingly charming in spite of its strong resemblance to the moon.

Even when the already existing elements of poetic themes such as arrangements of letters etc. are utilised, it will certainly not smack of a flaw so long as the poetic theme as a whole is shining with novelty.

Whatever theme it might be, so long as it produces the impression in the minds of people: 'Yes, this is a lovely and unique flash';

Though it might smack of earlier usages, a theme can very well be utilised by a good poet. He will never become an object of censure by so doing.

May words that appear (to critics) as full of manifold ideas and ambrosiac sentiments be freely spread out. Poets need have no compunctions in the flawless realm of their own.

The Goddess of Speech, Saraswati, herself will provide the desired ideas of a good poet whose mind is averse to borrowing the belongings of another.

Anandavardhana, from the Dhvanyāloka
translated by K. Krishnamoorthy

DHANANJAYA

Dhananjaya has received less attention than he deserves from students of literary theory in India. His special contribution cannot be appreciated in terms of his theoretical formulations in isolation from their cultural context. He is important because he happens to be the most notable opponent of Abhinavagupta's concept of *śantarasa.* He was also an opponent of Anandavardhana's *dhvani* theory, his argument being that aesthetic experience is a function of its reception, as Bharata had argued, rather than of the art-structure as Anandavardhana had argued. The ruling passion of Dhananjaya's theoretical work was to return to Bharata as much as to return to his contemporary literary practices.

Dhananjaya's work is called the *Daśarupa* since it discusses the ten types of drama known in his times. Bharata, some seven centuries before him, had intended to discuss the ten types as stated in the *Nāṭyaśāstra* (chapter 20, verses 1 & 2). Dhananjaya accomplished that plan by presenting an exhaustive catalogue of drama, though he is more partial towards the Nāṭak-drama and Prakaraṇ-drama.

If one had to think of a single critical text within the Indian tradition devoted entirely to drama, one has to point to the *Daśarupa.* It is exhaustive in its treatment of the subject. It is naturally a great help to historians of Sanskrit literature. Dhananjaya's work, together with that of his contemporary Rajasekhara, indicates that the theorists had the supporting branches of literary study, literary history and literary criticism, at their disposal. The details offered by him while building the network of definitions and descriptions in his compendium of drama presuppose a rich fund of critical and historical comment.

Daśarupa started attracting the attention of Indologists from the nineteenth century: and at the beginning of this century George Hass (1912) produced an impressive edition with translation of the *Daśarupa.* The excerpts given here are from Hass's translation.

Definitions and Descriptions in Drama

CLASSIFICATION OF DRAMA:

Dramas are classified according to Subject-matter, Hero and Sentiment.

The Subject-matter (*vastu*) is twofold. The main is known as the Principal Subject (*ādhikārika*), the subordinate as the Incidental Subject (*prāsaṅgika*). The possession of the desired result is called *adhikāra*, and its possessor is called *adhikārin*; that which contains an incident connected with him is called *ādhikārika* (Principal Subject). The Incidental Subject (*prāsaṅgika*) is a purpose of another person by means of which one's own purpose is incidentally furthered. When it is continuous it is called Episode (*patākā*, lit. 'banner'); when of short duration, Episodical Incident (*prakarī*). An indication by the mention of something extraneous, of a matter that is begun or is about to happen is called an Episodic-indication (*patākāsthānaka*), which is characterized by similar situations or attributes. This is also threefold, owing to a threefold classification into legendary, invented, and mixed subjects. The legendary variety of subject-matter is derived from legends of the past and the like; the invented is devised by the poet; the mixed arises from a combination of these two in accordance with a classification into gods, mortals, and the like.

ELEMENTS OF THE PLOT:

The Denouement (*kārya*) of the action consists of one of the three objects of human existence (*trivarga*); it is either simple or connected with one or both of the other objects. The cause of this Denouement is the Germ (*bija*), at first manifested as very small, but expanding in manifold ways as the action proceeds. When the secondary matter of the drama is interrupted, the cause of its being resumed (*accheda-kāraṇa*) is the Expansion (*bindu*). The elements designated as the Germ (*bija*), the Expansion (*bindu*), the so-called Episode (*patākā*), the Episodical Incident (*prakarī*), and the Denouement (*kārya*) — these are declared to be the five Elements of the Plot (*arthaprakṛti*).

THE FIVE STAGES OF THE ACTION:

There are five stages of the action which is set on foot by those that strive after a result: Beginning (*ārambha*), Effort (*yatna* = *prayatna*), Prospect of Success (*prāptyāśā*), Certainty of Success (*niyatāpti*), and Attainment of the Result (*phalāgama* = *phalayoga*). Beginning (*ārambha*) is mere eagerness for the obtaining of the more important result. Effort (*prayatna*) is exertion attended with great haste, when this result has not been obtained. Prospect of Success (*prāptyāśā*) is the possibility of succeeding, with means at hand, but also with fear of failure. Certainty of Success (*niyatāpti*) is the assurance of succeeding because of the absence of risk. Attainment of the Result (*phalayoga*) is the accomplishment of the entire result, as previously mentioned.

THE FIVE JUNCTURES:

There are five Elements of the plot (*arthaprakṛti*), parallel with the five Stages (*avasthā*) of the action; from these respectively arise the five Junctures (*saṃdhi*), beginning with the Opening (*mukha*). Juncture (*saṃdhi*) is the connection of one thing with a different one, when there is a single sequence of events. The five Junctures are: the Opening (*mukha*), the Progression (*pratimukha*), the Development (*garbha*), the Pause (*avamarśa*), and the Conclusion (*upasaṃhṛti* = *nirvahaṇa*). The Opening (*mukha*) is the origination of the Germ (*bija*), giving rise to various purposes and Sentiments; it has twelve subdivisions, because of its connection with the Germ and the Beginning (*ārambha*).

The twelve subdivisions of the Opening are: Suggestion (*upakṣepa*), Enlargement (*parikara*), Establishment (*parinyāsa*), Allurement (*vilobhana*), Resolve (*yukti*), Success (*prāpti*), Settling (*samādhāna*), Conflict of Feelings (*vidhāna*), Surprise (*paribhāvanā*), Disclosure (*udbheda*), Incitement (*bheda*), and Activity (*karaṇa*).

(These verses are followed by Dhananjaya's definitions of each of the above twelve types of the Opening.)

CHARACTERISTICS OF THE HERO:

The Hero should be well-bred, charming, liberal, clever, affable, popular, upright, eloquent, of exalted lineage, resolute, and young; endowed with intelligence, energy, memory, wisdom, skill in the arts, and pride; heroic, mighty, vigorous, familiar with the codes, and a just observer of laws.

THE FOUR TYPES OF HERO:

... the Hero is of four kinds, being light-hearted (*lalita*), calm (*śānta*), exalted (*udātta*), or vehement (*uddhata*). The self-controlled and light-hearted Hero (*dhīralalita*) is free from anxiety, fond of the arts, happy, and gentle. The self-controlled and calm Hero (*dhīraśānta*) is a Brahman or the like, possessed of the generic merits of a hero. The self-controlled and exalted Hero (*dhīrodātta*) is of great excellence, exceedingly serious, forbearing, not boastful, resolute, with self-assertion suppressed, and firm of purpose. The self-controlled and vehement Hero (*dhīroddhata*) is altogether dominated by pride and jealousy, wholly devoted to magic practices, and deceit, self-assertive, fickle, irascible, and boastful.

THE HERO AS LOVER:

When he has been captivated by another woman, the Hero may be (act) clever (*dakṣiṇa*), deceitful (*śaṭha*), or shameless (*dhṛṣṭa*) towards his previous love. A clever Hero (*dakṣiṇa*) is one that is kind to his previous love. A deceitful Hero (*śaṭha*) is one that hides the unfaithfulness. A shameless Hero (*dhṛṣṭa*) is one that lets the disfigurements on his body show. A faithful Hero (*anukula*) is one that has only a single lady-love.

Companions of the Hero:

The Hero of the Episode (*patākā*) is a separate person called Attendant (*pithamarda*), intelligent, assisting him, i.e., the Principal Hero, devoted to him, and possessed of his qualities in a lesser degree. Another companion is the Parasite (*vita*), who has but a single accomplishment, and the Jester (*vidūṣaka*), who is the fun maker.

The Opponent of the Hero:

The Opponent of the Hero is avaricious, self-controlled and vehement, stubborn, criminal and vicious.

Selection of the Principal Subject:

In a play in which the Hero is endowed with attractive qualities of the type known as self-controlled and exalted (*dhīrodātta*), glorious, eager for fame, of great energy, a preserver of three Vedas (*trayī*), a ruler of the world, of renowned lineage, a royal seer or a god — in that the incident for which he is renowned is to be made the Principal Subject (*ādhikārika*).

Adaptation of the Story:

Whatever in it, i.e. in the original story, is at all unsuited to the hero or inconsistent with the Sentiment is to be omitted or arranged in some other way. After determining upon the beginning and end of the play in this manner and after dividing it into five parts, the author should furthermore break up into small sections the division called Junctures (*saṃdhi*). The subdivisions should be sixty-four in number. In like manner, moreover, one should divide the incidents of the Episode (*patākā*), which should have one or more Sub-junctures (*anusaṃdhi*) less than the principal subject. ...One should insert the Episodical Incident (*prakarī*) without any Juncture. At the beginning of the play one should put an Explanatory Scene or an Act, according to the Appropriateness of the action. When after omitting an extensive part of the subject-matter that is required, but is without Sentiment, one wishes to present the rest, then one should put an Explanatory Scene (*viṣkambhaka*) at the beginning.

When, on the other hand, the subject-matter proceeds with Sentiment right from the start, then there should be at the beginning an Act following up the hints given in the Introduction. An Act visibly represents the doings of the Hero, is attended with inherence of the Expansion, and is based on the purposes, contrivances, and Sentiments of various kinds.

The principal Sentiment (*aṅgin*) is to be furthered by means of the Consequents (*anubhāva*), the Determinants (*vibhāva*), the Permanent State (*sthāyin*), and the Transitory States (*vyabhicārin*), taken up and dropped in turn. One should not make the Subject-matter too disconnected by the excessive use of Sentiment, nor should one overwhelm the Sentiment with matters relating to the Subject-matter or its embellishment. One Sentiment, either the Heroic or the Erotic, is to be made the principal Sentiment; all the other Sentiments should be made subordinate. The Marvelous Sentiment should be employed only in the Conclusion.

SENTIMENT AND ITS PRODUCTION:

Sentiment (*rasa*) results when a Permanent State produces a pleasurable sensation through the operation of the Determinants, the Consequents, the Involuntary States, and the Transitory States. Among these a Determinant (*vibhāva*) is that which causes the development of the States by its being recognised. Determinants are of two kinds, being divided into Fundamental Determinants (*ālambana*) and Excitant Determinants (*uddipana*). A Consequent (*anubhāva*), on the other hand, is an external manifestation that serves to indicate a feeling. ... A State (*bhāva*) which is brought about by emotional states such as pleasure and pain, is the realisation of such states. The Involuntary States (*bhāva sāttvika = sattvabhāva*) are separate, for, although in the category of Consequents, they are different from these just because of their arising from the inner nature (*sattva*); and this is the reason for the realization of such states. The eight Involuntary States are: Paralysis (*stambha*), Fainting (*pralaya*), Horripilation (*romāñca*), Sweating (*sveda*), Change of Colour (*vaivarṇya*), Trembling (*vepathu*), Weeping (*aśru*), and Change of Voice (*vaisvarya*). ... The Transitory States are those that especially accompany the Permanent State in cooperation, emerging from it and again being submerged in it, like the waves in the ocean.

Dhananjaya, from the Daśarupa
translated by George Hass

KUNTAKA

Kuntaka is known as the originator of the *vakrokti* school of Sanskrit literary theory. Historically, he occupies a place between Anandavardhana of the ninth century and Abhinavagupta of the later tenth century. These dates indicate that Kuntaka lived at a time when literary criticism in India was acquiring a great sophistication. Among his other able contemporaries were Dhananjaya and Rajasekhara. Considering the presence of these literary geniuses in his generation, the originality of Kuntaka's critical persuasions acquires a special significance. *Vakrokti* and *Alaṇkara* are the two schools of Sanskrit criticism which come very close in spirit to the twentieth century Western Formalism and New Criticism.

Vakrokti is a theory of poetry which perceives poetry essentially in terms of the language of its expression. It sees the poetic language as language of metaphor and suggestive communication. It is amazing to see how much Kuntaka (and his contemporary critics) knew about the language of poetry, and the sophistication and rigour of logic and argument in his writing.

The text reproduced here is from K. Krishnamoorthy's translation of the *Vakrokti - Jivita* (Karnataka University Press, 1977). Only the main points of Kuntaka's argument — the *karikas*, have been included, without giving the elaborations of these points — the *vṛttis.* For a commentary on the concept of *Vakrokti* refer to Krishnamoorthy's *Overview* included in the second part of the present volume.

Language of Poetry and Metaphor

My salutations to the goddess of speech, the dancer on the stage, of the moonlike face of master-poets, and giving a brilliant and beautiful performance with gestures, artful turns of speech.

In order to set forth the nature of beauty conducive to extraordinary delight, a fresh study of poetry is offered here, like an added ornament to it.

A poetic composition created with an eye to beauty is not only a means for the inculcation of values like righteousness, but also a delight to the hearts of the *elite*.

Participants in the affairs of life can come to appreciate the beauty of life-activity in a new light, viz. an appropriate pattern imposed by the poet, only by means of good poetry.

Apart from the enjoyment of the benefits of the four-fold values, there is the immediate sense of delight produced in the reader as a result of his enjoying the nectar of poetry.

The 'adornment' and the 'adorned' are distinguished artificially for the purposes of our enquiry, because this would be the only means to attain the ultimate goal. The truth of the matter, however, remains that the two together constitute poetry.

Poetry is that word and sense together enshrined in a style revealing the artistic creativity of the poet on the one hand and giving delight to the man of taste on the other.

That 'meaning' is what is signified, and 'word' is that which signifies, is so well known that it needs no elaboration. Yet, in the province of poetry, their true nature is as follows:

That unique expression which alone can fully convey the poet's intended meaning out of a hundred alternatives before him is to be regarded as 'word'. Similarly that alone which possesses such refreshing natural beauty as to draw the appreciation of delighted readers is to be reckoned as 'meaning'.

Both these are 'adorned'. Their adornment consists in the poetic process known as 'artistic turn of speech'.

For those rhetoricians who hold that 'natural description' is an ornament, what on earth remains for being ornamented?

It is impossible to state anything except in terms of its nature. An object without it is tantamount to a nonexistent idea.

If the body itself should be reckoned as ornament, what would be the other thing which it can adorn at all? Never does one climb upon one's own shoulder.

In the event of nature-description itself being regarded as an ornament, when another ornament is also added, the question arises whether the distinction between the two is manifest or unmanifest.

If manifest, there should be only 'separable union of figures', and if unmanifest only 'inseparable union of figures' everywhere. There should be no scope at all for the remaining figures of speech.

When it is so obvious that word and meaning are ever experienced jointly, what is the special import of mentioning it (in the definition)?

The *sāhitya* or mutual coherence between word and meaning in respect of beauty is nothing but a unique poetic usage, involving neither more nor less than the exact form of word and meaning required to make the whole beautiful.

Art in the poetic process is divisible into six categories. Each one of them may have numerous subdivisions, every subdivision striking one by a new shade of beauty.

Art in the arrangement of syllables, art in the base form of substantives, and also art in their inflection forms.

And art in a whole sentence admits of a thousand varieties. In it is included the whole lot of Figures of speech.

The 'beauty of section' and the 'beauty of work' will be treated now under the two heads, 'natural' and 'artificial', both yielding artistic delight.

Diction is the name given to the art of sentence-construction which is congenial to heighten inner and outer charm of both 'meaning' and 'word' and which is at the same time a partaker of the poetic process.

The quality delighting men of taste is something over and above the three elements so far considered, namely, 'meaning', 'word' and 'artful expression'. It has a unique beauty of unfailing appeal.

There are three styles which serve poets as high-roads. They are: (1) 'the element', (2) 'the brilliant' and (3) 'the mixed'.

That charming style where fresh words and meanings both blossom forth by virtue of the poet's undimmed imagination, where ornaments are few and yet lovely as they come in without efforts.

Where studious technical skill is superseded by the prominence given to the inner nature of things, where beauty is felt due to sympathy by men of taste who are experts in enjoying sentiments, etc.;

where the beauty is such that it eludes the critic's power of analysis, where the wealth of beauty reminds one of the supreme artistic creation of the universe by the Creator himself;

wherein every element of beauty is a result of the poet's imagination alone and succeeds in conveying flashes of gentle grace;

such is the style called 'the elegant' which master-poets follow like bees roving along the grove of full blown blossoms.

The first and the foremost excellence of the 'elegant' style is sweetness. It is vivified by the use of expressions which are lovely inasmuch as they are uncompounded.

The excellence called 'perspicuity' is that which brings out the poet's intent without any effort on the reader's part, which conveys the meaning in an instant as it were, and which is concerned with sentiments and artful speech.

When even a little beauty in respect of alliterative syllables and in the choice of diction results in the charm of syntax and contributes to the strikingness of style, we have the excellence called 'grace'.

That which is smooth on the ear, and capable as it were of intimate embrace by thought and which is a naturally sparkling shade of loveliness, is spoken of as having the excellence called classicality.

Wherein artistic beauty appears to be radiating brilliantly from within, in respect of both word and meaning, even at the time of the first manifestation of the creative imagination;

wherein poets pile up tropes upon tropes without a sense of satisfaction, like necklaces inlaid with gems;

just as the ornaments dazzling with lustrous beams of gems conceal a beloved's body and produce beauty;

so also, wherein the 'adorned' is made to acquire brilliance by virtue of the tropes brilliant in themselves and reflecting it through their own excessive beauty;

wherein even a trite subject is raised to a unique height of excellence merely by dint of artistic expression;

wherein everything is made to acquire altogether new features at his sweet pleasure by a master-poet in his vision by the power of his inventive genius;

wherein, further, the intended purport of the whole is communicated by a suggestive use of language which is distinct from the two well-known uses, viz., the communicative use of meanings and the denotative use of words;

wherein the real nature of things pregnant with sentiments is augmented with a novel beauty which is unique;

that style, whose life-breath is, verily, artistic beauty of expression, is termed the 'brilliant'. An element of imaginative flight or exaggeration will be invariably striking in it.

Such is the extremely impassable way trodden by learned poets. It is just like the path of sword-blades traversed by the cherished desires of brave warriors.

In this style a verbal 'sweetness' is maintained which is conducive to artistic brilliance. Relieved of loose texture, it becomes a means of producing compact beauty in diction.

The 'perspicuity' contained in this style is nothing but the use of uncompounded expressions which is well known in the tradition of poets, but which mostly assumes a touch, however slight, of 'floridity'.

When in a sentence other sentences are made to fuse with a coherence usually possible only in the case of the constituent words, we have another variety of 'perspicuity'. By words without elision of the final aspirates and in euphonic combination with each other, and by syllables which precede conjuncts, 'grace' is enriched.

'Classicality' in this style is a product of great artistic skill. Neither too tender nor too harsh, it wins the heart all the same.

Wherein the two styles, viz., the 'elegant' with its natural beauty and the 'brilliant' with its decorative effect both come to be blended,

where the whole host of qualities like 'sweetness' become grounded on the 'middling' mode of style so as to nourish a unique stylistic effect,

we get a third style, pleasing all tastes, and containing the best of both the other styles in competition as it were, which may be termed 'middling'.

It is this style which fascinates a class of fastidious poets who are fond of mixed variety in their art, like men-about-town, who are fond of fashionable dress.

That quality is known as 'propriety' by virtue of which the poetic subject gains in value in a most lucid manner; in fact it may be regarded as the vital essence of all poetic description.

An instance, wherein the matter on hand is concealed as it were by reason of the exquisitely charming nature of either the speaker or the listener, also deserves being regarded as an example of 'propriety'.

In the wide-ranging material before the poet, that which is pitched upon by the genius of the poet for its activity endows the whole with the quality of 'splendour'.

It is something attained by the full co-operation of all the constituent elements and it is something which surely results in an extra-ordinary aesthetic effect in the mind of connoisseurs; in short it is the whole and sole essence of poetry.

These twin literary qualities, very appealing in all the three styles permeate every element of poetry like word, sentence and the work as a whole.

Such are the three styles perfected only by a few poets in their earnest quest after perfection, after long, assiduous practice. The attainment of even a modest grounding in them has brought great reputation to them. Hereafter will be taken up for treatment the nature and scope of that unique and charming word-usage which is at once a happy sporting ground for all good poets and also an index of good taste.

II

One, two or more syllables used again and again at short intervals constitute the three forms of 'art in the arrangement of syllables'.

And consonants classified (i.e. 'ka' to 'ma' 25 in number) might combine with their nasals in alliteration; 'ta', 'la', 'na' etc. might be doubled and reiterated; or the rest might become conjunct with 'ra' etc. in alliteration. These also will shine by their harmony with the theme.

Sometimes alliteration without any interval too, employed artistically by the poet, contributes to high poetic charm because of variation in vowels.

When alliteration is effected without extra effort, when it is adorned with syllables which are not harsh, when it becomes appealing by discontinuance of earlier sound repetitions and by new choices for reiteration.

This alliterative art which directly exploits the beauty of syllables is seen to serve the cause of 'qualities' as well as 'styles' too; and it is this again which is meant by the ancients when they use the expression 'beauty of literary mode' (*vṛttivaicitrya*).

Rhyme ('yamaka') is a special type of it which consists in words of similar sound with different meaning, perspicuous and pleasing to the ear, and endowed with decorum, and which shines in specific places of the verse such as the beginning. Since its beauty is not of a different kind, it is not treated here at length.

When common denotation of words is seen to expand to include connotation of even impossible attributes imagined by the poet, or to include a hyperbolic excess of even an existing attribute as a result of the poet's intent to shower extraordinary belittlement or extraordinary glorification of the theme, we get what is called 'art in beautifying conventional sense'.

The use of a synonym which approximates most to the meaning intended, which can add to the beauty of meaning considerably, which can embellish the meaning by itself or its epithets coming to assume other shades of figurative body;

which by itself, contributes to a new lease of excellence, which hints at a meaning having almost inconceivable elements;

which contains embellishing figurative elements conducive to beauty, comes to be termed a 'superior art in the use of synonyms'.

Wherein even when the two are far from each other, a common attribute, however slight, is metaphorically superimposed in order to indicate that the resemblance is very close ...

... and which forms the basis for various pleasing and inventive figures headed by metaphor — such a type of poetic beauty is designated by the name 'beauty of metaphorical expression'.

If, as a result of the excellence of the epithet, beauty is added to the verb or the noun (in a sentence), it is to be classed as 'beauty in epithet'.

In order to achieve excellence of expression, when the subject of description is screened as it were by the use of pronouns and so forth, we have what is designated as 'beauty of concealment'.

The affix in the middle of a word often adds to the beauty of decorum in the subject described, by virtue of its own excellence. This may be regarded as another type of poetic beauty.

Beauty of augment and so forth contributes a new charm to style by making for a striking originality in respect of composition.

A usage where beauty of word-forms such as adverbial compounds shines forth may be deemed as an instance of beauty of '*vṛtti*'.

An example wherein an activity yet to be accomplished is described as already accomplished, illustrates 'beauty of *bhāva*'.

When two words in different genders are used to signify an identical object, a new kind of beauty will emerge which we may characterise as beauty of gender.

Even when other genders could be used, if the feminine is preferred, it contributes to beauty; since even the name of a woman is pleasing.

Although other genders are possible, when a specific gender is significantly used by a poet in harmony with the idea to be conveyed and this contributes to beauty, we have another form of this type.

Extreme capability of the subject, superiority to another subject who could perform the same action, a significant qualification of the action itself, beauty of metaphorical superimposition and concealment of the direct object etc. — these five which add charm to the idea described are regarded as the five forms of beauty in action.

When there is remarkable beauty due to the utmost propriety of time described, we have what is called 'beauty in the speciality of time'.

Treatment of one and all auxiliary 'instruments of action' as if they were pre-eminent by superimposing primacy on them and reducing the status of the really pre-eminent into that of an auxiliary so that some special shade of charm is infused into the artful poetic expression — a treatment which thus involves a reversal of status in 'instruments of action' — comes to be designated by the phrase 'beauty of instruments of action'.

When poets intent on achieving special poetic charm resort to transposition of numbers, we have what is known as oblique beauty of number.

When the (grammatical) first person or second person is required logically, instead of using it, the third person is used obliquely in order to gain poetic beauty, it should be regarded as 'oblique beauty of person'.

When both the *Atmane* and *Parasmai -pada* affixes are possible for a root, if a poet is seen preferring the one as against the other because of an aesthetic purpose, that may be designated as arresting beauty of '*upagraha*' or verb-affix.

Apart from the usual affix, when a new affix is superadded with an eye to striking beauty, it constitutes 'unique beauty of affix'.

In a poem where the preposition and indeclinables are employed only to suggest *rasas* as the sole essence of a poem as a whole, we have what may be called another type of 'word-beauty'.

When several forms of such literary turns occur together in such a way as to enhance the beauty of one another, they go to produce artistic charm reminiscent of myriad-faceted beauty.

Poetic speech is a veritable creeper, with words as leaves, forming the bases for (symmetrical) beauty striking with artistic turn adding to the wealth of feelings and sentiments in a most striking manner. May the bee-like connoisseurs appreciate it and collect the profusely fragrant and sweet honey, from the sentence-blossoms, and enjoy it with ever-increasing zest.

III

When the subject-matter is described in a way conducive to beauty by virtue of its own infinite natural charm and by means of exclusive artistic expressions, we may take it as an instance of creative beauty relating to content.

There is also another kind of artistic beauty. It glows with the natural as well as the acquired skills of the poet. It results in imaginative original creations which are extraordinary.

The artistic beauty of a sentence is something quite distinct from the wealth of beauty due to qualities and figures of speech in so far as they relate to artistic word and content belonging to one or the other of the (three) styles. In fact expressiveness of the sentence-form should be regarded as the essence of this beauty. It is an index of the unique skill of the poet even as the unique total appeal of a painting which is something quite distinct from the beauty of the individual elements that go to fashion it such as lovely canvas, lines, and colour shades.

Subjects of poetry described in all their undimmed propriety and beauty of nature come to be classed under two heads, namely, the sentient and the non-sentient.

Of these, the first class can be subdivided again under two heads — 'gods etc.', and 'lions etc.' These may be either primary or subsidiary in the poet's treatment.

The first, i.e., the primary kind, is made beautiful by a spontaneous presentation of emotions like love. The second is rendered lovely by a description of the animals etc. in a way natural to their species.

The secondary sentient ones and non-sentient ones become sources of delight when they are so described that they promote the rise of sentiments.

Poets should note that such is the body of content brimming with beauty and serving the purpose of their descriptive art which they should strive to adopt into their work.

There is also another kind of poetic content which becomes the subject of the poet's art: it will be replete with the means for the attainment of the fourfold values of life; and is worthy of emulation by the people as befitting in their daily life.

'Rasavat' is not an ornament because there is nothing palpable apart from it which is adorned by it, and because the literal meaning of that word itself is contradicted.

Nor is *preyas* (praise) adornment; for its opposite, viz., dispraise, also might be an adornment at that rate. And the use of accepted figures of speech (like the simile) along with 'praise' would have to be regarded as a case of two 'merged' or 'mixed' figures; and it should come to have an independent status too like other figures, even as instances not involving praise or eulogy.

In the same way, the characteristic of adornment is not found in *ūrjasvin* (lit. the high-spirited) and *udātta* (lit. the exalted), as well as twofold *samāhita* (lit. the abated).

When the subject matter is described in a way conducive to beauty by virtue of its own infinite natural charm and by means of exclusively artistic expression, we may take it as an instance of creative beauty relating to content.

There are two forms of poetic statement: One of them partially adds up to the beauty of the adorned; another suggests it primarily, remaining subservient itself and thus exhibiting itself as an adornment.

Now we shall set forth the nature of *rasavant* in such a way that it will become the life-essence of all adornments of figures of speech on the one hand and the quintessence of poetry itself on the other.

That adornment of figure of speech, which functions like *rasa* because it suffuses poetry with *rasa*, is designated as *rasavat* inasmuch as it causes poetic appeal to connoisseurs.

Any object, which illuminates such aspects of the things described as are full of propriety, undimmed, capable of delighting the connoisseurs and not contained in plain denotation of the word, should be considered as an 'illuminator' or *dīpaka*.

Dīpaka is two-fold: It may either be single or in a series. That is, one single object might illuminate many things, or many objects may illuminate many other things.

The second type (viz. *dīpaka* in a series) again is three-fold: 'several ones are illuminated by several', or 'one illuminates a second and that a third in a serial order' (or 'the illuminated ones will in their turn be illuminators')

Just as a verb referring simultaneously to more than one subject becomes appealing to the connoisseurs by reason of its adding beauty to the main theme described, so also an agent or subject (which has such a simultaneously multiple reference conducive to the beauty of the whole) should be deemed as a *dīpaka-alaṇkāra*.

That content which conveys similarity implicitly, by virtue of an essentially metaphorical usage of words, is termed 'metaphor' (*rūpaka*) since it involves a surrender of its own form in favour of another.

The similarity implied will be such that it will become a source of aesthetic charm in respect of poetic content. *Rūpaka* or metaphor is twofold: (1) extended to each individual part and (2) restricted only to some aspect.

The soul adornment (or figure of speech) is held by the wise to be threefold: 1. explicitly stated, 2. implied by indicators and 3. suggested.

By virtue of their creative imagination, poets are seen transforming metaphor to yield the highest poetic effect in such novel ways that new shades of figures are brought into relief thereby.

When an extraneous word-meaning or sentence-meaning becomes the main theme of a description in so far as it lends charm to the proposed subject on hand;

By virtue of similarity or some other relation between the two, the figure of speech will be designated 'Praise of the inapposite' (*aprastutapraśansā*).

When that which can be conveyed by quite a different sentence is conveyed by one sentence in such a way that it adds charm to the subject of description, the figure of speech involved is called 'euphemism' (*prayāyokti*).

Where we have outwardly dispraise stated in so many words but actually praise is suggested in such a way that it adds beauty to the subject primarily described, the figure of speech should be called 'Veiled Praise' (*Vyāja-stuti*).

Either by way of fancying or by way of similarity or by way of both, when the poet desires to convey the extraordinary nature of the subject under description,

and employs such indicative words as 'iva' (= 'as though') or leaves them to be understood suggestively from the context of the several words and meanings which take either of the forms 'It is like this' or 'It is like itself' ....

and which involves thus a coordination of the well-conceived matter on hand with a purport quite apart from it, we have the figure of speech called *utprekṣā* or poetic fancy.

When, in respect of an action, agency is attributed to one though it be really inactive since it so appears in the eyes of the percipient, because of its extreme likelihood in view of its unique natural endowment, (we have another kind of *utprekṣā* or poetic fancy).

Atiśayokti or hyperbole is that which is the vital principle underlying all figures and in which the aethetic qualities of the subject described are raised to a unique height of exquisiteness in a very artistic manner.

Sentiments, natural objects, and figures of speech — all of them reach their highest point of artistic beauty when their inherent brightness is so heightened by the element of hyperbole.

In order to invest rare beauty in the features of the subject described, if its similarity with another object, possessing the same features in a greater measure, is stated, we get the figure of speech viz. simile.

Simile is illustrated in various ways such as explicit mention of the common feature, an implicit reference to it by the sentence as a whole, and a use of express words like *eva* (= as); but in all these the predicate is the element which makes the simile aesthetic.

Though there might be similarity present in the subject of poetic fancy also, its main purport lies elsewhere.

The figure called '*upameyopamā*' involving mutual similitude between the '*upamāna*' and '*upameya*' should also be regarded as coming under this *upamā* only because *upamā* exists therein also and there is no separate definition possible for it.

Association of equals or *tulyayogitā* (admitted by some) is really no separate figure. We have in it two or more similar objects brought together, each one of them claiming equal attention as subjects of description, since primacy is not affirmed of any one of them specifically. Only one should serve as the primary subject described; and when more than one claim to be primary, how could one say which is the adorned and which the adornment?

In case it is held that, in this figure, all subjects are equally important as things meant to be described, or that they are really similar to each other, then these very conditions force us to conclude that the figure is clearly *upamā* and nothing else.

The learned think that *ananvaya* is on par with *kalpitopamā* or 'invented simile'.

Pushing out one thing and bringing in of another in its place cannot be deemed as any figure of speech, because the exchange is the same as before.

When two separate meanings come to be conveyed by the same words, that special function of equivocation in words will be deemed as a figure of speech, viz., *śleṣa*.

The learned say that the indicator of *śleṣa* is a new entity other than the paranomistic word, as well as the suggestive function of the whole sentence and also the expression such as *iva* sometimes.

One and the same word will be denoting two meanings here; between the word and the two meanings so denoted as if they were identical, similarity will be found to be the ruling principle behind such unique technique of the poet.

By the remembrance of similar-sounding words, we get at the meaning, first of the one and next of the other. Since sound or word gets lost as soon as it is produced, remembrance (of past impressions of meaning) alone should be held as governing all such (equivocal) denotation.

When there is similarity in respect of meanings conveyed by the specific word, and when the similarity in features of the two is also present, still if the features of the one are shown as singularly distinct from those of the other, with a view to bring about the excellence of the subject on hand, we get the figure of speech called *Vyatireka*. It is of two kinds — (1) explicitly stated and (2) suggested.

When a subject is described without clearly intending the effect of other figures like *upamā* but intending to bring out its distinctive excellence over or superiority to the well known features associated with it in the world, we have another type of figure: *vyatireka*.

We have *virodha* or paradox when the (apparent) contradiction between two statements is overcome in an ingenious way and the final meaning is made to become reasonable.

Samāsokti ('condensed metaphor') as well as *sahokti* ('description of concurrent occurrences') is not regarded as a figure of speech; for it happens to possess the features of another figure on the one hand and is devoid of poetic beauty on the other.

When, in order to enrich the beauty of the subject described, two subjects are simultaneously described in one and the same sentence, the learned regard it as a figure called *sahokti* or description of concurrent occurrences.

When another idea is pointed to on the basis of its factual similarity (to the idea on hand) without explicit use of expression like *iva*, we have *dṛṣṭānta* or poetic analogy.

On the basis of similarity between two main sentence-ideas or imports, when (along with the one on hand) the other one is also described, it should be understood as the figure *arthāntaranyāsa* or 'corroboration' because it corroborates the first idea.

Suggestion, by way of a denial, for the sake of aesthetic emphasis of the main subject-matter is to be regarded as *ākṣepa* or paralipsis.

All these three figures beginning with *dṛṣṭānta* will have two types, namely, (1) Relating to an idea yet to be stated and (2) relating to an idea already stated, depending upon the intention of the poet; (and the middle one may contain explicit indicators of corroboration or may not contain them).

In order to enrich the beauty of the effect, when it is imagined to be produced uniquely in some way other than the usual cause whose agency is denied, we have the figure of speech known as *vibhāvanā* or 'inscrutable effect'.

When a feature fancied as something allows room for the rise of other fancies too in such a way as to result in aesthetic charm, the figure of speech is designated *sasandeha* or 'poetic doubt'.

With the object of endowing a unique form to the subject matter described, when its actual nature or form is suppressed or concealed, we get the figure of speech known as *apahnuti* or 'poetic concealment'.

Just like words which join in a group to form a sentence, when figures of speech come to be mutually associated with each other in the production of a total impression of beauty, it may be regarded as an instance of the 'mixed' figure of speech.

When all the different figures noticed above get merged inseparably, and strike us in a sentence in various ways, the designation of *saṅkara* is given to such an instance of figurative beauty.

The other figures left out here are really not separate figures because they are either non-different from the ones defined or they are lacking in aesthetic charm.

Though counted as a figure of speech by ancient theorists, *yathāsaṁkhya* (or 'enumeration in a respective order') is not accepted by us as an independent figure because of both the reasons mentioned.

Artful speech of a good poet appeals to one's heart even like one's beloved: Both the beloved and poetic speech share common attributes, namely, possession of striking qualities like grace, alluring charm of word-usage or foot-steps, appeal of elegant but sparse ornaments, abundance of tasteful sentiment and tender-heartedness and elegance of expression.

IV

When we find the speakers giving vent to such expression as is replete with the beauty of unlimited enthusiasm and also capable of expressing their ideas powerfully; when the intended object at the end will remain inscrutable from the beginning (i.e., suspense remains constant till the denouement), the unique and boundless poetic skill underlying it all should be regarded as the poetic beauty of an episode.

When a poet is constructing a plot of his own, based though it might be on a well-known source, if he succeeds in infusing even a small streak of originality, the beauty gained thereby will be singular;

Even as an episode too can shine forth as the vital essence of the work as a whole, brimful of sentiments reaching their utmost limit.

An organic unity which strikingly underlies the various incidents described in different parts of the work leading to the ultimate and intended, each bound to the other by a relation of mutual assistance,

reveals the essence of creative originality which is most aesthetic only in the case of a very rare poetic genius who is endowed by nature with the gift of an extraordinary inventive imagination.

When even one and the same theme is again and again described in different places with a new touch of creative originality, and is made to radiate the glow of sentiments and figures of speech, it manifests a strikingly new mode of artistic beauty.

When integrated with the beauty of the plot, even the conventional themes, that come to be described in court-epics and so forth conforming to set patterns, attain a novel artistic beauty.

Another type of beauty in respect of Acts etc. is instanced when the beauty is so exclusive to an Act that it cannot be attained by any other Act, either preceding or following, in the play and the Act thus serves as a touchstone in its own way of the ruling sentiment in the play.

When the inventiveness of the poet in devising some other incident also ultimately contributes to add significance to the total plot, it should be regarded as another type of beauty of episode.

When actors, expert in the art of pleasing the audience, are seen to play the role of an audience themselves on the stage with other actors performing, such a play-episode within a play-episode may be regarded as illustrating a literary art which beautifies the entire drama exquisitely.

The art of the dramatic plot should be pleasing by the construction of delightful 'junctures' (*sandhis*); each of the parts should be organically related to other parts, the succeeding one following logically from the preceding one.

It should not be vitiated by any excessive craze for observing rules even when they are inopportune. Only in such cases, the episode will reveal a unique charm of originality.

When there is a departure from the enriched *rasas* of the source-book and a new delightful *rasa* is delineated by the poet at the conclusion of his work, so that the delight of the readers is ensured, we should regard it as beauty of a whole work.

When a good poet concludes his work with only such a select incident in his original source as promotes the singular prosperity of the hero depicted as an ideal character in all three worlds,

with the idea of avoiding the distasteful culmination of the story in the original, it should be regarded as another appealing form of beauty relating to a whole work. Supposing the even flow of the main story has been broken and its sentiment impaired by the intrusion of some incident whose connection with the main story is almost indiscernible; the poet might give the incident such a turn that it will become inevitable for the conclusion of the main story and thus maintain the unbroken course of *rasa* and invest his whole work with a very unique novelty thereby.

Again, though the hero is concerned in achieving primarily a single goal, when he is seen to attain incidentally many other equally great fruits,

which add up to make his glory shine very brilliantly, such an assemblage of his great achievements will contribute in another way to the beauty of a work as a whole.

Even if we let alone the artistic skill of the poet in devising original incidents or episodes, we find that he can display his unique art even in designating his main plot with a very significant title.

Even when great poets compose different literary works based on an identical theme, they are each seen to possess infinite individual beauty, each possessing distinctiveness from the others.

Whatever works might be composed by great poets who are able to instruct in new forms of political strategy, they may be taken as embodying literary beauty.

Kuntaka, from the Vakrokti-Jivita
translated by K. Krishnamoorthy

ABHINAVAGUPTA

With Bharatamuni and Anandavardhana, Abhinavagupta (10th–11th century A.D.) is among the very greatest in Indian aesthetics. He has a further distinction, which the two others do not have, namely, he is also one of the most important of the Kashmir Shaivite philosophers. His work is comparable, to think in comparative terms, to that of Immanuel Kant in the Western tradition. P.V. Kane remarks about Abhinavagupta that he was one of 'the most remarkable personalities of medieval India. He was a man of very acute intellect and was an encyclopaedic scholar. He had taken all knowledge for his province.'[1] Historically speaking too, Abhinavagupta stands at one of the most crucial moments of Indian history. He had completed his work by the end of the tenth century; and he retired into exile in a Kashmir cave about the same time as Mahmud of Ghazni began his raids on India. Thus, his life and philosophy represent the last great pinnacle of intellectual achievement in ancient India. 'In his eager search for knowledge, Abhinavagupta states that he resorted to teachers of *tarka* (Nyāya and Vaiśeṣika systems), and of Buddha, Ārhata and Vaiṣṇava doctrines. Abhinava was proficient in yogic practices, he believed that he had realized the Highest Reality (Śiva).'[2]

The concept of *Śàntarasa* posited by Abhinavagupta, and defended with an extraordinary logical rigour, reflects his visionary poetics. He argues: 'the eight *rasas* are like eight gods, and the *śānta* is like their highest centre, Siva.' But this insistence on transcendence as the highest value in literary aesthetics also reflects Abhinava's realization of the need to modify Bharata's formulation to suit the changing cultural ethos. Bharata's achievement in literary aesthetics is mainly of two types: 1) he synthesized the concept of poetry and the concept of drama, which were treated separately by his predecessors, and formed a common concept of literature; and 2) he combined theology, philosophy and criticism, which his predecessors had kept distinct as such. He was thus a great synthesiser.

The excerpt selected here is from J. L. Masson and M.V. Patwardhan on Abhinava's concept of *Śāntarasa* (*Śāntarasa & Abhinava's Philosophy*, The Oriental Institute, Pune, 1969, pages 120–143).

---

1 & 2: P.V. Kane, *History of Sanskrit Poetics,* Motilal Banarsidass, Delhi, 1971, pp. 236 & 240, respectively.

On *Śāntarasa:* Aesthetic Equipoise

The nature of *śānta* will now be explained according to those who follow the reading *nava rasāh* (nine *rasas*), instead of the reading *aṣṭau rasāh.* In this connection some say that *śama* is the *sthāyibhāva* of *śanta* and that it arises from *vibhāvas* such as ascetic practices, association with Yogins, etc. It can be represented on the stage by *anubhāvas* such as the absence of lust, anger, etc. Its *vyabhicāribhāvas* will be firmness, wisdom, etc. Others however do not accept this, because, they say, *śama* and *śānta* are synonyms. Nor do they wish to relinquish the figure of 49 *bhāvas* that was given by Bharata. Moreover, they say that it is proper for the *vibhāvas* such as the seasons, flowers, etc., to be connected with love, etc., which arise immediately after these *vibhāvas* are apprehended. But ascetic practices, Vedic recitation, etc., do not immediately give rise to *śānta.* Should one argue that ascetic practices, Vedic recitation, etc., are the immediate causes of the knowledge of the truth, then, since the knowledge of the truth which precedes *śānta* is their immediate effect, they cease to be the *vibhāvas* of *śānta.* Even the absence of lust, etc., cannot be the *anubhāva*, because it is not conclusive evidence of *śānta*, inasmuch as it is found to be present in *rasas* other than *śānta* as well, and because it cannot be combined with a stage-representation (*prayoga*). After all, it is not possible to display a cessation of activity. For example, even the *anubhāvas* sleep, a swoon, etc., can be shown by actions like breathing in and out, falling down, lying on the ground, etc. As for *vyabhicāribhāvas*, how can firmness of mind, etc., which is accompanied by a desire for the attainment of objects, be appropriate to *śānta*? Those to be instructed cannot be taught how to attain the knowledge of truth by means of a state of complete inactivity. Those people whose minds are pained by the sufferings of other people have not yet reached a state of tranquillity characterised by correct perception of the highest truth, but rather they are still caught in the turmoil of worldly life. Therefore *śāntarasa* does not exist.

The reply is as follows: Just as in this world there is the trilogy of *dharma*, etc., so also, it is quite well-known that *mokṣa* too is one of the goals of life, and it is found to be taught predominantly in the *śāstras* and in the *smṛtis* and *itihāsas*, etc., by specifying the means leading to its attainment. Just as the states of mind that are proper to love, etc. and expressed by such words as sexual love (*rati*) etc., by being made capable of being relished through the activity of the poet and the actor, are brought to the status of *rasas* such as *śṛngāra*, etc., in relation to the spectators who are possessed of the proper sympathetic response; in the same way, we ask you to tell us why the state of mind which is appropriate to the highest goal of man known as *mokṣa* cannot be raised to the status of a *rasa*? That state of mind just described is indeed the *sthāyibhāva* of *śānta*. But one must consider what its name is. Some say that it is complete detachment (*nirveda* — world-weariness) that is born from a knowledge of truth. For this detachment is quite different from the detachment that arises from poverty, etc., because its cause, viz. knowledge of the truth, is different. It was for this very reason — i.e., because *nirveda* is the *sthāyibhāva* of *śānta* — that it has been mentioned by Bharata midway between the *sthāyibhāvas* and the *sancāribhāvas* (i.e., *vyabhicāribhāvas*). Otherwise, i.e., if *nirveda* had not been intended by Bharata as the *sthāyibhāva* of *śānta*, the sage who had great regard for uttering an auspicious word at the commencement of a section of his work (*māngalika*) would not have mentioned *nirveda* at that place ... he would not have put the inauspicious word *nirveda* at the head of the list of *vyabhicāribhāvas*. When Bharata forbade the use of disgust (*jugupsā*) as a *vyabhicāribhāva* of *śṛngara*, he sanctioned by implication the interchangeability of the characters of the *sthāyibhāvas*, the *sancāribhāvas*, the *sāttvikabhāvas*, and the *anubhāvas*, in the case of all the 49 *bhāvas* as demanded by the requirements of a particular situation and as presented by the power of words and their senses. *Nirveda* arises from knowledge of the truth and overwhelms the other *sthāyins*. For only that emotion which is more highly stable than any of the other *sthāyins* such as love etc. which can tolerate co-existence with a variety of emotions, that alone (namely *nirveda*), they say, can overwhelm other *sthāyins*.

They also raise the following objection: if *nirveda* which arises from knowledge of the truth, is said to be the *sthāyibhāva* of *śānta*, ... in which case how could *vairāgya* (detachment) and similar other things (e.g. *samādhi*, which have been mentioned as *vibhāvas* of *nirveda*) be the *vibhāva* of *nirveda*? If one were to claim that detachment, etc., become the *vibhāva* of *nirveda* because they are the means of attaining to the knowledge of the truth, then it would mean that you are giving the name *vibhāva* to that which is the cause of another cause, and that would involve you in a great absurdity since *vibhāva* means the direct cause of a *sthāyibhāva* and not the distant or remote cause. Moreover *nirveda* is an attitude of rejecting everything, an attitude of not being attached to anything, and it would on the contrary be helpful to the emergence of the knowledge of the truth, far from being the effect of the knowledge of the truth, it would be a cause leading to it, because a detached person will strive in such a fashion that the knowledge of the truth arises in him. And *mokṣa* comes from a knowledge of the truth. It is not that one knows the truth, and then feels detached, and from that detachment *mokṣa* would arise. For Īśvarkṛṣṇa says:

'From detachment comes only *prakṛtilaya* (i.e. dissolution into the eight causes, *pradhana, buddhi, ahankāra* and the *pancatanmātras*, and not mokṣa)'.

Objection: Everywhere one sees a very great detachment on the part of those who know the truth. Even Patanjali has said:

'Thereafter from that knowledge of the truth (*puruṣakhyāti*) arises an extreme aversion to the *guṇas* (detachment)'. That is true (*bhavatyevam*). But Patanjali himself has said: 'Such detachment is really the highest state (*kāṣṭhā*) of knowledge.' Thus, then, knowledge of the truth (leading to aversion according to *Yogasutra* I.16) means nothing but knowledge of the truth reinforcing itself from stage to stage. And so *nirveda* is not the *sthāyibhāva* of *śānta*. On the other hand, knowledge of the truth alone would be the *sthāyibhāva*. As for right perception, which will be mentioned (by Bharata) while describing *nirveda* as a *vyabhicāribhāva*, as a *vibhāva* of *nirveda*, and which leads to the dissipation of the attitude of acceptance, for attachment to unworthy objects, on the part of a person who has been deceived by a delusion of long standing, as exemplified in the following stanza:

'In vain did I milk a bull mistaking it for a cow bending under the burden of her full udder; in vain did I embrace an ugly eunuch thinking him to be a young girl; in vain did I cherish a longing for a piece of glittering glass thinking it to be beryl. All this I did when bemused as I was, I bowed to you, a miser unable to appreciate merit.'

Well, that perception of truth has been mentioned as a *vibhāva* (cause of only the ordinary kind of *nirveda*) whose nature is sadness arising from a realisation of one's stupidity in wasting energy in a worthless cause. We will speak of this perception of truth there (i.e. in the seventh chapter while commenting on the section on *nirveda*).

Objection: 'Attachment to the sense-objects is rooted in false knowledge. It will cease when knowledge of the truth arises. This is what the revered *Akṣapāda* has said in his *Sutra* beginning with the words *duḥkhajanma* etc., when he says that knowledge of the truth is caused by the removal of false knowledge and that it is further the cause of *vairāgya* which is of the nature of the removal of all faults (*doṣa*) such as attachment to worldly pleasures.' 'So *nirveda* is the *sthayin* and *tattvajñāna* is a *vibhāva*).' Who says so? For *nirveda* is a certain state of mind which is characterised by a flow if sadness, whereas *vairāgya* is a higher form of detachment than is *nirveda*, for the latter is often used non-technically to mean simply '*weariness*' or '*disgust*'. Even granting that *vairāgya* and *nirveda* are identical, still Gautama placed it in the midst of several (other causes of *mokṣa*) and did not mention it as the immediate cause of *mokṣa* (for it is only the remote cause, and so it does not follow that according to Akṣapāda *nirveda*, that is, *vairāgya*, is the *sthāyibhāva* of *śānta*). Moreover to say that *nirveda* arising from *tattvajñāna* is the *sthāyibhāva* of *śānta* means that you are giving to *śama* the name *nirveda*. Reply: *śama* and *śānta* have been explained as synonyms like *hāsa* and *hāsya* (i.e. *sthāyibhāva* and *rasa*). But the synonymity in the case of *śānta* and *śama* is only apparent and not real. There is a real difference between *śānta* (the *rasa*) and *śama* (the *sthāyibhāva*), for *śama* is *siddha*, an accomplished fact, while *śanta* is *sādhya*, something to be accomplished; *śama* is *laukika*, worldly, while *śānta* is *alaukika*, other-worldly; *śama* is *sādhāraṇa*, ordinary, while *śānta* is *asādhāraṇa*, extraordinary. Therefore, *nirveda* cannot be the *sthāyibhāva* of *śānta*.

Others believe that only eight mental states have been mentioned (by Bharata), such as love, etc. Those same mental states when depending on extraworldly *vibhāvas* such as *śruta* (study of scriptures and especially of the *Upaniṣads*), which are different from the ordinary (*kathita*) *vibhāvas*, become indeed unusually lovely (*vicitra*). And from out of their midst one can become the *sthāyin* here, i.e., in the case of *śāntarasa*. Out of them (*tatra*), *rati* alone, having for its object one's own Self consisting of undisturbed bliss, is the means of attaining *mokṣa*. And so, that *rati* it self is the *sthāyin* in *śānta*. For it has been said:

'That man whose love is centred in the Self, who is gratified in his Self, and who takes all delight in the Self — for such a man there is nothing any longer to be accomplished.'

In the same way, any of the *sthāyibhāvas* beginning with *rati* and *hāsa* and ending with *vismaya* can be explained as the *sthāyibhāva* of *śānta*, because we find that a person attains to liberation if he realises the oddity of everything in the world (*hāsa*); if he sees that the whole world is lamentable (*śoka*); if he perceives the happenings in the world as harmful to his spiritual well-being, and angry with them, desires to conquer them; (*krodha*); if he resorts to extraordinary energy dominated by the absence of delusion in order to overcome worldly temptations (*utsāha*); if he feels afraid of all the objects of the senses (*bhaya*); if he feels disgust for young women, etc., though they are desirable for all other people (*jugupsā*); if he feels astonished at his unprecedented realisation of his own self (*vismaya*). And Bharata agrees with this position. For while Bharata enumerates particular *bhāvas* by using words like *rati*, etc., and includes thereunder other varieties of the same by using the word *ca*, he does admit their ability to lead to liberation, provided that they are the result of extraordinary causes (i.e. *vibhāvas*) different from ordinary causes. But in the case of those people who hold this view (namely that any one of the *sthāyibhāvas* such as *rati*, etc., can be the *sthāyibhāva* of *śānta*), the different *sthāyibhāvas* would cancel each other out and so not even one of them could be regarded as the *sthāyibhāva* of *śānta*. If it is said that the different *sthāyibhāvas* can be the *sthāyibhāvas* of *śānta* because of the different approaches leading to it, that is as good as already refuted. Further, because of the different *sthāyibhāvas* of *śānta* depending on the approaches of the persons concerned, there would be an infinity of *śāntarasas*. If it is said that there would be only one *śāntarasa* and not countless *śāntarasas* because of its being the cause of one single result, namely *mokṣa*, then even *vira* and *raudra* would have to be regarded as one *rasa* because both lead to one single result, namely destruction (of one's enemy). Others say that all the *sthāyibhāvas*, *rati*, etc., become merged together, just as different flavours merge together in a beverage, and when so merged they become the *sthāyibhāvas* of *śānta*. But because different states of mind cannot coexist at one time, and because some are mutually antagonistic, even this is not a very attractive thesis.

What then is the *sthāyibhāva* of *śānta*? The reply is as follows: knowledge of the truth alone is the means of attaining *mokṣa* and so it would be proper to regard that alone as the *sthāyibhāva* of *mokṣa*. Knowledge of the truth is just another name for knowledge of the Self. The knowledge of any object other than the Self is the knowledge of worldly objects. For anything that is different from the Self is nothing but non-self. Our teacher has dealt with this at great length. And we have gone into it in some detail elsewhere, and so at this moment there is no point in dilating. Therefore, the *ātman* alone possessed of such pure qualities as knowledge, bliss, etc., and devoid of enjoyment of imagined sense-objects, is the *sthāyibhāva* of *śānta*. Its status as a *sthāyibhāva* should not be explained in the same terms as the status, as a *sthāyibhāva*, in the case of other *sthāyibhāvas*; there is a great difference between the *ātman's* status as a *sthāyibhāva* and the other *sthāyibhāvas'* status as *sthāyibhāvas*. For *rati*, etc., which arise and disappear due to the emergence and disappearance of their respective causes, are called *sthāyibhāvas* in so far as they attach themselves for some time to the canvas (wall) in the form of the *ātman* which is of an unchanging nature relative to them. But knowledge of the truth is the canvas behind all emotions, and so it is the most stable of all *sthāyibhāvas*. It transforms all the states of mind such as love, etc., into transitory feelings, and its status as a *sthāyibhāva*, having been established by its very nature, need not be specifically mentioned. And therefore it is not proper to count knowledge of the truth separately in addition to the eight *sthāyibhāvas*. Between a lame bull and a dehorned bull, bullness which is the generic property present in both the bulls is not considered a third thing. And so the number, viz. forty-nine, of the *bhāvas* is not disturbed. Should one demand to know why then knowledge of the truth is separately considered as a *sthāyibhāva* by me, Abhinavagupta, we reply that it is so because it can be separately enjoyed. For whereas *rati*, etc., can be the subject of ordinary perception in their pure form, without being mingled with anything else, the nature of the Self is of course not the subject of ordinary perception in its pure form without being mingled with anything else, the way *rati*, etc., are. But even though in its pure nature it is of an indeterminate form, still when it is investigated at the time of the return from abstract meditation, it invariably appears as mingled with various mental states.

Or let it appear like that (i.e., let the nature of the Self appear as you say, soiled by the various mental states). Still you cannot consider as *sthāyibhāvas* all possible moods of the mind, for they are of no use so far as the eight *rasas* actually mentioned by Bharata are concerned. They rather deserve to be regarded as transitory feelings and not otherwise (i.e., not as *sthāyibhāvas*). And thus only can the statement (*praghaṭṭaka*) that there are in all forty-nine *bhāvas* be justified. This nature of the Self cannot be said to be transitory because it would be impossible, unimaginative (*avaicitryāvaha*) and improper. *Śama* is the nature of the Self. Bharata has designated it (i.e., the nature of the Self) by the word *śama*. If that same nature of the Self is called *śama* or *nirveda*, there is no objection. Only note that *śama* is a different kind of state of mind altogether. And this special *nirveda* is only apparently similar to the *nirveda* that arises from other causes such as poverty, etc. Although their causes are different, nonetheless, because they are similar, they are both called *nirveda*. This is similar to what takes place in love, fear, etc. Therefore the nature of the Self is itself the knowledge of the Truth, and it is also tranquillity. Further (*tathā ca*) *rati*, etc., are only particular dark colorations (*kālusyoparāgaviśeṣāh*) of the Self (or of *śānta*?). Having by means of continued concentration realised its form as being pure, though connected with them (i.e. *rati*, etc.), there is even at the time of withdrawing from meditation (*vyuthāna*), complete tranquillity of the spiritual aspirant, the *sādhaka*. As has been said: *praśāntivāhita samskārāt*. This entire collection of ordinary and extra-ordinary states of mind can become the helper of the major emotion known as knowledge of the Truth. Its *anubhāvas* are *anubhāvas* helped by *yama*, *niyama*, etc., and also the *svabhavābhinayas* which will be described in the three chapters beginning with *upāngābhinaya*. And so they (i.e., these *anubhāvas*) are concerned with *śāntarasa* itself. This itself is its nature (i.e., the nature of *śāntarasa*). The *vibhāvas* are the grace of God, etc. And love etc., which are soon to be completely destroyed, can be aesthetically enjoyed in *śānta* as subsidiary, momentary elements. Just as the *vyabhicāri* 'eagerness' appears as important in love during-separation or even love-during-union, as said in the phrase: 'love whose festivity never comes to an end', and just as *augrya*, a *vyabhicārin*, appears as prominent in *raudra*; and just as *nirveda*, *dhṛti* (firmness of mind), *trāsa* (fear) and *harṣa* (joy), though really *vyabhicāribhāvas*, appear as prominent in *karuṇa*, *vira*, *bhayānaka* and *adbhuta*; so in *śāntarasa*, *jugupsā* (disgust), etc., appear predominantly, since they are completely opposed to love. For the *mahāvrata* (ceremony) one carries about a human skull ..... (*tr.n.* obscure). At the time of begetting a son by a widow from her brother-in-law, anointment of one's own body with oil has been recommended with a view to creating a sense of disgust. For the man who has done all that must be done with regard to his Self (i.e., who has realised the true nature of his Self), his efforts are all for promoting the good of other people, and so his energy takes the form of an effort that is prompted by the wish to help others. This is a synonym for compassion, and it is very intimately connected with *śānta*. And so some people call *śāntarasa*, *ḍayāvira* (compassionate heroism) and some call it *dharmavira* (religious heroism) because of the intensity of this energy (*utsāha*) which becomes its *vyabhicāribhāva*.

Objection: 'Energy is based on egoism as its essence, whereas *śānta* consists primarily in a loosening of egoism.' Reply: It is not improper for an opposing mood to be a *vyabhicāribhāva* (in *śānta*), for we find, for instance, *nirveda* as a *vyabhicāribhāva* in love. In the verse 'With the forest-ground overgrown with grass as my bed' and other similar stanzas, we find a high degree of *utsāha* in helping others. There is no state that is devoid of *utsāha*. For in the absence of desire and effort, one would be like a stone. And so because one has understood the higher Self and the lower Self, there is nothing left to do with regard to one's own Self, and therefore, for those whose hearts are tranquil, to give their all-in-all, i.e., to give their bodies, for the sake of helping another is not contrary to *śānta*. 'One should preserve one's self', and such similar advice is meant in the sense of guarding one's body and is meant for those who have not realised their Self, because ascetics are not concerned with guarding their bodies at all. For it has been said:

'The life-breaths (*prānah*) are the cause of attaining *dharma*, *artha*, *kama* and *mokṣa*. When they are destroyed what is not destroyed? When they are guarded, what is not guarded? (i.e., all is guarded).'

In this stanza the motive (*nidāna*) for the preservation of the body is shown to be its capacity to achieve the well-known four goals of life. In the case of the man who has realised his Self however, it is often heard, in the context of *sannyāsa* that he should throw his body into water, fire or a pit. Thus the idea is that since somehow the body is to be renounced sometime or other, if it be given up for the sake of another, what would not be achieved? (i.e., so much is thereby gained). Should one argue that Jimūtavāhana and others were not ascetics, we should ask how that matters to us? Certainly they had attained to knowledge of the Truth. For it would be inconceivable that those who consider their body as their soul should abandon for the sake of others the very body which is to them their all-in-all, for in their case there would be no urge for *dharma*, etc. In a battle, a warrior has no intention of abandoning his body for a religious cause, but rather he enters the battle only in order to conquer his enemy. In suicide by jumping off a cliff, etc., the main purpose is the desire to attain a more beautiful body in the life to come. Therefore whatever deeds, beginning with the imparting of spiritual advice and culminating in renunciation of one's body, are performed in order to achieve the benefit of others and without reference to one's own benefit, are certainly inconceivable in the case of people who have not attained to a knowledge of the true nature of *Ātman*. And they i.e., people who do these deeds are also knowers of the Truth. For those who know the Truth, there is liberation in all the (four) stages (*āśrama*) of life. This is what is taught in the *Smṛtis* and *Śrutis*. As has been said:

'A man who is attached to worship of the gods, who is grounded in the knowledge of the Truth, who is gracious to guests, who, having performed the ceremonial rites to his ancestors (*śrāddha*), gives out wealth, even though he be (only) a house-holder, (this man) is freed.'

However (*kevalam*) in the case of Bodhisattvas, etc., although they have known the truth, there is, because of their religious or righteous actions springing from a desire to do good to others and expected by them to result in the benefit of others, a reappearance of a body appropriate to that (i.e., to those actions that they have performed).

Even in the case of *rasas* which occupy a subsidiary position in a poetic work, the attainment of 'repose' (i.e., aesthetic enjoyment) is met with, because that is only appropriate to their nature as *rasas*. For instance, in the *Rāmāyaṇa*, in the case of Rāma when he obeys his father's orders and goes into exile, repose is met with in this, though the aesthetic repose is only subsidiary. The same should be understood in the case of *sṛngara* and other *rasas* when they occupy a subsidiary position in a poetic work. Hence although *śāntarasa* has come to stay in the *Nāgānanda*, it is not the major *rasa*, because in that play the achievement of the three goals of human life (*dharma, artha* and *kāma*), with special emphasis on helping others, is the final result in the case of Jimūtavāhana. With this thought in mind, Bharata will say while defining a *nāṭaka*, that 'it is possessed of qualities such as wealth, flirtatious ways, etc.' This means that a dramatist should introduce into the *nāṭaka* all kinds of actions in which opulence and flirtation are predominant and in which emphasis is placed on the two goals of life, *artha* and *kāma*, because such actions have the charming purpose of winning a sympathetic response from all people (i.e., because such actions have a universal appeal). We will describe this in that very section dealing with the definition of a *Nāṭaka*. With this in mind, Bharata will not prescribe any *jātyaṃśaka* in *śānta*. Hence the view of some that *śāntarasa* does not exist in as much as Bharata has not prescribed any *jātyaṃśaka* in its case, is refuted.

Others however say: 'Jimūtavāhana saved an old woman who needed protection, and who said: "Oh son, who will save you?" He had no power. He wanted to harm nobody.' We agree with this. Should it be further argued that there is no power .... of Bodhisatvas (?). But the *śānta* does not teach by means of *kākatāliya* (*nyāya*) (?). Therefore it is proved: *utsāha* is principally intended in this play and therefore *vira* is the major *rasa*, and it is characterised by compassion. In the *Nāgānanda* other moods like love for Malayavati, detachment, etc., become subsidiaries according to the circumstances (*yathayogam*). As has been said:

tacchindreshu pratyayāntarāṇi saṃskārebhyāh

And so we have refuted the contention that *anubhāvas* cannot exist because of a complete absence of action in the case of a man who is *śānta*. When, however, one has reached the culminating state of *śānta* and all *anubhāvas* are absent, this *śānta* cannot be represented. In love and sorrow, etc., also, in the culminating stages, it is correct that there is no possibility of representation.

Sympathetic identification however is possible for those who have planted in them the *saṃskāras* that are the seeds of such knowledge of the Truth. As Bharata will say:

'People devoid of passion take delight in *mokṣa*'.

After all not everybody is always sympathetic to everything. For instance, a man whose nature is heroic will not sympathetically identify with a character in *bhayānaka*. Objection: 'How can a heroic type of person take any delight in such a presentation?' The reply is: in a work where this (*śānta*) is presented, surely there is one or other of the other *rasas* such as *sṛngāra*, *vira*, etc., since the work is intended to be useful to the goals of life other than liberation. Its aesthetic relish is grounded in *śānta* however. In *prahāsana*, etc., too, where *hāsya*, etc., are principal, the aesthetic relish is grounded in other *rasas* which arise in their wake (*anuniṣpādi*). According to some, the justification for the exposition of the different drama-types is the intention to cater to aesthetic enjoyment in the case of different kinds of spectators (*adhikārin*). Therefore *śāntarasa* does exist. And so in old manuscripts, after the passage 'we will show how the *sythāyibhāvas* develop into the *rasas*', is read definition of *śānta* in the phrase 'What is called *śānta* has for its *sthāyibhāva śama*', etc. In this connection, the aesthetic enjoyment of all *rasas* is similar to that of *śānta*, because it (i.e., this aesthetic enjoyment) is turned away from actual sense-object contact. (Because we are particularly concerned with one *rasa*, except that it is mixed with other latent mental impressions (vāsana) In order to indicate that it (*śānta*) is at the root of all *rasas*, it was named at the beginning. In ordinary worldly dealings, one does not mention separately a thing common to all, and so its *sthāyin* was not separately given. But even a thing which is common to a number of other things deserves to be separately reckoned by the discriminating man, and so it (*śāntarasa*) has become separate as the object of cognition in the form of aesthetic enjoyment of the spectator who is admitted to be a discriminating reader. In the *Itihāsas*, the *Purāṇas*, doctrines, etc., we hear of nine *rasas* as well as in the revered *Siddhāntaśāstra*. Thus it is said:

'He should display the eight *rasas* in the places alloted to the eight gods. And in the centre he should display *śāntarasa* in the place of the supreme God (Śiva).'

Its *vibhāvas* are *vairāgya*, fear of *saṃsāra*, etc. *Śānta* is known through the portrayal of these. Its *anubhāvas* are thinking about *mokṣa*-texts, etc. Its *vyabhicāribhāvas* include world-weariness, wisdom, contentment (*dhṛti*), etc. And as *bhakti* and *śraddhā* which are directed towards meditation on God and which are reinforced by *smṛti*, *mati*, *dhṛti*, are in any case (*anyathaiva*) helpful (to *śānta*), neither of them should be counted as a separate *rasa*. Here is a *sangrahakārikā on this matter:*

'*Śānta rasa* is to be known as that which arises from a desire to secure the liberation of the Self, which leads to a knowledge of the Truth, and is connected with the property of highest happiness.'

By the three adjectives qualifying *śānta* in this verse, the *vibhāvas, sthāyibhāva* and *anubhāvas* are shown respectively.

'Various feelings, because of their particular respective causes arise from *śānta* (a state of mental calm). But when these causes disappear, they melt back into *śānta*.'

In this verse and others it has been summarily shown that *śānta* is the source of all other *rasas*.

As for the statement that will be made by Bharata to the effect that in the *Ḍima* type of drama there are six *rasas*, excluding both *hāsya* and *śṛngāra*, here is what is meant: by giving the definition: 'It is based on a composition with an exciting *rasa*', there can be no question at all of *śānta*, as it is opposed to *raudra* which is predominant in the *Ḍima*. So what is the point of separately excluding it? Since *śānta* is impossible and since *Ḍima* has its source (i.e., since it is based on) an exciting *rasa*, what else can be excluded (but *śānta*)? Had he only said that it can be associated with six *rasas*, excluding *śṛngāra* and *hāsya*, (without adding the qualifying phrase *diptarasakāvyayonih*), *śānta* would not have been excluded. Objection: 'This quarter stanza (*diptarasakāvyayonih*) excludes *karuṇa, bibhatsa* and *bhayānaka* as predominant *rasas*.' This is not true, because when (he) says that the *Ḍima* is associated with the styles called *Sāttvatī* and *Ārabhatī*, they are automatically excluded since they belong to style *Kaiśiki*. But *śānta* uses only the *Sāttvatī* style, and therefore this qualification alone would not be enough to exclude it. And therefore the definition of the *Ḍima*, far from arguing against the existence of *śānta*, is evidence for its existence. *Śṛngāra* however would be possible in a *Ḍima* because demons make love in a violent manner. *Hāsya* is helpful to *śṛngāra* and therefore only their exclusion was specifically mentioned, because both are possible and only a possible thing can be excluded, but not an impossible thing such as *śānta*.

Because *śānta* is common to all *rasas*, it would be improper to name especially a colour or god that is appropriate to it, as one has done for the other *rasas*, but they have been invented by some. And so the reasonableness of *śānta* has been shown. Its true nature is *hāsya*. *Vira* and *bibhatsa* tend to lead towards it. Therefore there is in the case of *śānta* the advice about the practice of *yama*, *niyama*, meditation on God, etc. It stands to reason that it leads to a great result (i.e., *mokṣa*), as it eschews enjoyment of worldly objects (*anupabhogitayā*), that it is more important than any other *rasa*, and that it pervades the entire plot. And so enough of further elaboration.

What is the nature of its true relish? It is the following: The nature of the soul is tinged by *utsāha, rati*, etc., which are capable of imparting their peculiar tinges to it. It is like a very white thread that shines through the interstices of sparsely threaded jewels. It assumes the forms of all the various feelings like love, etc., which are superimposed on it, because all these things are capable of imparting their tinges to it. Even then (*tathābhāvenāpi*) it shines out through them, according to the maxim that once this *Ātman* shines, it shines for ever. It is devoid of the entire collection of miseries which consist in (i.e., which result from) turning away from the *Ātman*. It is identical with the consciousness of the realisation of the highest bliss. It takes its effect through the process of generalisation in poetry and drama. It makes such a heart (i.e., the heart of the sensitive spectator or reader) the receptacle of an other-worldly bliss by inducing a peculiar kind of introspection (*antarmukhāvasthābheda*).

There are only these nine *rasas*, because only they deserve to be taught, as they are useful to the four goals of life or are exceptionally pleasant. Therefore, what others say, namely that this restriction on numbers is because only these nine are well-known to enlightened literary critics, though other *rasas* are possible, has been refuted. This will be explained in the chapter on the *bhāvas*. It is wrong to say that affecion, with a *sthāyibhāva* of being moved (*ārdratā*) can be a *rasa*, because affection is nothing other than attachment, and all attachment culminates in *rati*, *utsāha* or some other such accepted *sthāyibhāva* ... For instance, the love of a child for its mother and father terminates in (i.e., can be included under) 'fear'. The affection of a young man for his friends terminates in *rati*. The affection, as of Lakṣmaṇa, etc., for his brother terminates in (i.e. can be included under) *dharmavira*. The same is true of the affection of an old man for his son, etc. The so-called *rasa* 'cupidity' with the *sthāibhāva* of 'greed' can be refuted in the same manner, because it will terminate in some other (*sthāyibhāva*) such as *hāsa* or *rati*. The same holds true of *bhakti*.

Abhinavagupta, from the Abhinavabhārati
translated by J.L. Masson and M.V. Patwardhan

JÑĀNEŚVARA

Jñāneśvara is to Marathi literature what Dante, his contemporary, is to modern Italian literature. He is considered by common consent to be the greatest poet, stylist and thinker in the seven-hundred-year tradition of Marathi poetry. His life and work are nothing short of a miracle. He is believed to have willed death at the age of twenty after completing his great work, the *Bhāvārthadīpika*, popularly known as the *Jñāneśvarī*. The poem is an elaborate commentary on the *Bhagavadgītā*, involving a verse-by-verse textual analysis, which Jñāneśvara composed as an offering to his teacher Nivṛttinath. Though it is not exactly the first Marathi poem, the *dīpikā* founded the tradition of Marathi poetry, and in the course of time acquired the status of the central canonical work in the Vārkari movement in Maharashtra.

At the time Jñāneśvara wrote it, writing in a new language like Marathi a philosophical commentary on a Brahminical scripture was an act of radical cultural departure. It was an important shot in the battle against the cultural hegemony of Sanskrit and high-caste Hinduism waged by the Bhakti poets all over India. As such, the *Jñāneśwarī* is couched in political, social and linguistic attitudes which, for the thirteenth century India, are remarkably progressive.

The text of Jñāneśwara's commentary on the *Gītā* employs the device of invocation, both at the beginning of the poem as well as at the beginning of the individual sections. It is in these invocatory parts that we get the poet's philosophy of language, poetry, style and readership. The abundance of imagery that surrounds his explication shows the wealth of his imagination. Extracts from these parts are reproduced here to represent the direction in which non-Sanskrit literature in India was moving during the early centuries of the second millennium. *Jñāneśvarī* deserves the credit of being the first critical text in modern Indian languages, though of course that is not its only and main achievement.

The *dīpikā* has been translated several times. The latest and the most readable translation is by Swami Kripānanda (State University of New York Press, 1989). It is in fact a revised version of the translation published by Pradhan and Lambert, which in turn was a reworking of the translation by R.K. Bhagwat (in two parts, Part I with S.V. Pandit, and Part II with V.V. Dixit). The extracts reprinted here from the original, i.e., the translation by R.K. Bhagwat (Jñāneśvarī English Rendering Publishing Association, Poona, 1953). Though the diction and syntax of this rendering is quite archaic, it is very close to the original.

Note: Several terms in this extract have been transliterated for the reader's convenience.

Invocations

... Oh Om, the Primeval being, the very form of Supreme Self, the subject-matter of the Vedas, be bowed to, All glory to it. Oh you, the form of self who can be known from self experience alone, I hail you. Oh God, you yourself are, as I, the humble disciple of Nivṛttināth, propound, that Gaṇeśa who is the very light of the understanding power of all, and (Oh hearers) hear this attentively. This entire Vedic literature is, as it were your own beautiful image, and its body in the form of orthography is shining flawlessly. The Smṛti Scriptures are the very limbs of that image, while the stanzas of the poetry are the very movements of the limbs, and the eloquence of the meaning is the pose of their beauty. The eighteen *Purāṇas* (mythologies) are like the jewelled ornaments and the principles (and truths) are the gems, the phraseology being the sockets in which the gems are set. The gentle and beautiful poetic composition is a colourful yarn and its ground in the form of literature is substantial and bright. See further: if these poetic dramas are planned with taste they can constitute jingling bells (*ghungarē*) that create a jingling sound in the form of meaning. And the principles and truths arrived at, as the result of an analysis of these dramas, if subjected to skilful tests — the resultant factors (*padē*) constitute the gems set on jingling bells. The ideology of the poets, Vyas and others, constitutes the belt (round the waist) formed of silken scarf, while the ends of its ornamental border glitter (above the jingling bells). The six different schools of (Hindu) philosophy that are called *ṣaḍdarshanē* (six points of view) are the six arms (of the image of *Gaṇeśa*) and for the same reason, the arms in the six hands differ from each other.

The logic (*tarkaśāstra*) is the battle axe: the *Nyāyaśāstra* (the doctrine of Social and Political Science) is *aṅkuśa* (elephant goad). The *Vedānta* is a sweet juicy pudding (*modak*). The broken tusk in one hand represents the mutilated doctrine of Buddhism, defeated as a result of the commentary by followers of the Nyāya philosophy. Proceeding in this order, it naturally follows that the logical debate that establishes Absolute Brahman is the bountiful hand (*varadahasta* of Gaṇeśa) and the establishment of religion is his hand stretched forth in reassurance or in token of favour (*abhayahasta*). Pure and right thinking is the straight (elephant) trunk helping to secure the Supreme unalloyed bliss of the Absolute. The talk that removes all differences (of opinion) is his complete (unbroken) and white tusk. *Unmeṣas* (the thrill of the lustre of knowledge) are the small glistening eyes of God Gaṇeśa — the remover of all obstacles. The introductory as well as the concluding portions of the *Mimāṅsa* (the Science of interpretation of Vedic texts) are the two ears on which hover the bees in the form of sages, taking the juicy honey (oozing from the temples). Duality and non-duality are the two temples glistening with corals in the form of philosophy and both these temples, being quite close to each other on the elephant head of Gaṇeśa appear as if equipoised and merged into one. Besides, the fragrant flowers in the form of the ten *Upaniṣads*, full of floral honey in the form of deepest and truest knowledge, appear beautiful on the crown. The syllable 'a' forms the two feet of Gaṇeśa, the syllable 'u', his big belly while the syllable 'm' — the grand crown of his head. The combination of these three syllables 'a, u, m' forming AUM (Om), covers up and comprehends all the truth revealed as Divine word or word Absolute, I therefore bow, through the grace of the good preceptor, the primary seed of the entire Universe. Now I bow to the world-attracting Śāradā (the Goddess of learning) who inspires the diverse and new expressions of literary beauty and who sustains and fulfils the desire for truth and beauty. Since the good Master who has taken me across to the other side of the ocean of the mundane existence is dwelling in my heart, I hold in high regard the quality of right thinking. Just as an application to the eyes of divine antimony confers on men the super-human power and enables them to see big underground treasures whereever they might cast their glance, or just as the possession of the gem 'Chintamani' fructifies all desires, in that way, I Jñāneśvara say, that I have, through the grace of Sri Nivṛttināth, become fully gratified in desires. Therefore a wise one should worship the preceptor and realise the status of one who has realised his highest duty. The watering of the roots makes the branches and leaves get fresh, or a dip in the ocean accomplishes the object of bathing in all the holy waters in the Universe, or the taking of nectar includes taking in all health-giving juices: in that way the preceptor who makes successful all my wishes — to that preceptor Nivṛttināth I bow again and again. Now hear the very grand and solemn tale. It is the very birth-place of all arts and enjoyments, or it is a garden of unique trees in the form of right thinking: or it is the very treasure of the Supreme truths which are the very roots of all happiness; or it is an ocean filled with the nectar of nine artistic sentiments (*navarasa* — Nine classes of emotions or feelings) — all these are this tale. Or this tale is the very place of salvation or the original fountain spring of all learning (*vidyā*) or the abode of all groups of Scriptures; or this tale is the mother home of all religious thoughts, the very heart-cherished thing of the virtuous people; and the treasure house of beauty of Goddess Sarasvatī: or the very Goddess in the form of the faculty of speech has revealed her grandeur in the form of this tale through her inspiration to the genius of sage Vyāsa. For all these reasons this tale is the very queen amongst the great Epics and source of grandeur of all literary works and from this has been secured the sweetness of the *Navarasas* (Nine *Rasas*) including romance, etc. Do hear one more special feature of this work. The glory of word-beauty has been rendered pure and refined through this tale and the tenderness of the highest wisdom of realisation of the Self has been enhanced. This tale has made talent wider or truth truer and the truth has become more tasteful and sweet, while the very consummation of happiness has been made more consummate. This has added sweetness to the sweet, beauty to romantic amours and supreme goodness to worthy things, thereby giving them more pleasing aspect. This tale has secured the essence of artistic perfection for arts, and unique glory to merit, and therefore the sins of king Janamejaya got easily washed out. Thinking a little longer it would appear that by this tale artistic patterns are made more artful and all qualities more lustrous. In short, just as the Universe appears more bright through the Sun's splendour, in that way the Universe has also got greatly illumined and adorned being pervaded by sage Vyāsa's genius, or just as seed sown in a fertile soil automatically grows extensively in that way all truths and subjects worth being known have come to fruitful perfection in the Bhārata Epic: or just as one living in a city naturally becomes well-informed, gentle, and refined in conduct, in that way the entire Universe has become bright and clear on account of Vyāsa's words: or just as the tenderness of beauty becomes specially visible in a woman in her early youth; or just as all trees and shrubs, big and small in the garden lands get abundance of growth at the advent of the spring season; or just as there appears nothing special in point of form in a molten lump of gold, but the real beauty comes in when it is converted into ornaments; in that way with the idea that the beauty of all varieties of patterns of one's liking could be expressed by studding them with ornaments in the form of Vyāsa's composition, all story writers have approached this tale, for inspiration and with the object of securing adequate position, all the mythologies have accepted even subordination, and have contributed in the form of sub-narratives to the great epic *Bhārata*, and therefore it is, that what is not contained in this epic, is not to be had anywhere else in the Universe; and this has led to the adage 'The entire world of literacy or universe of truth and beauty is rendered stale by being tasted by Vyāsa (*Vyāsocchiṣhta*).' In this way this eloquent tale has been told by sage Vaiśampāyan to the King Janamejaya — the narrative which is the very birth-place of the highest spirituality in the Universe. You should therefore hear this tale attentively — that tale which is unparalleled, supreme, full of great merit, unique, and the very home of Unity with the very essence of divinity. The portion named *Gītā* preached by Lord Kṛṣṇa to Arjuna is but a particle of the pollen dust of lotus flower in the form of the epic *Bhārata*; or this is the butter incomparable in quality in the form of *Gītā* that emerged through the churning process to which the talent of Sage Vyāsa subjected the ocean of truth. This butter by being successfully boiled in the fire of knowledge with careful thinking has been converted into flavoured ghee: that tale the spiritual vision of which the ascetics wish for, which is actually experienced by the saints and which is revered all over the three worlds, which transpired in due course in the *Bhīṣmaparva*, which is named *Bhagavadgītā*, which is praised both by God Brahmadeva and God Śaṅkara.

And which is taken in with great regard, by Sanat and others — the sweetness of such a story should be enjoyed with refined, equipoised mind by the hearers, in the way, the young ones of the bird cakor pick up with feeble mind the tender atoms of the nectar of the small phase of early moon in the 'Śarad' season. The narrative is preached without words (uttered), is experienced even before the senses come to know of it; its subtle truths are grasped even before its words actually fall into the ears. Just as the black bees carry away the flower dust from the lotuses even before the lotuses come to know of it, in that way becomes the state of hearers. Only the Kumudinī (Lotus-plant) possesses the skill of embracing the rising moon and to experience his love without even leaving her own place; in that way only that seeker, whose heart is calm and steady on account of serious and solemn temper can understand the *Gītā* truth. Therefore such saints as are worthy of taking their place by the side of Arjuna on the occasion of hearing the *Gītā* teaching, should kindly pay attention to this story. I might perhaps be considered a bit impudent, over-bearing through familiarity in saying this, yet such is really not the case. Oh hearers, you possess solemn and generous hearts, and therefore I have made this humble request at your feet. It is the nature of parents that they should feel happy at the prattling of their child, in that way since you have once accepted me and called me your own favourite, it is for you now to put up with whatever short-comings you may notice in me, without any such prayer coming from me: but I have committed another fault and it is of venturing to illumine, enlighten the meaning of the *Gītā* and I have therefore to pray you to hear attentively that illuminating comment. I have of my own accord made myself overbold, without weighing in my mind how difficult it is to carry successfully to its end this work. Could there stand any comparison between the brilliance of the Sun and that of the glow-worm? Or that I, an ignorant person, should embark upon the doing of such a thing, is like a lapwing trying to measure the depth of the ocean with her beak! Another thing: anyone thinking of holding in an embrace the entire sky, must himself be bigger than that sky: in that way the work I have undertaken is indeed simply beyond my scope. The grandeur of its meaning is well praised by God Śaṅkara who was once discoursing on the depth of the meaning of *Gītā*, to questions asked by Goddess Pārvatī who was dismayed and felt puzzled. God Śaṅkara then said 'Oh Bhavāni, the *Gītā* truth is as un-utterable and as perennially fresh as your own majestic appearance and beauty. This *Gītā* truth is the very word of the Almighty, whose very snoring of sleep threw up the *Veda* itself. How an insignificant, such a diminutive and a very dull thing as myself would fare in such a vast and limitless task (I have undertaken), in a region of profoundest mystery wherein even the *Vedas* lost themselves completely? How to bring within grasp such unbounded *Gītā* principles? And who could illumine this mighty flame of uncommon splendour? How can a small eye-fly hold in its fist the big sky? But even in this state I consider myself able enough, and the only authority on which I do so is the favour of good preceptor Nivṛttināth towards me, I, Jñāneśvara say. Without that support I am indeed — stupid and thoughtless: yet the lamp of the saint's kindness to me is brilliant and clear. Only in the *Parīs* lies the power by which iron is converted into gold; and so is the power of the ambrosia of bringing a dead pẹrson to life. If only the Goddess Sarasvatī is propitious, even a dumb one can command the faculty of speech: that way lies the power of certain things of bringing about certain results, and if these take place in that way there is no reason to feel any mystery of it. One who has got a mother like the desire-yielding cow (*kāmadhenu*) could never be in want of anything and it is for this reason that I have prepared myself to compose this work. My request therefore to you is 'It is up to you to make good whatever is defective and to drop out whatever is excessive in my work.' Now therefore attend here. I shall be able to talk only if you could make me talk in the way the puppet's movements depend upon the movements of the strings on which they are worked. In that way I am a favoured one of the Saints and the righteous and the protegé of their kindness. I have entirely delivered myself up unto them and they should adorn me with ornaments as they like. Just at this, the preceptor said 'Suffice now: there is hardly any need for you to ṣay all this: hasten up and turn your attention to the composition.' Jñānadeva felt extremely elated at the preceptor Nivṛttināth's words and he said 'Now hear with calm and patient attention.'

... Now, cleansing the heart and making it a boarded frame with feet *(caurañga)*, let there be installed on it the preceptor's feet (foot-prints). Filling the cavity formed by putting the hands side by side hollowing the palms *(añjulī)* in the form of union, with partially blown flowers in the form of all of sense-centres, let the floral oblations be dedicated at the feet of the preceptor. Let the body of the preceptor be smeared with fragrant sandal paste in the form of single-pointed desire (to render service), cleansed with water in form of deep devotion. Let the tender feet of the preceptor be adorned with jingling anklets prepared of gold in the form of unalloyed love. Let the preceptor's toes be adorned with rings in the form of deep and unswerving devotion. Let there be placed on the feet of the worthy preceptor, fully blown lotuses having eight petals constituted of the eight righteous feelings, laden with fragrance in the form of righteous joy. Let there be burnt before him incense in the form of conceit and let there be waved round him the lighted lamp (*niranjana*) in the form of the notion, 'I am myself Supreme Brahman'. Let the preceptor's feet be closely embraced with the feelings of complete identity. Let the feet of the preceptor wear the pair of wooden sandals in the form of my body and life and let enjoyment and liberation be waved around them. I should be eligible to render the service of the preceptor in such a way, that I should secure through such service all the qualifications for (attainment of) all the (four) objects of existence of man. The blaze of knowledge should go up straight to the abode of rest of Supreme Brahman in such a way that the faculty of speech is immediately transformed into the sea of nectar. Each letter (uttered) should have eloquence of such a type that crores of full-moons should be waved around it. When the East is dominated by the Sun it gives an empire of light to the entire universe; in that way the (faculty of) speech should be able to make a gift of Diwali-festival in the form of knowledge to the entire society of hearers. By offering service to the feet of the preceptor, the (faculty of) speech attains a unique luck — luck that brings out words from the mouth that make the divine resonance (*nādabrahma*) look small before them, and to whose level cannot come up even the dignity of the oneness of the Deity: — luck that makes the creeping plant of oration grow in abundance, so that the entire universe enjoys a lovely scenery of the spring season under its bower in the form of hearing; — luck that brings about the miracle of the words (oration) securing Supreme Brahman, which the mind along with speech were unable even to trace and they had to come back disappointed; — luck that makes it possible for the words to store in themselves the Supreme Spirit which is not intelligible to knowledge and also not securable by meditation. That the speech (of the disciple) is invested with such infinite beauty is due to the grace of the pollen of the lotus in the form of the dust of the preceptor's foot. What more should be said; it (preceptor's love) is not securable anywhere else but in the 'mother', declared Jñānadeva. (He said further) 'I am only an infant, while the preceptor is the mother with an only child, with the result that the flow of her affection turns solely towards me. Oh hearers, the preceptor has showered his kindness on me, in the way the cloud pours down all its waterstore for the sake of the bird Cātak. Therefore, even from the stray talk the unengaged mouth might indulge in, an eloquent discourse like that on the *Gītā*, emerges. When luck is favourable, even sand could be converted into gems, and when the longevity of life has not ended, even an assassin turns friendly. Were the master of the universe to be pleased and to give food for satisfying hunger, even small bits of stone turn into nectar (sweetened) rice when boiled. In that way when the good preceptor calls one his own, then even the mundane existence leads to liberation. Just see, did Lord Kṛṣṇa — the incarnation of Nārāyaṇa, the primeval man (purāṇa puruṣa — God) the one all-revered by the entire universe — did he permit the Pāndavas to be ever in want of anything? In that way, Śri Nivṛttināth brought up and exalted my ignorance to the same level with knowledge. But enough of this; I am overcome with feelings of affection while speaking. Whoever does possess knowledge to extol adequately the greatness of the preceptor? Now, through his grace, I am dedicating at the feet of you, saints, the interpretation of the *Gītā*. At the end of the Chapter XIV the Lord of the Union (of the individual soul with the Deity) declared, as an established truth, that the man of knowledge is as much the master of deliverance as the God Indra is of the riches of the Heavens; or that one who performs religious duties enjoined to Brahmins (*Brahmakarma*) throughout a hundred births, alone becomes God Brahmadeva and none else; or that the bliss of emancipation goes to the lot of the man of knowledge alone, in the way the light of the Sun becomes available only to the one having a vision, and to none else. Looking (mentally) round for one who becomes qualified to attain such knowledge, (the Lord) found only one such. The magical collyrium shows treasures hidden underground, but the seer must be one born with feet foremost. In that way there is no doubt that the mind must be very pure to enable knowledge to get deeply impressed oṇ it. The Lord has after careful consideration laid down as an established truth, that knowledge cannot be firmly impressed, unless there is asceticism. Lord Hari has further thought out how the mind can get asceticism. Should one come to know that food has been cooked mixed with poison, he walks away pushing aside (untouched) the plate (in which the food has been served). In that way, once the fact of the mundane existence being only transitory, is firmly impressed on the mind, asceticism, even though pushed away would closely follow you. The Lord is preaching in Chapter XV, how it (mundane existence) is transitory, by giving it the form of a sham tree. A (common) tree, if pulled out and re-planted with the roots upwards and the top downwards withers away; but this tree is not like that. With the aid of this simile (of a tree) the Lord has skilfully swept out clean the cycle of mundane existence. This Chapter XV is intended to prove the nullity of the mundane existence and to establish in one's self the truth of the proposition, viz., 'I am myself Supreme Brahman.' I am now going heartily to lay bare the secret of the Sacred Work (*Gītā*) and you do hear about it. The King of Dwārakā — the full moon, bringing into full tide the ocean of bliss — further said, 'Oh Son of Pāndu (there is) the semblance of the universe that obstructs the way leading to the abode of Supreme Self; this universe of vast expanse is not the mundane existence, this is the form of a giant tree, which is static. But is it not like other trees, that have their roots at the base and the branches upwards, and consequently it cannot normally be brought under control. However extensive the top, were an axe to be applied at the base or a fire applied there, the tree is cut at the base and topples down with its branches. But this tree cannot be easily felled down. Oh Arjuna, it is such a novel tale to narrate that all is extraordinary with this tree. The growth of this tree is all directed downwards. The Sun is at an immeasurable height, while his rays spread out downwards; in that way the growth of this tree is downwards in a very curious way. The floods of water occupy the entire cavity of the sky at the time of world dissolution; in that way every nook and corner of the universe is stuffed with this tree; or after sunset, the night gets fully stuffed with darkness; in that way the sky (space) is packed to its fullest capacity by this tree. It (the tree) bears neither any fruit that could be tasted nor any flower that could be smelt. What exists is this tree by itself all alone, Oh Son of Pāndu, it is top-rooted; yet is not (first) up-rooted and (then) placed in that (topsy-turvy) position; and consequently it is ever fresh and green. Even though truly called up-rooted, still, it has also got innumerable roots at the base. Owing to rank growth of grass (round about) there grow its branches in the tuft of its descending shoots (pārambyā). As in the case of Pimpaḷ, Vaṭa and other trees, similarly, Oh Dhanañjaya, it is also not the case that it has got branches only at the base. There appear in abundance branches on the top-side also. It looks as if the very sky has become its (tree's) foliage or the wind has taken the tree-form or the three different states (namely creation, sustenance and end) have appeared in incarnation (in the form of this tree). Such a big (world-tree), with its upwending roots has come into existence. What is its top, what are the marks of the base, how and why it is down-spreading, and how are its branches, what are the roots at the base, what and how are the branches in the upper region, and why it is called 'Áśvattha' — all these queries have been answered by that self-knowing God. All this I would make clear in select and choice phraseology, so that you will be able fully to realize it. Hear you, Oh lucky one; this is a befitting occasion for you; so you bear it attentively, creating ears (to hear) all over your body!

... Summarising thus the purport of the entire *Bhārata*-Scripture in one single verse, Saṅjaya delivered it into the hands of the Head of the Kurū Clan. The scope of fire is unlimited; yet in order to make up the want of the Sun (light) caused by sunset, it is utilized by simply kindling with it only one end of a cotton wick. In that way Brahman in the form of (articulate) sound is infinite in volume, it is transformed into (a finite volume and form of) one lakh and a quarter verses of *Bhārata*-Scripture. *Bhagavadgītā* made up of 700 verses, forms the quaint essence of the *Bhārata*-Scripture; and this last verse of the 700 verses, which represents the very perfection of Saṅjaya's dictum — Saṅjaya the disciple of Sage Vyāsa — it is an all-inclusive sum and substance of the entire *Gītā* scripture. One who holds fast this verse next to his heart will have conquered nescience, root and branch. These 700 verses constitute as it were so many foot-steps of the *Gītā* Scripture, and instead of calling them foot-steps, they might be taken as the ambrosia raining down from the sky in the form of *Gītā*-Scripture. Or, I rather feel that these verses are the very pillars of the Court (hall) of the King 'Supreme Self': or the *Gītā* might be likened to the Goddess described in the *Saptaśati* Scripture (Saptaśati - 700 verses) — the Goddess that got gladdened by giving absolution (by slaying him) to the demon named Mahiṣa — buffalo — in the form of infatuation. Therefore, one who becomes its devotee (servant) through mind, body and speech would be the sovereign King of the empire in the form of self-bliss: or these are the lustrous verses in the form of *Gītā*, that compete with and even excel the Sun in point of splendour, created by Lord Kṛṣṇa for fighting out the darkness in the form of nescience; or these verses constitute a bower of the vine (creeping plant), provided as a resting place for the weary travellers wending the path of wordly affairs; or this *Gītā* constitutes a lake in the form of Lord Kṛṣṇa's mouth, buzzing with black bees in the form of lucky saints that enjoy (honey in) the lotuses in the form of verses; or it appears to me that these (700) verses are none else but as many bards (*bandījan*) singing profusely the greatness of *Gītā*; or the *Gītā* is a town enclosed all-round by a (wall in the form of) 700 beautiful verses, wherein have come together to dwell all the Scriptures; or the verses are the out stretched arms of the devoted wife in the form of *Gītā*, coming to embrace her Lord — the Supreme Soul; or these (verses) are the black bees on the *Gītā*-lotus flower, or the waves on the ocean in the form of the *Gītā*, or the horses of the chariot in the form of the *Gītā* of Śri Hari; or these verses are an assemblage of (the floods of) all the holy waters come together into the holy Ganges, at the advent of the unique occasion (*parvaṇī*) of the planet Jupiter entering into the Zodiacal sign Leo (*Simhastha*) in the form of Pārtha (*nar*); or instead of being a row of verses they are the rows of gem 'Cintāmani' capable of attracting even ascetics' minds, or, of the Kalpataru trees planted to win pure meditation. Who could be able to trace, each one separately, of these 700 verses, every one of which excels every other (in point of greatness). There could exist no such terminology as 'milk-yielding' or 'dry' (lit. a cow that has recently calved or calved one year back) in regard to 'Kamadhenu' (Desire-yielding cow). It is meaningless to use these adjectives. 'In the front or in the rear' in regard to a lamp or 'younger or elder' in the case of the Sun, or 'deep and shallow' in the case of the sea of nectar: in that way *Gītā* verses should not be talked of as 'of the beginning', or 'of the end'. Could the Pārijātaka flowers be distinguished and classified as stale or as fresh? Where is the need of my maintaining that *Gītā* verses are all alike in point of greatness, none being more or less (great) than the other, since the *Gītā* knows no distinction such as its sense and its words — which convey the sense. It is generally known that in the *Gītā* Lord Kṛṣṇa is the 'sense' as well the 'word'. In the case of *Gītā* what is secured by understanding its import is also equally got by its verbal recital. With such bold dash this Scripture brings about complete identity between the sense and its vehicle the word, therefore now no topic is left on which I can expatiate and argue. In fact the *Gītā* is the literary and glorious image of Lord (Kṛṣṇa). Any other Scripture subsides within itself, i.e., loses its importance having exhausted its function, once it makes known its intended meaning. Such is not however the case with the *Gītā*. It is ever (without any wastage or destruction) Supreme Brahman in its entirety. Just see: how out of love for the entire universe the Lord made easily available to all, the Supreme Bliss of the Self, making Arjuna only the excuse. The Moon cools down the hearts of all three worlds, making the bird Cakor only the excuse; or Lord Śankara brought down to the earth the Sacred Ganges, with the object of cooling down the fever (heat) caused by the advent of Iron Age, (*kaḷi kāḷ*) making Sage Goutama only the excuse. In that way the cow in the form of Lord Kṛṣna has provided this milk in the form of *Gītā*, in sufficient quantity, to the entire universe, making Partha the calf. You will attain the Supreme state were you to concentrate on it (*Gītā*) heart and soul; not only that; but were you only to knead (i.e., set into motion repeatedly) your tongue with it, with the intent of reciting it, you would be strengthening your spiritual power all round, as soon as you hold to your lips the cup in the form of the recital of a quarter of the verse, just as the *parīs*, with a single dash (of its touch) converts iron into gold. Or were you to turn aside your face, without making the cup in the form of the recital to touch your lips, but simply turn your ears to it the mere falling of the *Gītā*-letters into your ears would also result in the same. In short, the *Gītā* gives nothing short of liberation, whosoever, either hears it, or recites it or comprehends its meaning in the way a generous donor never refuses (anything) to anyone. Therefore have recourse only to the *Gītā*, in the company (for help) of the learned: what will you gain by taking to other Scriptures? The subject matter (of the conversation) frankly carried on (discussed) separately (at different time and place) by Kṛṣṇa and Arjuna, has been rendered into such a simple form that anybody may understand it if he so wishes to. When a fond mother sits down to feed her child, she prepares the morsels of such size (so small) as could be easily swallowed by it; or just as the air which is infinite in extension and fitful in its motion is brought under control and made serviceable by an ingenious man with the contrivance of a fan. In that way that which could not be secured (grasped) through (ordinary) words, was converted into Anuṣṭupa metre and made so easy ... Were the pearls not to be created by rain drops of Svātī Nakṣatra (the 15th Lunar asterism), how could they appear to advantage on the person of beautiful (ones)? How could the ears hear the sound were the musical instruments not to send out any? How could one have fragrant smell, were there created no flowers at all? How could the tongue have sweet taste, were the dainties not to be sweet or how could the eye see itself (its reflection) were there to be no mirror at all? How could he (the seer) worship the preceptor were he not to appear in a manifested form? In that way who could have been able to grasp the infinite, Supreme Brahman, had it not been encompassed within the measure of 700 verses? The clouds continue to draw water (by the process of evaporation) from the sea, but the world looks to the clouds, not to the sea although it (the sea) is immeasurably wide! How could the ears and the mouth have been able to experience (enjoy) this theme, which is beyond the scope of the faculty of speech, had it not been composed into verses? That the Sage Vyāsa has stored up in the form of (*Gītā*) Scripture, the talk of Lord Kṛṣṇa, has been a great favour done to the universe and that same Scripture I am now making available in the Marathi language after closely scrutinizing every word of Śri Vyāsa. I, an insignificant being, am simply prattling on a subject, on which the imagination and intellect even of a sage like Vyāsa, beset with uncertainty proceeds haltingly. But this *Gītā*-Deity is so affable (simple). If he has accepted the floral wreaths in the form of the preaching of Sage Vyāsa, surely he would not say 'Nay' to the simple (bent) grass leaves (*dūrvādal*) from me! Herds of elephants go to rivers for water (to quench their thirst). Could the insignificant sand-flies be denied (the water there)? The young birds, getting new wings and not being able to fly efficiently (get fatigued in attempting to fly) and simply hover in that very sky (cavity), in which the mighty eagle speeds with magnificent sweeps. Because the swan walks so stately (on the earth), does it mean others should not walk in their own (crude) style? A pitcher, when dipped in a vast and deep lake etc., is filled with water according to its capacity; how can it prevent the mouth from holding a mouthful of water (*cuḷa*) according to its modest capacity? Because of its larger size a torch can shed a greater amount of light; does not the small wick also shed light according to its own (limited) power? The size of the reflection of sky on the sea-surface is in proportion to its (sea's) wide expanse; yet there is also its reflection on the surface of the small pond in proportion to its petty size. In that way, because the great talents like Sage Vyāsa and others deal with (move about in) this Scripture, I should forbear from stepping into it, does not stand to reason. Because aquatic animals of the size of the mountain Maṅdāra live in the sea, should not the other smaller fish, etc., even swim there? Aruna (the Sun's Charioteer) sees the Sun because of his close contact with the Sun; does not an ant living on the (distant) earth also see him? Therefore it cannot be said it is improper, that quite ordinary persons like us should compose *Gītā* in the people's dialect (*deśīkarē*). The father walks ahead while his child follows in his foot-steps (foot-marks); would not the latter reach the same place as the father reached? In that way, if I follow the track of Sage Vyāsa, enquiring of the commentators (Śaṅkara, Rāmānuja etc.) about the (correct) way, where else can I go and how can I fail to reach the proper destination, even though I might not be personally competent? Besides, the worthy preceptor — Nivṛttināth — that preceptor whose forbearance like that of the earth does not get sick of the quick and the still (movables and immovables) — whose ambrosia the Moon borrows and (therewith) cools down the universe — whose splendour is secured by the Sun for removing the darkness, and from whom the sea derives its supply of water, the water its sweetness, the sweetness its beauty, the wind its force, the sky its expanse, knowledge its bright and sovereign glory, the *Vedas* their eloquence and the happiness its fervour — in short, all things their (respective) forms and shapes — who places all under his obligations — that all powerful and worthy preceptor has entered into me and inspired me. What wonder is there then, that I should be enabled to preach in all its bearings the *Gītā* in Marathi idiom. That Hill-Koli (named) Ekalavya, who rendered service (i.e., worshipped) the very earthen idol on the hill-top in the name of its preceptor (Droṇācārya) made all the three worlds applaud his skill in archery: Trees (whose roots are) associated with (those of) sandal trees also become fragrant like sandal: Sage Vaśiṣṭha spread out his ochre coloured sheet of cloth (*cchaṭi*) by way of challenge as a substitute for the Sun; what of myself then? (In contrast to the inanimate sheet of cloth) I am a living being endowed with a virile mind and possess a preceptor so powerful that with a single glance (of his) he can elevate his disciple and enable him (disciple) to occupy the same status as he enjoys. With a vision already perfectly fine (clear) and in addition backed up by the (light of the) Sun, what is there that could not be seen? There the daily act of my continuous respiration is capable of yielding perennially new compositions (literary master-pieces): given the grace of the preceptor, are there any miracles that cannot be wrought, says Jñānadeva. For all these reasons I have preached the substance of the *Gītā*, through the medium of Marathi, in a style that would make all the people understand it. If one were to sing the Marathi version with great skill, there would not be found wanting an attraction in that singing. If therefore one were to sing it, it would be an adornment to his singing. Were one merely to read it (instead of singing it) in a simple way, even then, the *Gītā* would not be found any the less charming. An ornament even in an unworn state looks beautiful; would not its looking beautiful, in the state of being worn, be only in the fitness of things? The pearls if studded with gold lend it additional beauty; yet they do not look less beautiful by themselves even though not so studded: The fully blown flowers of the 'mogrā' plant during the spring season, are not deficient in fragrance whether (they are) unwoven (loose) or inwoven. In that way, I have composed in the 'Ovī' form of verses (*prabandha*) a type of metrical composition which when set to music appears to advantage and even without any musical element looks charming (if merely recited). In this 'ovī' form of composition, I have interwoven letters smelling the essence of Supreme Brahman, in a way that would make all including even children, understand it. It never becomes necessary to look up for any floral growth on a sandal tree for having fragrance; in that way, one gets into rapt concentration in spiritual meditation, as soon as he hears this versified composition (recited): What then if he hears a sermon on it? Will it not throw him into a state of ecstasy? While it is being recited, the erudition contained in it is invested with such a superb bloom that even a flow of nectar (if one be passing nearby) would not be able to attract towards itself the hearers' attention away from that (erudition)! This inborn poetic genius has become (as it were) the very abode of rest with the result that (mere) hearing (of the recital) conquers (i.e., proves more valuable spiritually than) constant study and meditation. Anyone will be able to secure the enjoyment of the select portion of the bliss of the self by hearing, which will nourish further the other sense-centres through auditory sense. The bird Cakor enjoys, through its inherent power, the Lunar rays — yet cannot any one (else) also avail himself of the Moonlight: In that way (although it is true that) only those that are fully qualified, can secure knowledge of the deep secret contained in this science of metaphysics, yet ordinary people even will enjoy happiness through this rhapsodical work. This is really all due to the glory of Sri Nivṛttināth. It is not (in fact) a composition, but is the glory of his favour. That secret which in immemorial times, the slayer of the demon Tripura (viz., Lord Śiva) whispered into the cavity of the ears of goddess Pārvatī, somewhere, where exactly we do not know, in the neighbourhood of the sea of milk — that very secret (knowledge) was secured by Machindranāth, while abiding secretly in the stomach of the alligator, living amidst the waves of the sea of milk. Machindranāth met Couranginăth, the limbless cripple, on the 'Sapta-Śṛngi' mountain; the latter got all his limbs restored to him as before as the result of Machindranāth's mere vision. Getting desirous of enjoying undisturbed, enrapt concentration in spiritual meditation (*samādhi*) Machindranāth gave over the profound mystery (*mudrā*) to Gorakhnāth – the very lake of lotus flowers in the form of the path of Yoga and the unique warrior capable of vanquishing the sense of objects, and installed him on his own spiritual throne, endowing him with all his powers. Gorakhnāth preached to revered Gaininăth the bliss of monism along with all its traditions, that had descended down from the very God Śri Śaṅkara. Gaininăth seeing that the 'Kali' age (*kaliyuga*) was swallowing up all beings, called on Nivṛttināth with a mandate, 'You do embrace the traditional lore (*saṁpradāya*) that has descended down to us through the chain of teacher and disciple from the Lord Śaṅkara — the love which I have fortunately received thus, and make haste (run fast) to protect all the beings that are being devoured by the Kali (strife personified).' Nivṛttināth, naturally kind and very tender-hearted, and having in addition got such a mandate from his preceptor, started like monsoon clouds to cool the universe. Then moved with compassion at the sight of the people in distress, he profusely showered on them the sentiment of tranquillity (note the pun on the expression *śāntarasa*) which means: (i) a liquid that has the power to soothe and cool anything and (ii) the 9th poetic sentiment of tranquillity, which, by generating aversion to mundane affairs, inclines a man to the path of salvation thus enabling him to shake off all worldly-cares and miseries under the pretext of putting together systematically the meaning of *Gītā*. The upshot of that activity is this book. On that occasion I stood before him, with a strong desire to take in (the *śāntarasa*), like the bird Cakor and that brought me the present (magnificent) success. In this way, the preceptor following the traditions imparted to me, through discourse on that subject, the treasure of (the knowledge of) enrapt concentration in spiritual meditation. Had it not been so, whence could I, who never recite nor read, nor yet know how to serve the preceptor properly, have secured such capacity? But remember that the preceptor, making me only a plea (an instrument) composed this work and protected the world. So whatever merits or flaws might have been penned (uttered) here as coming from a mere instrument (of the preceptor), should all be borne by you as would a mother. I hardly knew how to chisel a word most fittingly, how to broach and treat methodically a subject (problem), or what in fact the figures of speech are. In fact it was the good preceptor that did all the talk, making me only a mouthpiece, just as the dancing of a doll takes place according to the movements of the string or other mechanism on which it works. I am not quite particular about tendering an apology to you for any merits or demerits, since, I was intended by the preceptor merely as a conveyance for carrying the composition. And any deficiency (in it) that might stand out in the conference of you saints – were such deficiency not to be made up (by you), I would be all wrath with you in a spirit of affection (being accustomed to your indulgence). (If the inferiority – base condition – of iron is not removed at the touch to it) of *parīs,* whose fault would it be? The only part that a stream has to play is to flow and mingle with the Ganges; if it does not then get one with the Ganges, whose fault would it be? Therefore, now that I have luckily approached the feet of you saints, what more do I want in the world? Oh sires, through the grace of my preceptor I have been favoured by the close friendship of saintly men like you who have fulfilled all the ambitions of my life perfectly. Just see, having secured a parental home (*māher*) like you, I was enabled to carry quite happily to its successful completion this book – my cherished desire. It might become possible to cast entirely of gold the earth-globe, or, to create the seven mountains (*kulācal*) of Chintamani gems; or it might be easy to fill up the seven seas with nectar, or it would not be difficult to convert all the (minor) stars into as many moons; or to lay out and plant pleasure-gardens of 'Kalpataru' trees; but it would be very difficult to discover the hidden sense of *Gītā* by resolving its intricacies. Yet that 'I', a complete mute (dunce) has been enabled to expound the Scripture in the Marathi language in a way that could make all view (i.e., understand) it clearly; that I could swim across the vast sea in the form of this stupendous composition, and waved and paraded the banner of victory (in my hands) in the form of fame; that I could erect a temple in the form of the *Gītā* interpretations, the temple that looks like the mountain Meru with its enormous tops (*śikhara*) and therein install and worship the image of the preceptor: or that an infant that had missed its frank and guileless mother in the form of the *Gītā* teaching, and was wandering aimlessly, should be able to meet its mother again: The credit of all these acts of piety is due to you (the audience). I, Jñānadeva, proclaim to you all the saints that whatever I have said here is the net result of assimilating all your piety, and is not merely an empty talk (i.e., a thing to be trifled with). What more should I say to (you) all? That I have been shown (enabled to see) the festival of the completion of this work, is, (as I take it) the fruition of my life. I feel extremely happy that you fulfilled all my expectations to the full extent I confidently hoped of you. O Sires, you have created for me another universe in the form of this work and that makes us simply laugh (out of ridicule) at the Sage Viśvamitra. Where was the greatness in his creating for, and his giving importance to 'Triśaṅku', a mortal world simply for belittling God Brahmadeva! God Śambhu created the ocean of milk, getting charmed with Upamanyu; but it (sea) is not also fit to be compared (with this work) since it contained poison (which was later on churned out). The sun comes in hot haste for delivering the universe from the demon in the form of darkness who has devoured it; yet while doing so, he makes the people suffer from the (tormenting) heat. The moon pours out to cool down the heat-stricken universe; but being herself contaminated, she too is not worthy of being used as a standard of comparison with regard to this work. Therefore, I say, there is no other thing (in the world) that can bear comparison to this work, which meritorious achievement you saints have caused to be created in the three worlds through my agency. Nay, that this religious sermon, *kīrtana* (praising God with the help of music and singing), has reached its (successful) termination, is all your doing, what remains as my role in it, being that of only a servant.

...EPILOGUE

Now the Supreme Self should get itself propitiated by this sacrifice in the form of a literary production and should grant me in charity the only boon (*prasāya*) that the evil vision of the vile and wicked should drop all its crookedness and sting and they should develop a love towards good actions, and further there should be created fellow-feeling (towards one other) amongst the beings. May the darkness in the form of sins get destroyed and may the entire universe (people) conduct itself in the light of the rising Sun in the form of one's own (religious) duty; and may each and every being (as a class) get the fulfilment of each and every wish of his. Let the concourse of saints that shower down all that is propitious on the universe, appear and visit perpetually the aggregate of beings on this earth. These saints are as it were the blossoms of the moving (walking) 'Kalpataru' trees, or the inhabited places (towns) of sentient 'Chintamani' gems or the talking oceans of the nectar. May these saints who are uncontaminated Moons and heatless (cool) Suns be the constant kinsmen (*soyarē*) of all. In short, let all the three worlds be all happy and perfected (with the bliss of Monism), and let them render service eternally to the Primeval Male-Supreme Being. And especially those in this universe that (internally) live on (the constant study of) this work (*Gītā*) – may they have the perfect happiness both temporal as well as spiritual. Hearing this, the Lord of the Universe (in the form of the preceptor Nivṛttināth) said, 'This boon has been granted to you', at which Jñānadeva became very happy. There is in this 'Kali-age', the most holy in all the three worlds, and a very ancient place called 'Pancakrośa' (the modern town named 'Newāse'), on the southern bank of the river Godāvari, in (the province of) Maharashtra (modern Deccan), where there dwells the deity named 'Mahālaya' (known as 'Mohanirājā' in modern times the living thread (the root cause) of the universe. In this holy place rules most justly King Śri Ramacandra, the crown gem in the Soma Dynasty of the Kṣatriya race, and the very abode of all the arts. At this place, Jñānadeva, the Disciple of Nivṛttināth, – the follower of the traditional sect (School) of Mahesha (the Great God Śiva), gave the *Gītā* the garb of Marāthi (language). I, Jñānadeva, the disciple of Nivṛttināth, declare that this 18th Chapter is the pinnacle (*śhikhar*) of the beautiful dialogue named *Gītā*, that took place between Lord Kṛṣṇa and Arjuna (and is described) in the celebrated 'Bhīṣma' Parva (part) of the Great epic '*Mahā-Bhārata*', and which is the very essence of the 'Upaniṣads' and also the parental home of all the Scriptures, and in which (*Gītā* lake) the Supreme Swans – the Yogins – take resort, in the way do the swans in the lake (known as 'Manasa'). May the aggregate of beings derive complete happiness day by day from the wealth, in the form of the holy Scriptures. Jñānadeva composed (edited) this commentary (on the *Gītā*), in the year *śakē* (saka) 1212 and 'Sacidanandabābā', with great reverence became its writer (copyist).

Jñāneśvara, from the Bhāvārthadīpikā
translated by R.K. Bhagwat

AMIR KHUSRAU

Amir Khusrau (A.D. 1253–1325) was of Turkish origin; his ancestors had migrated to India a generation or two before his birth. Though a soldier by profession, he made a name for himself at an early age as a scholar and a poet. Appreciation came to him so early in his life that the famous saint at Delhi, Sheikh Nizamu'd-Din Auliya, took him under his spiritual care while Khusrau was still a boy. Khusrau served the Delhi court and had a long, though occasionally perturbed, career. He was prolific as a poet and composer. His contribution to Indian music and Persian and Hindi poetry is remembered by the common people in India even today. It is somewhat curious that though he was familiar with Sanskrit, and with Sanskrit literature on poetics, and though he was himself a poet of excellence, he did not translate any of the Sanskrit theoretical documents about poetry and literature. The fact that he wrote poetry in two languages, Persian and Hindi, and was familiar with several of the living languages of India of his times, shows that he believed literature to be a matter of creation in languages that are spoken and understood. His brief comments on India's multilingualism, learning and cultural excellence reveal a profound catholicity of taste. They also show his respect for bilingual literary practice and literary translations. Khusrau can be claimed as an exponent of what we today call Comparative Literature. The extracts included here are from his composition, *Nuh - Siphir* (1318) translated into English by R. Nath and Faiyaz 'Gwaliari' under the title *India As Seen By Amir Khusrau in 1318 A.D.* (Historical Research Documentation Programme, Jaipur, 1981). The verses included are from Nath & Faiyaz's Chapter IV: 15–17, 47–65, 78–83, 94–104; Chapter V: 1–3, 64–76, 82 (pp. 53–76).

Multilingual Literary Culture

... The Brahmans of India have greater wealth of philosophical thought than what Rumi had revealed to the World.

As nobody has tried to learn from the Brahmans, their learning has not been revealed to the world.

I have done a bit of research in this matter and, after winning their confidence, I have gained some insight into their secrets of learning.

... In order that you may not have an iota of doubt, I shall put up ten arguments (in support of my preference to Indian Wisdom and Learning). My first point is there is inestimable learning ('Ilm') in every nook and corner of India.

It is unfortunate that people outside India are not aware of its arts and sciences.

My second point is that the people of India speak different languages. But the people outside India cannot speak in Indian dialects.

The people of Khita (Chinese Turkistan), Mongols, Turks and Arabs are unable to speak Indian languages.

But we can speak any language of the world as fluently and effectively as a shepherd tends his sheep.

Our mastery over the languages is as assertive as is our capacity to conquer other lands.

But, no country has the courage to look at us aggressively.

My third argument is based on Wisdom. It is irrefutable and wise men will accept it.

Scholars come to India from all over the world, to learn its arts and sciences.

But the Brahman never went out of India to acquire knowledge. He did not consider it necessary to go out to improve upon his worth of learning or to seek judgement on it.

It is well known that a great scholar like Abu Ma'asir visited India. He was like a star from the Heavens and there was none comparable to him on Earth.

He came to India and resided in the ancient city of Banaras for ten years to acquire knowledge from the Brahmans.

He learnt Astrology so proficiently that he excelled all others. I believe, there is nobody who could have acquired so much knowledge as he did, though other scholars have also tried it at length.

Whatever he has written, it is with the ink of India. That is, it is all due to the knowledge he acquired in India.

Now I shall put up my fifth argument to convince those who challenge me. In the *Dimnā-Khalīlā* (*Pancatantra*), which is also an ancient work of India, there is only conversation of animals and birds.

Had there not been an excellent flight of imagination in this work, the world would not have acknowledged its merit.

Because it is such a marvellous and meaningful work, it has been translated into Persian, Turkish, Arabic and Dari.

This book was written in India and other languages have only borrowed it, in their own way.

Can there be a better Book of Wisdom than the *Dimnā-Khalīlā*? The scholars of the world derive inspiration from it.

My eighth argument is that Indian Music is overwhelmingly moving. We put fire of our heart and soul in it.

It is known to everybody in the world that there is nothing like Indian Music (it is *par excellence*).

Truly, musicians have come to India and they introduced some new features to it.

They learnt Indian Music and lent tempo to it.

In fact, they became proficient in this Art and made their own contribution to it.

But this was possible only after they stayed in India for more than 30 or 40 years.

However, the foreigners could not add anything to the basic principles of Indian Music.

My ninth argument is that our Music is so sweet that it captivates the wild deer and attracts it even in the face of the hunter's arrow.

When (the) wild deer hears the sound of sweet music, it stands hypnotized by its effect.

When the Hindu musician finds the deer standing helplessly hypnotized, out of compassion he bids it to move away.

But the deer is struck by the charm of Music and is so completely lost that it cannot move.

My tenth argument is that no wizard in the art of poetry like Khusrau (himself) exists under the Sun.

I have established India's superiority in the sphere of Knowledge and Learning. Now I will proceed to describe the beauty of Indian languages. These languages are such that I have also learnt and gained something from the common languages of the peasants of India.

I know it, I understand it, I can speak it and on inquiry I have been, to some extent, enlightened by it.

... one feature is common to all languages, that is, each one has a taste of its own.

Somebody claims his language to be the best, while the other thinks his own to be better than others.

Everybody is proud of his own language and does not admit superiority of any other one.

It shall be improper on my part to talk of Persian, Turkish and Arabic and beguile myself of their virtues.

One should talk of his own country. As I belong to India, it is only befitting that I also talk of the things Indian.

There is a different language in every corner of this land with its own system and technique.

Sindhī, Lāhorī, Kashmīrī, Kubrī, Dhur-Samundrī, Tilangī, Gūjar, Ma'abrī, Ghourī, Bengālī, Oudhi, Delhī and around it, within the boundaries of this land are the languages of India.

All these are Hindwī languages, languages of India since olden times and they are spoken by the people at large.

There is yet another language which is the best of all. It is the language of the Brahmans.

It is known as the Sanskrit since ancient times. Common people do not know its usage.

Only the Brahmans know this language. But every Brahman cannot claim to have mastered it.

Like the Arabic, the Sanskrit also has its grammar, definitions, system, technique and rules, and literature.

This language is a pearl among pearls.

Amir Khusrau, from Nuh-Siphir
translated by R. Nath and Faiyaz 'Gwaliari'

RUPA GOSWAMI

The *Bhaktirasāmṛtasindhuh* of Rupa Goswami is an important critical document on Bhakti poetry. Composed during the first quarter of the sixteenth century, it is one of his twenty or so literary/philosophical works. It was written in Sanskrit, though the literary context within which it was worked out was that of poetry in modern Indian languages. Keeping to the convention of illustrating theoretical premises by quoting from established literary texts, Goswami does indeed offer numerous examples of Bhakti from the *purāṇa* literature to support his taxonomy of Bhakti. But one can read between his lines a constant reference to the poetry of his own time. That the critic aimed at providing a compendium of literary styles and conventions of poetry as practised in his own time should be clear from the fact that he makes but one passing reference to the *Nātyaśāstra* and no reference at all to practically any other text on Sanskrit poetics. Clearly then, Rupa Goswami was not trying to explain Bhakti poetry in terms of the *rasa* theory as much as he was trying to explain the *rasa* theory in terms of Bhakti poetry as rooted in poetic practice in his own time. In his account, Bhakti is presented as the highest *rasa* because it brings to the *rasika* an experience which is aesthetically superior to the experience of *bramhananda*.

The conceptualisation of *bhaktirasa* and its incorporation in the gamut of the *rasas* established by Sanskrit poetics, are the two major developments in the tradition of Sanskrit poetics during the medieval period. Rupa Goswami's text, which achieves both these tasks, is therefore an important landmark in Indian literary theory. However, one is likely to be disappointed if one were to approach the *Bhaktirasāmṛtasindhuh* with the expectations trained by the philosophically rigorous criticism in the Sanskrit tradition. Rupa Goswami is primarily interested in describing Bhakti and its psychology. Besides, for him Bhakti in real life itself is a *rasa*, which is indistinct from the *rasa* in poetry. In spite of this confusion of categories, his account provides very valuable tools to understand the conventions of Bhakti poetry as practised in modern Indian languages during medieval times.

The translation used here is by Tridandi Swami Bhakti Hṛdaya Bon Maharaja, published by the Institute of Oriental Philosophy established by the Swami himself at Vrindavan. The translation was first published in 1965. The reader is likely to find this translation not very lucid. The translator has prepared it for the devotees, and he has added his own comments to the original text at numerous places. Besides, he does not treat the original text as a treatise having relevance to aesthetics. He looks upon it with utmost reverence as a text useful for spiritual upliftment of the masses. And yet, when read with this caution in mind, it does reveal the sense of revolt against the Brahminic aesthetics which shaped Rupa Goswami's vision of poetic delight. The excerpts presented here form a tiny part of the original text which runs nearly to a thousand verses. All oddities of the translation are preserved.

The *Bhaktirasa*

All glory to Lord Kṛṣṇa-candra, who is the Beauty of the Moon personified and who is the Embodiment of the ambrosia of Joy everlasting and immortal, called *Rasa*, and the radiance of Whose Body has subdued the two Gopīs known as Tārakā and Pāli or Pālikā, and Who has owned Śyāmā and Lalitā, the other two damsels, as His own, and Who is the most beloved of Rādhā.

... Oh Sanātana! ... may this Thy *Bhakti-rasāmṛta-sindhuh* glow or be manifest in all its brightness and lustre in my heart for all time by extinguishing the flame-like tongue of the Mīmāṅsakas.

... Exceptionally wonderful supernatural powers, long-enduring worldly and heavenly pleasures, long and lasting experiences of *Mukti* as *Brahmasukha* (felicity derived from knowledge and realisation of impersonal *Brahman*), and eternal and ever-progressive and supreme flow of transcendental felicity (from realisation of the Supreme Lord) are attainable by Bhakti in Lord Govinda (Kṛṣṇa), who is the Lord of all senses.

... Even with the slightest awakening of Bhāva-Bhakti in the heart of the Lord, the four objects of human pursuit, viz. *dharma* (relative duties offering heavenly pleasures), *artha* (mundane wealth), *kāma* (sensual pleasures or desires), and *mokṣa* (final emancipation or realisation of the self as identical with *Brahman*) become insignificant and as worthless as a straw.

Oh Lord of the Universe: The ocean of delight in which I have been plunged as a consequence of my immediate vision of Thyself makes even *Brahmānanda* or the delight of the Absolute Life of the Sankarite as a little pool created on the soil by the hoof-marks of cows.

... Even a little real taste in *Bhakti* is a passport to the understanding of the true nature of *Bhakti*, while mere argument has no sound foundation and does not conduce to the comprehension of the true nature of Bhakti.

BHAVA-BHAKTI

... The essential nature of *Bhāva-Bhakti* is of a particular form of absolute *sattva* quality which is far beyond and completely different from the *Māyik sattva-rājas -tamas* qualities ...

It has been said in the *Tantra* that the first stage of *Prema* is called *Bhāva*. There are partial manifestations of tears, horripilation, paleness, and other *Sāttvika-bhāvas* in *Bhāva-Bhakti*. This *'Bhāva'* has been stated in the *Padma Purāṅam*: 'Then the King Ambarīṣa was full of tears in his eyes being partially overwhelmed by meditating ... on the Lotus-Like Beautiful Feet of Lord Hari.' This *Rati*, i.e., *Bhāva* appearing in the mind of the devotee becomes one with the whole mental quantum of the devotee (just as fire set to an iron rod makes the whole iron rod look like fire itself), and in itself being self-manifest appears as if it has been made manifest in the heart by the mental faculties. Besides, *Rati* or *Bhāva* is itself enjoyment or object of taste and enjoyment, and yet at the same time it becomes the cause of the devotee's experiencing of the bliss of his Object, the Object of desire being Sri Kṛṣna...

The *Bhāva* or *Rati* appears in the hearts of rare and extraordinarily fortunate ones due to either intense ardour for spiritual practices or causeless grace of Kṛṣna and His devotees. But in most cases it is due to the profound application to or earnestness for one's spiritual practices that *Bhāva*, i.e., *Rati* is aroused in the heart ...

In the *Purāṇas* and Dramaturgy both *Rati* and *Bhāva* have been used in the same sense; here in Bhakti literature also they are conceived as equivalent to each other...

Those in whose hearts there has been bursting forth of the sprout of *Bhāva* shall have in its wake the appearance of the following signs in them without any doubt — forbearance, ensuring that not a moment is allowed to go in vain, i.e., there is no cessation of *Bhāva* in them, indifference to worldly enjoyments, unassumingness, i.e., having no vanity or pride, cherishing positive hopes or firm hopes of receiving the Lord's Grace, eager and anxious longing for the Beloved

Lord, ever relishing and chanting of the Name of the Lord, the attachment for the praise and eulogy of the glories of the Lord, and love to live in his dwelling place or realm...

The nature of this *Rati* is that it is always full of warmth, i.e., of an uncontrollable nature, and is the fast current of a very powerful and predominant bliss or delight. Therefore even though this *Rati* throws up, i.e. manifests the heat of all forms of *sancāri bhāvas* (the evanescent feeling of *Bhāva*, which strengthens the pervading sentiment), it is cooler and sweeter than crores of moons ...

Rupa Goswami, from the Bhaktirasāmrtasindhuh
translated by Tridandi Swami Bhakti Hṛdaya Bon Maharaja

KESHAVADĀSA

Keshavadāsa (A.D. 1555–1617) is a major poet of the Hindi tradition of poetry. Of the various works ascribed to him, *Kāvyapriyā, Rasikapriyā* and *Rāmacandrikā* were definitely written by him. The *Rasikapriyā* was written for the benefit of literary scholars. It offers a catalogue of poetic conventions and aesthetic assumptions accepted by the literary community of Keshavadāsa's time. It is, therefore, more a text of historical interest rather than of original theoretical interest. However, in its orientation it becomes representative of the sixteenth century Indian literary taste, and by implication, of the prevalent theoretical beliefs. At the same time, the *Rasikapriyā* follows a certain methodological discipline which has its roots in the *Bhakti* tradition of poetry and philosophy. Though Keshavadāsa's text offers definitions and descriptions of the conventional aesthetic categories such as *'nāyaka'* and *'nāyikā'* or *śṛṇgārā* and *virah*, he treats all *nāyakas* as forms of Kṛṣṇa and all *nāyikās* as forms of Rādhā. All *śṛṇgāra* is seen as an expression of love between Kṛṣṇa and Rādhā, a kind of cosmic affair. It is often believed that the medieval Indian aesthetics had posited a new theoretical category of *Bhakti rasa.* When we follow Keshavadāsa's text carefully, it becomes clear that *bhakti* was not an additional *rasa,* a new sentiment not known to Bharata, but that *bhakti* is an aspect of all sentiments described by Bharata and Abhinavagupta. *Bhakti rasa* is, in Keshavadāsa's meticulous rendering of it, a category of literary convention, loaded with metaphysics and folklore, which overlaps with all other aesthetic sentiments, *Rasas.*

The translation of the *Rasikapriyā* used here is by K.P. Bahadur (*The Rasikapriya of Keshavadasa: Translated into Verse,* Motilal Banarsidass, 1972, pp. 239–247). In the translation, as it would happen with any other translation of poetry, the musical quality of the original is lost. However, the extracts reproduced here may indicate the quality and concerns of Indian literary theory during the sixteenth century.

Kinds of Poetry

Says Keshavadasa all poetry
Is of four kinds, as poets do know,
Kaushiki, Bharati, Arabhati,
And Sattviki, which is the fourth.

Says Keshavadasa: where merriment
And love and tenderness combine,
Of simple words and happy sense.
That's poetry of Kaushiki kind.

(Example of poetry of the Kaushiki kind)

Some women to meet him essay,
Through go-betweens, and some enjoy
In their minds the bliss of sport: some take
Many a vow in sacred sports,
So that they may some converse make
With him, and hear his winning speech:
Some who as goddesses are, always
Do run to see him, and appease
All day the gods with gifts, I fear
Oh! bosom friend, that he's so dark.
What can I do? No sooner she hears —
She, my Krṣna's name, this woman laughs.

Says Keshavadasa: that verse in which
The sentiment heroic is,
And wonder too, and merriment;
Appealing to the mind whose sense —
That soul delighting poetry
is of the kind called 'Bharati'.

(Example of poetry of the Bharati kind)

The ear-rings of gold which she wears
Are verily the chariot's wheels,

The pendants which are glittering there
The banner which does greatly please:
Head ornament the charioteer.
The saffron lines on forehead laid
As though spokes are, and the nose-pearl
Is as it were the hub well made.
Her one glance does Śri Kṛṣna purchase!
Big eyes she has: and a gem shines
On her forehead, as if Kamadeva
On fishes' chariot were reclined!

Says Keshavadasa: that verse in which
The violent sentiment, and dread,
And loathing are, in which there is
Alliteration, and words have
Meaning diverse: such poetry
Should be considered 'Aribhati'.

(Example of poetry of the Aribhati kind)

Dense and dreadful clouds, rain-filled,
Whose splendour is of black and white,
Do thunder on the first and fifth
Of *Savan's* lunar days: the sky
They roam, these hideous messengers
Massive as elephants: all around
The lightning strikes! Braja women are
With awe filled by the fearful sound
Now that Śri Kṛṣna is far away
Grim horror stalks all people thus.
It seems as though all night and day
Death dances on the land of Braja.

Where wonder, valour, evenness,
All the three sentiments do merge
In equal measure, and the sense
Is understood as soon as heard,

That is considered by all men
To be the pure Sattviki verse.

(Example of poetry of the Sattviki kind)

The bosom companion says to another *nayika:*
'Oh! foolish girl, burn and destroy
Your million cravings and desires,
Oh! kindle not within your heart
A blaze that burns like Holi's fire!
The love of Radha and Śri Kṛṣṇa
Consider of the highest kind,
Kamadeva's and Rati's love even
Inferior to theirs I find,
Bhavaniji too cannot sow
Discord between them: not to speak
Of others: Sarasvati's glow
Before them too does little seem;
Though simple she considered is,
One are their souls, and thoughts, and minds,
Though separate are their bodies, still
Through ardent eyes the two are joined!'

Says Keshavadasa: thus I've portrayed
The sentiments of poetry, nine,
Now of their four faults I'll relate
But unto these give not your mind.

Defects of Poetry

Conflict, dryness, and nauseousness,
Contrariness, and the unwise,
Says Keshavadasa, these lack goodness,
So these the poets don't describe.

Where contrary sentiments, like love
And loathing, and awe, are described,

And violence too, and tenderness,
Are by poets mentioned side by side —
There the conflicting sentiment
Is by all men known to arise.

(Example of a verse with conflicting sentiment)

When laughing I converse, then all
Do laugh; when shorn of shame I see,
With loathing are they filled, and fall
Away from me; if words I speak
I am reproached, and if I long
For something, passion in me wakes —
So your advice to love him not
I kept in mind, Oh! friend, always,
Knowing that love will my heart not win,
And for a moment if my gaze
I chance to throw upon Śri Kṛṣṇa
To censure me men will not stay.

Where outwardly the lovers speak
With loving words, but in hearts hid
Their lies, deceit and duplicity,
That is the sentiment insipid.

(Example of insipidity in verse)

Whose mind in cunning is so steeped
On seeing this world, her do you tell
Love's riddle; Oh! so sad it is,
And laughable! ne'er have I heard
A co-wife could be thought a friend,
As with my eyes today I see!
So woman vain! I understand
With your heart you love not, but with speech!

Says Keshavadasa: where a poet tells
Of pleasures of sex in the midst of grief,

With relish; there is known to dwell
The sentiment which disgusting is.

(Example of the disgusting sentiment in verse)

The bosom companion says to the *nayaka*.
'To bathe, to give alms unto all,
To eat, drink, and with song console,
All this the *nayika* has forgot:
Her wisdom has fled, and her soul
Hard as a stool's top has been made!
Oh! lover fond, consider not
No sooner she on you will gaze
All pleasures she will leave unsought!
Thus anxious, dull your letter proved
Sweet words her please not — she who turns
From love, how will she laugh and look
When in her grief's furnace burns?'

Says Keshava where good and bad mix,
'Tis sentiment of opposites.

(Example of sentiment of contrariness in verse)

When Śri Kṛṣṇa said, 'Give me some milk,'
The cowherd girl thus made reply,
'I will not give it on credit,
If you should need it, friend, then buy,
And you will get!' Then he exclaimed,
'I am used to free milk, why should I?'
The cowherd maid said, ''tis the same
If I give or give not, for nigh
My home is where I soon will be!'
Śri Kṛṣṇa then said, 'Why do you fight?'
'When was there love 'twixt you and me?
I love to fight!' the maid replied:
Śri Kṛṣṇa then said, 'Will fighting make
Your milk sell?' And the girl said, 'if

It does not sell, I'll myself take
The milk, but you I'll never give!'

Where thoughtlessly those very things
Imagined are, and by poets described,
Which far from understanding lie,
That sentiment unseemly is.

(Example of impropriety in verse)

A danger of deception bright,
A casket of romantic love,
And beneficial to all life
As holy Ganga water, pure,
The treasure selfishness does hold,
The sources of good to others — like
The story of love's god in gold
Entangled— and outspreading wide
As stream of nectar: giving joy
To wise man: shaming Guara quite,
And Gira—which the hermits foil,
And creatures of the world, unwise—
A voice such as these, know my queen,
Is poisonous: thus do I well ween.

(The opposing sentiments)

Know tenderness, and merriment,
Love, loathing, valour, awe, to be,
Says Keshavadasa, such sentiments
As are opposing mutually.
So do I say: from the hateful
Is fear born, from love merriment:
From valour is the wonderful,
From horror follows compassion.
Says Keshavadasa, so I with care,
Have various sentiments described,
And lack of sentiment, and where
I've erred, may poets set it right.

(The significance of *Rasikapriyā*)

As lovers miserable appear
Without their loved ones, even so
Poets of the language are, I fear,
The Rasikapriyā*—who do not know.*
More knows he of love, who has read
The Rasikapriyā*, and knowledge gains*
Of sentiments, and practices,
And joy and salvation attains.

Keshavadasa, from the Rasikapriyā
translated by K.P. Bahadur

Al Badāonī

(Abdul-'l-Quadir Ibn-i-Mulukshah)

It is generally believed that Indian critics learnt the discourse of literary history from Western criticism. However, that assumption needs to be properly qualified. There indeed were forms of literary history practiced in medieval India; and several histories of literature were written in Persian from the fourteenth century to the end of the eighteenth century. The most accurate in factual details and the most readable in its style is Badāonī's *Tawārīkh*, a history of Persian poetry composed in India during the sixteenth century. Badāonī wrote it as a sequel to his general history of the reign of Akbar.

Badāonī's achievement is impressive for several reasons. First, he was clear about the aims of his history. Then, he is consistent in methodology employed to analyse poets and poems. And, finally, his standards of evaluation are uniform throughout the massive work. The three extracts presented here form, respectively, the 'introduction', a fairly detailed analysis of the contribution of the poet Faizī, and the 'Conclusion'. The first and the final sections throw light on his historiography, the middle one on his method of practical criticism. The English translation used is by Sir Wolseley Haig (Asiatic Society of Bengal, Calcutta, 1925). Haig was an outstanding scholar of Arabic and Persian, and a Professor of Arabic, Persian and Hindustani at the Trinity College, Dublin. The translator's notes have been retained here as they form material of value for understanding Badāonī's work and times.

Excerpts from the *Tawārīkh*

I will state at the outset[1] that as the author of the Tārikh-ī-Niẓāmī[2] has given an account of the nobles of the realm immediately after his history of the empire, and as most of them are now dead, and gone to perdition,[3]

[In no one have I seen fidelity,
If thou hast found one who possesses it convey to him my blessing.]

I will refrain from polluting the nib of my pen with a description of such worthless wretches, and will commence with the enumeration of some of the holy men of the age, for an account of noble men who have chosen the way of God is in every way to be preferred to an account of scoundrels and debauchees. And so will I not be a mark for threats and comminations.[4] ('Throw dust on the faces of those who praise without stint,' and again, 'may God protect us from the wickedness of tyrants.'[5]) An account of the base acts of the followers (of the Divine Faith),[6] with whose unclean existence the age is polluted may be thus described:-

Their letters do not spell sense,[7]
Nor do their thoughts tend in the direction of sense;
Think meanly of the base, and of those whose faith is weak,
Form the same estimate of the latter as of the former.
When one can call to mind one's friends,
And so make the heart a garden of sweet memories,
Pity were it to mention one's enemies
For that were to quit the sweet garden for the midden.[8]

The holy men by whose noble existence the reign of Akbar Shāh was adorned have now, for the most part, withdrawn, as the *'anqā*[9] retires to the mountains of Qāf, to the neighbourhood of the Great God. It is as though they had all conspired together to roll up and remove the baggage of life from this dwelling of care and deceit and to take up their abode in the home of joy and bliss. And now of that caravan not one remains to encourage stragglers.

'The mansions are deserted, temporary and permanent dwelling alike,'
'Nothing remains but owls and rubbish.'[10]

I shall begin with that class of men who were regularly employed in the Imperial service until[11] their fame reached such a pitch that it was as manifest as the sun at midday.

2: Shaikh Faiẓī, the Poet Laureate[12]

In many separate branches of knowledge, such as poetry, the composition of enigmas, prosody, rhyme, history, philology, medicine, and prose composition Shaikh Faiẓī had no equal in his time. At first he used to write under his well-known poetical name of Faiẓī, but later, imitating the title of his younger brother, whom the Emperor describes in writing as ʿAllāmī,[13] and in order to glorify himself, he chose a political name in the same measure, viz. Fayyāẓī,[14] but it did not suit him, and one or two months later, having packed up the baggage of this life, he took it from the world with the most bitter regret. He was a master[15] of malevolent activity, idle jests, conceit, pride and malice, and one epitome of hypocrisy, baseness, dissimulation, love of pomp, arrogance and ostentation. All Jews, Christians, Hindūs and fire-worshippers, not to speak of Nizārīs and Sabāḥīs held him in the very highest honour for his heresy, his enmity to the followers of Islām, his reviling of the very fundamental doctrines of our faith, his contemptuous abuse of the noble companions (of the Prophet) and those who came after them, and of holy Shaikhs, both dead and living, and of his unmannerly and contemptuous behaviour towards all learned, pious, and excellent men, both in secret and openly, and both by day and by night. Not content with this he used, despite the sacred faith of Muhammad (may God Bless and assoil him and his family) to regard all forbidden things as lawful, and all the injunctions of the sacred law as unlawful, and, with a view to washing away the stain of his ill-repute, which the waters of a hundred oceans (poured over it) till the day of judgement will not wash away, he used, in the height of his drunkenness, and while he was ceremonially impure,[16] to write a commentary[17] on the *Qur'ān* written entirely in words which contained no dotted letter, and his dogs[18] used to trample on it in all directions. At last, after all his denial of the truth, his obstinacy, his pride and his heresy, he hastened to the place to which he belonged, and went in such sort that I pray that nobody may see or hear of the like. When the Emperor went to visit him when he was at his last gasp, Faiẓī barked like a dog in his face, and the Emperor used to relate this story in open *darbār*, his face was swollen and his lips had become black, so that the Emperor asked Shaikh Abū-l-Faẓl what caused this blackness of the lips and suggested that Faiẓī had rubbed *misī*[19] on his teeth, as the people of India use to do, but Abū-l-Faẓl replied that this was not so, and that the blackness was caused by the blood which Faiẓī had been vomiting. But, without a doubt, the sufferings which he had already endured were very little considered with reference to his vice, his abuse of the faith, and his revilings of his holiness the last of the Prophets (may God bless him and his family, all of them). Many abusive chronograms were discovered for the date of his death. One was as follows:

> "When Faiẓī the atheist died an eloquent man uttered (as the date of his death) the words,
>
> 'A dog has gone from the world in an abominable state.' "[20]

Another said:

> "The date of the death of that carrion Faiẓī is fixed by the words 'The four religions of fire.' "[21]

Another found the following chronogram:

> "Faiẓī the inauspicious, the enemy of the Prophet,
> Went, bearing on him the brand of curses,
> He was a miserable and hellish dog, and hence
> The words 'what dog-worshipper has died' give the date of his death."

In the same strain was the chronogram:

> "The laws of apostasy have been overthrown."[23]
>
> And another wrote: "Faizi was an apostate."[24]

And to the same effect is the following:

> "Since he could not choose but go, there is no help but that
> The date of his death shall be found in the words, 'He is for ever in fire.'[25]

He wrote poetry for a period of exactly forty years, but it was all imperfect. He could set up the skeleton of verse well, but the bones had no marrow in them, and the salt[26] of his poetry was entirely without savour. His taste in lewd raving, in boastful verse,[27] and in infidel scribblings, is well known, but he was entirely devoid of any experience of the love of truth, of the knowledge of God, and of any idea of a painful longing for God, and "a favourable reception is the lot of enemies." Although his *divān* and *maṣnavī* contain more than twenty thousand couplets there is not among them one couplet that is not as much without fire as his withered genius, and they are despised and rejected to such an extent that no one, even in lewdness, studies his verse, as they do those of other base poets.

> "Verse which is wholly devoid of pith
> Remains, for all time, a rough draft."

And this is stranger still, that although he has spent the whole revenue of his *jāgīrs* in having his misleading lies written and copied, and has sent copies of them to all his friends, both far and near, nobody has ever taken a copy in his hand a second time.

Thy poetry has doubtless taken a lesson from the dignity of the veil,
For it displays no desire to come out of its private corner in the house.

The following few couplets are taken from his selected poems which he wrote as memorials of himself, and entrusted to Mirzā Niẓāmu-d-dīn Aḥmad and others:

"Cover not thy eyelashes[28] when thy eyes travel, like feet, (the road of love)
For stout wayfarers march with naked feet."
"Why dost thou cut my hand, thou sword of love? If justice is to be done
Cut out the tongue of the slanderer of Zulaikhā."
"When we cast our bounteous glance on those who sit in the dust
We distribute even to ants brains like those of Solomon."
"The flood of my tears will hardly turn thy heart of stone;
To turn this mill-stone the flood of Noah is required."
"O love, overthrow not the *Kaʿbah,* for there, for a moment,
Those exhausted in the faith of love sometimes take rest."
"O love, have I leave to remove from the shoulder of the sky
To my own shoulder the banner of thy power?"
"How long shall I stake my heart on the blandishments of the fair?
I will burn this heart and obtain a new heart.
Faiẓī, my hand is empty and the road of courtship is before me,
Perhaps I shall be able to pledge my *dīvān* for this world and the next."

The following is the opening couplet of a boastful ode, of which he was very proud:

"Thanks be to God that the love of beautiful ones is my guide.
I am of the religion of Brahmans and of the faith of the fire-worshippers."

The following couplet is also by him:

"In this land there is a sugar-lipped multitude
Who have mixed salt with their wine and are drunk indeed."
(Poet) say thyself in what part of his poetry there is any savour.

The following couplets are from the *Masnavi Markaz-i-Adwār* which he wrote in imitation of the *Makhzan-i-Khiyāl*[29] and which did not turn out fortunately for him:[30]

"To beg[31] for what aid I come to this door,
That I have become richer in heart and hand?
I asked for little, but my stock increased
Then, though I sat down, my footsteps advanced."

The following couplets are from his projected[32] *maṣnavī, Bilqīs-u-Sulaimān*:

I set myself again to place
The slit of my pen opposite to the window of my heart:
There comes from that window and enters this window[33]
That very light which serves as a guide to the soul,
Although from this court of injustice
The throne of the Sulaimān of my words[34] has gone on the breeze,
Yet it occurred to me to consider a plan
Whereby by means of spells, I might bind the demons in chains,[35]
Bind them, by what means I have, to the throne of my rhetoric,
And adorn that (throne) from the treasures of my mind."

The following is an enigma which he composed on the name of *Qādirī*,:[36]

"I will leave the mark from love's brand
Since it is a memorial in my heart, and is the only scar there."

When he was absent as an envoy in the Dakan I sent him two letters from the lower slops of the Kashmir mountains, informing him of the Emperor's disfavour towards me and of his refusal to admit me to his presence in order that I might pay my respects. In the petition which Faiẓī sent to court he recommended me to the Emperor's favour and Shaikh Abū-l-Faẓl was ordered to embody that petition in the *Akbarnāma* in order that it might be read as an example of what such documents should be. The following is a copy of that petition, which was dated on the 10th day of the month *Jamādīʾu-l-Awwal*, A.H. 1000 (February 23, 1592), and despatched from Aḥmadnagar to Lāhor:

'Refuge of the world! There lately came to me from Badāon two relatives of Mullā ʿAbdu-l-Qādir, in a very disturbed state of mind, weeping, weeping and tortured by anxiety. They told me that Mullā ʿAbdu-l Qādir had for some time been sick, and had been unable to keep his promise to attend at court, that some of the Emperor's officers had carried him off with force and violence,[37] and that they did not know what the end of the matter would be. They also said that the long duration of his sickness had not been reported to your majesty. Cherisher of the broken spirited! Mullā ʿAbdu-l Qādir has much aptitude, and he has studied what the *Mullās* of Hindustan usually study in the ordinary branches of learning. He acquired accomplishments under my honoured father, and I, your slave, have known him for nearly thirty-eight years. In addition to his acquirements in learning he has some skill in poetry, and good taste in prose composition, both Arabic and Persian. He has also acquired some knowledge of Indian astrology, and of accounts, in all their branches. He is acquainted with Indian and foreign music, and by no means ignorant of chess, both the two-handed and four-handed game,[38] and has some practice in playing the *bīn*.[39] In spite of all these acquirements he is endued with many virtues. He is not avaricious, has a contented mind, is not vacillating, is truthful, straightforward, respectful, unambitious, humble-spirited, meek, moderate in his requests, almost entirely devoid of the dissimulation so common at court, and entirely faithful and devoted to the Imperial Court. When the imperial forces were sent against Kūmbhulmer,[40] he, having requested permission to accompany them, went thither in the hope of offering his life to your majesty, and was in action and was wounded, and when the fact was reported he received a reward. Jalāl Khān Qūrci[41] first presented him at court, and said, when presenting him: "I have discovered for your majesty an *Imām*[42] with whom you will be well pleased. Mīr Fatḥu-'llah[43] also acquainted your sacred majesty, to some extent, with his affairs, and my respected brother[44] is also aware of his circumstances; but it is well known that "a grain of luck is better than a load of merit."

Since your majesty's court is the court of the just, your slave, acting as though he were present in person at the foot of the august throne, when he saw a helpless man suffering persecution, has represented the case to your majesty. Had he not represented it at this time he would, in a manner, have been guilty of insincerity and want of proper regard for the truth. May God (who is praised) deign to keep the slaves of your majesty's court constant in the path of truth, justice, and righteous dealing under the heavenly shadow of your majesty, their Emperor; and may He long maintain your majesty as their shelter, the cherisher of the miserable, the bestower of favours, the coverer of faults, with boundless wealth, glory, greatness and majesty, by the honour of the pure ones who dwell in the courts of God and the enlightened ones who rise betimes to praise him. Amen. Amen.

If any should ask me what rules of humanity and faithfulness I observe in so harshly reviling one who had so much goodwill for me and so much sincere friendship, and especially how it is that I, forgetful of the command, 'Mention not your dead but in connection with good,' have thus written of a man after his death, and have become one of those who disregard their obligations, I reply, 'All this is true, but what could I do?' The claims of the faith and the safeguarding of one's compact with God are above all other claims, and 'Love is God's and hatred is God's' is an established precept. Although I was for full forty years in the company of Faiẓī, yet after the gradual change in views, the corruption of his nature, and the disordering of his disposition and especially in his mortal sickness, our relations were changed, and as our association together became mere hypocrisy we were freed each of the other. All of us have our faces set towards that court where all disputes shall be decided. "On that day the intimate friends shall be enemies to one another, except the pious."[45]

Among the property left by Faiẓī were four thousand six hundred valuable bound books, all corrected, of which it might have been said with but little exaggeration that most of them were either in the handwriting of the authors or had been written in the authors' time. These became the property of the Emperor, and when they were presented before him he caused them to be catalogued in three sections, giving the first place to books of verse, medicine, astrology, and music; the middle place to works on philosophy, religious mysticism,[46] astronomy, and geometry; and the lowest place to commentaries, the traditions,[47] books on theology, and on all other subjects connected with the sacred law.[48]

Faiẓī wrote a hundred and one books, the *Nal-u-Daman*[49] and others, which he used to reckon. When he was near death he wrote, at the earnest solicitation of some of his friends, some couplets in praise of the Prophet (may God bless and assoil him), and of his ascent,[50] and incorporated them in the *Nal-u-Daman*.

The following couplets are taken from the conclusion of that work:

"O King of Kings,[51] who seekest after wisdom,
Wealthy as the sea and glorious as the sky,
The world is a banquet linked with joy,
The reign is the wine, which stupefies the heavens;
I am the minstrel singing melodies drawn from the veins of my heart,[52]
My pen is the sounding organ.
If from this banquet, in which thy conversation is the cup-bearer
I arise, my song will still remain.
The drinkers circulate the tale
That there is no[53] singer, and yet the assembly is full of song.
To-day, with my honey-sweet music
I am Bārbud, thou the Khusrav of the age.
Though I have polished my pen on the heavens
I am standing before thee on one leg.[55]
Look now on the arrangement of my mystical characters
And now on my long years spent in thy service.
This poem, which bears on its tongue the name of love
Takes thy name[56] to heaven.
I am the inebriating wine of true wisdom,
If I ferment no blame is mine.

I am the bell of thy caravan
And must surely be excused if I give forth sounds.
The reward of my handiwork is this (appreciative) eye,
Which I reckon among the gifts of God.
A hundred nightingales, drunk with love, have arisen, singing
That the rose of Persia has blossomed in India.
I have arrayed in splendour virgin thoughts
In the Ganja of my genius and the Dihlī of my mind.[57]
Before this, when my poems were all the current coin I had
Faiẓī was the name written on my signet;
Now that I am chastened by (spiritual) love
I am Fayyāẓī[58] of the ocean of superabundance.[59]
In thy reign, incomparable King,
Have I plucked from the bush of time the rose of good fortune.
The breeze of my genius has diffused the odour of roses over my banquet,
My cup has been filled to overflowing with the wine of delight;
I have sat laughing, like a cup of sparkling wine,
While the cupbearer, like the bottle, stood behind me
Drinking deeper draughts than either I or my good fortune,
My days have been good, but my means of spending them better.
My gardener has been happy, like thy reign,
For my basil plant has grown freely.
These four thousand jewels of pure water,[60]
Which I have stirred up with the water which is like fire,
Accept, for the lustre of the gems is all thine,
They were produced that they might be scattered round thy crown;
If I have scattered more than I have said
I have then reckoned my harvest without any deficiency.
From this ocean which, in its turmoil, rears its head to the highest heaven
Gems bubble forth on the crest of each wave.
Thus employed, in the art of arranging mystic sayings,
My speech has set itself to no mean employment.
Every pithy phrase with which my pen has charged itself
Has been brought by my heart from distant recesses.
My pen points out to me the road to inscrutable mysteries
Where a mountain of meaning best appears,
Hidden under phrases slight as a blade of grass.
This book is illuminated with my heart's blood.

Its allegories are filled to overflowing with true wisdom.
If its melodies be chanted in the mountains
Their sound will dance among the grains of flowing sand.[61]
I have woven from my swiftly travelling breath
Sacred threads for the Brahmans of the nine monasteries.
My thought, which stirs up mystic truths,
Is an ocean which produces gems from its waters.
This writing, which brings to the light the essence of all things,
Is but half the shadow of my pen.
Every truth contained in it is as water in the stream,
Every knotty saying is as the curl in lovely hair.
This poem is a pearl of which the price may be fixed
For it shows forth the felicity of both worlds;
This lovely idol from the workship of Āẕar[62] received
Its adornment in the month of Āẕar[63]
In the thirty-ninth year of the Imperial reign,
In the new Divine Era,[64]
When I reckoned up the years of the *Hijrī* era
I computed them to be a thousand and three *alifs.*[65]
This garden, which is full of thy perfume
Is but one rose of the plant of thy boundless wealth.
I have the prospect of the joy of another cup
In laying out four gardens more.[66]
If love thus consumes me entirely,
I shall make moonlight shine from my ashes.
The transparent glass of my heart is melted,
And I will give it, as a mirror, into the hands of the assembly.
The story-tellers of the market-place base their stories on their dreams;
But I have awoken from such stories.
This is the arena of those who have traversed the heavens
And in it valiant heroes are to be descried;
Scribes whose very breath breathes magic, with the points of their pens
Have completed the adornment of this epic.
I also, for the sake of making a name in the world,
Have with my skill in words made a talisman.
I melted down both my heart and my tongue
In displaying this picture to the world.
When my genius scattered its wit into pen,

The pen poured the water of life into the inkstand;
The Messiah saw musk in a moist bladder
And dried it with His breath.
Is this an inkstand filled with ambergris,
Or a censer emitting smoke of ambergris?
When this lofty dome (the sky) became my cradle
The year was 954 (A.D. 1547).[67]
Now that I have spent forty-nine years in this monastery
I have passed through the seventy-two sects (of Islām)
My meeting-place has been in the idol-temples of India,
The fire-temples of Persia have been in my heart.
With a hundred incantations and magical devices
Have I cleaned from the mirror of the king's heart the scum of rust.[68]
This day, among the great tribe of the ages
The sky beat the *naubat* for me on the roof;[69]
Eloquence, that king who has been my surety,
Has enthroned himself on my tongue.
I have become both the equal of the *amīrs*
And the prince of poets.
In every direction I go, uttering my wise words,
The ranks of mystic significations bow the knee to me.
Since love entered into my mind
I have become the adorner of the diadem which is over the
    nine thrones of the heavens.
The valiant swordsmen of the kingdom of rhetoric,
The archers of the battle of pretensions,
When they cast their eyes on my forces,
Cast down their shields in the field before me.
My pen, on account of my great fame
Writes as my autograph, 'He who is mighty in speech';
'The pride of the philosophers' is the writing on my forehead
'The greatest[70] of the poets' is the device on my seal.
The heavenly key has opened
To my thoughts the door of mystic significations.
When my breath gave birth to this poem
Khiẓr[71] came, and bestowed on me his length of days.
If the door has been opened before me
My poems have also been endued with long life.

If I reckon up all that both worlds can give
I find it to be but dust from the stour[72] which I have raised.
This pen, which has traversed the whole of my poem,
Drives its splinters under the nails of bad penmanship.[73]
See now the drift of this book, which shall last for ever,
See boundless wisdom concealed in (boundless) love.
Those who are not dumb before this splendour
Are men who are not admitted to the privy chamber of imagination.
As for him whose business is with words,
Let the age endow him with justice.
It is the practice of those of meagre wit
Ever to gibe at their contemporaries:
What of those who have fallen asleep, wrapped in the sheet of the earth?
Knowest thou what they said of the men of their time?
And those who shall obscure my light with smoke
Will I afflict in their eyes (with their smoke).[74]
Moreover, a time will come when I shall be no more,
And shall no longer be the nightingale of this garden;
Then those who struck a thorn into my rose
Shall sigh for sorrow over my shrine.
O thou who hast poured the lees of the draught into my pure wine
Pluck but a rose of the spring of justice,
Or else take my goods at my valuation;
Look to their worth and consider yourself fortunate in me.
In the morning, when I sing in this meadow
My melodies shed a hundred gardens of flowers.
I am humble as dust in the path of true appraisers
Who this day, despite the ungrateful,
When they opened this treasure from my stock.
Cast on it a glance which justly estimated it
And looked (with pity) on other unfortunates.
They, like the ocean, teemed with gems
And the diver who brought the gems to the surface
delighted in their commendation.
Art is intensely jealous of love
For I have compounded this poem with love's magic.
This pen is the source of great wonder
That from a dry reed such moist sweetness should flow.

This breath of mine is a monument to love,
For it is vapour which arises from my inward fervour.
Fayyāẓī on this incantation of thine
How long will thou dilate?
It is best that thou should'st bring thy tale to a close
Before thou becomest, thyself, no more than a tale.
O thou consumed with love restrain thy breath;
Have done with love's tale, have done!"

Conclusion

This is the account of some of those poets, most of whom were contemporary with the author and were writing during the time in which he was writing, and whose *dīvans* are current in this age and are circulated as examples. As for those who have leapt from the net of this memoir and are here neither described nor indicated by casual mention, I make them over to those who shall hereafter set foot in the plain of existence, for this series (of poets) is as endless as the *Burhán-i-Taṭbīq*,[75] and to comprehend them all within the limits of one age, or one short space of time is beyond the limits (of any capacity) and beyond the extremity (of its powers).

A maṣnavī.
"Two couplets one day scared my heart,
As the singer was chanting them to his guitar
Many Junes, Decembers, and Aprils
Will come after we have become dust and bricks,
While those who are now invisible to me
Will come and pass over my dust."

Praise be to God! My pen, in its atrabiliousness, has like a madman, dealt drily and coolly with everybody, and has poured out from the cup of its heart every drop of black bile which it had in its spot of original sin[76] and given forth from the columns[77] of its fingers all that came to its tongue, so that (I am not sure) what those who come after we will say when, in their search for treasure[78] they have hastened[79] in the tracks of the crows' feet of this impudent (pen),[80] or what answer I shall give in respect of all my idle gossip. I fear that in accordance with the saying, 'Thou shalt be treated as thou hast treated others' they will deal with me as I have dealt with these poets.

"Thou hast called me a promise-breaker, but I fear
That this accusation will be laid to thy charge on the day of resurrections."

But there is here a subtle distinction if the discriminating neglect it not, and it is this, that I have apportioned eulogy and execration according to the canon of the unmistakable sacred law and have bestowed praise and blame in accordance with my zeal for the faith, and my case is similar to that of the boor who entered a company seated at table and began to eat without any regard to the others, and collected all the dishes round himself. One of the company said, 'Sir, who are you, and why do you thus intrude upon us?' He replied, 'I am a Turk, and I am servant of the *dārogha*,[81] and I am hungry.' But if others, besides myself, should be jealous for the faith I shall not resent their criticism; nay, rather, my life is a sacrifice for those people who shall apprise me of my faults. But if they be not jealous for the faith let them hang their heads and hold their peace; for in truth the bird of my pen, with its sharp bill and its sublime flight, is in the position of that beast[82] which shall come forth as the first sign of the Judgment Day, for it stamps on the foreheads of the circumstances of the folk of this last age the words 'this one is a Muslim,' or 'this one is an infidel,' exalting some to God's mercy and setting apart others as accursed, and the saying of the prophet (may God bless and assoil him,) is clear on this point, 'O God, I have not blessed, and I have not cursed in my cursings any but him whom Thou hast cursed.'" It is related that that chief of the prophets (may God bless and assoil him while the sun and the moon shall rise) invoked curses on the polytheistic 'Arabs and on the chiefs of the Quraish, and particularly on one mentioned by name, for a whole month after he had been slandered[83] by the wicked, and said, 'O God, curse the infidels, who stray from Thy way, who make Thy prophet a liar, and who slay Thy saints. Thou art Lord of this world and the next. O God, preserve me in safety, and join me to the pious!' And, since the end is but a return to the beginning, there is, in these days when the faith is exiled (for 'the faith appears as a stranger, and verily, it has become as it appears') every occasion for the constant recital of the following prayer, 'O God, assist him who assists the religion of Muḥammad and forsake him who forsakes the faith of Muḥammad!'

The author of the Mirṣādu-l-ʿIbād[84] four hundred years ago uttered his complaint and said:

"O kings of the earth, hasten, all of you,
That you may catch the perfume which is all that is left of the faith!
Islam has gone from your hands, and ye heed it not;
Infidelity has captured the world, and ye sleep!"

Forsaking the custom of authors, who have in respect of each of their works, of whatever sort, a hundred hopes of favour from the age and from the people of the age, and, having dedicated a work to somebody, make it a means of being admitted to the intimacy of kings, of begging for rewards, and of attaining their objects I, without desire or expectation (of material gain but) seeking aid from God, trusting in Him, and firmly laying hold of the skirt of his universal favour and his bounty well-known in bygone times, have placed these, my first fruits, on the dish of speech merely for the sake of virtuosos among those to come, who may be desirous of, and anxious for, information regarding our times, that haply its flavour may please the palates of souls, and also that some relish from the morsels on the table of their favour may become the lot of the palate of the compiler of the work, who is, as it were, their gardener.

If thou drink wine, pour a draught out on the ground,
Fear not that sin which carries some gain to others.[85]

I shall now expalin what it was that originally led me to collect these fragments.[86] Since a complete revolution, both in legislation and in manners, greater than any of which there is any record for the past thousand years, has taken place in these days, and every writer who has had the ability to record events and to write two connected sentences has, for the sake of flattering the people of this age, or for fear of them, or by reason of his ignorance of matters of faith, or of his distance from court, or for his own selfish ends, concealed the truth, and having bartered his faith for worldly profit, and right guidance for error, has adorned falsehood with the semblance of truth, and distorted and embellished infidelity and pernicious trash until they have appeared to be laudable, confirming the truth of the verse, 'These are they who have purchased error at the price of true direction: but their traffic hath not been gainful,'[87] I am convinced that the people of succeeding generations who shall see their false fables and all their unprofitable prolixity will, in accordance with the saying, 'he who hears dispenses with the solution of his difficulties,' with another class of men, regretful not in the least, be perplexed, and will expect and await (something else), and therefore, that the veil may be drawn aside, it is incumbent on me, who am acquainted with some, at least, of the affairs narrated, and have even been intimately connected with these transactions, to place on record what I have seen and what I have heard, for my evidence regarding these things is that of any eye-witness who is certain of what he relates, and does not spring from mere supposition and guess-work ('and when can that which is heard resemble that which is seen?') in order that, on the one hand, my record may be an expiation of the writings,[88] past and present, which I have been compelled and directed to undertake, and, on the other, right may be proved to be on the side of the Muslim's and mercy may be shown to me.

'Perchance some pious man may one day put up a prayer for mercy for this
poor wretch.'

And when I examine the matter well I perceive that this rough draft, and other rough drafts like it, have all the merits of fair copies, for, in conformity with the couplet.

Reduce a word at once to writing.
For words slip suddenly for one's memory.

Something, at least, of what the author knows whether by having seen occurrences or by having heard of them, is (at once) entered in them and reduced to writing. At the same time to define such scribbling as literary compositions can, to do no more than justice, be nothing but mere boasting and vaunting, which are repugnant to refined natures, and so far am I from vain-glory and pride in this matter that I am-ashamed of them, and if I should attempt any lofty flights regarding them this base coin of mine, this worthless and contemptible merchandise, my faulty and inappreciated style, is sufficient to refute and falsify my claim.

In these matters nobody knowns me as well as I know myself.

A story by way of Moral.

A fox said to a camel, 'O uncle,
Tell me truly whence you come.'
The camel replied, 'Lo, I come from the bath
Where I have bathed my limbs in water hot and cold.'
The fox said, 'You have fine proof of what you say,
For both your forelegs and your hindlegs are very dirty.'

It is now high time for me to raise the hand of supplication to the court of that Providence who lacks nothing and who cherishes his servants, and to ask of Him that which shall be most expedient for me, although His glorious majesty is fettered by no expediency. I shall therefore conclude with the following supplications, which are free from all spaciousness and elaboration, and are (therefore) not far from the assurance of a favourable answer.

Supplications

O King, look upon us with the eye of acceptance and mercy! O Lord of all things, visible and invisible, compose us in the seeking of Thy will, and remove from our way, and from the way of all Muslims, all disunion, disquiet, and perplexity! Bestow Thy pardon and forgiveness on us in our time. Let Thy gracious favour and guidance both impel and lead us. Deliver us not up into the hands of our own disunion and leave us not to ourselves, neither entrust us with ourselves, but preserve us from our own wickedness, and bring our affairs and those of all Muslims to a happy conclusion in Thy pardon and acceptances. Pardon what we have done in the past and preserve us from what we would do in the future.

Whatever Thou bestowest on Thy servant, bestow on him faith.
Bestow on him adherence to Thy will.

Forsake us not in Thy wrath; let us not be occupied with any but Thee. Displace us not from Thy remembrance. If Thou shouldst question us we have no answer ready, if Thou art angry we have no strength to abide it. From Thy servant proceed faults and lapses, and from Thee all pardon and mercy. O Ancient of Days that changest not, and Glorious one without peer! O Hidden and Omniscient God, Thou that hearest and seest, that hast no need of description or explanation, our faults are many, and Thou knowest and seest us: grant unto us a good end, let us die Muslims, and join us to the pious; and bless and assoil Muḥammad and the race of Muḥammad, and all Thy prophets and apostles.

Look on me as though I were entirely free from disobedience,
Consider not mine offences, consider Thy mercy.
Ward off from me all the evils of the age,
Keep me afar from every evil that there is,
So direct for me all worldly affairs and religious matters,
That I may be free from want in both worlds.
By Thy favour Thou keepest me in safety
From the calamities and tumults of these latter days.
Thou accomplishest the desires of Thy poor servant,
Thou makest me a partaker of worldly and spiritual blessings.
Deliver me not helpless into the hands of mine own lusts,
But grant me protection from my dominant lusts.
Send me not as a beggar before any one,

My begging is at Thy door and no other.
Give me a portion of lawful gain,
Give me a corner apart from the worldly.
Pardon and veil my sin,
For it is Thou that veilest and pardonest sins.
Grant me knowledge of Thine eternal bounty.
Free me from ignorance and error.
Preserve me from companionship with the unworthy.
Cause me to meet with a pious and sympathetic friend.
Set my face on the road towards Thee,
Free me from all else but Thee.
Accomplish not my desire in any object
The end of which will bring me shame.
No one but Thee knows what is for my good.
Thou knowest my loss and my profit.
Enrich me with the treasure of contentment.
Give me ease in the joy of serving Thee.
Incline me not to objects of this world,
Make my heart cold to such desires.
So accustom me to thoughts of Thee
That I may think on no other but Thee.
Open before me the door of knowledge of Thee
And in that privy chamber impart Thy secrets to me.
Give me a cup from the flagon of love
And grant me, from that wine, a new intoxication
So fashion my inclinations to the world to come
That I may no more desire the things of this world.
Though death shall rend my upper garment
Let not the dust of this world settle on my lower garment.
When the sword of death cleaves my life,
When 'Azāzil[89] shall resolve to accept the faith,
Of Thy mercy cast one glance towards me,
Open in my face the door of Thy favour,
Declare to me the glad tidings of Thy gracious forgiveness.
That I may have rest in the sleep of death.
Grant unto me such power that, in that perplexity,
My cross-examination[90] may be easy to me.
When the people of this world set their faces towards the resurrection.

And raise their heads in bewilderment from the dust.
Captured, by their evil fate, in disobedience
Their faces blackened with shame for their sins,
When, in that confusion, in the heat of the Resurrection
Day,
The rocks shall become water from the fierceness of the
sun's rays,
When there shall not be, in all that plain full of grief
Any refuge but the shadow of the Most High
Of Thy bounty, O Creator, Lord of many claims,
Cast the shadow of Thy favour on my head!
When the balance of justice is brought into the midst
And the deficiency and excess of all shall be made apparent,
When I shall have in my company mountains of sin,
Beside which the mountains shall seem no larger than a blade of grass,
It is not impossible to Thine illimitable mercy
To weight down the scale of my obedience:
In that place of fear and confusion
When the records of each one's acts shall fly open
And my record shall be so black
That it will be impossible to enter any fresh sin therein,
Wash my record with the cloud of Thy clemency,
And, by that washing, raise me to honour:
When the fire of hell shall leap forth as a banner
To draw to itself all the people of the world
Pour, of Thy grace, some water on my fire
And bring me forth purified from that fire.
When over hell the narrow bridge[91] shall appear
And the people shall raise a shout for joy,[92]
That bridge, long as the dark nights of separation,
Soul-melting as the sighs from lovers' hearts,
Narrower than a hair,
Darker than the smoke of the night of separation,
Sharper than a sharp cutting sword,
Shooting forth tongues of flame like hell fire
If Thou take me not by the hand, woe is me,
For the nethermost pit of hell will be my place!
I bring no goods with me but hope,
O God, make me not hopeless of forgiveness!

Praise be to God, and thanks, that after all this smearing of myself with the smoke of the midnight lamp and all this fever of the brain I have gained freedom from this hasty work. Ah, how much distraction have I not suffered at the hands of these troubled times, before this valuable coin of time (to complete my work) and this priceless jewel (the work itself) was obtained.

Please God this work will, for a while, be preserved from the treachery of lack of preservation,[93] of faithlessness, or of evil guardianship, and will thus be safeguarded from the picking and stealing of the ignorant cutpurses of this age, and, being constantly hidden under the protection of God's guardianship, will receive the ornament of acceptance, and no damage will reach it from the evil eyes of squinting (rogues) of varying degrees,[94] the hands of impotent (foes) will fail to reach the skirt of the beauty of this creature of my wit, and whoever is not admitted to the knowledge of its secret will remain disappointed.

A thousand thanks to the God of the world.
For that I have entrusted my jewel to one who can appraise jewels.

It was the intention of my languid and secretive[95] heart and my wearied mind to gather together the *Key to the History of Kashmīr*,[96] and the histories of the Kings of Gujarāt, Bengal and Sind, with an account of the wonders of India, and to have them bound together in one volume with this, but that stuff did not match this, for ṣilk must be joined with silk. Therefore, on Friday, the twenty-third of the month Jamādī'u-ṣ-Sānī A.H. 1004 (March 5, A.D. 1595) I shortened the rope of prolixity and contented myself with writing this much. I composed the following verses with the object of giving, in an enigma, the data of its completion:

Thanks be to God, by whose clemency this Selection[97] has
arrived at completion.
When I sought the date of it from my heart (my heart) replied.
(It is) a selection which has no second.

Praise be to God whose assistance has enabled me to complete it, and blessings and peace be on the best of mankind, our lord Muḥammad, and on his family, and on his great companions, till the Day of Resurrection.

Al Badāonī, from the Muntakhabu-t-Tawārīkh
translated by Sir Wolseley Haig

TRANSLATOR'S NOTES

1. *Makhfī-na-mānad:* literally, "let it not be concealed," a common form of commencing a history.
2. Niẓāmu-'d-Dīn Aḥmad, vide *Āīn-i-Akbarī passim.* His history is generally known as the *Ṭabaqāt-i-Akbarī.*
3. Such expressions as this explain Badāonī's reason for keeping this history secret. The literal translation is "and have not been pardoned."
4. *I.e.*, "were I to mention these men at all I could only mention them in such a manner as would lead to my being persecuted, for I will not give praise where it is not due. I will therefore keep silence regarding them."
5. Two pious ejaculations in Arabic, the former, which is one of the *aḥādīs*, or traditional sayings of Muḥammad, denouncing flatterers, while the latter prays for protection from tyrants.
6. These are evidently the persons intended by the word *Ṭalbat.* Badāonī as a good Muslim was much scandalized by the strange freaks of the followers of this new religion of Akbar's.
7. The reference to the idiomatic use of the word *ḥarf* "a letter of the alphabet" as in the phrase *ḥarfzadan*, "to talk," is hard to reproduce in a translation. The meaning of the line is: "The letters (or sounds) of which their talk is composed do not spell (or make) sense."
8. *Gulkhan*: lit., 'dustbin,' otherwise 'the furnace used for heating a bath.' The unsavouriness of the latter would be due to the nature of the fuel used.
9. A fabulous bird, described as being "known as to name, but unknown as to body." Its abode is in Qāf, a mountain encircling the world, which may be described in much the same terms as is the bird. In practical, as oposed to mythical geography, the name is given to the Caucasus.
10. This Arabic couplet is clearly a parody on the opening couplet of the fourth *qaṣīdah* of the *sab'amo'alleqāt.* In the second hemistich the word *ṣum* appears in the text, and also in MSS (A) and (B). This does not make sense. I prefer to read *ṣum.*
11. *Bā* in the text, despite the clear meaning of the passage and the authority of both MSS.
12. Literally *Malik-al-sh'orā* (Poet laureate) 'King of poets', the official title given to him by Akbar in A.H. 997 (A.D.1580).

Shaikh Abū'l Faiẓ Faiẓī, one of the most learned men of Akbar's court, was the eldest son of Shaikh Mubārak of Nagor, and elder brother of the famous Abū-l-Fazl. He was born at Āgra in A.H. 954 (A.D. 1547). His acquirements in Arabic literature, the art of poetry, and medicine were very extensive, and he used to treat poor people *gratis.* As a young man he was regarded with suspicion and ill-treated by the orthodox in Āgra on account of his *Shī'ah* proclivities, and when he was summoned to court the orthodox believed, or affected to believe, that he was to be called to account for his heterodoxy, and carried him to court by force. He was however, very favourably received by Akbar, and in a short time became his constant companion and friend. He was instrumental, in A.H. 986 (A.D. 1578–79), in bringing about the downfall of Shaikh 'Abdu-n-Nabī the *Ṣadr*, who had been one of his persecutors. It is said that Faiẓī wrote a hundred and one books. In 1586 he planned a *Khamsah*, or collection of five epics, in imitation of the *Khamsah* of Niẓāmi. The first, *Markazu-l-Adwār*, was to consist of 3000 verses, and was to be an imitation of Niẓāmi's *Makhzanu-l-Asrār.* The *Sulaimān-u-Bilqīs* and the *Nal-u-Daman* were to consist of 4000 verses each and were to be imitations of *Khusrav-u-Shīrīn* and the *Lailā-u-Majnūn*; and the *Haft Kishwar* and the *Akbarnāma*, each of 5000 verses, were to correspond with the *Haft Paikar* and the *Sikandarnāma.* This great undertaking was never completed. Portions were written, and in 1594–95 Faiẓī, encouraged by Akbar, completed the *Nal-u-Daman* and presented a copy to the Emperor. The *Markazu-*

l-Adwār appears also to have been completed. Faiẓī translated from the Sanskṛt the *Līlavatī*, a work on arithmetic, and the *Bhagavad Gītā*. Faiẓī was sometimes employed as tutor to the Princes, and sometimes acted as an ambassador. He suffered from asthma and died on Safar 10, A.H. 1004 (Oct.15, 1595). He was a member of Akbar's 'divine faith.' Vide *Āīn-i-Akbarī*, i, 490 *et passim* and Badāonī, vol. ii. text pp. 260, 309, 365, *et passim*.

A long description of Faiẓī as a poet is given in the Āīn (i, 549) from which I give the following extracts: 'He was a man of cheerful disposition, liberal, active, an early riser. He was a disciple of the Emperor, and was thus at peace with the whole world.** He wrote for nearly forty years under the name of Faiẓī, which he afterwards, under divine inspiration, changed to Fayyāẓī.** His excellent manners and habits cast a lustre on his genius.** He composed many works in Persian and Arabic. Among others he wrote the *Sawāṭi ʻu-l-Ilhām* (*vide* p. 194 n.1)** Genius as he was, he did not care for poetry, and did not frequent the society of wits. He was profound in philosophy.** The gems of thought in his poems will never be forgotten. In the Ṭabaqāt he is thus described, "He is one of the greatest of learned men and Shaikhs and is much respected for his resignation to the Divine will and for his habits of solitary meditation. He has grown to maturity in the Emperor's service and has been honoured with the title of *Maliku-sh-Shʻarā*. In the art of poetry he is a prodigy, and he has written a work on ethics, entitled *Mawāridu-l-Kilam*, which contains no dotted letters, and he has also written a commentary on the word of God, which contains no dotted letters. It is known as the *Sawāṭi-u-'l-Ilham*. His *dīvān* contains over 15,000 verses and he has written some *maṣnavīs*. In poetry he is the chief of all poets of the age, and in prose composition he is alone and unapproachable. In branches of knowledge foreign to the Arabic, and in philosophy, medicine and many other sciences he has much skill. In universality of knowledge he has no equal. I have enjoyed intimate friendship with this most learned man of the time from my childhood up. His gentle disposition is equalled by his cheerfulness. His angelic nature imposes an obligation on all his contemporaries."

13. *ʻAllāmī* 'my very learned man,' a title bestowed on Shaikh Abū-l-Faẓl by Akbar.
14. *Faiyyāzī-Faiẓī* signifies 'abundance'; with the *yā-yi-nisbatī* added to it, as usual in a *takhallus*, it becomes Faizī. Faiyyāz is an intensive adjective formed in the same measure as *ʻAllām*, from the same root, and signifies 'profusely generous.' The *yā-yi-nīsbatī* converts it into a *takhallus*. The letter *yā* in Allāmī is, on the other hand, the sign of the first (singular) possessive pronoun in Arabic.
15. *Khayulā*. The word has perplexed the editor of the text, who says, in a plaintive footnote, *Sic*, in all three MSS.
16. *Janābat* 'Vir de quo egreditur semen coitus, lavabit aquâ omne corpus suum; et immundus erit usque ad vesperum.' Lev xv. The Muḥammadan law on this point was the same as the Mosaic. The obligation was contemptuously set aside by the 'divine faith'; *vide* Badāonī, ii, text p. 305.
17. The *Sawāṭiʻu-l-Ilham*, vide *supra* p. 194 and note 412.
18. Faiẓī was very fond of dogs.
19. A dentifrice used in India for blackening the teeth.
20. *Makkī az jahān raft ba ḥāl-e-qabīḥ*. 60 + 20 + 10 + 1 + 7 + 3 + 5 + 1 + 50 + 200 + 80 + 400 + 5 + 2 + 8 + 1 + 30 + 100 + 2 + 10 + 8 = 1003. One year short.
21. *Bachār mazhabnār* 2 + 3 + 1 + 200 + 40 + 700 + 5 + 2 + 50 + 1 + 200 = 1204. This chronogram gives two hundred years in excess. Badāonī perhaps thought that any stick was good enough to beat a dog with. The 'four religions of fire' were probably Judaism, Christianity, Hinduism, and Zoroastrianism, the 'divine faith' of Akbar being, perhaps, substituted for one of these.

22. *Cheh sag parastī murd.* 3 + 5 + 60 + 20 + 2 + 200 + 60 + 400 + 10 + 40 + 200 + 4 = 1004.
23. *Qāedah ilhad shikast.* 100 + 1 + 70 + 4 + 5 + 1 + 30 + 8 + 1 + 4 + 300 + 20 + 60 + 400 = 1004.
24. *Būd Faiẓī mulḥidī.* 2 + 6 + 4 + 80 + 10 + 800 + 10 + 40 + 30 + 8 + 4 + 10 = 1004.
25. *Khālid fil-nār.* 600 + 1 + 30 + 4 + 80 + 10 + 1 + 30 + 50 + 1 + 200 = 1007. Three years in excess.
26. *Maṣaliḥ.* 'Spices,' 'flavouring materials.'
27. *Fakhriyyāt.* Verses boasting of their own accomplishments in poetry are a favourite form of composition among Persian poets, and especially among Indian poets writing in Persian.
28. i.e. 'Veil not thyself.'
29. This is a mistake. The *Markazu-'l-Adwār* was written in imitation of Niẓāmī's *Makhzanu-'l-asrār, vide supra* p. 412 n.1
30. By this expression Badāonī appears to mean merely that he did not live to finish it.
31. *Darvīzah* in the text. The MSS. have *Daryūzah.* The difference affects neither the meaning nor the scansion.
32. *Mauhūm* 'imaginary.' The meaning may perhaps be that the poem was the work of Faiẓī's imagination, but I believe my translation to be correct. The poem was never finished. *Vide* p. 412 n.1.
33. *i.e*, the light is conveyed from the window of the poet's heart to the nibs of his pen, the slit between which is compared to another window.
34. *i.e.* the poet's words of wisdom.
35. As Sulaimān is said to have done.
36. The meaning of the passage may be, "an enigma which he addressed to Qādirī". I have not been able to solve the enigma.
37. *Bi-shiddat-i-tamām.* MS (A) substitutes *sharārat* (malice) for *shiddat.*
38. Akbar himself played both games. *Vide Aīn-i-Akbarī*, i, 308.
39. The *bīn* is a stringed instrument consisting of a narrow strip of wood connecting, and placed over the openings of, two dried gourds, spherical, or nearly so, in shape. Along the wooden bridge are stretched five or seven steel strings, which are played with a plectrum.
40. This place, the name of which is variously spelt by Badāonī, is Kūmbhalgarh, a fortress on the western border of the Udaipūr State in Rajputāna, about 40 miles north of Udaipūr city. *Vide* text, vol. ii. pp 227, 266. It was in April 1576 that Badāonī asked for and obtained leave to accompany this expedition.
41. Jalāl Khān Qūrcī was a commander of five hundred. He distinguished himself in the field and Akbar was much attached to him. He was murdered, in mistake for Shimāl Khān, early in 1576. *Vide Āīn-i-Akbarī* i, 475.
42. The reader and leader of prayers in the *musjid.*
43. *Vide* p. 216.
44. Shaikh Abū-l-Faẓl.
45. *Ala khilāyaomaēzinb'aza humb'az aduvun illal-muttaqīn Qur'ān,* c.xliii. The text A has *muttaqūn.*
46. *Tasavvuf* the doctrines of the Ṣūfis.
47. *Ḥadīs* (*ḥadīth*). the sayings of Muḥammad.
48. The classification indicates Akbar's contempt for orthodoxy, and evidently much shocked Badāonī's prejudices.
49. The text is corrupt here, and reads as though there were a hundred and one books of the *Nal-u-Daman,* which was not the case. From other sources, e.g. the *Mir'atu-l-'Ālam,* we know that Faiẓī was credited with the authorship of a hundred and one books in all. The *Nal-u-*

Daman is the story of the loves of Nala, King of Nishada or Mālwa, and Damayanti, daughter of the king of Vīdarbha, or Berar. Faiẓī's source of inspiration was the *Mahābhārata*, where the story is given at length.

50. *M'erāj* (*mi'rāj*). According to the belief of Musalmāns Muḥammad was caught up one night from Jerusalem to heaven, his means of conveyance being *Buzāq*, an animal smaller than a mule and larger than a ass. While in heaven he held 90,000 conversations with God, but on his return found his bed yet warm. This belief was one of those selected for ridicule by Akbar and the followers of the 'divine faith,' *vide* text, vol. ii, p. 316. If Faizī's recantation were genuine it must be regarded as, in some sort, a triumph for orthodoxy.
51. Akbar.
52. Literally 'bloody melodies' (*pardahā-yi-khūnī*). I believe the meaning to be that which I have given.
53. The text has, wrongly, 'thou art not (a singer)'. From the scansion it is clear that the simple negative (*not*) is the correct reading.
54. A celebrated musician at the court of Khusrav.
55. The attitude, in India, of a supplicant, or penitent.
56. *Ṭugrā (ṭughrā).* literally, 'thy royal sign manual.'
57. The reference is to the two great poets Niẓāmī of Ganja (in imitation of whose *Lailā-u-Majnūn* this poem was written) and Amir Khusrav of Dihlī. Faizī means to say that he has conceived poetical ideas which neither Niẓāmī nor Amir Khusrav ever conceived.
58. *Vide* p. 43. note 2.
59. Mr. Blochmann (*Āīn-i-Akbarī*, i, 549) charitably supposes 'the Ocean of Superabundance' to mean 'God's love,' as, indeed, it may; but it is just as likely to signify Abkar's generosity, or spiritual gifts.
60. *i.e.* the verses of the *Nal-u-daman.*
61. *Rēg-e-ravān* (*rīg-i-ravān*) commonly means quicksand. I take it to mean here the sands of mountain streams, as quicksands are not commonly found in the mountains.
62. The father of Abraham, said by the Musalmāns to have been a sculptor of idols.
63. The ninth month of the Persian solar year.
64. The era instituted by Akbar, beginning with the first year of his reign (A.H. 963 = A.D. 1556). In this era the years were solar, and the old Persian solar months were used. The era was instituted in 1582; *vide* vol. ii, text, p.306.
65. *i.e.* A.H. 1003 (A.D. 1594–95), the numerical value of the letter *alif* being one. There is a play on the words *alf* 'a thousand.' and *alif*, the letter *alif.*
66. *Scil.* the *Markazu-l-Adwār*, the Sulaimān-u-Bilqīs, the *Haft Kishwar*, and the Akbarnāma.
67. Faiẓī refers to his own birth in that year. *Vide* p.411, n.1. The next verse fixes the date of the completion of this poem.
68. It is obvious that this 'conclusion' of the *Nal-u-Daman* does not consist of the couplets written in praise of the prophet and on his ascent, mentioned on p. 422. Here Faiẓī, after boasting of his electicism mentions with pride his part in weaning Akbar from orthodoxy. The whole extract consists of the glorification of Akbar and the poet, chiefly the latter.
69. The *naubat* was the daily music played at stated hours over the gate houses of the emperor and some of the chief grandees.
70. Literally, 'the seal,' *i.e.* the last and greatest.
71. The guardian of the water of life.

72. 'Dust in motion.' I know of no *English* word by which to translate *gubār* (*ghubār*) 'dust in motion' as opposed to *gard* 'dust at rest'.
73. Faiẓī here praises his penmanship. Driving splinters under the nails is a well-known torture. The meaning of the verse is that other penmen will be tortured by envy owing to the excellence of his handwriting.
74. This verse may also mean, 'I will hold them excused, owing to (the badness of) their eyesight.'
75. I take this to be the name of a book. The words mean 'the demonstration of comparison.'
76. *Suvaēdā* (*suwaidā*) the black spot of original sin which the Musalmāns believe to be in every heart.
77. Jadāval: 'ruled columns.'
78. The text has *kajkāō* and MS (A) has *kanjkā* of neither of which can I make sense. *Kanjkāo*, the reading of MS (B), given as a variant in the text, is correct.
79. The text has *wadīdah.* The variant *dawīdah* given in the text on the authority of MS. (B) is correct.
80. *Zāgpāē kajkulā.* The letter h at the end of is *kulah* is not in the text.
81. Prefect of a town or village. In India, a police officer.
82. *Dabbatul arẕ*, the beast which, according to the Musalmāns, is to come forth as the first sign of the coming Judgment Day, touching the believers with the staff of Moses and marking the faces of the infidels with the seal of Solomon.
83. The text has *qunwat.* MS (A) has *qutwat.* Which appears to be the correct reading.
84. I regret that I have been unable to find mention of this book, or of the name of its author. The meaning of the title is 'a highway for (God's) servants.'
85. *i.e.* 'pour a draught on the ground that those who are dead and turned to dust may benefit by it.' The conceit is a favourite one among Persian poets and occurs in the 'tomb-song' of Hāfiẓ (ode 439, Jarrett's editiion), and frequently in the quatrains of 'Umar-i-Khayyām.
86. Literally 'potsherds.'
87. *Ūlāikal lazīna ashtarū-aẕ zalālat bil hudā famā rabīḥat tijaratahum, Qur'ān, ii, 15.*
88. Badāonī here refers to the works undertaken by him under the orders of Akbar, *viz.*: the translation of the *Mahābhārata* and the compilation of parts of the *Tārikh-i-Alfī*, (vide *Āīn-i-Akbarī*, i, 104, 199, and Badāonī, in text), 320, 399.
89. Satan.
90. After a corpse is laid in the grave it is visisted by Munkir and Nakīr, two black livid angels, of a terrible appearance, who order the dead person to sit upright and examine him as to his faith. If he answer rightly they suffer the body to rest in peace and it is refreshed by the air of Paradise, but if not they beat him on the temples with iron maces. They then press the earth on the corpse, which is tormented till the day of resurrection.
91. *Alṣirāt* (*aṣ-ṣirāt*) the bridge over the midst of hell, which is here graphically desribed, must be passed by all after the Judgment. Muḥammad and his Muslims will, with God's aid, pass rapidly over its path, narrower and sharper than the edge of a knife, but the unbelievers, following them, will lose their footing, and fall through the briars, which hedge it in on either side, into the flames of hell.
92. *Nishāṭ.* Joy does not, at first sight, appear to be an emotion suitable to the occasion. The meaning may be either that men will be overjoyed to see that hell is bridged at all, or that the devils in hell will rejoice to see that the bridge is so perilous.
93. Badāonī here declares his intention of keeping this work, the *Muntakhabu-t-Tawārīkh*, a secret. His anxiety that it should not become known during his life-time will be easily understood by anybody who has read it. He designed it to be a counterblast, in the interests of Islām, to the

writings of Abū-l-Faẓl and his elder brother Faiẓī, who had borne the chief part in leading Akbar into the paths of religious speculation and had so far succeeded in leading him away from orthodoxy as almost to persuade him that he was God. According to a statement in the *Mir'ātu-l-Ālam* the book was made public during the reign of Jahāngir, who showed his displeasure by disbelieving the statement of Badāoni's children that they had not known of its existence. Badāoni's work was certainly not known in A.H. 1025 (A.D. 1616), the tenth year of Jahāngir's reign, in which year the *Ma'āṣir-i-Raḥīmī* was written, whose author complains of the want of a history besides the *Ṭabaqāt* and the *Akbarnāma*.

94. Badāonī here does not hesitate to attack the highest.
95. The text here has *sāṭir* 'a butcher,' or 'butcherly,' which makes no sense. MS.(A) has *sātir* which I have translated. Badāonī apparently refers again to his intention of keeping his book a secret.
96. This was, apparently, the History of Kas͟hmīr, based on that of Mullā S͟hāh Muḥammad of S͟hāhābād, which Badāonī, by Akbar's order, compiled in A.D.1591. Vide vol. ii, text, p.374.
97. The letters of the word *intek͟hāb* ('selection') have the following values, 1 + 50 + 400 + 600 + 1 + 2 = 1054. If we subtract the value of the second letter, 50, we obtain the date 1004.

MIRZA ASADULLAH KHAN GHALIB

Mirza Ghalib (A.D. 1797–1869), who wrote poetry of extraordinary beauty both in Persian and Urdu, is probably as widely known an Indian literary figure as Kalidasa or Tagore. He was a legend in his own lifetime, whose fame had spread from Delhi to Calcutta. He lived during the period of decline of the Mughal empire, and though born in a prosperous family, he lived a life of ever multiplying penury. He was a witness to the fall and destruction of his beloved city, Delhi, in 1857. Though he never collected his poems, or even kept them properly, his influence on the poets of his generation and subsequent generations has been so pervasive that Ghalib at once stands out as the symbol of India's creativity during the period of cultural decline in the nineteenth century. His comments, like Keats's, on poetry and poets come to us through his letters, which have now been translated (*Ghalib And His Poetry*, by Sardar Jafri & Qurratulain Hyder, Popular Prakashan, Bombay, 1970) The letters included here are from pages 30, 32, 38, 40, 41, respectively. These letters bring out the social background to literature during Ghalib's times more effectively than any other document of the century does; but more than that they establish an attitude to creativity and literature, an attitude of healthy appreciation but not carried to any excess. The desolation of the social scene which characterises Ghalib's period also shows, by contrast, his abiding faith in poetry as a way of life, and poetry as ultimate freedom.

Poetry as Freedom

To 'Tufta'

... Why seek my permission to send me your poems? Do send them along although I am no longer a practising poet, like an aged wrestler can only teach the tricks of the trade. Don't think I am exaggerating. Can't write verse any more. I am amazed at my earlier work and wonder how I had composed all that.

April 12, 1858

* * *

To Mirza Hatim Ali Beg 'Mehr'

... I have never kept my poems with me. Nawab Ziauddin Khan and Nawab Hussain Mirza used to collect whatever I composed. Their houses were sacked, and their libraries destroyed. Now I yearn for my own poems. The other day a beggar, who has a good voice, got hold of a ghazal of mine from somewhere. When he showed me that piece of paper I wanted to cry ...

1858.

* * *

To 'Mehr'

... Among the poets Firdausi, among the mystics Hasan Basri and among the lovers Majnun ... they crown the lists in these fine arts. The pinnacle is reached when a poet becomes Firdausi, the faqir Hasan Basri and the lover Majnun ... Laila had died before him. You have survived your beloved ... The sons of the Mughals are incorrigible. When they love, they love with a vengeance and destroy the object of their passion ...

* * *

To Shiv Narain 'Aram'

... I am glad that *Dastambo*[1] has been sold. Who bought the copies — Englishmen or Indians? Bhai, the light has gone out of India. The land is lampless. Lakhs have died and among the survivors hundreds are in jail. Those outside cannot afford to buy books. I think the English must have bought its copies and it must have been sent to the Punjab. Fewer copies must have been sold in the Purab.

April 19, 1857

* * *

To 'Tufta'

... I find both Avicenna and Naziri to be futile. To live one's life one requires just a little happiness; philosophy, empires, poetry are all nonsense. If the Hindus had their avatars and the Muslims their prophets, so what? If you lived as a famous man or as a non-entity, what of it? One should have some means of reasonable livelihood, and good health. The rest is all illusion ... Soon this illusion may end too. My means of livelihood and my health may vanish and I may reach the state of Void. In this Silence in which I find myself now, I am not aware either of myself or of this world or the Hereafter. I duly answer questions, continue my dealings with others, but know that all this is delusion, not a river, but a mirage, not life but vainglory. Both

1 (Dastambo: Ghalib's account of the Mutiny, 1857)

you and I are fairly good poets. Agreed that some day we might become renowned like Saadi and Hafiz. But what did *they* gain that we would?

1859

* * *

To 'Majrooh'

Mir Nehdi, aren't you ashamed of yourself when you say in your couplet: 'Mian, this is the language of Delhi'. From the Jama Masjid to Rajghat Gate is all wasteland. If the debris were removed the place would look haunted ... And the people are still proud of Delhi's language! What a laugh. Where is Delhi? It is now a military camp.

1860

Ghalib, from his letters
translated by Sardar Jafri and Qurratulain Hyder

RABINDRANATH TAGORE

Tagore (1861–1941) belongs to World Literature and Indian Literature, as much as he belongs to Bangla literature. Being the only Indian recipient of the Nobel Prize for Literature (1913), a charismatic nationalist, and a member of the distinguished Tagore family, he is one of the few internationally known Indians. Along with Bankimchandra Chatterjee, Tagore ushered Bangla literature into the twentieth century by contributing copiously to all forms of writing: poetry, novel, story, drama, essay and criticism. In addition to being a first-rate writer, he was also a painter, a composer, and an educationist.

Tagore's uncommon popularity among the reading public is reflected in the fact that to this day he is the most frequently translated Indian writer. As with his contemporary Indian romantics, Tagore's standing as a writer has been questioned by every succeeding generation, the question having never been settled permanently.

All that he wrote was in Bangla, except the translations of his own works he made into English, and some of his critical essays. The *Essays* were in fact his lectures delivered at Oxford and in the U.S.A. during his tours. The essay selected for inclusion here is one such lecture, which is reproduced from the collection. *Personality: Lectures Delivered in America* (1917). Tagore's educational philosophy and his literary philosophy had an integral link, namely, his theory of personality. He believed that art is created out of a surplus of emotions. A close reading of the essay reveals that Tagore had his own brand of phenomenology, very well thought out and lucidly presented.

What Is Art?

We are face to face with this great world and our relations to it are manifold. One of these is the necessity to have to live, to till the soil, to gather food, to clothe ourselves, to get materials from nature. We are always making things that will satisfy our needs. Thus we are always in touch with this great world through hunger and thirst and all our physical needs.

Then we have our mind; and mind seeks its own food. Mind has its necessity also. It must find out reason in things. It is faced with a multiplicity of facts, and is bewildered when it cannot find one unifying principle which simplifies heterogeneity of things. Man's constitution is such that he must not only find facts, but also some laws which will lighten the burden of mere number and quantity.

There is yet another man in me, not the physical, but the personal man; which has its likes and dislikes, and wants to find something to fulfil its needs of love. This personal man is found in the region where we are free from all necessity, — above the needs, both of body and mind, — above the expedient of the useful. It is the highest in man, — this personal man. And it has personal relations of its own with the great world, and comes to it for something to satisfy personality.

The world of science is not a world of reality, it is an abstract world of force. We can use it by the help of our personality. It is like a swarm of mechanics who though producing things for ourselves as personal beings, are mere shadows to us.

But there is another world which is real to us. We see it, feel it; we deal with it with all our emotions. Its mystery is endless because we cannot analyse it or measure it. We can but say, 'Here you are.'

This is the world from which Science turns away, and in which Art takes its place. And if we can answer the question as to what art is, we shall know what this world is with which art has such intimate relationship.

It is not an important question as it stands. For Art, like life itself, has grown by its own impulse, and man has taken his pleasure in it without definitely knowing what it is. And we could safely leave it there, in the subsoil of consciousness, where things that are of life are nourished in the dark.

But we live in an age when our world is turned inside out and when whatever lies at the bottom is dragged to the surface. Our very process of living, which is an unconscious process, we must bring under the scrutiny of our knowledge, — even though to know is to kill our object of research and to make it a museum specimen.

The question has been asked, 'What is Art?' and answers have been given by various persons. Such discussions introduce elements of conscious purpose into the region where both our faculties of creation and enjoyment have been spontaneous and half-conscious. They aim at supplying us with very definite standards by which to guide our judgement of art productions. Therefore we have heard judges in the modern times giving verdict, according to some special rules of their own making, for the dethronement of immortals whose supremacy has been unchallenged for centuries.

This meteorological disturbance in the atmosphere of art criticism, whose origin is in the West, has crossed over to our own shores in Bengal, bringing mist and clouds in its wake, where there was a clear sky. We have begun to ask ourselves whether creations of art should not be judged either according to their fitness to be universally understood, or their philosophical interpretation of life, or their usefulness for solving the problems of the day, or their giving expression to something which is peculiar to the genius of the people to which the artist belongs. Therefore when men are seriously engaged in fixing the standard of value in art by something which is not intended in it, — or, in other words, when the excellence of the river is going to be judged by the point of view of a canal, we cannot leave the question to its fate, but must take our part in the deliberations.

Should we begin with a definition? But definition of a thing which has a life growth is really limiting one's own vision in order to be able to see clearly. And clearness is not necessarily the only, or the most important aspect of a truth. A bull's-eye lantern view is a clear view, but not a complete view. If we are to know a wheel in motion, we need not mind if all its spokes cannot be counted. When not merely the accuracy of shape, but velocity of motion, is important, we have to be content with a somewhat imperfect definition of the wheel. Living things have far-reaching relationships with their surroundings, some of which are invisible and go deep down into the soil. In our zeal for definition we may lop off branches and roots of a tree to turn it into a log, which is easier to roll about from classroom to classroom, and therefore suitable for a textbook. But because it allows a nakedly clear view of itself, it cannot be said that a log gives a truer view of a tree as a whole.

Therefore I shall not define Arts, but question myself about the reason of its existence, and try to find out whether it owes its origin to some social purpose, or to the need of catering for our aesthetic enjoyment, or whether it has come out of some impulse of expression, which is the impulse of our being itself.

A fight has been going on for a long time round the saying, 'Art for Art's sake', which seems to have fallen into disrepute among a section of Western critics. It is a sign of the recurrence of the ascetic ideal of the puritanic age, when enjoyment as an end in itself was held to be sinful. But all puritanism is a reaction. It does not represent truth in its normal aspect. When enjoyment loses its direct touch with life, growing fastidious and fantastic in its world of elaborate conventions, then comes the call for renunciation which rejects happiness itself as a snare. I am not going into the history of your modern art, which I am not at all competent to discuss; yet I can assert, as a general truth, that when a man tries to thwart himself in his desire for delight, converting it merely into his desire to know, or to do good, then the cause must be that his power of feeling delight has lost its natural bloom and healthiness. The rhetoricians in old India had no hesitation in saying, that enjoyment is the soul of literature, — the enjoyment which is disinterested. But the word 'enjoyment' has to be used with caution. When analysed, its spectrum shows an endless series of rays of different colours and intensity throughout its different worlds of stars. The art world contains elements which are distinctly its own and which emit lights that have their special range and property. It is our duty to distinguish them and arrive at their origin and growth.

The most important distinction between the animal and man is this, that the animal is very nearly bound within the limits of its necessities, the greater part of its activities being necessary for its self-preservation and the preservation of race. Like a retail shopkeeper, it has no large profit from its trade of life; the bulk of its earnings must be spent in paying back the interest to its bank. Most of its resources are employed in the mere endeavour to live. But man, in life's commerce, is a big merchant. He earns a great deal more than he is absolutely compelled to spend. Therefore there is a vast excess of wealth in man's life, which gives him the freedom to be useless and irresponsible to a great measure. There are large outlying tracts, surrounding his necessities, where he has objects that are ends in themselves.

The animals must have knowledge, so that their knowledge can be employed for useful purposes of their life. But there they stop. They must know their surroundings in order to be able to take their shelter and seek their food, some properties of things in order to build their dwellings, some signs of the different seasons to be able to get ready to adapt themselves to the changes. Man also must know because he must live. But man has a surplus where he can proudly assert that knowledge is for the sake of knowledge. There he has the pure enjoyment of his knowledge, because there knowledge is freedom. Upon this fund of surplus his science and philosophy thrive.

There again, there is a certain amount of altruism in the animal. It is the altruism of parenthood, the altruism of the herd and the hive. This altruism is absolutely necessary for race preservation. But in man there is a great deal more than this. Though he also has to be good, because goodness is necessary for his race, yet he goes far beyond that. His goodness is not a small pittance, barely sufficient for a hand-to-mouth moral existence. He can amply afford to say that goodness is for the sake of goodness. And upon this wealth of goodness, — where honesty is not valued for being the best policy, but because it can afford to go against all policies, — man's ethics are founded.

The idea of 'Art for Art's sake' also has its origin in this region of the superfluous. Let us, therefore, try to ascertain what activity it is, whose exuberance leads to the production of Art.

For man, as well as for animals, it is necessary to give expression to feelings of pleasure and displeasure, fear, anger and love. In animals, these emotional expressions have gone little beyond their bounds of usefulness. But in man, though they still have roots in their original purposes, they have spread their branches far and wide in the infinite sky high above their soil. Man has a fund of emotional energy which is not all occupied with his self-preservation. This surplus seeks its outlet in the creation of Art, for man's civilisation is built upon his surplus.

A warrior is not merely content with fighting, which is needful, but, by the aid of music and decorations, he must give expression to the heightened consciousness of the warrior in him, which is not only unnecessary, but in some cases suicidal. The man who has a strong religious feeling not only worships his deity with all care, but his religious personality craves, for its expression, the splendour of the temple, the rich ceremonials of worship.

When a feeling is aroused in our hearts which is far in excess of the amount that can be completely absorbed by the object which has produced it, it comes back to us and makes us conscious of ourselves by its return waves. When we are in poverty, all our attention is fixed outside us, — upon the objects which we must acquire for our need. But when our wealth greatly surpasses our needs, its light is reflected back upon us, and we have the exultation of feeling that we are rich persons. This is the reason why, of all creatures, only man knows himself, because his impulse of knowledge comes back to him in excess. He feels his personality more intensely than other creatures, because his power of feeling is more than can be exhausted by his objects. This efflux of the consciousness of his personality requires an outlet of expression. Therefore, in Art, man reveals himself and not his objects. His objects have their place in books of information and science, where he has completely to conceal himself.

I know I shall not be allowed to pass unchallenged when I use the word 'personality', which has such an amplitude of meaning. These loose words can be made to fit ideas which have not only different dimensions, but shapes also. They are like raincoats, hanging in the hall, which can be taken away by absent minded individuals who have no claim on them.

Man, as a knower, is not fully himself, — his mere information does not reveal him. But, as a person, he is the organic man, who has the inherent power to select things from his surroundings in order to make them his own. He has his forces of attraction and repulsion by which he not merely piles up things outside him, but creates himself. The principal creative forces, which transmute things into our living structure, are emotional forces. A man, where he is religious, is a person, but not where he is a mere theologian. His feeling for the divine is creative. But his mere knowledge of the divine cannot be formed into his own essence because of this lack of the emotional fire.

Let us here consider what are the contents of this personality and how it is related to the outer world. This world appears to us as an individual, and not merely as a bundle of invisible forces. For this, as everybody knows, it is greatly indebted to our senses and our mind. This apparent world is man's world. It has taken its special features of shape, colour and movement from the peculiar range and qualities of our perception. It is what our sense limits have specially acquired and built for us and walled up. Not only the physical and chemical forces, but man's perceptual forces, are its potent factors, — because it is man's world, and not an abstract world of physics or metaphysics.

This world, which takes its form in the mould of man's perception, still remains only as the partial world of his senses and mind. It is like a guest and not like a kinsman. It becomes completely our own when it comes within the range of our emotions. With our love and hatred, pleasure and pain, fear and wonder, continually working upon it, this world becomes a part of our personality. It grows with our growth, it changes with our changes. We are great or small, according to the magnitude and littleness of this assimilation, according to the quality of its sum total. If this world were taken away, our personality would lose all its content.

Our emotions are the gastric juices which transform this world of appearance into the more intimate world of sentiments. On the other hand, this outer world has its own juices, having their various qualities which excite our emotional activities. This is called in our Sanskrit rhetoric *rasa*, which signifies outer juices having their response in the inner juices of our emotions. And a poem, according to it, is a sentence or sentences containing juices, which stimulate the juices of emotion. It brings to us ideas, vitalized by feelings, ready to be made into the life-stuff of our nature.

Bare information on facts is not literature, because it gives us merely the facts which are independent of ourselves. Repetition of the facts that the sun is round, water is liquid, fire is hot, would be intolerable. But a description of the beauty of the sunrise has its eternal interest for us, — because there, it is not the fact of the sunrise, but its relation to ourselves, which is the object of perennial interest.

It is said in the Upanishads, that 'Wealth is dear to us, not because we desire the fact of the wealth itself, but because we desire ourselves.' This means that we feel ourselves in our wealth, — and therefore we love it. The things which arouse our emotions arouse our own self-feeling. It is like our touch upon the harp-string: if it is too feeble, then we are merely aware of the touch, but if it is strong, then our touch comes back to us in tunes and our consciousness is intensified.

There is the world of science, from which the elements of personality have been carefully removed. We must not touch it with our feelings. But there is also the vast world, which is personal to us. We must not merely know it, and then put it aside, but we must feel it, — because, by feeling it, we feel ourselves.

But how can we express our personality, which we only know by feeling? A scientist can make known what he has learned by analysis and experiment. But what an artist has to say, he cannot express by merely informing and explaining. The plainest language is needed when I have to say what I know about a rose, but to say what I feel about a rose is different. There it has nothing to do with facts, or with laws, — it deals with taste, which can be realized only by tasting. Therefore the Sanskrit rhetoricians say, in poetry we have to use words which have got their proper taste, — which do not merely talk, but conjure up pictures and sing. For pictures and songs are not merely facts, — they are personal facts. They are not only themselves, but ourselves also. They defy analysis and they have immediate access to our hearts.

It has to be conceded, that man cannot help revealing his personality, also, in the world of use. But there self-expression is not his primary object. In everyday life, when we are mostly moved by our habits, we are economical in our expression; for then our soul-consciousness is at its low level, — it has just volume enough to glide on in accustomed grooves. But when our heart is fully awakened in love, or in other great emotions, our personality is in its flood-tide. Then it feels the longing to express itself for the very sake of expression. Then comes Art, and we forget the claims of necessity, the thrift of usefulness, — the spires of our temples try to kiss the stars and the notes of our music to fathom the depth of the ineffable.

Man's energies, running on two parallel lines, — that of utility and self-expression — tend to meet and mingle. By constant human associations sentiments gather around our things of use and invite the help of art to reveal themselves, — as we see the warrior's pride and love revealed in the ornamental sword-blade, and the comradeship of festive gatherings in the wine goblet.

The lawyer's office, as a rule, is not a thing of beauty, and the reason is obvious. But in a city, where men are proud of their citizenship, public buildings must in their structure express this love for the city. When the British capital was removed from Calcutta to Delhi, there was discussion about the style of architecture which should be followed in the new buildings. Some advocated the Indian style of the Moghal period, — the style which was the joint production of the Moghal and the Indian genius. The fact that they lost sight of was that all true art has its origin in sentiment. Moghal Delhi and Moghal Agra show their human personality in their buildings. Moghal emperors were men, they were not administrators. They lived and died in India, they loved and fought. The memorials of their reigns do not persist in the ruins of offices and factories, but in immortal works of art, — not only in great buildings, but in pictures and music and workmanship in stone and metal, in cotton and wool fabrics. But the British government in India is not personal. It is official and therefore an abstraction. It has nothing to express in the true language of art. For law, efficiency and exploitation cannot sing themselves into epic stones. Lord Lytton, who unfortunately was gifted with more imagination than was necessary for an Indian Viceroy, tried to copy one of the state functions of the Moghals, — the Durbar ceremony. But state ceremonials are works of art. They naturally spring from the reciprocity of personal relationship between the people and their monarch. When they are copies, they show all the signs of the spurious.

How utility and sentiment take different lines in their expression can be seen in the dress of a man compared with that of a woman. A man's dress, as a rule, shuns all that is unnecessary and merely decorative. But a woman has naturally selected the decorative, not only in her dress, but in her manners. She has to be picturesque and musical to make manifest what she truly is, — because, in her position in the world, woman is more concrete and personal than man. She is not to be judged merely by her usefulness, but by her delightfulness. Therefore she takes infinite care in expressing, not her profession, but her personality.

The principal object of art, also, being the expression of personality, and not that which is abstract and analytical, it necessarily uses the language of picture and music. This has led to a confusion in our thought that the object of art is the production of beauty; whereas beauty in art has been the mere instrument and not its complete and ultimate significance.

As a consequence of this, we have often heard it argued whether manner, rather than matter, is the essential element in art. Such arguments become endless, like pouring water into a vessel whose bottom has been taken away. These discussions owe their origin to the idea that beauty is the object of art, and, because mere matter cannot have the property of beauty, it becomes a question whether manner is not the principal factor in art.

But the truth is, analytical treatment will not help us in discovering what is the vital point in art. For the true principle of art is the principle of unity. When we want to know the food value of certain of our diets, we find it in their component parts; but its taste-value is in its unity, which cannot be analysed. Matter taken by itself, is an abstraction which can be dealt with by science; while manner, which is merely manner, is an abstraction which comes under the laws of rhetoric. But when they are indissolubly one, then they find their harmonies in our personality, which is an organic complex of matter and manner, thoughts and things, motives and actions.

Therefore we find all abstract ideas are out of place in true art, where, in order to gain admission, they must come under the disguise of personification. This is the reason why poetry tries to select words that have vital qualities, — words that are not for mere information, but have become naturalized in our hearts and have not been worn out of their shapes by too constant use in the market. For instance, the English word 'consciousness' has not yet outgrown the cocoon stage of its scholastic inertia, therefore it is seldom used in poetry; whereas its Indian synonym 'chetana' is a vital word and is of constant poetical use. On the other hand the English word 'feeling' is fluid with life, but its Bengali synonym 'anubhuti' is refused in poetry, because it merely has a meaning and no flavour. And likewise there are some truths, coming from science and philosophy, which have acquired life's colour and taste, and some which have not. Until they have done this, they are, for art, like uncooked vegetables, unfit to be served at a feast. History, so long as it copies science and deals with abstractions, remains outside the domain of literature. But, as a narrative of facts, it takes its place by the side of the epic poem. For narration of historical facts imparts to the time to which they belong a taste of personality. Those periods become human to us, we feel their living heart-beats.

The world and the personal man are face to face, like friends who question one another and exchange their inner secrets. The world asks the inner man, — 'Friend, have you seen me? Do you love me? — not as one who provides you with foods and fruits, not as one whose laws you have found out, but as one who is personal, individual?'

The artist's answer is, 'Yes, I have seen you, I have loved and known you, — not that I have any need of you, not that I have taken you and used your laws for my own purpose of power. I know the forces that act and drive and lead to power, but it is not that. I see you, where you are, what I am.'

But how do you know that the artist has known, has seen, has come face to face with this personality?

When I first meet anyone who is not yet my friend, I observe all the numberless unessential things which attract the attention at first sight: and in the wilderness of that diversity of facts the friend who is to be my friend is lost.

When our steamer reached the coast of Japan, one of our passengers, a Japanese, was coming back home from Rangoon; we on the other hand were reaching the shore for the first time in our life. There was a great difference in our outlook. We noted every little peculiarity, and innumerable small things occupied our attention. But the Japanese passenger dived at once into the personality, the soul of the land, where his own soul found satisfaction. He saw fewer things, we saw more things; but what he saw was the soul of Japan. It could not be gauged by any quantity or number, but by something invisible and deep. It could not be said, that because we saw those innumerable things, we saw Japan better, but rather the reverse.

If you ask me to draw some particular tree, and I am no artist, I try to copy every detail, lest I should otherwise lose the peculiarity of the tree, forgetting that the peculiarity is not the personality. But when the true artist comes, he overlooks all details and gets into the essential characterization.

Our rational man also seeks to simplify things into their inner principle; to get rid of the details; to get to the heart of things where things are One. But the difference is this: the scientist seeks an impersonal principle of unification which can be applied to all things. For instance he destroys the human body which is personal in order to find out psychology, which is impersonal and general.

But the artist finds out the unique, the individual, which yet is in the heart of the universal. When he looks on a tree, he looks on that tree as unique, not as the botanist who generalises and classifies. It is the function of the artist to particularize that one tree. How does he do it? Not through the peculiarity which is the discord of the unique, but through the personality which is harmony. Therefore he has to find out the inner concordance of that one thing with its outer surroundings of all things.

The greatness and beauty of Oriental art, especially in Japan and China, consists in this, that there the artists have seen this soul of things and they believe in it. The West may believe in the soul of Man, but she does not really believe that the universe has a soul. Yet this is the belief of the East, and the whole mental contribution of the East to mankind is filled with this idea. So, we, in the East, need not go into details and emphasise them; for the most important thing is this universal soul, for which the Eastern sages have sat in meditation, and Eastern artists have joined them in artistic realisation.

Because we have faith in this universal soul, we in the East know that Truth, Power, Beauty, lie in Simplicity, — where it is transparent, where things do not obstruct the inner vision. Therefore, all our sages have tried to make their lives simple and pure, because thus they have the realisation of a positive Truth, which, though invisible, is more real than the gross and the numerous.

When we say that art only deals with those truths that are personal, we do not exclude philosophical ideas which are apparently abstract. They are quite common in our Indian literature, because they have been woven with the fibres of our personal nature. I give here an instance which will make my point clear. The following is a translation of an Indian poem written by a woman poet of mediaeval India, — its subject is Life.

> I salute the Life which is like a sprouting seed,
> With its one arm upraised in the air, and the other down in the soil;
> The Life which is one in its outer form and its inner sap;
> The Life that ever appears, yet ever eludes.
> The Life that comes I salute, and the Life that goes;
> I salute the Life that is revealed and that is hidden;
> I salute the Life in suspense, standing still like a mountain,
> And the Life of the surging sea of fire;
> The Life that is tender like a lotus, and hard like a thunderbolt.
> I salute the Life which is of the mind, with its one side in the dark and the other in the light.
> I salute the Life in the house and the Life abroad in the unknown,
> The Life full of joy and the Life weary with its pains,
> The Life eternally moving, rocking the world into stillness,
> The Life deep and silent, breaking out into roaring waves.

This idea of life is not a mere logical deduction; it is as real to the poetess as the air to the bird who feels it at every beat of its wings. Woman has realised the mystery of life in her child more intimately than man has done. This woman's nature in the poet has felt the deep stir of life in all the world. She has known it to be infinite, — not through any reasoning process, but through the illumination of her feeling. Therefore the same idea, which is a mere abstraction to one whose sense of the reality is limited, becomes luminously real to another whose sensibility has a wider range. We have often heard the Indian mind described by Western critics as metaphysical, because it is ready to soar in the infinite. But it has to be noted that the infinite is not a mere matter of philosophical speculation to India; it is as real to her as the sunlight. She must see it, make use of it in her life. Therefore it has come out so profusely in her symbolism of worship, in her literature. The poet of the Upanishad has said that the slightest movement of life would be impossible if the sky were not filled with infinite joy. This universal presence was as much of a reality to him as the earth under his feet, nay, even more. The realisation of this has broken out in a song of an Indian poet who was born in the fifteenth century:

There falls the rhythmic beat of life and death:
Rapture wells forth, and all space is radiant with light.
There the unstruck music is sounded; it is the love music of three worlds.
There millions of lamps of sun and moon are burning;
There the drum beats and the lover swings in play.
There love songs resound, and light rains in showers.

In India, the greater part of our literature is religious, because God with us is not a distant God; He belongs to our homes, as well as to our temples. We feel His nearness to us in all the human relationship of love and affection, and in our festivities He is the chief guest whom we honour. In seasons of flowers and fruits, in the coming of the rain, in the fullness of the autumn, we see the hem of His mantle and hear His footsteps. We worship Him in all the true objects of our worship and love Him wherever our love is true. In the woman who is good we feel Him, in the man who is true we know Him, in our children He is born again and again, the Eternal Child. Therefore religious songs are our love songs, and our domestic occurrences, such as the birth of a son, or the coming of the daughter from her husband's house to her parents and her departure again, are woven in our literature as a drama whose counterpart is in the divine.

It is thus that the domain of literature has extended into the region which seems hidden in the depth of mystery and made it human and speaking. It is growing, not only into history, science and philosophy, but, with our expanding sympathy, into our social consciousness. The classical literature of the ancient time was only peopled by saints and kings and heroes. It threw no light upon men who loved and suffered in obscurity. But as the illumination of man's personality throws its light upon a wider space, penetrating into hidden corners, the world of art also crosses its frontiers and extends its boundaries into unexplored regions. Thus art is signalling man's conquest of the world by its symbols of beauty, springing up in spots which were barren of all voice and colours. It is supplying man with his banners, under which he marches to fight against the inane and the inert proving his claims far and wide in God's creation. Even the spirit of the desert has owned its kinship with him, and the lonely pyramids are there as memorials of the meeting of Nature's silence with the silence of the human spirit. The darkness of the caves has yielded its stillness to man's soul, and in exchange has secretly been crowned with the wreath of art. Bells are ringing in temples, in villages and populous towns to proclaim that the infinite is not a mere emptiness to man. This encroachment of man's personality has no limit, and even the markets and the factories of the present age, even the schools where children of man are imprisoned and jails where are the criminals, will be mellowed with the touch of art, and lose their distinction of rigid discordance with life. For the one effort of man's personality is to transform everything with which he has any true concern into the human. And art is like the spread of vegetation, to show how far man has reclaimed the desert of his own.

We have said before that where there is an element of the superfluous in our heart's relationship with the world, Art has its birth. In other words, where our personality feels its wealth it breaks out in display. What we devour for ourselves is totally spent. What overflows our need becomes articulate. The stage of pure utility is like the state of heat which is dark. When it surpasses itself, it becomes white heat and then it is expressive.

Take, for instance, our delight in eating. It is soon exhausted, it gives no indication of the infinite. Therefore, though in its extensiveness it is more universal than any other passion, it is rejected by art. It is like an immigrant coming to these Atlantic shores, who can show no cash balance in his favour.

In our life we have one side which is finite, where we exhaust ourselves at every step, and we have another side, where our aspiration, enjoyment and sacrifice are infinite. This infinite side of man must have its revealments in some symbols which have the elements of immortality. There it naturally seeks perfection. Therefore it refuses all that is flimsy and feeble and incongruous. It builds for its dwelling a paradise, where only those materials are used that have transcended the earth's mortality.

For men are the children of light. Whenever they fully realise themselves, they feel their immortality. And, as they feel it, they extend their realm of the immortal into every region of human life.

This building of man's true world, — the living world of truth and beauty, — is the function of Art.

Man is true, where he feels his infinity, where he is divine, and the divine is the creator in him. Therefore with the attainment of his truth he creates. For he can truly live in his own creation and make out of God's world his own world. This is indeed his own heaven, the heaven of ideas shaped into perfect forms, with which he surrounds himself; where his children are born, where they learn how to live and die, how to love and to fight, where they know that the real is not that which is merely seen and wealth is not that which is stored. If man could only listen to the voice that rises from the heart of his own creation, he would hear the same message that came from the Indian sage of the ancient time:

'Hearken to me, ye children of the Immortal, dwellers of the heavenly worlds, I have known the Supreme Person who comes as light from the dark beyond.'

Yes, it is that Supreme Person, who has made himself known to man and made this universe so deeply personal to him. Therefore, in India, our places of pilgrimage are there, where in the confluence of the river and the sea, in the eternal snow of the mountain peak, in the lonely seashore, some aspect of the infinite is revealed which has its great voice for our heart, and there man has left in his images and temples, in his carvings of stone, these words, — 'Hearken to me, I have known the Supreme Person.' In the mere substance and law of this world we do not meet the person, but where the sky is blue, and the grass is green, where the flower has its beauty and fruit its taste, where there is not only perpetuation of race, but joy of living and love of fellow-creatures, sympathy and self-sacrifice, there is revealed to us the Person who is infinite. There, not merely are facts pelted down our heads, but we feel the bonds of the personal relationship binding our hearts with this world through all time. And this is Reality, which is truth made our own, — truth that has its eternal relation with the Supreme Person. This world, whose soul seems to be aching for expression in its endless rhythm of lines and colours, music and movements, hints and whispers, and all the suggestion of the inexpressible, finds its harmony in the ceaseless longing of the human heart to make the Person manifest in its own creations.

The desire for the manifestation of this Person makes us lavish with all our resources. When we accumulate wealth, we have to account for every penny; we reason accurately and we act with care. But when we set about to express our wealthiness, we seem to lose sight of all lines of limit. In fact, none of us has wealth enough fully to express what we mean by wealthiness. When we try to save our life from an enemy's attack, we are cautious in our movements. But when we feel impelled to express our personal bravery, we willingly take risks and go to the length of losing our lives. We are careful of expenditure in our everyday life, but on festive occasions, when we express our joy, we are thriftless even to the extent of going beyond our means. For when we are intensely conscious of our own personality, we are apt to ignore the tyranny of facts. We are temperate in our dealings with the man with whom our relation is the relationship of prudence. But we feel we have not got enough for those whom we love. The poet says of the beloved:

'It seems to me that I have gazed at your beauty from the beginning of my existence, that I have kept you in my arms for countless ages, yet it has not been enough for me.'

He says, 'Stones would melt in tenderness, if touched by the breeze of your mantle.'

He feels that his 'eyes long to fly like birds to see his beloved.'

Judged from the standpoint of reason these are exaggerations, but from that of the heart, freed from limits of facts, they are true.

Is it not the same in God's creation? There, forces and matters are alike mere facts — they have their strict accounts kept and they can be accurately weighed and measured. Only beauty is not a mere fact; it cannot be accounted for, it cannot be surveyed and mapped. It is an expression. Facts are like wine-cups that carry it, they are hidden by it, it overflows them. It is infinite in its suggestion, it is extravagant in its words. It is personal, therefore, beyond science. It sings as does the poet, 'It seems to me that I have gazed at you from the beginning of my existence, that I have kept you in my arms for countless ages, yet it has not been enough for me.'

So we find that our world of expression does not accurately coincide with the world of facts, because personality surpasses facts on every side. It is conscious of its infinity and creates from its abundance; and because, in art, things are challenged from the standpoint of the immortal Person, those which are important in our customary life of facts become unreal when placed on the pedestal of art. A newspaper account of some domestic incident in the life of a commercial magnate may create agitation in Society, yet would lose all its significance if placed by the side of great works of art. We can well imagine how it would hide its face in shame, if by some cruel accident it found itself in the neighbourhood of Keats's 'Ode on a Grecian Urn.'

Yet the very same incident, if treated deeply, divested of its conventional superficiality, might have a better claim in art than the negotiation for raising a big loan for China, or the defeat of British diplomacy in Turkey. A mere household event of a husband's jealousy of his wife, as depicted in one of Shakespeare's tragedies, has greater value in the realm of art than the code of caste regulations in Manu's scripture or the law prohibiting inhabitants of one part of the world from receiving human treatment in another. For when facts are looked upon as mere facts, having their chain of consequences in the world of facts, they are rejected by art.

When, however, such laws and regulations as I have mentioned are viewed in their application to some human individual, in all their injustice, insult and pain, then they are seen in their complete truth and they become subjects for art. The disposition of a great battle may be a great fact, but it is useless for the purpose of art. But what that battle has caused to a single individual soldier, separated from his loved ones and maimed for life, has a vital value for art which deals with reality.

Man's social world is like some nebulous system of stars, consisting largely of a mist of abstractions, with such names as society, state, nation, commerce, politics and war. In their dense amorphousness man is hidden and truth is blurred. The one vague idea of war covers from our sight a multitude of miseries, and obscures our sense of reality. The idea of the nation is responsible for crimes that would be appalling, if the mist could be removed for a moment. The idea of society has created forms of slavery without number, which we tolerate simply because it has deadened our consciousness of the reality of the personal man. In the name of religion deeds have been done that would exhaust all the resources of hell itself for punishment, because with its creeds and dogmas it has applied an extensive plaster of anaesthetic over a large surface of feeling humanity. Everywhere in man's world the Supreme Person is suffering from the killing of the human reality by the imposition of the abstract. In our schools the idea of the class hides the reality of the school children; they become students and not individuals. Therefore it does not hurt us to see children's lives crushed, in their classes, like flowers pressed between book leaves. In government, the bureaucracy deals with generalizations and not with men. And therefore it costs it nothing to indulge in wholesale cruelties. Once we accept as truth such a scientific maxim as 'Survival of the Fittest' it immediately transforms the whole world of human personality into a monotonous desert of abstraction, where things become dreadfully simple because robbed of their mystery of life.

In these large tracts of nebulousness, Art is creating its stars, — stars that are definite in their forms but infinite in their personality. Art is calling us the "children of the immortal," and proclaiming our right to dwell in the heavenly worlds.

What is it in man that asserts its immortality in spite of the obvious fact of death? It is not his physical body or his mental organization. It is that deeper unity, that ultimate mystery in him, which, from the centre of his world, radiates towards its circumference; which is in his body, yet transcends his body; which is in his mind, yet grows beyond his mind; which, through the things belonging to him, expresses something that is not in them; which, while occupying his present, overflows its banks of the past and the future. It is the personality of man, conscious of its inexhaustible abundance; it has the paradox in it that it is more than itself; it is more than as it is seen, as it is known, as it is used. And this consciousness of the infinite, in the personal man, ever strives to make its expressions immortal and to make the whole world its own. In Art the person in us is sending its answers to the Supreme Person, who reveals Himself to us in a world of endless beauty across the lightless world of facts.

Rabindranath Tagore, from Personality

SRI AUROBINDO

Poet, philosopher, mystic, political activist and nationalist, Sri Aurobindo (1872–1950) is quite an enigmatic and misunderstood figure of the modern Indian renaissance. He was educated from his early childhood in England, and when he returned to India at the age of twenty-one, he had to learn his mother tongue, Bengali, from a tutor employed for the purpose. In no time, however, Aurobindo had acquired mastery over Bengali, Sanskrit, Gujarati as he had done with respect to English, French and Italian earlier. The knowledge of so many languages, and his untiring zeal for reading, gave Sri Aurobindo familiarity with a vast body of world literature, such as perhaps only Goethe had before him. As such, he developed an extremely receptive attitude to literary forms and experiments, and acquired a catholicity of literary taste. This literary background, his anti-British political programme, and the visionary mysticism combined to produce Sri Aurobindo's curious critical masterpiece, *Future Poetry*. It is curious, for half of it is a synoptic history of English poetry, and the other half is a manifesto of mystical poetry. But the literary wisdom and critical insight pervading the volume have rarely been matched by any other critic or critical work in modern India.

Future Poetry is, after all, a serious book of literary criticism, though it has not had the reception it deserved. It is a book of criticism by a poet involved in writing a highly experimental kind of poetry. Besides, the ideas in it are not derived either from the West or from ancient India. They are Sri Aurobindo's own creation. The ideas present in Sri Aurobindo's criticism represent, generally speaking, the romantic mood in Indian literature of the early twentieth century. Two of his essays are included here. 'The Sources of Poetry' was written by him when he was barely twenty-five, when he had not yet turned a mystic. 'The Essence of Poetry' is a chapter, a crucial one, from *Future Poetry*. Both of these were originally written in English, which also seems to have become the major language of twentieth century Indian literary criticism.

The Sources of Poetry

The swiftness of the muse has been embodied in the image of Pegasus, the heavenly horse of Greek legend; it was from the rapid beat of his hoofs on the rock that Hippocrene flowed. The waters of Poetry flow in a current or a torrent; where there is a pause or a denial, it is a sign of obstruction in the stream or of imperfection in the mind which the waters have chosen for their bed and continent. In India we have the same idea; Saraswati is for us the goddess of poetry, and her name means the stream or 'she who has flowing motion'. But even Saraswati is only an intermediary. Ganga is the real mother of inspiration, she who flows impetuously down from the head of Mahadev, God high-seated, over the Himalaya of the mind to the homes and cities of men. All poetry is an inspiration, a thing breathed into the thinking organ from above; it is recorded in the mind, but is born in the higher principle of direct knowledge or ideal vision which surpasses mind. It is in reality a revelation. The prophetic or revealing power sees the substance; the inspiration perceives the right expression. Neither is manufactured; nor is poetry really a poiesis or composition, nor even a creation, but rather the revelation of something that eternally exists. The ancients knew this truth and used the same word for poet and prophet, creator and seer, *sophos, vates, kavi.*

But there are differences in the manifestation. The greatest motion of poetry comes when the mind is still and the ideal principle works above and outside the brain, above even the hundred-petalled lotus of the ideal mind, in its proper empire, for then it is Veda that is revealed, the perfect substance and expression of eternal truth. The higher ideation transcends genius just as genius transcends ordinary intellect and perception. But that great faculty is still beyond the normal level of our evolution. Usually we see the action of the revelation and inspiration reproduced by a secondary, diluted and uncertain process in the mind. But even this secondary and inferior action is so great that it can give us Shakespeare, Homer and Valmiki. There is also a tertiary and yet more common action of the inspiration. For of our three mental instruments of knowledge, — the heart or emotionally realising mind, the observing and reasoning intellect with its aids, fancy and memory, and the intuitive intellect, — it is into the last and highest that the ideal principle transmits its inspirations when the greatest poetry writes itself out through the medium of the poet. But if the intuitive intellect is not strong enough to act habitually, it is better for the poetry to descend into the heart and return to the intellect suffused and coloured with passion and emotion than to be formed directly in the observing intellect.

Poetry written from the reasoning intellect is apt to be full of ingenious conceits, logic, argumentation, rhetorical turns, ornamental fancies, echoes learned and imitative rather than uplifted and transformed. This is what is sometimes called classical poetry, the vigorous and excellent but unemotional and unuplifted poetry of Pope and Dryden. It has its inspiration, its truth and value; it is admirable in its way, but it is only great when it is lifted out of itself into intuitive writing or else invaded by the heart. For everything that needs fire rather than Light, driving-force rather than clearness, enthusiasm rather than correctness, the heart is obviously the more potent instrument. Now, poetry to be great must have either enthusiasm or ecstasy.

Yet the poetry that rises up from the heart is usually a turbid stream; our own restless ideas and imaginations mix with the pure inrush from above, and turbulent uprush from below, our excited emotions seek an exaggerated expression, our aesthetic habits and predilections busy themselves to demand a satisfaction greatly beyond their due. Such poetry may be inspired, but it is not always suitable or inevitable. There is often a double inspiration, the higher or ecstatic and the lower or emotional, and the lower disturbs and drags down the higher. This is the birth of romantic or excessively exuberant poetry, too rich in expression, too abundant and redundant in substance. The best poetry coming straight from the right centres may be bare and strong, unadorned and lofty, or it may be rich and splendid; it may be at will romantic or classical; but it will always be felt to be the right thing for its purpose; it is always nobly or rapturously inevitable.

But even in the higher centres of the intuitive intellect there may be defects in the inspiration. There is a kind of false fluency which misses the true language of poetry from dullness of perception. Under the impression that it is true and inspired writing it flows with an imperturbable flatness, saying the thing that should be said but not in the way that it should be said, without force and felicity. This is the *tamasic* or clouded stimulus, active, but full of unenlightenment and self-ignorance. The thing seen is right and good; accompanied with the inspired expression it would make very noble poetry. Instead, it becomes prose rendered unnatural and difficult to tolerate by being cut up into lengths. Wordsworth is the most characteristic and interesting victim of tamasic stimulus. Other great poets fall a prey to it, but that superb and imperturbable self-satisfaction under the infliction is his alone. There is another species of tamasic stimulus which transmits an inspired and faultless expression, but the substance is neither interesting to man nor pleasing to the gods. A good deal of Milton comes under this category. In both cases what has happened is that either the inspiration or the revelation has been active, but its companion activity has refused to associate itself in the work.

It is when the mind works at the form and substance of poetry without either the revelation or the inspiration from above that respectable or minor poetry is produced. Judgement, memory and imagination may work, command of language may be there, but without that secondary action of a higher than intellectual force, it is labour wasted, work that earns respect but not immortality. Doggerel and bastard poetry take their rise not even in the observing intellect but from the sensational mind or the passive memory guided only by the mere physical pleasure of sound and emotion. It is bold, blatant, external, imitative, vulgar; its range of intellectuality and imaginativeness cannot go beyond the vital impulse and the vital delight. But even in the sensational mind there is the possibility of a remote action from the ideal self; for even to the animals who think sensationally only, God has given revelations and inspirations which we call instincts. Under such circumstances even bastard poetry may have a kind of worth, a kind of inevitability. The poet in the sensational man may be entirely satisfied and delighted, and even in the more developed human being the sensational element may find a poetical satisfaction not of the highest. The best ballad poetry and Macaulay's lays are instances in point. Scott is a sort of link between sensational and intellectual poetry. While there are men mainly sensational, secondarily intellectual and not at all ideal, he will always be admired.

Another kind of false inspiration is the *rajasic* or fiery stimulus. It is not flat and unprofitable like the *tamasic,* but hasty, impatient and vain. It is eager to avoid labour by catching at the second best expression or the incomplete vision of the idea, insufficiently jealous to secure the best form, the most satisfying substance. *Rajasic* poets, even when they feel the defect in what they have written, hesitate to sacrifice it because they also feel and are attached either to what in it is valuable or to the memory of their delight when it was first written. If they get a better expression or a fuller sight, they often prefer to reiterate rather than strike out inferior stuff with which they are in love. Sometimes, drifting or struggling helplessly along that shallow and vehement current, they vary one idea or harp on the same imagination without any final success in expressing it inevitably. Examples of the *rajasic* stimulus are commonest in Shelley and Spenser, but few English poets are free from it. This is the *rajasic* fault in expression. But the fiery stimulus also perverts or hampers the substance. An absence of self-restraint, an unwillingness to restrict and limit the ideas and imagination is a sure sign of a *rajasic* ideality. There is an attempt to exhaust all the possibilities of the subject, to expand and multiply thoughts and imaginative visions beyond the bounds of the right and permissible. Or else the true idea is rejected or fatally anticipated by another which is or seems to be more catching and boldly effective. Keats is the principal exemplar of the first tendency, the Elizabethans of the second. The earlier work of Shakespeare abounds with classical instances. As distinguished from the Greek, English is pronouncedly *rajasic* literature and, though there is much in it that is more splendid than almost anything done by the Greeks, — more splendid, not better — a great deal even of its admired portions are rather rich or meretricious than great and true.

The perfect inspiration in the intuitive intellect is the *sattwic* or luminous inspiration, which is disinterested, self-contained, yet at will noble, rich or vigorous, having its eye only on the right thing to be said and the right way to say it. It does not allow its perfection to be interfered with by emotion or eagerness but this does not shut it out from ecstasy and exaltation. On the contrary, its delight of self-enjoyment is a purer and more exquisite enthusiasm than that which attends any other inspiration. It commands and uses emotion without enslaving itself to it. There is indeed a *sattwic* stimulus which is attached to its own luminosity, limpidity and steadiness, and avoids richess, force or emotion of poignant character even when these are needed and appropriate. The poetry of Matthew Arnold is often, though not always, of this character. But this is a limited inspiration. *Sattwic* as well as *rajasic* poetry may be written from the uninspired intellect, but the sensational mind never gives birth to *sattwic* poetry.

One thing has to be added. A poet need not be a reflective critic; he need not have the reasoning and analysing intellect and dissect his own poetry. But two things he must have in some measure to be perfect, the intuitive judgement which shows him at a glance whether he has got the best or the second-best idea, the perfect or the imperfect expression and rhythm, and the intuitive reason which shows him without analysis why or wherein it is best or second-best, perfect or imperfect. These four faculties, revelation or prophecy, inspiration, intuitive judgement and intuitive reason, are the perfect equipment of genius doing the works of interpretative and creative knowledge.

Sri Aurobindo, The Harmony of Virtue

The Essence of Poetry

In order to get a firm clue which we can follow fruitfully in retrospect and prospect we have proposed to ourselves, it will not be amiss to enquire what is the highest power we demand from poetry; or — let us put it more largely and get nearer the roots of the matter, — what may be the nature of poetry, its essential law, and how out of that arises the possibility of its use as the *mantra* of the Real. Not that we need spend a vain effort in labouring to define anything so profound, elusive and indefinable as the breath of poetic creation; to take the myriad-stringed harp of Saraswati to pieces for the purpose of scientific analysis must always be a narrow and rather barren amusement. But we do stand in need of some guiding intuitions, some helpful descriptions which will serve to enlighten our search; and to fix in that way, not by definition, but by description, the essential things in poetry is neither an impossible, nor an unprofitable endeavour.

We meet here two common enough errors, to one of which the ordinary uninstructed mind is most liable, to the other the too instructed critic or the too intellectually conscientious artist or craftsman. To the ordinary mind, judging poetry without really entering it, it looks as if it were nothing more than an aesthetic pleasure of the imagination, the intellect and the ear, a sort of elevated pastime. If that were all, we need not have wasted time in seeking for its spirit, its inner aim, its deeper law. Anything pretty, pleasant and melodious with a beautiful idea in it would serve our turn; a song of Anacreon or a plaint of Mimnermus would be as good as the *Oedipus, Agamemnon* or *Odyssey*, for from this point of view they might well strike us as equally and even, one might contend, more perfect in their light, but exquisite unity and brevity. Pleasure, certainly, we expect from poetry as from all art; but the external sensible and even the inner imaginative pleasure are only first elements; refined in order to meet the highest requirements of the intelligence, the imagination and the ear, they have to be still farther heightened and in their nature raised beyond even their own noblest levels.

For neither the intelligence, the imagination nor the ear are the true recipients of the poetic delight, even as they are not its true creators; they are only its channels and instruments; the true creator, the true hearer is the soul. The more rapidly and transparently the rest do their work of transmission, the less they make of their separate claim to satisfaction, the more directly the word reaches and sinks deep into the soul, the greater the poetry. Therefore poetry has not really done its work, at least its highest work, until it has raised the pleasure of the instrument and transmuted it into the deeper delight of the soul. A divine Ananda, a delight interpretative, creative, revealing, formative – one might almost say, an inverse reflection of the joy which the universal Soul has felt in its great release of energy when it ranges out into the rhythmic forms of the universe the spiritual truth, the large interpretative idea, the life, the power, the emotion of things packed into its original creative vision – such spiritual joy is that which the soul of the poet feels and which, when he can conquer the human difficulties of his task, he succeeds in pouring also into all those who are prepared to receive it. And this delight is not merely a godlike pastime; it is a great formative and illuminative power.

The critic – of a certain type – or the intellectually conscientious artist will, on the other hand, often talk as if poetry were mainly a matter of a faultlessly correct or at the most an exquisite technique. Certainly, in all art good technique is the first step towards perfection; but there are so many other steps; there is a whole world beyond before you can get near to what you seek; so much so that even a deficient correctness of execution will not prevent an intense and gifted soul from creating great poetry which keeps its hold on the centuries. Moreover, technique, however indispensable, occupies a smaller field perhaps in poetry than in any other art, – first, because its instrument, the rhythmic word, is full of subtle and immaterial elements; then because, the most complex, flexible, variously suggestive of all the instruments of the artistic creator, it has more infinite possibilities in many directions than any other. The rhythmic word has a subtly sensible element, its sound value, a quite immaterial element, its significance or thought value, and both of these again, its sound and its sense, have separately and together a soul value, a direct spiritual power, which is infinitely the most important thing about them. And though this comes to birth with a small element subject to the laws of technique, yet almost immediately, almost at the beginning of its flight, its power soars up beyond the province of any laws of mechanical construction.

Rather it determines itself its own form. The poet least of all artists needs to create with his eye fixed anxiously on the technique of his art. He has to possess it, no doubt; but in the heat of creation the intellectual sense of it becomes a subordinate action or even a mere undertone in his mind, and in his best moments he is permitted, in a way, to forget it altogether. For then the perfection of his sound-movement and style comes entirely as the spontaneous form of his soul: that utters itself in an inspired rhythm and an innate, a revealed word, even as the universal Soul created the harmonies of the universe out of the power of the word secret and eternal within him, leaving the mechanical work to be done in a surge of hidden spiritual excitement by the subconscient part of his Nature. It is this highest speech which is the supreme poetic utterance, the immortal element in his poetry, and a little of it is enough to save the rest of his work from oblivion. *Svalpam apyasya dharmasya*!

This power makes the rhythmic word of the poet the highest form of speech available to man for the expression whether of his self-vision or of his world-vision. It is noticeable that even the highest experience, the pure spiritual which enters into the things that can never be wholly expressed, still, when it does try to express them and not merely to explain them intellectually, tends instinctively to use, often the rhythmic forms, almost always the manner of speech characteristic of poetry. But poetry attempts to extend this manner of vision and utterance to all experience, even the most objective, and therefore it has a natural urge towards the expression of something in the object beyond its mere appearances, even when these seem outwardly to be all that it is enjoying.

We may usefully cast a glance, not at the last inexpressible secret, but at the first elements of this heightening and intensity peculiar to poetic utterance. Ordinary speech uses language mostly for a limited practical utility of communication; it uses it for life and for the expression of ideas and feelings necessary or useful to life. In doing so, we treat words as conventional signs for ideas with nothing but a perfunctory attention to their natural force, much as we use any kind of common machine or simple implement; we treat them as if, though useful for life, they were themselves without life. When we wish to put a more vital power into them, we have to lend it to them out of ourselves, by marked intonations of the voice, by the emotional force or vital energy we throw into the sound so as to infuse into the conventional word-sign something which is not inherent in itself. But if we go back earlier in the history of language and still more if we look into its origins, we shall, I think, find that it was not always so with human speech. Words had not only a real and vivid life of their own, but the speaker was more conscious of it than we can possibly be with our mechanised and sophisticated intellects. This arose from the primitive nature of language which, probably, in its first movement was not intended, – or shall we say, did not intend, – so much to stand for distinct ideas of the intelligence as for feelings, sensations, broad indefinite mental impressions with minute shades of quality in them which we do not now care to pursue. The intellectual sense in its precision must have been a secondary element which grew more dominant as language evolved.

The reason why sound came to express fixed ideas, lies not in any natural and inherent equivalence between the sound and its intellectual sense, for there is none, – intellectually any sound might express any sense, if men were agreed on a conventional equivalence between them; it started from an indefinable quality or property in the sound to raise certain vibrations in the life-soul of the human creature, in his sensational, his emotional, his crude mental being. An example may indicate more clearly what I mean. The word 'wolf', the origin of which is no longer present to our minds, denotes to our intelligence a certain living object and that is all, the rest we have to do for ourselves: the Sanskrit word *vṛka*, 'tearer', came in the end to do the same thing, but originally it expressed the sensational relation between the wolf and man which most affected the man's life, and it did so by a certain quality in the sound which readily associated it with the sensation of tearing. This must have given early language a powerful life, a concrete vigour, in one direction a natural poetic force which it has lost, however greatly it has gained in precision, clarity, utility.

Now, poetry goes back in a way and recovers, though in another fashion, as much as it can of this original element. It does this partly by a stress on the image replacing the old sensational concreteness, partly by a greater attention to the suggestive force of the sound, its life, its power, the mental impression it carries. It associates this with the definitive thought value contributed by the intelligence and increases both by each other. In that way it succeeds at the same time in carrying up the power of speech to the direct expression of a higher reach of experience than the intellectual or vital. For it brings out not only the definitive intellectual value of the word, not only its power of emotion and sensation, its vital suggestion, but through and beyond these its soul-suggestion, its spirit. So poetry arrives at the indication of infinite meanings beyond the finite intellectual meaning the word carries. It expresses not only the life-soul of man as did the primitive word, not only the ideas of his intelligence for which speech now usually serves, but the experience, the vision, the ideas, as we may say, of the higher and wider soul in him. Making them real to our life-soul as well as present to our intellect, it opens to us by the word the doors of the Spirit.

Prose style carries speech to a much higher power than its ordinary use, but it differs from poetry in not making this yet greater attempt. For it takes its stand firmly on the intellectual value of the word. It uses rhythms which ordinary speech neglects, and aims at a general fluid harmony of movement. It seeks to associate words agreeably and luminously so as at once to please and to clarify the intelligence. It strives after a more accurate, subtle, flexible and satisfying expression than the rough methods of ordinary speech care to compass. A higher adequacy of speech is its first object. Beyond this adequacy it may aim at a greater forcefulness and effectiveness by various devices of speech which are so many rhetorical means for heightening its force of intellectual appeal. Passing beyond this first limit, this just or strong, but always restraining measure, it may admit a more emphatic rhythm, more directly and powerfully stimulate the emotion, appeal to a more vivid aesthetic sense. It may even make such a free or rich use of images as to suggest an outward approximation to the manner of poetry; but it employs them decoratively, as ornaments, *alamkara*, or for their effective value in giving a stronger intellectual vision of the thing or the thought it describes or defines; it does not use the image for that profounder and more living vision for which the poet is always seeking. And always it has its eye on its chief hearer and judge, the intelligence, and calls in other powers only as important aids to capture his suffrage. Reason and taste, two powers of the intelligence, are rightly the supreme gods of the prose stylist, while to the poet they are only minor deities.

If it goes beyond these limits, approaches in its measures a more striking rhythmic balance, uses images for sheer vision, opens itself to mightier breath of speech, prose style passes beyond its province and approaches or even enters the confines of poetry. It becomes poetical prose or even poetry itself using the apparent forms of prose as a disguise or a loose apparel. A high or a fine adequacy, effectivity, intellectual illuminativeness and a carefully tempered aesthetic satisfaction are the natural and normal powers of its speech. But the privilege of the poet is to go beyond and discover that more intense illumination of speech, that inspired word and supreme inevitable utterance, in which there meets the unity of a divine rhythmic movement with a depth of sense and a power of infinite suggestion welling up directly from the fountain-heads of the spirit within us. He may not always or often find it, but to seek for it is the law of his utterance, and when he can not only find it, but cast into it some deeply revealed truth of the spirit itself, he utters the *mantra*.

But always, whether in the search or the finding, the whole style and rhythm of poetry are the expression and movement which come from us out of a certain spiritual excitement caused by a vision in the soul of which it is eager to deliver itself. The vision may be of anything in Nature or God or man or the life of creatures or the life of things; it may be a vision of force and action, or of sensible beauty, or of truth of thought, or of emotion and pleasure and pain, of this life or the life beyond. It is sufficient that it is the soul which sees and the eye, sense, heart and thought-mind become the passive instruments of the soul. Then we get the real, the high poetry. But if it is too much an excitement of the intellect, the imagination, the emotions, the vital activities seeking rhythmical and forceful expression which acts, without enough of the greater spiritual excitement embracing them, if all these are not sufficiently sunk into the soul, steeped in it, fused in it and the expression does not come out purified and uplifted by a sort of spiritual transmutation, then we fall to lower levels of poetry, and get work of a much more doubtful immortality. And when the appeal is altogether to the lower things in us, the mere mind, we arrive outside the true domain of poetry; we approach the confines of prose or get prose itself masking in the apparent forms of poetry, and the work is distinguished from prose style only or mainly by its mechanical elements, a good verse form and perhaps a more compact, catching or energetic expression than the prose writer will ordinarily permit to the easier and looser balance of his speech. That is to say, it will not have at all or not sufficiently the true essence of poetry.

For in all things that speech can express there are two elements, the outward or instrumental and the real or spiritual. In thought, for instance, there is the intellectual idea, that which the intelligence makes precise and definite to us, and the soul-idea, that which exceeds the intellectual and brings us into nearness or identity with the whole reality of the thing expressed. Equally in emotion, it is not the mere emotion itself the poet seeks, but the soul of the emotion, that in it for the delight of which the soul in us and the world desires or accepts emotional experience. So too with the poetical sense of objects, the poet's attempt to embody in his speech truth of life or truth of Nature. It is this greater truth and its delight and beauty and therefore a joy for ever, because it brings us the delight of the soul in the discovery of its own deeper realities. This greater element the more timid and temperate speech of prose can sometimes shadow out to us, but the heightened and fearless style of poetry makes it close and living and the higher cadences of poetry carry in on their wings what the style by itself could not bring. This is the source of that intensity which is the stamp of poetical speech and of the poetical movement. It comes from the stress of the soul-vision behind the word; it is the spiritual excitement of a rhythmic voyage of self-discovery among the magic islands of form and name in these inner and outer worlds.

Sri Aurobindo, from Future Poetry

B.S. MARDHEKAR

Mardhekar (1909–1951) is acknowledged as the most significant Marathi poet of the twentieth century, and as one of the pioneers of Indian modernism. He wrote some experimental fiction, in the stream of consciousness mode; but his reputation rests mainly on his contribution to the fields of aesthetics and literary criticism.

He wrote criticism in Marathi as well as in English. His major critical works were collected under the title *Arts and Man* and published posthumously. The essay reproduced here is from that collection. Mardhekar's criticism shows a keen interest in philosophy, logic and linguistics. In formulating his ideas, he followed the leading Western thinkers of his generation, mainly Croce, Collingwood and I.A. Richards. But, in spite of this influence, Mardhekar's theory of 'rhythm, contrast, balance' is his own. The Mardhekar Law of Beauty has haunted Marathi criticism for half a century; and almost all theoretical discussion in Marathi about literary beauty focuses on Mardhekar's views. If Marathi is one of the very few Indian languages in which the branch of philosophy known as Aesthetics has made any development, it is thanks to Mardhekar's pioneering of that branch. The essay by R.B. Patankar included in the second part of the present anthology, 'Aesthetics: Some Important Problems', offers a searching critique of Mardhekar's theory.

Though Western literary influence, and the English type of education had influenced the Indian critical climate in the early part of this century, it was not until Mardhekar did it that an unhesitating acceptance of the Western lead in literary criticism was accepted. Mardhekar is thus India's first 'modernising' critic. Hence his writing is important historically too.

Poetry and Aesthetic Theory

No one who ponders over the various problems of the aesthetic science and tries to seek light upon them from the writings of art critics and aesthetic philosophers will fail to be struck by the amount of confusion that has been imported into aesthetic theory by the fact that poetry has been treated as being on a par with the other fine arts. Such a conception, and the consequent temptation to treat the *Ars Poetica* as a representative art in the analysis, discussion and illustration of aesthetic problems, arise from causes which are not difficult to discern.

Poetry deals in words as carriers of emotional meanings. The intimate apprehension of emotional meanings is a biological necessity. Without the prompt apprehension of such meanings and the quick and proper reaction to them, the sentient being will not be able to maintain itself in the constant struggle for existence, nor succeed in perpetuating its species. The attraction of poetry, which helps the above process, is, therefore, quite natural, and its interest for human beings both widespread and perennial. Art critics and aesthetic philosophers, sharing this interest and moved by this attraction like the vast majority of human beings, with leanings primarily humanistic, tend almost invariably to resort to poetry while illustrating their analyses of aesthetic problems. Secondly, all discussion, and therefore, aesthetic discussion, must be carried on in words. Those, therefore, who have a special facility in handling and manipulating linguistic symbols, by the volume of their voice, their repetitions and the charm of their verbal expression, come finally to saturate men's minds with their opinions, and induce a sort of mental hypnosis in which these opinions are accepted without challenge.

The chief traffickers in this kind of soporific aesthetics are the poets. Either by explicit aesthetic formulation or by recording their own reactions before a work of non-literary art, both of which could not but be in terms of poetic (that is to say, non-aesthetic-emotional) experiences, they have brought the assurance of an apparently authentic certainty to what was before merely a tempting surmise, namely, the assumption that poetry is a fine art on the same level as painting, music, sculpture, dancing, etc.

This all too human prejudice in favour of poetry, and the natural inclination to regard poetry as a *typical* fine art instead of recognising that there is a hierarchy of order among the fine arts, have received their most powerful philosophical sanction from the intuitional aesthetics of Benedetto Croce. It is a significant indication of the 'pattern of criticism', to use a happy phrase of Mr. Eliot, which the Crocean aesthetics has set, that Croce's article on Aesthetics in the latest edition of the *Encyclopaedia Britannica* begins with the examination of a poem, a piece from Virgil, and that the first sentence of the second paragraph reads as follows:

'What has been said of "poetry" applies to all other "arts" commonly enumerated; painting, sculpture, architecture, music.'

As a reaction against the 'compartmental' and unrelated criticism of his predecessors, the setting up of the abstract Crocean conception of Art, as against the various individual fine arts and transcending them, might have been both necessary and opportune; but unless the exact content of this conception is determined by a rigorous logical analysis, its value as what Dr. Richards would call 'a speculative instrument' for the investigation of aesthetic problems is of the most dubious kind. Once transfer it from the purpose for which it is relevant to other issues, and you will immediately land yourself in a complete aesthetic mess. It will then seem to you to follow with an absurdly evident necessity that, for the purposes of aesthetic theory and the elucidation of aesthetic problems in all their manifold aspects, one art is as good as another; that poetry is no worse than painting and music no better than either. What is, however, denied here is *not* that there is nothing common to the various fine arts, but that an abstraction — made for a certain purpose and with certain metaphysical or otherwise subjective predilections — can be rightfully held valid for the whole field of aesthetic science and be elevated to the position of a supreme principle from which any inference is legitimate without much further ado. *L'estetica dell' una parola*, as we might describe the Crocean aesthetics without irreverence, even as Gentile has described the Crocean philosophy, *la filosofia delle quattro parole*, has, I humbly submit, sinned in this latter way.

The tendency to think of human life as of the highest value and the emotions which directly administer to its prolongation by ensuring its smooth and even flow as of paramount significance, reinforced by poetic utterances and justified by a philosophy, making of poetry the Ars Artis, has led to some unfortunate results in aesthetic theory. Since everyone understands, or thinks he understands, poetry, more or less, because its counters are his counters, and because the poet's experience differs from his experiences only in being more integral, less attenuated, and not *essentially*; and since there is a prima facie similarity between poetry and the other fine arts as both are in a strictly limited sense useless, the temptation is as obvious as it is compelling, to interpret all artistic creation and every aesthetic process in terms of those involved in literary production. The familiar facility with which such an interpretation can be given and the spurious, effortless and cheap joy which it is supposed to impart, soon turns what was once a temptation into a settled habit of mind.

Now in so far as poetry is a fine art (and it is not denied that it is a fine art, the contention merely being that it is not of the same order as the other fine arts), that is in so far as it yields an enjoyment that is aesthetic as opposed to the poetic or non-aesthetic-emotional (which means involving emotions that are in the last analysis either immediately or remotely instrumental), its products and processes must necessarily partake of the character of works of art and aesthetic processes. There is, therefore, nothing inherently absurd or illegitimate in the interpretation of the latter in terms of the former. Before, however, an interpretation of this type is essayed, it is absolutely essential that the literary processes and their products should be subjected to a stringent analysis and the nature of their terms adequately ascertained.

The next step is to equate these terms to exactly corresponding terms in similar aesthetic products and processes. Error may creep in either in the first or in the second step. Either the preliminary analysis is defective, or else there is a slight shifting in the placing of the terms of the one process against those of the other so that they do not really correspond. More often both these causes have combined to produce much false speculation and wrong aesthetic interpretation. Poetry thus conceived in ambiguous terms and poetical interpretation thus illegitimately extended have become a curse to aesthetic theory and a standing obstacle to the proper and full enjoyment of the other fine arts.

In order to detect where the ambiguity of the current analysis of the literary process and its products resides, and to realise the nature of the shift that has taken place in equating their terms to those of the aesthetic process, we cannot do better than examine the character of the middle term in those processes, that is of the 'medium' of poetry. For in poetry, as in every other fine art, a clear understanding of the nature of its medium is the beginning of appreciation. It is the prerequisite of any aesthetic which aspires to be scientific. To grasp the precise nature of the medium of any fine art is to furnish oneself with a speculative instrument of the utmost value, which can at once reveal what is relevant, and differentiate between what is not, like grain and chaff, when one undertakes criticism of that art.

Most of the errors, conflicts and confusion which are visible in the various aesthetic theories will be found ultimately to spring from a failure to define the concept of medium of art. Once you boggle over this concept, and fail to perceive the medium of any particular art, you will commit all the current fallacies. You will appreciate one thing in the comfortable delusion that you are appreciating something else. You will indulge in perorational aesthetics and believe that you have written a magnificent piece of acute art criticism. Fine phrases, although they cannot butter parsnips, are yet able to cover an incredible amount of faulty analysis, counterfeit enjoyment and mistaken enthusiasm.

Perhaps in the foregoing paragraph, while accusing others of a certain fault, I might appear to some to remain self-condemned for one very like it. Still more likely it is that I might appear to be making much ado about nothing. For no great philosopher is required to enlighten us on the question, what is the medium of poetry. The answer is perfectly simple: Words; though not, fortunately, 'Words, Words, Words!'

But the matter is not so simple and it is advisable to cite a philosopher. As seasoned a scientific thinker and as acutely clear-headed a psychologist as Prof Spearman has the following sentence on page 88 of his book, *The Creative Mind*:

> 'And as the former (painter) employs for this purpose (representation of the physical world outside him) the medium of pigments, so the latter (the literary artist) uses words and phrases.'

Immediately on the same we happen to read in the next paragraph:

'The beauty sought by the painter is, in the main, that of his medium'

the obvious implication being that the aims of the painter and the literary artist are different. No more comment is needed than the mere juxtaposition of these two statements. Such a juxtaposition at once reveals how great a source of misunderstanding a half-hearted, perfunctory and superficial analysis can become even in the hands of one who is nothing if not severely analytical. If Prof Spearman had gone sufficiently deep into the analysis of the medium of painting as well as that of the literary art, he would have come nearer to the truth in aesthetic theory and realised that the artistic aim of all the arts, painting and poetry included, is the same, namely, the revelation of the beauty of their several mediums. The differences between the various arts are the differences of their mediums. It is not that while painters seek the beauty of their medium, poets seek the beauty of something else.

That is a fairly recent book. But take one still more recent. Commenting on Prof Abercrombie's critical position that 'The inspiration is the poem; something self-contained and self-sufficient, a complete and entire whole', Prof Dewey in a footnote of his book, *Art as Experience*, asks significantly, presumably believing the question to be disarming, 'if it is already self-sufficient and self-contained, why does it seek and find words as a medium of expression?' Now here again, if the nature of the medium, that is, of words, had been duly taken into account, it would have become apparent that the question posed is as meaningless as a similar question about paper, pen and ink would be. It is, however, needless to multiply illustrations of this point.

Let us then examine the nature of the medium of poetry, that is, of words, as briefly as possible. A word has primarily two aspects: (a) Sensational and (b) Intentional. In the first instance, it is a phenomenon of sound, a complex of auditory sensations, a group of vowels and consonants. In language, however, these sounds are not significant in themselves but only as they serve as symbols for something else. They are in short subsidiary to the second aspect, the Intentional. The intentional aspect is the sole justification of the existence of that particular combination of vowels and consonants. Language arises out of the necessity of communication and immensely facilitates it. It is fashioned by man for the more efficient carriage of human intercourse, and answers to the incessant demand of ever increasing thought contents for easier handling.

The evolution of meaning is a process of constructive thought, which thought is essentially a function of a limited consciousness. It is the product of the interaction of the circumscribed consciousness with that within which it finds itself so circumscribed, and meaning has relevance and value for such a consciousness only. But the more frequent these interactions grow, the more various, the more complex they become, the less certain becomes the grasp of the circumscribed consciousness upon the meanings that emerge out of them, the more awkward, the more precarious its handling of them. A limited consciousness in its primary, least developed stages might perhaps be able to manipulate meanings themselves bodily but it has very soon to face the necessity of finding some convenient shorthand, abbreviated method of storing them for social currency. It is only when incipient thought gathers weight and volume and craves for definition that it crystallises itself into words.

The sensation or sound aspect of a word is symbolical of the intentional, and is only used as a manageable vehicle for it. The combination of the two aspects in a word is at once a boon to, and a bane of every limited consciousness. In a world where partial or divided consciousness, as of the human being, did not exist there would be no meanings at all. To a consciousness that is universal, everything would be its own meaning, every thing its own symbol. The division and combination of symbol and significance would be both impossible and unnecessary then. As we shall see presently, the necessity and nature of this division and this combination has not been sufficiently constantly nor sufficiently clearly kept in mind when equating the aesthetic to the literary process.

Now the intentional aspect of words or language can itself be further analysed into two aspects. Meaning, as a fact of mental life, has the two facets: (a) Cognitive and (b) Affective. It is, of course, a commonplace of psychology that there is no clear-cut division between the two, and it is only when someone fails to find some more original argument that he thinks it worth while reminding others of it. Yet the distinction between an experience that is predominantly intellectual and one that is predominantly emotional is not difficult to perceive. There are intellectual ideas, theoretical meaning and emotions, or emotional meaning.

We need remark here this easily observable though not sharply marked difference.

Next we have to recognise two subdivisions of the affective aspects or two categories of emotions. The first category we may call that of *pure* or *absolute* emotions, and group the second under the heading of *contingent* emotions. Pure or absolute emotions are the immediate accompaniments of the perception of the quality of any sensation, or of a pattern, a *Gestalt*, an organisation of relations. They are the necessary concomitants of any experience that is sensuous or formal, and do not derive from any 'experience of this world', as that expression is understood when we say that old men are more experienced than the young. I have used the word emotions, but strictly speaking the word should be in the singular. We may call this emotion 'aesthetic' and so distinguish it from the other group of contingent emotions which are 'poetic'. They are contingent because they depend upon a specific human world order. They are contingent upon the existence and persistence of a particular demand of the environment.

It is, as I stated above, only in so far as they facilitate human reactions to the existing environment and ensure survival, that they are of any value. If the environment changes so that certain reactions are found to be no longer necessary, then the emotions which had formerly served these reactions tend to disappear, gradually suffering and ultimately vanishing altogether. Those emotions, for example, which accompanied the relations of the two sexes in the old days of chivalry have lost their *raison d 'être* in our times. For in a world where there is municipal peace, and physical culture is no longer the exclusive prerogative of only a section of mankind, the sentiment of chivalry is superfluous, except in so far as it is demanded by the requirements of social etiquette or a sense of decorum – that is to say, by the intrinsic grace of the conduct in which it displays itself, or except in so far as it is helpful to sublimate the sexual impulse. That emotion of love which governs the relations between parents and children would tend to disappear in a state organised on the Soviet model, in which a Government department looks after old parents and little babies, because in such a state that emotion would lose its sole relevance. That the prospect of such a disappearance is instantly resented and seldom fails to rouse profound indignation is only a reflection of the way in which the self-protective mechanism in man works, and confirms the view of the contingent nature of this kind of emotions. And nothing can indicate more clearly how men are willing to deceive themselves into faulty intellectual positions in the interests of poetry than all the flowers of language and rhetoric, all the glowing paeans of praise and admiration bestowed upon the nobility of filial piety and dutifulness, in terms of which their resentment and their indignation usually manifest themselves.

We may call the contingent emotions 'interested' also, since they are indulged in simply because they are biologically significant and useful, whereas the aesthetic emotion is 'disinterested', and subserves no biological plan. Again the contingent emotions are merely 'instrumental': they promote ends that are outside the situations which realise the said emotions. In contrast, the aesthetic emotion is an end in itself; the end is fulfilled in the very moment in which the emotion is realised. It is thus significant on its own account.

To summarise the result of the foregoing discussion schematically:

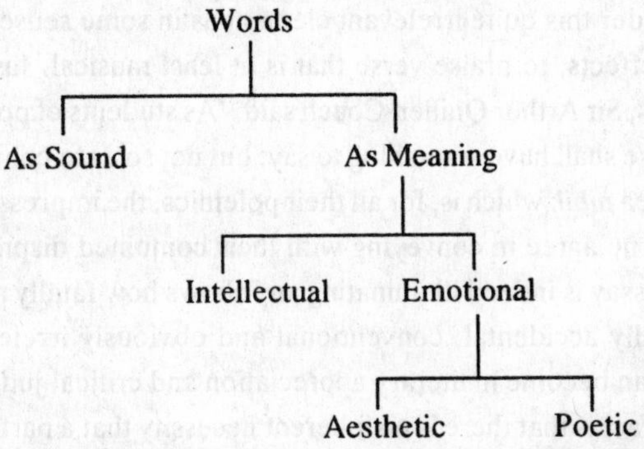

With the aid of the above analysis, I wish to maintain the proposition that words, as implying both sound and meaning, are not the medium of poetry. Words can be said to be the medium of poetry only if we understand by words 'emotional meanings of the poetic type'. A less ambiguous way of stating the position would be to say that emotional meanings are the medium of poetry. It is these meanings that the poet works with and that he manipulates, and neither sound nor intellectual ideas as ideas. To speak roundly of words being the medium of poetry is to smuggle in sound and ideas as mere cognitive facts, and that works havoc — as will be seen in the next paragraph — in aesthetic theory. Poets who are second-rate are so, either because they employ the medium of one art while fashioning a work of another art, and thus, aspiring to become musicians when they ought to think of remaining poets, fall between two stools; or else because intellectual ideas have not in them been turned into fuel for an emotional blaze. The latter of these points I shall not labour at all, since very few would be disposed to dispute it.

'Meditate often on these truths, that some time or other they may become your feelings'. And Sir Walter Raleigh, in his Wordsworth monograph, has spoken of the true mystic poet making thought the food of his emotions rather than emotions the food of his thoughts.

But despite the patent turns in the fortunes of Tennyson and Swinburne on the one hand, and of Browning on the other, the proposition that sound is irrelevant in poetry will be contested. Now I wish to state categorically that sound as sound has absolutely no place in poetry at all. That is the province of music. This proposition must be firmly grasped and never lost hold of. Sounds have only symbolic value in poetry, as carriers of emotional meanings, and not intrinsic value as in music.

Only in so far as it develops, adds to, or emphasizes the meaning for which it conventionally stands is the sound of a word either of significant or relevant in poetry. The besetting sin of second-rate poets and third-rate literary criticism is to consider this quite irrelevant element as in some sense a legitimate factor in poetic effects, to praise verse that is at least musical. Justifying Shelley to his students, Sir Arthur Quiller-Couch said: 'As students of poetry and its technique again, we shall have something to say; but not so as to convey that he was *vox et praeterea nihil*: which is, for all their polemics, the impression which Arnold and Swinburne agree in conveying with their combined dispraise and praise.' The whole essay is indeed illuminating and shows how fatally mischievous (because essentially accidental, conventional and obviously irrelevant) the element of sound can become in literary appreciation and critical judgment.

The fact is that there is no inherent necessity that a particular combination of sounds must express a particular meaning. The same meaning is expressed by different combinations of sounds in different languages, and sometimes even in the same language (as witness some of the synonyms, if not all). Conversely, the same combination of sounds may express different meanings in different languages or even in the same language.

The sound of the word 'murmur' is relevant in

'—murmur of flies on summer eves,'

because of its associations in an English mind; that is, because of purely accidental circumstances. There is nothing in the mere vowels and consonants which make up that word that necessitates either the meaning or the associations. The same combination of vowels and consonants will convey an altogether different meaning to a Maratha man. The sound sensations of the word 'wail' will in a similar way mean different experiences in English and in the Indian language Marathi. The same view of the function of sounds in language can be illustrated by the following pairs: French 'Paris' and Italian 'pari'; Italian 'para' and Marathi sound equivalent to the same; French pronunciation of 'bien' and a similar utterance in Marathi. Readers can easily supply more examples of this as well as of the other proposition that the same sounds may express different meanings in the same language, from any book on Phonetics.

This division between sound and meaning and the relevance of the latter alone in poetry is the core of the precept about the agreement of sound and sense in poetry. The misunderstanding of the nature of the medium of poetry is the cause of the ephemeral character of the commonly boosted 'sound poetry' of our day; for whenever an artist, and therefore a poet, allows himself to be seduced by an irrelevant or secondarily relevant aspect of that with which he works into playing false to his medium, he inevitably condemns himself to speedy oblivion. To go a step further, not only are sounds irrelevant in poetry and outside its scope, but even the recognition of a sound effect, if sufficiently subtle, is dependent upon and conditioned by the prior realisation of the pattern of its emotional meanings. The protocols to the sixth poem in Dr Richards's book, *Practical Criticism*, and the analyses they embody and the prosodic conclusions to be derived from them would be sufficient to convince the reader of the truth of the above assertion. Particularly illuminating in this respect are the comments on the delicate rhyming of the first two lines:

'Margaret! are you grieving
For goldengrove unleafing?'

Unless then the beauty of sounds is transmuted into the beauty of emotional meaning by the mechanism of associations or otherwise, poetry can take no cognisance of it. The quality of sound *qua* sound has no place in poetry. Many a rhymester could dribble out more melodious verse than that of even Shakespeare or Dante! And epic poets are greater than writers of lyrics not because they are more musical but because they achieve larger, more complex and withal more coherent organised wholes of emotional meanings. It is indeed a curious irony that in music, where sounds and sound patterns alone are significant, men will hunt after emotional meanings, while in poetry, which offers them emotional meanings, they will not rest until they have squeezed what little drop of music they can out of it.

The foregoing analysis is not original except for the thoroughness, emphasis and categorical way with which it discards the calm of pure sound in poetry. The most important thing is the next step: to demonstrate, and correct if we can, in the light of the above analysis, the shift that has taken place in relating the aesthetic process to the literary. We might write the aesthetic process schematically thus:

ARTIST: MEDIUM: BEAUTY:

Now we proceed to substitute the specific determinants of particular arts. First, let us take painting:

ARTIST: MEDIUM: BEAUTY:

PAINTER: VISUAL ASPECT OF WORLD: BEAUTY:

(colour, line, mass, etc.)

Then poetry:

POET: EMOTIONAL MEANINGS: BEAUTY:

The beauty of the medium is revealed by organising it, by using it in accordance with formal principles. Now to remember our Spearman. One is led to treat painting and poetry as having different ends only when one has no clear conception of the medium of either. If you say pigments are the medium of poetry, then you pave the way to unending ambiguity and confusion; for once you start including irrelevant factors in the middle term, why and on what principle would you stop at one point rather than at another? You attempt to write your painting process thus:

PAINTER: PIGMENTS: BEAUTY:

and then proceed to write your literary process. Your first two terms are:

POET: WORDS:

and you put MEANING as your third term, forgetting that this is already included in the second term in a way in which BEAUTY is not included in PIGMENTS. Another way of saying the same thing is this: taking the literary process first, you roughly analyse it in this way:

POET: WORDS: MEANING:

Then the corresponding aesthetic process is supposed to be somewhat like this:

PAINTING: PIGMENTS: MEANING:

The fallacy here lies, as can be easily seen, in the middle term. Pigments in the second process really correspond to the second and third terms put together in the first process. If you break up a term into two in the first process, you are logically bound to do likewise in the second. You must formulate your two processes thus:

POET: WORDS: MEANING: BEAUTY:

PAINTER: PIGMENTS: COLOURS: BEAUTY:

The common mistake is to seek the meaning of colours in pictures as you seek the meaning of words in poetry. But as words are meant for meanings, so pigments are meant for colours and not colours for meanings. Colours are not fashioned by men to signify something. No meanings, no words: but not No meanings, no colours in any intelligible sense of the terms. The word 'green' means green colour. If there had been no sensation of green that you wanted to communicate, there would never have come into being that particular combination of sounds to signify that fact. But greenness, the colour green, does not *mean*, in its own primary right, anything: it is just that colour. We come to associate certain ideas with greenness undoubtedly, but these are accretions: the green colour would still be green even if we forgot or eliminated all these associative factors. But if we forgot all the meaning of the word 'green', that combination of vowels and consonants would not exist in our vocabulary.

So, whereas meaning is subsidiary, associative phenomena merely in the case of colours, sound is subsidiary, associative phenomena merely in the case of meanings (of words). The real correspondence is not this:

MEANING: WORD: MEANING: COLOUR

but rather this:

MEANING: WORD: COLOUR: PIGMENT

You can ask what is the meaning of colour, only if you ask what is the meaning of meaning also:

PAINTER: PIGMENTS: COLOURS: MEANING:

POET: WORDS: MEANINGS: MEANING (of meaning)

This is perfectly legitimate, but then the question becomes not of meaning in the popular sense, but one of philosophical analysis, and in that case one has to refer to any book on the psychology of sensations and to Ogden and Richards's book, *The Meaning of Meaning*.

To summarise:

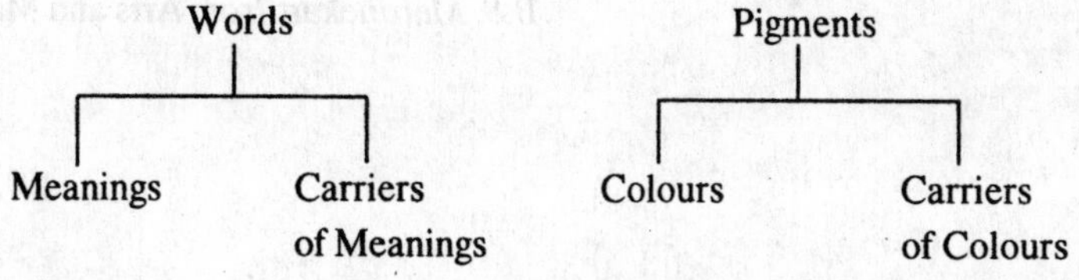

Or, thus:

MEANING + CARRIERS OF MEANING - WORD

COLOUR + CARRIERS OF COLOUR - PIGMENT

To grasp that the sensation aspect — that is, the sound aspect of words — is purely symbolical, is a vehicle for meaning even as oil or water paint is a vehicle for colour; that sound in the one case and oil or water paint in the other are in plain fact merely instrumental, and although indispensable without doubt as instruments, are not on that account essentially relevant to the nature of the creative process involved, is at once to detect the shift and understand its vitiating character. What has been discussed here in relation to painting applies to all the other fine arts in terms of their several mediums.

And if you can guard yourself against this shift, then there is no harm in treating the creative process deduced from poetry as typical of all arts. Thus you will save yourself from falling into the pitfall of the representational versus abstract art controversy. Nor will you then misconceive the aesthetic process, because you have initially yielded to the emotional potency of poetry and tried to construe the former in terms of that underlying the latter.

Such an unambiguous treatment of poetry together with an analysis of the mediums of the various fine arts will bring a systematic unity in aesthetic theory, and yield principles which will hold valid for the entire field of artistic creation without exception. Upon the foundations of such an analysis alone can you erect securely the science of aesthetics and rid critical judgments of their bewildering and conflicting diversity. The supposed gap between the appreciation of literature and of the other fine arts will be bridged not by a sleight of the philosopher's hand, but by discovering the identity of the underlying formal processes. But this can happen, and poetry cease to be a curse to aesthetics, only when we realise the doubly emotional character of poetry, that is, only when we learn to distinguish between emotions which are the medium of poetry and that specific *sui generis* aesthetic emotion to which poetry (or those mediumal emotions as organised) like all other arts gives rise; which aesthetic emotion is evoked by beauty, that is, by the perception of formal organisations, simply in virtue of their character of being formal organisations, instead of mere chaotic conglomerations.

B.S. Mardhekar, from Arts and Man

KRISHNA RAYAN

Krishna Rayan (b. 1918) is perhaps the only contemporary Indian critic to develop a 'theory' of literature by putting to use ancient Sanskrit poetics. While other interpreters of Sanskrit poetics and Indologists are engaged in presenting ancient theories in modern versions, Krishna Rayan has been exploring the possibility of 'modernising' Sanskrit poetics, in particular the *dhvani* theory. His explorations are presented through a series of critical works: *Suggestion and Statement in Poetry* (London, 1972), *Text and Sub-text* (London and New Delhi, 1987), *The Burning Bush* (Delhi, 1988) *and Sahitya, A Theory* (Delhi, 1991). In all these works the main contention of Krishna Rayan is that literature is distinguished from other forms of linguistic discourses by virtue of the complexity of literary language, and that complexity arises from the ability of literature to be 'suggestive'. It is here that he turns to the *Alamkara* school of Sanskrit poetics and to Anandavardhana's stylistics. Krishna Rayan is keen that his observations should have an applied value. Therefore, much of what he has written comes in the form of practical criticism, and shows a clear influence of the New Critics.

Krishna Rayan taught English at the National Defence Academy at Khadakwasla, and was a professor at various universities in Zambia, Nigeria and India.

The extract reproduced here forms a chapter in *Sahitya, A Theory* (Sterling, Delhi, 1991), pp. 7–16.

What is Literariness?

In *The Religion of Man*, Rabindranath Tagore describes *niśkāma-karma* (disinterested action) as the formula for harmonizing the Western emphasis on action with the Indian emphasis on *śānti* (inner tranquillity):

> According to the Gita, the deeds that are done solely for the sake of self fetter our soul; the disinterested action, performed for the sake of giving

up self, is the true sacrifice. For creation itself comes of the self-sacrifice of Brahma, which has no other purpose and therefore, in our performance of the duty which is self-sacrificing, we realize the spirit of Brahma. (Tagore tr. Radice 1987: 144).

The title of Tagore's poem '*Sankha*' ('The Conch') (Tagore, ibid: 77), the second and last stanzas from which are reproduced below, has an obvious reference to the conch blown on the battlefield by Krishna, supreme exponent of the ideal of disinterested action which the conclusion of the poem celebrates.

I came to the prayer-room with an offering of flowers neatly laid out,
Longing to end my long day's labours with heavenly quiet.
  I thought this time my heart's lacerations
  Would heal; I thought my ablutions
  Would purge me – till I saw the degradation
Of your great conch lying on the path, lying in the dirt.

* * *

When I looked to you for rest I received nothing but shame;
But dress me for battle now, let armour cover each limb.
  Let new obstructions chafe and challenge me;
  I shall take all blows and hurts unflinchingly;
  My heart shall drum redress for your injuries;
I shall give all my strength, win back your conch and make it BOOM.

The substantive difference between the two passages — as I hope to establish by the end of the essay — is not that one is in prose and the other in verse but that the second one is literature while the first is not. But what, in the meantime, is the difference between a literary text and a non-literary one?

The differentia of literary discourses as opposed to ordinary or standard discourse has been variously identified in terms of such oppositions as: fiction/truth; emotive/referential; aesthetic/utilitarian; deviation/norm; foregrounded/automatized. But literariness is best described (as it indeed has been, across the ancient/modern and East/West divides) as defined by the dominance of unstated, implied meaning. At one end of the scale is the affirmation cited in the opening verse of the *Dhvanyaloka*, the 9th century Sanskrit classic of literary theory: *kāvyasyātma dhvanih* (*dhvani* — i.e., suggested meaning; suggestion — is the essence of poetry or, more widely, of literature) — an affirmation refined elsewhere in the same treatise by describing dominance of suggested meaning as the defining characteristic of the best or truest poetry. At the other end of the scale are affirmations in recent or contemporary theories in the West. Paul de

Man, chief among the founding fathers of Anglo-American Post-Structuralism, declares that he 'would not hesitate to equate the rhetorical, figural potentiality of language with literature itself' (De Man 1979: 10) and cites a similar equation offered by Monroe Beardsley, a leading theoretician of the New Criticism, according to whom what distinguishes the language of literature is its being 'distinctly above the norm in ratio of implicit (or, I would say rhetorical) to explicit meaning'. (Bradby *et al* eds. 1973; 37)*

The oppositions presented here—rhetorical/logical or grammatical: figural/literal; and implicit/explicit — correspond to suggested/stated meaning (*vyangyārtha/ vācyārtha*). Suggested/stated also corresponds to connotation/denotation, imaginal/conceptual, latent/manifest or overt, and similar antinomies. These are hierarchical oppositions, with the first term in each pair specifying what in effect is the differentia of a literary text. The terms are not interchangeable, because each of them aims at particularizing a slightly different facet or aspect of literariness. But the term which subsumes all these without blurring the refinements they embody and which comprehensively designates the concept of literariness is, I think, 'suggested' (or 'suggestive' or 'suggestion').

Meaning was described initially in semiotics in terms of a definition of the sign which was based on a one-to-one correspondence between signifier and signified. The notion that the signified is thus locked into the signifier has since been displaced by increasingly revisionist notions that a signifier can have multiple signifieds, that a signified can become the signifier of another signified and so on in an infinite regression (altogether this is an old assumption), that the signified can 'slide incessantly' under the signifier, and even that there can be signifiers without signifieds. Thus the definition of the process of signification has moved away from denotation to polysemy (and beyond it to indeterminacy, undecidability, and dissemination). Once connotation and polysemy are accepted as the basis of signification and it is seen as a complex, flexible, loose process, it becomes identical with suggestion. By the same token, statement becomes identical with signification as originally described in terms of denotation.

Signification is a function of all language, literary or other, but when it is redefined as above and equated with suggestion, its two most essential characteristics prove to be figurality (i.e., discourse based on image or metaphor) and pregnancy (i.e., discourse based on impliedness of meaning). These are the very characteristics which the statements of De Man and Beardsley above declare

* De Man, however, also thinks that 'the rhetorical' or 'the literary' results when it is impossible to decide whether the literal or the figurative meaning of a passage should prevail.

between them to be the defining characteristics of literary discourse. What marks off the literary signifier from the non-literary signifier is its evasion of the signified and its imposition on the reader of the necessity of producing rather than recovering meaning. A literary text therefore (1) is pervasively image-based, and (2) generates plural meaning through such strategies of implication as gaps, minimalism, and a subtext.

As the quotation from Beardsley indicates, literariness is defined not by the exclusive presence of suggestion but by its preponderance over statement. However, this preponderance does not consist in a merely quantitative outweighing such as Beardsley's word 'ratio' might suggest but in a qualitative predominance. It should, that is to say, have absolute authority and pre-eminence in the text in the sense that the suggestive, and not the expository, components of the text will be constitutive of its identity and meaning. Nevertheless, the expository elements will be very much there, because *'rien que la suggestion'* was never more than a French Symbolist dream; statement in one form or another and for one reason or another is always present in literature, and it can even be claimed that the suggestion/statement dialectic is indispensable in most cases. Agyeya's novel *Apne Apne Ajnabi* (Hindi), for instance, is predominantly suggestive in design and style, structured as it is around two core images of existential isolation (i.e., a snowbound mountain cabin; and the remains of a bridge in the middle of a river in spate), underpinned by a chain of symbolic situations. Yet the novel has a statement component consisting either of linear narration in the classic realist mode or, in its extreme form, of philosophic exposition as in the following passage:

> Time is merely experience; it is history. In this context, a 'moment' is that in which there is experience but in which there is no history, which has no past or future, but is pure present, beyond history, uncorrupted by memory, freed from the course of events. Otherwise it is not a moment, because my living in a fragment of time, however small it may be, makes it relative to time, since it is living historically. It is then not a point but a line; a line has sequence, whereas a moment must be freed from that sequence. (Agyeya tr. Agyeya and Roadarmel 1967).

Propositional discourse of this kind is of little literary value, but the other form of statement in Agyeya's novel, i.e., linear narration, is legitimated by its function as a base supporting suggestion. This function is easily noticed in Tagore's well-known early poem *'Agaman'* which had an overt level of statement describing the arrival of *andher gharer raja* — the King of the Dark House:

Fling wide the doors and let him in to the lowly conch's room;
In deepest dark the King of Night has come with wind and storm,
  Thunder crashing across the skies,
  Lightning setting the clouds ablaze
Drag your tattered blankets, let the yard be spread with them:
The King of Grief and Night has come to our land with wind and storm.
(Tagore tr., Radice 1987: 72)

The event thus explicitly narrated is the suggestor of another, an unstated, event: namely, the dark, turbulent descent of the Universal Self and the terror and trauma of its violent invasion of the individual consciousness. This other event is the unnamed tenor and the dominant meaning in the poem.

The most important form of literary signification relates to the way the text 'means'. Ultimately the text is what the reader produces; primarily, however, it is so much language. It consists of linguistic units organized on progressively higher and more complex levels; the phonological, the lexical, the syntactic; then the discourse level, and beyond it, what may be called the text level. On the text level are verbal structures co-extensive with the whole work, such as style and metre, (and at a further remove from the primary linguistic units) imagery, narrative, character, and landscape. These textwide units are signifiers, formed of course on a much higher level of linguistic organization than the "acoustic image" which Saussure had described as the signifier, but their function is essentially the same. They are, moreover, structures which are intrinsic and internal in the text and are formal elements constitutive of its identity.

These signifiers have a common signified consisting in the reader's response to the text. The response to a literary text is, almost by definition, a predominantly affective one. Thus the reader's emotional experience is in fact the meaning of the text. Because the bond between the textwide signifiers and the reader's emotion is necessarily a loose, fluid, variable association (as will be explained in the next chapter), the process of signification here is a process of suggestion in a much truer sense than in other areas of literary signification. The reader's emotional response arises from the signifying structures in the text in precisely the same way as suggested meaning arises from statement. The verbal structures are the suggestors (*vyanjakas*); the reader's emotion (*rasa*) is the suggested (*vyangya*).

The question 'What is literariness?' can be refined as 'How does a literary text work?' The answer is: by the emergence of emotion-meaning from its verbal structures. This operation of suggestion is, therefore, more basic to a theory of literature than its other operation whereby meaning emerges from figuratively pregnant language. The two operations, however, are essentially the same, although it is important that they be kept distinct.

The verbal structures in a literary work pertain to its nature as fiction and are intrinsic to it, whereas its reference to reality, whether outer (i.e., society) or inner (i.e., the self), is extrinsic. This reference includes the beliefs stated, the information provided, and the social reality claimed to be reflected. The reader's interest in the work's authorial, historical, social, religious and moral dimensions is valid only to the extent that it is unavoidable in devoting the fullest attention to the intrinsic elements which evoke his response.

The authorial dimension includes the author's intention, his personal history, his beliefs, his historical context, his social milieu, and more comprehensively, his 'imagination'. S.K. De points out that Sanskrit literary theories, or most of them, contented themselves with analysis of textual features and devices and failed to relate them to the poet's imagination (*kavi-vyāpāra*) and personality (*kavi-svabhāva*). But what De regards as the chief failing of Sanskrit poetics is in fact its chief strength. Sanskrit theory focussed — as literary theories should and indeed today do — on the observable formal elements in the work, analysing them in relation to the reader's response; and it marginalized the creative imagination and the author's life, psychology, philosophy etc., as factors external to the experiencing of a work.

U.R. Anantha Murthy's novel *Samskara* (Kannada) is a case that shows how peripheral are the historical, social and religious dimensions of a literary work. The novel has, as pointed out by A.K. Ramanujan (Anantha Murthy, 1978: 115), certain anomalies and inaccuracies in the portrayal of Hindu mores; the central problem about the death-rite is no insoluble problem; the central figure, Praneshacharya, who is claimed to be a paragon of Hindu *dharma*, has in fact skipped an important *puruṣārtha*, i.e., *kāma*; and the picture of Brahminism is, according to some, a caricature. These discrepancies, however, are secondary and hardly matter; it is the intrinsic elements — imagery, narrative, characterization and language — that engage the reader's response, and the novel is able to win his emotional assent because of them.

It is such suggestive action by the internal structures that constitutes the literariness *per se* of the text. The critic's chief project then is to identify as far as possible the normal affective response to the work, examine each of the objective elements in it, analyse their interaction among themselves, and evaluate their effectiveness as suggestors of the reader's emotion which constitutes the meaning of the work.

Given this definition of his function, what will a critic do with Tagore's poem '*Sankha*' which we started with? He will be interested in the thematic concern of the poem - i.e., the philosophy of *niśkāma-karma* - only to the extent that such interest is inescapable in consciously formulating his emotional response to the work. He will be aware that the response is a composite one, made up of a sense of serenity (*śānta*), desired if not actually experienced, to start with, followed by a contrasting sense of heroic enterprise (*vira*). Building up these affective states are the formal elements. They are in two groups — the first (the quiet room, the offering of flowers, the prospect of a healed heart and a cleansed spirit) evoking serenity, or the hope of it; and the second (the armour, the drum, the conch) stirring the heroic emotion. There are other elements too that the critic will notice: the role of the narrator; the drama of entering the prayer room, only to quit it and don armour; and the rhythm, if he has access to the original. He will also notice how the poem is structured around the ambiguity of the conch symbol (i.e., the conch is sounded in a place of worship but also on the battlefield) whose overarching presence bridges the gap between the two moods and in a way reconciles them.

The critic will also be aware that these agents of suggestion whose operations define the literariness of the text are missing in the extract from *The Religion of Man* which is concerned exclusively to expound its theme (i.e., the concept of disinterested action) and does so necessarily through a discourse that is propositional, aiming at communication and eliciting a response which is cognitive rather than affective. The extract is therefore not a literary text.

Krishna Rayan, from Sahitya, A Theory

BIBLIOGRAPHY

Agyeya, 1967. *To Each His Stranger*, tr. Agyeya and Gordon C. Roadarmel. Delhi: Hind Pocket Books.

Anantha Murthy, U.R. 1978. *Samskara*, tr. A.K. Ramanujan. Delhi, Oxford University Press.

Bradley, Frank et al, eds. 1973. *Literary Theory and Structure*: Essays in Honour of William K. Wimsatt. New Haven: Yale University Press.

De Man, Paul. 1979. *Allegories of Reading*. New Haven: Yale University Press.

Tagore, Rabindranath. 1987. *Selected Poems*, tr. William Radice, Harmondsworth: Penguin Books.

SURESH JOSHI

What B.S. Mardhekar has been to Marathi, Suresh Joshi (1921–1986) has been to Gujarati. He is acknowledged as the leader of the avant garde writers in Gujarati during the post-Independence period. He brought Modernism to Gujarati literature. Though his impact was felt in almost all areas of Gujarati writing, his contribution to short fiction, literary prose and literary criticism has been the most remarkable.

Suresh Joshi gave to Gujarati literature an acute self-awareness. The main emphasis in his critical writings was on the processes of aesthetic transformation in literary transactions. He propagated a theory of fiction known in Gujarati as *Ghatanavilop*, which insisted on minimising the plot element and enriching the suggestive potential of language.

Joshi came into prominence in the post-Gandhian era of Gujarati literature with the publication of his short-story collection, *Grihapravesha* (1959). Apart from his own creative writings, he did much translation and literary periodical work that has enriched Gujarati literature. The present essay is taken from his collection of critical essays *Chintayami Manasa* (1983), for which he was given the Sahitya Akademi award. Incidentally, he refused to accept the award, saying that the book contained nothing more than some stray essays. On reading the essays, one tends to completely disagree with Joshi's self-assessment.

The essay quoted here has been translated into English specially for this volume by Upendra Nanavati.

On Interpretation

The first question which arises is: whether or not the term 'interpretation' is accurate. Literary terms often acquire currency, yet their indications take time to stabilize. Neither unanimity nor sufficient data exist about the term 'interpretation'. If Susan Sontag opposes it, Seymour Hersh favours it. In our terminology *artha* is not meaning, but *rasa*. Thus interpretation means an analysis of the aesthetic process and the obstacles in its realisation. What exactly do we do in the name of interpretation? Does the perception of meaning precede interpretation? How important is it to analyse language in order to understand a poet's linguistic activity?

Some critics maintain that interpretation is a hypothesis about the common structural principles based on the relationship between the components of a literary work. In other words, the analysis of the organising principles, the way various components are inter-related in a literary work, is the process of interpretation. In brief, interpretation is analysis of the structure of a literary work. Such an analysis can postulate the thematic as well as the semantic premises about a literary text. For some interpretation becomes an act of pointing at the suggested meaning of a literary text. For such an exercise the basic components of a literary text like images, characters, episodes etc. need to be arranged and explained in such a way that their mutual relationship becomes evident. 'The writer has this or that to say through this or that text', is but an aspect of interpretation. The complexity of interpretation cannot be summarised in such a single statement. The order of relationships of components in a literary text and the conceptualisation of the same order need to be differentiated. The explication of the attributes of a literary text does not amount to interpretation. A loose definition would be: 'Whatever a critic does to a literary text is interpretation'. But, is interpretation a description of the attributes and relationships among the components of a literary text? Or is it something more? What is the difference between description and interpretation? If there is any logical method in interpretation, what could it be? Do the style, images, symbols etc., effect aesthetic function or do they not? These problems too need to be considered.

A critic has said: 'We discover the text, but we don't dig it'. Often we stop short at the stated meaning of a text. Many a time the stated meaning itself may be aesthetically pleasing. Yet it has to be accepted that an exploration in the direction of implied meaning becomes necessary for aesthetic enjoyment of a literary text. For that 'digging' is necessary. Some hold that this digging itself is interpretation.

The day-to-day life cannot be lived merely with the help of stated meanings. There too one tends to use implied meanings. Since the frame of reference for language is the entire universe, there are infinite possibilities for the use of language. Words tend to combine and yield numerous shades of meaning. Often it so happens that the syntactic relationships in a verse are clear to us but the verse as a unit is not. Meanings and grammatical structures may be clear, yet ambiguity persists. We speak of the relationships between words or lines; however this 'between' actually refers to the space within the consciousness of the author or the reader. This space cannot be grasped instantaneously. Aesthetics is the discipline formulated to explain it. It charts various possible relationships like one object in place of another (Metaphor), one object grafted on the other (simile) etc. These intangible chains of separation and transfer do not quickly yield to logic or psychology. It is commonly believed that there is a direct link between what one wishes to say and its linguistic expression. Yet our linguistic communication shows that it is not such a direct relationship. We commonly come across persons who use polysemic words and double entendre. It is a curious phenomenon. Despite the prevalence of dictionaries and technical grammars of living languages one's perception of meaning remains opaque and uncertain. George Steiner has elaborately discussed this issue in his recently published book *On Difficulty*.

It is necessary to concede to Beardsley that the issue of interpretation or aesthetic experience is connected with understanding. It remains to be seen what exactly is implied when one says that a certain verse is obscure. Clarity of meaning is not expected of poetry. In fact clarity becomes inappropriate at a certain level of literary texts. Moreover it even tends to be an interference. Without getting into the interpretation of meaning, tone, environs, sentiments etc., one just has to allow them to invade one's consciousness.

Thus the perception of meaning, as Beardsley maintains, precedes its interpretation. When a Gujarati poet like Botadkar employs uncommon words, we can manage by referring to a dictionary. But in statements like 'This theorem is difficult' or 'this concept of Kant is difficult', the difficulty is not that of understanding the lexical meanings. In order to understand the conceptual framework, it is necessary to grasp the logical basis. In the case of poetry, if a poet employs archaism, dialect, slang, code language, or loan words, the difficulty can be overcome by obtaining information about such diction.

Here, we are not concerned with this difficulty alone. A poet is an alchemist offering new formulations by soldering words. He miraculously revives obsolete words using various phases of the extended history of semantic transformations and expansions. He also employs the language considered substandard or unacceptable by elitist norms. It may just be impossible for him to use language creatively in poetry, if he remains restricted by contemporary social norms. The flora and fauna unknown to the present urban society also make inroads into the universe of his poetic discourse. Moreover, as Coleridge says, words are like 'hooked atoms'. They merge into and combine with each other in a variety of ways. Exploring the past registers, a poet revives the usable ones, and offers fresh combinations. Breaking away the decadent moulds of language, he illuminates the semantic core. He relies on etymology too. Steiner compares this dynamism of words with that of molecules passing through a 'cloud chamber' effecting profound modifications and enrichment of meaning. Through synonymy, polysemy, etc. words acquire new contours. This process cannot be understood with the help of dictionaries and grammar. One has to take into account the evolution of a word to feel its life in poetry. Words are not auditory alone, they also have visual and tactile properties. One has to pay attention to all that a poet does to lift language above the level of common usage.

Aristotle maintained that 'metaphor is the instrument of the poet'. Howsoever abstract or subtle the matter may be, a poet gives it a concrete form, investing it with uniqueness. He revives the rich context of myths and connects one world with another. He extends the dimensions of reality, and therefore the context of poetry is always dynamic. Poetry employs material which supports, reflects and makes the implicit meaning unique. A poet keeps striving to recapture poetry that was, but has fallen to the level of statements. That is why a poet writes in his own language after internalising the tradition of poetry in it. If this does not happen it is impossible to create the climate congenial to the development of the essence of poetry. From heaven-hell or the fourteen *lokas*, to whispered secrets or the lore, a poet uses everything.

Therefore, without sufficient training, one cannot enjoy poetry. The twentieth century has added a lot to the raw material of poetry. The poetry of Holub, the Czech poet, has multiple references to science and technology. The field of poetry has become increasingly intellectual. We have moved away from the age of simple, emotive poetry. Poetry of the higher kind is charted across the total cultural canvas. Besides, poetry fuses together the raw materials of the unique contemporary sensibility, all its unusualness, opacity, and also incongruities. These enhance poetry which enriches all its contexts in its own fashion. Therefore, as Walter Benjamin says, 'Cruces and talismanic deeps in poetry cannot be elucidated now or at all times'. Besides, it is necessary to bridge the gap between certain texts and cultural contexts.

The obscurity resulting from the use of certain words or word combinations is not a great hindrance; but a more subtle difficulty arises. Our aesthetic pleasure is hindered either due to the variance in tastes, or due to some poetic flaw resulting from the inconsistency between the material of poetry and its poetic transformation. If the central context or theme of a poem is elusive or uninteresting it goes against our sensibility; or the references which we find aesthetically or ethically improper could be conceptually mixed up. Therefore comprehensive interpretation is called for. Only then can one truly ascertain the hindrances, and also the fact that we have not been susceptible to any prejudices. Yet another impropriety is possible; there may be some incongruity between the level of language and the quality of emotion, or between the poet's performative means and the native pulse. It cannot be said that such an incongruity is invariably undesirable. It will be in order, provided there is an aesthetic justification for it. What may be passable or appropriate in other genres of literature, may not often be so in poetry.

There may be a rational perception of the meaning of a text in us, leading to pleasure or displeasure; yet the autonomous existence of the text may not have been grasped and therefore the response to it could be blurred. Even when we have the necessary information about a text, we may still not be able to establish any rapport with it. This does not happen merely because of our likes or dislikes. We feel that our consciousness and that of the poet do not share common environs, and hence the text is not received as an aesthetic entity and we find it difficult to surrender to it. It may be agonising for us to mould our sensibility in correspondence with the form of sensibility reflected in the poetic text. This can obstruct the aesthetic pleasures.

It is said that our own culture is more interested in experience than in cognition. Excessive emotions may not hold their balance with rationality; the insistence on form or discipline may slacken; and the tendency to make combinations and parities may increase. Any discipline or method in writing may be seen as undesirable. There is no patience for arriving at an informed response in place of an instant and limited response. Because of these tendencies we have developed insensitivity towards several elements of contemporary art and literature. That is why our prejudices are intensified and our taste becomes increasingly shallow. This too has come as a reaction to what has happened in the past. Since the industrial revolution, Man's aesthetic sensitivity has gradually become blunt. In consumerist societies consumer goods and their trading became important; Bureaucracy reduced Man to a mere pawn. As a result the relationship between the craftsman and the creator snapped. The intensity of alienation has aggravated. Since the possibility of rebelling did not exist, the artist created the illusion of being exiled into himself. He preferred to escape an insensitive society, which resulted in his cultivating the tendency for semantic privacy. Around the same time, mass-media became a menace, and media propaganda destroyed the possibility of individual response. Newspapers, thrillers, pornography, comics, etc., pushed poetry into the background. The uniqueness of individual experience lost its value. Language lost its capacity to influence, and became cheap. Therefore poets began to seek that rare and untarnished word; and manifestos were brought out. Desperate attempts were made to revolutionise the cliche-ridden language. There are two strands in this reaction: there is an unconscious revolt against highbrow literature and its dominance; the tradition is sought to be disrupted by resorting to the marginal. The second strand supports the contention of Mallarmé who wishes to establish the primitive, incantative and magical element in place of the linear, realistic and this-worldly narrative. To use Heidegger's language this experience approximates 'the hidden presence of being in beings'. Our selfhood, lost through amnesia, has to be retrieved from the layers of the unconscious and the subconscious. The challenge for the poet is to make decadent and disused language intensely expressive of the contemporary human destiny. The German poet Paul Celan stated that it was impossible to write poetry after the genocide of Auschwitz, since to write poetry one had to use the same German language used by the killers. The reason is that in poetry it is not the poet who speaks, it is the language that speaks and manifests itself. Authentic poetry is that in which language manifests itself without any artifice; obviously, such poetry is rare.

A poet wishes to enliven language by the truth and intensity of his feeling. This gives his poetry freshness and novelty, which are not ephemeral. These qualities engender a profound insight which is both penetrating and nurturing. But the language with which a poet deals is the language of ordinary affairs; it is the language in which metaphors and similes have become cliches. How can poetry employ such language for its own ends? Many have gone to the extent of believing that a true poet could never put such soiled language to use. Since words are already devalued, how can a poet make them resound again? Therefore, he should create new coinages and idioms. Ezra Pound's pronouncement to poets was 'Make it new'. Dadaism, Surrealism, Futuro-cubism, etc., too, were engaged in similar efforts. Attempts were also made to distance language from meaning. Therefore, Beardsley's contention that no interpretation can be objectively unanimous is valid. He says: 'Interpretation is not verdictive'. If a reader wishes to traverse the unknown realm created by a poet, he has to know the semiotic code to experience the poet's realisation. Whatever is expressed through the semiotic code should be expressed in such a way that its mystery is not lost. In fact, language conceals rather than reveals. Therefore only the initiated have access to poetry. It is not meant for everybody. If it is accessible to everybody, it will lose its unparalleled lustre.

Many possible relationships exist between past and present, manifest and unmanifest. To locate, discover and invest them with aesthetic quality and appeal is an important aspect of poetic creativity. Therefore, the issue of how to interpret metaphors and similes, is an important one. It is not merely a question of locating or discovering relationships; it also relates to new relationships. How can these relationships be validated? These stylistic features become 'creative', not by semantic extensions, but by novel presentation of the universe. The novelty of stylistic features articulates new facets of the subject matter when the style itself succeeds. Yet no fresh point of view of the universe can claim having effected its transformation. The stylistic features are indicative of the direction of poetry, and they bring sophistication to our understanding of the universe; and in that sense, to an extent, the universe is renewed for us. The stylistic features yield fresh initiative to one's understanding of poetry and its historicity. Therefore analysis of stylistic features has a distinct place in the interpretation of poetry.

Borges has said that 'Oppression is the mother of metaphor'. Where there is dictatorship, there are bound to be restrictions on creative artists. Yet it cannot arrest their commitment to the truth and the authenticity of expression. It then becomes imperative to create what needs to be expressed, but in such a way that only the connoisseurs can grasp it, and the insensitive rulers cannot. In this situation what the artist manifests has to be really unmanifest. In these circumstances, instead of being indicative of the poetic meaning, the stylistic features effect its concealment. Thus, indirection becomes a function of signification, and, interpretation turns into an exercise in decoding. In India, literature created during the Emergency reflects this phenomenon. People's capacity for satire acquires poignancy, and the local or temporal attains the status of 'permanently poignant'. It is not true that such a need is felt only in a specific political context. It becomes necessary to adopt the strategies of concealment when the moral climate is unfavourable in order to protect the poetic emotion from puritanical objections, or else, because the poet himself prefers the privacy of emotions. For the poet, it is not an attempt at keeping his mistress concealed. Love becomes more aesthetic when it is secret. Love does not go hand in hand with publicisation. Refined taste is averse to publicisation. Often, lovers do not like to express their true sentiments to each other. Such ambiguity creates intensity and surprise in love. A poet uses ambiguity in poetry so that a reader is tempted towards '*digging*' it. We see poets employing strategies like creating deliberate hindrances in the meaning of poetry, so that grasping of it is deferred by avoiding easily identifiable patterns, by using complexity and obscurity, and by concealing the inner unity of poetry through apparently incongruous elements of diction and style. But, if there is no basis for the dialogue between a poet and his reader, how is interpretation possible?

Those who consider poetry magical and capable of epiphany think of the whole business of interpretation as a needless hair-splitting and hence redundant. Isn't it enough to allow the totality of poetry to sink into our consciousness, or to be sensitive to it? Nothing can be a substitute for poetry itself.

Those who advocate interpretation of the meaning of poetry, end up giving prose renderings. It may serve scholars to do so, but it does not necessarily enhance aesthetic enjoyment. Not criticism but immersion in a variety of poetry ultimately opens the world of aesthetics. People who comment on poetry, invariably get into the exercise of explicating what a poet has 'said', but they can be indifferent to what a poet has 'done'. Culture gains its value through poetry. Because poetry happens to represent the climax of the evolution of human consciousness, some regard it as a vehicle and a propagator of existing cultural values. Owing to this tendency among the intellectual leaders even the literates believe that the enjoyment of poetry is meant only for the initiated and turn away from it.

For those who hold the above view, the poetry of T.S. Eliot, which is meant for the learned, is the dried-up bed of the river *Saraswati*. This kind of poetry does not have that touch of magic. It is emphasised that poetry is creation and not imitation. Interpretations may cause the loss of spontaneity of a response and give rise to anti-art intellectualism. The desired immediacy in aesthetic experience is generally displaced in the name of interpretation. The tendency to reduce the totality of poetry to intellectual abstraction gradually constricts our capacity to experience. By and large, mediocrity dominates the business of interpretation. Instead of humble empathy with art, it shows an arrogant dissatisfaction. Actually, by way of interpretation a critic does not have to do anything but describe what is there in a poem, as it is.

These assertions too are extremes. Rarely does a poem get absorbed in the consciousness in a single reading or hearing. Nevertheless, interpretation must not render the aesthetic experience secondary.

Suresh Joshi, from Chintayami Manasa

translated by Upendra Nanavati

BHALCHANDRA NEMADE

Bhalchandra Nemade shot into fame as an avant-garde novelist when he was in his early twenties, soon after the publication of his first novel, *Kosala* (1963). Three more novels and two volumes of poems, *Melody* and *Dekhni*, have followed it during the last three decades. In spite of his meagre literary output, Nemade has exerted an influence on Marathi fiction, prose style and literary culture to an extent surpassed in the past only by B.S. Mardhekar (in poetry). In the initial phase of his literary career he was active in the Marathi 'little magazine' movement. Since then he has published a large number of critical essays, a collection of which has been published under the title *Tikaswayamvar* (1991) in Marathi; and another volume of essays on style, *Sahityachi Bhasha* was published in 1987. Nemade's critical position is popularly known as 'Nativism'. Nativism insists that literature be treated as a sub-system of the native culture, and that literature should represent the social reality. It also proposes realism and 'a writerly morality' as criteria of critical judgement. These views have, understandably, produced opposition as well as sympathy. Nemade has been a controversial critic. He is included here for the reason that he is one of the very few Indian critics of the present generation with a programme for literature, and an organic view of the literary and cultural past. The essay was first delivered as a conference paper in 1980 at Shivaji University, Kolhapur causing an unprecedented literary controversy, and was subsequently published in *Anushthubh*. It appeared in English translation in *Setu* Vol.II, No.1, 1985. The translation is by G.N. Devy. It has appeared in an abridged version in P.K. Rajan's *Indian Novel* (1989). The essay is an elaborate statement of the concerns of Nativism. It is also a model of Nativistic historiography.

The Marathi Novel 1950–75

In analysing the shaping forces and trends responsible for the unprecedented growth of the novel in Marathi during the post-Independence years, particularly since 1960, certain principles have been followed in the present essay:

1. In order to trace the origin of the prevalent trends, it is necessary to examine the cultural background of the nineteenth century which gave birth to the novel in Marathi as a literary form.
2. Since as a literary form the novel occupies a large verbal space and offers wide scope to each of its constituents, it is difficult to categorize novels or novelists representing various trends in their pure form. But criticism must have a clarity of thought. As a way out, it is necessary to bear in mind that criticism is a non-autonomous means.
3. While discussing the trends, conclusions about the individual works have been derived by applying the criteria of style and substance.
4. The present generation must have an unfailing nativistic awareness that the novel in Marathi is a creation of Marathi writers, who, in turn, are the product of the Marathi society. Further, the Formalistic, unintelligent practice of picking up all and sundry works of art from languages all over the world for a comparative assessment of works in Marathi—a tendency rife in our criticism —has to be avoided. It is dangerous for criticism to enter the comparative field without making an in-depth study of both the cultures compared. Culture is not a hot-house, but a soil-bound process; literature is not a theoretical construct but a living phenomenon.

The novel form has not received any serious critical attention except through some stray articles. Especially the problems related to the recent Marathi novel have rarely been discussed. Owing to the absence of definite critical canons an overwhelming confusion abounds in our novel-criticism. In the present essay, therefore, concepts have been explained wherever possible. The term *riti* is used for design-consciousness, and a formalistic, entertaining, affected and non-realistic aestheticism. 'Style' is used to mean the techniques employed creatively to shape the substance into a form through the medium (= language). Style is neither language, nor merely the treatment given to language. The term 'morality' is used in the sense of a personal value-scale. It does not have implications of a social, unvarying, impersonal morality. The term *kriti* is employed to indicate action, and *pratikriti* to indicate illusion or image.

1. *Three Basic Trends in the Marathi Novel: Origin*

Assuming that the forces that have shaped the novel in contemporary society can be identified in their pure form at their source, if we follow the historical reconstruction method and travel backwards in time, relating the cognate qualities of various trends, we can locate three basic trends. These trends are present in every period, in forms that continue to develop, change and interact. Perhaps the three trends are deep-rooted in our literary culture. This method naturally gives us an awareness of our tradition, and helps us in putting together its missing links. Though the three trends can be traced right back to the thirteenth century,[1] in what follows the discussion is confined to the novel form only.

a) The *Yamunaparyatan* Trend:

This trend is manifest in Baba Padmanji's *Yamunaparyatan* (1857), which is considered to be the earliest of the Indian novels resulting from the interaction between the Western culture and the native Hindu culture during the British period.[2] A novelist selects the theme as a verbal action with a specific moral angle in the context of the multi-faceted relation between the individual and the community. And, in keeping with the theme, style organizes the form through the medium of language using various techniques. Such type of verbal action can be seen in *Yamunaparyatan.* That Padmanji was a perceptive and versatile individual is evident from over sixty books on religious and social topics that he wrote. Whether the fact that the very first Indian and Marathi novel during the Indian Renaissance was action-oriented is a mere accident, or whether it reflects the strongest instinct of the Marathi society on its way to modernization, can be an independent subject for debate. The *Yamunaparyatan* trend has been present in the Marathi novel throughout its history (Padmanji, H.N. Apte, V.M. Joshi, Sane Guruji, Vibhavari Shirurkar, Bhau Padhye, Anant Kadam, Dinanath Manohar, and so on).

Prose literature is one of the important cultural activities emerging from an interaction between the restless, active British culture and the contemplative, passive Hindu culture during the nineteenth century. The Hindu writers, who had inherited a long tradition of poetry, found in the novel a new vehicle of expression which offered scope for social characters, themes and incidents. Prose is more open to the depiction of social life and to reason than poetry, and it is more active a medium. The nineteenth century gave rise to the feeling that the native culture was being smothered by a cultural encounter of a victor-victim character. Anthropologists call this phenomenon 'Nativism.'[3] Nativism articulates itself either through a sudden irrational explosion or else gradually through reason. The mutiny of 1857 was the former type of expression. When the Marathas realized the foolishness of trying in that direction, they adopted the latter path and organized various movements and activities based on reason. It could be said that the most effective of these was the creation of prose literature. The contributions of the nativistic essayists to this effort is well known (Jambhekar,

Lokhitwadi, Gunjikar, Phule, Chiplunkar, Tilak, Agarkar, V.R. Shinde, S.V. Kelkar, Savarkar, Sane Guruji, etc.) The novelists can be seen expressing the predominant dynamism of prose literature through the novel form. The novel has proved all the world over to be an important vehicle of social thought and dynamic expression. It has been so in Marathi too. However, in order to see why it did not gain in strength, we must refer to the other two trends.

b) The *Muktamala* Trend:

Manifest in Laxmanshastri Moreshwarshastri Halbe's *Muktamala* (1861), the trend has dominated the Marathi novel from the beginning. It is rooted in literary convention rather than in life. Owing to the inactive, affected, entertaining mode which the novels in this trend adopt, they seek the fictitious in or with the help of the real, and present it in a formalistic manner. They avoid action. (Halbe, Risbud, Jorvekar, N.S. Phadke, V.S. Khandekar, G.T. Madkholkar, P.B. Bhave, P.S. Rege, C.T. Khanolkar, Ranganath Deshpande, Madhav Kanitkar, Kakodkar, Yogini Jogalekar, Kusum Abhyankar, Chandrakant Khot, Baba Kadam, etc).

c) The *Mochangad* Trend:

The tendency manifest in *Mochangad* (1871) by R.B. Gunjikar, to create the illustration of a non-existent reality, has come to be the most popular in the Marathi novel since Independence, after a short spell of dormancy. This trend is predominantly imagistic. (Gunjikar, Haribhau Apte, C.V. Vaidya, Nathmadhav, Hadap, Ranjit Desai, V.S. Khandekar, Manmohan Natu, N.S. Inamdar, Shivaji Savant, G.N. Dandekar, Arnalkar, Dharap, Sinkar, etc.).

The first generation of English-educated Marathas started writing independent prose after 1857.[4] It appears that this generation was jointly influenced by the English novel and the decadent Sanskrit works such as those by Bana. The observation that Marathi novelists have derived their idea of human nature from English and Sanskrit literatures seems applicable even to the initial phase of the Marathi novel.[5] At the same time, the formalistic and affected manner of poetry fashionable in that period infected prose literature too. The romantical English novelists, who followed the generation of Defoe, Swift, Richardson and Fielding, more particularly Johnson, Goldsmith, Walpole and Scott of the early nineteenth century, and Dickens and Raynolds of the later nineteenth century, continued to exert a simultaneous influence on the novel in Marathi. The Mochangad trend was a combined product of the romanticality, the nativistic revivalism and the Marathi tradition of stylized re-telling of *Ramayana* and *Mahabharata*. This trend with its fixation on a glorious past, finds its expression at times through suspense, fantasy and horror. However, its main emphasis is on nativism. This goes to show that our society finds nativism indispensable even after Independence. The inspiration of the Muktamala trend can be seen coming from the formal structures of the works of the English novelists mentioned previously, as also from the literary taste nourished by the formalistic, affected poetry which the contemporary pundits wrote, and from the works of the decadent Sanskrit writers like Bana, Dandin and Kalidasa. It is no wonder then if the style of the novels in this trend is artificial. That the pundits who cultivated the trend had not read the realistic prose of the *Mahabharata*, the *Brahmanikas*, the *Arthasastra*, and of Patanjali is evident from the information we have about their scholarship.[6] It is well known how the thoughtful writers like Phule and others ridiculed the pseudo-scholarship of these pundits. Draupadi, Sita, Shakuntala were still their ideals; sexuality was their *sthayibhava* (permanent emotion), and a reactionary orthodoxy was their *vyabhicaribhava* (transitory emotion)! We shall see in the latter part of this essay how these symptoms recur in a predictable manner in the novels of the Muktamala trend even today. The symptoms are visible with extreme clarity at its origin. The author of *Manjughosha* (1867), Naro Sadashiv Risbud, writes in the preface to his immensely popular work (1868):

> If we view the thirty thousand years' history of Hindu life and family, we will notice that there has been few changes in them and there are no elements of fantasy in them... The event that brings about a radical transformation in an individual's life is marriage. Our present marriage system is simply shameful... If one were to write stories about this marriage system, or about several other things (in our culture), no fascinating virtues or vices of the Hindu character can be revealed; and it is precisely this that creates problems when one sets out to write a novel. It is not possible to entertain by writing things experienced. So, if one had to write for entertainment, one would naturally be controlled by fantasy.[7]

This preface reveals the secret of all Marathi novelists of the Muktamala trend right up to the present times. That 'there is no element of fantasy' in Hindu life, that the Hindu marriage system, which Risbud thinks is 'the greatest event bringing about a radical transformation' (though his actual concern is sex), is 'shameful' should have moved the writer to some action. On the contrary, he avoids action and turns to the fantastic, and laments the 'impossibility' of writing fiction. Avoiding *kriti*, action, turning to the fantastic, considering fascinating virtues and vices as the essentials of a novel, making entertainment the main purpose, and finally surrendering to fantasy have been the characteristics inherited to the last detail by the works of writers from Halbe and Risbud to the present day (Phadke, Khandekar, Madkholkar, Rege, Khanolkar, Khot). All of them have avoided *kriti* and embraced the non-real. Their novels have accepted the principle that writing about the contemporary reality will be non-entertaining, that sensuality alone can be entertaining, and that some perversions, vices must form the subject of fiction. Realism could not grow strong in Marathi due to this trend.

Should not the novelist play his role, not only in the context of the import of the novel, but also as a sensitive member of the society? Padmanji and Halbe were contemporaries. How is it that the former felt concerned about the agonies of tender widowed girls, whereas the latter remained unperturbed by them? Padmanji advocated re-marriage of widows through various scholarly books he wrote; and, moreover, through his novel he performed a verbal action too. Halbe, however, sidetracked the *kriti* by manipulating a meeting between Muktamala, the heroine, and Dhanshankar, her lost hushand who was taken to be dead, just a day before her head-shaving ritual. This is the patent way that *riti*-oriented novels employ to avoid action. Besides being escapist, this type forces the writer to be amoral as a human being, forcing him to the path from the real to the non-real. It is important to have a verbal action in a novel, whether it is progressive or orthodox. In order to avoid action, the writers of the Muktamala trend have to take recourse to the fantastic, formalistic, and entertaining claptrap. And our 'Art for Art's sake' formalistic and aestheticist critics have all along been justifying such 'art' by superficial and punditic criteria such as 'autonomy of art', 'self-sufficiency of art values', etc. This trend, of coure, loses the awareness of reality. Reason, which is an important aspect of prose and which appeals to the intellect, remains totally disused in it, in turn, causing several undesirable consequences. The novel has to accept an eccentric individualism and imagine perverse, non-existent sexual situations. Form becomes more important than import. The novel ceases to be productive and becomes merely an end-product. It forgets the specific time and space and enters a mystified world of fantasy. Among the reasons for the flourishing of this trend in Marathi can be counted its capacity to entertain, to win easy acclaim, financial gains and popularity, the unhealthy literary culture and false theories of criticism. The realistic novel did not deveop in Marathi before Independence as the Muktamala trend was going strong at that time. However, realism which values verbal action, appears to have gained momentum after 1960. The fact that no trends other than *pratikriti*, *riti* and *Kriti* (illusionistic, entertaining and activist, respectively) could even emerge in Marathi is closely related to the basic life instinct of Marathi society.

In the English novel there were several types of realistic trends, and works belonging to many of those had been translated into Marathi during the 19th century (*The Pilgrim's Progress–Yatrik Kraman,* 1841; *Robinson Crusoe, 1875; Gulliver's Travels–Galivar Yacha Vritant,* 1880–90 etc.). There were some other realistic trends available in Marathi itself as also in good classical Sanskrit literature. But it was not possible for these trends to strike root in the Marathi novel. Once in a while we see something like an allegory (*Aastik* by Sane Guruji, 1933), or else like the picaresque (*Niranjan* by Godse Bhatji, 1882 ?); but these trends did not survive as our writers could not afford to take their subject matter entirely from reality. Besides the tendency to import whatever was respectable in England dominated our writers from H.N. Apte who imitated Scott to B.S. Mardhekar who followed the footsteps of Joyce. And since most of the writers had little awareness of the native tradition, the Marathi novel remained just entertaining and *riti*-oriented till Independence. K.B. Marathe had described these formalistic novels as 'the pest of Marathi fiction' (1872); and later V.K. Rajawade observed that the novels of the *Manjughosha–Muktamala* type were consumed by 'elite rich, lazy and useless persons' (1902), supporting his observation with examples.[8]

2. *Language*

The British Government decided to spread new ideas in Hindu society by adopting the filtration method proposed in Macaulay's Minute (1835), the method of spreading new knowledge among the classes at the top first. Earlier on, the missionaries had started spreading the new knowledge among among all classes of the society. But this process was halted after 1857. As a result, it was only the urban Brahmin class that benefited from the new knowledge before Independence, and even after until the Congress Government opened schools and colleges in small towns and villages. The English-educated Brahmins did contribute to the development of Marathi literature and language during the nineteenth century;[9] but this developed literary language reflected only one segment of the social life. At that time, some of the anti-Brahmin castes like Prabhu and Shenavi had initially prevented the Marathi language from becoming totally Brahminical. However,as the number of Government recognized autonomous educational institutions increased,following Wood's Dispatch in 1854, the Brahmins acquired a monopoly over education. Many British officers had registered their deep resentment against this monopoly. But since the Government's policy was to neglect education, the field remained predominantly Brahminical even after Independence. The Marathi literary language was enriched during the nineteenth century primarily by the Education Department. In this Department, the Brahmins outnumbered the others. The Marathi used by these Brahmin producers of school-texts was drawn on a haphazard mixture of English and Sanskrit, and was just functional and artificial. The other Marathi register, epitomized in Chiplunkar's manner of writing which combined Johnson's style with Sanskrit mannerism, came to stay through newspapers and periodicals. As Marathi journalism has remained a Brahminical movement even to this day, journalistic Marathi has remained artificial and continues to draw on the English-Sanskrit combination.

The language of Marathi prose literature is largely underdeveloped. No previous generation laid bare this truth. The effects of this inferior quality of Marathi on the novel in it have been profound. It is on record that a responsible Marathi gentleman had told Monier Williams in 1858 that "there is not a single person here who can write good Marathi."[10]

Justice M.G. Ranade had said about the educated Brahmins that 'they practically lose touch with their people.'[11] Jotiba Phule has clearly described, giving instances, the 'holier than thou' attitude the Brahmins in positions of authority displayed towards others. V.R. Shinde has stated succinctly that 'authentic Marathi existed from Jnaneshwar to Tukaram. It somehow survived till the period of Lokhitwadi and Jotiba Phule. But Chiplunkar and Agarkar throttled it. Tilak and Haribhau Apte tried to resuscitate it, but theirs turned out to be the last attempt'[12]

Even after Independence, the school texts continued to force down the throats of students passages from the works of someone like S.M. Paranjape, who did not ever write good Marathi, as samples of stylistic excellence. If the children brought up in such a literary culture start believing that they cannot write such 'great' Marathi and stop writing altogether, or else start writing such artificial Marathi only, the language can have no hope of any development. Owing to these Anglo-Brahmin *samskaras* the Marathi language has come to be empty of expression. It has remained merely a register capable of expressing only predictable sentiments. Even today that development of Marathi seems difficult because of its twin enslavement to Sanskritized prose and to Anglicized vocabulary which is treated as a status symbol and has polluted the taste even of womenfolk.[13] The children of the urban, service-minded elite class are forced to go to English medium schools at a tender age. They become intellectually invalid and incapable of shaping language creatively and independently. This class cannot help the Marathi language. We should note that the universities, particularly the universities of Pune and Bombay, have done nothing to develop the Marathi language. Some activity has begun at the Governmental level; but that is not going to benefit the present generation.

Since perception of reality is dependent on language, it can be concluded that no authentic creative literature is possible through artificial Marathi. Artificial language distorts the dimensions of substance and form. Severely restricted themes alone can be presented through such language. It also encourages the *riti* trend excessively. A society which does not admit in its literature the language varieties of very large communities, castes, tribes and regions, automatically prevents the world-views, aesthetic ideas and values of those communities from entering literary activity. This results in a minority monopoly of literary taste.

As a matter of fact, from the times of Jnaneshwar and Mahimbhatta Marathi has the tradition of overthrowing the minority monopoly. Few of the pre-Independence writers realised this fact. But now the *riti*-oriented novel is on the decline; and with it also the 'whirlpool' style of H.N. Apte, the artifical claptrap of Phadke, the decorative manner of Khandekar and the ornamentation in Madkholkar have started showing signs of becoming stuff in the lumber room of history. This is the most significant achievement of the Marathi novel since 1960. Writers from all sub-cultures, sub-groups and regions have exploded the Anglo-Brahmin tradition and reduced the gap between the spoken word and the written word. The enriched Marathi language of post-1960 seems to have emerged from an integration of various caste and tribe language varieties. In respect of language, the works of Vyankatesh Madgulkar and other *gramin* (rural) writers, the 'little magazine' and the *dalit* (oppressed) literature movements have proved to be revolutionary. Ever since the Marathi Sahitya Parishad liberalised the minority rules of written Marathi, the written language and the spoken language have come closer. Today an atmosphere prevails in Marathi which enables any person belonging to any sub-group or any sub-culture to write with confidence. That the discernible effects of this nativistic style have started showing is evident from the fact that since 1960 at least one good novel was written every year: *Dhag,* 1960; *Rathachakra, Swami,* 1962; *Manus, Chakra,*1963; *Vaitagwadi, Indhan, Tarfula,* 1964; *Vasunaka,*1965; *Kalokhache Aang,* 1966; *Barrister Aniruddha Dhopeshwarkar,*1967; *Shidori, Devacha Shabda,*1968; *Aagresar,* such and so much prospering was not there before 1960 in the Marathi novel.

3. *Style and Form*

Style, which emerges from the synthesis of meaning, medium and techniques reflects the inborn imagination of the writer. The style of the Marathi novel before Independence was almost entirely born out of a blind imitation of English style.

Initially techniques like first person narration, third person narration, epistolary narration and flashback were imported; and as if this were not enough, Mardhekar brought in the stream of consciousness (*Ratricha Divas,* 1942; *Tambadi Mati* 1943; *Pani,* 1948) to conclude the pre-Independence period. No writer or critic seemed to have an awareness that in Marathi too there was a strong, though fragmented, tradition of prose style. This state of affairs continued even after 1950. Prof. S.R. Kulkarni discerned a continuous tradition of punditic prose.[14] Kusumavati Deshpande was not aware of this tradition but had an inkling of it.[15] Usually a victim-culture revives its past when it encounters an alien culture. But the Marathi critics started considering every writer belonging to the past to be a great writer. They did not leave out even the writers like Moropant. Such claims showed no sense of discrimination. R.S. Jog spent pages together to comment on the prose writings of S.M. Paranjape and N.C. Kelkar instead of writing on the great works of the Māhānubhava prose or the Bākhar prose.[16]

The reason for this critical bankruptcy is the undue emphasis that University courses give to English criticism. Sir Richard Temple hit on the truth when he remarked in 1882 that:

> the effect of this (English) education, direct or indirect, undoubtedly was in the first instance...to suppress the natural originality of the educated.[17]

This has happened invariably to all English-educated individuals. The style of the Marathi novel has not moved beyond literary fashions. That in Marathi we have not even begun to think seriously about style is in itself an evidence of what is being taught in the five universities in the state.

In depicting reality, an authentic touch of social life has an extraordinary importance. That touch was lacking in Marathi; and both in creative literature and in criticism imitating English models had become respectable. It was no surprise then if the literary style in Marathi became bookish. Chakradhar had a first-hand knowledge of the living practice of dumping the flat, light, odd-shaped corn-winnower on top of a fully loaded cart carrying household goods from one place to another. That is why when he forces his disciple Nagadevacharya to eat another bowl of sweets on a full belly, he jokingly states that 'a corn-winnower is no burden to a loaded cart.' Marathi style was deprived of these language references to social life during the British rule.

The statements such as: '*Kadambari* (the novel) is a native word but an alien concept' (P.V. Bapat, N. V. Godbole),[18] or 'Though Marathi literature has a history of eight hundred years, the novel in Marathi has a history barely of seventy years' (N.S. Phadke),[19] may be true; but the sense in which they are used in criticism is misguiding. The novel is not an entirely English form; its origin too is not English. If one were to search its origin, one would have to move from country to country and to refer to various writers and works like the *Decameron*, Bendelloe, the *Panchatantra*, and so on. Max Muller has established through research how the *Panchatantra* fables were transformed while migrating from India to Iran and then, through Baghdad and Constantinople, to all of Europe. Similarly Rawlinson has shed light on how Suvarnadevata in the original Hindu story later became Cinderella, and how literary forms all over the world carry the cultural imprint of the specific space and time to which they belong.[20] While relating formal principles to literary forms, it is necessary to bear in mind that literary forms as much belong to space and time as they transcend them. It may be, then, possible to realize that though the novel as a form of literature came to India through our contact with English, it is not entirely new in India as a form of writing.

It must be accepted that during the pre-Independence period no one had the imagination to relate us to this tradition. Besides to believe that the Aristotelian concepts of form, later developed by various tiny states of Europe, are worth imitating in preference to the aesthetic concepts concentrated in our multi-racial, multi-cultural, multi-communal and vast society is simply foolish. In none of our ancient literatures do we find such narrow concepts as unity and organicity. Any of our works like Ajanta, Ellora, the *Mahabhárata, Ramayana, Kathasaritsagara,* and even a second rate work like *Meghaduta* can illustrate the point. While formulating a concept of the novel, it is necessary to consider its nature as a form of writing. In fact, *Lilacharitra, Smrutisthala*, the Bakhars (historical chronicles), the biographies composed by Mahipati are all forms of writing very close to the novel. But nearly three generations of writers were wasted because of the unenlightened idea that the novel is only what our novelists did by imitating the English models. Since we lost the subtle concept of form, everyone including the novelists themselves indulged in a superficial classification such as Khandekar's 'Art for Life's sake' and Phadke's 'Art for Art's sake'. Actually, there is little qualitative difference on the formal level between Khandekar's idealism, humanity, freedom, purity, sublime love, sacrifice, love, yagna, and such other nice 'Sanskrit' ideas on the one hand, and on the other hand, Phadke's colourful saris, scents, perfumes, puff and powder, tennis, kisses, courtship, etc. Both of them are essentially formalistic, entertaining type of novelists. At the most one could say that as a stylist Phadke was a post-graduate if Khandekar was an under-graduate. In this conspiracy of writers and critics, the others who presented the form with a sense of style were dismissed as unreadable (S.V. Ketkar), or as children's writers (Sane Guruji), or else as humorists (C.V. Joshi); and the field of the novel was kept reserved for the monopoly of a couple of literary capitalists. N.S. Phadke states:

> Just as it can be said that the first generation of novelists was that of Haribhau Apte, the second of Phadke and Khandekar, and the third of Bhave, it is difficult to say that the subsequent generation of novelists is of any particular novelist... In the initial stages of the novel, Haribhau Apte reigned supreme; later Phadke and Khandekar reigned...but no present day novelist has done a similar incomparable work so that we could say that he rules over the literary situation.[21]

It needs no saying how ridiculous and childish the idea of 'ruling over' the literary situation is. In fact, it is really quite revolutionary that so many novelists have come to the forefront in recent times. If one were to think on the lines of Phadke's argument it would be logical to say that the 'fourth generation of novelists in Marathi is that of Kakodkar and Baba Kadam'!

It should be possible to differentiate the peculiarities of the novel from among the four distinct literary genres — short story, story, short novel and novel — on the basis of formal criteria. For us it has become necessary to understand the nature of the undesirable process of invasion of the novel by the short story form since 1950 which has prospered on the basis of its twisted subject matter in combination with its commercial potentiality.

The short story and long story are close to each other; the short novel and novel are similarly related. The present day Marathi criticism is inclined towards wiping out the clear formal distinction that exists between the two types, since the criticism is based primarily on the short story. The short story is a form of literature with restricted length and verbal space, which offers through a single-channel theme a limited, and therefore intense, perception of time and space. In the long story the limits of length and verbal space relax, though the theme remains single channel. Both short story and long story have their limits of maximum length.

The short novel is, in comparison to the above two forms, spatially extended and also thematically plural. Owing to its multi-channel theme it offers larger dimensions of time and space. In the novel, proportionately, several layers of theme combine; and it has a very vast range of expression and verbal space. As opposed to the short story and long story, the short novel and novel have their limits of minimum length. Owing to the complexity of themes they handle, they occupy expansive length of time and large areas of space, and at once transcend them to suggest a reality beyond space and time. This time-transcending suggestiveness of the novel removes all restrictions on the range of space it occupies.

In short, in each of these four forms the relation between the theme and the verbal space proves to be the differential quality. And it is essential to have a clear comparative perspective in order to understand the formal inter-relationships among these four forms. Here are some examples:

Short story — Long story: *Manus navache Bet — Tuti* (G.A. Kulkarni)
Long story — novel: *Avalokita — Savitri* (P.S. Rege)
Short novel — Novel: *Savitri — Andharwata* (P.S. Rege — Subhash Bhende)
Short story — Short novel: *Mandeshi Manase — Bangarwadi* (Vyankatesh Madgulkar)
Long story — Novel: *Garambicha Bapu — Rathachakra* (S.N. Pendse)

Thus the novel can be said to be a form of literature which has a large verbal space, a multi-layered and complex theme, and which, therefore, offers scope for a complex structure, characters and situations that incline more towards completeness than towards incompleteness. Owning to such characteristics it becomes possible for the novel to present a significant action in its fulness. It can contain and present a large-as-life social meaning, the life of a sub-culture or sub-group in detail, an entire cross section of a particular period or society, and can handle a social problem with all its entanglements. Its themes are self-sufficient and characters consistent and capable of existing on their own.

Several of the Marathi writers treated as novelists are in fact short story writers. On the other hand, some of those treated as short story writers are in reality novelists. This classification will save our criticism from being misguided, and help us to describe the true nature of the novel. The novel in Marathi does not present an authentic picture of reality because it has been working under the constraints of the short story such as poverty of themes, distortion of reality for the sake of concentrated effects, perverted, twisted and, therefore, shocking endings, and the mindless use of techniques, symbols, 'images' and language in general.

4. *Social Reality: Realism*

Realism means acceptance of the objective existence of the universe independent of the individual's existence; and the primary condition of realism in literature is the acceptance of the individual-society relationship from this perspective. The details that a novelist selects while structuring his meaning percolate to him from the various aspects of the individual-society relationship. Since the medium of expression for literature, which is language, belongs to a specific place and a specific time, and since it is available to an individual only as a social system, it controls the individual's cognition. The writer, therefore, has to abide by the sign-structure of meanings that society has determined. It will not be possible to depict reality in an uncontrolled way, and keeping only the individual in focus.

From the various undesirable trends referred to so far, it should be clear to us why realism has not been growing healthily in the Marathi novel. The most definite misconception our writers have is in respect of the individual-society relationship. There, they side-track the native culture, and take recourse to erroneous, imported generalizations. This leads them to move farther from the native tradition and to create an artifact of formalistic detail which is shorn of references to the outside context. This practice gives rise to false aesthetic tenets such as 'what is rare and tempting alone is beautiful'. Our writers were exposed to foreign values like individualism, etc., through the lone 'window on the world' to which they had access. Such values were bound to look quite attractive since they were seen outside their mundane social contexts. Our writers avoided seeing how awesome a sense of social responsibility lies hidden under the iceberg of individualism. They avoided seeing the entire spectacle since the whole of it was not attractive. This and such other values lured the novel too, since the readership shared the romantic fascination for these values, and since they came in handy for getting a cheap and quick popularity for the commercially-minded novelists. Even today, the 'stalwarts' among Marathi novelists cannot avoid the temptation of these Western values.

Colonized for a prolonged period of time, Hindu society has spent a longer period under enslavement than any other society in the world. When the culture values of the conquered society clash with the cultural values of the dominating society the former has to accept helplessly the values of the latter. This cultural invasion deprives one of the confidence to stand on his native ground with satisfaction as a human being. This is certainly the most dangerous consequence of cultural colonization. When Hindu society accepted Western values, all social systems—except the economic system—were reorganized on the pattern of the Western value systems. Since the British had come to India for economic exploitation, they left the economic system untouched in its old, medieval form, whereas they vowed to mould every other Indian system. This time-lag between the economic system and other value systems creates in the novel a strange kind of social unreality.

The realism in our literature such as of Tukaram and the others was reared on metaphysics. It crumbled down in the face of the new materialism. This materialism had not struck deep roots in our society from 1818 to 1950. As an instance, one could mention the fad of individualistic sexuality in the Marathi novel. When the English ideas of individualism entered our society of gentlemen who faithfully carried out the traditional duty of procreation to which their *dharma* had appointed them, the naked English values of freedom in the man-woman relationship found here a limitless blossoming. The very idea of love itself became a value. In countless acrobatic ways love began being expressed in fiction. In the Marathi novel romantic love was let loose from *Muktamala* to V.S. Khandekar, N.S. Phadke, G.T. Madkholkar, Gangadhar Gadgil, P.B. Bhave, P.S. Rege, C.T. Khanolkar, Yogini Jogalekar, and so on. We need not be surprised to see a writer like P.Y. Deshpande, who possessed some inborn imagination, getting engulfed in this wave. For, most of us hunger after sexual licentiousness; and what else can the mind of these lusty ones contain? However, it becomes necessary to create in the novel an economic background that will support the idea of romantic love, even if it does not exist in reality. This distorts reality to a large extent. Further, the themes are contrived as per the requirements of the form, and the necessary details follow automatically. It becomes necessary then to place the novel in an atmosphere that is congenial to love affairs to some extent: industrial cities, elite classes and colleges, love machinery like a bungalow, a good job, a car, etc. This follows the emergence of the urban writers who are familiar with only such an atmosphere. Their monopoly language becomes the received literary language. Then minority aesthetics is imposed on the larger society in a topsy-turvy manner. We can see in the Marathi novel a car accident leading to a love affair of delicate brows (*Jadugar*, 1927), the daughter of a prostitute playing the violin on the terrace of her house to lure Prabhakar, the hero, to her love (*Bandhanachya Palikade*, 1927), a political movement invariably giving rise to a love affair (*Krounchavadh*, 1942), and the love description written in Bombay but set in the natural surroundings of Ratnagiri district stooping to the level of a Hindi movie. It is a fact that love in our society is but an idea; and its meaning in literature is sexuality. We do not have in our society the necessary platforms for the man-woman relationship on which the Western society balances the idea of love. It is not possible to have them here while the economic system remains undeveloped. The compound word expression 'love-marriage' has been conclusively accepted in Marathi, though it does not exist in the original English, simply because the Marathi mind thinks of love as 'sexuality before marriage'.

By taking instances from various fields, it can be studied how the novel has tried to reduce the actual imbalance that exists in social life. For instance, G.T. Madkholkar employed socialism to ridicule Gandhism. The writer had in fact no concern for socialism. In the same manner several techniques (e.g. symbolism) and themes borrowed by our novelists from the West become, in fact, irrelevant to our social context. One can as much write a novel opposing our moral values (Bhau Padhye) as one can from the standpoint of native moral values (*Shyamchi Aai*, 1933). But the latter trend is to be rarely seen in the history of our novel before 1960. Unfortunately, *Shyamchi Aai* could not become *Pather Panchali* because its nativistic character was beyond the comprehension of P.K. Atre. And it is impossible that, considering what our literary culture is, it would create a Satyajit Ray.

5. *Trends from 1950 to 1975*

In addition to the three trends discussed above, which continue to be intact, some new trends seem to have emerged on their borders since 1950, either through an interaction between the three trends or as their direct off-shoots. The realistic and *kriti*-oriented Yamunaparyatan trend seems to be the most developed one at present. This may be taken as an indication of the end of the pathetic condition of realism in Marathi. Not only has the trend, interested in social problems and action, become more realistic, but even some new trends are emerging from it which deal with specific geographical regions, sub-community or sub-culture (seen as a segment of the larger society, the *dalits*, women, etc.), and with a new morality (opposed to the conventional entertaining tendency of writers and interested in realistic themes). The Mochangad trend too seems to have moved from history to mythology, biography and crime. In the Muktamala trend, sexuality has become more prominent, and the style more developed; but beyond that it shows no progress on the level of the subject matter. One can now think of the novel in terms of a spectrum ranging from the unrealistic and the fantastic to the realistic novel. Such a spectrum did not exist before 1950. This could be considered a good sign of the qualitative and quantitative growth of the Marathi novel.

The Novel Spectrum

Unrealistic

	1	Historical
Pratikriti-Oriented Mochangad Trend	2 3	Mythological Biographical
	4	Fantasy
Riti-Oriented ↕ Muktamala Trend	5	Sexual
Regional	6	Regional
Kriti-Oriented Yamunaparyatan Trend	7 8	Sub-Community Sub-Culture based Problem based
	9	New Morality based

Realistic

This spectrum will not be understood unless treated as a classification of hundreds of novels belonging to one period from the perspective of tradition. Again, it is important to look at the methodology of this spectrum only as a means of description. It is limited by the novels written during the present period. However, in the analysis of novels discussed hereafter other criteria have been applied; and those novels have been assessed independently. It is quite possible to employ another set of criteria to classify, grade and assess the novelists.

In a classification of this nature, a writer has to be assigned a place according to his overall trend. There could be a difference of opinion about the classification of certain novels depending on the individual critic's taste. Some novelists may fall in all the categories in the spectrum (e.g. G.N. Dandekar). It will also be seen that if one work of a given novelist falls under one category, another under another one, yet another falls under an altogether different category. This reflects on the commercial, careeristic mentality of Marathi writers. Rarely has a Marathi writer shown a life-long commitment to a particular literary philosophy or technique in order to make at least an inch of progress in that line. In this mixed crowd of good and bad coins, criticism cannot be expected to evolve and use precise canons. It is quite easy to detect in a single Marathi novel each and every literary technique perfected by writers all over the world through their life-long commitment. Used as readymade formulas, these techniques—symbolism, romanticism, realism, Freudian thought, existentialism, surrealism—are seen simultaneously co-existing as if fiction were a fun-fair of techniques. It could be said that very few Marathi writers show the awareness that writing is a consistent cultural activity.

The New Novel

This is the last branch in the development of the Marathi novel so far. The new novel, which originates in *Yamunaparyatan*, has an intimate relation with reality. It considers *kriti* to be an indivisible aspect of creation, and presents a new value scale about man in life. As such it distinguishes itself from the other trends because of its new morality.[22] It believes in selecting its subject matter from the contemporary life and ethos, and providing a thematic dimension to its style. Hence all constituent elements of this novel are supported by the theme; its content, characters, events, techniques, language, plot, narrative, style—all come to acquire an inherent thematic significance. Naturally, therefore, this trend in the Marathi novel has gained the highest significance in Marathi.

The novelists who could be included in the trend are: Udhhav Shelke (*Dhag*, 1960); Manohar Talhar (*Manus*, 1963); Bhau Padhye (*Dombaryacha Khel*, 1960, *Karanta*, 1961, *Vaitagwadi*, 1964, *Vasunaka*, 1965, *Barrister Aniruddha*

Dhopeshwarkar, 1967, *Agresar*, 1968, *Homesick Brigade*, 1974, *Rada*, 1975, *Vanava*, 1978); Manohar Shahane (*Devacha Rag*, 1968); A.V. Joshi (*Kalokhache Ang*, 1966); Prabhakar Pendharkar (*Are Sansar*, 1971); Kiran Nagarkar (*Sat Sakkam Trechalis*, 1974); Anant Kadam (*Kide*, 1971, *Strot*, 1977, *Pakharu*, 1979); Dinanath Manohar (*Robot*, 1976): all these are seen presenting the new morality through their fiction. At the same time Kamal Desai (*Ratrandin Amha...*, 1964) and several other story writers have stepped outside the constricted structure of the story and moved in the direction of the novel. These story writers too accept the new morality. Since the topic deserves independent discussion, it has not been taken into consideration here.

Besides these, some others inclined towards the *riti*-type sexuality—Jayawant Dalvi (*Swagat, Athang*), T.V. Sardeshmukh (*Bakhar Eka Rajachi, Uchhad*), H.M. Marathe (*Nishparna Vrikshavar, Kaleshar Pani*), Vasant Kanetkar (*Ghar*) — maintain a doubtful relation with this trend.

When this type of novel was born around 1960 it was born alien, since the established *pratikriti* trend and *riti* trend in vogue at that time were opposed to it in their scales of values. The novel with the new morality burst out like an explosion at a time when the innocent reader was misguided by a shameless mud-slinging that went on under the name of literary criticism; that criticism was a product of a literary culture crowded with journalistic publicity, flattering lectures, hooliganism in Sahitya Sammelans, rackets in literary taste, the formalist-aestheticist theories without rules by third rate reviewers, immoral literary activities as shown in *Kaleidoscope*, cheap popularity gained by erotic and *pratikriti* trend novels and such other things.[23] The new novel, which came up like an explosion, posed a radical challenge to the established Marathi literary taste; and it remains the only trend which has developed by its own merit alone. Perhaps for the first time after the thirteenth century we see a picture of an entire generation conscious of its ethical stand. This type of novel has been presenting the new morality without compromises, and has established its equation with a handful of knowledgeable readers; this is achieved within a literary culture which attaches importance to all other factors except the writer and the reader. It is this novel that made punditic Marathi criticism look into its canons for the first time during the last twenty years. The new novel expects a radical and total change in Marathi literary culture. Today we have clear indications that the change will be felt strongly when the new readers of the next generation start writing.

The new novel's confrontation with vitiated literary taste is evident in its subject matter as well as in its emergence itself. For instance Anant Kadam's *Strot* has numerous references to literature; Bhau Padhye's *Barrister Aniruddha*

Dhopeshwarkar discusses sex; Dinanath Manohar presents views about the writer's responsibility in his *Robot.* The theme and subject of the new novel can accommodate even a highly philosophic or radical ideology in its scope. Because of such extensive realistic grounding in the new novel, the web of *riti*-oriented novelistic conventions in Marathi crumbled. No novel before the new novel had such a conscious awareness of literature. The new novelists were the first to have the awareness of being responsible citizens of a sovereign nation in a new, post-Independence period. This position ruled out irresponsible, and eccentrically individualistic themes. The fundamental *kriti*-principle, which has survived from the time of Baba Padmanji till today, has broadened through the individual morality of the new novel. The linguistic *kriti* interested in the individual, more than that in the social, indicates the development of the *kriti*-trend.

The moral values found in the new morality vary from writer to writer. They do not adhere to a doctrine. This individual morality reflects impulses hidden deep inside the social psyche, because the novels of this trend articulate the fundamental impulses of the material life of the community. An exploration of these impulses without any compromise becomes possible only in a *kriti*-trend novel. They automatically percolate into the novel from its powerful subject-matter, the material culture of the society. Rickshaw pullers/drivers (*Manus*), workers (*Dombaryacha Khel, Karanta*), clerks (*Vaitagwadi*), loafers, unemployed children (*Vasunaka*), soldiers (*Robot*), rustic women (*Dhag, Manus*), Hindus-Muslims-Christians (Bhau Padhye, Dinanath Manohar, Uddhav Shelke), and such other sub-groups have upheld for innumerable years principles like tolerance, judiciousness, liberalism, personal and moral discrimination. These principles form the foundation of our culture. It is precisely these principles that the earlier novel did not know, because the subject matter of the earlier novel was not received from these sub-groups. Hence the limitations of the subject matter also became the limitations of the novel.

Since this novel has a limitless fascination for reality, at times the distinction between the real and the factual gets wiped out and a subject matter full of tedious particulars overwhelms the structuring process. Examples of such failures are: *Pakharu, Homesick Brigade* and *Virus* (Subhash Savarkar). But these victims of experimentation are bound to exist in Marathi which lacks a strong tradition of realistic depiction.

As much as this novel values the native tradition, so much it also values foreign contacts. This has enlarged the earlier Anglophile narrow literary culture. The literature of America and Europe has come closer to the new novelists in Marathi. Similarly the new contribution to Marathi by writers from a variety of castes and religions has enlarged the circumference of a secular society present in the novel, which was not present in the earlier novel. The number of concepts of literary worth also has increased. At present new concepts of literary excellence are being established and becoming acceptable. Therefore the conventionally imagined distance between life and literature is getting reduced. Literary taste has undergone a change which will not accept in a serious novel artificial characters, superficial subject matter and concocted episodes. All these achievements have been made by the new novel without help from the critics, or even in spite of them.

The protagonists of the new novels have often been described by Marathi criticism as 'Existentialist', 'Anti-hero', etc. There is, of course, no possibility whatsoever of these trends emerging and surviving in the Hindu social structure. Actually, these protagonists belong to the anti-colonial, nativistic tradition of Gandhi to Lohia in politics, and of Padmanji to Sane Guruji in literature. They do not have the counterfeit colonial currency of love, courtship, humanism, idealism, sublimity, etc. They do not have the bookish courage in sex which is necessary for 'hero'-ism. For the Hindu reality has no place for these things. The new novel which performed verbal *kriti* about the problems in the society-individual relationship did not rely too heavily on the characters; it rather focussed on the social envelope round the character and on the interdependence between the society and the individual. The statement that 'the other-interestedness of the protagonists of these novels is a new phenomenon' is valid only so far as the novel is concerned. Several Marathi poets from the thirteenth century down had experienced this other-interestedness. The Hindu cultural characteristic of taking interest in society was present in the earlier 'other-interestedness', as it is present now. The protagonists of the new novel prefer order to anarchy.

The structure of these fictional works is extensive, and their ending open. The principle of unity that they follow is not that of an apparent unity but of an essential, inner unity. They do not employ unrealistic, wooden characters. Since the language used is the ordinary, day-to-day spoken language, no falsified depiction of reality or sentimentality is possible. The emotionally high-pitched language of the *riti* trend punditic novels, and their formalistic, artificial events do not occur in the new novel. The narrative style in the new novel gives emphasis to irony; the narrators themselves also maintain an ironic point of view to their characters. Owing to this, the established Marathi convention of being pleased with one's own characters is almost finished. The convenient bias of the established Marathi novel too has been removed by the new novel. The journey of the Marathi novel from tribe to sub-community and from sub-community to society, which moves through Padmanji, Apte, and Sane Guruji, now seems to have turned, with the new novel, to humanity at large. Looking at the capabilities of Marathi society we can be happy about this journey. However, it must be accepted that the Marathi novel has still not been able to think of the entire human existence.

The best expression to the new trend is given by Bhau Padhye by writing earnestly and without compromise on a vast range of modern subjects in his novels from *Dombaryacha Khel* (1960) and *Karanta* (1961) — using the subject of the labour movement—to *Vanava* (1979)—showing the sex life of an ultra modern couple in a forest.[24] Padhye created a new field of literary taste through open structures and by selecting a variety of realistic themes. His Bombay dialect too is born out of his new realism, it is entirely free of poetical elements. It develops the narrative by employing a colloquial idiom expressed in sentences such as, "I felt my tummy was tight as a tyre" (*Vaitagwadi*); "The gossip continued *emni em*" (Marathi variation on a Bombay Gujarati expression meaning 'endlessly'), "The thread of his screw has worn out for the lass" (*Vasunaka*). The realism of content begins in it right from the selection of names: Dhopeshwarkar, Azad Chacha, Priyanvada — Malvika — Sharmishtha — Ivy — Clara, Dafya — Mamu — Ghoshya Koreta — Fari Bamford — Roshan — Nilima, etc. Padhye is basically a serious writer with socialistic morality (the starving tribals against modern couples busy in pornographic mischiefs — *Vanava*; emancipation of women — *Agresar*; Hindu casteism — *Vaitagwadi*; the marriage system, parentless children — *Barrister Aniruddha Dhopeshwarkar*; intense moral discrimination, respect for fallen women — *Vasunaka*). In comparison to any other Marathi novelist, Padhye shows a greater involvement with Bombay in his novels, loves it as if Bombay were his motherland; he has a profound love for all sections of the Bombay society, and he endows the topography of Bombay with a life. This humanitarian involvement is not found in any other novelist in Marathi after Sane Guruji. No character of Padhye uses the flashback technique, nor enters the area of day-dreaming. It is because of this that his prose style has a strong, coarse texture like that of jute-cloth. This makes it possible for his novel to contain varieties ranging from the loafers and the jobless of 'the loafers' toll post' ('*Vasunaka*') to the ultra-modern men and women, the ethics of life from the Valapa estuary to Malabar Hill:

"If you want to booze, do. Don't. That's your look out"; "At sunrise we would put on woollen trousers and gather in a company at Vasunaka to fool around. Had no other business. Neither had cricket, nor were we born brahmins to join the R.S.S. and do 'right turn, left turn'."

Barrister Dhopeshwarkar looks down upon his wife who forces him to move to a flat in a modern locality from his old house surrounded by trees. As a result of this powerful moral sense Padhye's *Rada* — a novel on the Shiv Sena — was suppressed so that its complete version would not reach the readers. Padhye puts forward a moral view even through the novels which have sex as their subject.

In this new novel, which has developed realism, the blunted tradition of the standard language was destroyed and a variety of dialects entered literature with confidence. A notable novel with this particular achievement is Manohar Talhar's *Manus* (1963). It develops through the Hindi spoken by two rickshaw driver friends in Amaravati, one a Hindu, the other a Muslim. It was just impossible that a theme like the one selected by Talhar could find a place in the novel written before 1960. The tolerant, liberal ordinary life depicted in this novel envelops in an emotional warmth women, men, upper-classes, lower-classes, policemen, hoteliers, goondas, brahmins, Hindus and Muslims; and it stands out with a native dignity. It shows in a new form the workers' life in which the concepts such as 'society' and 'individual' are inseparable.

Dhag (1960) achieves an unprecedented evocativeness through a regional register of Marathi. Kautik, a rustic woman, trying to survive firmly and hopefully through every single happy-sad day, and her inter-relations with the persons around her, together create a new symphony style in *Dhag*. Uddhav Shelke has depicted in a classic style the multiple facets of poverty in our society, and how living in poverty with honesty and dignity is one of those facets. Kautik, who encourages her husband to start a tailoring business instead of staying shamelessly with his brother, reveals the handsome build of the labour-class language when she remarks to her husband in the *Māhānubhav* style, "You cut grass, then why should I be shy of making the hay-rick?" This novel with its total acceptance of reality never loses the touch of the earth. Shelke admits sex in his novel only to the extent it actually exists in our society. Having moved out of the short story field, and having written (in 1960) a highly brilliant novel inaugurating the new novel trend, how he later became a commercial, *riti*-type, pornographic writer, can be understood only in terms of the diabolic nature of our literary culture.

Though *Are Sansar Sansar* (Prabhakar Pendharkar, 1971) and *Andharwata* (Subhash Bhende, 1978) discuss the social life in Bombay, they avoid being pornographic. When these novels are compared with the *riti* trend novels on a similar subject, it becomes clear that the *kriti* trend novel finds its moral backbone inevitable. *Devacha Shabda* (Manohar Shahane, 1968) tells through the particulars of daily life the psychological tensions of a woman who cannot conceive, and, in avoiding the touch of poeticality, displays an able prose style.

The period between 1960 and 1970 should be considered the period of the arrival of a native Marathi prose style. In this direction a notable novel is V.H. Pitke's *Shidori* (1969), which performs the miracle of creating a highly poetic prose style out of the dry subject matter about a sugar factory. Its plotting remains confined to the factory campus, the plot is filled with the particulars of the daily life there, and the novel creates a framework of a pure human perception. Therefore a defined time and a defined space create a distinct imprint of reality and produce a subtle poetic sensation. *Shidori* proves in an omnipotent manner that true poetic quality does not lie in lyrical-ornamental language, but in identification in body, speech and spirit with everyday-ness.

It is little wonder that the formalistic-aestheticist criticism in Marathi had to shut its mouth after so many more 'strange' novels had been written one after another.

In Dinanath Manohar's *Robot* the *kriti*-orientation becomes more intense. The fascination of the new novel trend for reality more than for the imaginary is seen more clearly after 1970. The trend moving in that direction appears to integrate the other branches of novel such as the problem-novel, the sub-culture novel, and the regional novel. In *Robot*, a modern consciousness, entering the military life, creates the entirely Anglicized framework of that life by analysing every particular; besides it also does a moral assessment of the modern military culture which leads humanity to that Genghis Khan path. Robot is an example of how the writer's *kriti* can achieve a fundamental social edification in a highly imaginative way owing to its new morality. Shekhu, the soldier, who comments, "*Arrey*, they turn us into machines so that their civilized world will remain secure. Destroy us as men so that they can live as men", is only passingly referred to later as a casualty in a 'wash out' platoon on the front. Since the narration has a steady compass of morality, these novels indicate a definite direction even when they give such stray particulars.

A further developed form of the realistic style is seen in Anant Kadam's *Kide* (1971) and *Strot* (1977). His style employs the first person narrative technique for a honest subjective analysis and for presenting layers of a sensitive, self-agonising sensibility. It is lucid, and uses short colloquial sentences. But since they have a social content, his novels assimilate the first person narrator as a constituent of their social orientation. In *Kide* he employs the stream of consciousness technique to portray a day in the life of a young, unwanted, unemployed man. He has been sacked from his job because of a conspiracy by his corrupt colleagues against his refusal to accept a bribe. Yet his reaction is not that of a self-indulgent bitterness. To feel frustrated out of unemployment also smacks of a Philistine selfishness; the protagonist of *Kide* tries to perceive the reality and become contemplative. One should not roll in filth but one cannot help it if others want to do so: from this stand, the confused, unemployed young man's stream of consciousness embraces the whole of society in its sweet devotion within an hour of its flow. This manner of avoiding bitterness in the new novel is worth studying. This novel proves by *kriti* that frustration is not helplessness, disillusionment is not pessimism. When the protagonist had a job, his parents showered affection on him, his mother fed him with delicacies. Having lost his job, and with it the affection from the family and status outside, this protagonist sits in a broken chair in the veranda and looks at the entire chawl, its family portraits human beings, their attitudes, the crowds in the street; and a vast image of their all being insects ('*kide*') emerges before him. This value scale is retained throughout the novel. A young man's place in the family is out of economic necessity. It is also true that it would not be possible to earn outside without corruption. The technique of the stream of consciousness is apt for a person caught in a dilemma of this kind. It projects the gigantic terrifying character of urban social life It is only the man who is in search of the self-identity that can realise this gigantic character of the city life. Gradually he discovers his *kriti* in this dilemma. Without informing anyone he disappears from his home.

In *Strot* too Kadam's transparent, pure style of using a self-searching narrator's simple narration expressing an intense realism, attempts an evaluation of social values from a liberal ethical perspective. This *kriti* is an instance of the obvious realistic attitude on increase through the new novel. For instance

> "... the other reason is that I belong to a certain caste. My neighbour does not mention this openly, but this is what he always wants to suggest. I just laugh. The other day I casually said to him that I like the Buddha's philosophy more than Krishna's. On this he got furious. Fought like an enemy. What crime did I do in saying so? I did not want to ridicule Krishna. But what I can do if I find Buddha more appealing? I read the *Gita*. Twice or thrice. I did not follow it. It did not attract me. *Dhammapada* I read. I understood it. It attracted me. *Gita* is great. The great might have said so too. But I may not be capable of understanding it. I might be on a lower level. But I have no fascination with it. This is not so out of hatred. There is no hatred in my mind. But my neighbour does not understand this. It hurts (*Strot*, p. 13, 1977)

This middle-class young man, wanting to live merely as a human, has no expectations from the world. He is disturbed due to his inter-caste marriage. He has no expectations beyond his poverty, family, wife, children, and an easily manageable employment. While his children eat and drink of a morning, he feels disturbed by the outcry of innumerable children reaching his ears. He has no bitterness when he tells his wife that he could not borrow money for her delivery after trying in every direction. At times he bestows a mysterious quality on reality:

"The other day one of the sons woke up shrieking, 'Mother, mother'. 'Mother, please do not die!', was what he repeated to the wife. She held him near her bosom for a long time and soothed him. He had a terrifying dream. The three year old child could not be convinced that it was only a dream even after much convincing." (*Strot*, p. 16)

This protagonist has no biases. But they exist in society. And it becomes difficult for him to face that. The new novel has presented a variety of verbal *kritis* of confronting the society.

Summing Up

While summing up this general survey, let us try to determine the nature of progress made by the Marathi novel during the period in question. It is very clear that the retreat of realism dating back to the emergence of the Marathi novel has come to an end. A new cycle of Marathi novel has begun around 1960. Progress can be judged on the basis of a new cycle within a given tradition (Croce).[25] Progress stops when no writer in a prevalent cycle can overtake himself. This situation existed in Marathi around 1950. Yet, the writers caught within the old cycle continued to write. In the intervening decade, the imminent cycle was arrested by the culture hatched and the criticism nurtured by the short story. (*Bali*, 1950; *Bangarwadi*, 1955). Therefore in this decade only the *pratikriti*-trend novels and the pornographic, *riti*-trend novels were written. Though the reviewers-professors-publishers-editors with their punditic taste tried hard to push the old cycle forward during the decade, a new cycle of the *kriti*-oriented trend with its various branches started emerging. The novelists belonging to the latter prevented the punditic criticism. They accepted realism, selected novel subject matter, and, avoiding the unrealistic individualism, bridged the gulf between the individual and society. They brought techniques of finding out significance in social life and activity. They invented new aesthetic ideas. The novelists of the past two decades (1960–80) have proved by their practice that beauty can be found in the existing reality, that it is not necessary to turn away from the contemporary world to fantasy, to the past, or to an imaginary unreality. The new novel has also proved that the novel calls for a greater support of *kriti* and morality than that of entertainment, for the novelist as an artist must perform the cultural function of preserving, cultivating and enlarging cultural values. Albert Camus has stated that "The novel is born simultaneously with the spirit of rebellion and expresses, on the aesthetic plane, the same ambition".[26] During the decade before 1960, an atmosphere was systematically created so as not to allow any writer to take such a responsible stand. The new novel opposed it by its advocacy of *kriti*. The commitment with which Baba Padmanji expressed in his novel his hopes for women's emancipation and opposition to casteism, once again can be seen becoming strong during the post 1960 period. The creators of today's Marathi novel have come from varied social strata and possess intense sensitivity. There is both a qualitative and numerical growth in all formal and contextual constituents of the novel. There are visible signs that the new novel will endear itself to the whole next generation. The Marathi novel has come to be native. This should be mentioned as the most valuable gain of the novel during this period.

But it would be being ignorant of the Marathi tradition to surmise on this basis that the future of the Marathi novel is bright. No critic from an undeveloped literary culture must make a statement like that. In Marathi, once in a while a good novel takes birth and, quickly, loses itself in history. (*Ranangan*, 1939). Later on its creator starts making films like *Sohrab Rustum*. Thereafter, even the critics in their infancy keep dropping its name as a literary fashion: this is one type of childishness. The other is that if a writer with an inborn creative talent emerges, he has to turn to writing rubbish (Uddhav Shelke). Once every score years someone like Justice Ranade down to Ashok Shahane has been exposing the inferior quality of Marathi literature. One cannot be sure if even this will continue for a long time. Rajwade, the historian, had said in 1902 that "novelists of fierce talent" are born, not made. But no one can have control over this factor, and therefore it is not enough just to have said so. Every generation, every literate society, needs novelists that will refine the sensibility of the society. That becomes possible in a healthy literary culture. Therefore it has now become necessary for Marathi criticism to devote itself to creating an atmosphere congenial to creative literature. Or else such surveys as the present one do not reach even a good bibliography. That a good bibliography is a more useful literary activity than irresponsible criticism can be easily proved by comparing Shankar Ganesh Date and the childish critics of this period. The Marathi generation which is caught between such backwardness on one hand and the creational dilemma as to whether a work of art narrates, or whether it is narrating itself, on the other hand, does not have a very promising future. After all the meaning of culture is 'growing', though we erroneously keep using the term *sanskriti* to express the concept. Our cultural responsibility is not fully discharged in merely discussing what has grown; to sow properly, to tend it and to destroy the pestilence of destructive tendencies are activities of greater cultural value. They are more deserving topics for discussion. There is little possibility of the situation changing for the better unless the next generation revolutionizes criticism and cures Marathi of its present poverty of taste.

Bhalchandra Nemade, from Setu *Vol. II, No. I, 1985*

translated by G.N. Devy

REFERENCES

1. Claude Levi-Strauss, *Structural Anthropology*, Vol.I, tr. Jacobson & Schoepf, Harmondsworth, Penguin Books, 1963, p. 21.
2. Ian Raeside, 'Early Prose Fiction in Marathi', *The Journal of Asian Studies*, August 1968, pp. 791–808.
3. Ralph Linton, 'Nativistic Movements', *Ralph Linton*, Adelin Linton and Charles Wagle (eds.), New York, Columbia University Press, 1971, pp. 112–7.
4. M.G. Ranade, 'A Note on the Growth of Marathi Literature, 1898', *The Miscellaneous Writings of the Late Hon' ble Justice M.G. Ranade*, 1915, p.14.
5. Gangadhar Patil, *Parisamvad* (Annual 1972) ed. V.R. Dhavle & V.D. Kulkarni, pp. 37–42.
6. Suniti Kumar Chatterji, *Indo-Aryan and Hindi*, Ahmedabad, Gujarat Vernacular Society, 1942, p. 102.
7. Naro Sadashiv Risbud, 'Preface', *Manjughosha* 1867/11th ed., Pune, Modern Book Depot, 1962, pp. 15–16.
8. K.B. Marathe, *Naval Va Natak Hyanvishayi Nibandha*, Bombay, 1872, p. 16; V.K. Rajwade, 'Kadambari', *Granthmala*, Kolhapur, V.G. Vijapurkar, 1902, pp. 15–16.
9. Anil Seal, *The Emergence of Indian Nationalism*, Cambridge, Cambridge University Press, 1971, pp. 89–93.
10. L.S.S. O' Malley, *Modern India and the West*, Chapter XVI, London, Oxford University Press, 1941, p. 585.
11. M.G. Ranade, *op. cit.*, p. 52.
12. G.M. Pawar (ed.), 'Preface', *Maharshi Vi. Ra. Shinde Yanchi Rojnishi*, Aurangabad, Marathawada Sahitya Parishad, 1979, p. 43.
13. Ashok Kelkar, *Marathi Bhashecha Arthik Sansar*, Aurangabad, Marathawada Sahitya Parishad, 1977, Chapter III.
14. S.R. Kulkarni, *Prachin Marathi Gadya: Prerana Va Parampara*, Bombay, Sindhu Publications, 1970, pp. 57–64.
15. Kusumawati Deshpande, *Marathi Kadambari: Pahile Shatak*, Bombay, Mumbai Sangh, 1953, p. 17.
16. S.R. Jog, *Marathi Vangmayabhiruchiche Vihangamalokan*, Pune, Poona University, 1959.
17. Sir Richard Temple, *Men and Events of My Time in India*, London, John Murray, 1882, p. 495.

18. P.V. Bapat & N.V. Godbole, *Marathi Kadambari: Tantra Va Vikas*, 3rd edition, Venus Prakashan, 1973, p. 3.
19. N.S. Phadke, 'Marathi Kadambarichi Vatchal', *Parisamvad*, Pune, Kulkarni Granthagar, 1972.
20. F. Max Muller, 'On the Migration of Fables', *Chips from a German Workshop*, Vol IV, London, Longman, Green & Co., 1907, pp. 412–89; H.G. Rawlinson, 'Indian Influence on the West', L.S.S.O' Malley, *op.cit.*, p. 536.
21. N.S. Phadke, *op.cit.*
22. Bhalchandra Nemade, 'New Morality in the Contemporary Marathi Novel', *Vagartha*, July 1977, pp. 1–5, reprinted in *Indian Literature*, Sept–Oct 1978, pp.34–8; L.G. Jog, 'Navi Marathi Kadambari', *Alochana*, Feb 1971, pp.17–35.
23. Bhalchandra Nemade, 'Halli Lekhakacha Lekhakrao Hoto To Ka?', *Vacha*-2, Aurangabad 1962, pp. 17–28.
24. Bhalchandra Nemade, 'Adhunik Marathi Kadambaritil Vastavachya Chitranachi Tantre Va Shaili', *Vangmayin Shaili Ani Tantra*, ed. M.D. Hatkananglekar, Kolhapur, Abhijat Prakashan, 1981.
25. Benedetto Croce, *Aesthetics*, tr. D. Ainslie, London, Vision Press, 1962, pp. 136–7.
26. Albert Camus, *The Rebel*, Chapter IV, 'Rebellion and the Novel', tr. A. Bower, Harmondsworth, Penguin Books, 1962, p. 224.

GAYATRI CHAKRAVORTY SPIVAK

Gayatri Chakravorty Spivak is, as was A.K. Ramanujan, an expatriate Indian. She teaches at Columbia University. She became famous with her translation of Jacques Derrida's *Grammatology* from French to English. The translation was prefaced by an elaborate and provocative 'Introduction', which has become a much quoted piece of literary criticism in recent years. Though Gayatri Chakravorty has been one of the most influential theorists in the US, she, like Edward Said, is deeply engaged in concerns related to her Third World identity. More recently, she has been writing/lecturing about feminism in the context of Indian culture and literature and translating the writings of Mahasweta Devi.

Mahasweta Devi is a significant Bangla fiction writer. Her stories and novels have been translated into many Indian languages, and also into English. She works with tribals and rural people of India, and writes about social reality. She received the Jnanapith award for her creative writing and the Magsaysay award for her social work. Though she has written about a variety of themes, in recent years she has come to be recognised in the Western world as a spokesperson for the underprivileged and for women. A shorter work on a similar theme is 'Stanadayini', which Gayatri Chakravorty has translated under the title 'Breastgiver'. The essay included here rests on that story, and tries to establish the subaltern perspective of woman/subject in Bangla society.

The original essay has appended the translation of 'Stanadayini' to it. It has not been possible to include the translation here for reasons of space.

A series of volumes under the title *Subaltern Studies* edited by Ranajit Guha was published during the 1980s and 1990s (Oxford University Press, Delhi). The '*subaltern studies*' provided a new historiographical perspective. Gayatri Chakravorty's essay forms part of one of the *Subaltern* volumes. It is reproduced here as it is generally considered to be a fine example of the employment of recent Western theory for discussing non-western positions.

"A Literary Representation of the Subaltern: Mahasweta Devi's *Stanadayini*", in *Subaltern Studies* Vol. V, Oxford University Press, Delhi, 1987, pp.91–134.

A Literary Representation of the Subaltern: Mahasweta Devi's 'Stanadayini'[1]

A historian confronts a text of counterinsurgency or gendering where the subaltern has been represented. He unravels the text to assign a new subject-position to the subaltern, gendered or otherwise.

A teacher of literature confronts a sympathetic text where the gendered subaltern has been represented. She unravels the text to make visible the assignment of subject-positions.

These two operations are similar but not identical. By way of a teaching strategy for Mahasweta Devi's 'Stanadayini' (Breast Giver), this essay circulates among the similarities and differences.[2] By its end I will hope to have importuned the reader at least to entertain the following propositions:

a. The performance of these tasks, of the bistorian and the teacher of literature, must critically 'interrupt' each other, bring each other to crisis, in order to serve their constituencies; especially when each seems to claim all for its own.
b. The teacher of literature, because of her institutional subject position, can and must 're-constellate' the text to draw out its use. She can and must wrench it out of its proper context and put it within alien arguments.
c. If thus placed in the arguments from Western Marxist-Feminism, Western Liberal Feminism, and French high theory of the female body, 'Stanadayini' can show us some of their limits and limitations.
d. This might have implications for the current and continued subalternization of so-called 'third world' literatures.

The essay will also touch upon the always tendentious question of elite methodologies and subaltern material. I suppose it needs to be said that the problem of 'what to do' about the gendered subaltern cannot be solved in any interpretive essay, historical or literary. An essay such as this one can perhaps give an idea of the extent and politics of the problem somewhat more soberly than invocations of the immediacy of the need for social justice or the ineluctability of a woman's domain.

I. *The Historian and the Teacher of Literature*

The production of historical accounts is the discursive narrativization of events. When historiography is self-consciously 'non-theoretical' it sees its task, with respect to rival historical accounts of the same period, as bringing forth 'what really happened' in a value neutral prose. Since the incursion of 'theory' into the discipline of history, and the uncomfortable advent of Michel Foucault, it is no longer too avant-garde to suspect or admit that 'events' are never not discursively constituted and that the language of historiography is always also language.

The fact that every object is constituted as an object of discourse has nothing to do with whether there is a world external to thought, or with the realism/idealism opposition. An earthquake or the falling of a brick is an event that certainly exists .... But whether their specificity as object is constructed in terms of 'natural phenomena' or 'expressions of the wrath of God', depends upon the structure of a discursive field. What is denied is not that such objects exist externally to thought, but the rather different assertion that they would constitute themselves as objects outside any discursive condition of emergence.[3]

The thought of 'how events exist' can itself be complicated in different ways via, say, Heidegger or particle physics; and I remain troubled by anything that claims to have nothing to do with its opposition.[4] Avoiding these perils, however, one might still posit an active relationship between historical and literary representation as discursive formations. With this in mind let us consider a celebrated passage in the early Foucault which establishes 'discourse' in the sense in which Laclau and Mouffe use it above.

The problem examined in the Foucauldian passage is not merely if *events* exist outside of discourse but also if language (sentences, propositions, signs) exists only to report events. Foucault is making a distinction between language as sentence, proposition and sign, and what he calls 'statement' (*enonciation*).

Among other things, a statement is 'the function of existence' of language 'on the basis of which one may ... decide ... whether or not (it) 'make(s) sense'.[5] A 'statement' involves the positioning of a subject (the place of the 'I'):

> The subject of the statement should not be regarded as identical with the author of the formulation. It is not in fact the cause, origin, or starting point of the phenomenon of the written or spoken articulation of a sentence... it is not the constant, motionless, unchanging arena (*foyer*) of a series of operations... It is a determined (*determinee*) and vacant place that may in fact be filled by different individuals.... If a proposition, a sentence, a group of signs can be called 'statement', it is not in so far as there had been (*dans la mesure ou il y a eu*) one day, someone to utter (*proferer*) them or to deposit somewhere their provisional mark (*en deposer quelque part la trace provisoire*); it is in so far as (*dans la mesure ou*) *the position of the subject can be assigned.* To describe a formulation qua statement does not consist in analyzing the relations between the author

and what he says (or wanted to say, or said without wanting to); but in determining what position can and must be occupied by any individual if he is to be the subject of it.[6]

This understanding of a statement does not entail ignoring what it is that sentences report or tell. It is the precondition for the analysis of how the what is made. That is what a 'discursive formation' is: 'the formation of objects, the formation of enunciative modalities, the formation of concepts, the formation of strategies.[7] Not even the simplest reporting or telling can avoid these manoeuvres. Foucault asks us to remember that what is reported or told is also reported or told and thus entails a positioning of the subject. Further, that anyone dealing with a report or a tale (the material of historiography or literary pedagogy) can and must occupy a certain 'I'-slot in these dealings. The particularity of this 'I'-slot is a sign. It may for instance signify a socio-political, psycho-sexual, disciplinary-institutional or ethno-economic provenance. Hence, Foucault uses the word 'assigned': 'the position of the subject can be assigned'. There may be a hidden agenda in covering over this rather obvious thing. For the purpose of this essay the 'I' - slots (subject-positions) to be kept in mind are: author, reader, teacher, subaltern, historian.

It is well-known that Foucault was finally disaffected from this project.[8] But many of the subalternist historians are, in my judgement wisely, working within its wider implications. One of these implications is that the archival or archaeological work of historigraphy might resemble a certain work of reading which is usually associated with literary interpretation if it is detached from its psychologistic or characterological orthodoxy. In this view it is as if the narrativizations of history are structured or textured like what is called literature. Here one must re-think the notion that fiction derives from the truth as its negation. In the context of archival historiography, the possibility of fiction cannot be derived.[9]

That history deals with real events and literature with imagined ones may now be seen as a difference in degree rather than in kind. The difference between cases of historical and literary events will always be there as a differential moment in terms of what is called 'the effect of the real'.[10] What is called history will always seem more real to us than what is called literature. Our very uses of the two separate words guarantees that.[11] This difference can never be exhaustively systematized. In fact the ways in which the difference is articulated also has a hidden agenda. The historians' resistance to fiction relates to the fact that the writing of history and of literature has a social connotation even when these activities do not resemble what we understand by them today; and that historiography and literary pedagogy are disciplines.

Mahasweta Devi's own relationship to historical discourse seems clear. She has always been gripped by the individual in history. Up to and including *Hajar Churashir Ma* (1973–4) her prose belonged to the generally sentimental style of the mainstream Bengali novel of the fifties and the sixties. To this reader it seems as if the vision of *Hajar Churashir Ma* - the bringing-to-crisis of the personal through a political event of immediate magnitude (the 'climactic phase of the annihilation of the urban naxalites') pushed Mahasweta from what was perceived as 'literary' or 'subjective' into an experiment with a form perceived as 'historical'.[12] The stories of *Agnigarbha* (collected in 1978) mark the site of this difficult move. In *Aranyer Adhikar* (1977) the prose is beginning to bend into full-fledged 'historical fiction', history imagined into fiction. The division between fact (historical event) and fiction (literary event) is operative in all these moves. Indeed, her repeated claim to legitimacy is that she researches thoroughly everything she represents in fiction.

Fiction of this sort relies for its effect on its 'effect of the real'. The plausibility of Jashoda ('Stanadayini'), a Draupadi ('Draupadi,' *Agnigarbha*), a Birsha Munda (*Aranyer Adhikar*) is that they could have existed as subalterns in a specific historical moment imagined and tested by orthodox assumptions. When the subalternist historian imagines a historical moment, within which shadowy named characters, backed up by some counter-insurgent or dominant-gender textual material, have their plausible being, in order that a historical narrative can coherently take shape, the assumptions are not very different. Those who read or write literature can claim as little of subaltern status as those who read or write history. The difference is that the subaltern as object is supposed to be imagined in one case and real in another. I am suggesting that it is a bit of both in both cases. The writer acknowledges this by claiming to do research (my fiction is also historical). The historian might acknowledge this by looking at the mechanics of representation (my history is also fictive). It is with this suggestion that I submit the following pages to the Subaltern Studies collective. I hope it will be admitted that my brief is very different from saying that history is only literature.

II. *The Author's Own Reading: A Subject Position*

By Mahasweta Devi's own account 'Stanadayini' is a parable of India after decolonization.[13] Like the protagonist Jashoda, India is a mother-by-hire. All classes of people, the post-war rich, the ideologues, the indigenous bureaucracy, the diasporics, the people who are sworn to protect the new state, abuse and exploit her. If nothing is done to sustain her, nothing given back to her, and if scientific help comes too late, she will die of a consuming cancer. I suppose if one extended this parable the end of the story might come to 'mean' something like this: the ideological construct 'India' is too deeply informed by the goddess-infested reverse sexism of the Hindu majority. As long as there is this hegemonic cultural self-representation of India as a goddess-mother (dissimulating the possibility that this mother is a slave), she will collapse under the burden of the immense expectations that such a self-representation permits.

This interesting reading is not very useful from the perspective of a study of the subaltern. Here the representation of India is by way of the subaltern as metaphor. By the rules of a parable the logic of the connection between the tenor and the vehicle of the metaphor must be made absolutely explicit.[14] Under the imperatives of such a reading the 'effect of the real' of the vehicle must necessarily be underplayed. The subaltern must be seen only as the vehicle of a greater meaning. The traffic between the historian and the writer that I have been proposing could not be justified if one devoted oneself to this reading. In order that Mahasweta's parable be disclosed, what must be excluded from the story is precisely the attempt to represent the subaltern as such. I will therefore take the risk of putting to one side that all too neat reading and unravel the text to pick up the threads of the excluded attempt.

This takes me to a general argument implicit within the study of the subaltern in the context of decolonization: if the story of the rise of nationalist resistance to imperialism is to be disclosed coherently, it is the role of the indigenous subaltern that must be strategically excluded. Then it can be argued that, in the initial stages of the consolidation of territorial imperialism, no organized political resistance was forthcoming. Through access to the cultural aspects of imperialism the colonized countries acceded to sentiments of nationhood. It was then that genuine anti-imperialist resistance developed.[15]

As in the case of the opposition between fact and fiction, there is a certain paratheoretical good sense in this. The exclusions that must operate in order to preserve that good sense are at least two-fold. First, if nationalism is the only discourse credited with emancipatory possibilities in the imperialist theatre, then one must ignore the innumerable subaltern examples of resistance throughout the imperialist and pre-imperialist centuries, often suppressed by those very forces of nationalism which would be instrumental in changing the geo-political conjuncture from territorial imperialism to neo-colonialism, and which seem particularly useless in current situations of struggle.[16] Secondly, if only the emancipatory possibilities of the culture of imperialism are taken into account, the distortions in the ideals of a national culture when imported into a colonial theatre would go unnoticed.[17]

Citizens of the nation must give something to the nation rather than merely take from it, the gist of Mahasweta's own reading of 'Stanadayini', is one of the many slogans of a militant nationalism. It can accommodate sentiments extending from '*sat koti santanere he mughdha janani, rekhechho bangali kore manush karoni*' (fond mother, you have kept your seven million children Bengalis but haven't made them human - Tagore) to 'Ask not what your country can do for you' (John F. Kennedy, Inaugural Address). In spite of the best possible personal politics, the reading Mahasweta Devi offers of her own story, entailing her subject-position as writer, signifies that narrative of nationalism that is perceived as a product of the culture of imperialism. This too obliges me to set it aside and to wonder what her text, as statement, articulates that must in its turn be set aside so that her reading can emerge..

III. *The Teacher and Reader(s): More Subject-Positions*

Mahasweta's text might show in many ways how the narratives of nationalism have been and remain irrelevant to the life of the sub-ordinate. The elite culture of nationalism participated and participates with the colonizer in various ways.[18] In Mahasweta's story we see the detritus of that participation.

In a certain sense we witness there the ruins of the ideas of parliamentary democracy and of the nation when bequeathed to the elite of a colonized people outside the supposedly 'natural' soil of the production of those ideas. Some of us would speculate that, used as a teaching tool (from within the subject-position of the teacher in a certain discursive formation), stories such as this can deconstruct those ideas even in their natural habitat. It is for us important that in 'Stanadayini' the piece of flotsam least susceptible to those ideas is the subaltern as gendered subject, a subject-position different from the subaltern as class-subject. In orthodox literary-critical circles the authority of the author's reading still holds a certain glamour. By way of Foucault I have therefore taken some pains to explain why I focus on the subaltern as gendered subject rather than as an allegorical seme for Mother India.

If 'the need to make the subaltern classes the subject of their own history (has, among other) themes.... provided a fresh critical thrust to much recent writing on modern Indian history and society', then a text about the (im)possibility of 'making' the subaltern gender the subject of its own story seems to me to have a certain pertinence.[19] Toward the end of this essay I will discuss the need to put the 'im' of 'impossible' in parentheses.

Accounts of history and literary pedagogy, as they appropriate and disseminate reports and tales, are two ways in which mind-sets are set.[20] The reading of

'Stanadayini' presented here, assigning the subject-position to the teacher/reader, can be helpful in combating a certain tendency in literary pedagogy that still shapes, by remote control, the elite in the most prestigious Indian educational institutions: the so-called radical teaching of literary criticism and literature in the United States and perhaps also in Britain.

This dominant 'radical' reader in the Anglo-US reactively homogenizes the Third World and sees it only in the context of nationalism and ethnicity. The dominant reader in India who is resistant to such homogenization, and who is to be distinguished from students of reading theory in elite Indian institutions, inhabits a reading practice that is indistinguishable from the *orthodox* position in the Anglo-US. This Indian reader, a faceless person within the sphere of influence of a post-colonial humanistic education (I use this awkward terminology because sociologists, economists, doctors, scientists, etc. are not outside of this sphere), takes this orthodox position to be the 'natural' way to read literature. The position is undergirded by the author's account of her 'original vision'. In this particular case that account (the reading of the story as a parable) would forbid the fulfilment of another assumption implicit in the orthodox position, the psychologistic or characterological assumption that we 'feel' the story as if it is gossip about non-existent people. The general reader can straddle such contradictions easily. The historians, anthropologists, sociologists and doctors among them can know or show that any group's perception of the 'natural' meanings of things may be discursively constructed through an erring common sense. When, however, it comes to their own presuppositions about the 'natural' way to read literature, they cannot admit that this might be a construction as well, that this subject-position might also be assigned. Given that this way of reading has been in control for at least a couple of centuries in post-Enlightenment Europe, and has served to distinguish our indigenous elite from the uneducated, to read thus certainly engages our affects.[21] I will not enter the abstruse arguments about the historicity or phenomenality of affects.[22] Nor will I suggest that there is a correct way to train our affects. Indeed, it is not only 'false consciousness' that is 'ideological'. A Foucauldian or, in this case, deconstructive, position would obligue us to admit that 'truths' are constructions as well, and that we cannot avoid producing them.

Without venturing up to the perilous necessity of asking the question of true readings or true feelings, then, I will propose an alternative. Let us jealously guard the orthodoxy's right to be 'moved' by literature 'naturally', and tremble before the author's authority. But let us also consider 'literature' as a use of language where the transactional quality of reading is socially guaranteed. A literary text exists between writer and reader. This makes literature peculiarly susceptible to didactic use. When literature is used didactically it is generally seen as a site for the deployment of themes, even the theme of the undoing of thematicity, of unreadability, of undecidability.[23] This is not a particularly 'elite' approach, although it may be called 'unnatural'. On the one hand Marxist literary criticism as well as a remark like Chinua Achebe's 'all art is propaganda, though not all propaganda is art' can be taken as cases of such a 'thematic' approach.[24] On the other hand some 'elite' approaches (deconstructive, structuralist, semiotic, structuralist-psychoanalytic, phenomenological, discourse-theoretical; though not necessarily feminist, reader-responsist, intertextual, or linguistic) can also be accommodated here.

(Any reader nervous about the fact that Mahasweta Devi has probably not read much of the material critically illuminated by her text should stop here.)

IV. *(Elite) Approaches: 'Stanadayini' in Marxist Feminism*

An allegorical or parabolic reading of 'Stanadayini' such as Mahasweta's own would reduce the complexity of the signals put up by the text. Let us consider another reductive allegorical or parabolic reading. This reading can be uncovered in terms of a so-called Marxist-feminist thematics. Peculiar to the orthodoxy of US Marxist-feminism and some, though not all, British varieties, these thematics unfold in a broadly pre-Althusserian way.[25]

Here is a representative generalization: 'It is the provision by men of means of subsistence to women during the child-bearing period, and not the sex division of labour in itself, that forms the material basis for women's subordination in class society.[26]

If one were teaching 'Stanadayini' as the site of a critical deployment of Marxist-feminist thematics, one would point out that the text reverses this generalization. The protagonist subaltern Jashoda, her husband crippled by the youngest son of a wealthy household, becomes a wet-nurse for them. Her repeated gestation and lactation support her husband and family. By the logic of the production of value they are both means of production. By the logic of sexual reproduction he is her means of production (though not owned by her) as the field-beast or the beast of burden is the slave's. In fact, even as it reverses the Marxist-feminist generalization I quote above, Jashoda's predicament also undoes, by placing within a gender-context, the famous Roman distinction, invoked by Marx, between *instrumentum vocale* ('the speaking tool' - Jashoda, the woman-wife-mother) and *instrumentum semi-vocale* (the working beast-Kangali, the man-husband-father).[27] This is worth noticing because one of the most important Marxist-feminist critiques of the labour theory of value is that it does not take sexual reproduction into account when speaking of social reproduction or the reproduction of labour-power.[28]

The political economy of the sexual division of labour changes considerably by the sale of Jashoda's labour-power, which is specific to the female of the species. One may even call this a moment of transition from one mode of social reproduction to another. Or perhaps one could call it the moment of the emergence of value and its immediate extraction and appropriation. These changes take place within extended domestic economy. One might therefore call it a transition from the domestic to the 'domestic'. 'Stanadayini' stalls the classic Engelsian-feminist narrative, which sees the family as the agent of transition from domestic to civil, private to public, home to work, sex to class. It should be pointed out that it also displaces the new Marxist-feminist critique of such a position (which I quote below) by bringing back the focus on the mothering female: 'The identification of the family as the sole site of maintenance of labour power overstates its role at the level of immediate production. It fetishizes the family at the level of total social reproduction, by representing generational replacement as the only source of renewal of society's labour force.'[29]

The emergence of (exchange) value and its immediate appropriation in 'Stanadayini' may be thematized as follows: The milk that is produced in one's own body for one's own children is a use-value. When there is a superfluity of use values, exchange values arise. That which cannot be used is exchanged. As soon as the (exchange) value of Jashoda's milk emerges, it is appropriated. Good food and constant sexual servicing are provided so that she can be kept in prime condition for optimum lactation. The milk she produces for children is presumably though 'necessary labour'. The milk that she produces for the children of her master's family is through 'surplus labour.' Indeed, this is how the origin of this transition is described in the story: 'But today, hearing from his wife about Jashoda's *surplus* (in English in the original) milk, the second son said all of a sudden, 'way found'. (p.259)

In order to keep her in prime condition to produce surplus, the sexual division of labour is easily reversed. Her husband is relegated to housework. 'Now take up the cooking at home and give her a rest', says the Mistress. 'Two of her own, three here, how can she cook at day's end after suckling five?' (p.260) This particular parabolic or allegoric reading is not necessarily disqualified by the fact that Jashoda's body produces a surplus that is fully consumed by the owners of her labour-power and leads to no *capital* accumulation (as it would have if the milk had been bottled and sold in the open market at a profit), although rearing children is indirectly an 'investment in the future'. Like the economy of the temple (which will provide the husband a patriarchal escape route), this domestic/ 'domestic' transition survives in a relatively autonomous way in the pores of a comprador capitalism whose outlines are only shadowily indicated in Mahasweta's story. If within this pre-capitalist surplus appropriation we assumed Jashoda's milk to be standing in for the 'universal equivalent' in the restricted 'domestic' sphere, we might get away with pronouncing that the situation is what Marx, with obviously unwitting irony, would describe as 'simple reproduction.'[30]

This account of the deployment of some Marxist-feminist 'themes' introduces a stutter in the presupposition that women's work is typically non-productive of value. I am not considering women's insertion into the labour-process. In that narrative woman is less than the norm of 'free labour'. I am half-fantasizing, rather, about an area where the product of a woman's body has been historically susceptible to idealization — just as, in the classical Marxian argument, the reason why the free (male) labourer becomes a 'proletarian' under capitalism is not that he has nothing but his body but that, his product, being a value-term, is susceptible to idealization. The commodity, by the same token, is susceptible to being transformed to commodity-capital.[31] Yet the word 'proletarian' – 'One who serves the state with nothing but his (*sic*) offspring' (OED) - continues to carry an effaced mark of sexuality. Am I then proposing to endorse some weird theory where labour-power is replaced by the power of gestation and lactation? Or am I suggesting that the study of this particular female activity, professional mothering, as it is to be found, for example, in Fanny Fay-Sallois's excellent *Les Nourrices à Paris aux XIX siècle*, be included in any study of the subaltern?[32]

I am suggesting both less and more. I see no particular reason to curtail the usefulness of classical Marxist analysis, within its own limits, by a tendentious requirement for uncritical inclusiveness. Any critique of strategic exclusions should bring analytical presuppositions to crisis. Marxism and feminism must become persistent interruptions of each other. The 'mode of existence' of literature, as of language, is where 'the task of understanding does not basically amount to *recognizing* the form used, but .... to understanding its novelty and *not* to recognize its identity... The understander, belonging to the same language community, is attuned to the 'linguistic form *not* as a fixed, self-identical signal, but as a changeable and adaptable sign... The ideal of mastering a language is absorption of signality by pure semioticity.'[33]

As the user, occupying different instituted 'I'-slots, understands the supposedly self-identical signal, always supposedly indicating the same thing, she persistently distances herself, in heterogeneous ways, from that monumentalized self-identity, the 'proper meaning.'[34] We can use 'Stanadayini', a discursive literary production, from the perspective of Marxist-feminist thematics by considering how it helps us distance ourselves from two self-identical propositions that ground much of subalternist analysis implicitly:

a) that the free worker as such is male (hence, the narrative of value-emergence and value-appropriation; the labour power specific to the female body is susceptible to the production of value in the strict sense);
b) that the *nature* of woman is physical, nurturing and affective (hence the professional-mother).

A good deal of feminist scholarship has reasonably and soberly analysed and revised these propositions in recent years.[35] I will consider two provocative examples at the end of this section. Such painstaking speculative scholarship, though invaluable to our collective enterprise, does, however, *reason* gender into existing paradigms.[36] By contrast, emphasizing the literariness of literature, pedagogy invites us to take a distance from the continuing project of reason. Without this supplementary distancing, a position and its counter-position, both held in the discourse of reason, will keep legitimizing each other. Feminism and masculism, benevolent or militant, might not then be able to avoid becoming opposing faces of each other.[37]

Resuming, then, our fabulation with Marxist-feminist thematics on the occasion of 'Stanadayini', let us consider Jashoda's 'alienation' from her breasts:

> She thought of her breasts as most precious objects. At night when Kangalicharan (her husband) started to give her a feel she said, 'Look, I'm going to pull our weight with these. Take good care how you use them'. Jashoda had forever scrubbed her breasts carefully with soap and oil, for the master's sons had put the nipples in their mouth. Why did these breasts betray her in the end? ..... Knowing these breasts to be the rice-winner she had constantly conceived to keep them filled with milk (pp. 260, 271, 275).

Just as the wage-worker cannot distinguish between necessary and surplus labour, so the gendered 'proletarian,' - serving the *oikos* rather than the *polis* with nothing but her (power to produce) offspring - comes to call the so-called sanctity of motherhood into question. At first Mahasweta broaches it derisively:

> Is a Mother so cheaply made?
> Not just by dropping a babe.

Finally it becomes part of Jashoda's last sentient judgement: 'If you suckle you're a mother, all lies. Nepal and Gopal (her own sons) don't look at me, and the Master's boys don't spare a peek to ask how I'm doing. The sores on her breast kept mocking her with a hundred mouths, a hundred eyes'. (p.271).

By contrast, her final judgement, the universalization of foster-motherhood, is a mistake: 'The doctor who sees her every day, the person who will cover her face with a sheet, will put her on a cart, will lower her at the burning ghat, the untouchable who will put her in the furnace, are all her milk sons' (p.276). Such a judgement can only be 'right' within the pieties of Mahasweta's own nationalist reading.

The Marxian fable of a transition from the domestic to the 'domestic' mode of social reproduction has no more than a strained plausibility here. In order to construct it, one must entertain a grounding assumption, that the originary state of 'necessary labour' is where the lactating mother produces a use value. For whose use? If you consider her in a subject-position, it is a situation of exchange, with the child, for immediate and future psycho-social affect. Even if we read the story as a proto-nationalist parable about Mother India, it is the failure of this exchange that is the substance of the story. It is this failure, the absence of the child as such, that is marked by the enigmatic answer-question-parataxis towards the conclusion: 'Yet someone was supposed to be there at the end. Who was it? It was who? Who was it? Jashoda died at 11 p.m.' (p.276).

By dismantling (professional) motherhood and suckling into their minute particulars, 'Stanadayini' allows us to differentiate ourselves from the axiomatics of a certain 'Marxist-feminism' which is obliged to ignore the subaltern woman as subject.

If Lise Vogel, from whom I drew my representative generalization, signals a certain orthodoxy, Ann Ferguson, in 'On Conceiving Motherhood', shows us a way out of it via the question of affect:

> Although different societies have had different modes of sex/affective production at different times, a cross-cultural constant is involved in different modes of bourgeois patriarchal sex/affective production. This is that women as mothers are placed in a structural bind by mother-centered infant and small child care, a bind that ensures that mothers will give more than they get in the sex/affective parenting triangle in which even lesbian and single parents are subjected.[38]

'Mothers will give more than they get.' If this broad generalization is broadened so that the distinction between domestic ('natural' mother) and 'domestic' (waged wet-nurse) disappears, this can certainly serve as a constant for us and can be a good tool for our students.[39] Yet it should also be acknowledged that such a broadening might make us misrepresent important details. A text such as 'Stanadayini', even if taught as nothing but sociological evidence, can shown how imprecise it is to write: 'In stratified class and caste societies, different economic classes and racial/ethnic groups may hold different sex/gender ideals, although when this happens the lower classes are usually categorized as inferior male and female types by nature'.[40] (I am referring, of course, to the class-subalternity of the Brahmin and the grotesque functioning of caste marked within subalternity. Jashoda is a complicit victim of all these factors.) It is possible that it is not only 'the relationship between the three domination systems (class, racial/ethnic, and sex/gender)' that is 'dialectical' but that in the theatres of decolonization the relationship between indigenous and imperialist systems of domination are also 'dialectical', even when they are variously related to the Big Three Systems cited above. Indeed, the relationship might not be 'dialectical' at all but discontinuous, 'interruptive'.

It is often the case that revisionist socialist-feminism trivializes basic issues in the Marxist system.[41] Ferguson writes, for example: 'My theory, unlike one tendency within classic Marxist theory, does not privilege the economic realm (the production of *things* to meet human material needs and the manner in which the social surplus gets appropriated) as the material base for all human domination relations.... The production of things and the production of people.... interpenetrate.'[42]

This is an excellent advance on generalizations such as Vogel's. But it is an oversimplification of Marx's view of the economic sphere. That sphere is the site of the production of *value*, not *things*. As I have mentioned earlier, it is the body's susceptibility to the production of value which makes it vulnerable to idealization and therefore to insertion into the economic. This is the ground of the labour theory of value. It is here that the story of the emergence of value from Jashoda's labour-power infiltrates Marxism and questions its gender-specific presuppositions. The production of people through sexual reproduction and affective socialization, on the other hand, presupposes mothers embodied not as female humans but only as mothers and belongs properly speaking to the sphere of politics and ideology (domination).[43] Of course it interpenetrates the economic sphere (exploitation), the sphere of the production of value, of the sustained alienation of the body to which the very nature of labour-power makes the body susceptible. In spite of the greatest sympathy for the mother, Ferguson's ignoring of the mother's body obliges her to ignore the woman as subject of the production of value. 'Stanadayini's lesson may be simply this: when the economic as such (here shown in terms of the woman's body) enters in, mothers are divided, women can exploit, not merely dominate. Ideology sustains and interpenetrates this operation of exploitation.

Anna Davin's meticulous 'Imperialism and Motherhood' shows us the development of sex/affective control within the context of class-struggle.

('Imperialism' and 'War' here are political signifiers used for ideological mobilization.[44] In Davin's account, the great narrative of the development of capitalism is untroubled by discontinuities and interruptions. She describes the construction of the British National Subject on the bodies of British mothers.[45] Public opinion is under active construction so that the working of the privates may be adjudicated. *Mutatis mutandis*, echoes of these arguments from eugenics and educated mothercraft can be heard among the Indian indigenous elite today. The space where Jashoda, burdened by her ideological production, nourishes her cancer, is not accessible to that narrative.

In Davin's essay the central reference point is class. The *oikos* is fully a metaphor for the *polis.* Foster-mothers are Virgin Mothers. Christianity, the official religion, gives a little help to the ideology of the secular state.

The lack of fit between this neat narrative and the bewildering cacophony of 'Stanadayini' permits us to ask: why globalize? Why should a sociological study that makes astute generalizations about sex/affective production in the United States feel obliged to produce a 'cross-cultural constant?' Why should a study that exposes gender-mobilization in Britain purport to speak on the relationship between imperialism and motherhood? Why, on the contrary, does 'Stanadayini' invoke the singularity of the gendered subaltern? What is at stake here? How are these stakes different from those of imperialism as such? The story will make us come back to these questions.

V. *Elite Approaches: 'Stanadayini' in Liberal Feminism*

There is a tendency in the US towards homogenizing and reactive critical descriptions of Third World literatures. There is a second tendency, not necessarily related to the first, to pedagogic and curricular appropriation of Third World women's texts in translation by feminist teachers and readers who are vaguely aware of the race-bias within mainstream feminism: 'Black and Third World feminist organizations are thus developing within different racial and ethnic communities as an attempt to resolve intra-community the social crisis of the family and personal intimacy presently occurring across racial/ethnic lines. Influential members and groups within the white women's movement are presently seeking to make coalitions with black feminists, in part by dealing with the racism within the white women's movement.'[46]

There are problems with this basically benevolent impulse which are increasingly under scrutiny.[47] The ravenous hunger for Third World literary texts in English translation is part of the benevolence and the problem. Since by translating this text I am contributing to both I feel obliged to notice the text's own relationship to the thematic of liberal feminism. This will permit me also to touch directly the question of elite approaches to subaltern material.

Resisting 'elite' methodology for 'subaltern' material involves an epistemological/ontological confusion. The confusion is not elite (ontology), so must the historian not *know* through elite method (epistemology).

This is part of a much larger confusion: can men theorize feminism, can whites theorize racism, can the bourgeois theorize revolution, and so on.[48] It is when *only* the former groups theorize that the situation is politically intolerable. Therefore it is crucial that members of these groups are kept vigilant about their assigned subject-positions. It is disingenuous, however, to forget that, as the collectivities implied by the second group of nouns start participating in the production of knowledge about themselves, they must have a share in some of the structures of privilege that contaminate the first group. (Otherwise the ontological errors are perpetuated: it is unfortunate simply to be a woman - not a man, to be a black - not a white; and to be subaltern - not elite - is only the fault of the individual.) Therefore did Gramsci speak of the subaltern's rise into hegemony; and Marx of associated labour benefiting from 'the forms that are common to all social modes of production.[49] This is also the reason behind one of the assumptions of subalternist work: that the subaltern's own idiom did not allow him to *know* his struggle so that he could articulate himself as its subject.

If the woman/black/subaltern, possessed through struggle of some of the structures previously metonymic as man/white/elite, continues to exercise a self-marginalized purism, and if the benevolent members of the man/white/elite participate in the marginalization and thus legitimate the bad old days, we have a caricature of correct politics that leaves alone the field of continuing subalternization. It is the *loneliness* of the gendered subaltern that is staged in 'Stanadayini.'

(The position that only the subaltern can know the subaltern, only women can know women, and so on cannot be held as a theoretical presupposition either, for it predicates the possibility of knowledge on identity. Whatever the political necessity for holding the position, and whatever the advisability of attempting to 'identify' (with) the other as subject in order to know her, knowledge is made possible and is sustained by irreducible difference, not identity. What is known is always in excess of knowledge. Knowledge is never adequate to its object. The theoretical model of the ideal knower in the embattled position we are discussing is that of the person identical with her predicament. This is actually the figure of the impossibility and non-necessity of knowledge. Here the relationship between the practical — need for claiming subaltern identity — and the theoretical — no programme or knowledge production can presuppose identity as origin — is, once again of an 'interruption', that persistently brings each term to crisis.)

By drawing attention to the complicity between hegemonic (here US) and orthodox (here Indian) readings, I have been attempting to attend to the continuing subalternization of Third World material. At this point I hope it will come as no surprise that certain version of the elite vs. subaltern position is perpetuated by non-Marxist anti-racist feminism in the Anglo-US in its attitude towards Third World women's text in translation. (The group covers the spectrum from anti-Marxism through romantic anti-capitalism into corporatism - I will call the ensemble 'liberal feminism' for terminological convenience.) The position is exacerbated by the fact that liberal feminist Third Worldist criticism often chooses as its constituency the indigenous postcolonial elite, diasporic or otherwise.

If Mahasweta's text displaces the Marxist-feminist terms of the analysis of domestic labour, it also calls into question this liberal-feminist choice. It dramatizes indigenous class-formation under imperialism and its connection to the movement towards women's social emancipation. In the strong satiric voice of authorial comment she writes of the patriarch Haldarkarta: 'He made his cash in the British era, when *Divide and Rule* was the policy. Haldarbabu's mentality was constructed then... During the Second War ... he helped the anti-Fascist struggle of the Allies by buying and selling scrap iron' (pp.255, 254). The mindset of the imperialist is displaced and replicated in the comprador capitalist. If 'East and West' meant a global division for the imperialist, within the minute heterogeneous cartography of this post-colonial space the phrase comes to indicate East and West Bengal. East Bengal (today's Bangladesh) has a phantasmatic status as a proper name, an indigenous division now merely alluding to the imperial and pre-imperial past. Haldarkarta identifies in no way with the parts of 'India' outside of this 'Bengal': 'he doesn't trust anyone -not a Punjabi-Oriya-Bihari-Gujarati-Marathi-Muslim' (p. 255).

This sentence is an echo of a well-known line from the Indian national anthem, an obvious cultural monument: 'Punjab-Sindhu-Gujarat-Maratha-Dravida-Utkala (Orissa) Banga (Bengal).' A national anthem is a regulative metonym for the identity of a nation. Mahasweta's mocking enumeration, describing the country metonymically even as it alludes to that regulative metonym, the anthem, measures the distance between regulation and constitution. This measure then reflects back upon the declarative sentence about secular India that opens the passage we are reading: 'He lives in independent India, the India that makes no distinctions among people, kingdoms, languages...' (p. 255). The reader cannot find a stable referent for the ill-treated Mother India of Mahasweta's reading.

Even in the archaic 'East Bengal' that seems to be the space of Haldarkarta's 'national' identity (Mahasweta's word is 'patriotism'), Dhaka, Mymensingh, Jashore - the celebrated cities, towns, areas are found wanting. 'Harisal', the man's birthplace, is claimed as the fountainhead of that most hegemonic construct, the cultural heritage of ancient India: 'One day it will emerge that the Vedas and the Upanishads were also written in Harisal'. (p. 256) Of course a lot of this relies for effect on the peculiar humour of the two Bengals. But surely to tie, as 'Stanadayini' does, this kind of molecular chauvinism to the divisive operations of imperialism is to warn against its too-quick definition as Hegel's 'childhood of history', transferred to Aderno's caution in *Minima Moralia* against 'pre-capitalist peoples', percolated into Habermas's careless admission that his defense or the ethicopolitics of modernism had to be, also, Eurocentric, or into Kristeva's impassioned call to protect the future of the European illusion against the incursions of a savage Third World.[50]

This appropriation of a 'national' identity is not the 'taking on (of) an essentialist temptation for internationalist purposes'.[51] Internationalist stakes are a remote presence here. This 'national' self-situation is marked by a contradiction, a failure of the desire for essence. First it seeks to usurp the origins of Brahminism, the Vedas and the Upanishads. Next it declares itself dissolved by a Brahmin: 'There's no East or West for a Brahmin. If there's a sacred thread around his neck (the sign of being a Brahmin) you have to give him respect even when he's taking a shit'. (p. 256). This two-step, standing in for identity, is a cover for the brutalizing of the Brahmin when the elite in caste is subaltern in class. (In the case of class-manipulation, 'poverty (is) the fault of the individuals, not an intrinsic part of a class society's; in the case of caste manipulation, the implicit assumption is the reverse: the Brahmin is systemically excellent, not necessarily so as an individual.)[52]

I have gone through the rich texture of the description of Haldarkarta as 'patriot' (nationalism reduced to absurdity) because, although he is a patriarch, it is through their access to the circuit of his political, economic and ideological production ('he had made his cash in the British era... his mentality was constructed then') that the Haldar women move into a species of reproductive emancipation seemingly outside of patriarchal control. Jashoda the 'proletarian' is only useful at the first stage:

> Jashoda's worth went up in the Haldar house. The husbands are pleased because the wives' knees no longer knock when they rifle the almanac. Since their children are being reared on Jashoda's milk, they can be the Holy Child in bed at will. The wives no longer have an excuse to say 'no'. The wives are

> happy. They can keep their figures. They can wear blouses and bras of 'European cut'. After keeping the fast of Shiva's night by watching all-night picture shows they are no longer obliged to breast-feed their babies. (p. 262)

But the transition from domestic to 'domestic' has no place in the greater narrative where women's ideological liberation has its class fix: 'In the matter of motherhood, the old lady's grand-daughters-in-law had breathed a completely different air before they crossed her threshold... The old man had dreamed of filling half Calcutta with Haldars. The granddaughters-in-law were unwilling. Defying the old lady's tongue, they took off to their husbands' places of work' (p. 263).

Another step, and we are free to fantasize an entry into the world of many of Bharati Mukherjee's heroines, Indian wives whose husbands' places of work are in the United States.[53] If they start going to school on the side, we have the privileged native informants of liberal Third Worldist Feminism. In 'Stanadayini' the Haldar daughters of this generation do not appear. Can we not imagine them going off to graduate school on their own, rebels and heroines suckled on Jashoda's milk, full fledged feminists, writing pieces such as 'The Betrayal of Superwoman':

> We must learn to be vocal in expressing, without guilt or embarrassment, what our careers mean to us. It is not something on the side that we can abandon at will to take up career moves of a husband that we were not included in discussing ... We must reach out to other women who think they are alone, share our experiences and be each other's support. We need to accept ourselves as Women Who Never Learned To Do Macrame and Do Not Plan Their Weekend Social Life until Friday Afternoon. We are sad. But we are glad. This is what we will always be.[54]

There is, of course, a complete absence of a sense of history or of subject position in this passage written by a woman of the Indian diaspora in the United States. Mahasweta's Jashoda dies in the nineteen eighties of the history that allows this diasporic woman to say 'this is what we will *always* be.' The critical deployment of liberal feminist thematics in Mahasweta's text obliges us to remember that 'we' in this passage might be parasitical not only upon imperialism (Haldarkarta) but upon the gendered subaltern (Jashoda) as well. Fiction and its pedagogy can here perform the ideological mobilization of a moral economy that a mere benevolent tracing of the historical antecedents of the speaker might not be able to. The two must go together as each other's 'interruption,' for the burden of proof lies upon historical research. It is to belabour the obvious to say that structures of logical and legal-model scholarly demonstrations alone cannot bring about counter-hegemonic ideological production.

It might be worth mentioning here that the left fringe of liberal feminism would like to correct Marxism by defining woman as a sexual class.[55] Again, it is possible to appreciate the situational force of this as an attempt to ensure that women's problems are not demeaned. But if this so-called correction is entertained theoretically then the call to unity might carry the imprint of the academic or corporatist class among women.

In this context, Mahasweta's own reading can be extended into plausibility. The granddaughters-in-law leave the household (a relic of imperialism) and thus deprive Jashoda of her means of livelihood, however grotesque. This can be decoded as the post-Independence Indian disapora, specifically as part of the 'brain drain'. It is a tribute to the story that no direct 'logical' or 'scientific' connection exists between this departure and Jashoda's disease and death, just as none can be established between the nature of Jashoda's labour and her end. Strictly speaking, whatever the pathology of her disease, what would have saved her is better medical care. I have tried to show so far that the pre-history and peculiar nature of her disease, since they involve unequal gendering, are crucial if 'Stanadayini' is to become a text for use.

Jashoda's story is thus not that of the development of a feminine subjectivity, a female *Bildungsroman*, which is the ideal of liberal feminist literary criticism. This is not to say that Jashoda is a 'static' character. To go back to my opening remarks, the development of character or the understanding of subjectivity as growth in consciousness is beside the point of this parable or of this representation of the subaltern. That road not taken is marked by the progress of the granddaughters-in-law. To place the subaltern in a subject position in her history is not necessarily to make her an individualist.

Inhabiting the shifting line between parable and representation, undoing the opposition between tenor and vehicle, Mahasweta's Jashoda also expands the thematics of the woman's political body. Within liberal feminism the feminist body politic is defined by the struggle for reproductive rights.

It is of course of central importance to establish women's right to practice or withhold reproduction. A text such as 'Stanadayini', by posing the double scene of Jashoda as both subaltern (representation rather than character) and parabolic sign, reminds us that the crucial struggle must be situated within a much larger network where feminism is obliged to lose the clear race-and-class-specific contours which depend upon an *exclusive* identification of Woman with the reproductive or copulating body. (Black and Hispanic working-class women in the US have already made this point with reference to the ignoring of enforced sterilization in favour of the right to abortion; but this is still to remain within the identification of women with the body defined minimally.) When the woman's body is used only as a metaphor for a nation (or anything else) feminists correctly object to the effacement of the materiality of that body. Mahasweta's own reading, taken too literally, might thus transgress the power of her text. But, in that shadow area where Jashoda is a signifier for subalternity as such as well as a metaphor for the predicament of the decolonized nation-state 'India', we are forced, once again, to distance ourselves from the identity of Woman with the female copulative and reproductive body.

In the story, having children is also accession to free labour, the production of surplus that can be appropriated with no apparent extra-economic coercion. (Almost incidentally, 'Stanadayini' undoes the line between consenting and coercive sexual intercourse (rape) without the facile reference to free libidinal choice.[56] As such the solution to Jashoda's problem cannot be mere reproductive rights but productive rights as well. And these rights are denied her not just by men, but by elite women as well. This is the underlying paradox of population control in the Third World.)[57] To oppose reproductive rights with the casuistical masculist pseudo-concern about the 'right to life' cannot be relevant here or elsewhere.[58] Yet to oppose productive rights with the so-called 'right to work' laws cannot be the only issue either, precisely because the subject here is female, and the question is not only of class but of gender.

Again, 'Stanadayini' can offer no precise answers, no documented evidence. Taught as a text for use, it can raise constructive questions, corrective doubts.

VI. '*Elite*' *Approaches:* '*Stanadayini*' *in a Theory of Woman's Body*

Used as a teachable text, 'Stanadayini' calls into question that aspect of western Marxist feminism which, from the point or view of work, trivializes the theory of value and, from the point of view of mothering as work, ignores the mother as subject. It calls into question that aspect of western liberal feminism which privileges the indigenous or diasporic elite from the Third World and identifies Woman with the reproductive or copulative body. So-called feminist 'theory', generally associated with developments in France of the last thirty years, is perceived as unrealistic and elitist by the two former groups.[59] I do not wish to enter that sterile quarrel. I submit that if 'Stanadayini' is made to intervene in some thematics of this esoteric theoretical area, it can show up some of the limits of that space as well.

I will keep myself restricted to the question of *jouissance* as orgasmic pleasure. If to identify woman with her copulative or reproductive body can be seen as minimizing and reductive, woman's orgasmic pleasure, taking place in excess of copulation or reproduction, can be seen as a way out of such reductive identifications. There is a great deal of rather diverse writing on the subject.[60] Mahasweta's text seems to be silent on the issue. I have heard a Bengali woman writer remark in public, 'Mahasweta Devi writes like a man'. I will therefore consider a man's text that is about women's silence: 'A Love Letter', by Jacques Lacan.[61]

In this essay Lacan gives a rather terse formulation of a point of view that he developed throughout his career: 'The unconscious presupposes that in the speaking being there is something, somewhere, which knows more than he does'.[62] If this is taken to mean that the subject (speaking being) is more like a map or graph of knowing rather than an individual self that knows, a limit to the claim to power of knowledge is inscribed. The formulation belongs with such experiments as those epistemographs (maps of stages of knowing rather than the story of the growth of an individual mind that knows) of Hegel that the early Lukacs used so brilliantly as charts of 'immanent meaning'; the Marxian notion of ideology; and the Barthesian notion of the writable text that is not readable as such.[63] Fredric Jameson has recently expanded this specifically Lacanian position into the 'political unconscious'.[64]

If we take Lacan at his word here, this knowing-place, writing itself and writing us, 'others' the self. It is a map of the speaking being that is beyond its grasp as other. Thought is where this knowing-programme, the mapping of knowledge, exceeds itself into and thus outlines the deliberative consciousness. Since this epistemograph is also what constitutes the subject (as well as 'others' it), knowing in this para-subjective sense is also being. (If we understand this being that-is-a-map-of-the-known as the socio-political and historical ensemble, collectively constituting the subject but not fully knowable, this would produce materiality preceding or containing consciousness.)[65] It is in this sense that Lacan writes: 'As against the being upheld by philosphical tradition, that is the being residing in thought and taken to be its correlate, I argue that we are played by *jouissance*. Thought is *jouissance* ... of being.'[66]

Thought, as *jouissance*, is not orgasmic pleasure genitally defined, but the excess of being that escapes the circle of the reproduction of the subject. It is the mark of the other in the subject. Now psychoanalysis can only ever conceive of thought as possible through those mechanics of signification where the phallus comes to *mean* the Law by positing castration is punishment as such. Although the point is made repeatedly by Lacan that we are not speaking of the actual male member but of the phallus as the signifier, it is still obviously a gendered position. Thus when thought thinks itself as a place that cannot be known, that always escapes the proof of reproduction, it thinks according to Lacan, of the *jouissance* of the woman.[67]

If one attempted to figure this out without presupposing the identity of the male-gendered position and the position of the thinking (speaking) subject, the singularity and asymmetry of woman's *jouissance* would still seem undeniable in a heterosexually organized world. It would still escape the closed circle of the theoretical fiction of pleasured reproduction-in-copulation as use-value.[68] It would still be the place where an unexchangeable excess can be imagined and figured forth. *This*, rather than male-gendered thought, is woman's *jouissance* in the general sense.

I cannot agree with Lacan that woman's *jouissance* in the narrow sense, 'the opposition between (so-called) vaginal satisfaction and clitoral orgasm', is 'fairly trivial'.[69] We cannot compute the line where *jouissance* in the general sense shifts into *jouissance* in the narrow sense. But we can propose that, because *jouissance* is where an unexchangeable excess is tamed into exchange, where 'what is this' slides into 'what is this worth' slides into 'what does this mean?' it (rather than castration) is where signification emerges. Women's liberation, women's access to autobiography, women's access to the ambivalent arena of thought, must remain implicated in this taming. Thus, to call Mahasweta's preoccupation in 'Stanadayini' with *jouissance* in the general sense 'writing like a man' is to reduce a complex position to the trivializing simplicity of a hegemonic gendering.

Jouissance *in general*: *Jashoda's body*: In 'Stanadayini' Jashoda's body, rather than her fetishized deliberative consciousness (self or subjectivity) is the *place* of knowledge, rather than the instrument of knowing. This cannot be an argument. Literary language, as it is historically defined, allows us no more than to take a persistent distance from the rationalist project, shared by the social sciences, radical or otherwise. This distancing is a supplement to the project. It could never have the positive role of an opposition. The role of Jashoda's body as the place where the sinister knowledge of decolonization as failure of foster-mothering is figured forth produces cancer, an excess very far from the singularity of the clitoral orgasm.

The speech of the Other is recorded in a cryptic sentence. It is a response to Jashoda's last 'conscious' or 'rational' judgement: 'If you suckle you're a mother, all lies... The sores on her breast kept mocking her with a hundred mouths, a hundred eyes'. (p. 271).

This is the only time the Other 'speaks'. The disease has not been diagnosed or named yet. The Other inhabits a hundred eyes and mouths, a transformation of the body's inscription into a disembodied yet anthropomorphic agency, which makes of the breast, the definitive female organ within this circle of reproduction, (a) pluralized almost-face.[70] (The metonymic construction common in Bengali colloquial usage should literally be translated 'in a hundred mouths' etc., 'meaning', of course, also *with.*) Does the Other agree or disagree with Jashoda's judgement about the identity of the mother, so crucial to the story? 'Mocking' tells us nothing.

Consider for a moment the phrase that I have translated 'kept mocking:' *Byango korte thaklo.*

The first noticeable thing here is the lack of synchronization between Jashoda's judgement and the response. The latter is sustained — '*kept* mocking' — as if Jashoda's remarks were merely an interruption. (We recall that the remarks had been made in the mistaken assumption that her husband was still in the room. Even as normal intersubjective exchange, it is a failure.) One may put discourse into the mouth and eyes of a displaced and disembodied Other. One cannot fabricate an intersubjective dialogue with it. The status of the cancer as the figuring of the *jouissance* of the subaltern female body as thought-in-decolonization is thus kept intact here.

Let us focus on the word *byango* - translatable loosely as 'mock (ery)'. The word *ango* - body (with organs) as opposed to *deho* - the body as a whole - makes itself felt within it. The Sanskrit source word *vyangya* meant, primarily, deformed. The secondary meaning - mockery - indicated the specific mockery that is produced by a contortion of the body, by deforming one's form. Modern Bengali has lost the sense that, in Sanskrit, would consolidate the reading that I am trying to produce: the implicit meaning that can only be understood through (gestural) suggestion.[71] When language de-forms itself and gestures at you, mocking significance, there is *byango*. The limit of meaning, the *jouissance* of the female body politic, is marked in this sentence.

This is altogether different from using the cancer simply as another metaphor invading the metaphor of the sexually undifferentiated body politic, listed in Susan Sontag's *Illness As Metaphor.*[72] It is interesting to see how different the history of cancer as metaphor is in the context of the last couple of centuries in the Anglo-US. The emphasis there is basically psychologistic: 'the disease is what speaks through the body, a language for dramatizing the *mental*'.[73] From within this history, Sontag calls for a 'demetaphorization' of the disease. This brings up two widely separated issues: philosophically, can anything be absolutely demetaphorized? - and politically, is it necessary in order to bring the theatre of decolonization into such a demetaphorized arena of reality, to drag it through the various stages of comprador capitalism, until it can graduate into 'expressive individualism' so that it can begin to qualify for demetaphorization? In other words the political aspect of this suggestion must confront us with the argument for 'development.' There can be no doubt that situational agents of 'development', especially counter-diasporic indigenous service professionals like 'Stanadayini's doctor, are often selfless and good. Yet it must be noticed that, if we were to read him characterologically, he would be the only character who had so internalized bureaucratic egalitarianism as to judge Jashoda by an absolute standard: 'The doctor understood that he was unreasonably angry because Jashoda was in this condition. He was angry with Jashoda, with Kangali, with women who don't take the signs of breast cancer *seriously* enough and finally die in this dreadful and hellish pain.' (p. 274)

Engaging the thematics of the *jouissance* of the female body, 'Stanadayini' can be read not only to show (a race-and-class-specific) gendering at work in Lacanian theory. It can also make visible the limits of a merely structural psychoanalytic strategy of reading.

In 'A Love Letter', Lacan rewrites 'I think; therefore I am' in the following way: 'There is ... an animal which finds himself speaking (taken to presume or entail 'thinking'), and for whom it follows that, by inhabiting (occupying with desire and mastery, *besetzend*, cathecting) the signifier, he is its subject'.[74] If one is sympathetic to the critique of the sovereign subject, one does not have trouble accepting this as a persistent caution. 'From then on', Lacan continues, 'everything is played out for him on the level of fantasy, but a fantasy which can perfectly well be taken apart so as to allow for the fact that he knows a great deal more than he thinks when he acts.'

Knowledge is played out or mapped out on the entire map of the speaking being, thought is the *jouissance* or excess of being. We have already drawn out the implication of this position in our discussion of Jashoda's body as the *place* of knowing in the text. But in order 'to take apart' the fantasy inhabiting this text 'perfectly' one would have to part company with the psychoanalytic scenario.

I have speculated elsewhere that a narrative of sanctioned suicide (rather than castration) might begin to limn a 'Hindu' phantasmatic order.[75] Rather than the stories of Oedipus (signification) and Adam (Salvation), the multiple narratives of situated suicide might then regulate a specifically 'Hindu' sense of the progress of life. (These narratives are 'regulative psychobiographies'.) When we begin to consider the question of a 'perfect' analysis, we have to analyse the subalternization of indigenous psychoanalysis, the establishment of its claim to scientificity (within which one must situate Lacan's critique), and its imposition upon the colonies, has its own history.[76] A question similar to some I have already posed emerges here also: should the access to hegemony of an indigenous (here 'Hindu') regulative psychobiography lie through the necessary access to an institutionalization, like that of psychoanalysis, entailing the narrative of imperialist political economy? Within feminist 'theory' we are caught in only the *gendering* rather than the overtly imperialist politics of psychoanalysis.

Given such matters, it might be interesting to measure the distance between Lacan's connecting of woman's *jouissance* and the naming of God on the one hand, and the end of 'Stanadayini' on the other. Lacan moves the question, 'can the woman say anything about *jouissance*?' asked by a man, to the point where the woman also confronts the question of the Other:

> for in this she is herself subjected to the other just as much as the man. Does the other know? ... If God does not know hatred, it is clear for Empedocles that be knows less than mortals... which might lead one to say that the more man may ascribe to the woman in confusion with God, that is, in confusion with what it is she comes from, the less he hates, the lesser he is, and since after all, there is no love without hate , the less he loves.[77]

At the end of Mahasweta's story Jashoda herself is said to 'be God manifest'. This is inconsistent with the logic of the rest of the narrative, where Jashoda is clearly being played by the exigencies of the Haldar household. It is also a sudden and serious introduction of the discourse of philosophical monotheism in what has so far been a satiric indexing of the ideological use of goddesses (*Singhabahini* or the Lion-seated) and mythic god-women (the 'original' Jashoda of Hindu mythology). Here at the conclusion the gender of the agent is unspecified. (The English translation obliges us to choose a gender.) Is it possible that, because Mahasweta Devi does not present this conclusion from a male-gendered position, we are not reduced to man's affective diminution when he puts woman in the place of God? Is it possible that we have here, not the discourse of castration but of sanctioned suicide? 'Jashoda was God manifest, others do and did whatever she thought. Jashoda's death also the death of God.' (p. 276) Does Jashoda's death spell out a species of *iccharmrityu* - willed death — the most benign form of sanctioned suicide within Hindu regulative psychobiography? Can a woman have access to *iccharmrityu* - a category of suicide arising out of *tatvajnana* or the knowledge of the 'it'-ness of the subject? The question of gendering here is not psychoanalytic or counter-psychoanalytic. It is the question of woman's access to that paradox of the knowledge of the limits of knowledge where the strongest assertion of agency, to negate the possibility of agency, cannot be an example of itself as suicide.[78] 'Stanadayini' affirms this access through the (dis) figuring of the other in the (woman's) body rather than the possibility of transcendence in the (man's) mind. Read in the context of *iccharmrityu*, the last sentence of the text becomes deeply ambivalent. Indeed, the positive or negative value of the statement becomes undecidable: 'When a mortal plays God here below, she is forsaken by all and she must always die alone'.

Over against what might be seen as the 'serious' laying out of the thematics of woman's *jouissance* in the general sense, there is rather a strange moment that might be read as indicating the inscrutability of woman's *jouissance* in the narrow sense.

'Stanadayini' opens with a general description of Jashoda as a professional mother. Immediately following, there is a brief narrative sequence, embedded in other, even briefer, references, the logical irrelevance of which the text is at pains to point out: 'But these matters are mere blind alleys. Motherhood did not become Jashoda's profession for these afternoon-whims'. (p. 253)

The sequence deals with the cook. Like Jashoda, she loses her job as a result of the youngest Haldar-son's clandestine activities: 'He stole his mother's ring, slipped it into the cook's pillowcase, raised a hue and cry, and got the cook kicked out' (p. 253). We do not know the end of her story. In terms of narrative values, the cook is the real marginal. It is in her voice that the inscrutability of woman's pleasure announces itself: (I am not suggesting that we should give in to our body's depradations and refuse to testify, just as — at the other end of the scale of cultural control - no one would suggest that the text about sex-affective production called *King Lear* invites people to go mad and walk about in storms. If what we are combating as teachers is liberal-nationalist-universalist humanism with its spurious demands for the autonomy of art and the authority of the author, we must be ready to admit that the demand that plots be directly imitable in politically correct action leads to the extravagances of 'socialist' or 'feminist' realism and a new Popular Front.)

In the voice of the marginal who disappears from the story, in between the uncaring 'do what you will' and 'what's there to tell', Mahasweta might be marking the irreducible inscrutability of the pleasure of the woman's body.[79] This is not the rhapsodic high artistic language of elite feminist literary experimentation. Escaping the reducible logic (including the authorial reading *and* the pedagogic interventions) of the story, this exchange is clothed in slang. As Gautam Bhadra has pointed out, it is in the unfreezable dynamic of slang that subaltern semiosis hangs out.[80]

What, indeed, is there to tell? The cook, a non-character in the story, could not have *intended* the rhetorical question *seriously*. It is almost as if what is told, the story of Jashoda, is the result of an obstinate misunderstanding of the rhetorical question that transforms the condition of the (im)possibility of answering - of telling the story - into the condition of its possibility.[81] Every production of experience, thought, knowledge, all humanistic disciplinary production, perhaps especially the representation of the subaltern in history or literature, has this double bind at its origin.

The influential French feminist theorist Julia Kristeva has proposed a rewriting of the Freudian version of the Oedipal family romance. She theorizes an 'abject' mother who, unequally coupled with the 'imaginary' father, offers a primary narcissistic model which allows the infant to speak.[82] The focus here is unwaveringly on the child - and since Kristeva is an apologist for Christianity - upon the Holy Child. If some details of the iconography of the abject mother seem to fit Jashoda's predicament, we should, I think, resist the seduction of a lexicon that beckons to a coherent reading by strategically excluding the entire political burden of the text. There can be no similarity between Kristeva's positing of a pre-originary space where sexual difference is annulled - so that a benignly Christian *agape* can be seen to pre-date eros on the one hand, and the sinister vision of the failure of social cement in a decolonized space where questions of genital pleasure of social affect are framed, on the other.[83]

One cannot of course compare analytical discussions of ideology with psychoanalytical reconstruction of interpellation.[84] Kristeva's discussions of the place of the Virgin within cultural Subject-representation and constitution are, however, so close to isomorphic generalizations that I think they might be productively contrasted to Mahasweta's critique of the nationwide patriarchal mobilization of the Hindu Divine Mother and Holy Child. Her treatment of an active polytheism focuses the possibility that there are many accesses to the mother-child scene.[85] The story plays itself out between two cultural uses of it. The figure of the all-willing Lion-seated, whose official icon of motherhood triumphant is framed by her many adult divine children, democratically dividing the governance of the many sectors of the manifest world, is reflected in the temple quarter of Calcutta. The figure of the all-nurturing Jashoda provides the active principle of patriarchal sexual ideology. As in the case of her earlier short story 'Draupadi', Mahasweta mobilizes the figure of the mythic female as opposed to the full-fledged goddess. Kristeva points at the Virgin's asymmetrical status as the Mother of God by constructing the imaginary father and the abject mother, Mahasweta introduces exploitation/domination into that detail in the mythic story which tells us that Jashoda is a *foster*-mother. By turning fostering into a profession, she sees mothering in its materiality beyond its socialization as affect, beyond psychologization as abjection, or yet transcendentalization as the vehicle of the divine.

VII. *Considerations Specifically of Gendering*

A few more remarks on the economy of the Lion-seated and Jashoda are in order here.

A basic technique of representing the subaltern as such (of either sex) is as the object of the gaze 'from above'.[86] It is noticeable that whenever Jashoda is represented in this way in 'Stanadayini,' the eye-object situation is deflected into a specifically religious discourse. In Hindu polytheism the god or goddess, as indeed, *mutatis mutandis* the reversed person, is also an object of the gaze, 'from below'. Through a programmed confounding of the two kinds of gaze, goddesses can be used to dissimulate women's oppression.[87] The transformation of the final cause of the entire chain of events in the first part of the narrative into the will of the Lion-seated is an example of how the latter is used to dissimulate Jashoda's exploitation. For the sufficient cause is, as we well know, the cheating and spoiled youngest Haldar son with the genital itch. In the following passage it is he who is the *subject* of the gaze, the object being the suckling Jashoda, a sort of living icon of the mythic Jashoda the Divine (Foster) Mother suckling the Holy Child. The man (the one above) thus masquerades as the one below, so that the subaltern can be dissimulated into an icon. Displaced into that iconic role, she can then be used to declare the will of the dominant Female, the goddess Lion-seated: 'One day as the youngest son was squatting to watch Jashoda's milking, she said, "There dear, my Lucky. All this because you swiped him in the leg. Whose wish was it then?" "The Lion-seated's", said Haldar junior.' (p.262)

Mahasweta presents Jashoda as constituted by patriarchal ideology. In fact her outspoken self-confidence in the earlier part of the story comes from her ideological conviction.[88] If the text questions the distinction between rape and consenting intercourse, Jashoda the subaltern does not participate in this questioning. 'You are husband', she will say, 'you are guru. If I forget and say no, correct me. Where after all is the pain?... Does it hurt a tree to bear fruit?' (She is given the same metaphor of the 'naturalness' of woman's reproductive function — one ideological cornerstone of gendering - when she reproaches the granddaughters-in-law for 'causing' the Old Mistress's death through their refusal to bear children.) She also accepts the traditional sexual division of labour: 'The man brings, the woman cooks and serves. My lot is inside out... Living off a wife's carcass, you call that a man?'

Mahasweta uses Jashoda the subaltern as a measure of the dominant sexual ideology of 'India'. (Here gender uniformity is more encompassing then class difference.) Over against this is a list of Western stereotypes, where a certain Western feminism ('Simone de Beauvoir' serves Mahasweta as a metonym) is also situated:

> Jashoda is fully an Indian woman, whose unreasonable, unreasoning, and unintelligent devotion to her husband and love for her children, whose unnatural renunciation and forgiveness have been kept alive in the popular consciousness by all Indian women... Her mother-love wells up as much for Kangali as for the children... Such is the power of the Indian soil that all women turn into mothers here and all men remain immersed in the spirit of holy childhood. Each man the Holy Child and each woman the Divine Mother. Even those who wish to deny this and wish to slap *current posters* to the effect of the 'eternal she,' - 'Mona Lisa, - La passionaria,' - 'Simone de Beauvoir' - et cetera over the old ones and look at women that way are, after all, Indian cubs. It is notable that the educated Babus desire all this from women outside the home. When they cross the threshold they want the Divine Mother in the words and conduct of the revolutionary ladies. (p. 260)

Here the authority of the author-function is elaborately claimed. We are reminded that the story is no more than the author's construction. The allusion to another school of Bengali fiction places the story in literary history rather than the stream of reality. In an ostentatious gesture, the author recovers herself and resumes her story: 'However, it's incorrect to cultivate the habit of repeated incursions into *by-lanes* as we tell Jashoda's life story' (p. 258). That Jashoda's name is also an interpellation into patriarchal ideology is thus given overt authorial sanction through the conduct of the narrative. In terms of that ideology, the fruit of Jashoda's fostering is the Krishna whose flute-playing phallocentric eroticism, and charioteering logocentric sublation of militarism into a model of correct karma, will be embraced in nineteenth and twentieth century Bengali nationalism as images of the private and the public.[89]

The end of the story undoes this careful distancing of the author from the gender-ideological interpellation of the protagonist. Even when Mahasweta Devi predicates her at the end by way of the defilement of institutional English on the name-tag for unclaimed corpses in the morgue ('Jashoda Devi, Hindu female'), a certain narrative irony, strengthening the author-function, seems still intact.[90] It is the three propositions at the very end that call into question the strategically well-advertised ironic stance of the author-function.

The language and terminology of these conclusive propositions remind us of those high Hindu scriptures where a merely narrative religion shifts, through the register of theology, into a species of speculative philosophy: 'Jashoda was God manifest, others do and did whatever she thought. Jashoda's death was also the death of God. When a mortal plays God here below, she is forsaken by all and she must always die alone' (p. 276).

One argument of Subaltern Studies has been that the subaltern as historical subject persistently translates the discourse of religion into the discourse of militancy. In the case of the subaltern as gendered subject, 'Stanadayini' recounts the failure of such a translation. It undoes the hierarchical opposition between the Hinduism of philosophical monotheism (largely bred in its contemporary outlines by way of the culture of imperialism) and that of popular polytheism. It suggests that the arrogance of the former may be complicitous with the ideological victimage of the latter. This is managed through making indeterminate the distinction between the author-function and the protagonist's predicament. If, therefore, the story (*enonce*) tells us of the failure of a translation or discursive displacement from religion to militancy; the text as statement (*enonciation*) participates in such a translation (indistinguishable now from its 'failure') from the discourse of religion into that of political critique.

'Stanadayini' as statement performs this by compromising the author's 'truth' as distinct from the protagonist's 'ideology'. Reading the solemn assenting judgement of the end, we can no longer remain sure if the 'truth' that has so far 'framed' the ideology has any resources without it or outside it. Just as in the case of the cook's tale, we begin to notice that the narrative has, in fact, other frames that lie outside a strictly authorial irony. One of these frames, we remember, renders the world's foster mother motherless within the text. The text's epigraph comes from the anonymous world of doggerel and the first word invokes *mashi pishi* - aunts - not mothers, not even aunts by marriage, but aunts suspended before kinship inscription, the sisters of the two unnamed parents, suspended also on the edge of nature and culture, in *Bangan*, a place whose name celebrates both forest and village.[91] If the narrative recounts the failure of affect, a counter-narrative (yet another non-story) of these curious affectless presumably fostering aunts threatens the coherence of our interpretation in yet another way.

It is the powerful title which holds together the reading that we have been developing in these pages. It is not 'Stanyadayini', the word we expect, meaning the suckler' or 'wet-nurse'. It is, rather, 'Stanadayini' - the giver of the breast, of the alienated means of production, the part-object, the distinguishing organ of the female as mother. The violence of this neologism allows the cancer to become the signifier of the oppression of the gendered subaltern. It is the parasite feeding on the breast in the name of affect, consuming the body politic, 'flourishing at the expense of the human host' (p. 276). The sentence is in English in the Bengali text, which allows for the word 'human'. The representative or defining human case, given in English and the objective language of science, is here female.

'Much Third World fiction is still caught in realism' (whereas the international literatures of the First World have graduated into language games) is a predictable generalization. This is often the result of a lack of acquaintance with the language of the original. Mahasweta's prose is an extraordinary melange of street slang, the dialect of East Bengal, the everyday household language of family and servant, and the occasional gravity of elegant Bengali. The deliberately awkward syntax conveys by this mixture an effect far from 'realistic', although the individual elements are representationally accurate to the last degree. (I have not been able to reproduce this in the translation). In addition, the structural conduct of the story has a fabulistic cast: the telescoped and improbable list of widespread changes in the household and locality brought about by the transition from domestic to 'domestic', the quick narrative of the thirty years of decolonization with its exorbitant figures are but two examples.

What is most interesting for my purposes, however, is that the text's own comment on realism in literature should be given in terms of gendering. Just as a naive understanding of a realistic style is that it is true to life, so is it a politically naive and pernicious understanding of gendering that it is true to nature. Mahasweta's rendering of the truth of gendering in realism is so deliberately mysterious and absurd that it is almost incomprehensible even to the native speaker. The reference is to Saratchandra Chatterjee, the greatest sentimental realist in Bengali literature. No ethnographic or sociological explication of the 'connotation' of 'wood apple nectar' would do the disciplinary trick here:

> Because he understood this the heroines of Saratchandra always fed the hero an extra mouthful of rice. The apparent simplicity of Saratchandra's and other similar writers' writings is actually very complex and to be thought of in the evening, peacefully after a glass of wood apple nectar. There is too much influence of fun and games in the lives of the people who traffic in studies and intellectualism in West Bengal and therefore they should stress the wood apple correspondingly. We have no idea of the loss we are sustaining because we do not stress the wood-apple-type herbal remedies correspondingly (p. 258)

Speaking in code, then, we might say that to diagnose all Third World literature in English translation, by way of a sanctioned ignorance of the original, as a realism not yet graduated into language-games, is a species of 'stress upon the wood-apple-type herbal remedies correspondingly.' Such a minimalizing reading would docket Mahasweta's story as nothing more than a 'realistic' picture of Indian gendering.

In his account of the Subaltern Studies Conference (January 1986) where an earlier version of this paper was read, and where Mahasweta presented her own reading of 'Stanadayini', David Hardiman comes to the following conclusion: '(Mahasweta's) down-to-earth style made for excellent theatre, with Gayatri being upstaged.'[92] I have obviously taken Mahasweta's reading, 'not unsurprisingly', as Hardiman writes, 'greatly at variance with Gayatri Spivak's', seriously enough to engage with it in writing; and I have commented elsewhere on the implicit benevolent sexism of some subalternist work.[93] This, however, is an explicit masculist gesture: turning women into rivals by making them objects of the gaze. Beyond this particular male voyeurism, beyond the ontological/epistemological confusion that pits subaltern being against elite knowing, beyond the nativist's resistance to theory when it is recognizably different from his own unacknowledged theoretical position, I hope these pages have made clear that, in the *mise-en-scène* where the text persistently rehearses itself, writer and reader are both upstaged. If the teacher clandestinely carves out a piece of action by using the text as a tool, it is only in celebration of the text's apartness (*être-a-l'-écart*). Paradoxically, this apartness makes the text susceptible to a history larger than that of the writer, reader, teacher. In that scene of writing, the authority of the author, however seductively down-to-earth, must be content to stand in the wings.

Gayatri Chakravorty Spivak, from Subaltern Studies, *Vol. V*

NOTES

1. I am grateful to Jill Matthews for a critical reading of this paper.
2. Mahasweta Devi, 'Stanadayini,' *Ekshan* (Autumn, Bengali year 1384). [A translation of 'Stanadayini' by the author of this essay was appended to the essay in its original place of publication. The references to the text are therefore references to the original place of publication . *Editor*]
3. Ernesto Laclau and Chantal Mouffe, *Hegemony and Socialist Strategy: Towards A Radical Democratic Politics*, tr. Winston Moore and Paul Cammack (London, 1985). p.108.
4. The two are nicely if somewhat metaphysically combined in Ilya Prigogine and Isabelle Stengers, *Order Out of Chaos: Man's New Dialogue with Nature* (Boulder, CO. 1984).

5. Michel Foucault, *The Archaeology of Knowledge and the Discourse on Language*, tr. A.M. Sheridan Smith (New York, 1972), p.86. Translations from all texts modified wherever necessary.
6. Foucault, *Archaeology*, pp.95–6. Emphasis mine.
7. Foucault, 'Discursive Formations,' *Archaeology*, p.31–9.
8. See especially Foucault, 'The Confession of the Flesh', *Power/Knowledge: Selected Interviews and Other Writings* 1972–1977, tr. Colin Gordon et al. (New York, 1980), pp.196–8.
9. Jacques Derrida, 'Limited inc: abc', *Glyph* 2 (1977), especially p. 239.
10. Roland Barthes, 'The Reality-Effect', in *The Rustle of Language*, tr. Richard Howard (New York, 1984).
11. The relationship between the two words that relate through this approximate differential is, of course, not 'the same' in all languages. There is, however, always a differential. In modern French and German, for example, the words for 'history' and 'story' being roughly the same, the manoeuvrings would be somewhat different from what we, writing in English, would argue. Ultimately the distinction is between the true and the sanctioned non-true.
12. Samik Bandyopadhyay, 'Introduction', in Mahasweta Devi, *Five Plays: Mother of 1084/ Aajir/Bayen/Urvashi and Johnny/Water* (Calcutta, 1986), p. xi.
13. Unpublished intervention, Subaltern Studies Conference, Calcutta, 9 January 1986.
14. 'The tenor is the gist of the thought concerning the subject (here India as Slave/Mother), and the vehicle is that which embodies the tenor — the analogy (here the specificity of Jashoda as subaltern)... by which the tenor is conveyed'. Sylvan Barnet et al., *A Dictionary of Literary, Dramatic, and Cinematic Terms* (second edition, Boston, 1971), p. 51.
15. This is the implicit grounding presupposition of Benedict Anderson, *Imaginary Communities: Reflections on the Origin and Spread of Nationalism* (London, 1983). For a review expressing the criticism that I here echo, see Ranajit Guha, 'Nationalism reduced to "Official Nationalism",' ASAA Review 9, 1 (July 1985).
16. See Edward W. Said, 'Culture and Imperialism' (the Clarke Lectures, University of Kent, December 1985; forthcoming).
17. See Partha Chatterjee, *Nationalist Thought and the Colonial World: A Derivative Discourse* (London, 1986). Uday Mehta, Assistant Professor of Government at Cornell University, is engaged in similar work on Lockean Liberalism.
18. David Arnold has examined some of the received wisdom on this issue in 'Bureaucratic Recruitment and Subordination in Colonial India: The Madras Constabulary, 1859–1947', *Subaltern Studies IV*.
19. Hardiman, '"Subaltern Studies" at Crossroads', *Economic and Political Weekly* (15 February 1986).
20. *Mutatis Mutandis,* Louis Althusser, 'Ideology and Ideological State Apparatuses (Notes Towards An Investigation)', *Lenin and Philosophy and Other Essays,* tr. Ben Brewster (New York, 1971), still seems the most authoritative account of this phenomenon. Disciplinary production such as historiography and literary pedagogy would probably fall between 'the educational' and 'the cultural ISA'-s (p.143).
21. See Terry Eagleton, 'The Rise of English', *Literary Theory: An Introduction* (Minneapolis, 1983).
22. The most spirited discussion of the historicity of affects is to be found in the debate on pornography in the United States. For a discussion of the phenomenality of affects see Robert C. Solomon, *The Passions* (New York, 1976). For a provocative suggestion about Freud's contribution to the latter issue, see Derrida, *Of Grammatology*, tr. Spivak (Baltimore, 1976), p. 88.

23. I am of course, describing deconstructive literary criticism when I cite these special themes. I take this position in spite of Derrida's cautionary words regarding the too positivistic use of 'themes' in an assessment of his own work ('The Double Session,' *Dissemination*, tr. Barbara Johnson, Chicago, 1981, p. 245). In fact, in 'Varieties of Deconstructive Practice,' a widely publicized paper which will eventually be forthcoming, I have distinguished Derrida's reading of literature from his reading of philosophical texts in terms of the issue of 'themes.' I mention this because that argument is also an issue of disciplinary production: of philosophy and literature, as here of history and literary pedagogy. For one of the most astute formulaic reductions of deconstruction to thematic reading, see Barbara Johnson, 'Teaching Deconstructively', in G. Douglas Atkins and Michael L. Johnson, eds., *Writing and Reading Differently: Deconstruction and the Teaching of Composition and Literature* (Lawrence, Kansas, 1985). For an example of my own excursion into thematizing 'affirmative deconstruction', see footnote 81 of this essay.
24. Quoted in Abiola Irele, *The African Experience in Literature and Ideology* (London, 1981), p.1.
25. In the US, anti-economistic 'cultural' Marxism, feminist or androcentric, faults Althusser's work because it apparently underplays the class struggle by structuralizing the mode of production narrative. In Britain the general impact of E.P. Thompson's critique, as reflected in *The Poverty of Theory and other Essays* (New York, 1979) diagnosed Althusser as using Hegel as a code-work for Stalin and betraying the spirit of Marxism by structuralizing the mode of production of narrative. On and around the issue of essentialism a certain alliance between British post-Althusserianism and British Marxist feminism may be found. The work of Toril Moi in *Sexual/Textual Politics: Feminist Literary Theory* (New York, 1985) would be a good example.
26. Lise Vogel, *Marxism and the Oppression of Women: Towards A Unitary Theory* (New Brunswick, 1983), p. 147.
27. Perry Anderson, *Passages from Antiquity to Feudalism* (London, 1974), p. 245.
28. Some well-known examples among many would be Mary O'Brien, 'The Politics of Materialism', in Kuhn and Wolpe, eds., *Feminism and Materialism: Women and Modes of Production* (London, 1978); Rosalind Coward, *Patriarchal Precedents: Sexuality and Social Relations* (London, 1983). See also Lydia Sargent, ed., *Women and Revolution* (Boston, 1981).
29. Vogel, *Marxism and the Oppression of Women,* pp.141–2. For a sound critique of the Engelsian-feminist position, see Coward, 'The Concept of the Family in Marxist Theory', in *Patriarchal Precedents.* It seems to me unfortunate that Coward's critique should be used to lead us back into Freud.
30. Karl Marx, *Capital*, tr. David Fernbach (New York, 1978), vol. 2, pp. 469–71.
31. Marx, *Capital*, vol. 2, pp.180 and 180ff., in general .
32. (Paris, 1980).
33. V.N. Volosinov, *Marxism and the Philosophy of Language*, tr. Ladislav Materjka and I.R. Titunik (New York, 1973), p. 68.
34. I am not arguing here for individual differences. On the social character of 'solitary self-experience', see Volosinov, *Marxism and the Philosophy of Language,* pp. 89–94. In a more essentialist form, assuming that there is such a thing as 'life in its immediacy', one might say, with Adorno: 'He (sic) who wishes to know the truth about life in its immediacy must scrutinise its estranged from, the objective powers that determine individual existence even in its most hidden recesses'. Theodor Adorno, *Minima Moralia: Reflections from A Damaged Life,* tr.E.F.N. Jephoott (London, 1974), p. 15. Institutional subject-positions are social vacancies

that are of course not filled in the same way by different individuals. All generalizations made from subject-positions are untotalizable.

35. See footnote 28 and, for the best-known examples, see Ann Oakley, *The Sociology of Housework* (Oxford, 1974) and the excellent documentation in Anne Ferguson, 'On Conceiving Motherhood and Sexuality: A Feminist Materialist Approach,' in Joyce Trebilcot, ed., *Mothering: Essays in Feminist Theory* (Totowa, NJ, 1984), an essay I discuss below.
36. For a discussion of feminist knowledge within existing paradigms, I have profited from listening to Susan Magarey, 'Transgressing Barriers, Centralising Margins, and Transcending Boundaries: Feminism as Politicised Knowledge', unpublished paper, conference on 'Feminist Enquiry As a Transdisciplinary Enterprise', University of Adelaide, 21 August 1986.
37. Here I am invoking one of the earliest deconstructive positions: that reversals of positions legitimize each other and therefore a persistent effort at displacement is in order. For the later suggestion of a distancing from the project of reason, see Derrida, 'The Principle of Reason: the University in the Eyes of its Pupils', *Diacritics* 13, 3 (Fall 1983).
38. Ferguson, 'Conceiving Motherhood', p.176.
39. In fact, Ferguson sees foster-mothering as one among many types of 'social mothering (adoptive mothers, step and foster mothers, older sisters, other mother surrogates) involving a second or different kind of mother-daughter bond' (p. 177). I discuss 'Stanadayini''s treatment of varieties of mother-child relationships later in the essay.
40. Ferguson, 'Conceiving Motherhood', p.156.
41. This is to be distinguished from uninformed anti-Marxist positions. I have in mind generalizations in such powerful essays as Catharine A. McKinnon, 'Feminism, Marxism, Method, and the State: An Agenda for Theory', in Nannerl O. Keohane, ed., *Feminist Theory: A Critique of Ideology* (Chicago, 1982); Luce Irigary. 'The Power of Discourse' and 'Commodities Among Themselves', in *This Sex Which Is Not One*, tr. Catherine Porter (Ithaca, 1985), pp. 82–5, 192–7; and Rosalind Coward, 'The Concept of the Family in Marxist Theory', in *Patriarchal Precedents.* It should be mentioned here that, in spite of her over-simplification of Marx's positions on value and ideology, Ferguson is generally politically astute in her assessment of the relationship between various domination systems in Euramerica.
42. Ferguson, 'Conceiving Motherhood', p. 155.
43. Hannelore Mabry, 'The Feminist Theory of Surplus Value', in Edith Hoshino Altbach et al., eds., *German Feminism: Readings in Politics and Literature*, tries interestingly to bridge to two spheres.
44. Anna Davin, 'Imperialism and Motherhood', *History Workshop* 5 (1978).
45. See Jennifer Sharpe, 'The Double Discourse of Colonialism and Nationalism: the Production of A Colonial Subject in British India', *Dissertation Abstracts* (University of Texas-Austin, forthcoming).
46. Ferguson, 'Conceiving Motherhood', p.175.
47. See Chandra Talpade Mohanty, 'Under Western Eyes: Feminist Scholarship and Colonial Discourses', *boundary* 2 12, 3/13, 1 (Spring-Fall 1984) and 'Feminist Theory and the Production of Universal Sisterhood', unpublished paper, conference on 'Race, Culture, Class: Challenges to Feminism', Hampshire College, December 1985; and Spivak, 'Imperialism and Sexual Difference', *Oxford Literary Review* 8, 1–2, 1986.
48. The discontinuities between the three domination systems are quietly revealed by the asymmetry in the articulation of the three pairs.

49. Antonio Gramsci, 'Some Aspects of the Southern Question,' *Selections from Political Writing: 1921–1926*, tr. Quentin Hoare (New York, 1978); Marx, *Capital*, tr. David Fernbach (New York, 1981), Vol. 3. p.1016.
50. Georg Wilhelm Friedrich Hegel, *The Philosophy of History*, tr. J. Sibree (New York, 1956), p. 105; Adorno, *Minima Moralia*, p. 53; Jurgen Habemas, 'A Philosophico-Political Profile', *New Left Review* 151; Julia Kristeva, 'Memoires', *L'infini*, 1.
51. Meaghan Morris, 'Identity Anecdotes', *Camera Obscura* 12 (1984), p. 43.
52. Davin, 'Imperialism', p. 54.
53. Bharati Mukherjee, *Wife* (Boston, 1975) and *Darkness* (Markham, Ontario, 1985).
54. Parvathy Hadley, 'The Betrayal of Superwoman', *Committee on South Asian Women Bulletin* 4, 1 (1986), p. 18.
55. One of the pioneering statements, Zillah Eisenstein's 'Developing A Theory of Capitalist Patriarchy and Socialist Feminism', in Eisenstein, ed., *Capitalist Patriarchy and the Case for Socialist Feminism* (New York, 1979), shows both the strengths and the weaknesses of this approach.
56. This is not in disagreement with the identification of rape with violence, as in Catherine A. McKinnon, *Sexual Harassment of Working Women: A Case of Sex Discrimination* (New Haven, 1979).
57. See Mahmoud Mamdani, *The Myth of Population Control: Family, Caste and Class in An Indian Village* (New York, 1973). For an unfortunate articulation of this contradiction, see Germaine Greer, *Sex and Destiny: the Politics of Human Fertility* (New York, 1984).
58. For an use of the phrase in a single-issue class-context see 'Right to Life, but ....' *Economic and Political Weekly* 20, 29, 20 July 1985, editorial.
59. This is a general feeling that is too pervasive to document satisfactorily. But notice the interesting undertone emerging in 'French Texts, American Contexts', *Yale French Studies* 62 (1981).
60. For representative pieces see Irigaray, 'When Our Lips Speak Together', *This Sex*; Monique Witting, *The Lesbian Body*, tr. David Le Vay (New York, 1975); Alice Schwarzer, 'The Function of Sexuality in the Oppression of Women', in *German Feminism*; and Spivak, 'French Feminism in An International Frame', *Yale French Studies* 62 (1981). I have not yet seen no.26 of *Les Cahiers du grif* (Paris/Brussels), entitled 'Jouir'.
61. In *Feminine Sexuality: Jacques Lacan and the ecole freudienne*, tr. Juliet Mitchell and Jacqueline Rose (London, 1982).
62. Lacan, 'Love Letter', p.159.
63. See, for examples, Hegel, *Aesthetics: Lecture on Fine Art*, tr. T.M. Knox (Oxford, 1975); George Lukacs, *Theory of the Novel*, tr. Anna Bostock (Cambridge, MA, 1971); and Roland Barthes, *S/Z*, tr. Richard Miller (New York, 1974).
64. Jameson, *The Political Unconscious: Narrative As a Socially Symbolic Act* (Ithaca, 1981).
65. It is possible to deduce Althusser's reading of Lacan in this way. See Althusser, 'Freud & Lacan', in *Lenin and Philosophy*.
66. Lacan, 'God and the Jouissance of Woman', in *Feminine Sexuality*, p. 142.
67. Derrida at once participates in and criticizes this gender-positioned definition of the object that cannot be known as the feminine thing when, in *Glas* (Paris, 1981) he abbreviates the Hegelian Absolute Knowledge (*savoir absolu*) beyond the grasp of the individual subject, as Sa. In French this is a possessive pronominal article which merely indicates that its object is feminine.
68. For a discussion of use-value as theoretical fiction see Spivak, 'Speculation on reading Marx: After Reading Derrida', in Derek Attridge et al., eds., *Post-Structuralism and the Question of History* (Cambridge University Press, forthcoming), pp. 39–40.
69. 'Guiding Remarks for A Congress', in *Feminine Sexuality*, p. 89.

70. For discussions of giving a face to the wholly other, see Derrida, 'Violence and Metaphysics: An Essay on the Thought of Emmanuel Levinas', in *Writing and Difference*, tr. Alan Bass (Chicago, 1978), and Paul de Man, 'Autobiography As De-facement', *Rhetoric of Romanticism* (New York, 1984).
71. Subhas Bhattacharya, *Adhunik Banglar Proyog Abhidhan* (Calcutta, 1984), p. 222.
72. Susan Sontag, *Illness As Metaphor* (New York, 1979).
73. Sontag, *Illness*, p. 43.
74. Lacan, 'Love Letter', p. 159.
75. In 'Can the Subaltern Speak? Speculations On Widow-Sacrifice', *Wedge* 7/8 (Winter/Spring 1985).
76. Franz Fanon's comments on 'Colonial War and Mental Disorders' are particularly pertinent here. See *The Wretched of the Earth*, tr. Constance Farrington (New York, 1963).
77. Lacan, 'Love Letter', p. 160.
78. Spivak, 'Can the Subaltern',p.123.
79. 'For the wish to sleep is the indeterminably significative tendency that is marking or repetition, and also the wish to forget about it, and to go on with the hypothesis that one is perceiving a meaningful form'. Cynthia Chase, 'The Witty Butcher's Wife: Freud, Lacan, and the Conversion of Resistance to Theory', revised version, unpublished paper, conference on 'Psychoanalysis and Feminism', State University of Illinois, 1–4 May 1986.
80. Suggestion made at Subaltern Studies Conference, Calcutta, January 1986. I believe it is a comparable impulse that prompts Derrida to place, in the right hand column of *Glas*, the torrential production of an unsystematizable slang in Jean Genet over against the definitive establishment of philosophical vocabulary in Hegel's work, treated in the left hand column of the book. See also my treatment of 'rumour' in *Subaltern Studies IV*.
81. Most rhetorical questions, such as the cook's 'What's there to tell?', imply a negative answer: 'Nothing'. Jashoda's story tells itself by (mis)understanding the question as literal and answering: 'this'. Such would be the morphology of 'affirmative deconstruction', which says 'yes' to everything, not as a proper negation which leads to a strategically exclusive synthesis, but by way of an irreducible and originary 'mistake' that will not allow it to totalize its practice. This affirmation is not the 'yes' of pluralism of repressive tolerance, which is given from a position of power. 'Stanadayini' as *enonciation* might thus be an example of an ever compromised affirmative deconstruction.
82. Kristeva, 'Ne dis rien', *Tel Quel* 90 (1981). I am grateful to Cynthia Chase for having brought this essay to my attention.
83. Incidentally, her method here is conservative, in that she annuls what was most radical in Freud's hypothesis, namely infantile sexuality. ('In the hands of post-Freudians, helped no doubt by hesitations in Freud's own account, orthodox assumptions reasserted themselves'. Jeffrey Weeks, 'Masculinity and the Science of Desire', *Oxford Literary Review* 8.1–2 (1986), p. 32.) She positivizes and naturalizes into a psychic scenario the pre-originary space that is no more than an unavoidable methodological presupposition.
84. Kristeva is openly anti-Marxist. By aligning her work with Althusser's - 'interpellation' is his notion of the subject's being 'hailed' in ideology ('Ideology and the state', *Lenin and Philosophy*, pp. 170–7) - I am giving her a benefit of the doubt.
85. See Kristeva, 'Stabat mater', in Susan Rubin Suleiman, ed., *The Female Body in Western Culture: Contemporary Perspectives* (Cambridge, MA, 1986). Generalizing about femininity on the avowed basis of monotheism, and dismissing 'progressive activism' as versions of 'feminine psychosis', this celebrated essay is a paean of motherhood sustained by thinly veiled autobiographical 'evidence' in the left hand column and sweeping historico-

psychoanalytic conclusions in the right about the 'virgin maternal' as 'coping with female paranoia' (pp. 116, 117, 114). With reference to Anne Ferguson's excellent essay, I had mentioned the sudden appearance of a 'cross-cultural referent' (see pp. 110) These quick and often misleading definitive moments invoking an imaginary 'Third World' influence feminist thinking. In Eisenstein, for example, the description of 'pre-capitalist society' where 'men, women, and children worked together in the home, the farm, or on the land to produce the goods necessary for their lives, (and) women were procreators and child-rearers, but the organization of work limited the impact of this sexual role distinction' (*Capitalist Patriarchy*, p. 30), would be instantly corrected by the account of gendering with the heterogeneity of decolonized space offered by 'Stanadayini'. In Kristeva, the Blessed Virgin appropriates re-incarnation in a flash; 'Mary does not die but rather - echoing Taoist and other oriental beliefs in which human bodies pass from one place to another in a never-ending flow (flux) which is in itself an imprint (calque) of the maternal receptacle (receptacle maternel) - she passes over (*transite*)' (Suleiman, *Female Body*, p. 105).

86. The question of the gaze has been most fully discussed in film theory. See, for example, Laura Mulvey, 'Visual Pleasure and Narrative Cinema,' *Screen* 16.3 (1975); E. Ann Kaplan, *Women and Film: Both Sides of the Camera* (Bloomington, 1984). See also Norman Bryson, *Vision and Painting: The Logic of the Gaze* (New Haven, 1983). I am grateful to Frances Bartkowski for suggesting this book to me.
87. See Spivak, 'Displacement and the Discourse of Women', in Mark Krupnick, ed., *Displacement: Derrida and After* (Bloomington, 1983), pp. 174, 179.
88. In this connection, see Temma Kaplan's interesting notion of 'female consciousness' in 'Female Consciousness and Collective Action: The Case of Barcelona, 1910–1918', in Keohane, ed., *Feminist Theory.*
89. For two examples, among many, consider Rabindranath Tagore, *Bhanusingher Padabali* (1921, Bengali year) and Bankimchandra Chattyopadhyaya, *Krishnacharitra* (1886).
90. I am grateful to Sudipta Kaviraj for having suggested to me that English is a medium of defilement in 'Stanadayini'.
91. It is immaterial to my point that there is an actual place by this name in Bengal.
92. Hardiman, 'Subaltern Studies', p. 290.
93. Spivak, 'Subaltern Studies', pp. 356–63.

AIJAZ AHMAD

The essay reproduced here was first published in *Economic & Political Weekly* (1992). A version of it, with slight variations, is included in Ahmed's substantial book *In Theory: Classes, Nations, Literatures* (Verso, London, 1992). The book, issued mainly for the use of Western readers, was immediately hailed as a major achievement in the area of post-colonial theory. The book has much in it that Indian readers will benefit by reading. Besides, it is written from the perspective of a post-colonial Indian Marxist, a perspective which recognises the immense diversity of materials and multiplicity of subjecthood covered by the current theories of colonial literatures. Mainly, Ahmad takes on Edward Said's version of Orientalism and shows the follies involved in Said's position. Therefore, the essay reproduced here anticipates the tone and the substance of *In Theory*.

With Homi Bhabha and Gayatri Spivak, Aijaz Ahmad is probably one of the most brilliant of Indian critics writing for international audiences. However, unlike the two others, Ahmad feels much more at ease with Indian literature and Indian languages. As such, his critical writing is less pedantic and more self-assured. Ahmad works as a Professional Fellow at the Nehru Museum in Delhi.

Orientalism and After

Ambivalence and Cosmopolitan Location in the work of Edward Said

> It needs to be said that criticism modified in advance by labels like 'Marxism' or 'liberalism' is, in my view, an oxymoron .... The net effect of 'doing' Marxist criticism or writing at the present time is of course to declare political preference, but it is also to put oneself outside a great deal of things going on in the world, so to speak, and in other kinds of criticism. (Edward W. Said, *The World, The Text and the Critic*, p 29)

I have written critically of Fredric Jameson in the past,[1] and substantial portions of what follows shall be highly critical of Edward Said. One reason simply is that with the passing away of Raymond Williams, Jameson and Said now are possibly the most siginificant cultural critics writing in the English language for the kind of work I do in this area, and I can scarcely find my own thought without passing through theirs. Disagreeing with Jameson had been easier. Writing from a Marxist position, I naturally share identifiable points of theoretical departure with Jameson even when—especially when—disagreements are on the most basic issues. Said is different in this regard. I disagree with him so fundamentally on issues both of theory and of history that our respective understandings of the world—the world as it now is, and as it has been at many points over the past two thousand years or so—are simply irreconcilable, which then leads, inevitably, to difference of local interpretation and local reading so numerous that no one article can possibly name them all.

These differences, both the general and the particular, are in any case the smaller part of my difficulty in writing about Edward Said. Much the larger difficulty resides, rather, with my sense of solidarity with his beleaguered location in the midst of imperial America. For, Edward Said is not only a cultural critic, he is also a Palestinian. Much that is splendid in his work is connected with the fact that he has tried to do honour to that origin; and he has done so against all odds, to the full extent of his capacity, by stepping outside the boundaries of his academic discipline and original intellectual formation, under no compulsion of profession or fame, in no pursuit of personal gain,in fact at frightening risks to himself, including threats of assassination. Said has decided to live with such risks, and much honour—very rare kinds of honour—attaches to that decision. How does one, then, register one's many disagreements from within this solidarity? For some years I have felt that one simply could not do that, that dissenting speech might be a betrayal of that solidarity. More recently, though, I have come to believe that such a position of willed neutrality is politically wrong, morally indefensible. Said, after all, continues to pursue his vocation in circumstances given to him. Those of us who admire his courage and yet disagree with him on substantive isssues also have to carry on our own critical pursuits—as if that gun, trained at him, was not there. Suppression of criticism, I have come to believe, is not the best way of expressing solidarity.

I

About the sense of that place, the question of that origin, Said has also written directly notably in his two books, *The Question of Palestine*[2] and *After the Last*

Sky[3], and in numerous articles. But the awareness of it is there—at times only on the margins, in some places very much foregrounded, and increasingly so with the passage of time—in many of the writings that have followed the publication of *Orientalism* in 1978.[4] It is likely, in fact, that when the dust of current literary debates settles, Said's most enduring contribution shall be seen as residing neither in *Orientalism*, which is a deeply flawed book, nor in the literary essays which have followed in its wake, but in his work on the Palestine issue, e.g. his seminal essay 'Zionism from the Standpoint of Its Victims'[5] the superbly inflected prose which he contributed alongside Jean Mohr's photographs in *After the Last Sky*, and generally the role he has played, with unrivalled energy and much salutary effect, in re-defining the issue of Palestine national liberation for western, especially American, intelligentsias. Even though the latter parts of *The Question of Palestine* were much weaker, one could see that in Said's own intellectual biography and in the history of his sentiments, the writing of *Orientalism* had been in some ways a preparation for the writings of that essay, on 'Zionism from the Standpoint of Its Victims'. One was in a sense grateful for that preparation, that will to settle the rage within, as much as possible, so that he could then speak, with scholarly precision and measured eloquence, about that most difficult place inside the self where the wound had once been, where the pain still was. And because one had already read *Orientalism*, the composure that Said had gained, the scruple he was now able to exercise, was all the more striking.

Orientalism marks such a radical break in Said's own intellectual carreer precisely because the writing of this book was an attempt at coming to terms with what it means for him to be a Palestinian living and teaching in the US, armed with not much more than a humanist intellectual training, a successful career as literary critic, and a splendid mastery over wide areas of European literary textuality. As he put it in the 'Introduction':

> My own experience of these matters is in part what made me write this book. The life of an Arab Palestinian in the West, particularly in America, is disheartening... The web of racism, cultural stereotypes, political imperialism, dehumanising ideology holding in the Arab or the Muslim is very strong indeed, and it is this web which every Palestinian has come to feel as his uniquely punishing destiny.[6]

That is one part of the purpose: to make manifest the many strands and histories of this 'web' confronting the Palestinian. But an equally personal and more nuanced undertaking was announced, with the aid of a quotation from Gramsci, two pages earlier (p. 25):

> In the *Prison Notebooks* Gramsci says: "The starting point in critical elaboration is the consciousness of what one really is, ... as a product of the historical process to date, which has deposited in you an infinity of traces, without leaving an inventory." The only available English translation inexplicably leaves Gramsci's comment at that, whereas Gramsci's Italian text concludes by adding that "therefore it is imperative at the outset to compile such an inventory" .... In many ways my study of Orientalism has been an attempt to inventory the traces upon me, the Oriental subject, of the culture whose domination has been so powerful a factor in the life of all Orientals.

This passage from Gramsci seems to have meant a great deal to Said, for it reappears at the beginning of his 'Zionism' essay. Several aspects of these two passages should therefore detain us. The first is that this was the first time in Said's writings that his personal voice has intruded so sharply, was positioned so centrally, in the definition of his scholarly project. As one returns today, some twenty years later, to Said's first two books, the ones on Conrad and Beginnings,[7] one notices the early mastery of style but one is also struck, from today's vantage point of the *tone of Orientalism*, by the essentially cerebral character of that earlier prose, by the fact that not much more than the mind is engaged, and the mind then seemed actually to have believed that, when it comes to intellectual inquiry, even in the human sciences, nothing other than the mind *need be engaged.* The emphasis here, by contrast, on one's own 'uniquely punishing destiny' and the intent, then, to prepare an 'inventory' of the traces—wounds, one might say—that the destiny has inflicted upon oneself, announces the emergence of a very different kind of prose, more personal and palpable, in which erudition is poised more or less precariously against the polemical verve.

But, why should this 'inventory' of traces take the form of a counter-reading of the western canonical textualities, mainly in the cognate areas of literature and philology, from Greek tragedy onwards? The reason was again a personal one, though it was really not connected with being a Palestinian. Said had been trained primarily in the classical mould of scholarship in comparative European literatures, in a milieu dominated by Auerbach and Spitzer, the German comparatists who had given to the discipline its stamp of high humanism of a very conservative kind, more or less Tory in orientation. It was the ghost of this precise canonicity which had to be laid to rest. The particular texture of *Orientalism*, its emphasis on the canonical text, its privileging of literature and philology in the constitution of 'Orientalist' knowledge and indeed the human sciences generally, its will to portray a 'west' which has been the same from the dawn of history up to the present, and its will to traverse all the main languages of Europe – all this, and more, in *Orientalism* derives from the ambition to write a counter-history that could be posed against *Mimesis*, Auerbach's magisterial account of the seamless genesis of European realism and rationalism from Greek antiquity to the modernist moment. If there is an absent anti-hero in Said's own counter-classic, it is Eric Auerbach. If Auerbach began with Homer, Said too must begin with Greek tragedy; and a special venom must be reserved for Dante because Dante, after all, is the hero of Auerbach's account. But ghosts of that kind are not so easily laid to rest, provided that you are sufficiently possessed by them.[8] Over the past decade or so, Said has recounted, most poignantly, over and over again, in several different texts, that moment in Auerbach's life when he, a refugee from fascism, sat in his lonely corner in Istambul, cut off from the European libraries of classical and romance languages, and wrote *Mimesis*, his loving summation of his beloved humanist knowledge of European literature at a time when he thought that the tradition itself was at the point of vanishing. In this narrative, to which Said returns again and again, Auerbach is the emblem of scholarly rectitude, a lone figure defending humanist value in the midst of holocaust, a scholar in the finest sense; also a surrogate figure, because this figure of an ultimate scholar writing his masterpiece in exile has, for Said, the stateless Palestinian and the ambitious author of *Orientalism*, a very special resonance. Outside this particular narrative of personal desolation and perseverance, however, Auerbach is also the master of European knowledge against which the counter-knowledge of *Orientalism* is assembled.

This paradoxical relationship with Auerbach, the individual master, is played out on a much more complex scale, in an equally paradoxical relationship with high humanism as such. In the field of cultural studies, Said is our most vivacious narrator of the history of European humanism's complicity in the history of European colonalism. The global history of humanism doubtless includes much besides that complicity, and it is of course eminently arguable that this narrative of the convergence between colonial knowledges and colonial powers simply cannot be, assembled in cultural studies as such, because histories of economic exploitation, political coercion, military conquest play the far more constitutive part; those other histories are the ones which provide the enabling conditions for the so-called 'Orientalist discourse' as such. But that argument we shall for the moment ignore. What is far more significant is that after Said has assembled the whole narrative of European literature, from Aeschylus to Edward Lane, as a history of literature's complicity in inferiorisation of the 'orient', and after he has identified the Enlightenment itself as an unified trajectory and master sign, of both orientalism and colonialism, he is of course faced with the problem of identifying some sort of agency that might undo this centuries-old tie between narratives of high humanism and the colonial project. At this point, we discover a peculiar blockage, for what Said now posits are the most ordinary, the most familiar values of humanist liberalism, namely, tolerance, accommodation, cultural pluralism and relativism, and those insistently repeated words: *sympathy, constituency, affiliation, filiation.* What is remarkable about this at times very resounding affirmation of humanist value is that humanism-as-ideality is invoked precisely at the time when humanism-as-history has been rejected so unequivocally.

These ambivalences about Auerbach and about humanism in general were problematic enough, but they were then complicated further by the impossible reconciliation which Said tries to achieve between that humanism and Foucault's discourse theory, which no serious intellectual would want to use simply as a method of reading and classifying canonical books because the theory itself is inseparable from Nietzchean antihumanism and the currently dominant anti-realistic theories of representation. The invocation of Foucault as the conceptual mentor we encounter early in the book (p. 3), as soon as Said is done with his three definitions of the object, orientalism, as such:

> I have found it useful here to employ Michel Foucault's notion of a discourse, as described by him in *The Archeology of Knowledge* and in *Discipline and Punish*, to identify Orientalism. My contention is that without examining Orientalism as a discourse one cannot possibly understand the enormously systematic discipline by which European culture was able to manage - and even produce—the Orient politically, sociologically, militarily,ideologically, scientifically, and imaginatively during the post-Enlightenment period.

This sense of affiliation with Foucault remians strong throughout *Orientalism*, and the prose of the book is replete with Foucaultian terminology: regularity, discursive field, representation, archive,epistemic, difference, etc. And yet one is not quite sure what the relationship of Said's thought with Foucault's really is.[9] Foucault surely knew how to be allusive, but underneath all his multiple enunciations one knows exactly what his agreements and diagreements with Marxism actually have been. His first and irreconcilable difference is that he locates Marx firmly within the boundaries of what he calls the 'western episteme'; in its epistemic construction, he says, the thought of Marx is framed entirely by the discourse of political economy as this discourse is assembled within that episteme.[10] From this purported philosophical difference, then, follows his equally clear disagreement with Marx on the issue of the principle that might govern historical narrativisation; he radically denies that narratives of history can be assembled at the twin sites of the state and economic production, which he deems to be the exclusive originating sites of Marx's historical narrative. I shall not here examine these preposterous propositions of Foucault, because I am at the moment interested only in the form of Foucault's resurfacing in Said's thought. For, after disagreeing with Marx on these fundamental premises, Foucault then goes on to specify both the spatial limits and the temporal constitution of the episteme he is engaged in. He insists that it is a *western* episteme; about the rest of humanity he makes no claims of knowledge. Second, he locates the constitution of this episteme, historically, in the processes that range from roughly the 16th century to the 18th. Foucault always sidesteps Marxist terminology, but he knows what he is talking about, namely, that emergence of bourgeois society which spans from primary accumulation up to the first industrial revolution. With the exception of *Histoire de la folie*, which he finished before working out his philosophical system in what became *The Order of Things* and *The Archeology of Knowledge*—with the exception of that one book, all the narratives he had assembled before 1978, especially the one in *Discipline and Punish* which Said here specifically mentions—all begin in that crucible of bourgeois beginnings. The episteme is western because it is located in a transition that occurred specifically in Europe, and the narrative of incarceration and surveillance which Foucault assembles and Said invokes is designed, precisely, to demarcate the boundary between the *ancien regime* and the modern.

Said uses Foucaultian terms as discrete elements of an apparatus but refuses to accept the consequences of Foucault's own mapping of history. If Foucaultian pressures force him to trace the beginnings of the 'Orientalist discourse' from the 18th century or so, the equally irresistible pressures of Auerbachian high humanism force him to trace the origins of this very 'discourse', in the conventional form of a continuous European literary textuality, all the way back to ancient Greece. In a characteristic move, Said refuses to choose and, as we shall demonstrate below, he offers mutually incompatible definitions of 'orientalism' so as to deploy both these stances, the Foucaultian and the Auerbachian, *simultaneously*. Now, the idea that there could be a discourse - that is to say, an epistemic construction—traversing the whole breadth of 'western' history and textualities, spanning not only the modern capitalist period but all the preceding pre-capitalist periods as well, is not only an un-Marxist but also a radically un-Foucaultian idea. The Foucault of *Discipline and Punish* simply would not accept that there is any kind of integral relationship between ancient Greece and modern western Europe, except that post-renaissance Europe begins to trace its lineage, in a more or less fantastic manner, from that antiquity while reversing most of the presuppositions prevailing in that antiquity. And, Foucault never speaks of a fully fledged discourse prior to the 16th century because what he calls 'discourse' presumes, as co-extensive corollary, a rationalism of the post-medieval kind, alongside the increasing elaborations of modern state forms, modern institutional grids, objectified economic productions, modern forms of rationalised planning. Said's idea that the ideology of modern imperialist Eurocentrism is already inscribed in the ritual theatre of Greek tragedy—or that Marx's passage on the role of British colonialism in India can be lifted out of the presuppositions of political economy and seamlessly integrated into the trans-historical orientalist discourse—is not only ahistorical in the ordinary sense but also specifically anti-Foucaultian in a methodological sense. And, from the 18th century onwards at least, Said traces the powers and densities of the 'Orientalist discourse' directly to what Foucault would designate as so many sites of the state—the Napoleonic invasion of Egypt, the French occupation of North Africa, the Anglo-French rivalries in the Levant, and so on—which Foucaultian positions would disqualify as constitutive sites of discourse. I do not normally agree with most of what I find in Foucault, but I must recognise that Foucault was on such accounts by and large careful in his procedures. It is not for nothing that Foucault never constructed the history of any discourse on the basis of master texts; Freud's psychoanalytic procedure has no privilege in Foucault's thought over the country priest who supervises the Catholic girl's confession. He always distinguishes *discourse* from canonical tradition, from mentality, from institution. His philosophical distinction between *discursive* regularity and *personal* statement, his historiographic preoccupation with specifying the *form* and *boundary* of discourse, his refusal to collapse one discourse into another—the discourse of incarceration into the discourse of sexuality, for example—are fundamental to his thought, and the prolixity of his prose stands in direct contrast to the austerity of his boundaries. Said observes none of those austerities.

One of the most rigid boundaries in Foucault's thought was drawn against humanism as such, which he retained until the last couple of years of his life, when there were some glimmerings of recantation. On this count, most especially, Said's procedures of 1978 are radically anti-Foucaultian and are taken directly from the high humanist traditions of comparative literature and philology, which have shaped his narrative method as well as his choice of texts. For, it is the proposition of this alternative, humanist tradition that (a) there is an unified European/western identity which is at the *origin* of history and which has *shaped* this history through its *thought* and its *texts*; (b) this seamless and unified history of European identity and thought runs from ancient Greece up to the end of the

19th century and well into the 20th, through a specific set of beliefs and values which remain eternally the same, only getting more dense; and (c) that this history is immanent in, and therefore available for reconstruction through, the canon of its *great books*. Said subscribes to the *structure* of this idealist metaphysic even though he obviously questions the greatness of some of those 'great' books. He duplicates, in other words, all those procedures even as he debunks the very tradition from which he has borrowed the procedures. Said's narrative here presumes, as Auerbach presumes, that there is a line of continuity between Aeschylus and the modern European; that this sense of continuity was itself fabricated in post-Renaissance Europe is something neither Auerbach nor Said (in *Orientalism* at any rate) would question. Like Auerbach, Said too is preoccupied with the canonical question, with tradition, with sequential periodisation. Auerbach *finds* humanist value in those books, Said finds only a lack; but both look for the same values, in the same books—or at least the same *kind* of books. He denounces with Foucaultian vitriol what he loves with Auerbachian passion, so that the reader soon begins to detect a very *personal* kind of drama getting enacted in Said's procedure of alternately debunking and praising to the sky and again debunking the same books, as if he had been betrayed by the objects of his passion. This way of alternating between inordinate praise and wholesale rejection was to endure far beyond *Orientalism*. For a more recent exercise of this procedure, the essay on Kipling may be cited,[11] where the criticisms of Kipling which Said offers are unsurprising since he only repeats, without acknowledgement of course, what has been said often enough by numerous critics on the left, but those familiar criticisms are then combined with surprisingly high and unwarranted praise for Kipling as a 'master stylist' so 'great', we are told, that

> as an artist he can justifiably be compared with Hardy, with Henry James, Meredith, Gissing, the later George Eliot, George Moore, Samuel Butler. In France, Kipling's peers are Flaubert and Zola, even Proust and the early Gide.

The list of novels with which *Kim* is then solemnly compared includes *Sentimental Education, The Portrait of A Lady,* and *Way of All Flesh*. It is not entirely clear why a minor novel, which owed its wide circulation only to colonial currency, has to be thus elevated—and made worthy of the attack—before getting knocked down.

The issue of trying to reconcile Auerbach with Foucault is indicative in any case of a whole range of problems that are at one methodological, conceptual as well as political. For, Said's work is self-divided not only between Auerbachian high humanism and Nietzchean anti-humanism (the issue of Nietzche I will take up later), but also between a host of irreconcilable positions in cultural theory generally, from the most radical to the most reactionary, ranging all the way from Gramsci to Julien Benda, with Lukacs and Croce and Matthew Arnold in between. This I should want to illustrate with some comments on Benda, whom Said has often praised as one of the exemplary intellectuals of this century. That Benda, a man possessed by notions of high aesthetics, would come in for that kind of praise is perhaps not entirely surprising, given Said's original training, his preference for high canonicity, and the aestheticist claim of being located beyond all 'isms'. What is far more surprising is Said's habit of equating Benda with Gramsci, which is I suppose one way of domesticating the revolutionary content of Gramsci's thought. One does not have to read far into *Treason of the Intellectuals*[12] to see (a) that the 'treason' that Benda speaks of is none other than the intellectuals' participation in what he calls 'the political passions'; and (b) that 'class passions' and 'racial passions' are for him among the worst, so that 'anti-semitism' and 'socialism' are said to be equally diabolical, while 'the working classes who even in the middle of the 19th century, felt only a scattered hostility for the opposing class' are castigated because in Benda's own time (i.e. 1920s) 'they form a closely-woven fabric of hatred from one end of Europe to another' (pp. 3–5). Benda then goes on to denounce dozens—literally dozens—of intellectuals, from all ages but especially from the modern age, who, in his opinion, 'have not been content simply to adopt passions ... They permit, they desire, them to be mingled with their work as artists, as men of learning, as philosophers, to colour the essence of their work and to mark all its productions. And indeed never were there so many political works among those which *ought to be the mirror of the disinterested intelligence*' (p. 67; emphasis added). There is thus boundless denunciation of all politics, especially socialist politics, in the name of 'the disinterested intelligence'; even poor Michelangelo is denounced for 'crying shame upon Leonardo da Vinci for his indifference to the misfortunes of Florence' while 'the master of the Last Supper' is commended for replying 'that indeed the study of beauty occupied his whole heart' (p. 47). One of Said's many laudatory comments on Benda runs, in turn, as follows:

> Certainly what Benda says about intellectuals (who, in ways specific to the intellectual vocation itself, are responsible for defiance) resonates harmoniously with the personality of Socrates as it emerges in Plato's *Dialogues*, or with Voltaire's opposition to the Church, or more recently with Gramsci's notion of the organic intellectual allied with the emergent class against ruling class hegemony... It is also the case, both Benda and Gramsci agree, that intellectuals

are eminently useful in making hegemony work. For Benda this of course is the *trahison des clercs* in its essence; their unseemly participation in the perfection of political passions is what he thinks is despairingly the very essence of their contemporary mass sell-out.[13]

The inflationary invocations of Socrates, Voltaire and Gramsci do not really help clarify what Said here really means, even as he ends with that Orwellian phrase: 'contemporary mass sell-out'. Gramsci, surely, means little if we subtract from his legacy his 'political passion'. And so fundamental is the tie in Benda's thought between anti-communism and a general hatred of the working class on the one hand, and 'the distinterested intelligence' and the 'study of beauty' on the other, that only a very conservative mind, essentially tory in its structure, would want to think of him as an exemplary intellectual. But then a mind of that kind would not normally want to associate itself with Gramsci. It is an index of Said's self-division that he would think of Benda, the rabid anti-communist, and Gramsci, one of the more persevering communists of the century, as occupying essentially the same political position.[14] And it is the listing of revolutionaries like Gramsci (in the more recent work such lists would get very lengthy indeed) which conceals how very traditionally literary-critical Said's thought actually is.

II

What is equally striking, as one looks back on the passage I quoted earlier, with a quotation from Gramsci embedded in it, is Said's own formulation—'In many ways my study of orientalism has been an attempt to inventory the traces upon me, the Oriental subject'—which summarises more or less accurately what the book is about, especially if we take literally the idea that the phrase 'inventory of traces upon me' here refers to Said's own quite specific grounding in—and ambivalent relation with—a very traditional and canonical conception of 'literature'. The significant move here in any case is Said's self-description as 'the oriental subject'. Such self-representations are always somewhat one-sided, and therefore somewhat hazardous, for anyone whose own cultural apparatus is so overwhelmingly European and who commands such an authoritative presence in the American university. The irony of such usages in Said's case are all the greater because any careful reading of the *whole* of his work would show how strategically he deploys words like 'we' and 'us', to refer, in various contexts, to Palestinians, third-world intellectuals, academics in general, humanists, Arabs, Arab-Americans, and the American citizenry at large.[15] More to the point, in any case, are the inflations that were to soon follow, on the heels of *Orientalism*. The cursory phrase 'the oriental subject' was then to be revamped in a number of radicalist strands in subsequent literary theory as 'the colonial subject' and, yet later, as 'the post-colonial subject'; Said's own highly tendentious uses of these latter terms shall be discussed below, when I come to discuss his schematic characterisation of C.L.R. James and George Antonius as the emblematic 'colonial' intellectuals, of S.H. Alatas and Ranajit Guha as the exemplary 'post-colonial' ones. The idea of the 'inventory of traces', eloquent and legitimate in itself, was to be inflated into the idea, by Fredric Jameson among others, that third world societies are *constituted* by the experience of colonialism and imperialism. Now, the notion of a 'colonial subject', or 'post-colonial subject' for that matter, of course *presumes* that we are indeed constituted by colonialism, then in quick succession by post-coloniality; if we are not *constituted* by colonialism then the term 'colonial subject' is theoretically meaningless.

The original Gramscian idea of an 'inventory of traces' presumes that there is a personality, a cultural location upon which the traces are inscribed; it presumes that there are other 'traces' into which *these* traces are woven, so that the personality that emerges out of this weave, this overlap, is conditioned not by a specific set of traces but by the whole of its history. What this original Gramscian idea could mean, for example, is that the Italian cultural formation cannot be read back from fascism or the Risorgimento or even the failure of the reformation, hence the unfinished character of the Italian renaissance; that it would have to be traced all the way back, historically, to the very moment of the ascendancy of the high church and of high Latin as the language of that church, as well as from the histories of subordinations following thereafter; in other words, histories, and therefore subjectivities, are constituted not by what Gramsci calls 'moments' but by the always accumulating processes of sedimentation and accretion. In relation to India, then, this original Gramscian formulation would mean, at the very least, that colonialism was doubtless a key 'moment', even in some specific areas a decisive 'moment', but the history of sedimentations which *constitutes* the Indian cultural formation includes much besides colonialism *per se*. I clarify this point here in order to emphasise that there is at least one major strand of literary theory which has developed under Said's influence—'colonial discourse analysis' —which is notable for its *separation* of the 'inventory of colonial traces' from other sorts of inventories, other sorts of traces. This, too, fits. Not only in the sense that if we *are constituted* by colonialism, then the only discourse that really matters is the discourse of the colonialist, but also because of the example that Edward Said himself had set in his book. For, a notable feature of *Orientalism* is that it examines the history of western textualities about the non-west quite in isolation from how these textualities might have been received, accepted, modified, challenged, overthrown or reproduced by the intelligentsias of the colonised countries, not as an undifferentiated mass, but as situated social agents impelled by our own conflicts, contradictions, distinct social and political locations, of class, gender, region, religious affiliation, etc. Hence a peculiar disjuncture in the architecture of the book. One of its major complaints is that from Aeschylus onwards the west has never permitted the orient to represent itself; it has represented the orient. That peculiar vision of human history I shall discuss below. But what is remarkable is that, with the exception of Said's own voice, the only voices we encounter in the book are precisely those of the very western canonicity which, Said complains, has always silenced the orient. Who is silencing whom, who is refusing to permit a historicised encounter between the voice of the so-called 'orientalist' and the many voices that 'orientalism' is said to so utterly suppress, is a question very hard to determine as we read this book. It sometimes appears that one is transfixed by the power of the very voice that one debunks.

In some limited sense of course, *Orientalism* belongs in a very particular genre, of which Said seems to be very conscious, considering that Julien Benda is one of his favourite authors. Developed mostly in France, though Nietzsche was a notable practitioner of it, this is the tradition of philosophers debunking the discipline of philosophy itself, and of intellectuals generally, for betraying the ethics of their vocation. Two of the books most influential in France during the inter-war years, *Treason of the Intellectuals* (1927) by Julien Benda and Paul Nizan's glorious polemic, *The Watchdogs* (1932) come immediately to mind, as does Regis Debray's more recent *Teachers, Writers, Celebrities* (1979). Said was doing for—in other words, against—his own discipline of comparative literature what they had done for theirs, which had been philosophy.

But we could actually push this matter of genre a bit further. For, part of the pleasure of the book, which caused anxiety in some circles, excitement in others, was its transgression of academic boundaries. Divisions of academic labour in the modern university are such that one is always pressed to disclose as to what it is that authorises one to speak: whether one is a sociologist, political scientist, historian, anthropologist, literary critic, or a mere interloper in defined and occupied territories. Attacks on Said on this count were numerous, joined, two years after this prolonged orchestration, by Bernard Lewis himself, one of the doyens of Zionist historiography, most recently at Princeton. The attack was unseemly on many counts, but the substantive point which Lewis raised was one of competence. What authorised Said to speak of Arab history and orientalist disciplines? What degrees did he have? Did he know such-and-such medieval Arabic dictionary? Did he know the meaning of such-and-such word in the whole range of Arabic lexicography over ten centuries? etc.[16] (In his elegant rejoinder, Said quite rightly ignored the issue of competence and authorisation, while concentrating on the issue that had gone unacknowledged in Lewis's attack, namely, that Lewis's scholarly pretence was itself a camouflage for Zionist allegiance.)

Orientalism was clearly not a book of middle-eastern studies, or of any established academic discipline, but it did belong, for all its academic sophistication, of a well known tradition of writing, and one that has been very dispersed through several genres: Cesaire's *Discourse on Colonialism* or Fanon's *Black Skins, White Masks* could be mentioned as famous predecessors. In the field of literature itself, and within even the Anglo-American tradition as such, there had of course not been the kind of systematisation that Said here offers, but there is actually a *very large* body of work which has previously analysed, as Said himself analyses Flaubert or Chateaubriand here, western canonical authors and their complicity in western colonial enterprises and ideologies. This question had been posed quite widely throughout the American and British universities, especially since the beginning of the Vietnam war, not to speak of France where the issue had been posed even earlier, in fields as diverse as literature and anthropology, thanks also to wars of liberation both in Indochina and Algeria. In the literary part of its undertaking, which is doubtless the largest part of the book, *Orientalism* thus belongs to a well known lineage. For, if we subtract the terminological and stylistic shifts, which often regulate our impressions of novelty and originality, Said's readings of individual authors like Nerval or Chateaubriand in the impressive middle sections of the book are politically not much more far-reaching than the kind of readings that were common during the 1960s, such as Jonah Raskin offers in *The Mythology of Imperialism.*[17] And, if one steps out of the Euro-American traditions, one is struck by the fact that neither the architecture of *Orientalism* nor the kind of knowledge that the book generally represents has any room in it for criticisms of colonial cultural domination of the kind that have been available in Latin America and even India, on an expanding scale, since the late 19th century. It is in fact one of the disagreeable surprises in *Orientalism* that it refuses to acknowledge that vast tradition, as old virtually as colonialism itself, which has existed in the colonised countries as well as among the metropolitan left traditions, and which has always been occupied, precisely, with drawing up an inventory of colonial traces in the minds of people on both sides of the colonial divide. When Said does return to this matter of what he might have owed to earlier critiques of colonialism and its cultural consequences for the colonies, in the well known essay '*Orientalism* Reconsidered',[18] he deploys a characteristically contradictory rhetoric. The dominant strain in the essay is that of royal contempt whereby all such efforts of the past are consigned to the dustbin of an undifferentiated 'historicism' which is itself declared to be twin as well as progenitor of imperialism as such. Thus, after debunking a loosely constructed genealogy which he calls 'historicism, that is, the view pronounced by Vico, Hegel, Marx, Ranke, Dilthey and others',[19] Said proceeds to posit the following:

> What, in other words, has never taken place is an epistemological critique at the most fundamental level of the connection between the development of a historicism which has expanded and developed enough to include antithetical attitudes such as ideologies of western imperialism and critiques of imperialism on the one hand, and, on the other, the actual practice of imperialism ....

All previous 'critiques of imperialism' are thus effortlessly conjoined with 'the actual practice of imperialism', thanks to the historicist contamination. So much for the intellectual capacities of national liberation struggles, which have often used at least the Marxist critiques of imperialism, not to speak of Gramsci's own historicism which Said often likes to invoke!

I must confess, though, that Said's irrepressible penchant for saying entirely contrary things in the same text, appealing to different audiences simultaneously but with the effect that each main statement cancels out the other, is in evidence in this essay as much as anywhere else. For, the sweeping statement which have just quoted stands in a curiously unresolved relationship with the following which we also find in this same essay:

> At bottom, what I said in *Orientalism* had been said before me by A L Tibawin (1961, 1966), by Abdullah Laroui (1976, 1977), by Anwar Abdel Malek (1963, 1969), Talal Asad (1979), by S H Alatas (1977a, 1977b), by Fanon (1969, 1970) and Cesaire (1972), by Panikkar (1959) and Romila Thapar (1975, 1978).

The most sweeping claim of originality is thus balanced against disclaimer of all originality; the most uncompromising attack on historicism is balanced against a list of authors among whom the majority would proudly associate themselves with historicism. The list of authors and dates is itself passing strange, I might add, since it is drawn up in the manner, more or less, of the post-modern pastiche. Tibawi, Laroui and Abdel Malek appear here probably because in his review of *Orientalism*[20] Robert Irwin had also raised the issue of Said's unacknowledged debts and had cited precisely these three writers. Then, as one turns to Said's actual citations of Romila Thapar, one finds that the only publications of hers that he seems to know of are the two textbooks on ancient and medieval India which Thapar did, very much on the side, for middle school pupils. The arrogance of a scholarship which presumes that Thapar's seminal work on Indian history is to be known only through her little textbooks is simply breathtaking. As for his other reference to an Indian writer in this list, the whole range of Said's citation—and he is copious in this matter—seems to suggest that the only significant book by an Indian writer that he had read until well after he had published *Orientalism* in 1978 was, precisely, K.M. Pannikar's good old *Asia and Western Dominance*.

Aside from the unclassifiability of genre, meanwhile, *Orientalism* had been notable also for the sweep, in fact, that few readers initially noticed that most of his references in the more substantial parts of the book were drawn from his training in comparative literature and philology. This was familiar territory for persons of similar background, but those were precisely the persons who were the most likely to resist the invitation to read this body of writing not as literature but as documents of an entirely different sort of archive, namely, the *Orientalist* archive, which *they* had thought was none of their business. The orientalist, on the other hand, into whose archive those other kinds of texts were being read, was equally displeased and bewildered, because he was being attacked but with no possibility of defending himself on what he had defined as his homeground—the ground of libraries, the comparison of medieval manuscripts, the labour of deciphering illegible manuscripts, the problems of establishing authentic texts and preparing the appropriate gloss, the learning of archaic languages, and bringing back the fruits of this labour for the enlightenment and edification of the public at large. The orientalist was, in his own eyes, a specialist, an innocent. As we well know the effect in both these fields, that of literature and of orientalism (specifically middle-Eastern studies), was electrifying, because the book did serve to open up, despite its blunders, spaces of oppositional work in these moribund fields. Meanwhile, for scholars working outside the academic fields of comparative literature, philology and orientalism, the contents of the book, the sort of documents it read, were largely unfamiliar in any case. That was novelty enough. But what was even more novel was, decidedly, Said's audacity of combination. Who, after all, had ever though that Lamartine and Olivia Manning, Chateaubriand and Byron, Carlyle, Camus, Voltaire, Gertrude Bell, the anonymous composers of *El Cid* and *Chanson de Roland*, Arabists like Gibb, colonial rulers such as Cromer and Balfour, sundry quasi-literary figures like Edward Lane, scholars of Sufism like Massignon,

Henry Kissinger—all belonged in the same archive and a deeply unified discursive formation! What was new, I must repeat, was the *combination*, the reach of erudition, the architecture of the book, the eloquence that went with it, even though the eloquence too had the tendency to be, at times, frightfully repetitive. What had happened in the past was that critics who had raised these issues with reference to modern British literature rarely knew much about 19th century French literature, and those who wrote about literature would rarely examine lexicography or the US state department, even though the imperialist design would often be at issue. Said assembled these varied strands into a single narrative line, and the sense of novelty in America, and British universities, therefore also in the Anglophone ex-colonies, was greatly enhanced by the fact that the most impressive part of the book, namely, its middle section where Said offers readings of individual authors, was preoccupied mainly with French writers. The book may not have added much to our knowledge of Edward Lane or Olivia Manning, T. E. Lawrence or Henry Kissinger, but its treatment of the Bibliotheque Nationale and Chateaubriand, Nerval and Flaubert, was surely unforgettable. (The power of the eloquence combined with the unfamiliarity of contents unfortunately had the effect, often enough, that Said's judgements were simply taken for granted as being true. Rare would be a reader of *Orientalism*, previously unfamiliar with Renan for example, who would then actually care to read Renan.)

Finally, the most striking novelty of *Orientalism*, which gave to it its essential prestige in avant-gardist cultural theory, was methodological: not simply its wide borrowing from the constituted academic disciplines but, far more crucially, its explicit invocation of Foucault, its declaration that the object of this study, namely, orientalism, was a *discourse*, and its insistence that this was the constitutive discourse of western civilisation as such, both chronologically, in the sense that we find it there already in the oldest European textualities, and also civilisationally, since it is by defining the 'orient' as the dangerous, inferiorised civilisational other that Europe has defined itself. There were two distinct consequences of this novelty. One was obviously the shift from Marx to Foucault, which was clearly very congenial to the post-modernist moment. The irrefutable fact about the period before Said's intervention is that aside from the more obscurantist and indigenist kinds of anti-westernist protests against European influence, the vast majority of the socially enlightened and politically progressive critiques of colonialism had been affiliated with either Marxism or, at least, with the general cultural anti-imperialism which Marxism, and the communist movement generally, had helped bring about. Said's break with that political tradition was sweeping indeed. Marx himself was dismissed in the book as yet another orientalist, Marxism was swept aside as an unsavoury child of 'historicism', and the insights which had originally emanated from that tradition were now conjoined with Foucaultian discourse theory. All this fell in very nicely, as the book appeared in 1978 and began its career in a world supervised by Reagan and Thatcher, with various kinds of anti-communisms and post-Marxisms which were to grip the most advanced sectors of the metropolitan intelligentsia during the period. Alongside these large theoretical and political shifts was the matter of a certain trans-historicity which, in claiming that Europe establishes its own identity by establishing the *difference* of the orient and that Europe has possessed a unitary will since the days of Athenian drama to inferiorise and vanquish non-Europe, made it possible for Said to assert that *all* European knowledges of non-Europe are bad knowledges because already contaminated with this aggressive identity-formation. This indeed was a novel idea. Numerous writers had previously demonstrated the complicity of European cultural productions in the colonial enterprise, but only the most obscurantist indigenists and cultural nationalists had previously argued—surely, no writer with any sense of intellectual responsibility and ever accepted—that Europeans were *ontologically* incapable of producing any true knowledge about non-Europe. But Said was emphatic on this point, and he mobilised all sorts of eclectic procedures to establish the point.

III

This issue of eclecticism should take us back into the text, starting with the very opening pages where Said offers not one but three—mutually incompatible—definitions of the term 'orientalism' itself, which he then tries to deploy, simultaneously, throughout the book. In his own words, first:

> Anyone who teaches, writes about, or researches the Orient—and this applies whether the person is an anthropologist, sociologist, historian, or philologist — either in its specific or in its general aspects, is an orientalist, and what he or she does in orientalism.

In this sense, then, orientalism is an inter-disciplinary area of academic knowledge, and the terms used here—anthropology, philology, etc.—would suggest that it is a *modern* discipline. But then, in the second definition, it becomes something much more than that, far exceeding academic boundaries, indeed a mentality traversing a great many centuries, if not a full-scale epistemology:

> Orientalism is a style of thought based upon an ontological and epistemological distinction made between 'the Orient' and (most of the time) 'the Occident'.... This Orientalism can accommodate Aeschylus, say, and Victor Hugo, Dante and Karl Marx.

We shall return to the difficulties of this particular inflation, and then to the matter of 'Dante and Karl Marx', at very considerable length later, but let me cite the third definition:

> Taking the late eighteenth century as a very roughly defined starting point Orientalism can be discussed and analysed as the corporate institution for dealing with the Orient in short, orientalism as a western style for dominating, restructuring, and having authority over the orient.

These three definitions come on two consecutive pages (pp. 2,3), and Aeschylus and Dante are in fact mentioned as examples of the orientalist 'style of thought' five lines before the 18th century is identified, in the third definition, as the 'roughly defined starting point'. Now, the demarcation of boundaries at the 18th century—and at the 'post-Enlightenment period' a few lines later—produces one kind of emphasis; but the naming of Aeschylus produces a very different sense of periodisation, which itself goes back to the opening paragraph where we had been told, in the very third sentence, that 'The Orient was almost a European invention, and had been since antiquity a place of romance ....' When did, then, this discourse of orientalism begin? Nor is this issue of periodisation a minor matter. On pp. 56–57, we get this crucial statement:

> Consider first the demarcation between Orient and west. It already seems bold by the time of the *Iliad*. Two of the most profoundly influential qualities associated with the east appear in Aeschylus' *The Persians*, the earliest Athenian play extant, and in *The Bacchae* of Euripides, the last one extant .... What matters here is that Asia speaks through and by virtue of the European imagination, which is depicted as victorious over Asia, that hostile "other" world beyond the seas. To Asia are given the feeling of emptiness, loss, and disaster that seem thereafter to reward Oriental challenges to the west; and also the lament that in some glorious past Asia fared better ....
>
> The two aspects of the Orient that set it off from the west in this pair of plays will remain essential motifs of European imaginative geography. A line is drawn between two continents. Europe is powerful and articulate; Asia is defeated and distant. Aeschylus *represents* Asia .... it is Europe that articulates the Orient; this articulation is the prerogative, not of a puppet master, but of a

genuine creator, whose life-giving power represents, animates, constitutes the otherwise silent and dangerous space beyond familiar boundaries ....

The 'Orientalist discourse' has already been set in motion, then, in the earliest of the Athenian tragedies, not in general but in the specific regularities which shall henceforth determine its structure: Asia's loss, Europe's victory; Asia's muteness, Europe's mastery of discourse; Asia's inability to represent itself, Europe's will to represent it in accordance with its own authority. The terms are set, and there is little that later centuries will contribute to the essential structure, though they will doubtless proliferate the discourse in enormous quantities. As Said puts it on p. 62: 'It is as if, having once settled on the orient as a locale suitable for incarnating the infinite in a finite shape, Europe could not stop the practice'. And: 'Only the source of these rather narcissistic western ideas about the orient changed in time, not their character'. This sense of an uninterrupted history of 'narcissistic' discourse is then made more dense with the discussion of figures like Dante who form a kind of bridge between ancient origins and modern repetitions, as I will clarify presently when I come to discuss Said's treatment of *Inferno*.

Now, if there really is this seamless and only incremental history of 'Orientalist discourse' from Aeschylus to Dante to Marx to Bernard Lewis, then in what sense could one take the 18th century 'as a roughly defined starting point'? In other words, one does not really know whether the 'orientalist discourse' begins in the post-enlightenment period or at the dawn of European civilisation, whether in the period of the battle of Plassey or in the days of the battle of Troy. This, then, raises the question of the relationship between orientalism and colonialism. In one sort of reading, where post-Enlightenment Europe is emphasised, Orientalism appears an ideological corollary of colonialism. But so insistent is Said in identifying its origins in European Antiquity and its increasing elaboration throughout the European middle ages that it seems to be the *constituting element*, trans-historically, of what he calls 'the European imagination'. In a revealing use of the word 'delivered', Said at one point remarks that orientalism *delivered* the orient to colonialism, so that colonialism begins to appear as a product of orientalism itself, indeed as the realisation of the project already inherent in Europe's perennial project of inferiorising the orient first in discourse and *then* in colonisation. This is of course doubly paradoxical, since Said is vehement in his criticism of 'Orientalism' for its highly 'textual' attitude, and yet in his own account imperialist ideology itself appears to be an effect mainly of certain kinds of *writing*.

But *why* has Europe needed to constitute—'produce' is Said's stark word—the Orient as 'that hostile other world' to 'animate' as he puts it, 'the otherwise silent and dangerous space' as 'one of its deepest and most recurring images of the Other' (p. 1). Well, because, 'European culture gained in strength and identity by setting itself off against the Orient as a sort of surrogate and even underground self' (p. 3). There are many passages of this kind, and Said borrows his language from so many different kinds of conceptual frameworks and intellectual disciplines that one is simply bewildered.[21] There is, for example, enough existentialism in Said's language, derived from identifiable Sartrean concepts, which stands in a peculiar relation with Derridean ideas of identity and difference, all of which is mobilised to posit in some places that the west has *needed* to constitute the orient as its other in order to constitute itself and its own subject-position. This idea of constituting identity through difference points, again, not to the realm of political economy in which colonisation may be seen as a process of capitalist accumulation but to a necessity which arises within discourse and has always been there at the origin of discourse, so that not only is the modern orientalist presumably already there in Dante and Euripides but modern imperialism itself appears to be an effect that arises, as if naturally, from the necessary practices of discourse.[22] That is one sort of difficulty. But there is another one as well, namely, that the matter of identity through difference doubtless points to the primacy of representation over all other human activities, but why must representation also *inferiorise* the other? Said again offers greatly diverse ideas, so that in quite a few places this inferiorisation is shown to be a result of imperialism and colonialism in the sense in which most of us would understand these words, but in another set of formulations, which draw their vocabulary from psycho-analysis, 'the west' seems to have suffered something resembling ego-anxiety whereby the ego is able to constitute its own coherence only through aggressive objectification of the other, so that what Said calls 'orientalism' appears to be a compulsive drive inherent in Europe's unitary *psyche*. So, when one comes upon statements like 'psychologically, orientalism is a form of paranoia' (p. 72), as one frequently does, there is reason enough to be disconcerted by the psychologising impulse but, even more, one then shudders to recall that, for Said, this 'paranoia' is constitutive of all European thought. These ways of dismissing entire civilisations as diseased formations are unfortunately far too familiar to us from the history of imperialism itself.

But let us return to the three definitions, especially the intermediate one which defines orientalism as 'a style of thought based upon an ontological and epistemological distinction between 'the orient' and (most of the time) the Occident'. It is rather remarkable how constantly and comfortably Said speaks, not only in this particular sentence but throughout the book, of a Europe, or the west, as a self-identical, fixed being which has always had an essence and a project, an imagination and a will; and of the 'orient' as its object, textually, militarily, etc. He speaks of the west, or Europe, as the one which produces the knowledge, the east as the object of that knowledge. He seems to posit, in other words, stable subject-object identities,as well as ontological and epistemological distinctions between the two. In what sense, then, is Said himself not an Orientalist, or, at least, as Sadel al-Azm puts it, an 'orientalist-in-reverse'? Said quite justifiably accuses the 'orientalist' for essentialising the orient, but his own processes of essentialising 'the west' are equally remarkable. In the process, Said of course gives us that same 'Europe'—unified, self-identical, trans-historical, textual— which is always rehearsed for us in the sort of literary criticism which traces its own pedigree from Aristotle to T.S. Eliot. That this Athens-to-Albion Europe is itself a recent fabrication as a whole range of writers from Amin[23] to Bernal[24] have recently emphasised, and any Aeschylus-to-Kissinger narrative is therefore also equally a fabrication (or a fabricated reflection of a prior fabrication), is something that seems not to have occurred to Said. The plain fact is that whatever Homer or Aeschylus might have had to say about the Persians or Asia, it simply is not a reflection of a 'west' or of 'Europe' as a civilisational entity, and no modern discourse can be traced back to that because the civilisational map and geographical imagination of the antiquity were fundamentally different from those that came to be fabricated in post-renaissance Europe. Parenthetically, we might emphasise again that Said does not say that 'orientalist' notions have been read *into* Greek and Latin texts; that the main regularities of the discourse are *already there* is central to Said's whole argument.

It is also simply the case that the kind of essentialising procedure which Said associates exclusively with 'the west' is by no means a trait of the European alone; any number of Muslims routinely draw epistemological and ontological distinctions between east and west, the Islamicate and Christendom, and when Ayatollah Khomeini does it he does so hardly from an orientalist position. And, of course, it is common among many circles in India to posit Hindu spirituality against western materialism, not to speak of Muslim barbarity. Nor is it possible to read the *Mahabharata* or the *dharmashastras* without being struck by the severity with which the *dasyus* and the *shudras* and the women are constantly being made into the dangerous, inferiorised others. This is not a merely polemical matter either. What I am suggesting is that there have historically been all sorts of processes—connected with class and gender, ethnicity and religion, xenophobia and bigotry—which have unfortunately been at work in all human societies, European and non-European. What gave to European forms of these prejudices their special force in history, with devastating consequences in the actual lives of countless millions and expressed ideologically in full-blown Eurocentric racisms, was not some trans-historical process of ontological obsession and falsity—some gathering of unique force in domains of discourse—but, quite specifically, the power of colonial capitalism, which then gave rise to other sorts of powers. Within the realm of discourse over the past two hundred years though, the relationship between the brahminical and the Islamic high textualities, the orientalist knowledges of these textualities, and their modern reproductions in western as well as non-western countries, have produced such a wilderness of mirrors, in which reflections are refracted in such diverse ways, that we need the most incisive of operations, the most delicate of dialectics, to disaggregate these densities.

Said's penchant for foregrounding the literariness of this so-called discourse gives rise to yet another kind of problem when he defines orientalism, in his third definition, as 'a western style for dominating, restructuring, and having authority over the orient'. The surprising word but also the key word here is *style* — which should save us from supposing that he might be talking of the political economy or the ideological constructs of colonialism and imperialism. For he says quite directly, on p.12:

> 'Orientalism is not a mere political subject matter or field that is reflected passively by culture, scholarship, or institution; ... nor it is representative and expressive of some nefarious 'western' imperialist plot to hold down the 'oriental' world.

So, we have at least some clue as to what orientalism is not: it is not what is commonly understood by colonialist — or imperialist — ideology. In the process, though, we come upon a strange discrepancy: it is a 'style' that has always spoken of occident and orient as victor and vanquished, a discourse which has always had a will to power, but it expresses no imperialist design; it is full of racism, jingoism, religious bigotry, but it has no will to 'hold down' anybody. So, it is hard to know what Said actually means, beyond, of course, the familiar Foucaultian trope of a power which permeates everything and reproduces itself copiously in all the pores of society and textuality but which has neither origin nor object nor an agency to which its processes could be traced, and which can be known only through the knowledge it produces but the knowledge itself can be referred not to the thing represented but to the truth-effect produced. Meanwhile, Said does give us clues as to what the book, *Orientalism*, is and how he wishes us to read it, and yet these clues tend also to cancel out each other:

> My analysis of the orientalist text therefore places emphasis on the evidence, which is by no means invisible, for such representations *as representations*... The things to look at are style, figures of speech, setting, narrative device, historical and social circumstances, not the correctness of the representation nor its fidelity to some great original.

The notable feature of this approach is Said's desire to combine very familiar emphases in literary-critical ways of reading ('style, figures of speech, setting, narrative devices, historical and social circumstances') with a post-modernist emphasis on 'representation as *representation*'. One of those ways of reading presses us toward the problematic of realism and mimesis, the other in the direction of non-mimetic, discursive, 'truth-effects', It would be unimaginably difficult if not altogether pointless, I should have thought, to refer a representation to its 'setting' and 'the historical and social circumstances' of its production and dissemination without raising, in some fundamental way, the issues of its 'fidelity' and 'correctness', for it is usally with reference to 'historical and social circumstances' that worthwhile distinctions between a representation and a misrepresentation are customarily made. I shall take up elsewhere this crucial issue of the primacy of representation as well as Said's inability to make up his mind whether 'orientalist discourse' is a system of representations, in the Foucaultian sense, or of misrepresentations, in the sense of a realist problematic. For, Said's use of this self-divided procedure leads to great many theoretical difficulties and political confusions which are then frequently replicated and even simplified in what had come to be known as 'colonial discourse analysis'. Let me say, meanwhile, that it is in the midst of all these difficulties—of definition, conception, periodisation, theoretical position and political uncertainty—that Said then launches on his reading of individual authors, most of which turn out to be the familiar canonical authors.

Many of these individual readings — of Nerval, for example, or T.E. Lawrence — are very good. One can actually say with fair certainty that, with the exception of those two magnificent opening chapters in *Question of Palestine*, where Said has handled extremely broad and complex issues altogether superbly, he still tends to be at his best when he is reading (closely) an individual canonical author, interpreting a particular canonical book, or at most preparing a focused critique of determinate issues in a particular academic discipline, such as anthropology, which has already had a great many very trenchant critiques that he can then borrow from in erudite and distinctive ways.[25] When he exercises this skill at his best, few living literary critics can match him, for he learned this skill of close reading in the pedagogical laboratory of 'new criticism'; has applied it in the wider and even more exacting field of comparatism; and now exercises it with his great wit, matchless erudition, power prose style, and generous liberal sympathies. This skill is his achievement — but a limitation, too. For, when he is at his weakest, such readings of individual authors can also be merely derivative or trite, as for example in his recent essay on *Kim*. The one on Jane Austen's *Mansfield Park* is better,[26] but Said's difficulties with the issue of gender are such that he can scarcely see that precarious ways in which women of (and around) the British propertied classes, who were doubtless complicitly benefiting from designs of empire, are nevertheless differentially located in mobilities and pedagogies of the class structure. Those are difficulties of a different kind, however. In *Orientalism* itself the largest difficulties occur when Said tries to fit rather complex matters in the unlinear 'orientalist' mode. This I should like to illustrate with some lengthier comment on his treatment of one author alone, namely, Dante.

IV

The transition that Said makes to Dante is *strategic* on at least two counts: Dante is the central, exemplary figure forming the bridge between antiquity and modernity; and, 'Dante's powers as a poet intensify, make more rather than less representative, these perspectives on the Orient' (p. 69). The theme of transhistorical continuity is stated unmistakably:

> ... as one surveys Orientalism in the nineteenth and twentieth centuries the overriding impression is of Orientalism's insensitive schematisation of the entire Orient.
>
> How early this schematisation began is clear from the examples I have given of Western representations of the Orient in classical Greece. How strongly articulated were later representations building on the earlier ones, how inordinately careful their schematisation, how dramatically effective their placing in Western imaginative geography, can be illustrated if we turn now to Dante's *Inferno* (p. 68).

There is thus an incremental history ('later representations building on the earlier ones'), 'inordinately careful' in its 'schematisation' which joins the 19th and 20th centuries with Dante and 'classical Greece'. Said is absolutely right, of course, in regarding the *Inferno* as a book mainly of *judgements,* and his initial comment on the poem turns, then, on Dante's treatment of Muhammed. This is predictable and unsurprising; Said is hardly the first to have noticed the inordinate horror of that passage. What is truly surprising is the way Said deals with Dante's far more complex treatment of, in Said's words, 'the great Muslim philosophers and Kings'.

Now, few readers of *Inferno* would find it possible to forget that Muhammed, the prophet of Islam, is found in the eighth of the circles of hell, eternally gyrating and eternally being cleft from brain to anus, in the worst punishment that Dante's prolific imagination could devise. This treatment of the prophet of Islam is, to put it mildly, indefensible, and I am entirely in sympathy with Said when he takes offence. The peculiarity in any case is that Ibn Sina ('Avicenna' in English, the Arab-Islamic philosopher best known for his expertise in empiricist physiology and medicine), Ibn Rushd ('Averroes' in English, the great Arab-Islamic philosopher of rationalist humanism), as well as Salah ad-Din (the 'Saladin' made famous by the crusades), are found in the *first* circle, in the company of Socrates, Plato, etc. Now, the presence of those figures from antiquity in this mildest of all circles in hell makes a certain sense within the Christian topography of punishments and sufferings, because they are heathens only to the extent that they came before Christ and therefore never had the benefit of Christ's teaching; this also explains the otherwise surprising decision on part of Beatrice to appoint Virgil, himself a heathen, as Dante's guide on this eventful tour. But, why Ibn Rushd? He came *after* Christ, therefore, had the choice to renounce the Islamic heresy, but did not! Dante never faces up to this question, and is benign towards Ibn Rushd despite this key difference between him and Socrates and company. One grasps the full force of this discrepancy only if one recalls that Ibn Rushd was a splendid rationalist whose books were banned in some places by the Inquisition, not because he was a Muslim but, explicitly, because he was a rationalist. How, then, does one explain the discrepancy in the *Inferno*? I would suggest that the discrepancy is to be understood in terms of the contradictions of Dante's own ideology, and that the contradictions stem from the fact that Dante powerfully represents that unfinished moment of transition in European thought wherein the medieval episteme is still there but in the process of being broken up and superseded by the humanist intellectual revolution which was the main theoretical contribution of the mercantilist phase of European capital. Muhammed is eternally undergoing the most awful punishment because predominant strands in medieval Christianity treated Islam as the most dangerous of all heresies and pronounced the prophet of Islam the worst of all heretics. Ibn Rushd, condemned by the authority of that same medieval Christianity through the awful powers of the Inquisition, was nevertheless greatly respected by mainly those who were to build toward the rising humanist revolution, with his books being copied and smuggled from one monastery to another. Still mired in the religious metaphysic, but unable to resist entirely the strain that was soon to blossom into a fully fledged humanism, and knowing that it was through its encounter with the labours of men like Ibn Rushd and Ibn Sina that a great many European thinkers were able to find their way into Greek thought in the first place, Dante tried to devise a topography of his hell that might do justice to these divided loyalities. An even more notable presence in fact is that of Salah ad-Din who, unlike Ibn Rushd, was to be much reviled by later centuries throughout Christendom, because he was in fact a commander of the Arab-Islamic forces that were ranged against the crusading Christians. Dante pays scant attention to that particular bigotry and delivers a 'judgement' on 'the great Muslim kings and philosophers' and on the prophet of Islam which is, from the viewpoint of orthodox Christianity, internally incoherent. The literary-critical point I am making is that one cannot read that passage about Muhammed outside this whole range of enormous complexity. The methodological point, in the Foucaultian language, is that one cannot detach a representation of Muhammed, which is produced in the discourse of Christian binaries between belief and heresy, and relocate that representation in the altogether different discourse of 'orientalism' which, if it exists at all and even though it may occasionally use religious forms of ideological interpellation, is a secular knowledge. Furthermore, Dante's treatment of Ibn Rushd, who is placed at least at par with Socrates, etc, and toward whom Dante is altogether more forgiving, shows that Dante makes a severe distinction between belief and heresy but none between occident and orient, as would be clear if Said were to actually reflect upon the fact that Judas, Brutus and Cassius do actually come even after Muhammed, in closer proximity with Satan himself. I might add that the treatment that Ibn Rushd receives in Dante's imagination, which does to the Muslim philosopher at least no physical harm in the real world, was not worse than the treatment he received in real life from Abu Yusuf, the Almohid king of Muslim Spain, who ordered him banished into exile and his books burned on charges of heresy. Said ignores such complexities at his own peril when he comments as follows, on p. 69.

> ... the special anachronisms and anomalies of putting pre-Christian luminaries in the same category of "heathen" damnation with post-Christian Muslims does not trouble Dante. Even though the Koran specifies Jesus as a prophet, Dante chooses to consider the great Muslim philosophers and kings as having been fundamentally ignorant of Christianity. That they can also inhabit the same distinguished level as the heroes and sages of classical antiquity is an ahistorical vision similar to Raphael's in his fresco *The School of Athens*, in

which Averroes rubs elbows on the academy floor with Socrates and Plato (similar to Fenelon's *Dialogues des morts* (1700–1718), where a discussion takes place between Socrates and Confucius).

References to Raphael and Fenelon further substantiate Said's great erudition but contribute no insight to the substance of the argument. That Said should require that kind of literalist historicity from confessedly allegorical work is also surprising; one might as well castigate Dante for putting himself and Virgil in the same historical time and in a purely fictitious place called hell. Matters are made worse by the way Said construes the meaning that 'ignorance' may have in the context of religious orthodoxy, for, not to believe in Christianity is for Dante (as not to *believe* in Islam would have been for Sa'adi and even Hafiz) the worst kind of ignorance — worse in the case of Ibn Rushd than Socrates because the former had the means to overcome that ignorance! The fact that 'the Koran specifies Jesus as a prophet' thus makes the matter of this 'ignorance' worse - though one would add, for the sake of a *modern*, irreligious discussion, that this reference to the status of Jesus himself in the literal word of the Koran is also irrelevant. What has been at issue in orthodox Islam is not the status of Jesus but of Christianity, and of how Jesus surfaces in Christian belief. For, if orthodox Christianity regards Islam as a heresy, orthodox Islam has historically regarded some of the main tenets of Christianity as altogether blasphemous: the idea of the trinity, the idea of Jesus as a *son* of God, the further idea that Mary was a *virgin*, the even more scandalous idea of the holy ghost. The legacy of the crusades lives, we might recall, on both sides of the orthodox divide.

V

Orientalism appeared in 1978, a rather precise point in the history of the world, in the history of the demographic composition and reorganisation of the political conjuncture in the United States, and in the history of intellectual productions in the metropolitan countries generally. Each of these aspects shall bear some comment because all this has some bearing on how books were now being read.

By 1978, the two great revolutionary decades, inaugurated—roughly speaking—by the onset of the Algerian war in 1954 and culminating in the liberation of Saigon in 1975, were over. The decisive turning-point had come in Chile in 1973, with the defeat of the Unidad Popular, but we did not then know it, because the liberation movements of Indochina and the Portuguese colonies in Africa were still in progress. The two revolutions of 1978, in Iran and Afghanistan, then made the shift unmistakable. For, the Khomeinite take-over in Iran was one of those rare conjunctures in which the revolution and the counterrevolution were condensed in the same moment. In Afghanistan, the last country to have a revolution under a communist leadership, history now repeated itself, in Marx's famous phrase, both as tragedy and as farce. If the Iranian revolution had signalled the decisive defeat of the left in West Asia and the rise to ideological dominance of Islamic fundamentalism in that whole region, the history-as-tragedy-and-as-farce in Afghanistan was to contribute considerably to the collapse of what socialism there had ever been in the Comecon countries, helping to pave the way to perestroika first in the Soviet Union, then on the global scale. The savage destruction of Baghdad, the worst since the Mongols sacked that city in the 13th century, was the gift of this global perestroika, making one recall Marx once more. As he famously put it in his correspondence on the Gotha Programme, capitalism does not lead necessarily to socialism, it may lead just as inexorably toward barbarism.

All that was to come later. What the end of the revolutionary decades did, however, was first of all, to shift the entire balance within the metropolitan countries further to the right. The Anglo-Saxon countries witnessed the rise to governmental power of the most reactionary kinds of ideologies, Reaganism and Thatcherism, movements for racial and social justice in the United States were beaten back, and the defeat of the miners' strike in Britain put an end to labour militancy there for years to come. Social democracy itself was soon to be defeated in Germany and the Scandinavian countries, while in Italy it submitted, under Craxi's leadership, to Christian Democracy, while PCI retreated and was then, after 1976, decisively disorganised; social democracy did come to power in France but survived by moving so far to the right that it renounced even the autonomist positions of high Gaullism. For the backward capitalist zones, developments were far too many and too clearly rooted in histories of particular countries to be summarised in so short a space, but what happened in our own subcontinent is indicative. The Bhutto-ite version of populist social democracy was first replaced, in 1977, by a fundamentalist military dictatorship and then fleetingly reappeared in a farcical form under his daughter's regime. In Bangladesh, the progressive content of the liberation struggle was dissipated quickly,leading to a regime of right-wing military officers who had previously served in the Pakistan army and had been trained at Fort Bragg in the United States; the widow of one those officers is currently the prime minister. In India, communism has been contained in its regional locations, the social compact based on Gandhian ideas of religious tolerance has been increasingly under attack, sometimes in the name of Gandhi himself; Nehruvian models of parliamentary democracy, secularist polity, planned economy, and non-aligned foreign policy have been emptied out of their content, and a whole range of disorientations since the Emergency, dating back again to the mid-70s, have moved the country and its entire political and social discourse cumulatively and decisively toward the right.

This global offensive of the right, global retreat of the left, and retreat also of that which was progressive even in our canonical nationalisms, is the essential backdrop for any analysis of the structure of intellectual productions and their reception in our time. For, it was within this reorganised global conjuncture that we have witnessed, in all the bourgeois countries, the ascendancy to dominance of an entirely new kind of intellectual within a formation which continued to call itself a formation of the left. The characteristic posture of these new intellectuals was that they would gain legitimacy on the left by constantly and fervently referring to the third world, Cuba, national liberation and so on, but would also be openly and contemptuously anti-communist; they would often enough not affiliate themselves even with that other tradition which had also descended from classical Marxism, namely, social democracy, nor would they be affiliated in any degree with any labour movement whatever; they would invoke an anti-bourgeois stance in the name of manifestly reactionary and propagated anti-humanisms enunciated in the Nietszchean tradition and propagated now under the signature of antiempiricism, anti-historicism, structuralism and post-structuralism, specifically Levi-Strauss, Foucault, Derrida, Glucksmann, Kristeva, and so on. It is in contrast to these reactionary anti-humanisms, across the whole spectrum of cultural theories, that the rectitude in careers of people like Raymond Williams turns out to be so exemplary.

I shall return to other kinds of determinations presently but this matter of Nietzschean anti-humanism is of some crucial interest here, in part because of the way Said's treatment of Marx, stands in tense balance with the authority of Nietzsche which is invoked indirectly through Foucault, and therefore structures the whole book around notions of representations and discourse, but also directly, in a crucial passage, on page 203. But, before getting to 203, we shall first have to take a detour through 272 and 273. For, on those two consecutive pages, we find two rather inconsistent statements, brief and stark. First, we have:

> as this book has tried to show Islam has been fundamentally misrepresented in the past ....

But then we quickly have on the next page:

> My whole point about this whole system is not that it is a misrepresentation of some Oriental essence...

Now, the substitution of the term 'oriental essence' in the latter sentence for the term 'Islam' in the former sentence may persuade one to believe that the two sentences are referring to two different things, or that they are not on the issue of (mis)representation, but what Said is actually doing is drawing closer to the Nietzschean idea that no true representation is possible because all human communications always distort the facts. For, what happens between these two sentences is that Said first raises the question: 'The real issue is whether there can be a true representation of anything'. In other words, is it possible to make true statements? There are powerful traditons, including the Nietzschean, which have denied such a possibility. There are other powerful traditions, including the Marxist, which have said that, yes, true statements are possible. Said's equivocation on the this key question is delivered in what appears to be a precise formulation, namely, that the line between a representation and a misrepresentation is always very thin. I should emphasise that this is not a personal statement on the part of Edward Said. Foucault would of course call this a discursive statement. What I would suggest is that this statement belongs directly in the Nietzschean phiolosophical tradition, and that Edward Said, who is here in the midst of writing a history of orientalism, is affiliating himself with a new kind of history-writing which is emerging more or less at this time ; which goes far beyond the empirical historian's usual interrogation of and skepticism about his source materials; and which enters the Nietzschean world of questioning the very factuality of facts, so that it will eventually force a wide range of historians around the globe — some of the Indian subalternists, for example — to start putting the word 'fact' in quotation marks.

With this clarification in hand, we can now turn to page 203. For, what Said say there is the following, with a quotation from Nietzsche embedded in the passage:

> (Orientalism's) objective discoveries — the work of innumerable devoted scholars who edited texts and translated them, codified grammars, wrote dictionaries, reconstructed dead epochs, produced positivistically verifiable learning — are and always have been conditioned by the fact that its truths, like any truths delivered by language, are embodied in language, and what is the truth of language, Nietzsche once said, but a mobile army of metaphors, metonyms, and anthropomorphisms — in short, a sum of human relations, which have been enhanced, transposed, and embellished poetically and rhetorically, and which after long use seem firm, canonical and obligatory to

a people : truths are illusions about which one has forgotten that this is what they are.

This image of language as the enemy of experience, this assertion that representation is always-already a misrepresentation, this shallow pathos about the impossibility of truthful human communication, is of course a familiar romantic trope which has undergone much aggrandisement first in those irrationalist philosophies of the late 19th century and the early 20th century which preceded the rise of fascism and then again, on a much wider scale, in the reactionary anti-humanisms which have dominated avant-gardist thought since the decisive defeat of the European labour movements and the consequent ascendancy of structuralism and post-structuralism; it is significant that these anti-humanisms should come to dominate American scholarship on the eve of the unprecedented imperialist consolidations of the present decade. That this form of irrationalism should surface so centrally in the very book which is doubtless the most influential among radically inclined cultural theorists today should give us, I believe, some pause. But it should also help us grasp some aspects of its enthusiastic reception and extremely widespread influence. For, in one range of formulations Said's denunciations of the whole of western civilisation is as extreme and uncompromising as Foucault's denunciations of the western episteme or Derrida's denunciations of the trans-historical logis; nothing, nothing at all exists outside epistemic power, logocentric thought, orientalist discourse—no classes, no gender, not even history, no site of resistance, no accumulated projects of human liberation, since all is repetition with difference, all is corruption, specifically western corruption, and orientalism always remains the same, only more so with the accumulations of linear time. The manichean edge of these visions — Derridean, Foucaultian, Saidian — is quite worthy of Nietzsche himself. But this vision, in the case of *Orientalism*, gains its authority further from the way it panders to the most sentimental, the most extreme forms of third-worldist nationalism. The book of course says nothing about any fault of our own, but anything we ourselves could remember, the bloodbath that we conducted at the time of the partition let us say, simply pales in comparison with this other power which has victimised us and inferiorised us for twenty-five hundred years, or more. So uncompromising is this book in its third-worldist passion that Marxism itself, which has historically given such sustenance to so many of the anti-imperialist movements of our time, can be dismissed, breezily, as a child of orientalism and an accomplice of British colonialism. How comforting such visions of one's own primal and permanent innocence are, one can well imagine, because, given what actually goes on in our countries, we do need a great deal of comforting.

But it is not within the so-called 'third world' that the book first appeared. Its global authority is in fact inseparable from the authority of the dominant sectors of the metropolitan intelligentsia who first bestowed upon it the status of a modern classic, while, perhaps paradoxically, its most passionate following within the metropolitan countries is within those sectors of the university, intelligentsia which either originates in the ethnic minorities or affiliates itself ideologically with the academic sections of those minorities. I have discussed elsewhere the connection between the emergence of the category of 'third world literature' and the key changes that occurred in the patterns of immigration from the late 1960s onwards, with substantial numbers of Asian immigrants being based now among the petty bourgeois and techno-managerial strata.[27] Those who came as graduate students and then joined the faculties, especially in the humanities and the social sciences, tended to come from upper classes in their home countries. In the process of relocating themselves in the metropolitan countries, they needed documents of their assertion, documentary proof that they had always been oppressed. Books that connected oppression with class were not very useful, because they neither came from the working class nor were intending to join that class in their new country. Those who said that the majority of the populations in Africa and Asia surely suffered from colonialism but that there were also those who benefited from it, were useless, because some of the new professionals who had come in this immigration themselves came from those other families, those other classes, which had been the beneficiaries; this question of the beneficiaries of colonialism would be posed by Said in very peculiar ways, in his invocation of Ranajit Guha, as we shall soon see. Among critiques that needed to be jettisoned were the Marxist ones, because Marxists had this habit of speaking about classes, even in Asia and Africa. What this new immigration needed were narratives of oppression that would get them preferential treatment, reserved jobs, higher salaries in the social position that they already occupied: namely, as middle class professionals, mostly male. *Orientalism* was for such purposes the perfect narrative. When, only slightly later, enough women found themselves in that same position, the category of the 'third world female subaltern' was found to be highly serviceable. I might add that this latter category is probably not very usable inside India, but the kind of discourse *Orientalism* assembles certainly has its uses. Communalism, for example, can now be laid entirely at the doors of orientalism and colonial construction; caste itself can be portrayed as a fabrication primarily of the Population Surveys and Census Reports, as Ronald Inden literally does[28] and Partha Chatterjee appears poised to do.[29] Colonialism is now held responsible not only for its own cruelties but, conveniently enough, for ours too.

Meanwhile, within the metropolitan countries, the emphasis on immigration was to continue getting strengthened. I have written previously on some aspects of this connection between post-modernism and migrancy,[30] but it is worth mentioning that the same theme surfaces with very major emphases in Said's latest essays, with far-reaching consequences for his own earlier positions, as we shall see.

The perspectives inaugurated in *Orientalism* served, in the social self-consciousness and professional assertion of the middle class immigrant and the 'ethnic' intellectual, roughly the same function which the theoretical category of 'third world literature', arising at roughly the same time, was also to serve.[31] One in fact presumed the other, and between the two the circle was neatly closed. If *Orientalism* was devoted to demonstrating the bad faith and imperial oppression of all European knowledges, beyond time and history, 'third world literature' was to be the narrative of authenticity, the counter-canon of truth, good faith liberation itself. Like the bad faith of European knowledge, the counter-canon of 'third world literature' had no boundaries either, neither of space nor of time, culture or class; a Senegalese novel, a Chinese short story, a song from medieval India could all be read into the same archive: it was all 'third world'. Marx was an 'orientalist' because he was European, but a Tagore novel, patently canonical and hegemonising inside the Indian cultural context, could be taught in the syllabi of 'third world literature' as a marginal, non-canonical text, counterpoised against 'Europe'. The homogenising sweep was evident in both cases, and if cultural nationalism was the overtly flaunted insignia, invocation of 'race' was barely below the surface, not just with respect to the United States, which would be logical, but with reference to human history as such. Thus, if 'orientalism' was initially posited as something of an original ontological flaw in the European psyche, Said was to eventually declare that 'in the relationship between the ruler and the ruled in the imperial or colonial or racial sense, race takes precedence over both class and gender .... I have always felt that the problem of emphasis and relative importance took precedence over the need to establish one's feminist credentials.'[32] The contemptuous phrase, 'establish one's feminist credentials' takes care of gender quite definitively as imperialism itself is collapsed into a 'racial sense'. In a Nietzschean world, virtually anything is possible.

VI

Said's inventions since the initial publication of Orientalism have doubtless been prolific and diverse. *The Question of Palestine* and *Covering Islam* as they came in quick succession thereafter, were explicitly conceived as volumes of a series inaugurated with *Orientalism*. *After the Last Sky* and *Blaming the Victims*, which came some years later, may also be considered as parts of that same integrated *oeuvre*. Surrounding this impressive array of books are essays, articles and reviews on cognate themes in a great many periodicals, political journals and newspapers, not to speak of unpublished interventions in scholarly conferences and public fora of various kinds, including very effective television appearances, so numerous that they could easily fill two or three volumes. Together, these writings constitute not only the most enduring though inevitably uneven part of Said's work but also, by any standards, the most persuasive insertion of a national liberation struggle into the American imagination which is otherwise substantially formed by Zionist-colonial presumptions. That remains true even though *Covering Islam*, which is not about Palestine, is, I think, Said's most forgettable piece of writing.

Almost equally extensive, though far more problematic and at times even disconcerting are Said's publications in the field of cultural studies. Central to this other work is of course his volume of 1983, *The World, The Text and the Critic*, which brings together essays written between 1969 and 1981. But there are also numerous other essays which have appeared in journals but have not yet been collected in a separate volume; a few of these, too, have been included in volumes edited by others. The book includes at least two major pieces, 'Raymond Schwab and the Romance of Ideas' and 'Islam, Philology and French Culture: Renan and Massignon' which are thematically connected with *Orientalism*, even though some of the formulations in those essays are considerably different; the essay on Schwab actually reads, in part, as something of a retraction of the extremities of *Orientalism*, without any overt suggestion to that effect.[33] Two other essays in the book, which are in fact the best known and the most influential, namely, 'Criticism between Culture and System' and 'Travelling Theory', were evidently written sometime after *Orientalism* and are notable not so much for explicating Said's preference for Foucault over Derrida as for his partial distancing of himself from Foucault. This distancing is facilitated by his reliance on criticisms of Foucault which had been framed already by Poulantzas[34] and Chomsky, whom Said cites directly, and part of what Said now says about Foucault is uncannily similar to some points I have raised above about *Orientalism* itself. The following from 'Travelling Theory', which is intended as reservations about Foucault and his notion of power applies almost exactly to Said and his conception of orientalism:

> Foucault's eagerness not to fall into Marxist economism causes him to obliterate the role of classes, the role of economics, the role of insurgency

and rebellion in the societies he discusses... The problem is that Foucault's use of the term *pouvoir* moves around too much, swallowing up every obstacle in its path ...., obliterating change and mystifying its microphysical sovereignty ... Foucault's history is ultimately textual or rather textualised; its mode is one for which Borges would have an affinity... they (his archaeologies) make not even a nominal allowance for emergent movements, and none for revolutions, counter-hegemony, or historical blocs.[35]

Since those two essays are only tangentially connected with the aspects of Said's work with which I am here the most concerned, I shall not offer any reading of the remarkable ambivalences one finds in them. It is in any event simply not possible within the space of an essay — even an inordinately lengthy essay such as this one — to give detailed accounts of each significant item in an output so substantial, distinctive and diverse.

This partial distancing from Foucault is in fact part of a number of shifts that have occurred in Said's more recent writings, which include a retreat from the Nietzschean position of all representations being misrepresentations, and admits, concomitantly, the possibilities of resistance from outside the colonial discourse. Meanwhile, his re-reading of both Foucault and Derrida, and his many convergences with diverse post-modernist positions, then culminates in the insistence that the double task of responsible knowledge is to resist the pressures both of the dominant culture as well as of what would now be increasingly known as 'system', 'theory', 'grand theory', 'disciplinary knowledge' and by several even more colourful epithets — referring frequently to Marxism in particular, but also to any other ways of being in the world which may seek to establish theoretical as well as narrative intelligibility of history as such, and which then identify collective agents (such as class, gender, nation) as bearers of resistance and political action. All such systems are rejected, in the characteristic post-modernist way, so that resistance can always, only, be personal, micro, and shared only by a small, determinate number of individuals who happen, perchance to come together, outside the so-called 'grand narratives' of class, gender, nation.[36] Ambivalences on this question are already notable in 'Travelling Theory', but even more representative in all this is the essay 'Opponents, Audiences, Constituencies and Community',[37] where Said first speaks derisively of 'the self-policing, self-purifying communities erected even by Marxist, as well as other disciplinary, discourses' and then goes on to specify what he considers as a key project that needs to be posed against, the 'disciplinary' character of Marxism etc.: 'to restore the non-sequential energy of lived historical memory and subjectivity to tell other stories than the official sequential or ideological ones produced by institutional power'. I am not quite sure what this last formulation actually means, but it would not be unfair to say, I think, that the sense in which Marxism is said to be 'self-policing, self-purifying', as well as 'disciplinary', 'institutional' and 'ideological' applies inescapably to feminism too. Theoretical eclecticism meanwhile gets increasingly out of control; sweeping, patently post-structuralist denunciations of Marxism can be delivered in the name of Gramsci, using the terminological language explicitly drawn from Althusser, and listing the names of communist poets like Aime Cesaire, Pablo Neruda and Mahmoud Derwish to illustrate the sites of resistance. Theory thus becomes what Roland Barthes called 'the free play of the Signifier'.

The largest shift, however, has been on the issue of nationalism, in the years immediately following the publication of *Orientalism*, Said's position was indistinguishable from straightforward third-worldist cultural nationalisms, and what we used to get was an unself-critical narrative of European guilt, non-European innocence. This has shifted dramatically, beginning in about 1984 and getting increasingly more strident in rejection of nationalism, national boundaries, nations as such, so that one now has reason to be equally alarmed by the extremity of this opposite stance. Characteristically, though, the most sweeping statements about 'nation' and 'state' as 'coercive identities' are frequently delivered alongside resounding affirmations of national liberation, Palestinian *Intifada* in particular, and the right of the Palestinian people to either obtain a nation-state of their own or, alternatively, to live as co-equals in a bi-national state. It is this growing ambivalence about nation and nationalism — combined with an even more surprising shift from a wholesale rejection of 'the west' to an equally wholesale assertion that the only authentic work that can be done in our time presumes (a) third world origin, but combined with (b) metropolitan location — which should bear some scrutiny. The intellectual cited as an exemplary figure of our time in this latest construction is of course Ranajit Guha — who is commended both for initial origin in the Indian upper class and for later location in the metropolitan university — but an autobiographical self-referentiality is here quite unmistakable.[38]

Among the numerous essays of Said which have appeared in journals over roughly the past decade but have yet not been collected into a single volume are a dozen or so that are thematically organised around the relationship between imperialism and (mainly) literature. Some of these happen to be on highly canonical figures (e.g., Jane Austen, Kipling, Yeats, Camus, Verdi); others are of more general import. Among the essays on individual figures, the one on Verdi[39] is my favourite, not because I wholly understand operatic language or have ever actually seen *Aida* but because I quite follow Said's highly convincing argument. With all the knowledge he accumulated in the course of writing *Orientalism*; with his great competence as a pianist and his passion for opera, he is peculiarly well situated to write about this masterpiece of European classical music which was composed especially for the opening of the Suez Canal, and he accomplishes the task with verve and rare wit. However, readings of particular authors I must again perforce skip, and it is from among essays that fall in the latter category, bearing a certain sweep of generalisation, that I should like to examine only two: 'Figures, Configurations, Transfigurations', cited earlier, and 'Third World Intellectuals and Metropolitan Culture', from *Raritan Quarterly*. Of these two, the 'Figures' essay appears to be chronologically earlier and was originally delivered as a lecture at the Conference of the Association for Commonwealth Literature and Language Studies, held at the University of Kent in August 1989. Such associations are usually very conservative and mindless affairs, so the radicalism of a great many things Said says in the essay is salutary. My interest in these essays is of a slightly different kind, however.

Both these essays, as several others in recent years, register some real advances over *Orientalism*. There had been, for example, no evidence until after the publication of that book that Said had read any considerable number of contemporary non-western writers. By contrast, references to principal figures of the counter-canon of 'third world literature' surface very regularly in his more recent writings, even though not even one of them has yet been treated with the hermeneutic engagement and informed reading which Said offers so often for scores of western canonical figures; in the rare event when Said actually refers to particular texts, as in the case of George Antonius or Ranajit Guha in the essay we shall discuss presently, none ever receives the kind of detailed scrutiny which Said routinely accords to a wide range of European writers ranging from Swift to Renan to Schwab to Kipling. His engagement both as activist and as scholar with the Palestine liberation movement has been extended, meanwhile, to regular expressions of solidarity with anti-colonial movements in general and a basic respect for figures associated with such movements. Similarly, the eloquence of his plea that the contemporary masters of western thought should extend humane attention and liberal sympathy to non-western writers, especially to those who have themselves taken up residence in the west, is undeniable.

These partial gains in the range of engagements and sympathies stands, however, in peculiar and paradoxical relation with the freshly-acquired but altogether irrepressible rage against the peoples, societies, national boundaries, reading communities and literatures of Asia, Africa, and 'the Islamic world'; the enormous privileging of a handful of writers, strictly those who now live in the west, over those societies and literatures; and the conception of the 'western centre' as the only site where 'contests over decolonisation' can now take place. The enormity of this shift is puzzling, to put it as kindly as possible. The continued American hostility toward the Arab world on the one hand, the sentencing of Rushdie by Ayatollah Khomeini on the other, combined with the failure of most people in Asia, Africa and the Arab world to do combat on Rushdie's behalf, seems to have given rise to an extraordinary fury against the west and non-west alike, with the figure of the lonely writer in the western city — and the uncommitted reader of novels in that same city — eventually emerging as the only figures of redemption.

VII

These ambivalences get played out fully only in the address on Commonwealth literature but some of the key formulations are found in the essay on 'Third World Intellectuals and Metropolitan Culture', which we shall take up first. The latter half of the essay consists of the entirely salutary recommendation that non-western writers be taken seriously by western readers. The main burden of the arguments rests, however, in a rather strange distinction between what get called 'colonial' and 'post-colonial' intellectuals; brief commentaries on four books to furbish this sweeping typology; and a resounding affirmation of the acquisition of western 'technique' and personal location in 'the western centre' as the prerequisites of 'insurgency' and 'contest over decolonisation'. Before we get to all that, however, it maybe useful to briefly indicate the breezy way in which generalisations get handled, as in the following rather interesting passage which opens the third paragraph:

> Resistance to imperialism does not, of course, only involve armed force or bands of guerrillas. It is *mainly* allied with nationalism and with an aroused sense of aggrieved religious, cultural, or existential identity. In its pantheon are great warriors like Abdel Qader of Algeria, prophets and priests like the Mahdi and Gandhi, a phalanx of nationalist writers — Tagore, Yeats, Neruda, Aime, Cesaire, Leopold Senghor — and dozens of intellectual figures like Marti, Mariategi, Fanon, Cabral and others, whose major role in the creation of an emergent and alternative discourse cannot be minimised (emphasis added for the word 'mainly')

Given that the Mahdi had declared himself a prophet, Gandhi clearly falls in the category of 'priests'. The affirmation of 'nationalism', here as in several other places, should be seen, meanwhile, in relation to the debunking of national identity which we shall see in the other essay. My immediate interest, however, is in the list — compiled in the genre of the post-modern pastiche — of nine names, joined to the infinite category of 'others', bringing together communists and anti-communists, pacificists and Marxists, five of whom actually either led or participated in guerrilla warfare, all mobilised to posit the idea that imperialism is *mainly* a cultural phenomenon to be opposed by an *alternative discourse*. What is important about Cabral evidently is his discursive position, not that he launched and led the armed struggle which led to the liberation of his country and contributed decisively to the liberation of all the Portuguese colonies in Africa, not to speak of the collapse of fascism in Portugal itself.

With this insight in hand, Said then goes on to specify a certain typology of two kinds of intellectuals: the colonial and the post-colonial. In all, he discusses four authors. In the category of the colonial intellectuals fall C.L.R. James, the Trinidadian communist and famous author of *Black Jacobins*, and the Arab nationalist historian, George Antonius, the author of the equally famous *The Arab Awakening*. In the category of post-colonial intellectuals come the Malaysian writer Alatas and the Indian writer Ranajit Guha. Between the four, the globe is nicely covered, as are political ideologies, notably Marxism and nationalism. Before going on to the theoretical import and arbitrariness of Said's usage in the context at hand, it is necessary to clarify what these terms, 'colonial' and 'post-colonial', actually mean in political thought. For, these are key analytic categories which are used for periodisation of history as regards the rule over peoples of particular countries by ruling classes of other countries; for the fundamental shifts that take place with decolonisation in forms of state and relations between different national formations, units of capital, classes and economies; for the internal re-organisation of state personnel, modes of governance and appropriation as well as in circulation of surpluses nationally and internationally, when sovereign regimes are constituted in former colonies. This analytic distinction rests upon the fundamental fact that the ruling class of a colony is located outside the colony and the colonial state is the instrument of that externally-based ruling class; with decolonisation, this structural feature of the dominated formation no longer applies and the formation therefore ceases to be colonial, regardless of any other kind of dependence. In political thought, these categories have a precise meaning because they refer not to the date of decolonisation but to identifiable structural shifts in state and society, and in the hierarchy of systemic determinations which structure that relation between the imperialist bourgeoisie and the direct producers of the imperialised but sovereign nation-state of what previously was a colony. To describe, on the other hand, a critic as 'post-colonial' simply because he/she came of age after decolonisation is a tautology; to ascribe a shared cultural attitude toward western dominance to all intellectuals who begin writing after decolonisation, and a structurally different attitude to all those whose intellectual formation was completed under colonial rule, regardless of their individual, social and political locations, is the sheerest idealism and a kind of a historical levelling unavailable for rational argument.

These categories, 'colonial' and 'post-colonial', have no analytic value, nor theoretical status, when they are mobilised to homogenise very complex structures of intellectual productions or the trajectories and subjectivities of individual writers and critics or broad intellectual strata, of the kind that Said suggests in his essay. For particular intellectuals or clusters of them, colonial cultural ambience can last far beyond the moment of decolonisation; for others, rejection of cultural dominance of the colonising country can take place, and often does take place, well before the actual dissolution of the colonial state. Careers of historians and teachers like Susobhan Sarkar, sociologists like A.R. Desai, militants and intellectuals like E.M.S. Namboodiripad, not to speak of D.D. Kosambi — mathematician, Sanskritist, anthropologist, historian of ancient India — span many years of both the colonial and the post-colonial periods, and none of them, let alone scores of others, display the kind of cut-and-dry characteristics that Said attaches so neatly to his category of 'colonial' and 'post-colonial' intellectuals. Kosambi started writing roughly at the same time as C.L.R. James, Irfan Habib roughly at the same time as Ranajit Guha; the kind of distinction Said makes tells us nothing about these other trajectories. He simply inflates differences of individual formation and attitude into meaningless global typologies.

What Said tells us is that colonial intellectuals, by which he simply means non-Europeans who wrote during the colonial period, be they nationalists or Marxists, always write within the cultural perspectives of European dominance, identifying themselves with European culture and thinking of the colonising country as 'mother country'. As Said puts it:

> For James and Antonius the world of discourse inhabited by natives in the Caribbean and the Arab Orient was honorably dependent upon the west... There is no sense in their work of men standing *outside* the Western cultural tradition, however much they think of themselves as articulating the adversarial experience of colonial and/or non-western peoples.

The generalisation which is intended here simply boggles the mind, for it is so obviously contrary to what one knows about numerous intellectuals of the colonial period who never thought of themselves as ever standing *inside* the western cultural tradition. Nor is one quite sure how Said can later describe Guha squarely as a 'post-structuralist' and at the same time designate him the exemplary 'post-colonial' intellectual standing *outside* the western cultural tradition; where, one wonders, is that line of demarcation between post-structuralism and the western cultural tradition! Post-colonial intellectuals are in any case said to be both outside western cultural tradition as well as having even a better command of the weapons of European critical thought; their real distinction is that they turn these weapons against their own tutors. No one in the past, during the colonial period, apparently did that! Criticism of the most fundamental aspects of Europe through critical methods learned initially in the European institutions was, one should have thought, a favourite pastime of a great many nationalists.

More significant nonetheless is Said's very special way of according absolute centrality to those intellectuals of non-European origin who command a high degree of technical competence and who have chosen, both in the colonial and the post-colonial periods, to locate themselves in the west:

> These figures address the metropolis using the techniques, the discourses, the very weapons of scholarship and criticism once reserved exclusively for the European, now adapted either for insurgency or revisionism at the very heart of the Western centre.

Both James (the 'colonial') and Guha (the "post-colonial") have written significant books, but to designate the writing of such books as acts of 'insurgency' appears excessive, not the least because words of that kind should be applied to the act of writing sparingly, lest not only acts but even words get devalued. Castro's writing of 'History Shall Absolve Me' or Mao's writing of 'The Human Report' were certainly acts of insurgency, as is the act of writing whenever it can constitute a challenge to the existing structure of rule and a risk to one's security, but scholarly works on events of the late 18th and early 19th century do not fall in that category. Guha did after all publish his study of the permanent settlement of the late 18th century, to which Said refers, some 16 years after decolonisation when enormous quantities of writing in India as well as Britain, during the colonial as well as the post-colonial periods, had demonstrated how much Indian agriculture had suffered from that settlement. What brings about such an inflationary tendency in Said's language here is probably the great importance that he attaches to the very act of 'addressing the metropolis ... at the very heart of the western centre', and it is probably this need to be 'at the very heart of the western centre' which accounts for the emphasis on 'the techniques, the discourses, the very weapons of scholarship'; if 'addressing the metropolis' is what one does, then one better have those 'techniques', those 'discourses'. (It should be pointed out in all fairness to Guha, though, that he moved permanently to 'the western centre' some years after writing the said book.) This migration of the superior scholar from non-western countries to the western ones is what Said calls 'the voyage in' and describes it in the following way:

> ... the voyage in constitutes a specially interesting variety of hybrid cultural work. And that it exists at all is a sign of adversarial internationalisation in an age of continued imperial structures.

That is a nice phrase: 'adversarial internationalisation'. Unfortunately, the novelty of the phrase serves to conceal the fact that there is usually no relationship between 'the voyage in' and any 'adversarial' activity. Earlier in the same paragraph Said speaks, inexplicably, of 'intellectual and scholarly work from the peripheries, done either by immigrants or by visitors, both of whom are generally anti-imperialist'. That is not even remotely accurate. The vast majority of 'immigrants and visitors' who go from 'the peripheries' to the 'western centre' in the United States are right-wing people, like Bharati Mukherjee, often even worse. Far from being 'generally anti-imperialist', they want to be part of the 'centre'; the last thing they want is 'adversarial internationalisation'. Said seems not to know the immigrant communities on whose behalf he speaks, and one does indeed need a great distance from the reality of those 'voyages', made overwhelmingly in pursuit of money and professional success, if one is actually able to formulate the following declarative, also in the same paragraph:

> The contest over decolonisation has moved from the peripheries to the centre.

The force of that work 'moved' takes one's breath away. The struggle against imperialism now simply does not take place in the countries that are actually imperialised; it is a movable feast, and it goes where the experts go! The 'contest over decolonisation' becomes in this kind of formulation mainly a literary and literary-critical affair, and the elite academic intelligentsia, anchored in the metropolitan university, claims for itself, in an amazing gap between fact and self-image, the role of the world's revolutionary vanguard. The statement is definitive enough, but we may still ask: why is Ranajit Guha deemed so uniquely endowed to represent the 'post-colonial' intelligentsia? The first formulation we get is the following:

Guha's book is, in ways that later post-structuralist writers (including Guha himself) would recognise, an archaeological and deconstructive study ...

Archaeology (Foucault), deconstruction (Derrida and friends) and post-structuralism generally seem thus to guarantee the personal affinity. And Said also approves of Guha's writing in his capacity as literary critic: 'narrative is replaced by irony', Said says admiringly of Guha's style and makes much of his postulate that 'post-colonial' history-writing of the kind that Guha practises has ceased to be built around narratives and is far more interested in language itself. Literary criticism, in other words, is the desired model for the writing of history. But what fascinates Said about Ranajit Guha above all is the issue of class origin, social and geographical location, and the accompanying mastery of research techniques and western knowledges. For, Said hardly talks about the substance of Guha's book and it remains unclear whether he has actually read it. What he talks about, rather, is the fact that Guha comes from a family that was notably a beneficiary of the same Permanent Settlement of which Guha then offers the fulsome critique; that he then moved to western countries to carry on technique and archive as the equal of any western scholar. In a rhetorical inflation characteristic of the contemporary third-worldist intellectuals located in 'the western centre', Said then goes on to erase the fundamental political distinction between immigration and exile when he simply declares Guha to be an 'exile figure'. With the personal choice one has utterly no wish to quarrel, and I surely neither know nor wish to judge the circumstances which lead any individual to emigrate from one country to another; those are strictly private matters. By the same token, however, it is best not to misrepresent personal preference as fate ordained by repression. Yet, the 'exile figure' is central to the persona Said ascribes to Guha. For, it is in this combination of comprador class origin, western location, exiled self, and mastery of techniques that Said locates the productive and oppositional energies of the subalternist project and its asserted ability to overturn the entire trajectory of all the schools and tendencies previously obtaining in Indian historiography.

The social context of this privileging of Guha is of some considerable interest. There are several references to *Subaltern Studies* in these essays but, with the exception of a passing reference to Guha's own introductory note in Volume One, Said does not even cite any of the individual texts that comprise this project, let alone any detailed engagement with the premises or products of the project or, especially, with what may signify its difference from — purported superiority over — other kinds of historiography in India. One is not sure what it is in the work itself that is being singled out for praise in this foregrounding. Even in the singular case of Guha, where a particular book is mentioned, namely, *A Rule of Property for Bengal*, two facts stand out. One is that it is an early work of Guha, published some two decades before the launching of the subaltern project, based upon his doctoral work within what one may loosely call the main traditions of Indian historiography, not entirely indifferent to premises shared with teachers like Susobhan Sarkar or rough contemporaries like Irfan Habib. It is significant that Said is so notably silent about Guha's more recent work in the actual subalternist mould.[40] Then, even with reference to *A Rule of Property* Said quotes only from the Introduction and only the biographical detail; it remains unclear whether Said is even interested in thinking of the book itself, in relation to the immense body of writing on the Permanent Settlement which has accumulated in India over the decades, before Guha's book and since. Given this pattern of invocation and affiliation, the actual content of what Guha or the general subaltern tendency actually does can hardly be an issue here, and all that matters is Said's own construction of it. One comes away with the impression that the paramount fact here is the structure of conversation, conference and personal encounter currently available in the American university, and the pre-eminence of the subaltern group in that particular milieu. This, then, is cemented by the matter of 'post-structuralism', all other recognisable traditions of history-writing in India have been, after all, self-confessedly 'historicist'. The main source of attraction is in any case the biographical one: class origin, privileged access to 'technique' and 'discourse', the imaginative construction of 'exile', and the subsequent relocation. The irony of this personally felt and highly valorised biographical detail nevertheless is that Said has given to us, with or without Guha's consent, the portrait of a typical upper-layer bourgeois; for, it is that kind of individual who has typically mobilised the accumulations achieved during the colonial period to acquire the most modern western technology, Swiss bank accounts, apartments and branch offices in the metropolitan centres, to launch upon collaborative competition with the metropolitan bourgeoisie, from the margins of global capitalism. In this account, Guha becomes for Indian historiography what Bajaj and Birla claim to have been for Indian industry: patriotic, albeit monopolistic, national bourgeois.

In according such primacy to metropolitan location Said is quite indifferent to the fact that not all subalternists have left the country, and there is of course a trenchant irony in the obviously paradoxical relationship between how the subalternist project would define itself and the way Said defines it, namely, as an upper class, emigre phenomenon at odds with its own class origin and metropolitan location. Suffice it to say that there is a very considerable resonance in this narrative of class origin, the migration as *a voyage in*, and preferred metropolitan location — the pleasures of self-exile much more often than forced exile — and the subsequent professionalisation and hybridisation ('cultural amphibians' is Said's laudatory term) — which far exceeds the terms of any personal choice that Guha might or might not have made, even though he is the one who gets singled out. For, one of the few features that these latter essays share with *Orientalism* is that they continue to speak of the existential situation — the class privilege, the presumed oppositional and beleaguered situation, the technical ability to collaborate as well as compete, the professional location — of the more privileged sections of the incoming immigrant in the United States. What is significant in terms of authorial intentions, meanwhile, is the fact that the turn from a wholesale denunciation of the west, so uncompromising in *Orientalism*, to an equally sweeping desire for a location in the west, which these latest essays assert, is now complete.

VIII

Predilections of this kind are what Said brings to the even more complex and internally far more riven essay, 'Figures, Configurations, Transfigurations', which is notable for its high estimation of western canonicity, its debunking of the non-west, its handsome praise for the civilising mission of English, its advocacy not only of literature's aesthetic pleasures but also its central importance as a vehicle for consuming the world. Reversals of a great many earlier positions are simply astonishing.

Said starts by commending the 'salutary and invigorating quality in the very notion of Commonwealth literature today', which is surprising for anyone on the left, since all that is wrong with the 'Commonwealth' begins wih the *notion* that it should exist at all. Said, however, sees in this construct an 'invigorating' civilisational mission, as follows:

> If configurations like Commonwealth or world literature are to have any meaning at all, it is ... because they interact ferociously not only with the whole nationalist basis for the compositions and study of literature, but also with the lofty independence and indifference with which it has become customary Eurocentrically to regard metropolitan western literatures.

Now, 'Commonwealth literature' is a construct pretty much of the British Council and is limited largely to its clients, who themselves construe it as a conglomeration of discrete 'national' traditions; the 'ferocity' Said imputes to it is at best imaginary. His ambivalent and self-cancelling remarks on literatures of Asia and Africa which surface in this same article I shall quote below, and it will become clear that what he means by 'world literature' is pretty much what Goethe actually meant and Arnold might have accepted, namely, a club of 'great books'. What is most pertinent in any case is the denunciation of 'the nationalist basis', which is a rather significant departure in this essay but should not be very surprising after our preceding analysis.

This civilising mission is said to reside, further, in the very global pre-eminence of the English language itself: 'What gives the actuality of Commonwealth literature its special force is that, of all languages today, English is, properly speaking, the world language'. (I am certain Said does not register, let along intend, the pun in 'properly speaking'.) Ngugi Wa Thongo, the Kenyan writer, is then invoked to make the point that this global circulation of English makes it possible for us to 'decolonise' our minds through study in the same language that was used to colonise us. This too is somewhat surprising, both because Ngugi has over the last several years made the point that in order to fully decolonise his mind he must rather write in Swahili and Kikuyu, and because this beneficent role of English as vehicle of enlightenment and world culture is, at the least, overstated. In present-day India, surely, English occupies a much more contradictory space; as at once a language for the production of knowledge, a means of connecting the country with currents around the world, both good and bad, as well as a line of demarcation, a cultural boundary between privilege and dispossession; for many among the literati, it is also the language of the Raj nostalgia. Said, however, is insistent on this point of the civilising ethos. He recounts a visit to a national university in one of the Gulf states and, having registered the fact that the English department attracted the largest number of students, goes on to bemoan two facts: that so many students took English not for its literature but as a technical language needed for professional advancement; and that 'English, such as it was, existed in what seemed to be a seething cauldron of Islamic revivalism'. Both these laments deserve some comment.

Said's main statement about the use of English in the Gulf states runs as follows:

> This all but terminally consigned English to the level of a technical language almost totally stripped not only of expressive and aesthetic characteristics but also denuded of any critical or self-conscious dimension. You learned English to use computers, respond to orders, tranmit telexes, decipher manifests and so forth. That was all.

Said's lament is quite unmodulated by any awareness that English has become a 'world language', a fact which he celebrates, not because of its 'aesthetic characteristics' or 'critical dimention'—i.e., not owing to its literature and literary critics—but because of its centrality in the administrative and capitalist enterprises in the most powerful empires of past and present, hence as a language of rule ('taking orders') and of command in global grids of telecommunications, airlines, administration, transnational corporations. The poor student whom Said so derides in fact makes a rational choice, in his own circumstances, in learning the technical aspect and ignoring the aesthetic one.

The main comment on the beleaguered situation of this 'world language' in the midst of a 'seething cauldron' runs, meanwhile, as follows:

> Either it is a technical language with wholly instrumental characteristics and features; or it is a foreign language with various implicit connections to the larger English-speaking world, but where its presence abuts on the much more impressive, much more formidable emergent reality of organised religious fervour. And since the language of Islam is Arabic, a language with considerable literary community and hieratic force, English seems to me to have sunk quite low ...

Against this debasement and overwhelming of the 'world language' by 'organised religious fervour' are ranged 'smaller literate groups that are bound together not by insensate polemic but by affinities, sympathies and compassion'. A particularly important member of these 'smaller literate groups' is Salman Rushdie, whom Said has defended most fervently, in this article as well as in every other public forum available for the defence, partly because 'That the novel dealt with Islam in English and for what was believed to be a largely western audience was its main offence'.

Said's way of posing English against Arabic is odd. In the Arab-speaking countries, surely, the characterisation of Arabic as the language of Islam (as of all else) may be substantially true, but insofar as he speaks constantly of larger things (Asia and Africa, Commonwealth literature, Rushdie and 'the Khomeini threat') it may be worth recalling that the vast majority of Muslims in the world speak or understand no Arabic. More to the point, any number of studies exist to show that the urban petty bourgeoisie which normally constitutes the cutting edge of 'organised religious fervour' in a number of countries is educated in English as much as in any other language; in the 'Islamic world', certainly, English-knowing professionals occupy key positions in such movements, and the representatives of orthodox Islam, who led the campaign against *Satanic Verses*.

in England knew English very well, while a great many knew no Arabic. And it is entirely to be doubted that such representatives of orthodox Islam, including the Irani clerics, would have been any the more forgiving if *Satanic Verses* had been written in Arabic, Farsi, Urdu or any other language, for Asian and other Arab readerships; what caused the outrage was the book's heresy, not its language of communication. Being written in English and for primarily western audiences became an issue only with regard to the money and power such facts normally represent, not to speak of the corrupting potential of that kind of money and that kind of metropolitan location, hero-worship, etc., made worse by the way the book got used by the (English-speaking) British and American states.

The touchstone for Said is provided by the issue of rising, or failing to rise, in Rushdie's defence. That most writers located in Asia and Africa failed to rise to this grand duty is said to indicate, then, that this intelligentsia is possessed, on the one hand, by networks of multinational information (CNN, NBC, etc.), and, on the other, complicities with their own states and regimes, with the result that

> in the relatively open environment postulated by communities of readers interested in emergent post-colonial Commonwealth and Francophone literature, the underlying configurations on the ground are directed and controlled not by processes of hermeneutic investigation, nor by sympathetic and literate intuition, nor by informed reading, but by much coarser and instrumental processes whose goal is the mobilisation of consent, the eradication of dissent, the promotion of an *almost literally blind patriotism* (emphasis added).

Those readers who are interested in 'Commonwealth literature', we are being told, 'postulate' 'open environments' but these readerly islands of literality are besieged by 'configurations on the ground' based on 'blind patriotism'; bureaucrats of the British Council, who have invented the category of 'Commonwealth literature', feel, I am sure, the same way. There is even a note of nostalgia. 'Environment' was once 'open', but 'intuition' has now ceased to be 'literature', and communities have become incapable of 'hermeneutic investigation' and 'informed reading'; what once had the potential of becoming refined has become 'much coarser'; the issue of the 'state' shall come up soon, but what is lamented here is 'the underlying configuration on the ground', i.e., the state of mass culture itself, exemplified by those students who read English for technical purposes ('instrumental process') and not for its aesthetic beauty (through 'hermeneutic investigation'). The Arnoldian problematic of culture and anarchy is here in full bloom. Once these 'communities' can be accused of lacking in all that the literary critic most values — literate intuition, hermeneutics, informed reading — they obviously become 'literally blind'. The evidence of this literal blindness of course is 'the quite stunning acquiescence of the Islamic world to the overall prohibitions and proscriptions as well as threats pronounced against Salman Rushdie', a lone genius whom an entire world ('Islamic world') fails to appreciate because of its blindness, its coarseness, its lack of hermeneutic finesse. Aside from the damning fact that they have come to regard English only as a 'technical language' which disregarding its 'aesthetic characteristics', the main problem of these communities is that they identify too closely with their state, not realising that 'the chief, most official, forceful and coercive identity is the state with its borders, customs, ruling parties and authorities'. We shall not comment here on the double-edged meaning of the word 'customs', but that a stateless Palestinian, longing always to have a state of his own, should describe the state — all states; the state as such — as a 'coercive identity' signifies a paradox too painful to bear comment. It is well to remember, however, that multinational capital registers exactly the same objection against the sovereign states of Asia and Africa; they have their governments, customs duties, borders, etc., so that free movement of capital and commodities is impeded. Of course, 'customs' also means signifying cultural practices; to have 'customs' of one's own in a non-European setting means having a hermeneutics of judgment which the metropolitan critic would not recognise as hermeneutics at all.

The price of not possessing hermeneutics but being enclosed within the borders and customs of Asian and African countries is not only that they fail to recognise a genius when they see one, Salman Rushdie in the case, but that the literature they themselves produce within those frontiers is fated to remain forever inferior.

> I think it is a mistake to try to show that the 'other' literatures of Africa and Asia, with their more obviously worldly affiliation to power and politics, can be studied respectably, that is, as if they were in actuality as high, as autonomous, as aesthetically independent and satisfying as French, German or English literatures. The notion of black skin in a white mask is no more serviceable and dignified in literary study than it is in politics. Emulation and mimicry never get one very far.

Naipaul, surely, never made a judgement more damning. The key word here is of course 'respectably'; people of Asia and Africa who produce literature within their own borders and according to their own 'customs' simply are not worthy of respect, becuase they are mimic men, all. In direct contrast, we get — from the author of *Orientalism*, no less — the characterisation of 'French, German and

English literatures' as not only 'high' but also 'autonomous', 'aesthetically independent' and 'satisfying'. Now, satisfaction is doubtless a personal matter, but may one ask: 'autonomous' and 'independent' of what? The whole point of *Orientalism*, one should have thought was that these literatures were not autonomous, that they were too complicit in colonialism to be spoken of primarily in terms of 'high' aesthetics.

All such mimicries (African and Asian literatures) and such coercive identities (the state, surely, but also nation, gender, class) need to be left behind. Once these are shed, the real business of literature can begin:

> The reader and writer of literature... no longer needs to tie him or herself to an image of the poet or scholar in isolation, secure, stable, national in identity, class, gender, or profession, but can think and experience with Genet in Palestine or Algeria, with Tayeb Saleh as a black man in London, with Jamaica Kincaid in the white world, with Rushdie in India and Britain, and so on.
>
> ... To paraphrase from a remark made by Auerbach in one of his last essays, our philological home is the world, and not the nation or even the individual writer.

Rarely has one come across in the latter half of the present century so unabashed a recommendation that the world, especially the 'Orient' — Palestine, Algeria, India — and indeed all the races, white and black, be consumed in the form of those fictions of this world which are available in the bookshops of the metropolitan countries; the condition of becoming this perfect consumer of course is that one frees oneself from stable identities of class, nation, gender. Thus it is that sovereignty comes to be invested in the reader of literature, fully in command of an imperial geography. All that seems to have changed since Auerbach made that recommendation, in the name of philology, is that London itself — Britain, the white world — has become an object among other objects of consumption, quite at par with India. This is the imperial geography not of the colonial period but of late capitalism: commodity acquires universality, and a universal market arises across national frontiers and local customs, while white trade rejoins the black trade. When cultural criticism reaches this point of convergence with the universal market, one might add, it becomes indistinguishable from commodity fetishism.

IX

So one returns, inevitably, to the question of Marxism. In the essay 'Secular Criticism', which serves both as dossier of his basic theoretical position and as Introduction to the book. *The World, The Text and the Critic*, Said had said:

> ... it may seem that I am an undeclared Marxist, afraid of losing respectability ...
>
> ... on the important matter of a critical position, its relationship to Marxism, liberalism, even anarchism, it needs to be said that criticism modified in advance by labels like 'Marxism', or 'liberalism', is, in my view, an oxymoron.
>
> The net effect of 'doing' Marxist criticism or writing at the present time is of course to declare political preference, but it is also to put oneself outside a great deal of things going on in the world, so to speak, and in other kinds of criticism (pp. 28–29).

But supposing that what Marxists write was not to be prejudged and already disparaged as 'doing', in the quotation marks; and supposing also that Marxism itself, when used alongside criticism, would be neither marked in similar fashion nor described as a 'label' — that is to say, if Said were to adopt a kind of direct phrasing that would accept responsibility for its own meaning, and not one so overwrought with mockery and polemic as to foreclose the possibility of serious argument — would it not be possible then to face the problem squarely? The problem of 'losing respectability' I shall not raise because that is always a personal and therefore very touchy matter, though I must confess I cannot help being reminded of the passage I quoted a little earlier, where Said declares that those 'other' literatures, Asian and African, cannot be read *respectably* as being at par with the European. Some other problems I may mention. The problem that one creates for the coherence of one's own thought when one refuses to acknowledge the full import of the fact that Gramsci was a communist militant, so that the word Marxist would quite accurately describe the nature of his understanding, and when one tries to claim, instead, that Gramsci was just another Julien Benda, another Matthew Arnold. The problem of accepting far too much from the dominant American ideology when one gives oneself the right to use the term 'Secular Criticism' as the title of the chapter, when 'oppositional criticism' can be recommended, when Guha can be lauded for being a 'post-structuralist writer', when one regularly takes recourse, in other words, to the common practice of putting two words together in order to specify lineages of theoretical or political position in all kinds of other situations — but the use of the word 'Marxist' before the word 'criticism' is declared oxymoronic. Why should one not attach the word 'Marxist' — not the label, but the word — and attach it consistently, without quotation marks, to all that Lukacs wrote after he had in fact become a Marxist, and then try to think through *his* Marxism, *one's own* Marxism if one has any, and Marxism *in general*? What sanctity attaches to the word 'criticism' which gets elevated by the terms 'oppositional' or 'secular' but gets defiled by the term 'Marxist'?

The larger issue, admittedly, is that of one's willingness, or lack of willingness, 'to put oneself outside a great deal of things going on in the world'. The pain of any ethical life is that all fundamental bondings, affiliations, stable political positions require that one ceases to desire, voraciously, everything that is available in this world; that one learns to deny oneself some of the pleasures, rewards, consumptions, even affiliations of certain sorts. This much Said must have himself learned through his consistent anti-Zionism. Why is Marxism singled out for this pain — and joy — of choosing? Rather, why is Marxism alone associated only with the pain, but not the joy and the ethical need, of choosing? Is is that the secular and the religious, even the Zionist and the anti-Zionist, can equally respectably partake of the imperial geography and the consumptions of 'a great deal of things', and it is only a fundamental acceptance of a Marxist position, with all its consequences, which entails an unbearable self-denial?

Like all political positions which are ethically viable, the Marxist one also closes off certain possibilities and opens up certain others. In choosing such a position, one chooses the closures, certainly, but one also chooses the potentialities. Said's warning, which is also a self-warning, that a choice for Marxism entails putting 'oneself outside a great deal of things' points towards a possible inventory of self-denials; it is a pity, though, that Said never takes stock of what Marxism might have made possible, nor of what one actually loses when one puts oneself *inside* too many things. Having access to 'a great deal of things' always gives one a sense of opulence, mastery, reach, choice, freedom, erudition, play. But resolution of the kind of ambivalences and self-cancelling procedures which beset Said's thought require that some positions be vacated, some choices be made, some of these 'great deal of things' be renounced.

Aijaz Ahmad, in Economic and Political Weekly *(1992).*

NOTES

(This essay is based on a chapter in my forthcoming book, *In Theory: Classes, Nations, Literatures* (Verso, London). Earlier drafts were presented in the Fellows' Seminar at the Centre for Contemporary Studies, Nehru Memorial Museum and Library, New Delhi, and subsequently in seminars at the Centre for Historical Studies, Jawaharlal Nehru University, as well as in the History department of Delhi University. The author is grateful for comments and criticisms offered by audiences at these distinguished institutions, in the course of subsequent discussions, formal and informal. For a related argument, see my 'Between Orientalism and Historicism: Anthropological Knowledge of India' in *Studies in History,* Vol.VII, No.1, January-June 1991, Delhi.)

1. See my 'Jameson's Rhetoric of Otherness and the "National" Allegory' in *Social Text*, Vol.17, Autumn 1978, New York.
2. Said, Edward W., *The Question of Palestine*, New York, Doubleday, 1980.
3. Said, Edward W., *After the Last Sky: Palestinian Lives*, New York, Pantheon, 1986.
4. Aside from scores of articles and interventions in the journalistic media, see in particular *Blaming the Victims: Spurious Scholarship and the Palestinian Question*, London, Verso, 1987; co-authored with Chrisopher Hitchens.
5. Said, Edward W., 'Zionism from the Standpoint of Its Victims' in the inaugural issue of *Social Text*, Winter 1979, later integrated into *The Question of Palestine*.
6. Said, Edward W., *Orientalism*, Vintage Books Edition, 1979, p.27. All subsequent references to the book shall be to this edition.
7. See, Said, Edward W., *Joseph Conrad and the Fiction of Autobiography*, Harvard University Press, 1966 and *Beginnings: Intention and Method*, Basic Books, 1975.
8. Twelve years after the publication of *Orientalism*, in his essay entitled 'Figures, Configurations, Transfiguration' in *Race and Class*, vol.32, No.1, 1990, where the title itself plays on the philological trope of 'figuration', Said uses the verb 'revere'.
9. For a scrupulous examination of Said's highly questionable uses of Foucault, though with very different emphases than mine, see 'On Orientalism' in James Clifford's *The Predicament of Culture*, Harvard, 1988.
10. Said of course locates Marx not in what Foucault calls the 'discourse' of political economy but in the *literary* ambience of what Said himself designates as an 'orientalist discourse', without even addressing the question, as any Foucaultian obviously would, whether or not statements, and their authors, can actually circulate so very freely between discursive fields which are otherwise mutually so distinct and discontinuous. For more on the treatment of Marx in *Orientalism*, see below.
11. Said, Edward W., '*Kim*, The Pleasures of Imperialism' in *Raritan Quarterly*.
12. Reference here and in subsequent quotation and pagination is to the Norton paperback edition of 1969, which is a reprint of the original 1928 translation by Richard Aldington.
13. Said, Edward W., *The World, The Text, and the Critic*, Harvard University Press, 1983, pp. 14–15.
14. As Raymond Williams once trenchantly remarked in a very different context, those who claim to be beyond all 'isms' rarely examine the 'ism' of their own 'criticism'. See Raymond Williams, 'The Crisis of English Studies', *New Left Review*, No. 129, Sept.–October 1981.
15. The latter pages of Said's famous essay, 'Representing the Colonised: Anthropology's Interlocutors' (*Critical Inquiry* No. 15, Winter 1989), which was delivered originally as an address at the 86th annual meeting of the American Anthropological Association of Chicago, November 21, 1987, may be usefully consulted for this use of the collective pronoun.
16. Lewis, Bernard, 'The Question of Orientalism' in *New York Review of Books*, June 24, 1982.
17. Raskin, Jonah, *The Mythology of Imperialism*, Random House, New York, 1971.
18. First presented at the Essex University Conference on 'Europe and its Others' in 1984, six years after the original publication of *Orientalism*, this essay, '*Orientalism* Reconsidered', had been reproduced widely, as, for example, in the American journal, *Critical Inquiry*, and the British journal, *Race and Class*, as well as in books, such as Barker, Hume, Iversen and Loxley (eds.), *Literature, Politics and Theory*, London, 1986.
19. Elsewhere of course, it is precisely Vico's 'historicist' statements which Said would invoke for high praise. See, for example, *The World, the Text, and the Critic*, pp. 290–91, where he explicates one of his favourite quotations from Vico, as well as the superb passage on p.

114 where he makes a crucial point about Vico's idea of history through a wonderfully inflected reference to Bach's *Goldberg Variations.*

20. See 'Writing about Islam and the Arabs: A review of E.W.Said, *Orientalism*' in *I and C*, No. 9, Winter 1981/82. It might be helpful to know that *I and C* was previously published as *Ideology and Consciousness*, but was then reduced to mere initials after the editors lost nerve about the categories of both 'ideology' and 'consciousness'.
21. Said keeps shifting, throughout the book, between one set of statements in which 'the Orient' is said to have 'always' served for Europe as the image of an absolute other, inferior and exotic and alien and insufferable because of this inferiority, and another set of statements which suggest that 'the West' has 'always' sought to represent 'the Orient' as a partial self-image, not necessarily inferior (e.g., 'To the Westerner, however, the Oriental was always *like* some aspect of the west; Indian religion was essentially an Oriental version of German Christian pantheism', p. 67). One might note, in passing, though Said does not say, that at least some of those romantics regarded the 'Indian religion' as the purer, higher form.
22. Variants of the following statement, for example, can be found throughout the book: 'To say simply that Orientalism was a rationalisation of colonial rule is to ignore the extent to which colonial rule was justified in advance by Orientalism, rather than after the fact' (p. 39).
23. Samir Amin's work on this question is far more extensive in Arabic but the relevant argument about epistemic unity both of the Mediterranean antiquity on the one hand, and of the Christian and Islamic theological bases on the other, is summarised also in his *Eurocentrism* (Monthly Review Press, New York, 1989).
24. Bernal demonstrates convincingly that the fabrication of ancient Greece as an originary and autonomous cultural formation, its sundering from the composite Mediterranean culture in which it had been placed overlappingly with Egyptian and Levantine antiquities, and its relocation as the fount of a west European history rather than at the confluence of Afro-Asiatic-European culture — i.e, the mapping of an Athens-to-Albion cultural grid which demarcates Europe from Asia — is a product really of the late 18th century onwards, after the main European interests (in both senses of the word) shift from Egypt to India and when the Indo-Aryan linguistic model gets going as the basic explanatory model for cultural unities and mobilities. See Martin Bernal, *Black Athena*: *The Afroasiatic Roots of Classical Civilisation, Volume 1: The Fabrication of Ancient Greece 1785–1985* (Rutgers University Press, New Burnswick, 1987).
25. For an erudite survey of a field, in which much originality resides actually in the way Said draws upon prior critiques, see his 'Representing the Colonised: Anthropology's Interlocutors' (*Critical Inquiry*, Winter 1989).
26. Said, Edward W., 'Jane Austen and Empire' in Terry Eagleton (ed.), *Raymond Williams: Critical Perspectives*, Polity Press, London, 1989.
27. See Chapter Two, 'Languages of Class, Ideologies of Immigration' in my forthcoming book, *In Theory: Classes, Nations, Literatures* (London, Verso).
28. See my 'Between Orientalism and Historicism: Anthropological Knowledge of India' in *Studies in History* (Volume VII, No. 1, January–June 1991) for detailed examination of Ronald Inden's *Imagining India* (Basil Blackwell, 1990).
29. See Partha Chatterjee, 'Caste and Subaltern Consciousness' in Ranajit Guha (ed.), *Subaltern Studies*, Vol. VI (Oxford, New Delhi, 1989).
30. See my 'Rushdie's *Shame*: Postmodernism, Migrancy and the Representations of Women' in *Economic and Political Weekly*, June 15, 1991.

31. See my essays referred to in notes 1 and 29 for detailed discussions of the theoretical category of 'third world literature'.
32. 'Media, Margins and Modernity: Raymond Williams and Edward Said', Appendix to Raymond Williams, *The Politics of Modernism: Against the New Conformists*, pp.196–97 (London, Verso, 1989). The transcript of that public discussion, and indeed the whole book, ends on that sentence about 'feminist credentials'.
33. This essay has also appeared as an introduction to Schwab's own *The Oriental Renaissance; Europe's Rediscovery of India and the East, 1680–1800*, translation of *Le Renaissance Orientale* (1954) by Gene Patterson-Black and Victoria Reinking (New York, Columbia University Press, 1984). The high praise Schwab receives in this essay makes curious reading when set against the vary marginal treatment he gets in *Orientalism* itself.
34. In his last book, *State, Power, Socialism* (New Left Books, London, 1978; translation by Patrick Camiller of *L'Etat, le Pouvoir, le Socialism*, published in Paris that same year), Poulantzas offers a critique of Foucault from a Marxist position but tries also to find common ground between the two. See, in particular the section on 'Law' in Part One and the one entitled 'Towards a Relational Theory of Power?' in Part Two. This critique, in the book that is theoretically the most eclectic in Poulantzas's overall *oeuvre*, was obviously not available to Said at the time of the writing of *Orientalism*.
35. *The World, the Text...* op. cit. pp. 244–46. This distancing from Foucault was then to be repeated in the more recent essay, 'Foucault and the Imagination of Power' in David Couzen (ed.), *Foucault: A Critical Reader* (Routledge, London, 1989), which too says less than what is there already in Poulantzas.
36. This emphasis on 'resistance' outside the 'grand narratives' is not notably different from the one that Foucault (partially aided by Deleuze) delineates in a great many places, including the two interviews published as the concluding chapters of Michael Foucault, *Language, Countermemory, Practice* (edited by Donald Bouchard, Cornell University Press, Ithaca, New York, 1977).
37. See Said, Edward W., 'Opponents, Audiences, Constituencies and Community' (*Critical Inquiry*, no. 9, 1982; printed in Hal Foster (ed.), *The Anti-Aesthetic: Essays in Post-Modern Culture*, Port Townsend, Washington, Bay Press, 1983, pp.135–59).
38. Editor of the series *Subaltern Studies*, and author most notably of *A Rule of Property for Bengal* (1963) and *Elementary Aspects of Peasant Insurgency in Colonial India* (1983), Ranajit Guha taught history for many years at Sussex in Great Britain before moving in 1980 to the Australian National University, Canberra.
39. See Said, Edward W., 'The Imperial Spectacle', *Grand Street*.
40. The more recent *Elementary Aspects* would be a closer approximation of the Subalternist approach ('post-structuralism', as Said designates it), but the monograph, *An Indian Historiography of India: A 19th Century Agenda and its Implications* (K.P. Bagchi, Calcutta, 1988), the superb essay, possibly Guha's best work in the past quarter century, entitled 'Chandra's Death' (*Subaltern Studies*, V, Delhi, 1987), and the recent, much lengthier and much more problematic essay 'Dominance Without Hegemony and Its Historiography' *Subaltern Studies*, VI, Delhi, 1989) would have been even more representative.

Part II
Interpretations

K. KRISHNAMOORTHY

Professor Krishnamoorthy has been a doyen of Sanskrit studies in India for the last five decades. He has published innumerable essays and books devoted to the discussion, interpretation and elaboration of critical concepts in Sanskrit poetics. Among his better known works are his editions with commentaries of Kuntaka's *Vakroktijivita* and Anandavardhana's *Dhvanyāloka*. Both have been used in this anthology. Professor Krishnamoorthy has also done a comparative study of Western and Indian aesthetics, and has commented on T.S. Eliot's criticism. His kind of scholarship, which is mainly interested in editorial finesse, is becoming extinct in contemporary Sanskrit studies. In this respect, he represents a whole generation of scholars such as S. K. De and P. V. Kane, of which he is the ablest example. The following pages form his entry to the encyclopaedic work edited by K. M. George, *Comparative Indian Literature* (Macmillan, Madras, 1984–86, pp. 1109–1126), and is used in the original as an exhaustive introduction to the section on Sanskrit literary criticism. This long essay is included here as a definitive commentary on the range and complexity of critical concerns in Sanskrit poetics. His bibliography should be of particular interest to students who wish to pursue the subject in greater detail.

Sanskrit Poetics: an Overview

Introduction

Sanskrit is not only the oldest of the Indo-Aryan languages, but also the repository of one of the most ancient literary records in the world, namely, the *Vedas* (2000 B.C.). One of the traditional names for this vast body of religious literature is *chandas* or 'pleasing metre', which underscores its pre-eminently poetic verse-form meant for recitation or chanting, preserving the original accents. *Rgveda* means the Veda of hymns; and the Vedic poets (*kavis*) were also seers (*ṛṣis*). We get references therein to speech (*vāk* or *sarasvatī*), personified as a goddess, who inspires the poet into a *furor poeticus*. The Vedic seers speak of their art often as a verbal craft 'like that of a carpenter fashioning out a chariot'. It is not unlikely that they had their own 'rules' (*śāstra*) of poetic composition; but they are not extant. In the Vedic age (c. 2000–800 B.C.), metres were invested with magical power and lauded as leading the chanter to heaven. We have also words like *kāvya*, *alaṃkṛti* and *rasa* in Vedic literature which became the key-terms of Sanskrit literary criticism in a later age; but they hardly have any critical significance in the Vedic texts.

Though modern scholars regard Vedic hymns as poetry, Indian tradition is reluctant to do so, because it accords the highest place of divine scripture (*śruti*) exclusively to the Veda while poetry (*kāvya*), by definition, is secular and of human authorship.

The next period (c. 800–200 B.C.) witnessed the rise of several intellectual disciplines (*śāstras*) to aid the understanding of the Veda. Etymology (*nirukta*) and grammar (*vyākaraṇa*) among them contain some incidental references to poetic devices like the simile (*upamā*), besides a few citations from folk-ballads or lyrics. Patanjali (150 B.C.) testifies to the aesthetic significance of the term *rasa* when he speaks of the actor in a drama as *rasika*, and also names a few folk-tales (*ākhyāyikās*) popular in his time such as *Vāsavadattā* and *Sumanottarā*. The Buddhist canonical work *Kavi-sutta* in Pāli speaks about four types of poets: (i) meditative (*cintakavi*), (ii) scholarly (*sattakavi*), (iii) inspired (*patibhanakavi*) and (iv) missionary (*atthakavi*). The treatment of prosody by Pingala as well as Bharata reveals numerous classical measures, based on quantity as well as stress. Inscriptions in the classical *kāvya* style are found as early as the Christian era; one of them (A.D. 150) expressly mentions prose (*gadya*) and poetry (*padya*), besides literary excellences such as clarity (*sphuṭatā*) and sweetness (*mādhurya*), as well as figures of speech (*alaṇkāra*). All this evidence indicates that the cultivation of different genres of poetry and drama went hand in hand with speculations on literary criticism round about the Christian era, though none of those early attempts is available to us today.

The two great epics of India, namely the Ramayana and the Mahabharata, are again ascribed by Indian tradition to poet-sages and are regarded not as models of pure poetry but as repositories embodying legendary history (*itihāsa*) as well as ideal ethical precept (*dharma*). Hence ancient Indian poetics (*alaṃkāraśāstra*) generally leaves them out of account; if they are alluded to once in a way, it is only to derive support from their example and not from their precept on literary theory.

Nāṭyaśāstra

However, the earliest treatise available to us is the *Nāṭyaśāstra* ascribed to sage Bharata (c. A.D. 200). It is a kind of encyclopaedia on dramaturgy, histrionics, dance, music, etc., and its concern with poetry proper is very cursory indeed. Yet, it gives us almost all the pivotal concepts of Sanskrit criticism which were to engage the attention of some of the best poet-critics and scholars of India for well over sixteen centuries. These are: *rasa-bhāva, aucitya, guṇa, doṣa, alaṃkāra, vṛtti* and the literary genres. In the domain of drama, however, its treatment is most exhaustive; and its norms regarding plot, characters, sentiments and style in as many as ten types of plays, have remained basically unaltered even after the lapse of so many centuries.

The Names and Nature of Sanskrit Poetics

Usually, all early writers on the subject — Bhāmaha (c. 600), Daṇḍin (c. 700), Vāmana (c. 750), Udbhaṭa and Rudraṭa (c. 800) — call their treatises by the name *Kāvyālaṇkāra* or *Kāvyalakṣaṇa*, i.e. 'the embellishment or hallmark of poetry'. Some earlier names which are known only by references are *Kriyākalpa* and *Kriyāvidhi* which mean 'rules of the poetic art'. The designation *sāhitya-vidyā*, 'theory of literature', is a later one (c. 900). It emphasizes the perfect concord of sound (*śabda*) and sense (*artha*) as the *sine qua non* of literature. But the latest and most commonly used name is *Alaṃkāra-Śāstra*, 'science of beauty', because the work *alaṃkāra* in Sanskrit means not only a means of beautification but also beauty itself. This usage became current when poetics adopted the scientific methodology and terminology of allied disciplines like grammar, prosody, dramaturgy, erotics, logic and philosophy in the discussion of its basic concepts, especially after Ānandavardhana (c. 850), who was a philosopher of the first rank besides being a masterly poet-critic and who, for the first time, gave in his aesthetic theory of *dhvani* (implied or suggested meaning) an equal status to drama and poetry, and who blazed the trail for applied or practical criticism of not only select literary pieces but also whole works. The formal and normative approach to poetry is replaced here by an aesthetic perspective, and he represents the dividing line between old (*prācina*) and new (*navya*) poetics. His original insights and illuminating observations paved the way for an age of systematization which includes celebrated names like Kuntaka (1000), Mammaṭa (1150), Vidyānātha (1300), Viśvanātha (1350) and Jagannātha (1650).

The systematized classics of these authors were studied throughout India and there are dozens of commentaries on them, almost from every province, which restate the discussions often in the light of new considerations.

Literary Genres

The major literary genres or *kāvya*-forms mentioned by Bhāmaha are: (1) art-epic in several cantos (*mahākāvya*), (2) drama (*abhinayārtha*), (3) prose-chronicle (*ākhyāyikā*), (4) romantic tale (*kathā*), and (5) smaller verse-units or single self-contained verses (*anibaddha*). To these should be added *campū* or mixed composition in ornate prose and verse on an exalted theme first mentioned by Daṇḍin. From time to time further subdivisions came to be noted, especially under the categories (4) and (5).

Kathā (Tale)

1. *Upākhyāna*: an episodic story in a larger work.
2. *Ākhyāna*: an episodic story, sung and enacted by a bard.
3. *Nidarśana*: didactic bird-and-beast fable.
4. *Pravalhikā*: a story in dialogue form.
5. *Matallikā*: a story satirizing society.
6. *Maṇikulyā*: a story involving an initial puzzle.
7. *Parikathā*: a tale narrating several adventures.
8. *Khaṇḍakathā*: a partially narrated well-known story.
9. *Sakalakathā*: a complete story of a hero's life.
10. *Upakathā*: an incidentally recounted story.
11. *Bṛhatkathā*: a vast repository of tales.

Anibaddha (small verse-units)

1. *Muktaka*: a self-contained stanza.
2. *Sandānitaka*: two run-on stanzas.
3. *Viśeṣaka*: three run-on stanzas.
4. *Kalāpaka*: four run-on stanzas.
5. *Kulaka*: four to fourteen run-on stanzas.
6. *Kośa*: anthology of independent verses composed by oneself and/or others. *Śataka* (century), *Pancāśikā* (fifty)
7. *Samghāta*: a short poem by a poet on a single subject consisting of several stanzas.
8. *Saṁhitā*: a collection of poems on different subjects.

Again, we have a number of divisions under the head of light literature (*Kṣudraprabandha*) in later works:

1. *Udāharaṇa*: alliterative and rhythmic prose paragraph with a metrical beginning and end.
2. *Cakravāla*: rhythmic prose-paragraph (following an initial verse), each component being a vocative and embodying the device of making the last word in a compound identical with the initial word of the next.

3. *Bhogāvali*: prose sections of eight or four uniformly structured sentences, beginning and ending with a stanza and containing the vocative form *deva* at the head of each unit, and describing beauties in Nature.
4. *Birudāvali:* eulogy, a bombastic parade of royal titles to serve as content in the form of *bhogavali* above.
5. *Tārāvali*: a poem in twenty-seven stanzas.
6. *Karambhaka*: a poem containing stanzas in Sanskrit as well as other languages.
7. *Ratnāvali*: a poem in nine stanzas.

So also, drama (*rūpaka*) has a number of types and sub-types which can be conveniently classified in tabular form.

It should be noted that Sanskrit literary criticism is primarily schematic and formal; and a critic is expected to judge a given work by first determining the genre to which it belongs and whether it successfully fulfils all the classical norms governing it. The basic principles underlying the tabulated norms of the different literary genres are indeed broad and simple. These relate to common elements which any literary analysis or appreciation of given works should perforce include:

> (1) plot, (2) characters, (3) *rasa* (sentiment) and *bhāva* (emotional state), (4) style: (i) *guṇas* and (ii) *alamkāras*, (5) judgement of literature-defects (*anaucitya* or *doṣa*), (6) gradations of beauty in literature, (7) *dhvani* (suggested meaning), (8) *pratibhā* (creative imagination), (9) *sahṛdaya* (critic with literary taste), (10) defence of poetry and criticism, (11) *vakrokti* (oblique expression), and (12) specimens of practical criticism.

But these involve in-depth studies in such varied, yet related, branches of learning as linguistics, semantics, psychology, grammar, aesthetics, logic and philosophy and raise even the eclectic discipline of poetics (*Alaṃkāraśāstra*) to a prestigious and independent status in the scheme of Sanskrit studies. Incidentally, a treatment under these broad heads will meaningfully include all the important concepts of the discipline such as *alaṃkāra*, *guṇa*, *rīti*, *rasa-bhāva*, *dhvani*, *vakrokti* and *aucitya*-cum-*anaucitya* and will help avoidance of needless repetition.

Theme and Technique of Plot-construction (Vastu-samvidhāna)

Whatever the literary genre, the theme serves as its very body or backbone. In the highest forms of poetry and drama, namely, *Mahākāvya* (art-epic in several cantos) and *Nāṭaka* (play extending to several acts), it is not so much an invented story which matters, but a plot structured in a well-ordered form. The more familiar to the audience, the better it serves to catch their aesthetic attention because they can concentrate more pointedly on the author's technique or masterly art in the arrangement of various incidents or scenes. The five noticeable divisions (*sandhis*) in a good plot are: (1) opening (*mukha*), (2) progress (*pratimukha*), (3) complication (*garbha*), (4) disentanglement (*vimarśa*), and (5) happy conclusion (*nirvāhana*). It will be seen that this kind of constructive skill endows an otherwise uninteresting story with suspense, surprise and artistic appeal. The action (*kārya*) does not move along a predictable line; its progress is deliberately made uneven and crisscross till the climax, when there is a sudden turn of events which removes the obstacles and eventually brings about the intended happy end. Corresponding to the uneven progress of the incidents, there will be uneven stages (*avasthās*) in the endeavours of the hero before he succeeds, and these are termed: (i) commencement (*ārambha*), (ii) effort (*prayatna*), (iii) possibility of gaining the end (*prāptyāśā*), (iv) certainty of reward (*niyatāpti*), and (v) successful attainment (*phalāgama*). Metaphorically, the main theme may be said to correspond to the seed (*bīja*), the water-drop (*bindu*) that nourishes it, and the fruit (*phala*) with two intervening accessories of sub-plot, namely, parallel incident (*patākā*) and episode (*prakarī*). Thus in the story of Rama, if Rama's coronation is regarded as the end, we first find incidents in favour of it, then unforeseen obstacles leading to complications, with possibilities of hope with the alliance of Sugrīva, certainty with the feats of Hanuman and happy conclusion after Rāvaṇa is slain. A good plot then involves a conflict, external or internal.

Characters

Much of the human interest in literature is due to characters created by writers. A mechanical analysis of these can yield only the broad types we actually find in the masterpieces and they need not be construed as normative. High (*uttama*), middling (*madhyama*) and low (*nīca*) characters; each of them has a place if they are judiciously brought in where they belong according to the demands made by the genres. A villain, a rake, a jester and a courtesan fit in best in a low comedy like *Prahāsana*; but would be out of place in a serious play or art-epic whose loftiness demands semi-divine heroes and heroines. Realism has little scope in the rarefied atmosphere of these great and idealistic literary forms. Similarly, love-lyrics are so varied in range that they demand a great diversity of maidens in love. The broad types of 'heroes' and 'heroines' are indicated in *Alaṃkaraśāstra* to provide guidelines to poets and critics.

Heroes

(i) General characteristics:

good manners, sweet temper, generosity, capability, lively speech, popularity, eloquence, noble birth, steadiness, youthfulness, sharp intellect, dynamism, accomplishment in the arts, heroism in battle, firmness, radiance, learning and religiousness.

(ii) Four broad types:

(1) exalted hero (*dhīrodātta*), e.g. Rāma.

(2) bumptious hero (*dhīroddhaṭa*), e.g. Bhīma.

(3) sportive hero (*dhiralalita*), e.g. Vatsarāja.

(4) calm hero (*dhīra-śānta*), e.g. Cārudatta.

(iii) Different stages of love in the above heroes:

(1) Courteous (*dakśiṇa*): one who feigns sincere love to his first wife when he is really in love with another woman, e.g. Agnimitra.

(2) Discourteous (*śaṭha*): one who does not care for the feelings of the first woman, e.g. love in Amaru's love-poem *Amaruśataka*, (c. A.D. 800), verse 109.

(3) Callous (*dhṛṣṭa*): one who does not care even to hide his tell-tale indications of guilt, e.g. the lover in *Amaruśataka*, verse 60.

(4) Devoted (*anukūla*): one who is completely devoted to one woman (i.e. wife) only, e.g. Rāma.

(iv) Associates of heroes:

(1) Hero of sub-plot (*pīṭhamarda*), e.g. Sugriva.

(2) Cavalier (*vita*), e.g. Śekharaka in *Nāgānanda*.

(3) Jester (*vidūṣaka*), e.g. Vasantaka in *Svapnavāsavadatta*.

(v) Hero's rival:

(1) Anti-hero (*pratināyaka*), e.g. Rāvaṇa.

Heroines

(i) Three types:

(1) Wedded wife (*svīyā*), e.g. Sita for Rāma.

(2) Another (*anyā*), e.g. Sita for Rāvaṇa.

(3) Courtesan (*sādhāraṇa-strī*), e.g. Vasantasenā.

(ii) Sub-types of wedded wife:

(1) Guileless (*mugdhā*), e.g. Pārvati in *Kumārasambhava*, VIII, 2.

(2) Youthfully excited (*madhyā*), e.g. *Śiṣupālavadha, VI*, 19.

(3) Love-mad (*pragalbhā*), e.g. *Amaruśataka*, verse 64.

(iii) Further classes of the last two:

(1) Bold (*dhīrā*).

(2) Timid (*adhīrā*).

(3) Partly bold and partly timid (*dhīrādhīrā*).

(iv) These six kinds, again twofold ($6 \times 2 = 12$):

(1) First wife (*jyeṣṭhā*) e.g. Vāsavadattā.

(2) Second wife (*kaniṣṭhā*) e.g. Ratnāvalī.

(v) Two types of 'another':

(1) Virgin.

(2) Married woman.

Extra-marital love in the main plot is strictly prohibited. However, there is no such restriction about love relating to a virgin.

(vi) Eight stages of love common to all types of heroines:

(1) One whose husband is under her control (*svādhinapatikā*).

(2) One who puts on her best show while receiving the lover (*vāsaka-sajjā*).

(3) One who suffers the pangs of separation (*virahotkanṭhitā*).

(4) One who is jealous of her husband's extra-marital love (*khaṇṇitā*).

(5) One who regrets her spurning the lover in a flurry (*kalahāntaritā*).

(6) One who has been deceived by her lover who misses his promised assignation (*vipralabdhā*).

(7) One whose lover is far away (*proṣita-priyā*).

(8) One who sallies forth on her own to meet her lover (*abhisārikā*).

(vii) Retinue of heroines:

maid-servants, friends, washerwomen, half-sisters, nuns, artists, etc.

Such detailed classifications indicate not only a minute literary analysis of a vast range of good literary works on the part of the theorists, but also their keenness in offering practical guidelines to new writers by posing before them the technical points which they should keep in mind while exercising their choice. Had they not gone so minutely into details, poets might have thought that blind conformity to broad types of characters would be enough to produce a standard play or poem. But the numerous subdivisions made in the types of heroes and heroines from several angles cannot but convince the poets that what is expected of them is highly individualized or 'round' characters and not 'flat' types. New permutations and combinations possible throw a challenge to genius instead of curbing originality. Like the rules of grammar and of prosody, rules of poetics too serve ultimately an aesthetic purpose, though apparently tedious and boring. Here again, the principle of propriety (*aucitya*) comes to play an important part in determining the choice of particular heroes, heroines and their companions in keeping with the kind of plot on hand and sentiment (*rasa*) intended. They held rasa by serving as the very foundation (*ālambanavibhāva*) for the rise of emotions. Further, the proper psychological and physical responses of characters to the stimuli provided in the plot become aesthetic to the spectator as these responses shed their raw implications on life; because literature is not a copy but a stylized shadow *sui generis.* These responses then come to be termed *anubhāvas* or aesthetically distanced ensuants of *rasa* or sentiment.

Rasa and *Bhāva*

Perhaps these are the two key-terms in Sanskrit literary criticism which have led to endless controversy among scholars, ancient and modern. In fact, they challenge precise translation into another language because some regard them as objectively present in the poem or play, while others regard them as aspects of the subjective experience of the reader or spectator, and most philosophers raise *rasa* to a transcendental and spiritual level in their attempt to solve the difficulties which arise when it is viewed as an empirical experience.

Rasa is the very essence of all literature. It vitally animates all the constitutive elements of literature from within; and even like life in a living body, its existence cannot be gainsaid though it eludes our sense-perception. *Rasa* means 'sap', 'juice', 'taste', 'supreme joy', 'mental feeling' and 'aesthetic enjoyment'. All these shades of meaning somehow get fused in its ultimate connotation. So understood, it is the *ultima thule* (ultimate end) of all literature, the highest aesthetic value which is an end in itself. It can be attained only by a few gifted souls with hearts akin to the poets' (*sahṛdayas* or *rasikas*) because it is highly imaginative on the one hand and spiritual on the other. It is a state far from one's personal likes and dislikes, loves and hates. It is a disinterested, impersonal, contemplative state of ecstasy, *sui generis.*

Even granting all this, the critic cannot disown his responsibility of logically accounting for his enjoyment of literature in terms of its constituent elements. He will have to declare the reasons why he deems one work a success and another a failure. This intellectual activity on his part may presumably be post-ecstatic. But at this level he can convincingly show how each of the basic elements of the given literary work — plot, character and style — is endowed with an organic unity by the genius of the creative artist. This unity is conditioned by one *aṅgi-rasa* or ruling sentiment in the midst of other seven or eight subordinate ones, when the given work is an art-epic or a play or a romantic tale. In self-complete stanzas which breathe but a passing mood, we surely have no scope for fully delineated *rasas*. Therefore we should talk of their vital essence as *bhāva* and not *rasa*. Thus from the ineffable heights of spiritual *rasa* (in the singular) we come down to the level of diverse *rasas* and *bhāvas* which partake somehow of both subjectivity and objectivity. Yet these are not life emotions; they are only emotions embodied in literature or literary emotions. In life all emotions and mental states (*cittavṛttis*) are fleeting; but in literature at least some emotions can be delineated in a way more abiding and lasting and hence the term *sthāyibhāvas*. They are just nine and their corresponding aesthetic counterparts are the nine *rasas*:

Sthayibhāvas	*Rasas*
(1) Love of sexes (*rati*)	the erotic (*śṛngāra*)
(2) Laughter (*hāsa*)	the comic (*hāsya*)
(3) Sorrow (*śoka*)	the pathetic (*karuṇa*)
(4) Heroic energy (*utsāha*)	the heroic (*vīra*)
(5) Fear (*bhaya*)	the frightful (*bhayānaka*)
(6) Anger (*krodha*)	the furious (*raudra*)
(7) Disgust (*jugupsā*)	the odious (*bībhatsa*)
(8) Wonderment (*vismaya*)	the marvellous (*adbhuta*)
(9) Dispassion (*śama*)	the tranquil (*śānta*)

It will be observed that while the names of *sthāyibhāvas* are nouns, those of *rasas* are adjectives. That is because they accompany the aesthetic experience of the connoisseur, the common denominator of all the emotional states or *bhāvas* delineated at length in the literary work outside as located in characters and, at the same time, rooted within the connoisseur's heart as primordial instincts. Only the above eight or nine mental states can permit of such elaborate delineation in literature, as they represent the most universal emotions in man. Other fleeting moods and feelings (listed as 33) group themselves with one or the other of these abiding states when delineated in literature. So while *bhāva* is a name commonly applicable to all mental states, they denote only passing moods when used alongside of the term *rasa* because it is none other than *sthāyibhāva* itself raised to a delectable and aesthetic level. Hence technically *bhāva* is tantamount to *vyabhicāri-bhāva*.

Vyabhicāri-bhāvas (33)

(1) Revulsion (*nirveda*)
(2) Anguish (*glāni*)
(3) Suspicion (*śaṇkā*)

(4) Jealousy (*asūya*)
(5) Arrogance (*mada*)
(6) Fatigue (*śrama*)
(7) Lassitude (*ālasya*)
(8) Wretchedness (*dainya*)
(9) Worry (*cintā*)
(10) Stupefaction (*moha*)
(11) Remembrance (*smṛti*)
(12) Steadfastness (*dhṛti*)
(13) Shame (*vrīḍā*)
(14) Fickleness (*capalatā*)
(15) Joy (*harṣa*)
(16) Agitation (*āvega*)
(17) Foolishness (*jaḍatā*)
(18) Pride (*garva*)
(19) Despair (*viṣāda*)
(20) Eagerness (*autsukya*)
(21) Sleep (*nidrā*)
(22) Forgetfulness (*apasmāra*)
(23) Dreaminess (*supti*)
(24) Wakefulness (*vibodha*)
(25) Indignation (*amarṣa*)
(26) Dissimulation (*avahittha*)
(27) Ferocity (*ugratā*)
(28) Decision (*mati*)
(29) Sickness (*vyādhi*)
(30) Madness (*unmāda*)
(31) Death (*maraṇa*)
(32) Terror (*trāsa*)
(33) Doubt (*vitarka*)

In life all these and many more are merely 'mental states with their attendant pleasures and pains. But when delineated in literary characters they become aesthetic, exclusively enjoyable, and are called by the technical term *bhāva* (short form of *vyabhicāri-bhāva*). In short lyric poems, by and large, these find independent expression and become no less enjoyable than the dominant emotions (which are termed *rasas*) delineated in art-epics and major plays. Hence when the emotions are to be referred to at the aesthetic level often they are termed *rasa-bhāvas* or *rasādis*. The latter expression *rasādi* includes, besides *rasas* and *bhavas*, their semblances (*ābhāsas*), their germination (*udaya*) and cessation (*śānti*) as well as commingling (*śabalatā*) with other mental states.

With this background, we are now in a position to understand the significance of Bharata's *locus classicus*, namely the *rasa-sutra*. It crisply states: '*rasa* results when there is a harmonious fusion of the three elements in drama, namely, *vibhāvas*, *anubhāvas* and *vyabhicāri-bhāvas*'. In the language of analytical theorists, all these elements and *rasa* come under the broad category of *artha* or content of literature, as distinguished from *sabda* or its linguistic form. Thus one can speak of *rasa* as the *kāvyārtha* or poetic content par excellence. Even tragic and odious emotions presented in literature become as aesthetic as pleasurable emotions because of the very nature of art-experience which is supra-mundane (*lokottara*) by definition.

Style

While the above findings are applicable in their entirety to drama which is a composite art made up of several elements like music, dance, painting and histrionics, a more formal structural analysis is required as a supplement to give us a complete idea of the art of poetry. The whole and sole medium of literature is language, and its natural qualities deserve exploitation to serve poetic ends, and new artistic patterns of expressive thought and language merit a close analysis. All these come under the broad category of style, which is indeed unique to every poet depending on his innate temperament, genius, talent and practice; yet we can distinguish some broad types of style in literature. Indeed, in this field too, Indians have shown an astoundingly remarkable flair for formal analysis. This may be set out as follows:

Poet's *rasāveśa* > *Kāvya*	end: rasa of reader	1. Simple (*vaidarbhī*)
Techniques: Stylistic arrangement (*rīti, mārga, bandha, racana, saṃghaṭanā, vṛtti*) including use of *samāsas*		2. Ornate (*gauḍī*)
of sound-form (*sabda*)	and of sense-content (*artha*)	
figurative (*alaṃkāra*)	qualitative (*guṇa*) and figurative (*alaṃkāra*)	
1. Alliteration (*anuprāsa*)	1. Vigour (*ojas*)	1. Simile (*upamā*)
2. Chime (*yamaka*)	2. Sweetness (*mādhurya*)	2. Metaphor (*rūpaka*)
3. Pun (*śleṣa*), etc.	3. Lucidity (*prasāda*), etc.	3. Hyperbole (*atiśayokti*)
		4. Paradox (*virodha*), etc.

(i) *Gunas (Literary Qualities)*

It should be noted that genuine poetry springs from the poet's afflatus of *rasa* and culminates in the *rasa* of the reader. But this is achieved by a conscious and deft technique involving selection and arrangement into a rhythmic pattern of syllables, short and long compounded words, sentences, etc., with an eye to their sweetness or harshness, lucidity or pedantry, not only in respect of sound-effect but also sense-effect, in conformity with the overall *rasa* or *bhāva* in question. These qualitative considerations are significantly termed *gunas* (of *śabda* and *artha*). Their number is usually given as three; but some theorists mention as many as 10. Some take them as rooted in sound and sense only (e.g., Daṇḍin); others opine that they belong to style (e.g., Vāmana). A few hold that they are really properties of *rasa* though they appear to be of sound and sense (e.g. Ānandavardhana); still others find them inherent in the nature of the creative poet (e.g., Kuntaka). But all are agreed on the point that they form the most significant and conspicuous ingredients of style, accounting for its clearly discernible variations like the delicate and the ornate, though each might be appealing in its own way. Originally, the two styles were named after regions, namely, the North (*Gauḍī*) and the South (*Vaidarbhī*); but later they were renamed the Delicate (*Sukumāra*) and the Ornate (*Vicitra*). A happy mixture of the two was recognized as a third known as *Pāncālī* or the 'Middle' (*Madhyama*). In critical judgement, the former was usually held to be the more natural and spontaneous and hence more appealing than the latter achieved by great labour. the words *mārga, bandha, saṃghaṭana, vṛtti, racanā*, etc. are more or less synonyms of *rīti* interpreted broadly as stylistic arrangement.

(ii) *Alaṃkāras* (Figures of Speech)

To the Indian analytical mind, discovery of new figures of speech was indeed the most favourite preoccupation for several centuries. They are devices for avoiding the obvious and achieving aesthetic form in respect of sound as well as sense, by turns of expression as well as poetic conceits. The underlying principle of all figures is therefore described as *vakrokti* or oblique expression. It is universally accepted that it is an activity of the exclusively poetic imagination, involving original turns of thought and language. It sees likenesses in things different (simile), talks of one as another (metaphor), fancies non-existent comparisons (*utprekṣā*) and indulges freely in exaggeration (*atiśayokti*). It means two or more things simultaneously (*śleṣa*) and revels in paradox (*virodha*). It notices strange and minute aspects of everything in nature (*svabhāvokti*); it overturns logic and reverses the roles of cause and effect (*vibhāvanā*) and makes impossible things possible (*asaṃgati*). It adduces parallels between remote objects (*dṛṣṭānta*), gives telling illustrations (*nidarsana*) and indulges in strange generalizations (*arthāntaranyāsa*). Doubt (*sandeha*), remembrance (*smaraṇa*) and even illusion (*bhrānti*) become delectable. It juxtaposes incompatibles (*viṣama*) and applauds by censuring (*vyajāstuti*). It overtly speaks of irrelevant subjects like birds and beasts when it covertly means something else most relevant (*anyokti*). It uses epithets with special significance (*parikara*) and even adopts word patterns like chain (*śṛnkhala*), iteration (*mālā*), respective reference (*yathāsaṃkhya*), and so forth.

These and many more are all happy devices of thought invented by a creative mind as the natural medium for poetry, however remote they may be from routine ways of expression in life. Since they all serve to beautify the thought, they are regarded as *arthālaṃkāras*. As many as a hundred of them have been defined and illustrated in the classical texts, and each one of them is subjected to further subdivisions, sometimes as many as thirty.

On the other hand, there are sound patterns too, artistically devised by the poet, such as alliteration (*anuprāsa*), chime (*yamaka*) and play upon words (*śleṣa*). These come under the head *śabdālaṃkāras* or figures of sound.

The importance of *guṇas* vis-à-vis *alaṃkāras* is self-evident. The *guṇas* are more intrinsic to poetry because they are intimately bound up with *rasas* while *alaṃkāras* are like external ornaments. Hence while the imagery of *alaṃkāras* is extremely desirable in poetry so long as they appear as spontaneous effusions of a creative genius suffused with *rasa*, they become sources of revulsion when indulged in excess because their artificiality is then obvious, and they mar *rasa*. There can be good poetry even without an obvious figure of speech; but not without poetic quality or style.

The formalist approach of the early theorists accommodated even *rasa-bhāvas* under a class of *alaṃkāras* or *guṇas*, in the field of poetry. In the opinion of later thinkers, this indicates a lack of philosophical judgement on their part. If virtually all figures are variations of the referential use of language, how can *rasa-bhāvas* —which, by definition, are undenotable but only suggestible—ever be classed on a par with simile and metaphor? This defect is remedied by the *dhvani* theorists, by regarding *rasa* as the soul of poetry, while figures are ornaments of its body.

Judgement of Literature

(i) Defects *(anaucitya* or *dosa)*

In the classical tradition of Indian literary criticism, 'Defects' constitute an important concept, because all the rules of the discipline are concerned with an ideal literary work, absolutely free from blemishes of every kind. There is no writer who is silent over them. Though they are sometimes mentioned as negations of *guṇas* or literary merits, the most common view is that they are positive blemishes of poetic beauty and obstacles that block aesthetic experience. What deserves to be noted is that there are no absolute defects (*nitya-doṣas*) in poetry as in grammar, since impropriety of any kind is relative to the context. Even a merit so-called may turn into a defect if it rings as inappropriate in a given context. Hence, determination of *doṣas* demands a high degree of literary sensibility from the critic, and poetry cannot be judged mechanically.

Usually, defects are brought under five heads: 1. word, 2. part of a word, 3. sentence, 4. subjects and 5. *rasa*.

Dissonance (*duḥśrāvatva*), obscenity (*aślīla*), improper denotation (*anucitārtha*), archaism (*aprayukta*), vulgarity (*grāmya*), lack of full significance (*apratīta*), ambiguity (*saṃdigdha*), far-fetched meaning (*neyārtha*), distorted meaning (*nihatārtha*), wrong meaning (*avācaka*), forced meaning (*kliṣṭa*), opposite meaning (*viruddhamatikṛt*), reversal of the roles of subject and predicate (*avimṛṣṭavidheya*) are listed as common defects of word, word-part and sentence.

Harsh syllables (*pratikāla-varṇa*), *visarga(h)* deleted or changed (*lupta-hata-visarga*), excess or shortage in words required and repetition (*adhika-nyāna-kathita-pada*), gradual decline in emphasis (*patat-prakarṣa*), hiatus or obscenity and loss of euphony (*viśleṣa-aślīla-kaṣṭatā*) in word-combination (*saṃdhi*), wrong order in the placement of words and in the use of clauses, unintended equivocation, omission of required words, wrong constructions of compound words, wrong pauses in composition, etc., are said to be other defects that might vitiate sentences.

Absence of significance (*apuṣta*), disorder (*duṣkrama*), vulgarity (*grāmya*), self-contradiction (*vyāhata*), obscenity (*aślīla*), obscurity (*kaṣta*), monotony (*anavīkṛta*), illogicality (*nirhetu*), opposite sense (*viruddha*), ambiguity (*saṁdigdha*) repetition (*punarukta*), misrepresentation of well-known facts in various fields of knowledge (*khyāti-viruddha* and *vidyāviruddha*), incompleteness (*sākāṇkśatā*), incompatibility (*sahacārabhinnatā*), reversal of order (*asthānayuktatā*), erroneous presentation of particular as general and vice-versa (*aviṣeśe viṣeśa*), etc., are listed as defects tainting meaning (*artha*).

It will be observed that these flaws mostly relate to errors in grammar, syntax and composition and arise from an inadequate equipment in general knowledge, rules of logic and commonsense on the part of the poet. They are all classed as defects because Sanskrit composition, in its very nature, is expected to represent the highest classical standard attainable in all respects. Want of genius on a poet's part may be pardoned, but not lack of learning.

But overriding all these is the aesthetic standard of propriety dictated by *rasa*. While the defects earlier mentioned might mar only individual parts of a poem, impropriety in the delineation of *rasa* or *bhāva* mars the work as a whole. Briefly, these shortcomings are:

(1) Stating the intended *rasa*, etc. by name instead of suggesting it in the proper way.
(2) Elaborating the accessories of a *rasa* which is opposed to the one on hand.
(3) Rendering the comprehension of *vibhāvas*, etc., difficult by excessive attention to figures of speech, etc.
(4) Untimely elaboration or attenuation of *rasa*.
(5) Treatment of the same *rasa* over and over again.
(6) Lack of sufficient attention to the dominant *rasa*.
(7) Inordinately excessive treatment of secondary *rasas*.
(8) Violation of the canons governing different types of characters.
(9) Attribution of wrong traits to the subject.

These flaws as well as the ones noted earlier, it should not be forgotten, are never absolute, but relative and functional in character. With proper discretion, a poet can not only remove their repulsiveness, but can actually turn them into positive merits. Thus a mad man is best described when his talk is rambling, incoherent and vulgar. A person in a fit of fury should use harsh language to be effective. An obscene hint sounds quite proper in the mouth of a prostitute. Once in a way, a learned speaker may allow himself difficult and technical language. When a character is swayed by sudden bursts of passion or wonder, he can flout the rules of propriety, and so forth.

Nor is it all; poets are indeed encouraged to adopt freely in their works certain poetic conventions though they flout the norms of commonsense.

(ii) Poetic conventions *(kavisāmayas)*.

These may be briefly indicated here under convenient heads, particularly those relating to our earth, ignoring the ones about heaven and the netherworld.

(a) *Describing non-existent things as existing.* Lotuses bloom in all rivers; swans reside in all waters; mountains contain gems; cobras contain gems in their heads, etc.
(b) *Existing things described as non-existent.* Malati flowers do not bloom in spring; sandal trees do not have flower and fruit; Aśoka trees have no fruit.
(c) *Restricting the existence of things to certain localities.* Pearls are found only in the river Tāmraparṇī; sandal trees are found only in Malaya mountain.
(d) *Abstract ones treated as concrete.* Darkness can be pierced by a needle; moonlight can be filled in a jug.

(e) *Inventions of fancy*. The *cakora* bird subsists only on moonbeams; the *cakravāka* gets separated from its mate at night; fame is white and infamy dark; anger and love are red; the god of love bears a sugarcane bow furnished with five flowery arrows and strung with a string of bees; women have a line of hair above the navel, etc.

These conventions, taken along with the legends and myths provided by the puranas, lend an atmosphere of unique grandeur to classical Sanskrit poetry; and they have become cliches of all Indian literature.

Gradations of Beauty in Literature

As explained above, poetic beauty (*saundarya*) is a total complex made up of several elements, some relating to form, some to content, many to style and quite a few to traditional conventions. Several manifestations of beauty in its synthetic aspect are noticed by poets, etc.:

(1) Sensuous beauty of sublimity perceived in the objects of Nature (*prakṛti-saundarya*).

(2) Beauty of sublimity (as of heroes and heroines) in man's emotions and actions as embodied in characters (*āśraya-saundarya*).

(3) Beauty inherently present in the poet's raw material, i.e., sound or sense (*sahaja*).

(4) Beauty in the technique adopted by a poet (*āhārya*).

(5) Beauty in the creative imagination of a poet (*bhāvikatva*).

Bhāsa (A.D. 200) quotes a maxim that 'beauty is that which pleases all' - while Kālidāsa (A.D. 350) and Bhāravi (A.D. 550) agree that inherent beauty needs no decoration. Kālidāsa also adds significantly that beauty in outer objects may not delight always, because it is also dependent on the mood of the beholder. When the mood is attuned properly, even a light distortion of a beautiful object may prove appealing. Thus we come to Māgha's (A.D. 680) final description of beauty as that which retains its freshness of charm every time it is viewed.

Dhvani

These insights of poets lack logical precision. It was Anandavardhana (A.D. 850), the doyen of Indian theorists, who remedied this defect by taking the analogy of a beautiful damsel. There are no doubt charming features in each of her flawless limbs, but what enchants an onlooker is her overall grace of personality (*lāvanya*) which is quite distinct from the perfection of parts. This overall beauty in literature is defined by him as *dhvani* or suggested meaning.

Dhvani is a higher kind of beauty because it is grasped at the highest level of sensitivity on the part of the connoisseur, after he has ceased attending to beauties of form and content for their own sake. The ordinary functions of language, namely primary denotation (*abhidhā*), secondary implication (*lakśaṣa*) and even purport (*tātparya*) of a sentence as a whole after constructing the words properly, become only means to serve the ultimate end of manifesting *dhvani*. Since *dhvani* is the sole meaning intended by the poet at one end and realized by the man of taste at the other, it deserves to be regarded as the very soul or vital essence that gives life to all the other aspects of literary beauty. In short, *dhvani* is what is beautified by all the other elements analysed by specialists of poetry - be it *guṇa*, *rīti*, *alaṃkāra* or *vṛtti*.

The range of *dhvani* is so vast that it not only covers all aspects of beauty noticed earlier, but goes far beyond them. If the entire world of nature and human thought can be described as *vastu* (subject), the *vastu* suggested in poetry is but one branch of *dhvani*. If all artistic or imaginative turns of expression can be termed *alaṃkāra* (embellishment), suggestion of associated imagery forms the second broad division of *dhvani*. But the imperial throne in the palace of *dhvani* is reserved for *rasa* because it is *dhvani* par excellence. Emotions and feelings can never be evoked in any way other than suggestion. This is true only when *rasa* reigns supreme in a given work. Such *dhvani-kāvya* will be automatically judged as a poem of the best grade, because it is an unmistakable and irrefutable index of a poet's creative art at its highest watermark. The credit for having provided room, in their wide aesthetic analysis of *rasa*, not only for the beautiful (*śṛṇgāra*), but also the sublime (*adbhuta*), the grand (*dhirodātta's Vīra*), the comic (*hāsya*), the ugly (*bībhatsa*) and the pathetic (*karuṇa*) cannot be denied to Sanskrit theorists. Everything is grist to the poet's mill and even the ugly and the repulsive can be transformed by the art of poetry into aesthetic experience.

The whole gamut of aesthetic experience is thus very sensitively traversed, the crown being reserved for spiritual ecstasy or *śānta* which may be described paradoxically as passionless passion or boundless calm. No wonder that the great mystic that he was, Abhinavagupta (c. A.D. 1000) went to the extent of recognizing *śānta* as the mainspring of all other *rasas*. Bhavabhuti (c. A.D. 700) seems to suggest that pathos deserves that pride of place; Bhoja declares that the all-embracing subjective ego's self-regard (*abhimāna*) comes to be technically termed *śṛṇgaṝa* and hence it should be regarded as the source of all other *rasas*. These divergent opinions do not affect the soundness of the dictum that the best order of poetry is constituted by *rasadhvani*; and even ordinary *vastu* and *alaṃkāras* come to be invested with a new halo of charm when they are suggested instead of being plainly stated, a charm that entitles them to rank on a par with *rasadhvani* itself. On deeper analysis, the latter too will open up their secret alliance with *rasa*, since nothing in the world can enter the realm of poetry without becoming a partner in *rasa*, at least as an indirect *vibhāva*.

It would be a mistake if one thinks that enjoyment of suggested *rasa* is a long-drawn-out process of reflective thinking. In fact, it flashes forth across the mind of the critic so quickly that he cannot notice any time-sequence intervening between his comprehension of the plain meaning and the suggested meaning. What *dhvani* demands from the critic is poetic sensibility and nothing else.

In the best or first-grade poetry discussed above, though we have stressed the dominance of *rasa* as vital, the invariable accompaniment of suitable *guṇas* and *alaṃkāras* therein should not be belittled; for, if *rasa* is the soul, *guṇas* and *alaṃkaras* constitute the very 'body' of poetry. How can there be a soul without a body? But the body should not distract attention from the soul. This is *aucitya* or propriety. All elements of structural beauty must become subordinate in order to let the aesthetic *rasa* have free play.

In actual practice, however, this ideal is not often realized. The structural elements often outshine the *rasa* and other forms of *dhvani*. In rare instances, even a suggested *vastu* might outshine a suggested *rasa*. Then the latter loses perforce its claim for the highest honour. To accommodate all such border instances, *dhvani* theorists speak of another class of poetry called 'poetry of subordinated suggestion' (*guṇībhūtavyaṇgya*). In the world of literature, this class is no less wide than the first; and the critic enjoys it too, not as the next best, but as good poetry for a different reason. A reader might even prefer this kind to the earlier, according to his taste.

Though the literary masterpieces in Sanskrit can all be brought under the first or the second of the classes of poetry, there would still remain a vast body of literary work unaccommodated under them. These laborious lucubrations of boring 'experts' teeming with tedious verbal exercises and riddles would, strictly speaking, fall outside the purview of poetry. But for courtesy's sake they may be given the lowest place called *Citra* (colourful portrait) when ancient; but this does not entitle a modernist to be recognized as a poet.

Thus an adoption of the theory of *dhvani* will enable one to grade literary works and attempt applied criticism by providing him a workable yardstick, not only for evaluating short poems, but even whole epics and plays. The connoisseur trained in the dialectics of *dhvani* will unerringly lay his finger on the poet's major lapses, if any, and will also convincingly demonstrate the plus points to the poet's credit, basing his judgement not so much on the poet's blind conformity to 'rules' but on his lively innovations in theme as well as technique.

Pratibhā (Creative Imagination)

It follows from the above considerations that Indian criticism makes heavy demands on the poet's creative originality, however trite his borrowed theme be. In the making of a poet, *pratibhā* or creative imagination is always given the highest importance; it is said to be an innate gift with which one is born. No amount of learning or assiduous practice can succeed if this primary requirement is not present. On the nature of *pratibhā* the observations made by Abhinavagupta's teacher, Bhaṭṭa Tauta (c. 950) have become classical:

> It has been remarked that no non-sage can be deservingly called 'poet'; a sage will be worth his name only by virtue of his vision. By vision we mean that insight into Truth about all the manifold objects in the world and their varying states. One can win the distinction of a being a 'poet in the sciences' if he possesses this vision of Truth. But in common usage the world accords that title exclusively to one who possesses both vision and imaginative expression. Thus though Valmiki was highly gifted with an abiding clear vision, he was not hailed as a poet by people until he embodied it in an epic.

Sahṛdaya (Critic with Literary Taste)

In order to be receptive enough to such rare creations of poetic *pratibhā*, it goes without saying that an equally rare gift of sensibility or good taste is expected in the critic also. That is why Anandavardhana insists on reminding us time and again that his doctrine of *dhvani* is a document based on the felt aesthetic experience of *sahṛdayas* or critics with good taste. Abhinavagupta goes a step further and declares the essential identity in the natures of the gifted poet and the gifted critic. Literally, *sahṛdaya* means 'one with a kindred heart'; but Abhinavagupta would prefer to think that the spirits of the ideal poet and the ideal literary critic are one and the same, not just similar. The names are two; but the spirit is one. Hence mere grammarians, dry logicians and science specialists have no right to attempt literary criticism. In the nature of things, it is the task of more gifted souls who have an aesthetic taste.

Defence of Poetry and Criticism

Poetry in Sanskrit originated as a handmaid of religion, to judge from our premier epics. The *Ramayana* and the *Mahabharata* were valued highly as popular and pleasing re-presentations of the ethical codes laid down in law-books. But soon secular poetry grew, adding a new sensuous dimension which proved more popular, and this aroused serious protests from orthodox philosophers. Rajasekhara (980) sums up their objections in his *Kāvyamimāmsā*: Poetry should not be taught because (1) it teaches untruth, (2) it teaches immorality and (3) it abounds in obscenity. His line of defence, however, is far from convincing because he merely refers to the point that even the Vedic scriptures are tainted with these very blemishes.

But Bhaṭṭa Tauta gives an effective rejoinder. He states:

> Surely, there is no real existence of sense-objects at all in the world of poetry because it is an imaginary one. How, then, can you complain that passions are profoundly excited by poetry?
>
> Should you urge that the dominant emotion delineated in poetry is itself the object, well, your position contradicts the nature of aesthetic experience wherein the emotion is not felt as objective.
>
> If you should say that 'aesthetic experience' itself is passion, you fail to distinguish once again between aesthetic emotion and sexual passion. If you persist in holding that the vicious effect proves the viciousness of the cause, we have only to ask you back how a character like Sita can ever be an object for the love of two or more persons.
>
> Hence our stand is this: just as dust is used to clean up a dusty mirror, passion is utilized to remove passion in the critic.

In addition to this claim that immediate aesthetic joy or *rasa* is an end or value in itself, standard theorists are seen stating that literature indirectly serves to help people in realizing all the four recognized values of life, namely, morality (*dharma*), material prosperity (*artha*), worldly pleasures (*kāma*) and spiritual emancipation (*mokṣa*). Unlike the ordinances of the law-books in regard to these which might repel the student by their dryness, literature sugar-coats the bitter pill of instruction by way of alluring *rasas* and is thus eventually more effective. Such pleasing instruction in literature is compared to the sweet and winsome influence of a beloved (*kāntāsammita*). To these are added the prospects of everlasting fame, wealth and religious merit that a poet might well aspire for. In fact, religious theists of a later age (1250–1850) regarded multifaceted *bhakti* itself as the 'overall *rasa*'.

Vakrokti

Deriving inspiration from the *dhvani* theory, Kuntaka (c. A.D. 980) developed his theory of vakrokti, 'oblique expression', to serve as an aid to practical criticism. His approach is eminently practical and he cannot accept the self-contradictory assertions of Anandavardhana that *rasa* may be sometimes dominant when it is termed *dhvani* and sometimes auxiliary when it is called an *alaṃkāra*. If *rasa* is the soul and *alaṃkāra* is the body of poetry, strict logic demands that the soul must perforce be always dominant and can never brook any subordination. Again, Anandavardhana had admitted two types of beauty in poetry in his scheme - the stated (vācya) and the suggested (*vyangya*) and recognized two classes of poetry depending on the relative preponderance of one over the other. But Kuntaka cannot accept such gradations of beauty in poetry, accepted as good by discerning critics. The only distinction logically possible in aesthetics is that of poetry from non-poetry. And there might be innumerable ways open to the poet for endowing his expression with beauty. So according to Kuntaka, the broadest principle which can do justice to all the categories of literary theory including *dhvani* (in all its varieties) is only *vakrokti* which might admit of innumerable varieties. A poem may be beautiful for more reasons than one; and it should be the task of the critic to be on the lookout for all the diverse elements that contribute to the poem's beauty as a whole. Except for these differences in principle, there is complete agreement between *rasa-dhvani* and *vakrokti* theorists who pioneered practical criticism of literature in Sanskrit.

Practical Criticism

The earlier writers on the subject had mostly contented themselves with illustrating their rules by their own made-to-order examples. Even the few who took the trouble of selecting right examples from accepted masterpieces of literature did not attempt literary assessment of whole works. Nor did celebrated commentators on particular poems like Mallinātha (1300) deem it their concern to attempt such literary criticism in detail. Hence the pioneering efforts in this neglected but most important field of applied criticism by Anandavardhana and Kuntaka deserve more than a passing notice here.

Two Specimens

(i) Ānandavardhana on the *Rāmāyana* and the *Mahābhārata*. 'In the *Rāmāyana* indeed, Vālmiki has embodied the dominant sentiment of pathos as is evidenced by his own declaration "sorrow has taken the form of a stanza". It has indeed been maintained as predominant till the very end of the work because the poem closes at the point of the irreparable loss of Sita.

In the Māhābharata too, which combines both the elements, instruction and poetry, it will be seen that its çonclusion on a note of despair consequent on the miserable deaths of Vṛṣṇis as well as the Pāndavas, devised by the great sage Vyāsa, reveals his primary intention of preaching the moral of renunciation through his work and throws light upon the fact that he intended final emancipation as the foremost of human values, and calm (*śānta*) as the most predominant sentiment in the work as a whole.

(ii) Kuntaka on Kālidāsa's *'Sakuntala'*. 'In a whole literary work too, an attainment of aesthetic effect owing its origin to the inventive power of the poet will present a new shade of charm even like a new touch-up given by a painter to an old faded portrait.'

For example, in the play *Abhijñana-śākuntalā*, we see in the hero so faint a recollection of the sweet impression of Śakuntalā's matchless beauty in her exquisite youth as soon as he sees her (in Act V) when she removes her veil that it does not rule out the possibility of his rejecting her as a wife of another person. Śakuntalā does everything to revive his memory by relating intimate incidents of their first honeymoon when both were filled with deep love for each other, incidents which are at once so intimate and delicate that they are bound to infuse confidence. The reason why Dushyanta is unable to recognize her even after listening to it is a mystery left unexplained in the original *Mahābhārata*. For explaining it adequately with a cogent reason, the poet has invented the episode of the curse of sage Durvāsas. Durvāsas is a sage blind to all soft feeling and highly irate by temperament, one who flies into a rage even at the slightest lapse. In that episode of Durvāsas, it is seen that Śakuntalā is completely overwhelmed by the excruciating pangs of her first separation from her lover; and as she is lying in her cottage in such a state, there comes this great sage to her doorstep, and flies into a fit of anger at being unnoticed and pronounces a curse:

He whom you are thinking of with such raptness
That you cannot see even me, a sage arrived,
Let him not recall you, though reminded,
Like one drunk who cannot, a statement his own (tr. IV. I)

Such is the curse flung upon Śākuntalā. And at once the sage starts moving out. Yet when he is appealed to by the two friends of Śakuntalā, the great sage yields to the extent of limiting the duration of his curse to the sight of the signet ring given to Śakuntalā by the king. And when Śakuntalā is on her way to meet her spouse, the ring adorning her tender shoot-like finger slips down without her notice and falls into the waters of a stream which she had entered for bathing. Mistaking the glittering glow of the ruby set in the ring for a fresh lump of flesh, a fish swallows it. In course of time, the fish gets killed by a fisherman who catches it and the ring recovered by him is at last presented to the king himself. Such an art of plot-construction may surely be regarded as the best medium for delineating literary sentiment. Thanks to it, the entire play has acquired a unique beauty.

Again, in due time, we have the incident of the song outwardly reviling the bee, whose inner significance is caught by the king, though his memory has been blacked out by the curse of the sage; deep down in his mind we notice that traces are still left of the old love on account of which he is very much upset.

Seeing things lovely and hearing sounds sweet,
If a happy man should get perturbed,
It means his mind is recalling unawares
The deep impressions of a former birth. (tr. V.2)

Here such a recollection of his beloved (so deep down in the subconscious), at once guileless and charming, appeals very much to the hearts of connoisseurs. What is more, she is turned down later; her story about the ring is dismissed as false; the account of her marriage with him and pregnancy, given by Sage Kanva's disciple, is discredited, and the king is seen in a fit of anger. Then, even transgressing the limits of natural shyness, Śakuntalā's veil is removed from her face suddenly. Yet the king is under the illusion that she is another's wife. Though her bubbling youthful charm, superior to that of all the women seen by him so far, impresses him highly, and though her narration, sweet like the notes from a lyre, of intimate incidents of their mutual love - like their pleasurable excursions in the penance grove - arouses his appreciation, still he shows the rudeness of rejecting her. Such rudeness too becomes understandable only by the intensity of his later repentance at the termination of the curse, a repentance which is indicative of the depth of his unmitigated love for her in his heart. and it is most appealing to the connoisseurs. and in devising the end of the curse, the poet prefaces it with a description of the intense wretchedness of the mental state of the king, who is now frenzied with the pangs of unbearable separation from his beloved Śakuntalā, after the slow return of his memory of the forgotten incidents. Synchronizing with it comes the recovery of the lost ring too which again delights the readers very much. The chamberlain of the king observes: 'Gone are all his personal decorations'. (VI. 6–7).

All these epithets given to the king in suffering are full of artistic beauty. There is artistic beauty of 'number' in the word *gotreṣu* (where the plural is aesthetically used to refer to the name of a single rival in love). They all add to the aesthetic appeal of the situation. When the king, looking at the picture of his beloved drawn by himself, speaks gallantly of the sweet recollection of his love, his words bear the deep impress of his darling:

O bee, if you dare to touch any more
My darling's lip as red as 'bimba' fruit,
..... I shall jail you in a lotus bud. (tr. VI.20)

the speech finds a ready echo in our hearts.

If the exquisite episode invented by the genius of the poet were not there in the play, the unbearable fact of the king's forgetting his wife without any reason would become a blemish as much in the play as in the original story of the Mahabharata itself.

BIBLIOGRAPHY

SANSKRIT

1. Abhinavagupta, *Abhinavabhārati*, vol.I, Oriental Institute, Baroda, Baroda, 1956.
2. ———, *Dhvanyāloka-locanā*, Chowkhamba, Banaras, 1940.
3. Anandavardhana, *Dhvanyāloka*, Karnataka University, Dharwar, 1974.
4. Bhamaha, *Kāvyālankāra*, Wallace Printing House, Tanjore, 1927.
5. Bharata, *Nāṭyaśāstra*, vols. I-IV, Oriental Institute, Baroda, vol. I, 2nd ed., 1956; Vol. II, 1954; Vol. III, 1954; Vol. IV, 1964.
6. Dandin, *Kāvyādarṣa*, Bhandarkar Oriental Research Institute, Poona, 1970.
7. Dhananjaya, *Daśarūpaka*, Adyar Library, Madras, 1969.
8. Hemachandra, *Kāvyānuśāsana*, Nirnayasagar Press, Bombay, 1934.
9. Jagannath, *Rasagaṇgādhara*, Nirnayasagar Press, Bombay, 1888.
10. Kuntaka, *Vakroktijīvita*, Karnataka University, Dharwar, 1977.
11. Mammata, *Kāvyaprakāśa*, vols.I–II, Calcutta Sanskrit College series, vol.I, 1958; vol.II, 1961.
12. Rajasekhara, *Kāvyamimāṃsā*, Oriental Institute, Baroda, 1924.
13. Rudrata, *Kāvyālankāra*, Nirnayasagar Press, Bombay, 1886.
14. Udbhata, *Kāvyālankārasārasaṇgraha*, Bombay Sanskrit Series, Poona 1925.
15. Vāmana, *Kāvyālankārasūtravṛtti*, Nirnayasagar Press, Bombay, 1953.
16. Vidyanātha, *Pratāparudrīya*, Sanskrit Education Society, Madras, 1970.
17. Visvanātha, *Sāhityadarpaṇa*, Chowkhamba, Banaras, 1947.

ENGLISH

1. De, S.K., *History of Sanskrit Poetics*, Firma K.L.Mukhopadhyaya, Calcutta, 1960.
2. ———, *Some Problems of Sanskrit Poetics*, Firma K.L.Mukhopadhyaya, Calcutta, 1959.
3. Gerow, Edwin, *Indian Poetics*, 2nd ed., Otto Harrassowitz, Wiesbaden, 1977.
4. Kane, P.V., *History of Sanskrit Poetics*, Motilal Banarsidass, Delhi, 1961.
5. Krishnamoorthy, K., *The Dhvanyāloka and its Critics*, Kavyalaya, Mysore, 1969.
6. ——, *Essays in Sanskrit Criticism*, Karnataka University. Dharwar, 1964.
7. ———, *Studies in Indian Aesthetics and Criticism*, D.V.K. Murthy, Mysore, 1979.
8. Kuppuswamy Sastri, M., *Highways and Byways of Literary Criticism in Sanskrit*, KSRI, Madras, 1945.
9. Raghavan, V., *Some Concepts of Alaṇkāraśāstra*, Adyar Library, Madras, 1942.
10. ———, *Bhoja's Śṛṇgāra-Prakāśa*, Punarvasu, Madras, 1963.
11. ———, *The Number of Rasas*, 2nd ed., Adyar Library, Madras, 1967.
12. Raghavan, V. and Nagendra, *An Introduction to Indian Poetics*, Macmillan, Madras, 1970.
13. Vijayavardhana, G., *Outlines of Sanskrit Poetics*, Choukhamba, Varanasi, 1970.
14. Warder, A.K., *Indian Kāvya Literature*, Motilal Banarsidass, Delhi, 1972.

PERIODICALS

1. Chaudhury, P.J., 'The Theory of Rasa', *Journal of Aesthetics and Art Criticism*, vol. XXIV, 1945, pp. 145–149.
2. Choudhury, I.N., 'Indian Poetics: A Study in Perfection', *Indian Horizons*, vol. XXIV, 1975, p. 6.
3. Gerow, E. and Aklujkar, A., 'On Śāntarasa in Sanskrit Poetics', *Journal of the American Oriental Society*, vol. 92, p. 80.
4. Honeywell, J. A., 'The Poetic Theory of Visvanatha', *Journal of Aesthetics and Arts Criticism*, vol. XXVII, no. 2, 1968–69.
5. Jhanji, Rekha, 'Bharata on Aesthetic Emotions', *British Journal of Aesthetics*, vol. XVIII, 1978, p. 66.
6. Krishnamoorthy, K., 'The Canon of Angi-rasa', *Indological Studies* (University of Delhi), vol. III, no. 2, 1975, pp. 101–9.
7. Kulkarni, V. M., 'The Conception of Sandhis in the Sanskrit Drama', *Journal of the Oriental Institute*, Baroda, vol. V, 1955–56, pp. 369–402.
8. Mukherjee, R., 'Rasa as a Spring of Art', *Journal of Aesthetics and Art Criticism*, vol. XXIV, 1965, pp. 91–96.
9. Pandey, K. C., 'A Bird's-eye View of Indian Aesthetics', *Journal of Aesthetics and Art Criticism*, vol. XXIV, 1965, pp. 59–73.
10. Ruth Katz and Arvind Sharma, 'The Aesthetics of Abhinavagupta', *British Journal of Aesthetics*, vol. XVII, 1977, p. 258.
11. Subrahmaniam, K., 'A note on the concept of a Critic in Sanskrit Poetics', *British Journal of Aesthetics*, vol. XXVIII, no. 4, 1978, pp. 368–9.
12. Thampi, G. B. M., 'Rasa as Aesthetic Experience', *Journal of Aesthetics and Art Criticism*, vol. XXIV, 1965, pp. 75–80.

M. HIRIYANNA

Ever since Bharata postulated his theory of *rasas*, the exact number of *rasas* has been a debated issue. The more orthodox view has been that there are only eight *rasas*, while another view proposes nine *rasas*. Both these have found able advocates over the centuries. The ninth disputed *rasa* is named the *śāntarasa*, which has been closely analysed by Abhinavagupta in his chapter on that topic. The issue has been raised in the twentieth century once again. The most scholarly commentary on it was written by V. Raghavan in his *The Number of Rasas* (The Adyar Library, Madras, 1940). Raghavan's work is a compendium of views, for and against the inclusion of *śānta* in the gamut of *rasas*. A lucid summary of Raghavan's comments is included in M. Hiriyanna's *Art Experience* (Kavyalaya, Mysore, 1954). A long extract from it (pp. 62–4) is reproduced here.

The Number of Rasas

Owing to the uncertainty of our knowledge of the early phase of Indian classical literature, it is not possible to say when poets began to portray this *rasa*. The ascetic and mystic elements, however, which form its distinctive basis, are very old features of Indian life; and they were highly valued by those who followed the teaching of the Veda as well as by those who did not. So we may assume that the *śānta* attitude found expression in literature quite early; and this is corroborated by the works of Aśvaghoṣa even if, on account of its chronological indefiniteness, we leave out of consideration the *Mahābhārata*, the useful example given of the *śānta rasa*. As regards writers on poetics, the earliest to recognise it definitely, so far as our knowledge at present goes, was Udbhaṭa. Possibly its recognition by them was even earlier. Bharata's view in the matter is somewhat doubtful, by reason of the unsatisfactory character of the *Nāṭyaśāstra* as it has come down to us. Some manuscripts of it mention only eight *rasas*, but others nine. The weight of evidence bearing on the point seems, on the whole, to be on the former side; and Dr Raghavan adduces several convincing arguments to show that the references to this rasa in Bharata are all spurious. But it should be added that the *Nāṣyaśāstra* contains nearly all the essential points necessary for a theoretical formulation of it.

Before we pass on to the aesthetic aspect of the question, it is desirable to distinguish the emotive content or theme of a literary work from the aesthetic sentiment which, according to the prevalent Indian view, its idealised presentation evokes in the reader or the spectator. Thus in the case of the *Śākuntala*, Duṣyanta's love for Śakuntalā forms the chief theme while the emotion, which it awakens in us as we witness the drama enacted, is *śṛngāra*. When we ask whether *śānta* can be a *rasa*, we mean whether situations in life involving the quietistic sentiment lend themselves to be similarly dealt with in literature. If they do, then *śānta* is a *rasa*; otherwise it is not. The practice of great poets like Kālidāsa, which is after all the true touchstone in such matters, shows that *śānta* situations can certainly be thus delineated in literary works. In the last act of his play, just alluded to, Kālidāsa describes the tranquillity and holiness of Mārica's hermitage in a manner which affects us most profoundly. But, however splendidly depicted, the *śānta rasa* occupies only a subordinate place there; and a doubt may therefore arise whether it can be the leading sentiment in a work, i.e., whether it can be portrayed in such a manner that it will impress us at the end as the predominant element in the unity of *rasas* which, according to the Indian view, every work of art is expected to achieve. Some of the works of Aśvaghoṣa, to whom I have already referred, show that it can be so represented. The *Mahābhārata* also, at any rate in its present form, illustrates the truth, as set forth by Ānandavardhana in his masterly way in the last section of *Dhvanyāloka*.

Yet there were theorists who denied that the *śānta* could be an art emotion. It is hardly necessary to examine their arguments when we have the practice of great poets and the opinion of great art critics to the contrary. But a reference should be made to one of them which appears, at first sight, to possess some force. This argument is that the attitude of mind for which *śānta* stands is altogether a rare one, and that its representation in art cannot therefore appeal to more than a very few. The objection, it is obvious, is based on the supposition that the test of true art is in the wideness of its appeal. The advocates of *śānta* brush this argument aside usually by saying that such questions are not to be decided by a plebiscite; but, by thus admitting the narrowness of its appeal, they seem to give up their position. Their conclusion is that *śānta* as a *rasa* is irresistible. Indeed, it would have been a strange irony of circumstance if Indians, of all, had excluded it from the sphere of art. The way in which this particular objection is met, however, is not satisfactory. May it be that the contention that the appeal of *śānta* is only to a very few is wrong? No unwonted occasion in life — whether it be one of joy or one of sorrow — passes without bringing home to man the supreme desirability of spiritual peace. It means that the need for such peace is fundamental to the human heart; and this conclusion is confirmed by the pure satisfaction which the contemplation, for example, of the images of Buddha in meditative repose brings to many. If so, the *śānta* mood is by no means uncommon; and the *śānta rasa* need not be an exception to the rule that the appeal of art is general. What is uncommon is the capacity in man to capture that mood and cultivate it, so that it may come to prevail over all other moods; but this deficiency does not matter so far as art is concerned, for it has the power of itself to enable him to attain, albeit only for a while, the peace of spirit which, as an old Indian critic has observed, even a *yogin* has to strain himself long to win.

A. K. RAMANUJAN

A. K. Ramanujan (1929–1993) is better known as a poet in English and Kannada, and a translator from Kannada and Tamil, than as an anthropologist, linguist and critic. His more important literary criticism has come to us through his memorable prefaces and afterwords to his remarkably well wrought translations. Before going to Chicago in 1963, Ramanujan taught English at Belgaum and Baroda. He was Professor of Dravidian Linguistics at Chicago, when he died in July 1993. The commentary on *Tolkāppiyam* included here is culled from his introduction to translations from Tamil, *Poems of Love and War* (Oxford University Press, Delhi, 1985, pp. 235–68).

It is marked by a rare lucidity and understanding of the subject. It is also included to indicate the significance of *Tolkāppiyam* in the theoretical canon of Indian literature, and to disabuse the student of the commonly held idea that Sanskrit poetics was all that there was in ancient India.

Indian literary criticism is a story woven through many languages, and the Tamil strand in it is of as much importance as the Sanskrit one, since Tamil is the mother of three other literary languages: Kannada, Telugu and Malayalam. Hence *Tolkāppiyam* has a special place in the history of Indian literary theory. Ramanujan's commentary on it has done great service to the cause of modern interpretation of ancient Tamil poetics.

On Ancient Tamil Poetics

Akam and Puram

Akam and *pu̱ram* are ancient, complex words. To understand them is to enter Tamil poetics, and much that is crucial to Tamil culture. According to *A Dravidian Etymological Dictionary*, they are also current in all the South Dravidian languages and in Telugu and Tulu. In classical poetry, as we have seen, *akam* poems are love poems; *pu̱ram* are all other kinds of poems, usually about war, values, community; it is the 'public' poetry of the ancient Tamils, celebrating the ferocity and glory of kings, lamenting the death of heroes, the poverty of poets. Elegies, panegyrics, invectives, poems on wars and tragic events are *puṟam* poems.

The *Tolkāppiyam* distinguishes *akam* and *puṟam* as follows:

> In (the five phases of) *akam*, no names of persons should be mentioned. Particular names are appropriate only in *puṟam* poetry. (*Tol.* 57)

The dramatis personae for *akam* are types, such as men and women in love, foster-mothers, girl friends, etc., rather than historical persons. Similarly, landscapes are more important than particular places. The reason for such absence of individuals is implicit in the word *akam*: the 'interior' world is archetypal, it has no history, and no names of persons and places, except, now and then, in its metaphors. Love in all its variety (with important exceptions) – love in separation and in union, before and after marriage, in chastity and in betrayal – is the theme of *akam*.

There are seven types of love, of which the first is *kaikkiḷai* or unrequited love, and the last is *peruntiṇai* or mismatched love. (*Tol.* 1)

Peruntiṇai, or the 'major type' (as the *Tolkāppiyam* somewhat cynically calls it), of man-woman relationship is the forced loveless relationship: a man and a woman, mismatched in age, coming together for duty, convenience, or lust. At the other extreme is *kaikkiḷai* (literally, the 'base relationship'), the one-sided affair, unrequited love, or desire inflicted on an immature girl who does not understand it. Neither of these extremes is the proper subject of *akam* poetry. They are common, abnormal, undignified, fit only for servants.

> Servants and workmen are outside the five *akam* types (of true love), for they do not have the necessary strength of character. (*Tol.* 25–26)

Most of the *akam* anthologies contain no poems of unrequited or mismatched love; only *Kalittokai* (e.g., "The Hunchback and the Dwarf", discussed below) has examples of both types. They follow none of the formal constraints on theme and structure that are characteristics of the *akam* poems.

Of the seven types, only the middle five are the subject of true love poetry. The hero and heroine should be "well-matched in ten points" such as beauty, wealth, age, virtue, rank, etc. Only such a pair is capable of the range of love: union and separation, anxiety, patience, betrayal, forgiveness. The couple must be cultured; for the uncultured will be rash, ignorant, self-centred, and therefore unfit for *akam* poetry.

The Five Landscapes

The *Tolkāppiyam* opens its outline of *akam* poetics with a statement about the world of the poems:

When we examine the materials of a poem, only three things appear to be important: *mutal* (the "first things", i.e., time and place), *karu* (the "native elements"), and *uri* (the "human feelings" appropriately set in *mutal* and *karu*). (*Tol.* 3)

"Place" is first divided into four kinds of regions, which are constituted by combinations of the five elements, earth, water, air, fire, sky (or space). Each region is presided over by a deity and named after a characteristic flower or tree:

mullai, a variety of jasmine, represents the forests overseen by *Māyōn*, "the Dark One", the dark-bodied god of herdsmen (Viṣṇu);

kuṟiñci, a mountain flower, stands for the mountains overseen by Ceyon, "the Red One", *Murukaṉ*, the red-speared god of war, youth and beauty;

marutam, a tree with red flowers growing near the water, for the pastoral region overseen by *Vēntaṉ*, "King", identified with the rain god (Indra);

neytal, a water flower, for the sandy seashore overseen by *Varuṇaṉ*, the wind god. (*Tol.* 5)

A rather special fifth region, *pālai* or desert waste, is overseen by *Koṟṟavai*, a demonic goddess of war, according to later writers. *Pālai* is supposedly a green desert tree that is unaffected by drought. *Pālai* has no specific location, for it is thought that any mountain or forest may be parched to a wasteland in the heat of summer.[3]

Time is divided into day, month and year. The year is divided into six "large time units", the six seasons: the rains (August-September), the cool season (October-November), the season of evening dew (December-January) the season of morning dew (February-March), early summer (April-May), and late summer (June-July). The day is divided into five "small time units": morning, midday, evening, nightfall, the dead of night. Some would add a sixth, dawn.

Particular "large time units" and "small time units" are associated by convention with particular regions.

Mullai country is associated with the rainy season and evening;

kuṟiñci, with the season of evening dew and midnight;

marutam, with the later part of night and the dawn;

neytal with the twilight or evening;

pālai with summer, the season of morning dew, and midday. (*Tol.* 6–12)

Each of the five regions or landscapes is associated further with an appropriate *uri* or phase of love. (The phases of war are discussed below.)

Lovers' union is associated with *kuṟiñci*, the mountain;

separation with *pālai*, the desert;

patient waiting, with *mullai*, the forests;

anxious waiting, with *neytal*, the seashore;
the lover's infidelity and the beloved's resentment, with
marutam, the cultivated agricultural region or lowland. (*Tol.* 16)

Of these five, the first is clandestine (*kaḷavu*), before marriage; the fifth occurs after marriage. The other three could be either before or after marriage. *Pālai*, separation, includes not only the hardships of the lover away from his love, his search for wealth, fame, and learning, but also the elopement of the couple, their hardships on the way, and their separation from their parents.

We may note a few features of the native categories of the Tamil system. First things (time and place) and native elements are distinguished from *uri* (appropriate human feelings and experience); the systematic symbology depends on the association between these two sets. They are distinct, yet co-present. They require each other; together they make the world. *Mutal* and *karu*, first things and native elements, are seen as the "objective correlatives", or rather the correlative objects,[4] of human experience. It is also significant that in this Tamil system, though gods are mentioned, they are only part of the scene; they preside, but as natives of the landscape.[5] There seems to be no creator-creature relation in the early anthologies.

In the *karu*, "things born into, or native to, a region". No clear distinction is made between nature and culture; among the native elements of a landscape are listed flora, fauna, tribes as well as arts, styles, instruments. Furthermore, the *Tolkāppiyam* (582 ff.) considers all native elements, especially all animate beings, as part of a continuous series[6] graded by degrees of sentience:

Things without any sentience: stones, water, etc.
Beings with one sense (touch):
grass, trees, creepers
Beings with two senses (touch and taste):
snails, shellfish
Beings with three senses (touch, taste, smell):
termites, ants
Beings with four senses (touch, taste, smell, vision):
crabs, lobsters, beetles, bees
Beings with five senses (touch, taste, smell, vision, hearing):
birds, beasts, and uncultured people
Beings with six senses (touch, taste, smell, vision,
hearing, mind): human beings and gods.

In poetry, says the *Tolkāppiyam*, the above categories are both used and crossed, say, in figures like metaphor and personification. Time may become a winged bird, a bird may be seen as a messenger of love, and love may be felt as a river in flood. As some philosophers would say, a metaphor is a "category mistake". A special figure (called *bhrāntimadalaṅkāra* in Sanskrit) depends on one thing being mistaken for another. George Hart (1975: 275–77) discusses this figure and points out that, historically speaking, it occurs first in Tamil and later in Sanskrit poetry. Here is a Tamil example:

What Her Girl Friend Said to Her

These fat cassia trees
are gullible:
the season of rains
that he spoke of
when he went through the stones
of the desert
is not yet here
though these trees
mistaking the untimely rains
have put out
long arrangements of flowers
on their twigs
as if for a proper monsoon.

Kōvatattaṉ,
Kuruntokai 66

The heroine is waiting for her lover's return; he has promised to return by the first rains. Cassia trees usually flower at that time and signal the season of rains. Here the girl friend is asking the heroine to be patient—not to be mindless and deluded like the cassia trees. Trees have only one sense (touch) and mistake an untimely sprinkle for the real monsoon. The woman should use her other senses, not make the same mistake.

Such a figure always involves animals (which lack mind, the sixth sense), or plants (which have only one sense) as in the above poem. This way of thinking prevents the use of some well-known figures of speech. For instance, the kind of "pathetic fallacy" that directly attributes mind of animals and objects is quite rare in Tamil poetry (except in ironic contexts, or where the speaker is overwhelmed by feeling). However, animal behaviour may suggest witnesses; for only human beings have the sixth sense to see such parallels, their poetry, and their irony.

According to both the Indian and the Western traditions, every sign is a union of signifier and signified (e.g., Saussure 1959: 65–67). In the Tamil system of correspondences, a whole language of signs is created by relating the landscapes as signifers to the *uri* or appropriate human feelings.

In this world of correspondences between times, places things born in them, and human experiences, a word like Kuṟiñci has several concentric circles of meaning: a flower, the mountain landscape, lovers' union, a type of poem about all these, and musical modes for these poems. But its concrete meaning, "a mountain flower" is never quite forgotten.

A conventional design thus provides a live vocabulary of symbols; the actual objective landscapes of Tamil country become the interior landscapes of Tamil poetry. Chart 1 tabulates some of these features. It would be useful, initially at least, to refer to the list of symbols when reading the poems.

The *Tolkāppiyam* takes care to add that "birds and beasts of one landscape may sometimes appear in others": artful poets may work with an "overlap of genres" (*tiṇaimayakkam*); they may even bring in war imagery to heighten the effects of an *akam* poem. The *Tolkāppiyam* further states that the above genres are not rigidly separated; the time and place appropriate to one genre may be fused with the time and place appropriate to another:

> Anything other than *uri* or the appropriate mood may be fused or transformed. (*Tol.* 15)

The following poem is a good example of this mixture of landscapes.

What She Said

The bare root of the bean is pink
like the leg of a jungle hen,
and herds of deer attack its overripe pods.

For the harshness
Of this season of morning dew
there is no cure
but the breast of my man.

Allūr Naṉmullai
Kuṟuntokai 68

The season is morning dew (*kuṟiñci*), but the bird mentioned is a jungle hen (*mullai*), the beast is a deer (*mullai*). The mixture of *kuṟiñci* (lovers' union) and *mullai* (patient waiting) brings out effectively the exact nuance of the girl's mood, "mixing memory and desire" in a kind of montage.

Chart 1. Some Features of the Five Landscapes

	LOVERS' UNION	PATIENT WAITING, DOMESTICITY	LOVER'S UNFAITHFULNESS, "SULKING SCENES"	ANXIETY IN SEPARATION	ELOPEMENT, SHIP, SEPARATION FROM LOVER OR PARENTS
Characteristic flower (name of region and poetic genre)	*kuriñci*	*mullai* (jasmine)	*marutam* (queen's-flower)	*neytal* (blue lily)	*pālai* (desert tree)
Landscape	mountains	forest, pasture	countryside, agricultural lowland	seashore	wasteland (mountain or forest parched by summer)
Time	night	late evening	morning	nightfall	midday
Season	cool season, season of morning dew	rainy season	all seasons	all seasons	season of evening dew, summer
Bird	peacock, parrot	sparrow, jungle hen	stork, heron	seagull	dove, eagle
Beast (including fish, reptile, etc.)	monkey, elephant, horse, bull	deer	buffalo freshwater fish	crocodile shark	fatigued elephant, tiger or wolf lizard

(Contd...

Chart 1. Some Features of the Five Landscapes *(Conts...)*

	LOVERS' UNION	PATIENT WAITING, DOMESTICITY	LOVER'S UNFAITHFULNESS, "SULKING SCENES"	ANXIETY IN SEPARATION	ELOPEMENT, SHIP, SEPARATION FROM LOVER OR PARENTS
Tree or plant	jackfruit, bamboo, *vēṅkai* (kino)	*koṉṟai* (cassia)	mango	*puṉṉai* (laurel)	*ōmai* (toothbrush tree) cactus
Water	waterfall	rivers	pool	wells	waterless wells, stagnant water
Occupation or people	hill tribes, guarding millet harvest, gathering honey	plowman	pastoral occupations	selling fish and salt, fisherfolk	wayfarers, bandits

This is not an exhaustive list; only a few of the elements that appear frequently in the poems are given here. The Tamil names of gods, heroes, clans, musical instruments, and kinds of food have been omitted.

This chart first appeared in the *The Interior Landscape* (Ramanujan 1967). For a more complete table, see Singaravelu (1966:22), or Zvelebil (1973:100).

Thus, for poetry, the hierarchy of components is inverted; the human elements (*uri*), the native elements (*karu*), and the first elements (*mutal*) are in a descending order of importance for a poet. Mere nature description or imagism in poetry would be uninteresting to classical Tamil poets and critics, for it could not "signify"; it would be a signifier without a signified, a landscape (*mutal* and *karu*) without an *uri*, an appropriate human mood.

Poetic Design

The conventions make for many kinds of economy in poetic design. Consider the following poem:

What She Said

Bigger than earth, certainly,
higher than the sky,
more unfathomable than the waters
is this love for this man
    of the mountain slopes
    where bees make rich honey
    from the flowers of the kuṟiñci
    that has such black stalks.

Tevakulattar
Kuṟuntokai 3

The *Kuṟiñci* flower and the mountain scene clearly mark this as a *kuṟiñci* poem about lovers' union. The union is not described or talked about; it is enacted by the "inset" scene of the bees making honey from the flowers of the kuṟiñci. The lover is not only the lord of the mountain; he is like the mountain he owns. Describing the scene describes his passion. The *kuṟiñci*, being a plant that takes about twelve years to come to flower, carries a suggestion assimilating the tree to the young tropical heroine who speaks the poem. The *Tolkāppiyam* calls this technique of using the scene to describe act or agent, *uḷḷuṟai uvamam*, hidden or implicit metaphor.

Furthermore, the poem opens with large abstractions about her love: her love is bigger than earth and higher than the sky. But it moves toward the concreteness of the black-stalked *kuṟiñci*, acting out by analogue the virgin's progress from abstraction to experience. We may remember that this progression (from the basic cosmic elements to the specific component of a landscape) is also the method of the entire intellectual framework behind the poetry: moving from first elements to native elements to human feelings. the poem in the original opens with earth, sky, and water, moves through the native elements of the mountain landscape (slopes, bees, *kuṟiñci*) and ends with a human feeling, *naṭpu*, "love".

Evocations designed like these may be seen in poem after poem. *Uḷḷuṟais* – let us call them insets – of the natural scene (somewhat like G. M. Hopkins's inscape) repeat the total action of the poem. Here are two clear examples from a sequence:

What She Said

In his place, mother,
mud-spattered spotted crabs
sneak into holes at the root
of the nightshade.
        O what's the point
        of his marrying me then
        with sweet talk,
                and saying
        these other things now?

In his country,
spotted crabs
born in their mother's death
grow up with crocodiles
that devour their young.
Why is he here now?
And why does he
take those women,
        a jangle of gold bangles
        as they make love,
only to leave them?

Ōrampōkiyār
Aiṅkuṟunūṟu 22, 24

These are *marutam* poems, poems about infidelity, set in the fertile, well-watered countryside. In the first, he has done to her what the crabs do to the nightshade – sneaked into the hole and gnawed at the root. In the second, the spotted crabs and crocodiles of his region, cannibals all, kill and eat the dear kin they ought to love and protect – like the man himself.

Metaphor and Metonymy

A word about the theory of *uḷḷuṟai uvamam* or insets. An inset is an implicit comparison. All explicit markers of comparison are suppressed. The *Tolkāppiyam* says that explicit comparison belongs to worldly usage (*ulakavaḻakku*), whereas implicit metaphor belongs to poetic usage (*ceyyuḷvaḻakku*).

There are other distinctions to be made: (a) An inset is a correlation of the landscapes and their contents (*karu*) to the human scene (*uri*), (b) Unlike metaphor in ordinary language, an inset is a structural feature within the poem; it integrates the different elements of the poem and shapes its message, (c) Unlike metaphor and simile, it often leaves out all the points of comparison and all explicit markers of comparison (e.g., "like", "as"); such an omission increases manyfold the power of the figure. As we have seen in the poems, image intensifies image, associations flow into each other. These "montage" and "dissolve" effects are aided by the flowing syntax of the language, (d) The inset is essentially a "metonymy,"[7] an in presentia relationship, where both terms are present, where the signifier and the signified belong to the same universe, share the same "landscape". Both are parts of one scene. Such a metonymy, rather than metaphor, is the favorite poetic figure of the classical Tamils. Metaphor implies diversity ("seeing similars in dissimilars" said Aristotle), to be unified by comparison. Poetry for the Tamils does not unify a multiverse but expresses a universe from within, speaking through any of its parts. The man belongs to the scene, the scene represents the man. Adapting a remark of Kenneth Burke's (1945: 6–7) in another context, we may say, "There is implicit in the quality of a scene the quality of the action implicit in it .... one could deduce the details of the action from the details of the setting." This kind of 'metonymous metaphor', based on an entire formal scheme, is a special feature of classical Tamil forms.

But then complex insets are not used everywhere in the poems; they are specifically preferred in the most structured of Tamil poetic genres – the fivefold *akam*; they are not used in the *peruntiṇai* (the mismatched affair), nor preferred in the heroic *puṟam* poems.

The Tamil theory of comparison deserves an essay to itself. I shall content myself here with only one more feature. All comparisons, says the *Tolkāppiyam* (276), whether explicit or implicit, involve terms of comparison. These terms may refer to shape, colour, action, or result. Examples abound in the poems I have quoted. Like the comparisons between crab and lover, that between cobbler and king is based on action; when the bare root of the bean is pink like the leg of a jungle hen, the points of comparison are colour and shape. If we consider colour and shape as special cases of sensory attributes in general, we can include comparisons based on touch, taste, etc., which occur in the poems, e.g. "sweeter than milk and honey". Of course, through colour, shape, action, and result, these comparisons convey much more. Usually, several terms are present in any comparison. For instance, in the poem at the beginning of the last section, the emphasis is on the action of the bee and the resulting honey. The shapes of the flower and the bee also suggest obvious sexual images.

The Personae

The *dramatis personae* in *akam* poems are limited to a small number: the hero, the heroine, the hero's friend(s) or messengers, the heroine's friend and foster-mother, the concubine, and passersby. In the *puṟam* poems, the poets mostly speak in their own person, though there are a few exceptions.

No *akam* poet speaks in his own voice; and no poem is addressed to a reader. The reader only overhears what the characters say to each other or to themselves or to the moon. A poem in this tradition implies, evokes, enacts a drama in a monologue.

The situations (*tuṟai*) when a hero or heroine or one of their companions may speak out, and to whom, are closely defined. For example,

> The girl friend of the heroine may speak out on the following occasions: when the heroine, left behind by her lover, speaks of her loneliness; when she helps them elope; when she begs the hero to take good care of the heroine; when she tries to dissuade the parents from their search for the runaway couple, or consoles the grieving mother... (*Tol.* 42)

An interesting convention usually restricts the imagery for different speakers within the poems. The heroine's images are mostly confined to what surrounds her house, or to the wonder of discovering his landscape or to hearsay and fantasies about it. The concubine or the heroine's girl friend or foster-mother have more ranging images: they are of a lower class, and their experience is wider. The man's imagery has even greater range. Apparently there are no limits to his experience, and therefore to his imagery. Thus the range of imagery, its quality or content, its very narrowness or width of choice, indirectly characterizes speaker and social class.

The Two Proprieties

The *Tolkāppiyam* speaks of "two kinds of proprieties: those of drama and those of the world." The conventional proprieties outlined so far are of the mode of drama. The situations of real life in the real world are governed by another set of proprieties. The strategy of the poet is to deploy both, to keep the tension between the forms of art and the forms of the world.

A highly formal scheme of landscapes that have neither name nor history bears within it the real land, the vivid particulars of bird, beast, insect, drumbeat, and waterfall.

A little-known book in Tamil by a botanist (Cāmi 1967; see also Varadarajan 1969) documents one's constant sense that these poets knew their fauna and flora; their botanical observations, for instance, are breathtakingly minute and accurate. In these poems, over two hundred plants of all the five Tamil regions are named, described, used in insets and comparisons. Root, stem, bark, bud, petal, inflorescence, seasons, special kinds of pollination, etc., are observed and alluded to. And their properties are aptly used to evoke human relationships.

We may ask, as the Tamil commentators do, why did the poets pick the *kuṟiñci* as the one flower that will name the mountain landscape and the mood of first love? Though such signs are symbols, cultural assignments, arbitrary conventions, they are half-motivated by botanical facts: the *kuṟiñci* plant, of the *Strobilanthes* genus, grows only 6,000 feet above sea level; so it is the mountain flower par excellence. Botanical calendars kept for over a century on South Indian hills like the Nilgiris show that a *kuṟiñci* plant comes to flower only from nine to twelve years after it is planted – this identifies it with the tropical virgin heroine who comes to puberty at the same age.

Kuṟiñci plants flower all at once on the mountain slopes, covering them with millions of blossoms, certainly a great symbol for the suddenness and the overwhelming nature of first love. It is a "honey" flower, rich in honey. The bees that frequent it frequent no other, thus making what bee-keepers call "unifloral honey", which is as rich as it is rare and pure. Furthermore, the *kuṟiñci* is fiercely competitive – it permits no other tree to grow in its neighbourhood.

Thus is the real world always kept in sight and included in the symbolic. These poets would have made a modern poet like Marianne Moore (1951:41) happy: they are "literalists of the imagination", presenting for inspection in poem after poem "imaginary gardens with real toads in them."

A Language Within Language

In a sense, the tradition of conventions does everything possible to depersonalize the poetry of *akam*. It gives all that can be given to a poet, and makes of poetry a kind of second language.

The poet's language is not only Tamil: landscapes, the personae, the appropriate moods, all become a language within language. Like a native speaker he makes "infinite use of finite means", to say with familiar words what has never been said before; he can say exactly what he wants to, without even being aware of the ground rules of his grammar. If the world is the vocabulary of the poet, the conventions are his syntax – at least one of the many kinds of poetic syntax.

The lyric poet likes to find ways of saying many things while saying one thing; he would like to suggest an entire astronomy by his specks and flashes. Toward this end, the Tamil poets used a set of five landscapes and formalized the world into a symbolism. By a remarkable consensus, they all spoke this common language of symbols for some five or six generations. Each could make his own poem and by doing so allude to every other poem which had been, was being, or would be written in this symbolic language. Thus poem became relevant to poem, as if they were all written by a single hand. The spurious name *Caṅkam* ("Fraternity," "Community") for this poetry was justified not by history but by the poetic practice.

Puram Poetry

The language of *akam* is only half the story. The scheme should include the *puṟam* poems, as well as the mismatched and the one-sided love affairs that define by contrast the tight structure of the fivefold *akam*.

The *puṟam* poems correspond to the *akam* poems in many ways. The *Tolkāppiyam* finds a *puṟam* parallel for every one of the seven genres of *akam*. Six of them are named after a flower or a plant. For instance, *vākai*, the *sirisa* tree of the desert region, lends its name to the *puṟam* genre depicting ideals of achievement – parallel to it is *pālai* in love poetry, which depicts a lover going through the wilderness in search of wealth, fame, etc. Commentators elaborate on the correspondences further. Why should the *kuṟiñci* (union) phase of love correspond to *veṭci* (cattle raids) in war? Because, say the commentators, they both have to do with first encounters, are clandestine, take place at night on hillsides. Chart 2 displays one set of *akam/puṟam* correspondences.

Though these correspondences are in the rhetoric, however, they are not always active in the poetry. The landscapes are not consistently used as "insets", nor are the distinctions clear. The poem on the cobbler and the king, for instance, is considered a *vākai* poem (in praise of kings, etc.), and is a counterpart of *pālai* (desert: separation, hardship); but the images in the poem do not belong to the desert at all, but to the *mullai* (forest, pasture: waiting, marriage): rains, laburnum, evening, and childbirth. Of course, the colophon could be wrong, or wrongly transmitted, for the *mullai* images could fit very well with the parallel *vañci* (preparation for war). By and large, though, the *puram* divisions are not as clear as the ones in *akam*. For instance, the last two classes (*kāñci* and *pāṭān*) are not clearly distinguished from the rest. *Pāṭān* is a large mixed class, and does not

Chart 2. Puram/Akam Correspondence

	Akam	Situation/Theme	Puram	Situation/Theme	Common Features
1.	*kuriñci*, a mountain flower	first union	*veṭci*, scarlet ixora	cattle-lifting, prelude to war	night, hillside; clandestine affair
2.	*mullai*, jasmine	separation (patience)	*vañci*, a creeper	preparation for war, invasion	forest, rainy season; separation from loved ones
3.	*marutam*, queen's flower	infidelity (conflict)	*uḻiñai*, a cotton shrub	siege	fertile area (city, etc.), dawn; refusing entry
4.	*neytal*, water lily	separation (anxiety)	*tumpai*, white dead nettle	battle	seashore, open battle-ground, no season; evening; grief
5.	*pālai*, desert tree	elopement, search for wealth, fame, etc.	*vākai*, sirissa tree	ideals of achievement, victory	no particular landscape; praise
6.	*peruntinai*,[a] "major type"	mismatched love	*kāñci*, portia tree	struggle for excellence; endurance	no particular landscape; struggle
7.	*kaikkilai*[a] "base relation"	unrequited love	*pāṭān*,[a] "praise"	elegy, praise for heroes, asking for gifts, invective	no particular landscape; a one-sided relationship

[a]Not the name of a tree or a flower.

bear the name of a tree or flower as the others do. Later writers add more separate classes, include in *puram* the classes of mismatched and unrequited love, and add a "general" class (*potunilai*) to make a twelvefold *puram*. By then only the "ideal fivefold", from *kuriñci* to *pālai*, is considered *akam*, "interior". Yet in reading *akam* and *puṟam* together one is struck as much by the common world they share as by the differences.

Whereas *akam* poems tend to focus on a single image, *puṟam* images rush and tumble over one another. Yet, as in the following *puṟam* poem, the same flowers and landscapes speak of war and peace, of fertility and desolation:

Where the Lilies Were in Flower

Fish leaping
in fields of cattle;

easy unplowed sowing
where the wild boar has rooted;

big-eyed buffalo herds
stopped by fences of lilies
flowering in sugarcane beds;

ancient cows bending their heads
over water flowers
scattered by the busy dancers
swaying with lifted hands;

queen's-flower trees full of bird cries
the rustle of coconut trees,
canals from flowering pools
in countries
with cities sung in song:

but your anger
touched them, brought them terror,
left their beauty in ruins,
bodies consumed by Death.

The districts are empty, parched;
the waves of sugarcane blossom,
stalks of dry grass.
The thorny babul of the twisted fruit
neck to neck with the giant black babul.

The she-devil with the branching crest
roams
astraddle on her demon,
and the small persistent thorn
is spread in the moving dust
of ashen battlefields.

Not a sound, nothing animal,
not even dung, in the ruins of public places
that kill the hearts of eager men,
chill all courage,
and shake those who remember.

But here,
the sages have sought your woods.
In your open spaces, the fighters play
with bright-jewelled women.

The traveler is safe on the highway.
Sellers of grain shelter their kin
who shelter, in turn, their kin.

The silver star will not go near
the place of the red planet; so it rains
on the thirsty fields.
Hunger has fled
and taken disease with her.

Great one.
Your land blossoms
everywhere.

Kumaṭṭūr Kaṇṇaṉār:
on *Imayavarampaṉ Neṭuñcēralātaṉ*
Patiṟṟupattu 13

The plant names are familiar: e.g., sugarcane, lilies, *marutam* or queen's-flower. The poem clearly falls into two parts, celebrating the destructive and protective functions of a king. The first part celebrates the fertility of the pastoral, agricultural, and seashore landscapes (cows, sugarcane, lilies, etc.); the middle part shows how they have been ravaged and turned into a *pālai* wilderness (the thorny babuls, etc.) by the war. The third section praises the king's own flourishing kingdom (forests and fields).

The *akam/puṟam* correspondences are not strict, but still close enough to allow us to integrate the two genres. Such correspondences should not be frozen into an exact taxonomy, for the Tamils never do so – they always make room for "overlap of classes" (*tiṇaimayakkam*) and "left-over classes" (e.g., *potunilai*).

Taken in the large, the two genres, poems of love and war – *akam* and *puṟam* – complement one another: contrasted in theme, mood, and structure but unified by imagery. Together, they make the classical, "bardic" Tamil world. This is why the same poets could write both *akam* and *puṟam* poems. Some poems explicitly place love and war together:

A Leaf in Love and War

The chaste trees, dark-clustered,
blend with the land
that knows no dryness;
the colors on the leaves
mob the eyes.
    We've seen those leaves
    on jeweled women,
    on their mounds
    of love.
Now the chaste wreath lies slashed
on the ground, so changed, so mixed
with blood, the vulture snatches it
with its beak,
thinking it raw meat.
    We see this too
    just because a young man
    in love with war
    wore it for glory.

Veṟipāṭiya Kāmakkaṇṇiyār
Puṟanāṉūṟu 271

The green leaves of the chaste tree were used as leaf-skirts by women and as laurels by warriors. So it is emblematic of *kuriñci* (union) in love and *uliñai* (battle) in war; the mere juxtaposition brings the irony home sharply.

One more contrast should be noticed. Through *akam* means "interior," *puram*, "exterior," *akam* poetry, which a modern reader might expect to be the most private and personal expression, is the most formally structured genre in the Tamil tradition; as we know, no names, individuals, or places are usually allowed here, only classes, ideal types; for in this inner world there are no names or individuals. *Puram*, the so-called "public poetry", is allowed names, places, expression of personal circumstances in a real society, a real history, and a certain freedom from the necessities of poetic convention both in insets and in the landscapes. Thus it is the "public" *puram* poetry that becomes the vehicle of personal expression and celebration of historical personages. Indeed, when a woman speaks in her own voice about her love, the poem is placed in a *puram* anthology (e.g., p.119).

Love, Mismatched

Quite in contrast to both *akam* and *puram* genres as we have defined them stands the mismatched affair or *peruntiṇai*. Here is an example from *Kalittokai*, probably the latest of the eight anthologies.

The Hunchback and the Dwarf:
A Dialogue

Hunchback woman,
the way you move is gentle
and crooked as a reflection
in the water,
what good deeds
did you do that I should want you so?

O mother! (she swore to herself) Some
auspicious moment made you dwarf.
so tiny you're almost invisible.
you whelp born to a man-faced owl,
how dare you stop us to say
you want us? Would such midgets
ever get to touch such as us!

Lovely one,
curvaceous,
convex
as the blade of a plough,
you strike me with a love
I cannot bear.
I can live
only by your grace.
(Look at this creature!)
You dwarf, standing piece of timber,
you've yet to learn the right approach
to girls. In high noon
you come to hold
our hand and ask us to your place.
Have you had any women?

Good woman,
Your waist is higher

than your head, your face a stork,
plucked and skinned,
with a dagger for a beak,
listen to me.
If I take you in the front, your hump
juts into my chest; if from the back
it'll tickle me in odd places.
So I'll not
even try it. But come close anyway and let's touch
side to side.

Chi, you're wicked. Get lost! You half-man!
As creepers hang on only to the crook of a tree
there are men who'd love to hold this hunch
of a body close, though nothing fits. Yet, you lecher.
you ask for us sideways. What's so wrong
with us, you ball, you bush of a man.
Is a gentle hunchback type far worse than a cake
of black beans?

But I've fallen for you
(he said, and went after her).
O look, my heart,
at the dallying of this hunchback!
        Man, you stand
        like a creepy turtle stood up by somebody,
        hands flailing in your armpits.
        We've told you we're not for you. Yet you hang around.
        Look, he walks now like Kama.

Yes, the love-god with arrows, brother to Cama.
Look at this love-god!
            Come now, let's find joy,
you in me, me in you; come, let's ask and tell
which parts we touch

I swear by the feet of my king.

All right. O gentle-breasted one. I too will give up
mockery.
        But I don't want this crowd in the palace
laughing at us, screaming when we do it,
"Hey, hey! Look at them mounting,
leaping like demon on demon!"
            O shape
of unbeaten gold, let's get away from the palace
to the wild jasmine bush. Come,
let's touch close, hug hard
and finish the unfinished,
then we'll be
like a gob of wax on a parchment
made out in a court full of wise men,
and stamped
to a seal.
            Let's go.

Marutaṉiḷanākaṉār
Kalittokai 94

Note the unheroic, even antiheroic, mock-heroic quality of this unlovely couple, looking not for love but frankly for sex; the folk-like bawdiness, the earthy humour. There are no sunset landscapes, though the poem is classified as *marutam*. Ploughs, herons, turtles and wild jasmine jostle in it. In a single phrase like "You whelp born to a man-faced owl", many categories are undone. The piece makes comedy and poetry by violating over and over the decorum of *akam* poems. The metaphors are bold, explicit. The two persons are not even young – one of them is "a stork, plucked and skinned". This is *peruntiṇai*, the "major type", depicting the common human condition, love among the misfits with no scruples regarding the niceties of time or landscape; moving from mockery to coupling in the course of a conversation. Their misfit is evident even in their bodies' lack of fit. And they are obviously servants. We have also shifted from the dramatic monologues of *akam* and *puṟam* to dialogue and interaction, from lyric to comic drama. As in drama, the characters and their speech change: the hunchback begins with a royal we in her rejection and ends with an I in yielding; her mocking exclamations to herself drop off.

If the *akam* has the most tightly structured symbolic language, the *peruntiṇai* is free and realistic, with real toads in real cesspools.

We have not spoken of one genre: the *kaikkiḷai*, onesided or unrequited love. There are not many classical examples of unrequited love. Here is one, from *Kuṟuntokai*:

What He Said

When love is ripe beyond bearing
and goes to seed,
men will ride even palmyra stems
as if they were horses;
will wear on their heads the reeking cones of the erukkam bud
as if they were flowers;
will draw to themselves
the laughter of the streets;
and will do worse.

Pēreyiṉ Muruvalār
Kuṟuntokai 17

The most significant observation on *kaikkiḷai* (not found in the *Tolkāppiyam* but in later commentaries) is that such expression of one-sided love is appropriate only to religion. Postclassical Tamil devotees, preoccupied with their unrequited love for their god, in a cloud of unknowing, created the most poignant poems of *kaikkiḷai*.

Thus the four genres (*akam*, *peruntiṇai*, *kaikkiḷai*, and *puṟam*) cover and formalize the main possibilities of Tamil lyric poetry. They define each other mutually. A great deal of Western love poetry would probably be described by the ancient commentators as the one-sided *kaikkiḷai*; a great deal of modern poetry, fiction, and black comedy as love among the misfits or *peruntiṇai*—exploring the unheroic, the antiheroic, and presenting the ironies of impotence.

Poem becomes relevant to poem within the five *akam* landscapes and across the four genres as well.

Akam and Puram as Poetic Devices

Akam ("interior") and *puṟam* ("exterior") are not only thematic divisions. The paired opposition is pervasive in Tamil poetry and culture. The two key categories are related to each other by context and by contrast. The various meanings to be found in the *Tamil Lexicon* can be paired as follows:

Akam	*Puṟam*
1. interior	exterior
2. heart, mind	body surfaces and extremities, e.g. back, side, arms
3. self	others
4. kin	non-kin
5. house, family	houseyard, field
6. inland, settlement	area far from dense human habitation, e.g., jungle, desert
7. earth	farthest ocean
8. love poems – no names of places or persons	poetry about war and other than (well-matched?) love, a "public" poetry, with names of real people and places
9. Codes of conduct appropriate to *akam*	Codes of conduct appropriate to *puṟam*

The meanings complement each other systematically, as we move from context to context, for each meaning of *akam*, there is a corresponding sense of *puṟam*. It is characteristic of this poetry and its poetics that the meanings seem to expand and contract in concentric circles, with the concrete physical particular at the centre, getting more and more inclusive and abstract as we move outward. The context picks and foregrounds one or another of these circles of meaning.

A poem moves along these various senses of *akam* and *puṟam*: this movement is one of the forms of the poem. In the course of such interplay, *akam/puṟam* contrasts such as inner/outer, self/other, nature/culture, household/wilderness become part of the form as well as the content of the poem.

For instance:

What He Said

In this long summer wilderness
    seized and devoured by wildfire,

if I should shut my eyes
    even a wink,
I see
    dead of night, a tall house
    in a cool yard, and the girl
with freckles
    like kino flowers,
hair flowing as with honey,
    her skin a young mango leaf.

Ōtalāntaiyār
Aiṅkuṟuṉūṟu 324

The poem consists of a number of movements from *puṟam* to *akam*, from the faraway wilderness to the inhabited house, from the outer landscape to the fantasy inside him; it also moves from the wildfire and noonday sun (*pālai*, desert, separation) to dead of night, the girl, the yellow kino flowers, and hair glistening as if with honey (all *kuṟiñci* images of lovers' union). Yet the whole poem stays with the palai mood of a lover in a desert faraway from his beloved.

Other subtleties should be noted: "seized and devoured by wildfire", an attribute of the outer wilderness, is also suggestive of the speaker's inner state. Where he is, is what he is: a scene/agent ratio (in Burke's terms); a metonymy, an *uḷḷuṟai*. He is contained by the wilderness devoured by wildfire; and he also contains it within him. But when he closes his eyes, he contains the house of his beloved in fantasy. We should also remember that *pālai* is one phase of a cycle –

he is going away from his woman "for education, work, earning wealth, war" – all *puṟam* concerns. Among the relations between *akam* and *puṟam*, household and the world, one should include the rhythm of a man going out into the world and coming back into the family. Only a warrior who dies or an ascetic who renounces doesn't return – both are themes for *puṟam* poems. He passes through the *pālai* wilderness on his way to do "the world's work", and survives by remembering his home and woman, in the heat and wildfire of the outer desert and the inner. Of course, heat and wildfire for the separated lover have sexual overtones.

In reading these poems, one need not explicitly trace *akam/puṟam* shifts. They guide our responses subtly, surprising us often, by turning inside out. *Akam* and *puṟam* are part of the very choreography of poetic moves in Tamil poems. As one learns the "second language" of these poems, one also learns to sense the "ins and outs"; one follows the rhythms without labeling them, as one soon learns to read the language of cassias and tigers and waterfalls without running to a glossary of symbols.

Looked at in this way, each poem is a structure and a process. While *akam* and *puṟam*, and the five landscape genres, are opposed to each other as overall genres, and clearly defined as such, within each poem they work as phases, change points. One might even think of the action of each poem as a crossing of thresholds, across genres: the above pālai poem crosses from the outer landscape to the interior one, and also from the wilderness to the human settlement. Each of the genres enacts a characteristic crossing of the *akam/puṟam* oppositions.

Typically, the movement of *akam* poems is a crossing from outer to inner; from outer body to the heart within, in memory or imagination (*kuṟiñci*); from sea to land (*neytal*), from warfield to home (*mullai*); from home to wilderness in actuality, from wilderness to home in memory (*pālai*); from the concubine who is no kin, who lives on the town's outskirts, to home, wife, and kin (*marutam*).

Puṟam poems, like the following, tend to start inside a house (*akam*) and move, like the tiger, out into the world (*puṟam*):

> You stand against the pillar
> of my hut and ask:
> Where is your son?
> I don't really know.
> My womb was once
> a lair
> for that tiger.

You can see him now
only in battlefields.

Kāvaṟpeṇṭu
Puṟanāṉūṟu 86

Often the poetic moment is actually poised on the threshold, though a figure in the poem may move (actually, or in imagination) from outer to inner. Many *marutam* poems are literally enacted at the door which is shut in the face of the unfaithful returning husband. The most extraordinary of these "door-shutting" (*vāyil maṟuttal*) poems moves from *puṟam* to *akam*, from the public realm of townsmen, kinsmen, and the wedding ceremony, step by step to the privacy of the bedroom and finally to the ultimate *akam* or "interior" of the bride's private parts:

What He Said
after a quarrel, remembering his wedding night

Serving in endless bounty
white rice and meat
cooked to a turn,
        drenched in ghee,
to honored guests,
and when the bird omens were right,
at the perfect junction
of the Wagon Stars with the moon
        shining in a wide soft-lit sky.

wedding site decorated, gods honored,
kettledrum and marriage drum
sounding loud the wedding beat,

the women who'd given her a bridal bath
– piercing eyes looking on, unwinking –
suddenly gone,
her near kin
strung a white thread on her
with the split soft-backed leaves
of the *sirissa*,
and with the *aruku* grass,

its sacred root a figurine,
its buds cool, fragrant,
dark-petaled, blue
as washed sapphire,

brought forth by the thundering skies
of first rains in valleys
where adolescent calves
feed on them.
they brought her to me
decked in new clothes,
rousing my desire
even in the wedding canopy,
wedding noises noisy as pounding rain

on that first night,

and when they wiped her sweat,
and gave her to me,
she splendid with ornament,
I said to her

who was body now to my breath,
chaste without harshness,
wrapped all over in a robe
new, uncrushed,

"It's hot. Sweat is breaking out
on that crescent, your brow.
Open your robe a little,
let the wind cool it,"
and even as I spoke,
my heart hasty with desire,
I pulled it off

and she stood exposed,
her form shining
like a sword unsheathed,
not knowing how to hide herself,

cried Woy!
in shame, then bowed, begged of me,
as she loosened her hair
undoing the thick colorful wreath
of broken lily petals

and, with the darkness of black full tresses,
hand-picked flowers on them
still luring the bees,

hid
her private
parts.

Viṟṟūṟṟu Mūteyiṉaṉār
Akanāṉūṟu 13

Before we leave the manifold of *akam/puṟam*, we must note some more ways in which the two genres differ. Only the full cycle of love between well-matched lovers is called *akam*; all else, including ill-matched love, the life and death of heroes, their relations to land, clan, enemy, and bard, were called *puṟam*. The Tamil world was divided between family, or "household" (one meaning of *akam*) and the "kingdom", the outer world. Women were central to the former, as heroes (named kings and chieftains and unnamed warriors) were central to the latter. In an *akam* anthology like *Kuṟuntokai*, only 62 poems are assigned to the man, but 180 to the woman, 140 to her girl friend, 14 others to women characters like foster-mothers and concubines. In a *puṟam* anthology like *Puṟanāṉūṟu*, hardly a handful are spoken by women—about 18 songs are about or by women characters, mothers, wives, or widows of heroes. I am not counting the songs by women poets, such as the 13 by Auvaiyār (e.g., *Puṟanāṉuru* 101-4), which she sings not as a woman but as a bard about her patron.

In many *akam* poems, a woman's body is suggestively present to our senses – the smell or texture of her hair, the shape of her breast, her brow, her mound of love or black-snake pubis, her leaf-skirts, the conch-shell bangles, her teeth like rice sprouts, her skin like young mango leaf, her great shoulders and red-streaked eyes, and in one poem even the taste of her saliva – yet a woman is never described in more than one or two details in each poem. We do not hear much about the man's appearance; we know more about what he has and about his country's scenery than about him. As we hear about her glittering bangles and ornaments, we also hear of his bright spear, his horses, chariots, garlands, anklebands, sometimes a chest enlarged by the drawing of bows. His spouse's chastity and virtue are also a chieftain's ornaments and his magical shields against disaster, as effective as his own "upright scepter" (*ceṅkōl*, as contrasted with *koṭuṅkōl* "crooked scepter"). It is significant that in the *akam* poems, rarely is the woman seen as the mature mother of a grown man, as she is in the *puṟam*. As in other heroic milieus, women bards, and poems in women's voices, enlist filial and familial feeling in the cause of war – especially that most compelling of family feelings, a mother's pride (or shame) about her son.

NOTES

[Notes 1 and 2 in the original refer to matter not included in this extract. *Ed.*]

3. This fact adds further subtlety to the symbolism. *Pālai* (wasteland) associated with separation can happen even in the heart of union (*kuṟiñci* or mountain landscape).
4. "Objective correlatives" (Eliot 1950), and what I have called correlative objects, are very different things: the first are sought and found by individual poets, the latter are given by the culture in which the poets dwell.
5. From now on, I translate *tiṇai* as "landscape." But *tiṇai* has several meanings: "class, genre, type", as in *akattiṇai* "the akam genre." In a more specific sense, *tiṇai* is a complex concept defined in the poetics for Tamil poetry: a genre is represented by a region or landscape, its nature and culture, and the human feelings associated with them—in short, an entire ecosystem used for poetic expression. "Landscape" is a convenient metonymy for the whole cluster of notions. Like the Tamils, we will also use the names *kuṟiñci*, *mullai* etc. for the landscapes and the genres associated with them.
6. This series is clearly reminiscent of the Jain "ladder of life" of *ekendriya* ("one sense"), *dvendriya* ("two-sense"), etc., all the way to the gods. See Zimmer (1960:277) for an exposition of this Jain system. Though several such Jain elements are found or "borrowed" in the Tamil texts, their use is not Jain at all; its thrust is not metaphysical, religious, nor does it imply an ethic of nonviolence. Instead, it adds one more "concrete" figure to the poetry. The subject of Jain ideas in early Tamil literature merits exploration.
7. My use of "metaphor" and "metonymy" follows Jakobson (1971:254–7), whom I find suggestive. As I show below, the categories cannot be mutually exclusive, nor can all figures be divided into these two super-classes. For a cogent criticism, see Genette (1982).

BIMAL KRISHNA MATILAL

After studying at Calcutta and Harvard, B.K. Matilal (1935 - 91) taught at the Universities of Toronto, Pennsylvania, Chicago and California (Berkeley). Between 1976 and 1991, the year of his death, he was the Spalding Professor of Eastern Religions and Ethics at Oxford and a Fellow of All Souls College.

Among his more important publications are *Logical and Ethical Issues of Religious Belief* (University of Calcutta, 1982), *Logic, Language and Reality* (Motilal Banarsidass, 1985), *Perception: An Essay on Classical Indian Theories of Knowledge* (Clarendon Press, Oxford, 1986) and *The Word and the World* (Oxford University Press, Delhi, 1990).

Matilal occupies a very important place among academic philosophers dealing with India as a field of study. Unlike his predecessors in the field, Matilal avoids being confined to speculative philosophy alone. In the tradition of Russell and Wittgenstein, he engages his attention in the language of philosophy and the philosophy of language. We see in his work a fruitful combination of profound understanding of modern philosophical schools and methods and an intimate knowledge of Hindu and Buddhist classics. It is therefore that Matilal is able to illuminate modern Western linguistics in the light of Buddhist theories of perception as well as to bring back into intellectual currency the *sphoṭa* debate between Bhartṛhari and Nāgarjuna–Dinnāga. The extract reproduced here forms a chapter in Matilal's *The Word and The World* (pp. 84–98).

Bhartṛhari's View of Sphoṭa

I

The *sphoṭa* doctrine has been most prominently associated with Bhartṛhari. But scholars have held different views about the exact significance of this concept in Bhartṛhari's thought. The situation if further complicated by the fact that later grammarians attribute a much crystallized and ostensibly different doctrine of *sphoṭa* not only to Bhartṛhari but also to Patanjalī.

Early Indologists (Keith, 1928, 387; De, 1925, 180) described *sphoṭa* as a mysterious or mystical entity, and this was probably due to its association with Bhartṛhari's notion of *śabda-brahman* or the Eternal Verbum (Sastri, 1959). But this was a mistake. In spite of its metaphysical underpinning which M. Biardeau (1964, 268) rightly emphasized, there is a linguistic treatment of the concept well-documented by Bhartṛhari himself, and other grammarians. Brough (1951, 34) and Kunjunni Raja (1969, 97–148) were right to stress the point that *sphoṭa* was not a mysterious entity. There is another dispute that is connected with it; whether the *sphoṭa* in Bhartṛhari is simply the linguistic sign in its aspect of meaning-bearer (Brough, Kunjunni Raja), or whether it represents an abstract class of sounds sorted out and extracted by the listener from gross matter (Moshi, 1967, 40). Cardona (1976, 302) thinks that Brough's thesis should be modified since Bhartṛhari also talks about *varṇa-sphota*, which refers to a sound unit of the language system, not to any meaning-bearing speech unit. Iyer (1969, 158–9) has, however, refuted Joshi's rather sweeping comment that Bhartṛhari's *sphoṭa* had nothing to do with the meaning-bearing speech unit. In *Mahābhaṣya-dīpikā* Bhartṛhari reinterpreted Patanjalī's use of the word *śabda*. This was noted by Patanjalī as the meaning-bearing element in the *Paspaśā* section. Bhartṛhari glossed this as *sphoṭa* and characterized it as eternal.

II

In *Vākyapadīya* Bhartṛhari clearly develops the threefold doctrine of *sphoṭa* related to letters or phonemes, words and sentences. This is explicitly mentioned in the *Vṛtti*. Sometimes he uses *śabda* and *sphoṭa* interchangeably, which might have been the source of confusion. The *sphoṭa* is further described as partless and indivisible, and as devoid of internal sequence. A *pada-sphoṭa*, i.e., *sphoṭa* identified as a word, seems to be a meaning-bearing unit. But, for Bhartṛhari, the *vākya-sphoṭa*, i.e., the *sphoṭa* in the form of a sentence, is the most important. In the second *kāṇda* of *Vākyapadīya*, he deals with various definitions of the sentences, and finally concludes that a sentence is a sequenceless, partless whole, a *sphoṭa*, that gets 'expressed' or manifested in a sequential and temporary utterance. This is also the primary meaning-bearing element.

For Bhartṛhari, however, this is a wrong term: 'meaning-bearing unit'. *Sphoṭa* is the real substratum, proper linguistic unit, which is identical also with its meaning. Language is not the vehicle of meaning or the conveyor-belt of thought. Thought anchors language and language anchors thought. *Śabdanā*, 'languageing', is thinking; and thought 'vibrates' through language. In this way of looking at things, there cannot be any essential difference between a linguistic unit and its meaning or the thought it conveys. *Sphoṭa* refers to this non-differentiated language-principle. Thus I believe that it is sometimes even incorrect to ask whether *sphoṭa* is or is not the meaning-bearing speech unit in Bhartṛhari's system.

III

Bhartṛhari begins the discussion of his theory by a reference to the distinguishing of the two aspects of language by his predecessors. In verse 1.44 he says that the linguists comprehend two types of *śabda* among the *upādāna śabda*, 'linguistic sound': one is the causal root of its manifestation and the other is applied, being manifested, to convey meaning. Of these two, the second is the linguistic unit properly understood, it is the real language, while the first is what 'manifests' or 'expresses' it. Bhartṛhari, and following him some later grammarians, related this duality to what I shall call the *sphoṭa-nāda* distinction of language. *Nāda* manifests *sphoṭa* and *sphoṭa* conveys meaning. We need to explain such expressions as 'manifests' and 'expresses'. The *sphoṭa* is an indivisible unit, a partless, sequenceless whole, which is connected with the verbal dispositional ability of the speaker or the hearer. For the sake of communication between language-users, *sphoṭa* needs to be made explicit, i.e., potentiality must be actualized, so that the bearer may receive it. This cannot be done without *nāda*, the sequential utterances of sound-elements. This is how the *nāda* becomes the causal factor for making *sphoṭa* explicit. The speaker cannot but utter *nāda* in a particular sequence, and *nāda* therefore reveals *sphoṭa* in this way appears (falsely) to have parts and temporal sequences just as the moon reflected in wavy waters appears to be wavy and disintegrated. Since the *nāda* is also identified with the *sphoṭa,* certain spurious features are superimposed on the *sphoṭa*.

The sounds uttered by the speaker make the real linguistic units, primarily a sentence, explicit, but this is the sphota of the speaker. *Sphoṭa* is also shared by the hearer, and as a result the hearer's *sphoṭa* is 'awakened' by the utterance of the speaker. This awakening of the hearer's *sphoṭa* is what is called the comprehension by the hearer of the sentence uttered. This is what is meant by the claim that the sentence uttered must 'already be present' in the hearer. From the point of view of the speaker, however, the *sphoṭa* 'already present in him' will be the causal condition for the *nāda* or the sequential word utterance, which will convey the *sphoṭa* to the hearer.

The metaphysical view of Bhartṛhari is that whatever is called *śabda*, 'language' and *artha*, 'meaning', 'thought' or 'things meant', are one and undifferentiated in their pre-verbal or potential state. Before the utterance, it is argued, the language along with whatever it conveys or means is like the yolk of a peahen's egg. In that state all the variegated colours of a full-grown peacock lie dormant in potential form. Later these colours are actualized. Similarly in the self of the speaker or hearer, or whoever is gifted with linguistic capability, all the variety and differentiation of linguistic items and their meanings exist as potentialities, and language and thought are identical at that stage. Bhartṛhari even believes that the nature of the self is nothing but identical with the nature of language-thought. This state of complete identity of language with thought is called the *paśyantī* stage of language. Before the proper articulation of the sound-sequence or utterance, there is another 'intermediate' stage (called *madhyamā vāk*) where the language and the thought it conveys are still one and undifferentiated, but at this 'pre-verbal' stage the speaker sees them as differentiable. In other words, he recognizes the verbal part, which he is about to verbalize either to himself or to another, as distinct and separable from the *artha*, 'meaning' or 'thought'. This perception impels him to speech which results in the *nāda-sphoṭa* differentiation.

It may be useful to quote here some relevant verses of Bhartṛhari to underline the *sphoṭa-nāda* distinction.

Verse 1.44: Linguists (*śabdavidaḥ*) comprehend two types of *śabda* among linguistic *śabda*. One is the *nimitta* of the sound and the other designates the object or meaning.

Commentary: In the sequenceless nature of the speech (*vāk*) both powers, the power to be articulated in sound (audible form) and the power to convey meaning, lie intermixed.

Verse 1.46: Just as light/fire (*jyotiḥ*) resides in the *araṇi* stick and (being manifested) becomes the cause for manifesting other objects, *śabda* resides likewise in the Mind (inner faculty, *buddhi*) and (being manifested) becomes separately the cause for manifesting the meaning ('as well as itself' added in the commentary).

Verse 1.48: Since *nāda* (sound) arises in sequence, *sphoṭa*, which has neither a former nor a latter stage and which is sequenceless (*akrama*), is apprehended (through *nāda*) and appears to be having a sequence as well as parts.

Verse 1.49: (Thus, properties of *nāda* are transferred to the *sphoṭa*.) The reflected image (of the moon, for example) although it resides in a separate location, seems to share the operation (i.e., movement of the waves in water) of objects in a separate location; *sphoṭa* being manifested in *nāda* shares the properties of nada in the same way.

Verse 1.52: A figure being grasped by a single awareness is painted on a canvas (part by part) into another complete, unitary figure (for the viewer to grasp it in one sweep). Similarly in *śabda*, too, all these three stages are found.

Verse 1.53: The speaker apprehends beforehand the entire *śabda*, with regard to which the hearer's awareness also arises.

Verse 1.55: Just as fire has both powers – the power to be the object of manifestation and the agent of manifestation – all *śabdas* individually have both powers likewise. (Fire in manifesting itself manifests others; *śabda*, too, in manifesting itself manifests others.)

Verse 1.56: (For this reason) *śabdas* do not convey meaning without themselves being the objects of our awareness. They cannot manifest or reveal the meanings simply by their existence, if they (themselves) remain unapprehended.

Verse 1.57: Hence, when from indistinct utterance, the form of the *śabda* is not apprehended, one asks 'what did he say?' But when the senses reveal objects, those senses do not need to be apprehended themselves.

IV

How is the *sphoṭa-nāda* distinction comprehended? Or, we may rephrase the question: how is 'language' comprehended? We have seen that Bhartṛhari has posited three stages of language or speech. The first stage, where there is complete identity of language and thought, is called the *paśyantī* stage; we can call it 'non-verbal'. The 'intermediate' stage, where despite the identity of thought and language their difference is discernible, can be called the 'pre-verbal' stage. And the third, the *vaikharī* stage, can be called the 'verbal' stage. This is how the matter stands from the speaker's point of view. But how does the hearer comprehend it? Bhartṛhari states four different views on this point.

According to some, *sphoṭa* is cognized as identical with the sound or *nāda*. One who grasps the *nāda* grasps the *sphoṭa* at the same time. Since basically the sound or *nāda* is identical with the *sphoṭa*, and they are so to say only two sides of the same coin, the grasping of one cannot be distinguished from that of the other. In other words, he who has not grasped one has not grasped the other. The commentator has supplied a beautiful analogy to elucidate the point. When a piece of crystal is placed near a red *japā* flower, the piece (of crystal) cannot be grasped or perceived without the colour red, for it now certainly appears red because of the proximity of the red flower. The *sphoṭa* is likewise comprehended along with the *nāda* that manifests it, one grasps the bits of language as sound or utterance, i.e., the *sphoṭa* as the *nāda*. It is not clear whether this analogy can be taken to imply that the *nāda* is only a superimposed feature of the *sphoṭa*, the real language. For, the piece of crystal is only apparently red due to the conditional superimposition; in reality it is colourless. If the implicit idea is that the *nāda* or sound is an inessential, conditionally superimposed feature of the *real language* or the *sphoṭa*, then I do not think this would be in exact accord with the doctrine of Bhartṛhari. Perhaps the analogy is not to be taken too far. It may be that simply the identification of the *nāda* with the *sphoṭa* is what is implied. In that case, this may well be Bhartṛhari's own view. The analogy between a piece of crystal and a bit of language was again used by Bhartṛhari in *kāṇda* 3 of *Vākyapadīya*. But the purpose of that analogy was probably different. It was to illustrate a point of Bhartṛhari's semantics. Objects meant by bits of language are only created by the language, for language is autonomous just as a piece of crystal is believed to be autonomous (according to the pre-scientific theory of light) in the sense that it 'reflects' objects by according an autonomous status to them (the reflector modifies the object in its own way). This analogy has been used with great ingenuity by R. Herzberger in her exposition of Bhartṛhari's semantics (Herzberger, 1986, 50–3). However, in the context of our comprehension of the *sphoṭa* through *nāda*, the 'crystal' analogy might serve a slightly different purpose. We grasp the *sphoṭa* as reflected in the *nāda*, and as almost identical with the *nāda* itself, just as we grasp redness as presented by the piece of crystal, not in any other way.

Bhartṛhari refers to a second view held by some: that the comprehension of the *sphoṭa* does not require the comprehension of sounds or *nāda* as a condition. A tentative argument is given in favour of this view. We know that when we cognize an object, say a pot, through visual perception, we do so through the instrumentality of the faculty of vision, the eye, and it is an established fact that we do not need to know the properties or features of the eye-organ itself. The fact that we *have* the eye-organ is enough, for this only is relevant for the knowledge of the object. Similarly we comprehend the *sphoṭa* through the instrumentality of *nāda*, sounds. Patanjalī has contended that sound is the attribute of the *sphoṭa*. Now when the *sphoṭa* is presented through sounds, we comprehend it right away even prior to our cognition of all the sound-symbols, though the latter is indicative of the former. In other words, in this view the cognition of the sounds themselves is not needed prior to our cognition of the *sphoṭa*. Bhartṛhari has criticized this view, saying that as long as the sounds are uttered they are also directly perceived by our sense of hearing. Hence it is impossible to comprehend the *sphoṭa* without comprehending the sounds. The view, as its stands, is indeed peculiar. Perhaps the upholders of this view were unconsciously arguing in favour of a distinction between sound-tokens and sound-types, and they accordingly wanted to say that we do not need to cognize the sound-types over and above the sound-tokens prior to our comprehension of the *sphoṭa*. Sometimes, it may be pointed out, we comprehend the *sphoṭa* even when only a part of the relevant sound-token is heard.

The third and fourth views mentioned by Bhartṛhari were also obscure. There were a few thinkers who apparently believed in the metaphysical existence of the *sphoṭa* but maintained that it could not be amenable to perception. The reason adduced further confounds the issue, for it is said that the distance that separates the *sphota* from the cognizing hearer makes the *sphoṭa* imperceptible. The upholders of the fourth view understood the matter in another way. Distance cannot make the *sphoṭa* imperceptible but can render it rather indistinguishable. In other words, since distance does not remove the object from the field or perception, it can render the *sphoṭa*, like an object at a distance, indistinguishable from the environment. Thus, we fail to perceive *sphoṭa* as a distinct entity. Bhartṛhari obviously rejected these views, and it is difficult to make sense of their notion of *sphoṭa*.

There is an obvious problem when we say that the sequential and atomic *nāda*-units in combination reveal or manifest the indivisible, impartite *sphoṭa*. The problem is similar to the problem of perception: how do the parts present the whole? If they present it *partially*, then the whole will never be presented in one sweep and this will cast doubt upon the contention about the reality of the whole over and above the constituents out of which it is formed. For the grammarians, the *sphoṭa* is a whole and it is a metaphysical entity, neither an object of construction, nor an abstraction. So the question arises: How do we perceive it from the utterance of a divisible and sequential sound-stretch? How is the unity perceived through the presentation of plurality? Thus by stating that the sound-stretch manifests the *sphoṭa* we do not explain much or answer the crucial question: How? For surely separate efforts are required to produce different sounds and they are produced in succession. At which point exactly is the unity that we call *sphoṭa* comprehended? If the unity is cognized at every instant from the beginning, then there is the fault of repetition and redundancy. If it is by the last (utterance of the) sound-unit then all the preceding units (or their utterances) are superfluous, for they have been destroyed at the time of comprehension.

Bhartṛhari answers this objection as follows: For the sake of convenience, let us use the illustration of a word-*sphoṭa* '*gauh*' (the cow). There is a unity here, the word. But the four sound-units or letters, *g, a u* and *h*, present the *sphoṭa*, each individually. Bhartṛhari says that each letter here is the medium of manifestation of the unity, the whole *sphoṭa*. The problem of repetitiveness or redundancy is avoided by postulating a difference or a distinct property (*viśeṣa*) each time in the resulting awareness or comprehension. The first letter (or the first sound-unit) shows the whole, but very indistinctly. It becomes gradually clearer and progressively better understood through successive stages until the last unit is uttered. Although the earlier units disappear when the last unit is reached, the memory-impressions left behind by those earlier units are in the hearer and each time there is a qualitative difference in the memory-impression (*samskāra*). The *sphoṭa* itself does not admit of any qualitative or quantitative difference, addition or subtraction, but the *impression* or image of it may be imperfect and different, due to the imperfect nature of the human intellect. Our memory-impression may be dim or partial, clear or unclear, on various occasions, but the object, *sphoṭa*, will always shine in its undimmed glory.

It may be further argued that Bhartṛhari's explanation of the comprehension of *sphoṭa* is unsatisfactory. For certainly the letters of sounds, *g, a, u* and *h*, reveal themselves only individually. That is, we perceive each unit as it is produced. When we produce *g* or *a*, it must be perceived as *g* or *a*. But *gauh* is not *g* or *a*. The *sphoṭa* is not identical with any of the individual sound-units. To perceive something *x* as what it is not, is to misperceive *x*. We call it error. It is somewhat unparsimonious to first postulate an entity like the *sphoṭa* of *gauh* and then claim that it is only misperceived in the first, second or third letter, *g, a, u*. Besides, each misperception is based upon recognition of some similarity between the object present and the object superimposed. In the present case, it is difficult to obtain any satisfactory account of such a series of misperceptions. Bhartṛhari gives a bold reply to this criticism which also has the metaphysical underpinnings of his *sphoṭa* doctrine. He says that just as the cognition of the lower numbers, 'one' and 'two', is the means for understanding a higher number, say, 'three', although they are each distinct and different, similarly, comprehension of the *sphoṭa*, either *a pada-sphoṭa* or *a vākya-sphoṭa*, is invariably conditioned by the cognition of the so-called constituents, either the sound, *g, a, u, h* or the word-elements 'Devadatta' and 'goes' (in the *sphoṭa* as a sentence 'Devadatta goes'). This presupposes an understanding of the Vaiśeṣika theory of numbers. According to this theory, numbers are distinct from one another and they constitute separate entities, and all numbers higher than one are produced by a sort of 'connective-comparative' cognition called *apekṣābuddhi.* This is the notion that brings many unities under one number or another. When two things are present, one cognizes both as 'this is one and that is one'. This is the 'connective-comparative' cognition that gives rise to the awareness of 'two' or duality, and similarly with each succeeding number. In this theory understanding of the previous number is the conditioning factor for the awareness of the higher number. Similarly understanding of the distinct sounds or distinct word-elements is the means for the awareness of the combined unity, the *sphoṭa.* Besides, Bhartṛhari claims that for the *sphoṭa*, or what he would call the *real* language, to convey some meaning to the hearer, it is an essential and unavoidable condition that it be made explicit through the sequential and transitory *nada* elements. Just as an episode of knowledge cannot be known or talked about without any reference to what it represents or what is known by it, similarly the *sphoṭa* cannot communicate or convey any meaning (or be known) without its being manifested through the sequential *nāda* or speech. To have a clear perception of a tree, for example, we must proceed from a distance step by step when the vague and indistinct blur gradually gives way to a distinct shape and identity. Similarly the *sphoṭa*, through steps or sequences, is distinctly understood and identified. Bhartṛhari claims that a man who has mastered the *śabdayoga* or obtained the light of the Eternal Verbum (some sages have apparently succeeded in this) can perceive or understand the *sphoṭa* clearly when the first sound is heard, just as a man with perfect vision or unlimited power of sight (if such a man exists) can see the tree distinctly even from a distance. Comprehension of the *sphoṭa* is equivalent to such a distinct vision of reality.

V

Bhartṛhari has noted also that there is no unanimity among his predecessors regarding the real nature of the *sphoṭa.* He refers to several earlier views. According to one, the *sphoṭa* is the *universal* manifested by the individuals which are *nāda* elements or sounds. The *sphoṭa* is thus the class, of which sounds would be members. The commentary quotes a line from the *Mahābhāṣya* of Patanjali, where the word *sphoṭa* is used in the sense of the universal. It is the universal of the word *gauḥ*, not the universal called *word-ness.* We may call it the word-form, realized through the sequential utterance of the sounds. Some later commentators (cf. *Bhaṭṭoji*) apparently have taken the class-*sphoṭa* theory as Bhartṛhari's own. But this is a mistake, and the claim of some modern scholars to the effect that *sphoṭa* is nothing but a postulation of a unitary word-universal should be rejected. Another view mentioned by Bhartṛhari regards *sphoṭa* as an impermanent entity, produced by the initial sounds resulting from the contacts and separations of the vocal organs. The initial sounds themselves constitute the *sphoṭa*, they do not manifest it. But these sounds, despite being momentary, produce further sounds which thus spread in all directions, gradually decreasing in intensity, and reach the hearer's organ as *nāda*. The sound produced initially is the *sphoṭa*, other sounds produced in reverberation are 'sound-produced' sounds (*dhvani* or *nāda*). Another view modifies this position, in that it understands both *sphoṭa* and *nāda* to be produced simultaneously through contacts and disconnection of vocal organs. They are like the flame and the light of a lamp. We produce both the flame and the light at the same time. The light 'travels', so does the reverberation. The flame is fixed in one place, and so is the *sphoṭa*, according to this view. None of these views would be acceptable to Bhartṛhari. His idea of *sphoṭa* is different, as already described.

Bhartṛhari draws another interesting distinction between two types of sounds in this connection. They are called the 'primary' sounds (*prākṛta*) and the 'derived' or 'transformed' sounds (*vaikṛta*). The usual way to take the 'primary' sounds is to refer to the linguistically relevant sound-sequences which the speaker intends to produce and the hearer expects to hear. It is the shared 'speech' which manifests *sphoṭa* (where the *sphoṭa* can be *prakṛti*, the 'original', and hence the *prakṛta* is the manifestor of the 'original'). These primary sounds are not abstractions, but *ideal* particulars which have sequences, duration and other qualities-all specified by the particular language system. The long sounds should be long, of required length, the short vowels should be short and so on. But this must be conceived as divested of all personal idiosyncrasies or 'mannerisms' of the speaker who utters them. It is the norm. The non-linguistic concomitants of any utterance are to be separated from this notion of 'primary' sound. This type of sound is also said to be identified with the *sphoṭa*, though of course wrongly, for the *sphoṭa* is conceived as a sequenceless, durationless and partless whole. In other words, one (wrongly) cognizes the *sphoṭa* as united with this 'primary' sound-series.

The 'secondary' or 'transformed' sounds may therefore be taken to be the individual instances of utterance that either reverberate or continue to show the individual peculiarities of the speakers, various differences in intonation, tempo, pitch, etc. The description here is a bit obscure, for it is also said that the manifestation of the *sphoṭa* still continues to happen or take place (after the first manifestation by the 'primary' sounds) with the help of the 'transformed' or 'secondary' sounds. 'Difference in the speed of utterance' (*vṛttibheda*) is also a factor in the 'transformed' sounds. They continue to manifest the *sphoṭa* again and again uninterruptedly for a longer period. They are said to resemble the light of a lamp which travels and continues to reveal the object as long as the lamp is lit. If this analogy is not very helpful, we may try another characterization. It is said that the slow utterance of a short *a* sound does not turn it into a long *a* sound, nor does speedy utterance of the latter turn it into the former. The primary sounds *a* or *a* are unchanged although the speed becomes a factor in the 'transformed' sound. In his commentary on the *Mahābhāṣya*, Bhartṛhari again refers to this distinction, but the matter there is further complicated by a reference to the two kinds of primary sounds (Iyer, 1969, 171). Kunjunni Raja's description of the 'primary' sound as the acoustic image or the abstract sound pattern is much too influenced by a knowledge of modern linguistics (Kunjunni Raja, 1969,120). That the 'transformed' sound may be just 'reverberations' after the utterance (of the primary sounds) which reveal the *sphoṭa* is a possible interpretation which receives support from Helaraja in his commentary on the third *kāṇda* of the *Vākyapadīya*. But by 'reverberation' we need not think of the echo or returning sound but extend its sense to include the continuous producing of the sound-series after the initial sound is produced by the impact of the vocal organs. This may presuppose the Vaiśeṣika theory of sound, according to which the first sound is produced by impact, etc., and is believed to be a momentary entity, which dies at the next instant but nevertheless generates another *similar* sound-individual, which in its turn generates another before being destroyed in the next moment, and so on. This process continues for a while and then stops (on reaching the hearer's organ). How long the process will continue and how far it will 'travel', will depend upon the intensity of the originally produced sound. Bhartṛhari does not contribute to the Vaiśeṣika theory of sound-production, but it seems that he would accept this process of sound-travel with one crucial change made in the theory – instead of talking about production of a new sound at every moment, we should talk about the new manifestation of the same sound at every moment during its persistence.

VI

Bhartṛhari's philosophy of language is ultimately grounded in a monistic and idealistic metaphysical theory. He speaks of a transcendental word-essence (*śabdatattva*) as the first principle of the universe. His *sphoṭa* doctrine is finally aligned with the ultimate reality called *śabda-brahman*. A self-realized person attains unity with the word-principle – a man of perfect knowledge. There is no thought without language, no knowledge without word in it. Consciousness vibrates through words, and such vibrating consciousness or a particular cognitive mode motivates us to act and obtain results. Hence language offers the substratum upon which human activity is based. Language and meaning are not two separate realities such that one *conveys* the other. They are in essence the two sides of the same coin. The *sphoṭa* is this unitary principle where the symbol and what is signified are one. To understand each other's speech and to communicate, we do separate the inseparable, the sound and its sense. This is only instrumental to our mutual understanding. At the ultimate level, they are one. Bhartṛhari talks about three kinds of *sphoṭa*: letter-or sound-*sphoṭa*, word-*sphoṭa* and sentence-*sphoṭa*, but his primary interest lies with the sentence-*sphoṭa*. He underlines the importance and primacy of the sentence in language analysis in the second *kāṇda* of *Vākyapadīya*.

The sentence is the unit of communication. According to Bhartṛhari it is a unity, a whole, and not the result of joining together smaller units called words. The sentence-meaning is likewise a whole, not constituted by word-meanings put together. The Mīmāṃsakas apparently believed that the sentence and the sentence-meaning are produced by joining the smaller units, words and word-meanings together. Bhartṛhari examines five different definitions of the sentence put forward by the Mīmāṃsakas.

1. The sentence is a 'collection' (*saṃghāta*) or words, and each word has a certain meaning of its own. When it is used in a sentence, it conveys the same meaning. But when the words are linked in a sentence, then, through mutual linkage, an additioṇal meaning is given to the whole unit. Thus the sentence-meaning is the 'mutual linkage' (*saṃsarga*).
2. The sentence is the 'sequence' (*krama*) of words, and the sentence-meaning belongs to this sequence. But since sequence is a property of time, one has to superimpose it upon the linguistic units called words.

Both views uphold an extreme form of atomism and are ascribed, later on in history, to the Bhaṭṭa school of Mīmāṃsakas. This Bhaṭṭa theory has been nicknamed *abhihitānvaya*, 'designation followed by (syntactic) connection', theory. In simple language, it means: words designate their meanings and then the meanings are brought together to give the sentence-meanings.

3. A sentence must have a finite verb, and we may even say that the finite verb is the sentence, for all the other words would be required in any case to be connected with the verb. Hence if we understand the verb, we understand the sentence, all the other *kāraka*-words being understood. The sentence-meaning, on this view, is of the nature of an action or process. It is the dependence of the meanings of other words on that of the verb that makes the sentence-meaning possible.
4. Even the very first word can be called the sentence, for the meaning of the sentence is already contained in, though only vaguely or partially expressed by, the first word.

5. A further modification of the above view is that each word in the sentence contains the whole sentence-meaning, though it is only partly revealed by it.

These last three views are supportive of a sort of contextualism. Words may have isolated meanings, but when they are in isolation they cannot express such separate or isolated meanings or meaning-atoms. Each word in connection with another word has a designation (meaning), which we should call 'connected designation'; it designates a connected entity. This is ascribed later on to the Prābhākara school of Mīmāṃsakas, and nicknamed *anvitābhidhāna*, 'connected designation'. The idea is that since, in order to talk about a word, we talk about a word used in some sentence or other, its meaning cannot be known in isolation. We must necessarily talk about the word's contextual meaning or rather its meaning in connection with the meanings of other words in the sentence.

Bhartṛhari refutes all these five notions of the sentence, and rejects both atomism and the sort of contextualism that has been defended by the second group of Mīmāṃsakas. He puts forward instead a holistic framework and argues that a sentence might be understood as an indivisible *sphoṭa*. The sentences as well as their meanings are indivisible units. It is for the sake of convenience as well as for facilitating our learning and understanding of a language, that we break the wholes into parts and smaller units and correlate words and word-meanings. The indivisible sentence is either internal to the language-user (any member of the speech-community) or external to him. It is externalized through its manifestation in speech or *nāda*. And through such manifestation it *appears* to have divisions (and this is true of both the sound-aspect and the meaning-aspect), although essentially it remains indivisible. In other words, appearance of divisibility of sentences and sentence-meanings is deceptive. It is like the 'cognition of multiplicity' (*citra-jñāna*). Although the cognition in such cases is one and indivisible, one sees plurality in it. A drink from the punch-bowl will have a plurality of flavours and tastes, but it is one and a unique drink – a whole.

Bhartṛhari underlines this indivisibility aspect by offering three more definitions of the notion of the sentence in addition to the five already mentioned.

6. The sentence is the class of the sequences of words, or the universal resident in the sequence of words. Or,
7. It is the whole string of words without any divisible part.

Both these definitions refer to what has been called the 'external' *sphoṭa* above. The former regards the sentence as a universal while the later regards it as a particular whole. Technically the later grammarians called them the *jāti-sphoṭa* and the *vyakti-sphoṭa*, respectively.

8. The last definition refers to what has been called 'internal' *sphoṭa*. The sentence is a whole piece of cognitive awareness.

These three so-called definitions may be just recognition of the three different levels of the realization of the same *sphoṭa* or three different ways of capturing the same reality, *sphoṭa*, the sentence. The sentence-meaning in all these cases is declared to be given by *pratibhā*, i.e., by a 'flash of understanding' of what is being communicated. This flash of understanding is also declared to be holistic. We do not obtain it bit by bit. That is why some people are said to understand the meaning of the sentence even before the utterance of the whole sentence.

Several points are not made clear here. The correlation between the 'external' and the 'internal' *sphoṭa* must be a crucial factor here. For, an ordinary sentence with indexicals, be it in the form of a universal of the sound-sequence or a concrete and particular sound stretch, will have to have a different *sphoṭa* as the speaker, time and place change. This distinction can be maintained by associating the external sound-pattern with the 'internal' *sphoṭa* of the speaker, which reveals itself to him at a particular time and place. This question has not been raised in this way and therefore the answer has not been given or discussed. Besides, if the *sphoṭa* is the *real* language or a particular language system, as Bhartṛhari seems to imply, we must apply the word 'language' in an extended sense, not to a system or string of sound-units having sense, but to what is only made explicit in a system-of-sound-units, not, that is, to the *nāda* exclusively, but to what is 'manifested' by *nāda*, the *sphoṭa*.

BIBLIOGRAPHY

Bhaṭṭoji-Dīkṣita, *Śabdakaustubha*, Vol. I, ed. Rāmakṛṣṇa Śāstrī; Vol. II, ed. Vindheśvarī Dvivedin and Gaṇapati Sāstrī Mokate, Chowkhamba Sanskrit Series, Varanasi, 1898–1917.

Biardeau, M. *Theorie de la Connaissance et Philosophie de la Parole dans le Brahmanisme Classique*, Paris, 1964.

Brough, John. 'Theories of General Linguistics in the Sanskrit Grammarians', *Transactions of the Philological Society*, 1951, 27–46.

Cardona, George. *Panini : A Survey of Research*, Mouton & Co., The Hague and Paris, 1976.

De, S. K. *Studies in the History of Sanskrit Poetics*, Luzac & Co., London, 1925.

Herzberger, R. *Bhartṛhari and the Buddhists*, Studies of Classical India Series No. 8, D. Reidel Publishing Co., Holland, 1986.

Iyer, S. *Bhartṛhari*, Deccan College, Poona, 1969.

Joshi, S. D., *The Sphoṭa-nirṇaya of Kaundabhaṭṭa*, Poona, 1967.

Keith, A. B. *A History of Sanskrit Literature*, Oxford University Press, Oxford, 1928.

Kunjunni Raja, K. *Indian Theories of Meaning*, Adyar Library, Madras, 1969.

Sastri, G. A. *The Philosophy of Word and Meaning*, Sanskrit College, Calcutta, 1959.

R.B. PATANKAR

R.B. Patankar, who was Professor of English at the Bombay University till 1986 and taught aesthetics and criticism, is a bilingual critic. His major work is in Marathi, and related to Marathi literature and criticism. Two of his monumental books, *Saundaryamimansa* (1972) and *Kantche Saundaryaśastra* (1984) have already acquired the status of critical classics in Marathi. He has a volume of essays in English, *Literature and Aesthetics* (1968). Patankar has published some practical criticism too, mainly dealing with modern Marathi fiction.

During the three decades of his active critical career, Patankar gave Marathi criticism a certain climate of concerns related to conceptual clarity and terminological and methodological precision. He writes criticism about criticism; and as such, it was natural that he engaged himself in analysing the ideas of Western origin and Indian tradition. The *Saundaryamimansa* is such an examination and re-statement of ideas, concepts and terms.

The most important contribution of Patankar lies in his critique of Marathi literary aesthetics. The essay reproduced here was published in the *Journal of Arts & Ideas* No.6, January-March 1984. It raises serious and fundamental issues related to the tradition and identity of Indian criticism. These issues will have immediate relevance to literatures in other Indian languages too.

Aesthetics: Some Important Problems

Aesthetics is a much-respected, almost awe-inspiring subject in Maharashtra today. People are enthusiastic and inquisitive about it. A large number of articles and books are being written on the subject. Many people have claimed that Marathi writing on aesthetics has a significant contribution to make to world aesthetic thought. Such claims, not infrequently made, are wild. The fact of the matter is that we have not made any contribution to any discipline that is included in the general category known as Humanities. That is why nobody has made similar claims about our contribution to any social science (on the theoretical plane); or to ethics, epistemology, metaphysics. Nobody appears to have evinced the slightest interest in these subjects. It is indeed a great wonder that so much should have been done in aesthetics alone and absolutely nothing in any other field. This is all the more surprising because some of these neglected fields should have been our main preoccupation. But let us pause a little and ask: by what criteria is it to be judged whether we have actually achieved anything significant in the sphere of aesthetics?

To begin with we have to ascertain whether the necessary infrastructure, of the right variety and quality, was already there, to make the emergence of new aesthetic systems possible. This infrastructure has at least three aspects:

(A) There should exist new and powerful movements in different Arts, clamouring for new theoretical formulations which they hope would do better justice to them than the older, outmoded ones. Do such movements exist in today's (or yesterday's) Maharashtra? At least in the field of literature the picture is not very heartening. Absence of greatness in modern Marathi literature is a theme to which critics from B.S. Mardhekar (who, incidentally, was our first modern aesthetician) have repeatedly turned, and nobody has challenged this estimate of modern Marathi literature. This observation has certain theoretical implications. Aesthetic theories are conceived and grow in the womb of a living, developing art tradition. The aesthetician or the theoretical critic cannot take the place of the parents; his is a much humbler task, that of watching the steady growth of the foetus, to help it in this process, till it comes out in the world in a perfectly normal, healthy condition.

(B) Aesthetic theoretical structures are usually present in the language of practical criticism in an implicit form. The second precondition for the emergence of a new aesthetic theory therefore is the existence of a strong critical tradition. If criticism is to be good, the critic must have absorbed his literary tradition and have the ability and the inclination to explore all the minutiae of new literary works which he is faced with. He is expected to have acquired certain intellectual skills, because he has to study the aesthetic data supplied by a work of art and on that basis reason his way to evaluative judgment. From where does a critic get these intellectual skills? Of course, from the community, that is, if there is a strong intellectual tradition in it.

(C) The existence of this tradition is the third precondition that a community which boasts of having created new aesthetic theories must satisfy. Our practical criticism, by and large, has degenerated into smart, verbally titillating chat or verbal pyrotechnics. The content of our critical articles is usually meagre. Very often they tell us more about the critic than about a literary work. Critical articles which combine a comprehensive range and attention to minutiae are already an extinct species. Entertaining chat about books/authors has taken the place of serious articles. Anyway, what can one expect from the butterflies and grass-hoppers who today go by the name of literary critics? Things are in very bad shape in the province of intellectual, discursive prose. We just do not have a tradition of intellectual prose. A Lokamanya Tilak here and a Dr Ketkar or Tarkateerth Laxmanshastri Joshi there do not constitute a tradition. Even if we assume that these few are our peaks, we must not forget that peaks by themselves do not constitute a mountain-range. A recent debate among Maharashtrian intellectuals about the merits of a history of Western philosophy in Marathi was both entertaining and saddening. Equally saddening is the Lawande-Patankar-Rege debate about Kant's relationship with Expressionism. All the debate shows is that we cannot yet distinguish between instruction and entertainment. The biting, exasperated attacks made by Prof. M. P. Rege on the poor quality of discursive prose in Marathi have had no effect, every writer complacently assuming that it was the others who were being attacked. We are *baddha* and, as always happens, we do not know that we are *buddh.* This intellectual poverty is not restricted to the field of literary criticism and aesthetics; it is present in every academic field.

The conclusion is obvious. If new aesthetic theories of world significance have begun to appear in a cultural group, even in the total absence of relevant traditions in the arts, criticism and discursive prose-writing, we are victims of an illusion. Extreme intellectual naivete alone is responsible for the Marathi fantasy – a world full of aesthetic *Pushpaks.*

Excessive importance is attached in Maharashtra to aesthetics because of an elementary misconception about the nature of the subject. It is believed that man can create an original aesthetic theory even if he is not deeply steeped in any artistic tradition and in all the important material on the subject; what one needs is nothing except original talent. But all this is a big illusion. Most Marathi thinking on the subject takes place within the Western framework. Aesthetics in the West is an age-old game. The first moves were made by Plato and Aristotle; later Kant and Hegel joined the game; it is being played today by people of similar calibre. Aristotle and Kant – or their eastern counterparts, Shankuka and Abhinavagupta – are giants; the present day Marathi theoreticians are to them what pebbles are to mountain peaks. What contribution can we hope to make to a game which was started and kept going by Aristotle and Kant? And this without first acquiring the preparatory materials and skills? We are qualified to make only a hesitant move and retire. If one is deluded into believing that one has done something more than this, one should, as a corrective, carefully read again – or, as would be the case with many, for the first time – Aristotle, Kant, Shankuka, Abhinavagupta. One will then realise that our so-called original theories have been suggested in passing by these great minds. As our scholarship develops, the illusions about our achievements will progressively melt. Once people realize the need for adequate knowledge – of art and theory – they will desist from writing on the subject on the strength of a brief acquaintance with an Osborne or a Santayana.

We shall have to modify a little our earlier statement about the absence of the threefold preparation needed for the creation of an aesthetic system. It is of course a fact, that we do not have any vigorous traditions. However, *occasional* attempts to move in the right direction appear to have been made. An occasional essay in practical criticism, which is comprehensive and which also goes into minutiae, a good critical survey of the literature of a particular period, an able treatise on a subject like imagery provide some, although meagre, evidence in support of this. But as these attempts try to exceed their present limits, difficulties crop up. For now we are forced to face questions about our basic conceptual structure. Within which structure have we been functioning? What are our valuational criteria? What is our aesthetic tradition?

Everything that has taken place in India since ancient times obviously does not belong to our (i.e. modern Maharashtrians') *today*. By the 12th century A.D. the vigorous Sanskrit traditions in imaginative and critical literature dried up. Today's writer cannot claim to have a living and comprehensive relation with them either on the creative or the critical plane. If we try to re-establish a relation with these there are two types of formidable obstacles in the way. It is true that we do now and then come across *Pundits* who discuss the Sanskrit poetic theories on an academic plane. But nobody would analyse a modern Indian play on the basis of the Sanskrit structuring principles of *sandhis* and *sandhyangas*. Nor do we get a detailed analysis and evaluation of a modern play in terms of *ālambana* and *vibhāvas*, *anubhāva*, *uddīpana*, *vyabhicāribhāvas*. Occasionally, we run into a critic who says that a particular novel is suffused with the *karuṇa rasa*. But he does not use the concepts of *vibhāva*, *sthāyibhāva*, *sādharaṇīkarṇa*. If the modern critic's responses do not spontaneously get articulated in the old Sanskrit theories, if these theories are not already there in the womb of the creative and critical processes of a modern man, these theories cannot be legitimately claimed to be part of our *today*. Secondly, the concepts which we spontaneously use today do not appear to have received due attention and emphasis in Sanskrit poetics. Sanskrit theoreticians agree that *rasas* are closely related to *puruśārthas*, the four ultimate goals of life. But Sanskrit poetics does not tell us how to discuss the moral problems presented in a contemporary novel, and, further, how to evaluate that novel in the light of this discussion. A play is today regarded as valuable on the ground that it gives an original and deep insight into life. These evaluations cannot be made from within the framework of Sanskrit Poetics. The above difficulties, it may be noted in passing, are not present, at least not in this degree, in the Greco-Roman framework. There is obviously nothing wrong in being proud of being Indians, but we should be more cautious in making claims on behalf of our Indian heritage. Indianness is a changing concept. We must constantly keep in mind that we are *today's* Indians and bear only a limited resemblance to our forefathers of the ninth or tenth centuries.

From the mid-nineteenth century onwards we imported through the medium of English some Western literary forms. We cultivated them partly in the Western and partly in our own ways, impoverished them and very rarely and in a negligible way enriched them. It was therefore only natural that we used the Western conceptual framework for the analysis and evaluation of literary works produced within these imported structures. These Western conceptual structures in the process of being assimilated in our changing identity, ultimately replaced our older structures. We should therefore frankly admit that today we spontaneously work within the Western framework, both as creative writers and as critics. To ask us to use theories like that of *rasa* will be a form of cultural tyranny. If we spontaneously begin to create literary works similar to those our forefathers created a thousand years ago, we shall equally spontaneously adopt the pre-Mammata critical framework. It will then not be necessary to persuade us to do this; we shall do it because we shall have no other alternative.

We were influenced most by the nineteenth century – and to some extent by the eighteenth century – English literature. We read even Shakespeare through nineteenth-century English eyes. The critical theory of this period was part of a long tradition of critical thinking from the Greek days to the modern age. This tradition, it is true, underwent changes, some of them major ones; but at no period was there a complete break. The artistic tradition in whose womb this theoretical tradition grew has also been in existence for over two thousand years. It also underwent major changes; but there was never a *complete* break. It looks as if the Greco-Roman tradition got lost in the Dark Ages. But it will not be a totally unwarranted guess to believe that it must have been alive at the deeper levels, maybe hibernating for a long period. The guess is not wild because if we do not accept it, we cannot explain the energetic re-awakening of the tradition during the Renaissance. There has been an equally long *intellectual* tradition in the West. This shows how the present West enjoys long and vital traditions of art, art-criticism and intellectual efforts in all fields. This explains the advance the West has made in different fields like aesthetics, moral and social philosophy, epistemology, logic, philosophy of science, metaphysics. Had this infrastructure been present in India we would have witnessed an equal advance in these and other fields. There is something to learn from this contrast. If we start in earnest to build the infrastructure today, in due course we shall be able to produce, if not the ethereal *pushpaka*, at least a couple of screws which might perhaps come in handy when we start making an aeroplane.

The first step that we have to take is to reject artificial aesthetic frameworks, accepted or assembled on a rarefied theoretical level, and attempt a spontaneous, undistorted, honest response to a literary work. If we analyse this response we shall begin to discern in it a conceptual structure and corresponding structural principles in its correlative, i.e. the literary work itself. This is sure to happen because the nature of a literary work and our spontaneous response to it are inter-dependent. In the principles underlying these structures there usually is a natural tendency towards universal expansion. To seek unity in multiplicity, to bring the largest possible diversity under a unifying principle is part of an inalienable human nature. One should not therefore feel surprised if a literary theorist who, after discerning expression of emotion as the most prominent feature in *some* poems, should try to extend it to all literature, and further to all arts. It is precisely here that one needs to exercise extreme caution; the complexity of human life calls for this caution; and yet the temptation not to exercise it is very strong. This reminds one of what Kant calls the transcendental illusion. At the time of sunrise or sunset the sun appears larger than it does at noon. We know that the size of the sun does not really undergo a change at the time it rises or sets. But even when this knowledge is firmly established in us we (including the scientists) continue to see that the size has changed. The theoretician in literature is subject to a similar illusion when he assumes that there *must* be *one* principle common to all literature. He has therefore to reconcile the impulse to unity with the awareness of multiplicity.

The insight that people have in the arts, if they have it at all, is usually restricted to one art or one of the varieties of a particular art, rarely to two. Let us suppose that a theoretician has obtained a genuine insight into fiction *and* drama. The concept of 'Probability' plays a significant role in them – at least in some of their varieties. Probability here is usually taken to mean statistical probability. If out of 100 cases *x* is followed by *y* in ninety cases it is taken as very probable that in the 91st case *x* will be followed by *y*. In a realistic novel to show that *x* follows *y* is to adhere to the principle of probability. In order to adhere to this principle the writer has to compare how things and events are connected in reality and in their literary representation. The claim that a representation of reality approximates truth depends upon whether the representation corresponds to the reality that it purports to represent. When the theoretician wants to extend the principle of probability to a non-literary art, for example, music, he is faced with a problem. How can the structure of a musical piece be compared with the structure of reality? A novel can be, and very often is, realistic. But it cannot be said that a musical piece is realistic. How can the principle of probability be applied to music? How can we decide that at a particular point in a musical piece, A is more *probable* than B? It is sometimes suggested that, between A and B, that which coheres better with the other constituents of the musical piece is *more probable* than the other. But this sense of probability is different from the sense of probability discussed earlier. Correspondence between reality and the artistic representation of reality appears to have been replaced by internal coherence in the constituents of the artistic whole. Two different theories of truth (correspondence theory and something like coherence theory) are implied in these two contexts and they ought not to be mixed up.

Once we have completely changed the meaning of probability to suit the context of music, can we still apply the term (in its changed sense) to literature? We can use it legitimately in its changed sense only while talking about fairy-tales. If its application is extended to realistic literature there will be chaos. It is possible to argue that the concept of probability in both its senses is applicable to a literary work. Does not Aristotle mention: (a) beginning-middle-end and (b) probability-necessity as two structuring principles in tragedy? Although this may be conceded, it must not be forgotten that dramatic representation can claim to be 'more philosophical than history' *only* on the basis of the second principle mentioned above. What is true of the concept of probability is equally true of the concept of rhythm. Can this concept which has spontaneously emerged in the art of music, and where alone it is certainly legitimate, be really applied in its original sense to the novels of Dostoevsky? One can of course apply it if one has placed a wager to do it and if one is willing to do violence to facts. Anything is possible for a 'clever' or a rash man. Such a man can, for example, prove that one common principle is present in things as different as Napoleon, the blue sky, a stone quarry, and cholera germs. The question is not what we *can* do; it rather is what we naturally, spontaneously do. In most contexts it will be seen that when a concept is transferred from its field of birth to another field it usually involves metaphorical extension of meaning to a large extent. If this is true, what is common to the two fields is only *one word*, but *not one* self-identical *concept.* To forget this is to extend an invitation to theoretical confusion.

We see here an amazing thing which is perhaps peculiar to a naive community like ours, adding to this confusion. The conceptual structure inherent in music will/can be discerned only by a musician and a discerning music critic. They alone are competent to tell the world what the nature of rhythm is and what its place is in the total conceptual structure underlying the musical world. But in our community it is mostly people whose acquaintance with the world of music is very slight who are found talking eloquently about the principle of rhythm and the nature of music as a whole. The loquacious critics working in the field of literature appear to be talking with equal authority on music, painting, and all the other arts. The musicians and music-critics do not know how to talk glibly about things as literary artists and critics do; they therefore are, or till recently have been, silent about their art. But it is a welcome sign that things are changing. Musicians and music-critics, who alone are competent to talk with authority about music are at last becoming vocal. Let us hope they in their turn do not make the mistake that literary critics have been making all along.

People who have attained some degree of sophistication and discipline in other intellectual fields show a surprising degree of naivete when they deal with concepts pertaining to the arts. That is probably because they do not pay equal attention to all aspects of the function of aesthetics; some are perhaps not aware of all these aspects or their importance. The aim of aesthetics is to analyse the statements which critics make about works of art and the concepts embedded in these statements. This analysis includes the study of (a) the logical peculiarities, and (b) the content/substance of the relevant concepts. Many people ignore (a) altogether and approach (b) directly, but soon get tied up in theoretical knots. It is therefore more fruitful if due attention is paid to (a) right from the beginning.

I shall illustrate my point with the help of a book called *Gārambichā Bāpu.* Soon after we have started reading it we realise that the book is a narrative – but it does not narrate what happened to actual men and women; it narrates fictional happenings; that it is a *novel* and it ought be read as a novel. This shows how classification is present right from the beginning of our process of reading anything. In other words, we do not merely read a book, we read it as a member of some kind/class.

Two questions arise here: the first is about the theoretical legitimacy of the process of classification and the second is about the concept *novel.* Some people hold that classification is in literary criticism only for practical convenience, but that such classification into literary forms or kinds has no *theoretical* justification.

Benedetto Croce has taken this extreme position. He holds that the librarian, for his own convenience, classifies books and places them in different cupboards, which are then labelled as *Drama*, *Novel*, or *Miscellaneous*. Then begins the search of the theoretician who assumed that because all books in a particular cupboard are called 'Novels', they must share some principle or essence in common that needs to be discovered. We should thank our stars that critics have not as yet set out to look for the common essence of books placed in the cupboard labelled 'Miscellaneous'. Croce thus ridicules the concept of literary/artistic classification because, according to him, Art is a Genus which has members in it, but no species. But this is evidently wrong. Just as there cannot be an Indian who is not at the same time a Maharashtrian, a Gujarati, a Rajasthani, there cannot be a work of art which is not at the same time a painting, a literary work, a musical piece; there cannot be a literary work which is not a novel, a lyric, a play. Only a professional philosopher, particularly of the older school, will ask 'how do we identify a work of art, as a work of art'? A non-philosopher reader will ask a more specific question; 'Is the book that I am reading a novel? How can I know for certain that it is one? In some respects it is like *Jādugār*, *Kulābyāchi Dāndi*, but then...' It is only the latter, the more specific question that is important in the context of our discussion. And it presupposes classification. The problem of literary classification is important for another reason also. When we realise that the book we are reading is a novel a definite range of expectations is created in us; different expectations are created, if we know that the book is a play; they become more specific if we realize that it is a musical play. Definite expectations are created if we know to which form of literature the book we are reading belongs, because definite conventions are associated with definite forms. It is these conventions which, in a sense, define the limits of a form. Although they change in the course of history, it never happens that they are totally absent. Till now we have been considering the problem from the reader's point of view. What is true of a reader is equally true of a writer. By the time a writer is completing the first page of what he is writing he becomes (however vaguely it might be) aware of the range of the literary kind in which he is writing. To cite an example from another field, a musician does not just begin to sing, he begins to sing a *Khyal* in a particular *Raga*. The process of learning and teaching music presupposes the concept of *Raga*; it is present with different degrees of explicitness in the teacher and the learner. It seems that the concept of a literary kind and a literary work are logically interconnected right from the moment the latter is conceived.

Evaluation of literary works is possible only because certain conventions and certain expectations with regard to them exist in a community. If we know that we are reading a social-realistic novel, we also know what to expect and what not to expect from it. We have already read many novels of the kind, their impressions have been synthesized and ordered in our minds, complex and elastic criteria for judging them have also been formed. This concept-value-criteria complex enables us to read a social-realistic novel as a social-realistic novel, and also judge whether it is successful. At the same time we also look for newness, conscious departures from traditional conventions, experiments with regard to the substance, its comprehensiveness and subtlety, the work's organization, technique, style, diction. For a literary work owes part of its value to its being new, different; both of these concepts (newness and difference) are relative and not absolute. Difference presupposes similarity; and newness implies the existence of conventions, tradition, history. Awareness of literary classification is a necessary but not a sufficient condition for the production and criticism of a literary work. Our problem is how to accommodate in our conceptual structure both the universal and the particular.

We shall now address ourselves to the second of the two questions raised above. It is about the nature of concepts like that of the novel which a critic cannot avoid using. We must bear in mind the fact that it is far more difficult to decide whether a particular piece of writing is a novel, than to decide whether a particular animal is a dog, because concepts like 'novel', 'play', 'tragedy' are not rigidly closed as the concept 'dog' is. One cannot identify permanently usable criteria of these concepts. It is generally held that the novel as a form emerged in England around the eighteenth century. Right from the start it was not a rigidly closed concept; for one cannot identify an essence common to the earliest well-known novels like *Robinson Crusoe*, *Pamela*, *Tom Jones*, *Roderick Random*, *Tristram Shandy*; they appear to be related to each other by a network of similarities and differences. With the addition of new novels this network became wider and more complex. We cannot predict today how and in what direction this network will grow. A form like the novel becomes complex also on account of the introduction in it of certain features which are more characteristic of other forms. For example, occasionally the presence of dialogue in a novel becomes so pronounced that one is continuously reminded of the concept of drama. The combination of drama and music in Marathi musical plays is well known. Sometimes the element of 'action' in a short story is overwhelmed by that of free meditation, with some event as an excuse, and then it becomes very difficult to decide whether the story is really a story and not a meditative personal essay. This is, of course, a border-line case. The point to remember is that in other, everyday contexts also borderline cases exist, but they do not render the concept of classification invalid or unusable. For example, we can meaningfully use the concept of family-relationship, although it is difficult to decide whether one's second cousin is to be called a family-relation. The elasticity of the concept has proved to be useful, for we can go beyond one's brother and call one's first cousin a relation.

Since concepts like the novel or the drama are open in a large measure, a critic sometimes comes to the conclusion that he can dispense with such concepts altogether. But he soon realizes that they are not dispensable. He then goes to the opposite extreme and tries to impose rigid discipline on these relatively open concepts; with a determined will he looks for the differentia of the novel, the drama, etc., and sooner or later announces that he has discovered them. For him all that now needs to be done is to use the differentia in the vast variegated field of concrete literary works. The relationship between theoretical criticism and criticism of particular literary works is conceived here as similar to that between science and technology. But this is a foolish error. The expressions 'practical' or 'applied' criticism commonly used by critics are highly misleading. A critic worth the name does not apply any abstractly conceived principles to concrete literary works. To try to apply such principles is to accept slavishly a discipline imposed from outside. Critics, whatever they may profess on the plane of theory, do not, indeed cannot work under an externally imposed discipline. Things of course work out differently if an extremely clever theoretician meets a group of extremely loyal, but less clever followers. They together can prove to be a disaster. But ordinarily a practising critic accepts complexity as a given fact and deals with it successfully. But the same complexity scares him stiff as soon as he rises to the level of theory. But if he were to study the logical features of the concepts he uses he would realize that all concepts do not have identical logical features. They are useful and usable precisely because of the differences among them. For analysing some concepts the Platonic one-essence model is adequate; for some others the Wittgensteinian family-resemblance model is more suitable. So long as human life continues to be what it is we cannot avoid using different models for analysing different concepts.

Till now, we have been discussing the validity of certain concepts, like kinds of literature and have examined their logical features. The concepts are being constantly used and they make literary criticism possible. Keeping them at the centre, we shall now try to move a little in two directions. On the one hand we shall consider concepts with scope wider than that of the novel or the drama. At the same time we shall try to evaluate the extent of usefulness of these concepts of ever-widening ranges for the analysis and evaluation of individual literary works.

We shall, however, not look for the most general features of works of art or aesthetic objects as such. The differences among the arts and aesthetic objects will show anybody that our decision is sensible. We shall confine ourselves to concepts of a middle range. Poetry or literature considered as a whole might prove to be a good choice. In modern times some critics have tried to explore and formulate the distinguishing marks and structuring principles of poetry and literature. They have tried to do it in two ways. First, some theoreticians have placed literature in a large class which contains, besides literature proper, such categories as dreams, day-dreams, myths, fairy tales, contents of the racial unconscious, and ritual. That these critics who give great importance to these non-literary products should pay special attention to disciplines like psychology and anthropology, is very natural. There is no doubt that these extra-literary aids are important. But a word of caution is necessary here. We do not need these aids in the case of all literary works. In order to analyse some, we are not required to go beyond the level of everyday consciousness and explanation in terms of established conventions and common sense. The wisest strategy in these cases is not to go beyond these. If in some cases we are required to use extra-literary aids we should acquire adequate mastery over them. This needs to be emphasized, for Indians today appear to be averse to scholarship of any kind. Further, in the case of literary works where the use of these aids is found to be indispensable, it is also often discovered to be inadequate. Both *Oedipus Rex* and *Hamlet* are explained with a large amount of success with the help of Freudian theories. Dr Ernest Jones's explanation of Hamlet's delay in avenging his father's murder is much more satisfying than many other explanations offered so far. But it is evident that the theory which explains equally adequately *Oedipus Rex* as well as *Hamlet* cannot by itself explain how they differ from each other. For this purpose, we shall need some other explanation. In order to determine the nature and value of any individual literary work we need not one, but *many* principles, theories and criteria.

We shall now turn to the second of the two above mentioned ways. A school of criticism known as 'New Criticism' was in vogue in the UK and USA for quite some time from the 1920s or 30s. Critics of this school start from the assumption that poetry or literature is a variety of linguistic discourse. In order to identify the nature of this variety, they contrast it with some other readily identifiable variety. Language as it is used in science invariably serves the necessary purpose. Literature evidently does not belong to the scientific variety of discourse. Scientific discourse is then used as a negative analogue to determine the features of literary discourse. For example, consider the dichotomy I.A. Richards has arrived at.

Scientific language is used to describe reality; literary (poetic) language is used not to describe anything, but to express and/or induce emotions. When Cleanth Brooks says that the language of paradox is the language of poetry he too has in mind a similar contrast between two varieties of linguistic discourse.

These critics claim to have also discovered the structuring principles peculiar to poetry (literature); these are: reconciliation of opposites, paradox, ambiguity, irony, etc. One does come across literary works characterised by these. But it might prove to be an exaggerated claim that *all* literary works exemplify them. On the other hand it can be shown that these structuring principles are not peculiar to literature alone. For example, one does not find them in many poems of Wordsworth. And, on the other hand, examples of paradox and irony can be seen in plenty outside literature, even in everyday life. Some of these critics see conflict as the central principle of literary works and try to show how the conflict between good and evil, life and death, light and darkness is at the core of different literary works. It is easy enough to show such conflicts in all literary works. But, if the type of principles mentioned above are treated as the sole differentia of all literature, the differences between various forms of literature are easily lost sight of. If a lyric by Donne, a Shakespearean tragedy like *King Lear*, and a Dostoievskian novel like *The Brothers Karamazov* can be identified with the help of one distinguishing mark alone, where is the need for the existence of different forms such as the lyric, the drama, and the novel? But we have already seen that the differences between forms of literature are important. The critics who recommended and, to some extent practised the above method evidently had in their mind poetry, or, to be more precise, short, lyrical poems. That the lyric is an important form of literature is of course a fact. But to treat it as a paradigm for all literature in all its aspects is patently wrong. If one treats any other form as a paradigm, it will be equally wrong. The above critics gave the central place to lyrical poetry and used the conceptual framework, which is perhaps adequate for it, for the criticism of all literature. But one does not ordinarily find in a lyric such elements as strong characterisation, elaborate plot construction, or descriptions on a large scale. Naturally, elements like imagery take the place of plot, characterisation etc., in lyric. But if we approach a novel like *War and Peace* with a conceptual structure in which imagery occupies the central place, the result will obviously be disastrous.

We discussed above the place in literary criticism of classes broader than the novel. R.S. Crane, a prominent neo-Aristotelian critic, has taken strong exception to the use in criticism of classes with ever-widening scope. In his book *The Language of Criticism and the Structure of Poetry,* Crane maintains that every act of criticism necessarily takes place within a framework; which framework to choose from among the many that are available depends on what the critic is aiming at. If he is aiming at (a) understanding and (b) evaluating *individual* literary works, frameworks which relate to the most general features of literature will be of little use to him. For a critic who has this aim in mind, Crane recommends the Aristotelian framework which will enable him to arrive at the knowledge of the individual literary work, and to grasp its individual structuring principle.

Aristotle himself, in his *Poetics*, has discussed two forms of literature: tragedy and epic. He has analysed tragedy in detail and has thus provided a model for analysing forms of literature. A neo-Aristotelian critic like Crane would not be hostile to the concept of literary forms. But it is probable that he might be opposed to the use of classes with a broader scope. Crane's contention most probably will be that the concept of forms of literature is not useless, but it is inadequate. That Crane is right becomes clear in all contexts where the value of individuality is recognised. Where individuality is not regarded as valuable, classification of individuals is enough. But in the modern concept of man individuality is included as an inalienable constituent. We adopt a similar attitude to a large number of man-made things. This is certainly true about individual literary works. This uniqueness partly constitutes the source of its value.

That every literary work has its own unique, non-repeatable structure and expression is a well-known tenet of the Kant-Hegel aesthetic tradition. Once this is accepted, it follows that the criterion for evaluating a literary work lies within itself. Kant has distinguished between determinate and reflective judgement. The function of judgement is to create unity in diversity. When the synthesizing concepts and principles are already given, the judgement is determinate; on the other hand, it is reflective when the unifying principle is still to be discovered. It is the reflective judgement that is operative in aesthetic experience. For, here the unifying principle is not given, it is to be discovered. Every manifold that is to be synthesized will need its own synthesizing principle. To operate with a unifying principle common to different manifolds amounts to replacing reflective by determinate judgement. But Kant was determined to avoid this. For otherwise the aesthetic experience would be transformed into cognitive experience, and would lose it autonomy. We experience a peculiar internal tension in the Kantian analysis of aesthetic experience. Kant comes very close to recognising the existence of concepts in aesthetic experience; but till the end he does not explicitly say that concepts are present.

There is only one possible way out of the predicament of the Kantians. They should accept the existence of concepts in the experience of beauty and art, and at the same time assert that these concepts are very often not closed, but admit of openness up to a point. Some of these concepts are rooted in particular arts and are usually confined to them; consider for example, concepts like *Bhairavi, Mālkauns, Khyāl, Thumri, Pancham*,.... It will not always be possible to find concepts which are born in a particular art and are confined to it alone. The possibility of finding them is greater in music than in literature. Once we admit that concepts in the field of art are to some extent open we shall also have to admit that the items which come under them are not exactly identical. Classes here are like families, the members of which are linked together by similarities and differences. It also follows that no two works of art are exactly identical in respect of substance, structuring principle, mode of expression; identity is not expected to be there; and even if we expect it, we shall never succeed in discovering it. Partial similarity is all that we can expect to find; and we do find it. And it is this partial similarity which makes teaching and learning possible within the framework of an art-tradition. If a structuring principle which is really not repeatable in any measure is possible in theory at all, then at least in practice it is well nigh impossible to be able to discern it in any work of art created in the past or to be created in the future. According to Absolute Idealists, if one wants to know the real character of a thing one will have to study all its *relations* with all the other things in the Universe, because the character of the thing we desire to know is determined exactly by these relations. It is theoretically impossible for any man to accomplish this task. The knowledge obtained by any *finite* knower will necessarily be incomplete, so long as he is finite; the object of his knowledge will also be incomplete on account of the same finiteness. This applies to a work of art as it does not to all the other things in the world. A work of art will be incomplete so long as it is finite. It will be complete only when it covers the whole Universe; and paradoxically it is only then that its principle of organization/expression will be really unique. In order to experience such a work of art the critic will himself have to be the infinite *Brahmananda* (the blissful experience of total identification with the Universal spirit) or to be *Brahmānanda-sahodara* (the twin-brother of *Brahmānanda*). As knowers, moral agents, and aesthetic appreciators, we are finite; and the objects we deal with are also finite. It is therefore logically impossible to find in the human world a principle of organization/expression which will get completely absorbed in one work of art. So long as the present situation (created by our finiteness) continues to be the same, the distinctions between concepts and their examples, classes and their members, traditions and individual works of art as well as their interdependence will have to be accepted.

We have been discussing problems pertaining to Form primarily because Marathi critics happen to be preoccupied with them. With all this, their first spontaneous responses to literary works are about the content of these works. Let me illustrate this point with the help of two short stories, both written by one author, sharing an equal degree of technical finesse. The first story depicts a dispute between a group of students and the Hostel Warden. One of the agitating students has gone on a hunger strike; tension is mounting every day. The Warden's wife intervenes at this stage and lovingly coaxes the boy to end the fast. At the same time she prevails upon her husband to give up his office. The second story depicts the mental torture that a woman, caught in a trying situation, is experiencing. She is a married woman and has recently become a mother. In fact this should have been a moment of great satisfaction and joy to her. But it is just at this moment that she comes to know about a hereditary disease in her parents' family – in each generation somebody in the family is afflicted with psychosis. She also realizes that she herself has a kink in her personality. This sudden realization unnerves her. Now the only earnest prayer that she, a mother, wishes to offer is that the child should not be tainted by the hereditary disease in her family, that the child should turn out to be the offspring of her husband alone, that it should belong only to its father's family and inherit nothing from the mother's side. The deeply painful conflict in her mind is powerfully depicted in the story. The first story is escapist like a day-dream and is, on that account, mediocre. The convincing depiction of the heroine's mental anguish makes the second story valuationally superior. We called the first story mediocre and the second story good mainly because the content of the first is, as content, valuationally much inferior to that of the latter. The Marathi reader needs to be reminded that we have called the second story *good* and not *great*. A Marathi critic, who moves about wearing certain theoretical blinkers, does not mind content-oriented criteria for judging *greatness* in literature; but he is opposed to using this variety of criteria for judging *goodness* in literature. When we do not have these blinkers on, we spontaneously give due importance to the content while deciding whether a particular piece of writing is a *good literary* work. But when a critic rises to the theoretical level, he regards as invalid all content-oriented criteria. Kant, while writing about the art of painting in his *Critique of Aesthetic Judgment*, gives all importance to design and almost no importance to the colours; and that was a serious error on his part. A similar, a more serious mistake is being made by contemporary Marathi writers on literary theory when they do not attach due importance to the quality of the content of a literary work in determining whether it belongs to the category of literature and in giving their verdict on its goodness as a literary work; the other aspect of their mistake consists in the excessive importance they give to the structure of a literary work. As a matter of fact a literary work derives its value from various sources such as the merits of the content, diction, style, metre, plot-construction, and so on. It seems Marathi critics are oblivious to this fact. That is why, even after you have analysed and evaluated all the above aspects of a story they will persist in saying: 'all this is very fine; but you have not yet told us what makes this story a *work of art.* At least now you will have to admit the importance of Form. For ultimately it is Form alone which is the deciding factor.'

This argument is based on an assumption whose truth is taken as self-evident. It is assumed that there is a well demarcated class called Art; that it has a definite distinguishing characteristic to mark it off from all that is not Art. You cannot hope to find it in the aspect of content, because there is little similarity in the content of the different arts. In literature we get content in the sense of *meaning* which is expressed through words. Content *in this sense* is not present in an abstract painting; there, in the place of expressed meaning, what we get is an organization of colours, etc. On account of such basic differences it is impossible to get at anything common in the content of works of art. The only way out is to concede that the common distinguishing characteristic of all arts can be found only in the aspect of Form; we should therefore look for it only there. As this common characteristic or principle is supposed to cover all works of art it is sure to be extremely abstract. 'Unity in diversity', 'harmony-contrast-balance' can be cited as examples of such abstract, all-comprehensive principles.

One can understand the difficulty before the people who accept the above assumption. They do not feel confident that by concentrating their attention of the content of works of art they will be able to clearly mark off art from non-art. It is, of course, true that the task is difficult; but it is not impossible as they think it to be. If we make a determined effort we shall be able to discover the dividing lines between the two fields. They might not have the certainty and precision that obtain in natural sciences; but they will be found to be adequate for doing practical criticism successfully and fruitfully at least in the case of most literary works. Let us take an example. Suppose that we are reading Laxman Mane's book *Uparā*. Before we had read it we knew almost nothing about the Kaikādi tribe, whose life it depicts. The book has made a substantial addition to our general awareness of tribal life. The range of our experience and understanding has been widened. But that is not all; more important than this is the fact that the structure of our customary emotional and ethical responses has been shaken. We have realized the nature of the high degree of tension and hostility that is generated when an inter-caste marriage takes place; we have also realized how tenaciously the caste-system continues to live on at all levels in our society. This social insight creates in us a mixed response, consisting of indignation, helplessness, a variety of despair, and along with these there is the intense realization that it is imperative to fight for social justice. This complex response is wholly content-oriented. It is exactly for these content-oriented reasons that we found the book to be so good. A difficulty needs to be taken note of at this stage. *Uparā*, we saw, gives an insight into our social life. Can we not get the same insight elsewhere too, for example through a book on sociology? A sociological book, it will have to be conceded, will certainly give us an insight into society; the insight will be characterized by precision and certainty also, if disciplines like statistics have been made use of. But the insight that a sociological book can give will not be of the same nature as the insight that *Uparā* gives. Sociological studies give us knowledge of reality on the plane of abstraction. Individuals have no room in these studies except as examples. When we read *Uparā* or Daya Pawar's *Balutan* we feel as if we are watching actual actions of real people taking place before our eyes. What we see *suggests* general propositions about our social life. But books like these do not *transcend* individuality of either persons of events in order to give us abstract formulations about reality as scientific books do.

Secondly, the mode of presenting information in a scientific book is not necessarily attractive. In a literary work it is presented in such a way as would create interest even in a common man. Further, the information contained in a scientific treatise is, as far as possible, kept away from emotions and values. These two elements are present in a large measure in most literary works. It is true that some modern writers consciously use an emotionally neutral style in their stories and novels. They rely rather on particular arrangements of the events, characters, situations in their novels to convey to the readers new insights and evaluations. This reliance on particular skilful arrangements of the constituents of literary works to give insights into life can be regarded as one more distinguishing mark of literary works.

We must however never forget that it may prove impossible to discover the principle that makes all literary works beautiful/good/powerful. It may be the case that all literary works do not share any one principle in common; again, if there is one, there may be no unanimity about it among critics. Let us consider a couple of examples. Some of the characteristics which were mentioned above in the context of literary works – e.g. that they are interesting, give importance to the particularity of events and characters – can be found in journalistic writing also. But is the latter, on account of this, to be admitted to the category of literature? But it may be pointed out as negative evidence that most journalistic writing is characterized by sensationalism, use of a cliche-dominated style, a tendency towards simplification, absence of neat organization, incapacity to provide a broad human context to events. That is why many critics will refuse to give the name of literature to most journalistic writing.

Suppose, following Warren and Wellek, we say that in literature the events, facts, characters all belong to the plane of *fictionality*, and that we make no positive or negative ontological claim about their actual existence. Science and history, on the other hand, give us information about events and facts which actually exist/existed in the real world. This distinction, however, may not be found to have universal applicability. If fictionality is regarded as the distinguishing mark of literature, what do we do with an autobiographical literary classic like Laxmibai Tilak's *Smrutichitre*? Some literary theorists try to overcome this difficulty by advising the readers to treat actual facts described in such works as if they were fictions. But then it would amount to conceding that the actual facts in that case have attained literary excellence without belonging to the plane of fictionality.

Till now we have been trying to look for content-oriented criteria of evaluating literary works. If we now turn our attention to the aspect of the expression of this content, we might be able to identify characteristics which will mark off literature from non-literature. It is possible to get a sufficient number of such characteristics if we pay attention to diction, qualities of style like *Prasāda*, *Ojas*, *Mādhurya*, and principles such as *Dhvani*, *Vakrokti* and *Alankāra*. If we are analysing a novel, we should keep in mind the different points of view from which events in a novel can be narrated, and the different ways in which they can be organized. But such comprehensive analysis of literary works has become a rarity during the last many years – perhaps during the last three or four decades.

Adequate knowledge of the individuality of persons, things, and situations can be obtained, valuational decisions in their regard can be made without losing sight of their individuality, if we bring to bear upon them a complex and flexible structure of various concepts and criteria used simultaneously. This is what we actually do in everyday life. In spite of the fact that this way of dealing with things has proved to be successful in our everyday life, we insist on trying to discover and use only one self-identical criterion in the field of literature; there seems to be something very odd about this insistence. It is better to solve a fresh problem in a fresh way with the help of the organized, ordered experiences we have stored in our mind, than to depend on some single so-called distinguishing mark of literature. If we do not want to lose the capacity to appreciate new literary works, we must, with firm determination, set aside the *Essentialist Fallacy* (the *one-term one-essence fallacy*), and resist the inclination to accept misleading simplifications, in any event to accept the assumption that all works of art have one common essence. If we accept this assumption there is every danger that while looking for the so-called common essence of all art in a literary work, we might forget that it is a *literary work*.

It should be clear from the general trend of the argument stated so far, that just as we must not fall a prey to the Essentialist Fallacy while thinking about the nature of works of art, we must also protect ourselves from that fallacy while considering the nature of the *experiences* induced by works of art. That different works of art, in the various fields of art, give rise to experiences which are different, sometimes strikingly different, from one another is a matter of everyday observation. It is therefore very surprising to see how people who are otherwise levelheaded, can readily assume that all art experiences are identical in nature. *Premā Tuzā Rang Kasa?* will create in us a healthy, pleasant mood; we shall find *King Lear* profoundly disturbing; *Antigone* might leave us feeling disturbed and baffled; The *Tempest* will *transport* us beyond the turmoils of the real world to the peace and tranquillity of a make-believe world. The *Mahābhārata* will create in us *Kshamā* and *Nirveda*, a state of non-attachment with regard to the phenomenal world. There can be no doubt that all these are valid literary experiences. The differences among them are so obvious, that if somebody thinks that he can discern a common principle in all of them he should be regarded as a victim of a conceptual illusion.

Sometimes aestheticians tell us that all art experience is characterized by delight/rapture, detachment and an all-absorbing concentration, verging on identification with the art-object. It is necessary to examine this assertion closely. First of all, all-absorbing concentration is not peculiar to art-experience alone. We can find it in various activities which have nothing to do with art; e.g. in watching a cricket match, working in our garden, playing cards, killing mosquitoes which disturb our sleep .... We know that everyday experiences are pleasurable or non-pleasurable, or they contain both pleasure and non-pleasure. But it is claimed by most Sanskritists, that the *Rasa* experience is necessarily pleasurable. Our own experience while watching plays does not lend support to this. One has only to consider the *Bībhatsa* and *Bhayānaka-Rasas* to see why our actual experience cannot support the Sanskritists' claim. It is argued that in the *Rasa* experience, the *Sattva* predominates, and the *Rajas* and *Tamas* are weakened; this inevitably renders the *Rasa* experience pleasurable. This argument is not based on actual experience, but on a particular metaphysical theory. And we need not accept the argument as valid or convincing unless we have already accepted that particular metaphysical theory. Perhaps there is some point in saying that the *Tamas* is weakened while we are watching a work of art. This is likely to happen because we are on the conscious plane and are all the while alert. But this point needs deeper probing. It is very likely that the *Tamas* is in ascendence when we are reading an escapist romance which takes us away from reality. Again, we cannot assert with certainty the *Rajas*, the principle at the basis of all our actions, is weakened in a literary experience. We shall return to this point later in the context of our discussion of the concept of Detachment.

A mention has already been made in this paper of the ontological status of a work of art and an aesthetic object. According to Kant in the context of aesthetic experience we are not supposed to claim that the object of our experience actually exists. This Kantian view seems to have been accepted by a large number of the later aestheticians. So far as the aesthetic experience is concerned, it makes no difference whether the aesthetic object actually exists or is only an illusion, an appearance. Once a person accepts this Kantian position, i.e. once he withholds the ontological claim he thinks that he has thereby ruled out the possibility of any commerce with the aesthetic object from the cognitive and the practical points of view; he cannot now look upon it even as something agreeable. Once he has excluded these approaches, it follows that in the aesthetic context his attitude is, and can only be, that of detached contemplation.

This line of thinking is convincing only up to a point. As there is no ontological continuity between the art world and our everyday world, we (who belong to the everyday world) cannot touch anything that belongs to the art world. But the converse is not true, at least not true in all respects. Things in the art world can, and often do, affect us, despite the ontological difference between the two worlds. Things in the art world do move us emotionally, and, to a certain extent, move us as practical agents also. To cite an example, we cannot dissuade Othello from killing Desdemona; but at the same time it is true that we are as much disturbed by the murder of the innocent Desdemona as we would be by the murder of an innocent woman in the actual world. This shows that characters in a play have the capacity to induce in us real-life emotions. Secondly, our response is not merely emotional. In the context of many literary works our response includes different elements such as our capacities to know, to think, to act, and to act morally; it comprehends our total value-system. And in the context of these literary works 'detachment' merely means absence of overt action with regard to the *characters* in literary works, and perhaps also non-involvement of the empirical self.

Let us probe further the concept of Detachment. In the context of many literary works 'detachment' signifies only absence of overt action with regard to the *characters* in a literary work. Action is closely related to desires. Desires are of two types. One type of desires can be satisfied only if items of a definite class are made available; for example, thirst can be quenched only with water or liquids which resemble it in relevant respects; nothing else will serve the purpose. On the other hand certain elastic desires are satisfied by a very wide range of heterogeneous objects. Love (*Rati*) is one such desire; the range of its objects includes union with the beloved as well as separation from her and the poignant lamenting over the separation. That is why Sanskritists mention *Vipralambha Shringāra* along with *Sambhoga Shringāra*. The actual presence of the beloved, her memory, her image, a handkerchief presented by her, thinking about her, thinking about even a fictional character can satisfy *Rati* in varying degrees. The escapist romantic literature that appears in popular magazines available in circulating libraries will bear ample testimony to this. The satisfaction of desires is thus seen not to have been ruled out by the ontological difference mentioned above. The problem of the cognitive aspect of literary experience will have to be tackled in a slightly different way. If the elements in a literary work and the organizational principles which synthesize them are similar to their counterparts in actuality (in spite of the ontological difference between them) we shall obtain an insight into reality through a literary work. This will naturally awaken our cognitive faculty and also our faculty of moral judgement.

Judgements such as '*Uparā* has given a new social awareness', '*Koslā* has given us an insight into the mind of a whole generation', 'when we saw the recent film *Ākrosh* we were convinced that it is imperative to fight against the present social structure although it is extremely difficult to undertake this fight', 'the universal destruction shown in the *Mahābhārata* fills our mind with despair' are regarded as valid *critical* judgements only because we accept the validity of content-oriented criteria of literary excellence. Moral, cognitive, and intellectual elements spontaneously enter these judgements and their legitimacy is not ordinarily challenged. But it is not enough to say only this; it is *necessary* to go a step further. In the context of some literary works it is necessary that these elements should find a place in our judgements about them. If, while reading some of the stories in *Maraṇ Swasta Hot Āhe,* the value structure of the reader is not even slightly disturbed, it will have to be said that his response falls short of completeness. An analogy might help us here. Suppose a film director has to decide whether to give the role of a particular character to a certain actor; the character is to be shown as drowning in a river and crying out for help; if the actor's urgent appeal for help proves to be effective the film director will give him the role. This is all that is expected from the director in the present context. But suppose the same director is strolling along the bank of a river and he hears the same appeal for help from a man who is really drowning. If, in this changed context also, the director's response does not go beyond, 'excellent performance; he should get an assignment in the new film', it will have to be regarded as a response which is totally irrelevant and incomplete in the changed context. Only if he had rushed to the rescue of the drowning man would the response have been relevant and adequate. The relevance and adequacy of the response depends upon the context in which it is made. Just as this is true about real life contexts, it is true also about literary contexts. A particular story by Baburao Bagul gives a jolt to our value-structure. Its excellence as *a good story* lies precisely in its capacity to give this sort of jolt. And in feeling this jolt lies, in a very large measure, the fullness and the relevance of our response as a literary response. On the other hand the excellence of an *Abhang* sung by Bhimsen Joshi early in the morning lies in its capacity to create in us mental repose; and in the context of such an *Abhang* the mental repose constitutes the fullness and relevance of our response. It may be appropriate, relevant, and valid to approach works of art of certain types only with one aspect of our personality; on the other hand, it will be appropriate, valid and relevant to approach with our total personality some other types of works of art. We can keep our ethical value-structure outside an art gallery and enjoy an exhibition of abstract paintings. But, if we keep our value-structure out, it may turn out to be impossible to read *Koslā* and to respond to it adequately. If reading *Koslā* does not affect our general view of reality and our value-structure, it only proves that we have read the novel as a proof-corrector reads any printed material.

It should be evident from the above analysis that so far as novels, stories, plays are concerned, our spontaneous and almost entire response is often content-oriented. But this does mean that the consideration of form plays no part in the process of reading and evaluating a literary work. At some stage or the other in our content-oriented study of a literary work we are inevitably led to the analysis of form. Here we should bear in mind two points. Firstly, how much importance form has in comparison with content depends upon the particular Art, the particular province in that art, and the particular work of art we have in mind. Secondly, 'form' does not only mean the principle of organization of a work of art as it is generally taken to mean in Marathi today. Form has other meanings as well; e.g. form of literature, expression (of some semantic content), arrangement of the elements of a plot.

According to some so-called Formalists in Marathi a work of art becomes a work of art only on account of its form, by which they mean some specific principle of organization. It has already been suggested above that this view cannot be accepted in the context of literature. We shall now discuss in some detail the reasons for saying so. While talking about an abstract musical composition we need not go beyond sound-units and their organization. But this cannot be the case with literature, our response to which, as we saw earlier, is mainly content-oriented. In the context of literature we have to consider two different concept-pairs: (a) semantic content and its expression, and (b) constituents like character, situation, events, ideas, emotions, etc., and their organization. Let us remind ourselves of one point before we proceed further. A literary work owes its existence as a literary work in a large measure to a content of a certain quality that it embodies. While we are looking for the features of the form of a literary work we shall have to keep this fact constantly in mind. To forget the demands of the content will be a big blunder.

B.S. Mardhekar has argued that emotive meaning is the medium of literature. Let us grant for the sake of discussion that this is true. According to Mardhekar the literary artist's aim is to create a beautiful work of art in this medium; in other words the literary artist aims at organizing emotive meanings in accordance with the three laws of rhythm, viz. harmony, contrast, and balance, which, Mardhekar claims, constitute beauty in art and nature. Generally, other relations (e.g. psychological) also exist between emotive statements. We take them for granted and do not take special note of them in the aesthetic context. Mardhekar has not shown any logical connection between these other relations and the three laws referred to above. We may therefore ignore the former and concentrate on the organization of emotive meanings in accordance with three Mardhekarian laws. Let us now consider the following passage from *Gārambicha Bāpu*, the famous novel already referred to above 'And they were then laughing with abandon... their eyes dimmed, their ears felt slapped and they felt faint at that sight.... Excessive enthusiasm, excessive attachment, attraction without a cause, despair and pain also without any cause... see how happy Bapu is; he has no recollection; no pain.' Mardhekarians will point out that the first two sentences are related by contrast; the third on one side and the fourth and the fifth on the other are also linked by contrast. If we take the group of the first two sentences and the group of the next three sentences, we will discern the relation of balance between them. Besides, the three units in the second sentence are linked together by harmony; the first three units of the third sentence have one, and the last two units of the same sentence have an additional relation of harmony. The first three units and the last two units in the same sentence are held together by the relation of contrast. As the organization of the different sentences in the passage is in accordance with the laws of harmony, contrast, and balance, it inevitably follows that the passage is a beautiful configuration.

But, to be honest, the above sentences are not taken from one single passage at all. But if they are read together it is possible that they might appear to be interrelated according to some laws e.g. by logical or psychological laws and create an impression that they constitute one passage. If we want to keep the laws of beauty completely separated from laws irrelevant to beauty, we must see to it from the beginning that these non-aesthetic laws do not get a chance to enter the aesthetic experience at all. Is not this separation artificial? Perhaps, yes. But we have a good precedent. In his discussion of Hedonism, Plato has made a distinction – which also looks artificial – between pleasure and consciousness of pleasure. There should be no logical difficulty if, following Plato's example, we isolated the three aesthetic laws from other, i.e. non-aesthetic laws. As an experiment let us consider the following sentences in which this separation has been consciously made: 'Kakasaheb looked very angrily at the clerk. Elizabeth glanced at Browning with smiling eyes. Justice Ranade and others sent petitions to the kindly government. The Peshwas rejected outright the Nizam's proposal regarding a treaty'. There is contrast between the first two sentences, and also in the next two sentences. There is balance between the first two and the latter two sentences. Again there is harmony in the first and the fourth, and also in the second and the third... all this can be shown. The Marathi Formalist will be immediately convinced that the above four sentences constitute a beautiful configuration. The real question is about the response and judgement of readers like us who do not wear the Mardhekarian theoretical blinkers. We shall certainly refuse to look upon this group of sentences as beautiful; we shall also go further and regard this attempt at bringing these four disconnected sentences together as the height of folly. So far as literature is concerned, content is not something whose presence is to be taken for granted only to be conveniently forgotten while formulating an aesthetic theory. Whatever may be true of other arts, form cannot be the only necessary pre-condition of the existence of the literary art; the presence of content of a certain quality is a much more important pre-condition. Finally, it must never be forgotten that 'form' must not be narrowly interpreted as Mardhekarians tend to do. Our critics, let us hope, will also turn their attention to the other things signified by 'Form'; this is most likely to happen as the study of forms of literature and stylistics strikes deeper roots in our soil.

There is perhaps one difficulty in Marathi critics' admitting the importance of content in literature. At least on the plane of theory this difficulty appears to be formidable. Giving importance to content, some critics feel, will lead to the devaluation of literature as art. The content of a literary work brings with it values of our everyday life, thus lowering art to the position of an instrument to establish and promote these life-values. We shall see that this fear is baseless if we consider the question not in the context of particular values like Plato's Wisdom, Courage, Temperance, Justice, but in the context of a larger and more general question: what makes life as a whole valuable? There are many possible answers to the above question. Suppose we accept the theory of value advocated by the utilitarians and I.A. Richards; the life in which the largest number of important impulses are satisfied, and which involves the least frustration of them, will then become the most valuable. Now suppose that we are able to prove that while reading literature that maximum number of important impulses are satisfied and the minimum number of them are frustrated. It will follow from this that reading literature does not lead to valuable life; it is in itself a way of living valuable life. Here we are making use of valuable life as a criterion of literary excellence; but that does not make us advocates of didactic literature. Suppose knowledge is an inalienable part of valuable life. If literature gives insights into different sides of life, it automatically becomes valuable on that account. If we accept that the knowledge that literature gives is different from – not higher or lower than – the knowledge that science gives, the cognitive aspect of literature will be seen to possess intrinsic (and not instrumental) value. From this it should be clear that by bringing Art close to life we do not devalue art. Some arts can be completely divorced from life (e.g. abstract designing); they might consequently claim and enjoy autonomy. Literature can never get the autonomy that these arts can claim and get. So long as literature cannot be deconceptualised, the present situation will not change. Literature need not be given the lowest position in the hierarchy of Arts on this account. To be fraught with concepts is just a peculiarity and not a defect of literature. If we avoid the Essentialist Fallacy we shall realize that literature is only different from other arts in some respects; it is neither superior nor inferior to other arts.

So far we were doing two things. We were studying some important problems in aesthetics. We were also considering the step that the Marathi critics and aestheticians have to take in order to make a genuine contribution to this discipline. We saw at the outset that aesthetics is the study of the logical features and the content of the concepts which spontaneously appear in our critical judgements. We discussed (a) whether concepts are present in our experience of works of art, (b) whether they are closed or open concepts; (c) how they are related to evaluation. We also discussed the nature of some important concepts in the context of literature. We considered the similarities and differences between literature and the other arts, the relation between content and form in literature, the importance of content in literary works, the problem of the autonomy of literature, and other similar substantive questions. Literature being life-values-oriented, we discussed in some detail the nature of the content-aspect of literature.

Now that we know something definite about the nature of aesthetics, it should not be difficult for us to see and evaluate what the Marathi critics and aestheticians have been able to do, and what they have not been able to do. Theories of beauty grow in the womb of art-traditions, they begin to become explicit in criticism, and if there is a strong intellectual tradition in the community, they can be formulated with logical rigour. If we resist the temptation of indulging in self-glorification and decide to face reality, we shall have to admit that nothing significant has been done in any of the three fields: aesthetics, criticism and creative writing. It is a saddening realization that this all-round poverty is not a recent phenomenon in Maharashtra; it has been there for decades. That there should spring into existence new aesthetic theories in this atmosphere of poverty seems to be almost inpossible. We shall have to come to the same conclusion about all disciplines that are given the general name of 'Humanities'. It is only when society is vibrating with life and vigour in all its aspects, traditions and institutions that the possibility is created for the emergence of new theoretical systems. Great problems arise only in such a living society; and the traditions in that society throw up great men endowed with genius to tackle them. No such problems have arisen in our art-tradition; and we have not produced great geniuses to tackle them.

To be honest, we shall have to begin at the beginning. Artists should try to be conscious of what they are trying to do; while they are endeavouring to attain self-awareness as artists, they should also communicate their findings to society. On the other hand, the art-critics must put away blinkers of arbitrary theories and examine their genuine and spontaneous responses to works of art. Mere enthusiasm is not an adequate equipment for art-critics; they must also have a well cultivated sensibility, necessary scholarship, tenacity and seriousness of purpose. They must acquire the intellectual skills necessary for formulating their responses explicitly and with logical precision. Criticism should be directed to a work of art and neither to the artist nor to the critic. It is necessary to examine carefully the complex theoretical structure that emerges from what the self-conscious artists and well-equipped critics say about works of art; one must do this with deft fingers, and while doing this delicate operation one must scrupulously avoid using the clumsy instrument called 'one-art: one-essence fallacy'. We must explore whether the same or analogous concepts are found to exist in different arts. It is needless to emphasize the importance of academic integrity in the whole process. It is here that we can hope to get much help from the Western aesthetic theories. We must of course resist the temptation to rely only on somebody like Clive Bell or Collingwood or Osborne, just because their books are easily accessible. The Western aesthetic structure is very comprehensive, complex, and well-built. It has received solid support from art-tradition on the one hand and the tradition of philosophical thinking on the other. It is necessary to study in detail the different constituents of this vast structure, to evaluate them, to examine their mutual bearings with regard to one another, to contruct a conceptual map. It is for them to ascertain where *we* and *our theories* can be placed on this map. All this will require a long time. We shall need, besides untiring patience, a well-developed ability to think on the abstract, philosophical plane. The number of people gifted with this specific ability is much smaller than we suppose. It is certainly not universal; further, it is not necessarily seen in people who are intelligent in other ways. No single individual will be able to cope with all the tasks listed above. It is in fact a sort of project that only a group of researchers, scholars, critics, philosophers can tackle. While this work is being done on the plane of theory, we must at the same time maintain continuous and direct grass-root contacts with literature, by functioning as practical critics with all the necessary equipment and substantial help from our native common sense.

That Maharashtrian critics and aestheticians should have wasted about thirty years in dealing with a particularly weak, small branch of the great tree of the aesthetics of the Kantian-Hegelian tradition bears ample testimony to their naivete and all-round ignorance. They were deluded into believing that this weak branch has great importance in world aesthetic thought. To give it a slight jolt was thought to be an event of international significance; to give it some support was also regarded as an equally significant event. If we had devoted even half of this time to the study of the Kantian-Hegelian tree itself perhaps we would have been able to produce a small corpus of theoretical writing of good quality. Thirty years is a small period in the entire history of Maharashtra. If we have our feet planted firmly in reality, and if we make all-round, honest, and determined efforts along proper lines, it is probable that an aesthetic theory which we can legitimately call *our own* may emerge in the next fifty or hundred years. When we call an aesthetic theory our own, it is implied that it is the creation not of any one individual, however brilliant he may be, but of a whole art tradition, a whole socio-cultural group. Let us hope that during this period an equal amount of work of good quality will have been done in natural sciences and humanities, and all sensible people will have been convinced that these other fields of inquiry are more important than aesthetics. Aesthetics will then get its due place; even if it turns out to be low, it will be its legitimate place.

SUDHIR KAKAR

Sudhir Kakar has the distinction of being one of India's small and select band of psychoanalysts. He is easily the most prominent of his type in his generation. He has brought the experience gathered at the analyst's couch to bear upon his probing inquiry into the 'Indian' psyche. Though all his writings and researches have focused attention primarily on the Indian Hindu (except in his study of Hyderabad's Muslim community), he can be said to be the modern India's Freud, whose method of analysis Kakar follows. However, Kakar shows a very acute awareness, not seen among literary critics, that European formulations have to be suitably modified before they are put to use in the Indian cultural context. Trained under Eric Erikson, Kakar has taught in universities in Europe, the U.S.A. and India, and has held various prestigious fellowships. Among his important publications are, *The Inner World, Shamans, Mystics and Doctors, Intimate Relations, Tales of Love, Sex and Danger* and *The Colours of Violence. The Inner World*, which is a study of the psychology of childhood, has an unconventional analysis of religious cults related to Shiva and Krishna. In his discussion of the Krishna cults, Kakar offers very valuable understanding of the psychology of *bhakti*. It is reproduced here as a psycho-analytic guide to the medieval literature of *bhakti*. It is not, in the original, intended to be literary criticism. But it does serve as an example of the recent developments in interdisciplinary discourse, which has contributed to theoretical thought in Indian literary criticism.

Cults and Myths of Krishna

In a country of many religious cults and variety of gods, Krishna is unquestionably the most popular. Worshipped throughout the subcontinent, among men and women of different castes and sects, among traditional orthodox Hindus as well as among modern 'secular' Indians, Krishna is the focus of Hindu devotionalism.

Krishna is usually portrayed as a blue-complexioned child full of pranks and mischief, or as a youthful cowherd wearing a crown of peacock feathers whose beauty entrances all who see him or hear the irresistible call of his flute. This is his present version. Two thousand years ago, when Krishna first moved into the Hindu pantheon, the god was a more sober and austere deity. In the *Mahābhārata*, for instance, he is the wise adult and helpful teacher and counsellor. His nature began to undergo a transformation around A.D. 500 in the *Harivamśa* (the genealogy of Hari or 'Krishna') which stressed Krishna's early years as a wilful, mischievous child and as the youthful, divine lover of the *gopis*, the cowherd girls. The later Krishna texts, *Vishnu Purāṇa*, *Padma Purāṇa*, and *Brahmavaivarta Purāṇa*, are fascinated by, and focus upon, these aspects of the god: Krishna's freedom and spontaneity as the eternal child, the youth-Krishna's surpassing beauty and the seductive power of his haunting flute which breaks down human resistance to the appeal of the divine lover.[1]

The cult primarily associated with Krishna, with its stress on *bhakti* or devotional activity, has faithfully reflected the change in the nature of the god. Whereas the bhakti of *Mahābhārata* and *Bhagavad Gitā* is staid and pietistic, its devotion channelled through a life of discipline and strict adherence to ethical and social norms, in the medieval *bhakti* cults and down to the present day, *bhakti* is no longer a pale and austere affair but rather emphasizes intoxication and uninhibited response to the dark god, a release from the constraints and precepts of orthodox Hinduism.

Devotional activity, practiced in groups composed of male and female devotees together, takes many forms. In festivals, processions, gatherings at temples, the devotees sing, dance, enact the legends of Krishna's childhood and youth, and chant his glories with an emotional fervour radically different from the meditative contemplation and emotional asceticism enjoined by other traditional Indian methods of enhancing spiritual experience. Krishna *bhakti* is a vision of the divine that is free and spontaneous, boisterous and anarchical. As it happens, as I sit writing this late at night in an old section of Bombay, the open-air theatre next door is putting on a Krishna festival to the music of stringed instruments, drums and the voices of several hundred devotees. The festival is a ten-day affair that starts each day at around nine in the evening and continues well into the early hours of the morning. Fervent discourses on Krishna by learned pundits are interspersed with communal singing of songs of praise accompanied by an abandoned, mesmerizing drum beat. The whole effect, 'liturgical' and dramatic, is an intended one, perfected over the centuries to enhance the individual's *bhakti*. For as Krishna himself puts it:

Till the pores of the body do not spill over with joy, till the mind does not dissolve, till tears of bliss do not begin to flow and the mind does not dissolve in a flood of devotion, until then there is no possibility of purification for the devotee. He whose voice breaks with emotion, whose mind has dissolved and flows only in one direction, who does not stop crying for a moment yet sometimes breaks out in loud laughter, who leaving shame bursts into loud song and begins to dance, such a devotee not only purifies himself but the whole world.[2]

This invitation to abandon self-control and self-consciousness perfectly captures the ecstatic nature of the Krishna cult. For Krishna is not one of those father-gods who primarily evoke attitudes of filial reverence in their worshippers – Krishna invites the devotee to fuse with him: he gives permission for joy. In psychological terms, he encourages the individual to identify with an ideal primal self, released from all social and superego constraints. Krishna's promise, like that of Dionysus in ancient Greece, is one of utter freedom and instinctual exhilaration.

The psycho-social meaning of *bhakti* is that it provides for, and actually uses, 'democratic' fantasies in which the inner and outer repression exacted by life in a rigidly structured and highly stratified social order are lifted. Traditional codes of conduct, and relationships between social groups, between generations, and especially between the sexes, are abrogated in Krishna worship. To illustrate this, I would like to quote passages from an anthropological report of the annual *Holi* festival in a north Indian village. *Holi* is of course an extraordinary celebration, a special ritual event.

It does not represent the everyday ritual of Krishna devotees, and it is a vivid counterpoint of their chaste daily life. Or perhaps, this 'obscene and depraved saturnalia' (as the disapproving British called *Holi*) illuminates Krishna devotion in much the same way that an individual's 'nervous breakdown' sheds light on his 'normal' personality, by revealing latent conflicts and laying bare the fundamental structure of the psyche.

McKim Marriott, the American anthropologist who did field work in a village of Uttar Pradesh, captures *Holi*:

As the moon rose high, I became aware of the sound of racing feet: gangs of young people were howling '*Holi*!' and pursuing each other down the lanes... Pandemonium now reigned; a shouting mob of boys called on me by name from the street and demanded that I come out. I perceived through a crack, however, that anyone who emerged was being pelted with bucketfuls of mud and cow-dung water. Boys of all ages were heaving dust into the air, hurling old shoes at each other, laughing and cavorting 'like Krishna's cowherd companions' – and of course, cowherds they were.[3]

As the day of *Holi* advances, the action becomes more frenzied, and at the same time subtly changes as the boundaries between the sexes dissolve. Women become the 'attackers' while the men turn into willing victims: the traditional roles of the one who pursues and the one who endures (and invites) pursuit are over-turned in that cathartic exuberance that often accompanies the breakdown of exaggerated repressive conventions; in this case, rigid sex-role differentiation:

> As I stepped into the lane, the wife of the barber in the house opposite, a lady who had hitherto been most quiet and deferential, also stepped forth, grinning under her veil, and doused me with a pail of urine from her buffalo... I witnessed several hysterical battles, women rushing out of their houses in squads to attack me and other men with stout canes, while each man defended himself only by pivoting about his own staff, planted on the ground, or, like me, by running for cover....[4]

Moreover, the aggression inevitably pent up in an inner world whose social boundaries are defined by the intransigent hierarchical systems of caste and family finds some release in this 'festival of love':

> Who were those smiling men whose shins were most mercilessly beaten by the women? They were the wealthier Brahman and Jat farmers of the village, and the beaters were those ardent local Radhas, the 'wives of the village', figuring by both the real and the fictional inter-caste system of kinship... The boldest beaters in this veiled battalion were often in fact the wives of the farmers' low-caste field labourers, artisans or menials — the concubines and kitchen help of the victims ... six Brahman men in their fifties, pillars of village society, limped past in panting flight from the quarter staff wielded by a massive young Bhangin, sweeper of their latrines.[5]

Nor do erotic impulses languish during the celebration of *Holi*, although the expression of eroticism is not always sexual in the sense of adult genital intercouse. Rather, the 'erotic' activity of *Holi* suggests the sexuality of the very young child. Obscene words and gestures, the smearing of loved ones with urine and dung, the throwing of mud, are as characteristic of the *Holi* festival as furtive, impetuous adultery. The ritual *Holi* dance in the Bundelkhand and Vraja areas of northern India in which two men respectively take the parts of a prostitute and an ascetic equipped with (what else!) a short crooked staff or horn, is harmless compared to many others shocking to even the most flamboyant imagination. In this particular village, 'There was one great throng of villagers watching an uplifted male dancer with padded crotch writhe in solitary states of fevered passion and then onanism; then join in a remote *pas de deux* with a veiled female impersonator in a parody of pederasty, and finally in telepathic copulating — all this to a frenzied accompaniment of many drums.'[6]

The *Holi* festival, then, with its exuberant polymorphous sexuality and insubordinate aggression momentarily obliterating all the established hierarchies of age, sex, caste and class, is an idealization and elevation of instinctuality and an apt celebration of Krishna who, of all the Hindu gods, is accorded the greatest permission for instinctual indulgence. To a psychologist who must necessarily forsake the mystical explanations of legends describing Krishna's sixteen thousand wives, his unrestrained amorous dalliance with the village *gopis*, his voracious childhood hunger for milk, butter and curds and his completely amoral attitude towards stealing them, as well as his general inability to bear any kind of frustration, Krishna is all impulse and appetite, a highly narcissistic being who incidentally benefits mankind while pursuing his own libidinous desires.[7] The cult of Krishna affords his devotees all manner of fantasied instinctual gratification through an unconscious identification with him.

The popularity of the Krishna cult has not only a psychological but also a social rationale — namely, its promise of salvation to the dispossessed classes. By rejecting the conventional Hindu axiom that a person's birth, social status and caste membership govern his chances of reaching *moksha*, the Krishna cult actively welcomes and even recruits the participation of oppressed castes and classes in its devotions and ceremonies, an utterly unorthodox state of affairs. The sole criterion of merit in Krishna worship is the extent and intensity of devotion. As Krishna says in the *Bhāgavata Purāṇa*, the closest Indian equivalent to the New Testament, 'The practice of yoga, knowledge and science, living in *dharma*, prayer or ascetic renunciation are none of them as successful in obtaining me (the godhead) as is the daily increase in loving devotion',[8] and, more specifically, 'I believe that even a Brahmin equipped with twelve qualities (wealth, family status, knowledge, yoga, intellect, etc.) who has turned his face away from the lotus feet of god (Krishna) is inferior to the *chāṇḍāla* (outcaste) who has laid his mind, speech, work, wealth and life at god's feet; that *chāṇḍāla* saves his whole family while the Brahmin, arrogant of his station, cannot even save himself.'[9]

Numerous other passages in the *Bhāgavata Purāṇa* are critical of the arrogance of high castes, and historically the Krishna cult has always drawn its support from the social and economic groups that were 'despised by the rest of society, but their poverty and distress made them naturally sympathetic to a devotional religion based on faith and simplicity.'[10] Although its appeal to the oppressed classes would be seen as a particularly sinister form of opium by most Marxists, many other modern Hindus sympathize with a religion that implicitly rejects the traditional interpretation of *Karma* in that it views members of socially and economically disadvantaged groups compassionately rather than as erstwhile sinners getting their just deserts. In any case, the democratic practices of the Krishna cult set it apart from other forms of Hinduism in which many holy men who preach other-wordly values seem to accept only the rich and the powerful into their company or their *āshramas* as favoured devotees, and rationalize the favour they show to the chosen few in terms of the workings of the impersonal *karma* principle.

Whereas I have so far explained the popularity of the Krishna cult in terms of its promise to release both the repressed instincts and the oppressed classes, a consideration of the *myths* surrounding Krishna's childhood leads us back to the world of psychological experience as it is magnified in cultural imagery, for the Krishna myths highlight the main themes in Indian inner life. Filtered through the decorous symbolism of art and folk-tale, these myths present modern psychic conflicts and their fantasied resolutions in a socially congenial form. As Jacob Arlow has pointed out, whereas an individual's dreams are meant to be forgotten after they have performed their nightly task of relieving instinctual pressure, myths are designed to be remembered and repeated in order that the sharing of unconscious fantasies may confirm and consolidate the mutual identification of members of the society to whom the myths appeal.[11] In myths, the terrific wishes and impulses of unconscious fantasy are defused by the very fact of the fantasy's becoming collectively shared rather than remaining an individual burden, and by the simple device of its being externalized and projected onto mythical heroes and heroines.

In the Indian family. . ., the male child's early experience diverges significantly from his sister's. So too, we find, do the myths of a single god such as Krishna, who is equally popular with both men and women, diverge; there are 'masculine' and 'feminine' Krishna legends. In spite of certain elementary features in common, all Krishna myths do not serve equally as a projective vehicle for the unconscious fantasy of both men and women. Whereas the cult in its rituals and festivals extends a promise of freedom and parity, both social and sexual, to both men and women, and indeed often has an even stronger appeal for women given the confined and constrained life that is their lot, the mythology surrounding a truly universal god must also appeal to both sexes. The enduring claim of the god Krishna to the devotional love of both sexes reflects in part the fact that, unlike others in the Hindu pantheon, Krishna enjoys a more explicit 'dual mythology'. In addition to the legends that elaborate the inner world of Indian men, the god of love is surrounded by lore that evokes, and responds to, the longings of Hindu women. This differentiation of 'masculine' and 'feminine' myths about a single god-hero is rarely made in psychological analyses, embedded as they are in a venerable patriarchal tradition of myth-interpretation that simply ignores women in such undertakings. The Krishna myths, however, show both faces; the myths of Putanā, Kāliya-Nāg, Agāsur and the lifting of Mount Govardhan are predominantly masculine in their orientation and appeal, while the Krishna-Yashoda and Krishna-Radha legends seem to be primarily, though not exclusively addressed to women.

Krishna, the reincarnation of Vishnu, the Preserver of the Hindu trinity, is said to have been born to rid the earth of the tyranny and oppression of King Kamsa, According to legend, Kamsa, informed of the prophecy that the eighth child of his uncle's daughter would one day slay him, confined his cousin and her husband in a prison and killed all their offspring as soon as they were born. But Krishna, the eighth child, was smuggled out of the prison and taken to live with foster parents in another part of the kingdom. Kamsa, learning of the infant Krishna's escape and yet ignorant of his exact whereabouts, instructed the demoness Putana to kill all the boys born in the kingdom during the month in which his cousin had expected the birth of her child. Putana went around the kingdom, obediently carrying out her master's orders. Transformed into a beautiful woman, with a deadly poison smeared on her nipples, she finally came to the house where Krishna lived in the remote region of Gokula. Pretending an upsurge of maternal love and relief that she had at last found him, she took Krishna from his foster mother and gave him her poisoned breast to suckle. Krishna sucked so hard that he not only drank all the milk Putana had to give, he also sucked her life away. The maternal monster swooned, with Krishna's mouth still at her breast, and as she fell dead, she resumed her original hideous form. The legend concludes that Putana nevertheless attained *moksha* since she had acted as a mother, albeit a malevolent one, to the infant-god.

The Putana myth contains several themes, such as the attempt to kill the infant god, that occur in the mythologies of other civilizations.[12] Krishna's suckling feat has a parallel in the ancient Greek account of Heracles sucking so hard at Hera's breast that she throws him off in agony, the milk spurting out of Heracles' mouth to form the Milky Way.[13] Yet the psychologically critical thematic items in the Putana myth that are perhaps unique to Hindu culture are the poisoned breast, the fight for survival between the malevolent mother and the voracious infant, and the capital punishment and subsequent redemption of the 'bad mother'.

The secret fantasy of poisoned milk, of nourishment that kills, originates early in life when the separation between child and mother takes place.[14] The elevation of this fantasy, which is occasionally encountered clinically, to the status of myth for a whole culture indicates the intensity of inner conflict associated with this separation in the Indian setting. On the one hand, the poisoned breast symbolizes the child's loss of familiar protection and nurturing of his mother, an experience of 'overall loss' and alienation intensified by the physical fact of the final weaning that may take place as late as the third or fourth year of a child's life, thus coinciding with the 'second birth'. If this coincidence is attended by the birth of a new baby, the psychological injury is likely to be compounded. The 'favoured son' finds himself a small, awkward involuntary novice subjected to a peculiar form of exile among the older boys and grown men of his own family. His emotional hunger for the milk of love, which but lately flowed in abundance, can become physically unbearable. His (confused) rage is necessarily projected outward onto the mother who is thus transformed in fantasy into a hostile and threatening figure, while the boy's own voracious need is also projected onto the 'oral image' of the devouring mother. This archaic mechanism of projection — 'It is not I who wants to kill my mother for frustrating me, but she who wants to destroy me for my ravenous need for her' — is part of the unconscious fantasy that 'feeds' the symbol of the poisoned breast. The child's need to repair the severance and restore the nurturing is, however, only one aspect of the conflict between his need for his mother and his anger at her. For he is also subject to a biologically-rooted developmental push towards becoming an independent and 'individuated' person, separate from his mother. Putana's poisoned breast thus symbolizes the Indian boy's critical psycho-social dilemma: how to receive nurturing without crippling his own budding individuality. This universal developmental dilemma is aggravated in the Indian setting (it creates an insoluble conflict for some Hindu men) because of the profound, often unconscious reluctance of the Hindu mother to 'release' the male child, to let him go in an emotional sense, for as we have seen, he is the psycho-social guarantor of her own identity.

In this regard, the fantasy of poisoned milk or poisoned breast resembles the 'double bind' in certain cases of schizophrenia in which the mother is perceived by the child to have given a contaminated love.[15] That is, unconditional maternal love and empathy, responsive to the child's needs, are missing; the price of the mother's nurturing being that the child remain an extension of her person and a fulfiller of *her* needs. The legendary Putana thus represents the dangerous 'schizophrenagenic' mother who has her son in an emotional clinch in which neither can let go; the mother wields the weapons of 'love', maternal solicitude and self-sacrifice, with an unconscious virtuosity that keeps the son in ambivalent emotional thraldom. Yet we must remember that although the imagery of the poisoned breast reflects the dark side of the legacy of the prolonged, intense mother-son relationship in India, this same relationship is decisive in rooting Hindu personality in the rich soil of trust and devotion and sensual care. After all, Krishna not only survives, he positively thrives.

The Putana myth underplays the sexually threatening aspect of the 'bad mother' discussed earlier. Although secondary to the theme of poisoned maternal love, the theme of maternal sexuality and its impossible aims is by no means absent. For we need not subscribe to the view that the killing of maternal monsters is always a disguised form of incestuous intercourse[16] to recognize that Krishna's avid fastening of his mouth to Putana's nipple, not releasing it till Putana falls down lifeless, is an act of oral sexual violence that combines both the infant's excitement and his anger. This image may be construed as a fantasied fulfilment of the mother's sexual demands and at the same time a grim revenge on her for making such demands at all.

Those who would reject this interpretation as a far-fetched 'wish fulfilment' concocted by a psycho-analytic interpreter irreverently predisposed to locate sexuality everywhere will no doubt be taken aback by the following rendition of the Putana legend by Kanhaiyalal Munshi, a devout Hindu writer on philosophical and religious themes who cannot even remotely be suspected of conscious awareness of the sexual content of the suckling scene:

> She (Putana) found her heart bounding in joy. In a transport of ecstasy, she hugged Krishna again. Her repressed maternal instinct burst out, as if it was a roaring flood. And she felt that her skin had become wet. Milk – in that moment of sudden transport – had oozed out of her generous breasts. Her bodice was drenched.
>
> Her body and mind and soul were now craving for this child. Wild ill-assorted thoughts ran beneath her transport. She must take this lovely boy to her breasts ...
>
> The insistent promptings of her heart were: 'Take this lovely boy to your breast. You are a wicked, miserable woman. You have never seen joy before, joy which thrills your whole body and mind with mad delight. This is your moment — the moment for which your life and the lives of your husband and children can be staked. Take this boy to your breast!.' Putana had no command over herself. Torn by ecstatic longing for the boy and forgetful of the poison which she had applied to her breasts, she took Krishna on her lap. He struggled to wriggle out, laughing all the time. She lost control of herself...

She felt as if her mind was stopping. Was she swooning with delight? Yes, all she wanted was that Krishna, Yashoda's boy, should suck this milk, her life, her hope and her all, if he so chose. 'Yes, I give you all, my beloved child.' The thought flashed across her mind 'I am yours'.[17]

Krishna's destruction of Putana and her subsequent redemption, as a 'purified' being, represents one solution of the son's conflict. By killing the 'bad' mother in fantasy, the son obliterates the overweening and sexually ravenous maternal images in his psyche and leaves the benign, protective one intact. This is the only way he can survive as an individual, for libidinal as well as aggressive energy must be ransomed before he can engage in adolescent or adult relationships of intimacy; the 'bad mother' must die in order that the son's capacity for individuation and for sexualizing (and loving) others, may emerge. In the Putana myth, this emptying of the 'bad' mother of her life-giving sensuality and sexual vitality, as well as the necessary establishment of boundaries between her and her son, is condensed into a single, pungent image. As Putana falls down lifeless, her hideous demonic body suddenly begins to emit a pleasing perfume, the exciting smells that infuse the maternal embrace, the odour of her skin and sweat, the smell of milk around her nipple are neutralized, transformed, and rendered benign.

The myths of Agāsur and Kāliyā-Nag are variations on one or the other of the themes in the Putana myth. The monster Agasur lies in wait, its huge mouth open and ready to swallow the child Krishna and his friends as they innocently walk into its mouth; Krishna kills Agasur by bursting out of its throat. The gaping-jawed monster of the legend is a symbolic projection of the child's own hunger for sustenance while its murder presents the elimination of these intense infantile needs, the end of orality.

The myth of the serpent Kāliyā-Nag is a more 'developed' version of this fantasy, in the sense that here the passions projected onto the 'bad mother' are not annihilated but appear capable of being tamed and controlled. Like all serpent myths,[18] the myth of Kāliyā-Nag of the poisonous pool lends itself to interpretation at many different levels. The story goes that Kāliyā-Nag, the king of the cobras, lived with his wives and brood in a pool of water so poisoned that anyone drinking it immediately fell dead. The child Krishna dived into the poisoned pool, and swimming towards the serpent, lassoed its hood with a rope. The serpent put up a furious struggle but was finally subdued. As Krishna triumphantly dragged the serpent out onto the shore, he was followed by the king cobra's wives and children who pleaded with the child-god to spare the life of their husband and father. Krishna explained that he did not wish to kill Kāliyā-Nag but simply to subdue him and cleanse the pool of his poison.

In this myth, Krishna represents the Hindu ideal of the strong ego, one that must struggle with instinctual drives in order to contain and transform them rather than make futile attempts to destroy and deny them. One must, the legend seems to say, dive into the unconscious pool of instinctuality and confront its awesome nature, an instruction from the ancestors reminiscent of the yogic injunction to plumb the depths of the waters of *chitta* in order to know the self. At another level, Kāliyā-Nag represents the mother's passions, or, more accurately, the son's own anxieties and affects triggered by his (conscious and unconscious) perceptions of her, anxieties that must be laid to rest without destroying the life-giving maternal image in the psyche. The subjugation of the serpent represents a resolution of this dilemma, by means of which the son takes a developmental step forward towards adulthood and 'genitality', relatively free from the 'poisonous' incestuous passions of infancy.

The Putanā, Agāsur and Kāliyā-Nag myths may be seen as a cultural elaboration of 'pre-genital' fantasy. That is, these myths incorporate collective infantile wishes and anxieties common and paramount during the first two or three years of the infant's life. By contrast, the lifting up of Mount Govardhan represents the later, oedipal stage of psycho-sexual development when the male world, represented by the father and the other men in the family, first intrudes upon the dyadic intimacy of Hindu son and mother. In this myth, the child Krishna tries to convince the villagers of Vrindavana that their annual rites to placate Indra, the king of the gods, are a shameful act of submission and cowardice, and that they should instead have a festival that celebrates the fields, rivers, trees — mother earth — and that pays homage especially to Gaumata ('Mother-cow'), who is their main source of livelihood and sustenance. With much trepidation and fear of the father-god's wrath, the villagers finally accept Krishna's suggestion, Incensed at this show of disrespect and the turn to the 'mother', Indra lets loose his fury on the hapless cowherds. The sky explodes with thunder and lightning and torrents of rain descend on the village, threatening to wash away the villagers and their livestock. The child Krishna lifts up the mountain Govardhan on his little finger and holds it above the earth as a protective roof till Indra's anger is spent and he becomes reconciled to the new festival.

The Govardhan myth lends itself to a straightforward oedipal interpretation; the male child, although frightened, withstands the veritable thunder and lightning of the father's presumed anger, survives the fantasied threat of being drowned in the huge urethral flood which that giant certainly seems capable of letting loose, and emerges from the contest victorious, ready to retrieve and celebrate intimacy with the mother. There are other corroborative elements that point to the myth's ontogenetic origin in the little boy's proud oedipal fantasies about his newly discovered tumescence, such as the phallic impudence of lifting up a mountain on one's little finger. But once again, in Hindu mythology even oedipal legends close with a characteristic gentle benevolence: neither of the parties to the conflict is blinded, maimed, castrated or killed. Since fathers of Hindu families have never been perceived as terrible avengers, that final, irrevocable act of violence is simply not germane.

The rebellion and dark passions that characterize the myths of Putanā, Agāsur and Kāliyā-Nag are missing from those Krishna myths that I have called 'feminine'. Some of these legends recount the tricks played by Gopal, the Babe-Krishna, on his foster-mother Yashoda, her anger at his mischief and ultimate forgiveness in an orgy of hugs, kisses and the inevitable 'overflowing of maternal milk'. On one occasion the *gopis* come to complain of Krishna's pranks:

> O Yashoda! This boy of yours has become much too mischievous. He sets the calves free even when its not time to milk the cows. When we scold him, he only laughs out loudly. He not only steals our curds and milk for himself, but feeds them to the monkeys. He breaks our pots. When he does not find anything to eat in our houses he teases our children and makes them cry. Even if we hide our milk pots, he always seems to know the hiding place and when we are busy elsewhere in the household, he comes and steals the milk and curds. Not content with his brazen stealing, he pees all over our freshly swept houses. Look at him standing there, pretending to be such an innocent![19]

But even while the *gopis* complain, they cannot take their eyes off the child's lotus face; they are fascinated by his beauty. A flood of affection and joy rises in Yashoda's heart as she sees their admiration of her son, and she begins to laugh, unable to scold, let alone chastise, the boy.

The rest of the legends, celebrated in centuries of devotional poetry, deal with Shyam, the Youth-Krishna, and his love-play with the *gopis*, especially Radha, his chosen consort. whose love for the youthful god is so great that she flouts parental prohibitions and social disapproval to be together with her god-lover. The love of Radha and Krishna which has been one of the central features of the cult from the eleventh century A.D. to the present, is celebrated in legends and poems as an idyllic affair beyond the norms of traditional courtship. It is full of playfulness and joy, of mock quarrels and passionate reconciliations in which Radha often takes the initiative. Thus in the following passage from the *Rasikapriya*:

> Radha came smilingly to Krishna and sang him a tale of love. She then asked him to explain to her the meaning of some of the sequences in the story: the simultaneous partaking by the lovers of the nectar of each other's mouths, and other parts of the body which in consequence suffered amorous injuries by nails and teeth. Enclosing him in an embrace, she also asked him, on an

> oath, what mode of embracing the lovers in the tale had adopted. Thus did Radha herself make up her quarrel with her lover today.[20]

In another poem by Kaviranjana, Radha sets aside traditional feminine modesty and takes the active part in their love-making:

> Her massive locks are dishevelled. She is the goddess of amorous sports embodied and incarnate. Their passionate love is excessive. So the girl behaves as a man.... Her vase-shaped breasts are turned upside down, as if the god of love is pouring out the nectar of life. Over them the hands of the dearest (lover) have been placed, as if (a pair of) *chakravakas* are sitting over (a pair of) lotuses. Bangles and bells at her girdle are jingling, as if the band of joy has been struck by the company of the god of love.[21]

One of the central features of the 'feminine' Krishna legends is the infantilization of the god and, implicitly, of the ideal male by Indian women. In striking contrast to the masculine identification with Krishna, Hindu women perceive and experience him primarily as an ideal son – mischievous, irresponsible and intrusive in a delightful, almost thrilling way. At the same time, Krishna's very playfulness reflects the deep sensual comfort and security of the idealized bond of intimacy between Hindu mother and son. In contrast with the ripe sexuality stimulated in fantasy and exaggerated in certain rituals and festivals of his cult (such as *Holi*), Krishna, the god of the legends, is the saviour of women not as an adult male and lustful partner but as the son who is vital to the consolidation and confirmation of a Hindu woman's identity around the core of motherliness. The legends of Youth-Krishna as the lover of Radha do not alter the intensity of the Indian woman's emotional investment in her son but rather serve simply, elegantly, to incorporate the fantasied fulfilment of her sexual desire for him. For we must remember that Rạdha was years older than Krishna and fell in love with him when she was already at the age of marriage, while he was still only a young boy. Radha-Krishna legends are thus illustrative of the Hindu woman's unconscious fantasy of her son as her lover and the complementary male fantasy, incorporated in Putanā and other myths, of the sexually ravenous mother. The masculine and feminine myths of Krishna thus neatly dovetail to highlight the dominant concerns and fantasies of both Hindu men and women.

NOTES AND REFERENCES

1. For a description of the essence of Krishna, see David R. Kinsley, *The Sword and the Flute: Kali and Krishna*, Berkeley: University of California Press, 1975, Chapter I and II. For an

account of the early and medieval forms of the Krishna cult, see S.C. Mukherjee, *A Study of Vaishnavism in Ancient and Medieval Bengal*, Calcutta: Punthi Pustak, 1966. See also Nicol Macnicol, *Indian Theism*, 2nd edn., Delhi: Munshiram Manoharlal, 1968.
2. *Bhagavata Purana* (my translation), XI. 14. 23–24. It is an interesting parallel that the 'gift of tears' was also a special mark of saintliness in medieval Catholicism.
3. McKim Marriot, 'The Feast of Love', in M. Singer (ed.), *Krishna: Myth, Rites, and Attitudes*, Honolulu: East–West Centre Press, 1966, p. 202.
4. *Ibid.*, pp. 203–4.
5. *Ibid.*, pp. 210–11.
6. *Ibid.*, p. 204.
7. The *Govind-lilamrita* is explicit on this point: Krishna was dancing. He paused and admired the girls. He kissed some of them on the cheeks and lips, looked at others with desire, and fondled the breasts of others, marking them with his nails. In that game of *rasa* he had sexual intercourse with Radha and others, and thus had intercourse with himself. Cited in Kinsley, op.cit., p. 53.
8. *Bhāgavata Purāṇa*, XI, 14.20.
9. *Ibid.*, VII.9.10.
10. Thomas J. Hopkins, 'The Social Teachings of the *Bhāgavata Purāṇa*', in M. Singer (ed.), *Krishna: Myths, Rites, and Attitudes*, p. 22.
11. J.A. Arlow, 'Ego Psychology and the Study of Mythology', *Journal of the American Psychoanalytic Association*, 9, 1961, 379.
12. Otto Rank, *The Myth of the Birth of the Hero*, New York: Brunner, 1952.
13. I am indebted to Philip Slater's analysis of the Heracles myths for an elucidation of certain parallels in Krishna legends. See Slater, *The Glory of Hera*, Boston: Beacon Press, 1966, Chapter XII.
14. In this context, see Melanie Klein, 'Bemerkungen uber einige schizoide Mechanismen', *Das Seelenleben des Kleinkindes*, Hamburg: Rowohlt Verlag, 1972, pp. 101–25.
15. The standard works on the double-bind theory of schizophrenia are Gregory Bateson *et al.*, 'Towards a Theory of Schizophrenia', *Behavioral Science*, 1, 1956, 25–164; and T. Lidz *et al.*, *Schizophrenia and the Family*, New York: International University Press, 1966. For a detailed discussion of the oral-narcissistic conflict mentioned here, see J. N. Rosen, *Direct Analysis*, New York: Grune and Stratton, 1953.
16. Henry, A. Bunker, 'Mother Murder in Myth and Legend', *Psychoanalytic Quarterly*, 13, 1944, 198–207.
17. Kanhaiyalal M. Munshi, *Krishnavatara*, Vol. I, Bombay: Bharatiya Vidya Bhavan, 1967, pp. 65–7.
18. 'Homeric Hymn to Apollo', quoted in Slater, op.cit., p. 139. Serpent myths are ubiquitous in the mythologies of most societies. The symbolic range of these myths and the many different levels at which these symbols can be interpreted exemplify both the possibilities and the limitations of psychological analysis of myths. For discussions of the symbolism in serpent myths see Joseph Campbell, *The Hero With a Thousand Faces*, New York: Meridian Books, 1956; Joseph Fonterose, *Python: A Study of the Delphic Myth and Its Origins*, Berkeley: University of California Press, 1959; and R.F. Fortune, 'The Symbolism of the Serpent', *International Journal of Psychoanalysis*, 7, 1926, 237–43.
19. *Bhāgavata Purāṇa*, X. 8. 26–31.
20. Cited in Kinsley, *op.cit.*, p. 47.
21. *Ibid.*, p. 50.